The Latin Church in the Crusader States

Bernard Hamilton

The Latin Church in the Crusader States

The Secular Church

VARIORUM PUBLICATIONS LTD

London 1980

British Library CIP data

Hamilton, Bernard
  The Latin Church in the Crusader states.
  1. Roman Catholic Church in Syria — History
  2. Latin Orient — Church history
  I. Title
  282'.5691   BX1627.3

  ISBN 0-86078-072-4

Published in Great Britain by

  Variorum Publications Ltd.
  20 Pembridge Mews London W11 3EQ

Printed in Great Britain by

  Galliard (Printers) Ltd
  Great Yarmouth Norfolk

VARIORUM PUBLICATION VP1

CONTENTS

CONTENTS

To Janet

PREFACE

The history of Frankish Syria has not hitherto proved very attractive to ecclesiastical historians. Important monographs have been written on special aspects of the history of the Latin church there, but there has been no general treatment of this subject except for W. Hotzelt's *Kirchengeschichte Palästinas im Zeitalter der Kreuzzuge, 1099–1291*, (Cologne 1940), which deals only with the kingdom of Jerusalem and concentrates chiefly on the activities of the Latin patriarchs. The present book has been written in an attempt to fill this gap in crusader studies.

I have not dealt with the military orders, except in so far as they exercised patronage in the secular church, because excellent studies of them already exist, nor have I written about the monastic establishment of Latin Syria, since adequate treatment of that topic would require a separate volume. I have been concerned solely with the history of the secular Latin church and of its relations with eastern-rite churches.

When rendering Arabic names into English I have, as a general rule, used the forms adopted in the Pennsylvania *History of the Crusades*, omitting diacritical marks which would be an affectation in a general work of this kind. For Greek names I have generally used Latin forms which are more familiar to English readers. I would not claim to have been completely consistent in either case, since sometimes I have considered it more helpful to use a form which is immediately recognisable to an English reader rather than one which is technically more correct.

My particular thanks are due to Professor J. Riley-Smith who read the manuscript of this book and made many valuable suggestions about the ways in which it might be improved; and also to Dr M.C. Barber who undertook the considerable labour of editing it. Since I have not in all cases acted on the advice which either of these scholars has given, they should not in any way be held responsible for mistakes which occur in the text. The faults of this work are exclusively my own.

I have received much help from many people in the course of my work. My thanks are particularly due to the Ecclesiastical History Society for giving me the opportunity to read preliminary drafts of some of my chapters as papers at their summer conferences. I am also grateful to the British Academy for making me a generous grant which enabled me to visit some of the sites about which I have written. While in Israel I received much help from the Revd John Wilkinson, Director of the British School of Archaeology in Jerusalem, and from Mr Kevork Hintlian of the Armenian Convent in Jerusalem. But my thanks are specially due to my medieval colleagues in the department of History of the University of Nottingham who, at some cost to themselves, have made time available to me to complete the writing of this book. I would also like to thank Mrs Turner and the staff of Variorum Publications for their courtesy and help at all stages of preparing this work for publication.

I wish to thank the staff of the following libraries who have assisted me: the Vatican Library and Archives; the Royal Library, Valetta, Malta; the British Library; the Warburg Institute; the University of London Library; the Institute of Historical Research; the London Library; Dr Williams's Library; and, not least, the University of Nottingham Library.

But my chief thanks must be given to my family for their continuous support: to my mother, who encouraged me in this work in its early stages, but who has, regrettably, not lived to see its completion; and to my wife, who has borne with good humour the antisocial hours and moods in which writing this book has involved me, and to whom, in gratitude, it is dedicated.

Bernard Hamilton

Nottingham,
Spring 1980

1. THE FIRST CRUSADE AND THE EASTERN CHURCHES

It was not part of pope Urban's intention when he launched the first crusade to set up Latin churches in the Levant. Writing to the people of Flanders shortly after the council of Clermont he stated:

> the heathen in their fury have laid waste the churches of God in the east, causing great distress by their attacks, and, moreover, have brought into oppressive bondage the holy city and its churches, made glorious by the passion and resurrection of Christ. This situation is intolerable. Being much distressed by the proper concern which we felt about the news of this disaster, we visited France and asked most of the princes of that land and their subjects to free the churches of the east . . . [1]

By the churches of the east the pope did not mean the separated churches, the Armenians, Maronites, Jacobites and Copts. The western church regarded these confessions as heretical and, with the exception of the Armenians,[2] the holy see had had little contact with any of them in the centuries immediately preceding the crusades and was probably not very well informed about them. The eastern churches to which the pope referred were the Orthodox patriarchates of Constantinople, Antioch, Alexandria and Jerusalem which, together with that of Rome, were traditionally believed to make up the Catholic church. To this it might be objected that although the papacy had conceived of the church in these terms in the early years of the eleventh century such a view was no longer tenable after the breach between Rome and Constantinople in 1054. The events of that year had indeed had serious consequences for Rome's relations with all the Orthodox churches, not only with that of Constantinople. The patriarch of Antioch was at that time a political subject of the Byzantine emperor, who was also regarded by the Fatimids of Egypt as the natural protector of their Orthodox subjects in the patriarchates

---

1. H. Hagenmeyer, ed, *Die Kreuzzugsbriefe aus den Jahren 1088–1110*, Innsbruck 1901, p 136, no 2.

2. Gregory VII corresponded with the Armenian catholicus: E. Caspar, 'Das Register Gregors VII', bk II, *ep* 31, *Epistolae selectae in usum scholarum ex MGH separatim editae*, 2 vols, Berlin 1955, II, p 167; B. Hamilton, 'The Armenian Church and the Papacy at the time of the Crusades', *ECR*, 10, 1978, pp 61–2.

of Alexandria and Jerusalem. But as recent examinations of the period between 1054 and the first crusade have shown, neither Rome nor the Orthodox regarded the breach as final.[1] There had been equally serious divisions between the eastern and western churches before, during the Iconoclast controversy of the eighth century and the Photian controversy of the ninth century, neither of which had proved irreparable, and churchmen in the second half of the eleventh century seem to have been hopeful of finding a solution.

Good relations between Rome and the Orthodox world could, however, only be restored with Byzantine co-operation, and the Byzantine attitude towards the papacy was ambivalent. As Runciman has observed, the Byzantine church viewed with disfavour and, it might be added, incomprehension, the revolution which at that time was transforming the papacy and leading it to claim universal temporal as well as spiritual jurisdiction.[2] The Byzantine emperors, on the other hand, were anxious to maintain friendly diplomatic relations with the popes who, since 1059, had been feudal overlords of the south Italian Normans: the Normans posed a threat to the eastern empire which it was thought papal influence might mitigate.

Gregory VII had attempted to harness Byzantine political goodwill in the interests of church unity. He won the favour of the emperor Michael VII by averting a Norman invasion of Macedonia, and then suggested that he should lead an army to the east in person to deal with the Seljuk threat in Asia Minor. Gregory added that during this campaign he would preside at an oecumenical council in Constantinople to bring about the unity of the churches. This was the genesis of the crusading concept, but nothing came of it at the time because the outbreak of the investitures' controversy in 1075 kept the pope occupied in western Europe. Gregory subsequently destroyed any goodwill which he might have built up at Constantinople by excommunicating first Nicephorus III (1078–81) and then Alexius I (1081–1118) for supplanting Michael VII, and by giving his full support to the Normans when they invaded the Byzantine empire in 1081.[3]

1. S. Runciman, *The Eastern Schism*, Oxford 1955, pp 68–92; R. Mayne, 'East and West in 1054', *CHJ*, 11, 1954, pp 133–48; G. Every, *The Byzantine Patriarchate (451–1204)*, 2nd ed, London 1962, pp 144–58; F. Dvornik, 'Constantinople and Rome', in *CMH*, IV(I), *The Byzantine Empire*, ed J.M. Hussey, Cambridge 1966, pp 460–5.

2. Runciman, *Eastern Schism*, pp 71–2, 80.

3. For Gregory VII's crusading correspondence and the literature arising from it, C. Erdmann, *The Origin of the Idea of Crusade*, trans with additional notes, M.W. Baldwin, W. Goffart, Princeton 1977, pp 164–70. On Gregory's support for the Normans in 1081, Caspar, 'Register', bk VIII, *ep* 6, vol II, p 524.

When he became pope in 1088 Urban II inherited the ambivalent legacy of Gregory VII in regard to the eastern churches. Although Urban's methods differed greatly from those of Gregory, the aim of the two popes was not dissimilar. Like Gregory, Urban wanted the papacy to become the paramount temporal and spiritual force in the Christian world. Urban's authority was only recognised in part of the west, since the western emperor and the majority of his subjects had for some years given their allegiance to an antipope, Clement III. This factor was probably decisive in convincing Urban of the need to seek a *rapprochement* with the eastern empire and church, since his position in the west would be greatly strengthened if eastern Christendom recognised him as lawful pope.

In 1089 he sent the cardinal archbishop of Reggio and the Greek abbot of Grottaferrata to Constantinople with authority to lift the excommunication of the emperor and with a request that the Latin churches in the city be reopened. This overture was welcomed by Alexius Comnenus, who saw in the pope a useful political ally, and who convoked a synod of the Byzantine church to discuss relations with the Roman see. The synod found that the pope's name had been omitted from the diptychs of Constantinople through oversight, and that no synodical decision had ever been made on the subject. The Latin churches of Constantinople were reopened, but the approach of the patriarch, Nicholas III, remained cautious. He stated that in view of the length of time which had passed since the pope's name had been commemorated at Constantinople the pope should either come in person to the east to discuss the matters at issue between the churches, or should submit in writing a detailed profession of faith. Urban certainly did not accept the first of these alternatives, and it is considered unlikely that he submitted the required profession of faith, although there is no certain evidence on this point.[1] Yet as a result of these negotiations good diplomatic relations were restored between the pope and the Byzantine emperor although, it would seem, full religious unity was not restored between Rome and the churches of the east.

This was the situation when in March 1095 envoys came from Alexius I to the council of Piacenza to ask the pope to help recruit western knights to serve in Alexius's army against the

---

1. W. Holtzmann, 'Die Unionsverhandlung zwischen Kaiser Alexios I und Papst Urban II im Jahre 1089', *BZ*, 28, 1928, pp 28—67, the correspondence is not complete. Runciman, *Eastern Schism*, p 76, considers it unlikely that Urban sent the required profession of faith.

Seljuk Turks.[1]   It was this appeal which led Urban eight months later to preach the first crusade at the council of Clermont. The crusade was, of course, in part an affirmation of the Hildebrandine concept of papal temporal authority: the pope placed himself at the head of the armies of Christendom in their fight against Islam, a role which in the west since the time of Charlemagne had traditionally belonged to the emperor, but which the schismatic Henry IV was unable to fulfil. The crusade was an eminently practical demonstration of papal power, since it led to the withdrawal of large numbers of fighting men from the authority of feudal rulers for an indefinite period of time under the command of the church.

But the pope also wished the crusade to be an instrument for promoting unity between Rome and the Orthodox churches. The avowed aim of the expedition was to free the churches of the east, particularly the holy places of Jerusalem, from the infidel. Urban was thus reviving the plan of Gregory VII to lead an army against the Turks. Unlike Gregory he did not propose to lead the expedition in person: he delegated that task to his legate, bishop Adhémar of Le Puy. Nor did he suggest that a council should be held at Constantinople during the campaign to restore church unity: perhaps as a result of his correspondence with the patriarch Nicholas he had a greater awareness than Gregory VII had had of the reserve with which Byzantine churchmen viewed the reformed papacy. His plan, as it can be discerned through the policies of his legate during the crusade, was a more gradual one. He sought to gain the goodwill of the Byzantine emperor, a necessary pre-condition for any progress in the achievement of church unity, by sending the military aid which he wanted. But he also wished to allay the fears which Orthodox churchmen entertained about the autocratic exercise of the Roman primacy, by instructing his legate scrupulously to respect the rights of the Orthodox hierarchy. For if it could be established in the course of the crusade that the pope was not seeking to interfere in the jurisdiction of the Orthodox patriarchs, then the greatest single obstacle to the recognition of Urban by his eastern colleagues would have been removed, and the cause of church unity greatly advanced.

Bishop Adhémar was thus entrusted with a delicate mission, but so long as he lived the pope's wishes were scrupulously observed.[2] Unfortunately nothing is known about his negotiations with the

1. Bernold of St Blaise, 'Chronicon', *MGH SS*, V, p 462; D.C. Munro, 'Did the Emperor Alexius I ask for aid at the Council of Piacenza?', *AHR*, 27, 1922, pp 731 *seq.*

2. J.A. Brundage, 'Adhémar of Puy: the bishop and his critics', *Speculum*, 34, 1959, pp 201–12.

patriarch Nicholas III of Constantinople, because Adhémar was injured in a skirmish while travelling through Macedonia and had to spend some weeks at Thessalonica recovering from his wounds. Consequently he did not reach Constantinople until the main armies, and with them the chroniclers of the crusade, had left for Asia Minor.[1] Yet it may be inferred that relations between legate and patriarch were cordial. Adhémar certainly raised no objection to the princes on crusade taking the oath which the emperor required of them: that they would restore to him all the lands they conquered which had formerly been part of the empire, and that they would hold any other lands which they conquered as fiefs of the empire. The territories referred to in the first part of the oath would seem to have been those which the empire had ruled before the Seljuk invasions, and therefore to have comprised Asia Minor, Antioch, Edessa and the lands of Syria north of the Dog river, though not Palestine.[2] This oath obviously determined the kind of ecclesiastical settlement which the legate tried to implement: there could be no question of setting up a Latin hierarchy in regions which were to be restored to full imperial control, while in those areas which were to be held as fiefs under imperial suzerainty it is unlikely that the emperor could have been expected to agree to the substitution of a Latin for an Orthodox hierarchy.

The crusade captured large parts of Asia Minor in 1097 and the terms of the oath were scrupulously observed. This territory was handed over to imperial representatives and no Latin fiefs were established there.[3] Asia Minor formed part of the patriarchate of Constantinople and the patriarch's jurisdiction was respected: no attempt was made by the legate to appoint any Latin bishops in this area. Initially the same policy was followed in north Syria, which the crusade reached in the autumn of 1097.

North Syria formed part of the patriarchate of Antioch, but the crusaders initially made contact with the southern patriarch, Symeon II of Jerusalem. He was a Byzantine Greek, who had been appointed sometime in the 1080s, but when the crusade

1. Le 'Liber' de Raymond d'Aguilers, ed J.H. and L.L. Hill, Documents relatifs à l'histoire des Croisades publiés par l'Académie des Inscriptions et Belles Lettres, IX, Paris 1969, pp 39, 42. The editors argue that this source places Adhémar's arrival in Constantinople before the point at which Raymond of Toulouse took the oath to Alexius (p 42, n 3) but the text does not imply this.

2. Anna Comnena, Alexiad, X, 9, ed B. Leib, 3 vols, Paris 1937–45, II, pp 220–6. These were the lands which had formed part of the empire before the Seljuk invasions.

3. It is doubtful whether the fief of Coxon can be considered as Latin. The crusaders granted it to a Provençal knight, Peter of Aups, to hold of the emperor, but although a Frank, Peter was already in Alexius's service. Gesta Francorum et aliorum Hierosolimitanorum, IV, 11, ed and trans R. Hill, London 1962, p 25.

arrived he was living in exile in Byzantine Cyprus where he had taken refuge from the oppression of the Artukid Turks who were ruling Jerusalem.[1] Symeon appears to have been the author of a treatise against the use of unleavened bread in the Eucharist, a Latin usage to which the Orthodox were traditionally opposed, but Symeon's work, it would seem, was written in defence of Orthodox practice, which had been attacked by a member of the western community in Jerusalem, and is not in itself evidence of a deep-rooted hostility towards the Latin church.[2]   Certainly Symeon made no difficulty about co-operating with the pope's legate.   The Byzantine government must have been responsible for establishing contact between Symeon in Cyprus and Adhémar who had accompanied the crusade on its overland route through Asia Minor.   This contact was probably achieved when the Cilician ports were captured by the crusaders in September 1097 and lines of communication opened between Cyprus and the main crusader force at Marash.[3]

It is not known whether Symeon II came in person to the crusader camp, or whether he sent representatives, but negotiations between him and the legate were sufficiently advanced for a joint communiqué to be issued by them from the camp near Antioch on 18 October 1097. This took the form of an encyclical letter to 'the faithful dwelling in the regions of the north', reporting the progress of the crusade and urging that all those who had taken the cross but had failed to set out should be excommunicated unless they fulfilled their vows by the following Easter. It also related that the patriarch had had a vision of Christ who had told him that all who took part in the crusade would appear before Him wearing crowns at the Last Judgment.[4]   In January 1098 a second letter was addressed to the western church by 'the patriarch of Jerusalem, the bishops both Greek and Latin, and the whole army of the Lord and of the church'. It is, perhaps, significant, that the legate is not specifically mentioned in this letter. Further information is given about the progress of the crusade, but the letter is chiefly an appeal for reinforcements, and it ends with a solemn warning:

1. V. Grumel, *Traité d'Etudes Byzantines*, I. *La Chronologie*, Paris 1958, p 452; Albert of Aix, 'Historia Hierosolymitana', VI, 39, *RHC Occ*, IV, p 489.

2. B. Leib, 'Deux inédits sur les azymes au début du XIIe siècle', *OCP*, 9, 1924, pp 85–107; Runciman, *Eastern Schism*, pp 89–90.

3. Liaison was effected at Marash on 15 October 1097 between the main army and the Cilician contingent. H. Hagenmeyer, *Chronologie de la première croisade (1094–1100)*, Paris 1902, p 101, no 195.

4. Hagenmeyer, *Kreuzzugsbriefe*, pp 141–2.

unless those who have taken crusader vows come and fulfill them, I, the apostolic patriarch, and the bishops and all the orthodox hierarchy excommunicate them and completely sever them from the communion of the church, and do you likewise, so that they may be denied Christian burial unless they have stayed behind for some valid reason.[1]

These letters show that Adhémar recognised Symeon as lawful head of the church of Jerusalem and as in full communion with the western church: a schismatic could not have threatened western Christians with excommunication. The legate can only have adopted this policy with the prior consent of the pope. Equally, Symeon would have had no reason to co-operate with the crusaders unless he had supposed that they would restore him to his see when they recaptured Jerusalem. He would not have given his moral support to the expedition had he thought that it intended to supplant him by a Latin patriarch when it captured the holy city. The premature death of Adhémar of necessity means that the sincerity of his dealings with Symeon must remain a matter of speculation, but the presumption that he intended to acknowledge him as lawful patriarch when Jerusalem was captured receives some support from his treatment of the other Orthodox patriarch, John IV of Antioch.

Like Symeon, John was also a Byzantine Greek, and had been a monk at Oxeia. He had been appointed patriarch in 1091[2] and was living in Antioch when the crusade laid siege to it. Probably because the crusade was at this stage working in conjunction with the Byzantine emperor, the Turkish governor of Antioch persecuted the patriarch who was an imperial nominee. His cathedral was desecrated and he was suspended from the walls of the city in an iron cage during the siege. He survived this treatment and when, after eight months, the city finally fell to the crusaders, the legate restored the cathedral to Christian worship, enthroned the patriarch there, and recognised his canonical authority over all the clergy in his patriarchate, Latin as well as Greek.[3] In this he does not seem to have met with any opposition from the crusaders, which may indicate that John IV was viewed with sympathy by the rank and file of the army because of his sufferings at the hands of the Turks.

The position of the Latin clergy at Antioch under the terms of Adhémar's settlement was analogous to that of the Latin clergy of Jerusalem who served the needs of western pilgrims before the

1. *Ibid.*, pp 146—9.
2. Grumel, *Traité*, p 448.
3. Albert of Aix, V, 3, *RHC Occ*, IV, p 433.

first crusade:[1] they would observe their own rite, but acknowledge the canonical authority of the Orthodox patriarch. This was the only acceptable religious settlement in the context of the political settlement which was envisaged when the crusaders captured Antioch. By the terms of their oath to the emperor the princes were committed to restoring the city to Byzantine control, and, after the relief army from Mosul had been defeated, envoys were sent to Alexius in July 1098 asking him to come and take possession of Antioch.[2] Hitherto the main crusade had worked harmoniously with Byzantium, and had restored to Alexius all lands which had formerly been part of his empire in accordance with the oath they had sworn. Even leaders like Baldwin of Boulogne, who had seized Edessa by a piece of shrewd pragmatism in March 1098, had not contravened the oath: no imperial representative had been present who could raise the matter of the emperor's rights, so the question of keeping the oath had not arisen.[3] In ecclesiastical affairs Adhémar had restored the Orthodox patriarch of Antioch and been punctilious in respecting the canonical rights of the Orthodox patriarch of Jerusalem.

This conciliatory policy towards the Byzantine empire and the Orthodox churches was abandoned by most of the crusaders in the late summer of 1098. Adhémar, the architect of this policy, died on 1 August 1098 during an outbreak of plague[4] and nobody else was present with the army whose authority was universally recognised. Shortly after this the crusaders learned that the emperor had abandoned his march to Antioch and left them to deal single-handed with a numerically superior Muslim relief force and they considered themselves to be absolved from their obligations to him. The only crusader leader who whole-heartedly wished to preserve the Byzantine alliance after that time was Raymond IV of Toulouse, but he was overruled.[5]

The abandonment of a policy of political and military co-operation with the Byzantine emperor by the crusader leaders was bound to make the implementation of pope Urban's ecclesiastical policy very difficult. The Orthodox hierarchies of Antioch

1. Sta Maria Latina and its annexed hospital and convent had been founded some fifty years before the first crusade, WT, XVIII, 5, *RHC Occ*, I, pp 824—6.

2. *Gesta Francorum*, X, 30, ed Hill, p 72.

3. Matthew of Edessa, 'Chronicle', *RHC Arm*, I, p 38; Fulcher of Chartres, *Gesta Francorum Iherusalem peregrinantium*, I, 14, ed H. Hagenmeyer, Heidelberg 1913, pp 203—15; J. Laurent, 'Des Grecs aux Croisés, étude sur l'histoire d'Edesse', *Byzantion*, 1, 1924, pp 410—49; J.B. Segal, *Edessa, the Blessed City*, Oxford 1970, pp 225—9.

4. Hagenmeyer, *Chronologie*, pp 182—3, no 308.

5. Account of the quarrel over Antioch in S. Runciman, *A History of the Crusades*, 3 vols, Cambridge 1951—4, I, pp 236—62.

and Jerusalem were Byzantine Greeks and their readiness to co-operate with the crusade would necessarily be subject to strain if there were any conflict between the crusader leaders and the emperor. In the autumn of 1098 such a conflict had not become overt, but the crusader leaders, now that Adhémar was dead, were uncertain what kind of ecclesiastical policy they should pursue. This is clear from the letter which the princes sent to the pope on September 11 informing him of the legate's death. They did not mention the restoration of John IV in Antioch, but instead made an unusual suggestion:

> What, therefore, seems more proper in all the world than that you, who are the father and head of the Christian religion, should come to the original and chief city where the Christian name was used, and bring to a conclusion on your own behalf the war which is yours? For we have beaten the Turks and the heathen, but we do not know how to defeat the heretics, the Greeks and Armenians and Syrian Jacobites. We therefore continually entreat you, our dearest father, that you, our father and ruler, will come to the city which is yours, and that you, who are the vicar of St Peter, will sit on his throne and then you will find in us obedient sons, acting rightly in all things, and you will be able to root out and destroy all heresies, of whatever kind they are, by your authority and our strength.[1]

This is a blueprint for the Latinisation of the Orthodox churches in Syria, suggesting that the pope himself should occupy the throne of St Peter at Antioch. It is chiefly interesting because it shows how great a gap there was between the views of the pope and his advisors about the nature of the church and those held by the mass of western Christians. The pope's view did not differ greatly from that of the Orthodox world: the Catholic church consisted of a pentarchy of patriarchates of which Rome was one. Where the pope and the Orthodox differed radically was in their respective interpretations of the role of the holy see in that community. The mass of western Christians, on the contrary, thought of the Catholic church as co-extensive with the Latin church and regarded other forms of Christianity as deviant and almost certainly heretical. This view was almost universally held in the crusader army and it created a climate of opinion which was inimical to the kind of ecclesiastical settlement in Syria which Urban II and Adhémar of Le Puy had envisaged.

Had communications between Rome and Syria been better the

---

1. Hagenmeyer, *Kreuzzugsbriefe*, pp 141–2. Runciman, *Eastern Schism*, p 102, suggests that by Greeks the princes meant Greek-speaking Paulicians. This construes the tolerance of the crusaders too generously: the plain sense of the text is Orthodox Greeks.

outcome might have been very different, but it was difficult for shipping to cross the Mediterranean between October and March, so although the pope appointed a new legate on learning of Adhémar's death, he did not reach Syria until the following year and by that time the situation there had changed radically. Although the crusaders made no change in the government of the church of Antioch while they were waiting for a reply from the pope, they did begin to appoint Latin bishops in Syria. The first occasion when this occurred was in September 1098 when Raymond of Toulouse captured the important city of Albara to the south-west of Antioch. A Provençal priest, Peter of Narbonne, was nominated bishop and was given half the city and its territory. His appointment was an irregular one in terms of canon law since there was no chapter of canons to make the formal election: Peter owed his elevation to the decision of the count of Toulouse who took the advice of his chaplains and lay commanders.[1] This was not intended to diminish the authority of the Orthodox patriarch of Antioch, for Raymond IV, almost alone among the crusader leaders, still maintained that Antioch should be restored to the Byzantine emperor, and this entailed the maintenance of the religious settlement which Adhémar had imposed there. Albara was not an Orthodox see, so that there was no conflict of jurisdiction involved in the new appointment,[2] and, according to a contemporary western source, Peter was immediately sent to Antioch to be consecrated by the Orthodox patriarch whose canonical authority was thus openly admitted.[3]

It would seem that the reason for Peter's appointment was political and social rather than ecclesiastical. In the late eleventh century the rulers of western Europe depended on the services of the clergy to carry out the work of secular government and customarily delegated extensive secular powers to bishops. But Orthodox bishops could not assume secular responsibilities of that kind because they had not been trained to do so. There was no need in the Byzantine world for clergy to be involved in the work of government because the eastern empire possessed a class of lay administrators for which there was at that time no parallel in the western world. It is therefore arguable that the crusaders, as soon as they began to conquer territory in Syria and to set up a form of

1. Hagenmeyer, *Chronologie*, pp 188–9, no 316.

2. See chapter 2 below.

3. *Gesta Francorum*, X, 31, ed Hill, p 75, states that John IV consecrated Peter. This contemporary source is to be preferred to William of Tyre who said that Peter was consecrated by Bernard, first Latin patriarch of Antioch, WT, VII, 8, *RHC Occ*, I, pp 288–9. When William wrote it may have seemed inconceivable that a Greek patriarch should consecrate a Latin bishop.

administration there modelled on that of the west, would have been obliged to appoint some Latin bishops to help in the work of government. The bishop of Albara was clearly expected to administer the city on behalf of the count of Toulouse rather than deal with the spiritual needs of its inhabitants, for only the garrison were Latin Christians and a chaplain would have performed those duties adequately.

The appointment of a Latin bishop in an Orthodox patriarchate was not in itself a cause of schism provided that he acknowledged, as the bishop of Albara did, the authority of the patriarch, any more than the appointment of Greek bishops in the Latin provinces of south Italy at this time was a cause of schism in the western church. Nevertheless, the appointment did act as a focus of popular discontent with the religious settlement. Raymond of Aguilers, chaplain of Raymond of Toulouse, relates that Peter's appointment was popular with the rank and file of the Provençal army: 'all the people gave thanks to God because they wished to have a Roman bishop in the eastern church to look after their affairs'.[1]

It is, perhaps, symptomatic of the mood of the army that, when in 1099 the crusade finally moved south, neither the patriarch of Jerusalem nor any representative of his travelled with them. As is well known, the crusaders marched directly to Jerusalem and did not attempt to capture any of the cities in the regions through which they travelled. On 3 June they reached Ramla, which had been abandoned by its garrison, adjacent to which was the basilica of Lydda, principal shrine of the military patron, St George. This place had a dual importance, as a cult-centre and as a route-centre, for it stood at the junction of the Ascalon and the Jerusalem-Jaffa roads. Any army coming from Egypt to relieve the garrison of Jerusalem would pass through Ramla and the crusaders therefore had to guard the city. The princes adopted the same expedient which they had used at Albara: a general assembly of the army chose a Norman priest, Robert of Rouen, as bishop of Lydda, to serve the shrine and govern the city.[2] As a bishop Robert occupied a position of authority in the eyes of the western garrison of Lydda which he would not have enjoyed as a simple priest, and this meant that an experienced nobleman did not have to be detached from the army to take over the command of the city. The appointment of Robert of Rouen, while not in itself prejudicing the final

---

1. Raymond of Aguilers, ed Hill and Hill, p 92.
2. *Ibid.*, p 136; Albert of Aix, V, 42, *RHC Occ*, IV, p 461; Fulcher of Chartres, I, 25, s 13, ed Hagenmeyer, p 277.

decision about the government of the church of Jerusalem, created another precedent for the latinisation of the Orthodox churches of Syria and Palestine.

Jerusalem fell to the crusaders on 15 July 1099. Eight days later Godfrey of Bouillon, duke of Lower Lorraine, was elected ruler but refused a formal coronation, saying that he would not wear a crown of gold in a city where Christ had worn a crown of thorns.[1]   At this time the see of Jerusalem was deemed to be vacant. The Orthodox patriarch, Symeon II, died in Cyprus at about the time that Jerusalem was captured, but it is by no means certain that the crusaders were aware of this when they came to choose a patriarch.[2]   There seems to have been no doubt in any of their minds that the church of Jerusalem should be ruled by a Latin: Adhémar's recognition of Symeon was ignored, and no attempt was made to consult the Orthodox canons of the Holy Sepulchre who were living in Cyprus.

In the absence of a canonical body of electors the crusaders devised an *ad hoc* procedure: on 1 August the senior clergy met together to chose a Latin patriarch from among themselves. This highlighted one of the chief problems which faced the crusaders in initiating a policy of Latinisation in the Orthodox churches of Syria, that of an absence of suitable personnel. A great patriarchal see like Jerusalem required an incumbent who had wide administrative experience, a bishop, or the head of an important religious house.   There was, however, nobody of that calibre available.   The only bishop who had come on the crusade and survived to take part in the siege of Jerusalem was the south Italian bishop of Martirano, whom Ralph of Caen described as 'scarcely more learned than the uneducated mass of the people and all but technically illiterate'.[3]   The bishop perhaps himself recognised his own inadequacies, and gave his full support to the successful candidate, Arnulf.[4]

Arnulf was probably in his mid-forties and was a native of Chocques in the diocese of Thérouanne.[5]   He was a controversial

1. J. Riley-Smith, 'The Title of Godfrey of Bouillon', *BIHR*, 52, 1979, pp 83–6, has convincingly argued that there is no reliable contemporary evidence that Godfrey assumed the title of Advocate of the Holy Sepulchre.

2. Albert of Aix, VI, 29, *RHC Occ*, IV, p 489.

3. Ralph of Caen, 'Gesta Tancredi in Expeditione Hierosolimitana', c 110, *RHC Occ*, III, p 683.

4. Raymond of Aguilers, ed Hill and Hill, p 154, refers to the bishop of Martirano as 'huiusce rei inventor vel centor et administrator' when describing Arnulf's election.

5. 'Versus de viris illustribus diocesis Tarvanensis qui in sacra fuere expeditione', E. Martène, U. Durand, eds, *Veterum Scriptorum … collectio*, 9 vols, Paris 1724–33, V, 539–40; R. Foreville, 'Un chef de la première Croisade: Arnoul Malecouronne', *BHCTH*, 1954–5, pp 378–9.

figure. Raymond of Aguilers complained that he was 'the son of a priest, was only in minor orders, and had such a bad reputation that the common people made up bawdy songs about him while the army was on the march'.[1] There clearly was some substance in these charges: Arnulf later had to obtain a dispensation from pope Paschal II so that he could exercise episcopal functions despite the canonical impediment of his birth, and he had to clear himself on oath before the same pope about charges that he had kept two mistresses, whom the pope named.[2] But this was only one side of Arnulf's character. He was also a learned man, who had been tutor of Cecilia, daughter of William the Conqueror and abbess of the Holy Trinity, Caen, and of Ralph of Caen, chaplain, and subsequently biographer, of prince Tancred of Antioch.[3] He came on crusade as chaplain to Robert, duke of Normandy, Cecilia's brother, and was admitted to be a gifted popular preacher.[4] But in addition to popular esteem, aristocratic patronage and wide learning, Arnulf occupied a place in the crusade which made him the obvious choice as first Latin patriarch of Jerusalem.

Twenty-five years ago Richard drew attention to a passage in the chronicle of Saint-Pierre-le-Vif which describes how Urban II appointed Arnulf and Alexander, chaplain of Stephen of Blois, as ancillary legates when he met the north French army travelling through Italy in 1096.[5] Alexander returned to the west with Stephen of Blois before the fall of Antioch, so Arnulf was the only legate left with the crusade after Adhémar's death. The description which Ralph of Caen gives of Adhémar's commending the crusaders to Arnulf's care as he lay dying would therefore seem to be grounded in fact, although he was not an eye-witness of this event.[6] Certainly it was Arnulf who arranged the trial by ordeal of Peter Bartholomew, the Provençal visionary, on Good Friday 1099.[7] Yet, although Arnulf had enjoyed the confidence of

1. Raymond of Aguilers, ed Hill and Hill, p 154.
2. de Rozière, pp 11–13, no 11.
3. Guibert of Nogent, 'Historia quae dicitur Gesta Dei per Francos', VII, 15, *RHC Occ*, IV, p 232; Ralph of Caen, preface to 'Gesta Tancredi', *RHC Occ*, III, p 604; Foreville, 'Arnoul', *BHCTH*, 1954–5, pp 382–5.
4. Ralph of Caen, c 110, *RHC Occ*, III, p 683.
5. J. Richard, 'Quelques textes sur les premiers temps de l'Eglise latin de Jérusalem', *Mémoires et documents publiés par la Société de l'Ecole de Chartes*, 12, *Recueil de Travaux offerts à M. Clovis Brunel*, 2 vols, Paris 1955, II, pp 420–30.
6. Ralph of Caen, c 94, *RHC Occ*, III, p 673.
7. Arnulf is also said to have preached to the crusaders on the Mount of Olives during their penitential procession round Jerusalem, Peter Tudebode, *Historia de Hierosolymitano Itinere*, ed J.H. and L.L. Hill, *Documents relatifs à l'histoire des Croisades publiés par l'Académie des Inscriptions et Belles-Lettres*, XII, Paris 1977, p 138; for his part in the trial of Peter Bartholomew, Raymond of Aguilers, ed Hill and Hill, pp 116–20.

Urban II and bishop Adhémar, he did not share their views about the canonical status of the eastern churches. One of his first acts as patriarch was to expel all eastern Christians from the Holy Sepulchre and to confide the shrine entirely to the ministrations of Latin clergy.[1] Duke Godfrey endowed a chapter of canons to serve the cathedral, presumably chosen from the Latin clergy who had accompanied the crusade.[2] This act of triumphalism accurately reflected the mood of the crusader army. They had won Jerusalem without the help of any other Christian power and in the face of odds which, in human terms, appeared insuperable. Their victory was a manifest sign of God's favour, and it was therefore fitting that the holy city should be made subject to the Latin church to which the crusaders belonged.

Arnulf's election took place without reference to the pope, but the evidence suggests that he was not consecrated bishop at that time[3] and it seems likely that he was considered patriarch-elect until papal ratification of his appointment was received. Fulcher of Chartres, the chaplain of Baldwin I of Edessa, who was in Jerusalem at Christmas 1099 and therefore had every opportunity to be well-informed, considered that the patriarchate was vacant before December 1099 pending a papal decision, an opinion substantially shared by William of Tyre.[4] Urban II could not adjudicate on the matter of Arnulf's appointment for he died on 29 July 1099 before news of the success of his crusade and the abandonment of his religious policies by its leaders could have reached him. He was succeeded by Paschal II who was to prove far less friendly towards the Byzantine empire and the Orthodox churches than his predecessor had been.

The legate whom pope Urban had appointed to replace Adhémar reached Syria in September 1099. This was Daimbert of Pisa, a man of about the same age as Arnulf and, like him, reputed to be well-educated and a good preacher.[5] He was a man of wide experience. He had become bishop of Pisa in 1088, and four years later the see was raised to an archbishopric in his honour by Urban II, who also granted him metropolitical jurisdiction over the church of Corsica. In accordance with the spirit of

1. *Ibid.*, p 154.
2. Fulcher of Chartres, I, 30, s 2, ed Hagenmeyer, p 308; Albert of Aix, VI, 40, *RHC Occ*, IV, p 490.
3. Foreville, 'Arnoul', *BHCTH*, 1954–5, p 379, n 3. In 1112, when he was again appointed patriarch, Arnulf issued a privilege 'eo die quo consecratus fui', *CGOH*, no 25.
4. Fulcher of Chartres, I, 30, s 2, ed Hagenmeyer, p 308; WT, IX, 15, *RHC Occ*, I, p 387.
5. He became bishop in 1088 and was therefore probably born in the 1050s. For his learning and eloquence Ralph of Caen, c 140, *RHC Occ*, III, p 704.

the Gregorian reformers Daimbert supported the commune of Pisa in its struggle against the nobility of the city and succeeded in negotiating the right of the commune freely to elect its consuls. He accompanied pope Urban to Clermont, took the cross, preached the crusade in Pisa and raised 120 ships there. But in 1098 the pope sent him as legate to Alfonso VI of Castile, so that he was unable to come to Syria until the following year, when he travelled east with the Pisan fleet.[1]

Daimbert's policies towards eastern Christians differed so radically from those of Adhémar that Krey was led to question whether he enjoyed legatine powers at all or whether he merely possessed authority when he reached Jerusalem because he was the senior-ranking Latin prelate there.[2] This thesis is not tenable, because in a charter of 1101 prince Tancred speaks of Daimbert as 'sent by God through the agency of the apostolic see to the regions of the east'.[3] Daimbert must have been appointed by Urban II to succeed Adhémar, because Paschal II was not elected pope until 13 August 1099, long after the Pisan fleet had left the west.

There is no clear information about Daimbert's attitude towards the Orthodox churches: his views about them may not theoretically have been very different from those of pope Urban. He was, however, politically hostile to the Byzantine empire. There were two reasons for this. By the time Daimbert left the west it was rumoured that the Byzantines had betrayed and ill-treated the crusaders. Such reports were often ill-founded, but they did little to create an atmosphere of goodwill towards the eastern empire.[4] Moreover, as archbishop of Pisa, and one who was very closely identified with the interests of the commune, Daimbert had little reason to favour the Byzantines who had granted a monopoly of trading rights with the west throughout the empire to Pisa's commercial rival, Venice. On their way to the east the Pisan fleet raided the Greek islands and when they arrived in Syria joined Bohemond in laying siege to the Byzantine-held city of Latakia and were only persuaded to desist by the remonstrances of crusader leaders who were returning to the west, who deplored war between Christians and who also needed Byzantine co-operation to return home.[5]

1. M.L. Gentile, 'Daiberto', *Enciclopedia Italiana,* Rome 1949, XII, 230.
2. A.C. Krey, 'Urban's Crusade, success or failure?', *AHR,* 53, 1948, pp 240–2.
3. Paoli, pp 200–1, no 166.
4. In June 1098 Alexius I wrote to Oderisius of Montecassino to deny allegations of Byzantine hostility towards the crusade which were already circulating in the west, Hagenmeyer, *Kreuzzugsbriefe,* pp 152–3, no 11.
5. Anna Comnena, XI, 10, ed Leib, III, p 45; Albert of Aix, VI, 55–8, *RHC Occ,* IV, pp 500–3.

Daimbert and the Pisan fleet accompanied the two northern princes, Bohemond of Antioch, and Baldwin of Edessa, duke Godfrey's younger brother, when they came to Jerusalem at Christmas 1099 to fulfil their crusader vows by praying at the Lord's Sepulchre. One of Daimbert's functions as legate was to review the appointment of Arnulf as patriarch. He received complaints about him, and presided at a council of clergy at which these charges were examined. Arnulf was found guilty and was removed from office. It is usually said that Arnulf was deposed[1] but it might be more accurate to say that his election was not confirmed. The office of patriarch being vacant once more, Daimbert was chosen to fill it.[2] He had the support of Bohemond of Antioch, but perhaps more persuasive than this was the presence of the Pisan fleet with whose help in the months that followed the port of Jaffa was fortified, thus securing the lines of communication between the infant state of Jerusalem and the western world.[3] But it was not political expediency alone which recommended Daimbert to duke Godfrey and the Franks of Jerusalem. He seemed ideally qualified to be patriarch, for he had a wide experience in politics, diplomacy and administration and was well-esteemed by the holy see.

Soon after his enthronement Daimbert, at the request of Bohemond and Baldwin of Edessa, consecrated four Latin bishops to sees in north Syria: Benedict of Edessa, Roger of Tarsus, Bartholomew of Mamistra, and Bernard of Artah.[4] Since all these dioceses were in the patriarchate of Antioch, Daimbert was showing scant respect for the rights of the Orthodox patriarch, John IV, although he may have considered that his legatine authority empowered him to interfere in the administration of another patriarchate. He made no attempt, however, to attack John of Antioch himself.

John's position at Antioch was rapidly becoming untenable for quite different reasons. In the spring of 1100 war broke out between Bohemond and the emperor Alexius who laid claim to the territories of Antioch, and whose fleet seized the coastal cities of Cilicia from the Franks. John IV was a Byzantine Greek and Bohemond was unwilling to leave him as head of the church in his state and virtual second-in-command of the city of Antioch

1. E.g. Runciman, *Crusades*, I, p. 305; H.E. Mayer, *The Crusades*, Oxford 1972, p 66.

2. Hagenmeyer, *Chronologie*, pp 273–4, no 439.

3. *Ibid.*, pp 276–7, no 443.

4. Ralph of Caen, c 140, *RHC Occ*, III, p 704; 'Historia Belli Sacri', c 135, *RHC Occ*, III, p 226.

while he was absent on campaign. In the summer of 1100 John left the city and retired to his monastery of Oxeia. The Franks chose to regard this as an act of voluntary abdication, but John's own account of events leaves no doubt that he considered that he had been expelled.[1] His eviction from Antioch was an embarrassment to later Frankish historians: he had undoubtedly suffered greatly for the faith at the hands of the Muslims and he had been restored to power by a papal legate. He deserved better treatment from the Franks than he obtained, and his deposition was imposed by a lay ruler who had not referred the matter to Rome. William of Tyre, who described John as 'a true confessor of Christ', found a tactful way of discussing his deposition: 'when scarcely two years had passed, realising that a Greek could not conveniently rule over Latins, he left the city and went to Constantinople'. In his place Bohemond, presumably with the advice of his clergy, appointed Bernard of Valence, who had been bishop of Adhémar's chaplain, and whom Daimbert had recently consecrated as bishop of Artah.[2]

The enthronement of a Latin patriarch in Antioch marked the total abandonment of Urban II's policy of co-operation with the Orthodox churches. Such a plan could only have been successful if the crusade had continued to work in harmony with the Byzantine empire. When the emperor Alexius made his understandable, but in the long term ill-judged, decision to retreat from Philomelium in June 1098 instead of marching to the relief of the crusaders beleaguered in Antioch, the pope's policies were doomed to failure. It is doubtful whether bishop Adhémar, had he lived, could have withstood the mounting pressure of anti-Byzantine, and, by extension, anti-Orthodox feeling in the crusader army. Certainly his successor as legate, Daimbert, made no attempt to do so, although he did not act overtly against the settlement which Adhémar had established at Antioch. Pope Urban's own death removed the only man who was powerful enough to stem the growth of Latin hierarchies in the patriarchates of Jerusalem and Antioch, for his immediate successors did not share his vision of the shape which a united Christendom might have under papal leadership, one in which the Orthodox patriarchs occupied a central place.

---

1. V. Benechewitch, *Catalogus Codicum Manuscriptorum Graecorum qui in Monasterio Sanctae Catherinae in Monte Sinai asservantur*, St Petersburg 1911, p 279.
2. WT, VI, 23, *RHC Occ*, I, pp 274—5.

2. THE ESTABLISHMENT OF A LATIN CHURCH AT ANTIOCH

When they first encountered a bewildering variety of eastern Christians at Antioch in 1098 the crusader leaders made no distinction between the Orthodox and members of the separated eastern churches. This view did not last, and by the time they decided to establish a Latin church in Syria they had revised their earlier opinion in conformity with the official teaching of the western church which held that the Orthodox, unlike other eastern Christians, were full members of the Catholic communion. The crusaders therefore regarded the Latin bishops whom they appointed as heirs of the Orthodox prelates whom they had dispossessed. Religious animosity played no part in the crusaders' decision to latinise the Orthodox churches for, like pope Urban, they believed that the Orthodox formed part of the one, holy, Catholic church to which they themselves belonged. What they disputed was Urban's contention that it was proper for an Orthodox bishop to exercise spiritual authority over Latins. Had the crusaders regarded the Orthodox as schismatics they would have adopted a different policy towards them and have treated them in the same way as they did the separated eastern Christians, the Armenians, Jacobites and Maronites, to whom they granted virtual religious autonomy. In Antioch, it is true, it might have proved necessary for political reasons to depose Byzantine Greek bishops, but they could have been replaced by bishops chosen from the native Orthodox community rather than by Latins. This did not happen because the Franks made no distinction between Orthodox and Latins in religious terms. For a variety of reasons, all of them secular, the crusaders considered that bishops should be chosen from their own race. In addition to the factors already discussed was the overriding consideration that the Franks had come to Syria as conquerors. The thought of being spiritually subject to Orthodox bishops drawn from a subject race was as little acceptable to them as the appointment of Indians to Anglican bishoprics would have been to the British rulers in nineteenth-century India.

Yet although the Franks appointed Latin bishops to Orthodox sees they did not disturb the lesser Orthodox clergy. Orthodox parish priests and Orthodox monasteries retained complete religious freedom and were in full communion with the Latin church, though subject to the canonical authority of Latin bishops. Their position will be considered in more detail later in this work, but the toleration which the Franks showed to them demonstrates that they had no religious antipathy towards the Orthodox. They were quite prepared to leave in office Orthodox clergy who did not occupy a central place in secular government, who did not constitute a threat to the security of their states, and who did not exercise spiritual authority over Franks.

The Latins' claim to be the heirs of the Orthodox in Jerusalem and Antioch was decisive in shaping the ecclesiastical settlement which they made in Syria. If they had decided to establish new Latin churches in the east they could have founded bishoprics where they were most needed without reference to earlier practice, but this was not the case. At both Jerusalem and Antioch they took over Orthodox ecclesiastical records, among which were lists of the dioceses over which the respective patriarchs ruled.[1] These lists bore almost no relation to the realities of Orthodox organisation in the late eleventh century: they dated from the sixth century, and the majority of Orthodox sees did not survive the Arab conquest of Syria.[2] It is easy to understand why the Orthodox continued to publish these lists for 500 years after they had ceased to have any practical application. They were a religious minority within the Arab empire, subject to various humiliating civil disabilities, and they took courage, as such minorities often do, from remembering the time when they had enjoyed great power and prestige. It is, at first sight, more surprising to find that the Latins viewed these archaic lists with equal enthusiasm. They translated them not only into Latin, but also into French.[3] The reason for this is that they could use the lists as an effective form of publicity. If the Latin patriarchs of Jerusalem and Antioch listed the scores of dioceses over which they had theoretical jurisdiction, their power appeared much more impressive than it would have done had they recorded only those sees which were filled which, throughout much of this period, were less than a dozen in each patriarchate. The papacy, similarly,

1. Tobler, Molinier, I, pp 323—43.

2. S. Vailhé, 'Une "Notitia Episcopatuum" d'Antioche du Xe siècle', *EO*, 10, 1907, pp 90—101; 'La "Notitia Episcopatuum" d'Antioche du patriarche Anastase, VIe siècle', *ibid.*, pp 139—45; 'Les recensions de la "Notitia Episcopatuum" d'Antioche du patriarche Anastase', *ibid.*, pp 363—8; Charon, II, pp 223—9; R. Devréesse, *Le Patriarcat d'Antioche depuis la paix de l'Eglise jusqu'à la conquête arabe*, Paris 1945, pp 103—7.

3. Latin lists, Tobler, Molinier, I, pp 323—43; Old French lists, Michelant, Raynaud, pp 11—19.

found it useful to emphasise how extensive its jurisdiction was in the churches of the east, and the future pope Honorius III recorded in the *Liber Censuum* of the Roman church in 1192 that there were 153 cathedral churches in the patriarchate of Antioch, which he likened to the miraculous draught of fishes.[1]   The reality, however, was very different.

A tenth-century list of the suffragans of Antioch, dating probably from the reconquest of north Syria by Nicephorus Phocas and John Tzimisces, records only nineteen sees, all of which were in the coastal cities.[2]   Although there is no extant list of Orthodox sees in the eleventh century, the situation does not seem to have changed substantially by the time of the first crusade.   Thus the Franks could not adopt the simple expedient of replacing Orthodox bishops by Latins; they had, in most cases, to set up a church organisation *ex nihilo* in areas where one had not existed for centuries.   Nevertheless, in most cases they conformed very closely to the pattern set out in the sixth-century lists. Indeed, the chief innovation which the Latins made in the ecclesiastical administration of Syria was in the size of dioceses. Orthodox dioceses were on the whole very small by comparison with those of the west: the Franks therefore tended to amalgamate several Orthodox sees in one Latin diocese.   James of Vitry, bishop of Acre in the early thirteenth century, explained why this policy had been adopted by the church of Jerusalem, and the reasons he gave no doubt obtained in the church of Antioch as well:

> . . . many other cities in the promised land . . . before the time of the Latins . . . may have had bishops of their own . . . yet on account of their number and their poverty the Latins have subjected many churches and many cities to one cathedral city, lest the dignity of a bishop should be made cheap.[3]

The establishment of a Latin church of Antioch depended on close co-operation between the patriarch and the secular princes. The pope ratified the appointment of the patriarch by sending him a *pallium*,[4] but apart from this Rome took no part in the appointment of archbishops and bishops unless an appeal were made to the pope against the nomination of a particular candidate.

1. P. Fabre, L. Duchesne, G. Mollat, eds, *Le Liber Censuum de l'Eglise romaine*, 3 vols, Paris 1910–52, I, p 239.
2. Charon, II, pp 233–5.
3. James of Vitry, *HO*, p 98.
4. Ralph, the second Latin patriarch, at his election took Bernard's *pallium* from the altar and wore it, WT, XIV, 10, *RHC Occ, I*, p 620.

The appointment of bishops was formally in the control of cathedral chapters, but in practice they chose the candidate whom the secular ruler favoured, though the ruler would normally take the advice of the patriarch about this. The patriarchs of Antioch had to deal with three independent rulers: the princes of Antioch (whose dominions in the early years of the century included Cilicia), the counts of Edessa and the counts of Tripoli, for all three states came under the ecclesiastical jurisdiction of Antioch. In fact the decisive influence in the establishment of the Latin church of Antioch was the patriarch, Bernard of Valence, who reigned for thirty-five years, during which time a succession of rulers held power in each of the three northern states.[1]

Bernard's rise to power might justly be described as meteoric. He came from Valence in the Rhone valley, and had accompanied bishop Adhémar on crusade as one of his chaplains. He held the see of Artah for six months in 1100 before being appointed to the chair of St Peter at Antioch, a dignity which ranked fourth in the entire Catholic world, since its holder took precedence over all clergy except the pope and the patriarchs of Constantinople and Alexandria. Bernard had very little experience to qualify him for such a position, yet he proved to be a wise choice. He had physical courage, and in the early years of his reign he accompanied the armies of Antioch into battle, riding on a mule: though he does not seem to have taken any part in the fighting, he was, nevertheless, exposed to considerable danger.[2] He was loyal to his friends: he arranged for the ransoming of prince Bohemond, who had appointed him, from the Danishmendid Turks in 1103 against the wishes of Tancred who was regent of Antioch during Bohemond's captivity.[3] His piety was of a conventional kind: he was a benefactor of the Hospital of St John of Jerusalem.[4] He was also capable of assuming secular responsibilities. He took charge of the defence of the city of Antioch in 1119 after prince Roger and the entire army of the principality had been annihilated at the *Ager Sanguinis* until Baldwin II arrived with reinforcements; and in the years that followed, until Bohemond II came to take over the government in 1126, his influence in the affairs of the

1. At Antioch: Bohemond I, Tancred, Roger of the Principate, Bohemond II; at Edessa: Baldwin I, Joscelin I, Joscelin II; at Tripoli: Raymond IV of Toulouse, William-Jordan, Bertrand, Pons.

2. At the attack on Harran in 1104, WT, X, 29, *RHC Occ*, I, p 444; Ralph of Caen, cc 148, 150, *RHC Occ*, III, pp 710–11.

3. Ralph of Caen, c 147, p 709.

4. *CGOH*, nos 5, 102.

principality was considerable.[1]   By this time he had become a
respected elder statesman in the northern principalities, and he
helped Baldwin II to mediate peace between Bohemond II and
Joscelin I of Edessa in 1128.[2]   In his last years he was again
influential after the death of Bohemond II and during the minority of the princess Constance.[3]   He died towards the end of
1135:[4] William of Tyre describes him as a 'vir grandaevus' at that
time, and although his exact age is not known it seems likely, in
view of the length of his pontificate, that he was in his seventies.
William of Tyre describes him as 'a simple and God-fearing man',
and it seems, from what is known of his career, to be a fair assess-
ment.[5]   Bernard was in many ways typical of the first generation
of bishops in Frankish Syria. He was not very well educated,[6]
he does not appear to have had any outstanding qualities as a
diplomat, an administrator or a churchman, and he had certainly
received no training commensurate with the responsibilities of
the high office which he was required to fill. A similar man in
western Europe, unless he had the backing of very powerful
patrons, would probably have had an undistinguished career.
But, being placed in a position of authority, Bernard showed
himself to be more than adequate for the requirements of his
office: the secular government of Antioch owed much to him for
the way in which he assumed responsibility during times of crisis,
and he gave the church of Antioch a structure which it had lacked
when he came to power.

In 1100 there were five Latin dioceses in the patriarchate of
Antioch: Albara, which had been set up by Raymond of Toulouse,
Edessa, erected at the wish of count Baldwin, and Bohemond's
three foundations, the sees of Tarsus, Mamistra and Artah. Artah,
of course, fell vacant when Bernard of Valence was translated to
the patriarchate. It had not been the seat of a bishop in Orthodox
times, and was one of the few new dioceses set up by the crusaders
in north Syria. The reason for this innovation must have been a
military one. Artah was an important fortress to the east of
Antioch, which guarded the approach roads to the Orontes valley

---

1. Baldwin II of Jerusalem was regent of Antioch from 1119—26, but during his
absences in the south and his captivity the patriarch's influence was paramount,
Runciman, *Crusades*, II, pp 154—75.

2. WT, XIII, 22, *RHC Occ*, I, pp 590—1; MS, XV, 2, vol III, p 224.

3. Officially after Bohemond II's death first Baldwin II and then king Fulk were
regents of Antioch: neither of them stayed there for long and 'authority there was
represented by the ... patriarch Bernard'. Runciman, *Crusades*, II, p 198.

4. He is last mentioned on 2 August 1135, de Rozière, pp 166—7, no 86.

5. WT, XIV, 10, *RHC Occ*, I, p 619.

6. William of Tyre normally uses the word *simplex* to refer to men with little
formal education.

from Muslim-held Aleppo, and its bishop doubtless acted as the representative of the prince of Antioch.[1] Bernard of Valence appointed a new bishop there, but the see is very poorly documented and little is known about it in detail.[2]

At Albara Peter of Narbonne remained the bishop for most of Bernard's reign,[3] but his position needed to be regularised. In Orthodox times Albara had formed part of the province of Apamea, whose archbishop ranked fourth among the metropolitans of Antioch.[4] Tancred captured Apamea from the Muslims in 1106, and if there was an Orthodox bishop there he was expelled.[5] Soon after this the patriarch made Peter of Narbonne a metropolitan archbishop and transferred his see to Apamea. This happened before 1110, for in a charter issued in that year by count Bertrand of Tripoli Peter is called both archbishop of Albara and archbishop of Femia, which is a Latin form of Afamiyah, the Arabic name of Apamea.[6] The archbishops continued to use the two titles of Albara and Apamea interchangeably for some years, but the traditional usage won out in the end, and the last recorded use of the title archbishop of Albara dates from 1144.[7] The translation by Bernard of this see to Apamea is an indication of his determination, which informed his ecclesiastical policy throughout his reign, to restore in so far as was possible the hierarchy of Antioch as it had existed in its Orthodox heyday.

In the case of Edessa there was no conflict between ecclesiastical tradition and contemporary politics. Edessa was the seat of government in its county and had been in Frankish control since 1098: it was also the third of the metropolitan sees of Antioch.[8] Count Baldwin I needed a Latin bishop to take spiritual charge of his Latin subjects, and to assume command of the city when the count was absent, and in 1099 he had appointed

1. This see was set up by Bohemond I, not by a patriarch. The prince clearly considered it of strategic importance and wanted a Latin feudal bishop to represent him there.

2. 'S. Arthasiensis episcopus', de Rozière, p 167, no 86.

3. Peter is last mentioned in 1119, WT, XII, 10, *RHC Occ*, I, p 526, but should, perhaps, be identified with the unnamed bishop of Albara of 1123, Ibn al-Qalanisi, *Chronicle*, extract trans H.A.R. Gibb, *The Damascus Chronicle of the Crusades*, London 1932, pp 168–9. His successor, Serlo, is first mentioned in 1140, WT, XV, 16, *RHC Occ*, I, pp 683–5.

4. Tobler, Molinier, I, p 332.

5. This see had been restored in the tenth century, Charon, II, p 234.

6. de Rozière, p 194, no 98.

7. *CGOH*, no 144. Delaville Le Roulx dated this document 1142. For the correct date, J. Riley-Smith, *The Knights of St John in Jerusalem and Cyprus, c 1050–1310*, London 1967, p 56, n 1.

8. Tobler, Molinier, I, p 332.

archbishop Benedict. Edessa is not recorded as an Orthodox see in the tenth-century list of the suffragans of Antioch, but since the city was in Byzantine hands from 1032—87 it seems likely that an Orthodox bishop was appointed during that time. If he was still there when the crusaders arrived, they expelled him. Archbishop Benedict is last recorded in 1104.[1] He was succeeded by Hugh, in whose appointment Bernard of Antioch must have had some share, who was enthroned by 1122[2] and held office for the rest of Bernard's reign.

The two other dioceses to which Latin incumbents were appointed before Bernard's pontificate were both in Cilicia, those of Tarsus and Mamistra. Bohemond had made these appointments, and his choice of dioceses would seem to have been dictated by military rather than by ecclesiastical considerations. Tarsus guarded the southern approach to the Cilician Gates, an important pass which a Byzantine army might use should it attempt to attack Antioch. Similarly, Mamistra commanded the Cilician approach road to the Syrian Gates which controlled communications between Cilicia and Antioch. It was common sense to place in these key cities bishops who were nominees of the prince of Antioch. In Orthodox times there had been three archbishops in Cilicia: those of Tarsus, Mamistra and Adana, of whom the archbishop of Tarsus had been the most important, ranking second among the metropolitans of Antioch.[3] All three sees had had Orthodox incumbents in the tenth century. It is not certain whether they remained there after the Turkish conquest of 1090, but, if they did, the Latins expelled them.[4] There was therefore no conflict between Bohemond's appointments and the ecclesiastical traditions of Antioch and Bernard made no innovations there. The third see of Adana was not revived but probably merged with that of Mamistra. Archbishop Roger of Tarsus, Bohemond's nominee, ruled until 1108 at least[5] but by the end of Bernard's reign he had been replaced by archbishop Stephen.[6] Bohemond's nominee at Mamistra, archbishop Bartholomew, had a much shorter reign:[7] by 1108 he had been succeeded by an

1. WT, X, 29, *RHC Occ*, I, p 444; Albert of Aix, IX, 39—40, *RHC Occ*, IV, p 615; Ralph of Caen, cc 148—9, *RHC Occ*, III, p 710.

2. Letter to archbishop of Rheims, *PL*, 155, 877—80.

3. Tobler, Molinier, I, p 332, 'sedes secunda, Tarsus'; p 337, 'metropolitani per se subsistentes . . . Mopsuestia, Adana'.

4. Charon, II, p 234.

5. Müller, p 3, no 1; the unnamed archbishop of Tarsus in 1110 is probably Roger, Albert of Aix, XI, 42, *RHC Occ*, IV, p 682.

6. de Rozière, p 167, no 86.

7. He may be the unnamed archbishop of Mamistra in 1103, Albert of Aix, IX, 16, *RHC Occ*, IV, p 600.

archbishop R who appears only once as a charter witness.[1] He cannot be identified with Ralph of Domfront, who held the see at the end of Bernard's reign and who succeeded him as patriarch, since all the evidence suggests that Ralph was a comparatively young man at the time of his translation to Antioch, which he would not have been had he been archbishop of Mamistra for almost thirty years.[2]

In the early years of Bernard of Valence's pontificate Raymond IV of Toulouse was attempting to carve out a lordship for himself in the Muslim-held lands south of the principality of Antioch. He intended to make Tripoli the capital of his state and, although he died before that city fell, he nominated a south Frenchman, Albert, or Hubert, abbot of St Erard, to be its first bishop.[3] His reasons for making this appointment were the same as those of count Baldwin in appointing a Latin archbishop of Edessa. Tripoli was an Orthodox see and had had a bishop in the tenth century.[4] If there was an Orthodox bishop in residence when the Franks finally captured the city in 1109 he was driven out and bishop Albert was installed in his place. The appointment of a Latin bishop of Tripoli, though not marking a break with Orthodox tradition, nevertheless raised certain practical problems. Traditionally Tripoli was a suffragan see of the church of Tyre, but Tyre remained in Muslim hands until 1124 so that no Latin metropolitan could be appointed there. In these circumstances Bernard of Antioch made the church of Tripoli immediately subordinate to himself.[5]

In Bernard's pontificate a Latin bishopric was set up at Marash. This city, which commanded the approach roads to Antioch through the Anti-Taurus mountains, had been restored to the Byzantines by the leaders of the first crusade in 1097 in accordance with their oath to the emperor.[6] In 1104 it was annexed by Bohemond who was at war with Byzantium and a Latin see was instituted there before 1114, in which year the first Latin bishop

1. Müller, p 3, no 1.

2. Ralph is first mentioned in 1135, Kohler, p 130, no 21.

3. Albert of St Erard appears as a member of Raymond IV's court at Tripoli in 1104, *RHC Lois*, II, pp 479—80, *chartes*, no 1. His appointment as bishop, William of Malmesbury, *Gesta Regum Anglorum*, IV, 388, ed W. Stubbs, 2 vols, London 1889, *RS*, 90, II, p 458, where he is wrongly called Herbert.

4. Charon, II, p 233.

5. William of Tyre makes it clear that from the beginning the patriarch of Antioch had jurisdiction over the county of Tripoli, WT, XI, 28, *RHC Occ*, I, pp 502—5.

6. The crusaders left the Armenian governor, Thatoul, whom the Byzantine authorities recognised, in charge at Marash. Matthew of Edessa, 'Chronicle', II, 17, *RHC Arm*, I, p 50.

was killed in an earthquake.[1]   Marash had been an autocephalous archbishopric in the sixth century, but there is no evidence that there was ever a bishop there after the Arab conquests.[2] It would seem that the Franks were motivated more by military considerations than by ecclesiastical ones in reviving this see, since it was in the interests of the prince of Antioch to nominate a bishop who could take charge of this strategically important city.

The Armenian scholar, St Nerses of Lampron, states that the Franks founded an archbishopric at Kesoun, which was situated between Marash and the Muslim emirate of Samosata.[3] Although this is confirmed in no western source there seems no reason to doubt that it is true, for Antioch is very poorly documented in the early years of Frankish rule.   Kesoun was an independent Armenian principality which was annexed by Baldwin II of Edessa in 1116, and he or his successor may well have wished to place a bishop there as his representative, even though the city had not been a see in Orthodox times.

Bernard of Valence was also responsible for appointing a Latin bishop in the coastal city of Jabala to the south of Antioch. This had been an autocephalous archbishopric in Orthodox times, an Orthodox bishop had been restored there in the tenth century, and one probably remained there until the Frankish occupation.[4] The city was captured by Tancred in 1109 and a Latin bishop was probably appointed soon afterwards: he is first recorded in a document of 1115.[5]   He was an immediate suffragan of the patriarch.

After the fall of Tripoli in 1109 the entire north Syrian coast from Beirut to Seleucia was in Frankish hands. This was the one area where there had been Orthodox bishops before the Frankish conquest and where a transition from Orthodox to Latin bishops might most easily have been effected. It is therefore surprising that, except in Tripoli itself, where a Latin bishop was appointed by the count for political reasons, as has been discussed above, no Latin diocese was set up to the south of Jabala for some twenty years. The reason for this delay was a dispute about jurisdiction.

1. Walter the Chancellor, 'De Bello Antiocheno, Bello Primo', Art I, *RHC Occ*, V, p 83.
2. Tobler, Molinier, I, p 338, listed under its classical name, Germaniceia.
3. St Nerses of Lampron, 'Reflections on the Institutions of the Church and explanation of the Eucharistic Mystery', extracts, *RHC Arm*, I, p 577.
4. Charon, II, p 234.
5. Walter the Chancellor, 'De Bello Antiocheno', I, art V, *RHC Occ*, V, pp 91–2; J. Richard, *Le Comté de Tripoli sous la dynastie toulousaine (1102–87)*, Paris 1945, p 58, n 3, argues that Jabala was not a see but was confused by later scholars with the see of Gibelet. This opinion is untenable: both sees are named in the official papal list, Fabre, Duchesne, Mollat, *Liber Censuum*, I, p 239.

In the Orthodox tradition the ecclesiastical province of Tyre formed part of the patriarchate of Antioch. Its archbishop ranked first among the metropolitans of Antioch and ruled over thirteen suffragans, from Acre in the south to Tortosa in the north.[1] This system, which had been devised when the whole of Syria formed part of the Roman empire, created difficulties for the Franks. For the political boundary between the kingdom of Jerusalem and the county of Tripoli was fixed just north of Beirut and cut through the middle of the province of Tyre.

No problem arose when the Franks captured Acre in 1104, because no bishop was appointed there at that stage, but when Sidon and Beirut fell to Baldwin I in 1110 some ecclesiastical provision had to be made for them. Nobody denied that they formed part of the province of Tyre, but Baldwin I was naturally reluctant to concede that Tyre should be subject to the patriarch of Antioch over whom he had no control. The matter was referred to Rome by the king and the patriarch of Jerusalem and in 1111 they received a favourable reply from Paschal II who ruled that the ecclesiastical boundaries of Jerusalem and Antioch should follow the newly-established political frontiers between the Frankish states.[2] On this authority the patriarch of Jerusalem nominated a Latin bishop to Beirut: he was not consecrated because Bernard of Valence lodged an objection at Rome, stating that Tyre had traditionally formed part of his patriarchate. The pope replied to this tactfully, stating that he intended no derogation of the rights of the church of Antioch, but standing firm by his earlier judgment.[3] Bernard of Valence was not satisfied, and sent envoys to the papal council of Benevento in 1113 to raise the matter again. One observer at least was troubled by their appearance: 'two men', he reported, 'whose hair and beards were matted and waved, not, as it would seem, by design, but through neglect, threw themselves at the pope's feet'.[4] This comment suggests that already by the early years of the twelfth century the Franks in Syria were adopting different fashions from those prevalent in the west. The pope substantially upheld his earlier ruling: Baldwin I should keep control of the churches in his kingdom, which should come under the jurisdiction of the patriarch of Jerusalem, but Bernard of Valence should control those churches which clearly could be proved to belong to the church of Antioch. By this the pope presumably meant the diocese of Tripoli and the other

1. Tobler, Molinier, I, pp 331–2.
2. *PL*, 163, 289–90, nos 323–4; WT, XI, 28, *RHC Occ*, I, p 502.
3. *PL*, 163, 303–4, no 346; WT, *loc. cit.*, Baldwin, elect of Beirut, *CGOH*, vol II, p 899, no 4.
4. Pflugck-Harttung, II, p 205, no 247.

former Orthodox dioceses in that county.[1]   Bernard of Valence continued to press his claims to the province of Tyre and in 1118 Paschal II wrote to Baldwin I urging him to respect the traditional rights of the patriarch of Antioch, though not giving any specific injunctions about what form this should take.[2]

Rowe has traced the stages of this dispute and argues that, except in the case of Tripoli, no suffragans were consecrated in the province of Tyre until after that city was captured in 1124.[3] In 1127 the patriarch of Jerusalem consecrated an archbishop of Tyre, and pope Honorius II not merely confirmed this appointment, but also ordered that all the suffragans of Tyre should give canonical obedience to their archbishop who should be subject to the patriarch of Jerusalem.[4]   Bernard of Valence refused to accept this decision, which would have deprived him of ecclesiastical control over the county of Tripoli which he had exercised for a quarter of a century.   Indeed, it seems to have been at the point when an archbishop was nominated for Tyre that Bernard decided to create two new Latin bishoprics in the north of the province. These were at Tortosa, where a Latin bishop is first recorded in February 1128,[5] and Gibelet, the classical Byblos.   This see is exceptionally poorly documented in the twelfth century: the earliest evidence of a Latin bishopric there comes from 1138[6] but it seems probable that this was set up at the same time as Tortosa as part of the ecclesiastical reorganisation of the county of Tripoli. Both sees had been Orthodox bishoprics before the first crusade.[7]   Bernard of Valence refused throughout his life to obey the pope's injunction in regard to the province of Tyre: the bishops of Tripoli, Tortosa and Gibelet remained directly subject to him as their metropolitan and did not acknowledge the archbishop of Tyre.[8]

At about the same time as the subdivision of the Latin diocese of Tripoli was being carried out a similar reorganisation took place in the archdiocese of Apamea.   The Franks captured Rafaniyah in the north-west of the county of Tripoli in 1126 and immediately appointed a Latin bishop there.[9]   In the sixth century this city

1. *PL*, 163, 316, no 359; WT, XI, 28, *RHC Occ*, I, p 502.
2. *PL*, 163, 316—17, no 360; WT, *loc. cit.*
3. J.G. Rowe, 'The Papacy and the Ecclesiastical Province of Tyre', *BJRL*, 43, 1960—1, pp 160—90.
4. WT, XIII, 23, *RHC Occ*, I, pp 591—3.
5. *CGOH*, no 82.
6. de Rozière, pp 5—6, no 7; *RR*, I, p 44, no 175.
7. Charon, II, p 233.
8 WT, XIV, 13, *RHC Occ*, I, p 624.
9. Delaville Le Roulx, 'Inventaire des pièces de Terre Sainte de l'Ordre de l'Hôpital', *ROL*, 3, 1895, no 8, a document of 1128 in which bishop Gerald mentions his predecessor, Aimery.

had been a suffragan see of Apamea, but there does not seem to have been an Orthodox bishopric there in the twelfth century.[1] The erection of this see seems to have been another instance of the way in which strategic considerations, in this case the need to guard an important frontier town, dictated the religious settlement, so that the ruler might be represented by a bishop whom he helped to choose.

The small coastal city of Valania was also a suffragan see of Apamea, and probably did have an Orthodox bishop at the time of the Frankish conquest.[2] The city was captured by the Franks in 1109, but it is not clear when the first Latin bishop was appointed. The earliest record of one is found in a document of 1163, which mentions a former bishop, Gerald, who had died before the document was written.[3] It is therefore possible, though necessarily unproven, that the see of Valania was created at about the same time as that of Rafaniyah.

Towards the end of Bernard of Valence's long reign the huge archdiocese of Edessa was subdivided. The lands of Edessa west of the Euphrates had formerly been part of the province of Hierapolis, which ranked fifth in dignity among the metropolitan sees of Antioch.[4] Hierapolis itself was in Muslim hands throughout the crusader period, and the Frankish see of Hierapolis was therefore fixed at a place which the Franks called La Tulupe, but which Cahen has identified with Duluk, the classical Doliche, which had formerly been a suffragan see of Hierapolis.[5] A Latin archbishop of this province is first mentioned in two documents of 1134[6] which suggests that it had only recently been established then. Duluk is very near Tell Bashir, the Frankish capital of western Edessa,[7] and the date of its foundation suggests that it was set up by count Joscelin II of Edessa as an ecclesiastical centre for the western half of his state soon after his accession in 1131.

When Bernard of Valence died in 1135 the number of Latin bishoprics in the patriarchate had risen from five to fourteen. He cannot, of course, be given all the credit for this, for the foundation of a new diocese was a political as well as an ecclesiastical decision. What is remarkable about Bernard's pontificate is

1. Tobler, Molinier, I, pp 332–3.
2. Charon, II, p 234.
3. Paoli, pp 40–1, no 39.
4. Tobler, Molinier, I, p 333.
5. C. Cahen, *La Syrie du nord à l'époque des croisades et la principauté franque d'Antioche*, Paris 1940, p 115.
6. Kohler, p 129, no 19; *CGOH*, no 104.
7. WT, XVII, 17, *RHC Occ*, I, p 786.

the absence of friction between him and any of the thirteen rulers
who held power in the three northern states during that time.[1]
The close co-operation which existed between the patriarch and
the princes must have been important in devising an ecclesiastical
settlement for the northern states, and the Latin church of
Antioch took shape very largely under Bernard's guidance.
Wherever possible he followed the Orthodox tradition in deciding
on the location of new dioceses.[2] But perhaps his greatest contribution to the development of the Antiochene church was the firm
stand which he took about the province of Tyre. It is true that he
did not succeed in gaining control of Tyre itself or of its suffragan
sees in the kingdom of Jerusalem, but against the wishes of the
papacy he preserved the sees of Tyre in the county of Tripoli as
part of the patriarchate of Antioch. This had important consequences, for the county of Tripoli was to prove the most enduring
part of the Frankish dominions in north Syria.

The second Latin patriarch of Antioch, Ralph, was a very different kind of man from Bernard of Valence. He came from
Domfront in southern Normandy,[3] but nothing is known about
his early career except that by the end of Bernard's reign he had
been appointed archbishop of Mamistra.[4] When the patriarchate
fell vacant the senior Latin clergy met with the canons of Antioch
to choose a new primate. Ralph was not present at the meeting,
although he was in Antioch, but while the rest of the clergy were
conferring together he was acknowledged patriarch by popular
acclaim and enthroned in St Peter's basilica. As he was already
in bishop's orders he did not need to be consecrated, and he took
Bernard of Valence's *pallium* from the altar and invested himself
with it as a sign that his jurisdiction was valid.[5] The method of
his election was unique in the history of the Latin church in Syria
and the closest parallel to it in the recent history of the western
church was the election of pope Gregory VII.

William of Tyre, who had met Ralph of Domfront when he was
a boy, gives a vivid and not unsympathetic account of him:

> The Lord Ralph was a tall, handsome man. His eyes slanted a little, but
> not excessively so. He was not very well-educated, but was a fluent
> speaker and a cheerful companion and had good manners. Because he
> was very generous he gained the favour both of the knights and of the
> middle classes. He was not good at keeping promises and agreements

1. This number includes the regencies of Baldwin II and Fulk.
    2. Only Artah and Kesoun had not been Orthodox sees. Artah was made a see
before Bernard's accession.
    3. WT, XIV, 10, *RHC Occ*, I, p 619.
    4. de Rozière, p 167, no 86; Kohler, p 130, no 21.
    5. WT, XIV, 10, *RHC Occ*, I, p 620.

that he had made and would say first one thing and then another. He was a complex character, cunning, cautious and discerning. His one weakness was that he would not take back into favour those whom he had rightly antagonised when they wished to make their peace. He was called arrogant and conceited, and this was true.[1]

It is easy from this description to see why Ralph was popular with the laity, but popularity alone was not usually enough to secure a senior church appointment in the Frankish east. Normally such appointments were made by the lay ruler, using the mechanism of canonical election. That this could be by-passed in Ralph's case was due to the unusual political situation which obtained at Antioch in 1135.

Bohemond II had died in 1130 leaving as his heir a young child, Constance. Bohemond's widow, Alice, the sister of queen Melisende of Jerusalem, wished to act as regent, but she did not have the support of the baronage of Antioch who appealed to her brother-in-law, Fulk of Jerusalem, to take charge of the principality. Fulk came to Antioch in 1135 and agreed with the barons to send to the west for a husband for the young princess Constance, who could take over the government in his wife's name. The favoured candidate was Raymond of Poitiers, younger son of the duke of Aquitaine, to whom envoys were sent in the lifetime of Bernard of Valence.[2] While these negotiations were being conducted, in the winter of 1135–6, queen Melisende, who had recently been admitted to a full share of power in the kingdom of Jerusalem, persuaded her husband to relinquish the regency of Antioch in favour of her sister, the dowager princess Alice.[3] Alice's position was, however, weak, since she did not have the full support of the baronage, and this would explain why she did not attempt to oppose the appointment of Ralph as patriarch since he was the barons' candidate and she wished to avoid a confrontation with them that she might not win.

The election was irregular and in normal circumstances the pope might have been expected to intervene. This did not occur because the papacy itself was in a very difficult situation. Innocent II, who had been elected in 1130, was recognised in the Frankish east, but his rival, Anacletus II, who had been elected at

1. *Ibid.*, XV, 17, p 686.
2. *Ibid.*, XIV, 9, pp 618–19.
3. *Ibid.*, XIV, 20, p 636, dates this while the negotiations for Raymond's marriage were in progress. On Melisende, see H.E. Mayer, 'Studies in the History of Queen Melisende of Jerusalem', *DOP*, 26, 1972, pp 102–13; B. Hamilton, 'Women in the Crusader States; the Queens of Jerusalem', in D. Baker, ed, *Medieval Women*, Oxford 1978, pp 149–51.

the same time, was acknowledged by Roger II, king of Sicily. The Frankish population of Antioch were chiefly south Italian Normans, Roger of Sicily was the closest male kin of the princess Constance, and Innocent II may well have considered that any attempt on his part to challenge the validity of Ralph of Domfront's election would drive the church of Antioch to transfer its allegiance to the antipope who had Sicilian support. Ralph did not seek papal confirmation of his office, and is, indeed, reported to have had little respect for the holy see but to have considered his own see of Antioch, also a Petrine foundation, equal in authority to that of Rome.[1]

In 1136 prince Raymond arrived in Antioch, and Ralph exploited the political tensions which his coming generated to his own advantage. He lulled princess Alice into a sense of false security by assuring her that Raymond had come to marry her, not her daughter, but at the same time he made a bargain with Raymond that he would solemnise his marriage to Constance if the prince did liege homage to him as patriarch for the principality. Raymond, who was anxious to exercise full power, agreed to these terms: Ralph performed the marriage, Raymond became prince of Antioch, and the princess Alice, presented with a *fait accompli*, retired to her dower-lands at Latakia.[2]

At first the patriarch and the prince worked together harmoniously. It was at this time that the final measures were probably taken for the organisation of Latin dioceses. In Ralph's reign a Latin bishop of Latakia is first recorded.[3] This city was the chief port in north Syria, and, after changing hands frequently in the early years of Frankish settlement, it had been permanently incorporated in the principality of Antioch in 1108. It had been an Orthodox archbishopric, and Orthodox archbishops would seem to have remained there until the Frankish conquest.[4] It was in the patriarch's interest that proper provision should be made for the government of this important city, but the measure would also have suited prince Raymond, for Latakia was the residence of princess Alice, who was a possible focus for those discontented with his rule, and a bishop of that city who was nominated by the prince could inform Raymond of any treasonable activities on the part of his mother-in-law.

---

1. Roger II of Sicily was first cousin of Bohemond I of Antioch. Ralph's reported views on the Petrine status of Antioch, WT, XV, 13, *RHC Occ*, I, pp 678–9.
2. *Ibid.*, XIV, 20, XV, 12, pp 636–7, 676–7. The 'Eracles' says that Raymond 'fist au patriarche Raoul homage lige', *ibid.*, p 676.
3. *Ibid.*, XV, 16, p 683.
4. Charon, II, p 234.

It is also from Ralph's reign that the first evidence comes of the establishment of a Latin archbishopric at Corice.[1] Cahen is clearly correct in identifying this with Quris, the classical Cyrrhus, rather than with Corycus on the Cilician coast, since William of Tyre states that this archbishopric was in the county of Edessa.[2] Once again the patriarch followed Orthodox precedent, for in the sixth century Cyrrhus had been an archbishopric without suffragans.[3] This see must have been established in conjunction with Joscelin II of Edessa, with whom Ralph was on friendly terms.

So far Ralph had shown himself to be a skilful diplomat and had greatly increased his own power and the prestige of the church of Antioch. The chief source on his fall from power is William of Tyre, but William was writing many years later and shows little awareness of the complexities of the political situation in which Ralph was caught up. He explains Ralph's downfall simply in terms of the antagonism which Raymond of Poitiers felt towards him for making him do homage for the principality. Such an explanation is too simple, and in any case it does not entirely fit the facts, but it would be inappropriate in this work to give more than a brief resumé of the full reasons for Ralph's deposition. It is hoped to publish separately a more detailed examination of the circumstances.

One factor which Ralph could not have foreseen, but which totally changed the balance of power that he had established, was the military intervention of the Byzantine emperor, John II Comnenus. This seems to have taken the entire Frankish east completely by surprise, and with reason, since no Byzantine emperor had campaigned in north Syria for well over a century. John Comnenus brought his army to Cilicia in 1137. This province had become independent of Antioch under Armenian rulers in 1132, although no attempt seems to have been made to evict the Latin bishops from Tarsus and Mamistra.[4] The Latins were occupying Orthodox, not Armenian, sees and the Armenians had no love for the Orthodox or for the Byzantine empire. John Comnenus annexed Cilicia and expelled the Latin bishops,

---

1. WT, XV, 16, *RHC Occ*, I, p 683.
2. *Ibid.*, XV, 14, p 681; Cahen, *Syrie*, p 315. P. Fedalto, *La Chiesa Latina in Oriente*, II. *Hierarchia Latina Orientalis*, Verona 1976, p 96, wrongly identifies this see with Corycus in Cilicia.
3. Tobler, Molinier, I, p 337.
4. S. Der Nersessian, 'The Kingdom of Cilician Armenia', in Setton, II, pp 636–7. Archbishop Stephen of Tarsus is recorded in 1135, de Rozière, p 167, no 86, and 1140, WT, XV, 16, *RHC Occ*, I, p 683. Gaufridus, or Gaudinus, was appointed to succeed Ralph of Domfront at Mamistra in 1135, de Rozière, pp 171, 177, nos 88–9.

replacing them with Orthodox ones.[1]   He then marched on
Antioch and demanded the homage of Raymond of Poitiers.
After consulting king Fulk of Jerusalem, who advised him to
submit,[2] Raymond did homage for his lands to the emperor in
the late summer of 1137.[3]   It was widely supposed, and not without reason, that the emperor would require the restitution of an
Orthodox patriarch in Antioch[4] and thus Ralph's position became
doubly insecure: by doing homage to the emperor, albeit against
his own inclinations, prince Raymond had ended the legal fiction
that Antioch was a fief of the church, but it also seemed possible
that Ralph would be deposed in favour of an Orthodox patriarch
as part of the political settlement.   It may be inferred that at this
point Ralph wrote to the pope complaining about the threat
which the Byzantine presence in north Syria constituted to the
Latin church, for on 28 March 1138 Innocent II wrote an
encyclical to all Latin Christians serving in the Byzantine army
forbidding them to take part in an attack on Antioch or any other
Frankish city under pain of excommunication.[5]

Intervention by the patriarch at this time must have been highly
embarrassing to prince Raymond: the Byzantine armies were still
in north Syria and could not be disregarded, neither could the
growing power of Zengi, ruler of Aleppo and Mosul, who might be
held in check by a joint Byzantine and Frankish alliance.   It seems
to have been this reason which led Raymond of Poitiers to encourage archdeacon Lambert of Antioch and canon Arnulf to appeal
to the pope against Ralph of Domfront with whom they had had
a violent quarrel about church property.[6]   Ralph had to go to
Rome to answer the charges against him and was thus unable to
intervene in the affairs of Antioch.

Ralph faced serious accusations.   In addition to the specific
complaints made by Lambert and Arnulf he was also accused of
simony, incontinence and of having been irregularly elected.[7]
Nevertheless, Ralph was well received by the pope, for whatever

1. Odo of Deuil, *De Profectione Ludovici VII in Orientem*, bk IV, ed and trans V.G.
Berry, New York, 1948, p 68.
2. Orderic Vitalis, *The Ecclesiastical History*, XIII, 34, ed and trans M. Chibnall,
vols 2–6, Oxford 1969–78, VI, pp 502–6.
3. Nicetas Choniates, *Historia, De Iohanne Comneno*, ed J.A. Van Dieten, 2 vols,
Berlin 1975, *Corpus Fontium Historiae Byzantinae*, XI (I and II), p 27.
4. In 1108 Alexius I had made Bohemond I agree to the restoration of a Greek
patriarch at Antioch, Anna Comnena, *Alexiad*, XIII, 12, s 20, ed Leib, III, p 134. Gibb,
Damascus Chronicle, p 245, states that Raymond agreed to the restoration of a Greek
patriarch in 1138.
5. de Rozière, pp 86–7, no 47.
6. WT, XV, 12, *RHC Occ*, I, pp 677–8.
7. *Ibid.*, XV, 16, p 684.

his other defects may have been he was a strenuous upholder of the rights of the Latin church in Syria against what the pope regarded as Byzantine aggression. Moreover, the long papal schism had just come to an end: Anacletus II had died in 1137 and his successor, the antipope Victor IV, had abdicated in May 1138. Innocent II was thus for the first time the undisputed head of the western Church and was anxious to restore peace throughout Latin Christendom. He therefore treated Ralph leniently, granted him a *pallium*, which regularised his election, and agreed to appoint a legate who should come to Antioch and adjudicate in the dispute between the patriarch and the canons. Ralph had won over the pope, but he must have realised that the final decision about his future would rest with Raymond of Poitiers, on whose advice the legate would rely when he came to Syria. The patriarch therefore sought a new ally, and found one in Roger II of Sicily with whom he stayed on his way home. He returned to Antioch in the spring of 1139 with an escort of Sicilian galleys.[1]

This was a dangerous game to play. Roger II was powerful and, like the patriarch, hostile to Byzantium. But he was also heir-presumptive to the principality of Antioch and therefore a potential threat to Raymond of Poitiers.[2] Ralph may well have reckoned that if he had such a powerful supporter the prince of Antioch would not dare to depose him, but it was equally possible, as the sequel was to show, that the prince might be forced to secure his deposition precisely because he was too powerful and because his loyalty was suspect. By the time Ralph reached Syria the political situation had changed. The emperor John and his troops had withdrawn, having campaigned against the Muslims. The presence of Byzantine troops had acted as a deterrent to Zengi, which lasted as long as John Comnenus lived; their departure had removed the threat to Raymond's control of Antioch.[3] Raymond was therefore much more securely in power than he had been a year earlier and viewed the prospect of Sicilian intervention in the affairs of Antioch with disfavour. He refused to allow Ralph into his dominions and the patriarch sought refuge with count Joscelin of Edessa.[4]

1. *Ibid.*, XV, 13, pp 678—9.
2. Constance of Antioch was the only living descendant of Bohemond I. Roger II of Sicily had made good his claim to be heir to the lands of Bohemond's younger brother, Roger of Apulia, when his line became extinct in 1127, and was the nearest in line of succession to the principality of Antioch. On Roger's relations with Byzantium, P. Lamma, *Comneni e Staufer*, 2 vols, Rome 1955—7, I, pp 24—39.
3. J.M. Hussey, 'Byzantium and the Crusades, 1081—1204', in Setton, II, pp 132—4; H.A.R. Gibb, 'Zengi and the fall of Edessa', *ibid.*, I, pp 458—60.
4. WT, XV, 14, *RHC Occ*, I, pp 680—1.

Raymond subsequently relented and allowed Ralph to return to Antioch, probably when he learned that the pope's legate, the archbishop of Lyons, had arrived at Acre.[1]   At this stage an accommodation might have been reached between the prince and the patriarch. Certainly Ralph's enemies tried to make their peace with him, probably at Raymond's suggestion.   Lambert was reinstated as archdeacon of Antioch, but Ralph refused to receive canon Arnulf back into favour, holding him, rightly it would seem, responsible for many of his own troubles.   Raymond of Poitiers clearly thought that it would be impossible to work with a man of this imperious temper and encouraged Arnulf to appeal to the pope once more.[2]

Because the archbishop of Lyons had died, Innocent II sent a new legate to Syria, Alberic, cardinal of Ostia. The date of his mission has been disputed, but a consideration of all the evidence shows that it occurred in 1140.[3] The cardinal convoked a council at Antioch on 30 November 1140 to investigate the charges against Ralph. This was attended not only by the Latin bishops of Antioch, but by a delegation from the southern kingdom, led by the patriarch, William of Jerusalem, and comprising also the archbishops of Caesarea and Tyre and the bishops of Bethlehem, Sidon and Beirut.[4]   The majority of bishops were hostile to Ralph: on the whole the three archbishops of the county of Edessa, whose ruler was well-disposed towards the patriarch, took his side, whereas the more numerous bishops of Antioch followed the lead of their prince in opposing him. The Jerusalem delegation might have been expected to remain impartial, but it is doubtful whether they were, since the whole question of the ecclesiastical obedience of the province of Tyre had been raised again in Ralph's reign and, like his predecessor, Bernard of Valence, he had defied the pope and withheld the obedience of the three bishops of Tripoli from the archbishop of Tyre.[5] By doing this he had antagonised not only the archbishop of Tyre, but also the patriarch of Jerusalem.

There seems no reason to doubt the assertion of William of Tyre that the council condemned Ralph because it was coerced by Raymond of Poitiers. Only one bishop, Serlo of Apamea, spoke in the patriarch's favour: he merely said that he refused to sit in judgment on his canonical superior, but the legate took massive retaliation against him, excommunicating him and degrading him

1. He died at Acre soon afterwards.
2. WT, XV, 15, *RHC Occ*, I, pp 681–2.
3. See Appendix below.
4. WT, XV, 16, *RHC Occ*, I, p 683.
5. *Ibid.*, XIV, 13, pp 624–5.

from the orders of bishop and priest. Ralph himself refused to attend the court, less, it would seem, because he questioned the legate's right to hear the case, than because he feared coercion from the prince's soldiers. He enjoyed great popular support in Antioch, but it was not enough to save him from arrest by the prince's troops when he failed to appear before the synod on the third day of its session. On 2 December he was declared deposed and was imprisoned in the monastery of St Symeon.[1] Some years later, probably in 1144, he escaped from captivity and fled to Rome where he appealed against his deposition to the pope.[2] His case was reopened and this time judgment was given in his favour, but he died (naturally it was said as a result of poison), before he could return to north Syria.[3]

Ralph of Domfront was clearly a very gifted man and an attractive personality, but his abilities would have been more valuable in a lay ruler than in a prince of the church. His career is symptomatic of the problem which faced rulers throughout Latin Christendom in the twelfth century when making church appointments: they needed men with secular abilities to whom they could delegate some of the routine work of government and who could deputise for them in a crisis, but it was difficult to find men with these qualities who were not also ambitious for temporal power. Ralph's reign was short, much of it was spent in litigation with the prince, and he had little opportunity to undertake work of a purely ecclesiastical kind. In so far as the opportunity to do so arose he behaved in a conservative way. When establishing new sees he respected Orthodox traditions; in the dispute about the province of Tyre he continued the policies of Bernard of Valence; in his opposition to the restoration of a Greek patriarch in Antioch he followed the policy which all popes had adopted since the death of Urban II; even in persuading Raymond of Poitiers to hold Antioch as a fief of the church he was merely following the precedent which had been established by the patriarch Daimbert in the case of Bohemond. Yet, although in ecclesiastical affairs his short reign showed a strong continuity with the work of his predecessor, in other ways it produced a lack of harmony among the small Frankish ruling class in north Syria at a time when unity was essential in the face of growing

1. *Ibid.*, XV, 16–17, pp 684–6.

2. William of Tyre says merely that Ralph was 'in monasterio diu detentus', but his escape would seem to be connected with the sending of Hugh, bishop of Jabala, to Rome by the patriarch Aimery in 1144–5, Otto of Freising, 'Chronica', VII, 33, ed A. Hofmeister, *MG-H SS rerum Germanicarum in usum scholarum*, Hanover, Leipzig 1912, pp 363–5.

3. WT, XV, 17, *RHC Occ*, I, p 686.

Muslim power.

During Ralph's term of office the organisation of the Latin church of Antioch reached its final form: no new sees were subsequently established there. In the first forty years of the twelfth century the Franks had made a genuine attempt to restore the patriarchate of Antioch as it had existed before the Arab conquest, using the sixth-century episcopal lists as their guide. They failed to gain control of eight of the thirteen provinces which had once formed part of the patriarchate: Amida (Diyar-Bakr), Sergiopolis, Theodosiopolis, Damascus, Homs, and Bosra in distant Arabia Petraea, remained in Muslim hands; the province of Anazarba in Cilicia was disputed between Byzantines and Armenians; while Seleucia of Isauria had in the eighth century been transferred from the jurisdiction of Antioch to that of Constantinople.[1] The remaining five provinces, Tyre, Tarsus, Edessa, Apamea and Hierapolis were either partially or totally in Frankish hands, and in all of them metropolitan archbishops were appointed, although it is true that Tyre and part of its province was removed from the jurisdiction of Antioch by papal fiat. In the case of Tyre, Apamea and Antioch itself suffragan sees were founded, and it is likely that a similar policy would have been followed in the other provinces as well if those areas had remained in Frankish control for longer.

The church of Antioch suffered a great deal from the resurgence of Muslim power in north Syria after Ralph of Domfront's deposition. It was guided in that troubled period by Aimery of Limoges, who succeeded Ralph as the nominee of Raymond of Poitiers. Aimery had grown up in France, but had come to Antioch because his uncle, Peter Armoin, was castellan of the city. According to William of Tyre the patriarch Ralph appointed Aimery dean of Antioch in order to secure his support in his struggle with the prince, but Aimery, while accepting the office, gave his loyalty to Raymond.[2] He is recorded as dean in two documents of April 1140[3] and was chosen to succeed Ralph soon after his deposition although he was only in subdeacon's orders. William of Tyre describes him as 'illiterate and of doubtful moral character',[4] but this

1. Charon, II, p 235. The province of Seleucia was transferred to Constantinople by Leo III in the eighth century and restored to Antioch after the Byzantine reconquest of 968. In the twelfth century it was an Orthodox province although it is uncertain whether it formed part of the patriarchate of Constantinople or of the Orthodox patriarchate of Antioch.

2. WT, XV, 18, *RHC Occ*, I, p 688.

3. de Rozière, pp 171, 177, nos 88–9.

4. 'hominem absque litteris, et conversationis non satis honestae', WT, XV, 18, *RHC Occ*, I, p 688.

judgment is not confirmed in any other source and must therefore be treated with some degree of caution. William had a reason for disliking Aimery: he was archbishop of Tyre while Aimery was patriarch and, like his predecessors, Aimery refused to relinquish his control over the churches of Tyre in the county of Tripoli, a matter about which William had strong feelings.

The early years of Aimery's pontificate cannot have been easy. It is true that he had the support of prince Raymond, but the bishops of Edessa were supporters of the deposed patriarch Ralph. When Ralph escaped from prison and went to Rome in person to appeal to the pope, Aimery's position as patriarch was called in question. He sent the bishop of Jabala to represent him at the curia, but apparently lost the case and it was only the timely death of Ralph which left him undisputed head of the church of Antioch.[1]

But by that time he was already showing himself to be a political realist who placed the interests of the whole Frankish community in north Syria above the narrow sectional interests of the Latin church. Before he came to power, Zengi of Mosul had captured the Latin cathedral city of Rafaniyah on the frontier of Tripoli. Bishop Gerald had escaped, and was still alive in 1139, when he witnessed a charter.[2] He is mentioned in no later source and it must be presumed that he died soon afterwards. Aimery of Limoges did not appoint a successor to him, even though a substantial part of the diocese remained in Christian hands. These lands, including the fortress of Crac des Chevaliers, were given to the Hospital of St John by Raymond II of Tripoli in 1144, together with Rafaniyah itself if it could be recaptured from the Saracens.[3] In the absence of a diocesan this territory was virtually exempt from the patriarch's jurisdiction, but Aimery, who could have nominated a new bishop to represent him there, did not do so, and was willing to acquiesce in the creation of what was, in effect, a palatinate lordship of the Hospital; it must be supposed because he considered that this was what was demanded by the defence needs of north Syria.

In his dealings with the Byzantine emperor Aimery was just as intransigent as Ralph of Domfront had been. The emperor John returned to Cilicia in the autumn of 1142 and on this occasion demanded the surrender of the city of Antioch. This was probably a tactical mistake, since it hardened Raymond of Poitiers and the Frankish barons of Antioch in opposition to his

1. *Ibid.*, XV, 17, p 686; Otto of Freising, 'Chronica', VII, 33, pp 363–5.
2. *CGOH*, vol II, p 901, no 7.
3. *CGOH*, no 144, see note 7, p 23 above.

demands, whereas they would probably have been ready to agree to renew homage to him. Aimery did not wish to see Antioch in Byzantine hands either, since that would certainly have meant the restoration of an Orthodox patriarch there. The bishop of Jabala was empowered by the prince and the patriarch to convey to the emperor their total rejection of his terms. John could not attack Antioch in the winter, but it was only his unexpected death in a hunting accident early in the following spring which saved Antioch from a Byzantine siege. His designated heir, Manuel, who was with him on campaign, had to return to Constantinople to be crowned and to assume control of the government.[1]

The Byzantines did not return to Syria for many years, but their departure, while relieving the government of Antioch of certain problems, created others. Zengi of Mosul had undoubtedly been deterred from attacking the Franks by John Comnenus's exercise of suzerainty in north Syria. Once John was dead he had no further reason for restraint. On Christmas eve 1144 he captured Edessa and archbishop Hugh, the Latin metropolitan, was killed in the crush of people who were trying to take refuge in the citadel after the walls had been breached.[2] The Muslims subsequently occupied all the lands of eastern Edessa as far as the Euphrates. The assassination of Zengi in 1146 gave the Franks no respite, for his son, Nur-ad-Din, was an equally efficient ruler, and in 1147 captured much of the land of Antioch to the east of the Orontes including the cathedral city of Artah.[3] The fiasco of the second crusade, which reached Syria in 1148, showed the Muslims that they had nothing to fear from western relief forces, and the defeat of the army of Antioch and the death of prince Raymond of Poitiers at the hands of Nur-ad-Din in 1149 opened the way for a new round of Muslim conquests in the north.

In 1149 Nur-ad-Din captured Apamea, one of the metropolitan sees of Antioch,[4] and the lands of northern Antioch and western Edessa were attacked simultaneously by the forces of Nur-ad-Din and those of Masud, Seljuk sultan of Iconium and Kara Arslan, the Artukid prince of Hisn Kaifa. Marash fell in 1149 and, although the Latin bishop was given a safe-conduct by the Muslim conquerors, he was killed while travelling to Antioch.[5] When Joscelin II of Edessa was captured by one of Nur-ad-Din's

1. Otto of Freising, 'Chronica', VII, 28, pp 354–5; Hussey in Setton, II, pp 134–5.
2. WT, XVI, 5, *RHC Occ*, I, pp 711–12; MS, XVII, 2, vol III, pp 260–2; *Anon 1234*, 'HC', c 415, p 94; Gregory the Priest, 'Continuation of the Chronicle of Matthew of Edessa', *RHC Arm*, I, p 158.
3. Ibn al-Athir, 'Sum of World History', *RHC Or*, I, pp 461–2.
4. H.A.R. Gibb, 'The Career of Nur-ad-Din', in Setton, I, p 516.
5. MS, XVII, 10, vol III, p 290.

lieutenants later that year, his wife, Beatrice, sold her remaining castles in western Edessa to the Byzantine emperor, Manuel, but his troops were unable to hold them and by 1151 all of them had passed into Muslim hands.[1] The Muslims thus gained control of the Latin sees of Hierapolis, Quris and Kesoun.[2]

Thus within ten years of Aimery's becoming patriarch the number of Latin sees subject to him had been halved. Among the churches which were lost were all the metropolitan sees: both the Cilician archbishoprics were in Byzantine hands and had Orthodox incumbents who did not recognise the Latin patriarch of Antioch, while the Muslims held the metropolitan see of Apamea and the three archbishoprics of Edessa. The only sees which remained in Frankish control were the six coastal bishoprics of Latakia, Jabala, Valania, Tortosa, Tripoli and Gibelet. Aimery was a pragmatist: he did not attempt artificially to sustain the prestige of the church of Antioch by nominating titular bishops to the sees which were in Muslim or Byzantine hands. The only exception to this rule was the archdiocese of Apamea. This was a special case, since although the Franks never regained control of the cathedral city much of the diocese remained in their hands, and throughout Aimery's reign archbishops were appointed to this see.[3] Possibly this was a matter of administrative convenience, since a metropolitan archbishop of Apamea with few administrative duties in his own diocese could deputise at need for the Latin patriarch of Antioch.

This is the context in which Aimery's dispute with a papal legate, Guido, cardinal of Florence, occurred. Guido reached the Holy Land in 1149, shortly after the death of prince Raymond, and convoked a synod at Jerusalem. The patriarch of Antioch replied that he was unable to attend because of the political situation in north Syria, and also forbade any of his suffragans to represent him. This caused particular problems for the bishop-elect of Tripoli, whom the cardinal summoned by name, but who, acting on Aimery's instructions, refused to attend. His election was quashed by the legate and he had to go to Rome in

1. F. Chalandon, Les Comnènes: Jean II Comnène (1118–43) et Manuel I Comnène (1143–80), 2 vols, Paris 1912, II, pp 422–6.

2. WT, XVII, 17, RHC Occ, I, p 789.

3. CGOH, no 474 records archbishop Gerald of Apamea in 1174–5. An archbishop of Apamea was present in Limassol in 1191 at the marriage of Richard I of England and Berengaria of Navarre, The Chronicle of the Reigns of Henry II and Richard I, ed W. Stubbs, 2 vols, London 1867, RS, 49, II, p 166; Chronica Magistri Rogeri de Houedene, ed W. Stubbs, 4 vols, London 1868–71, RS, 51, III, p 110. The archdiocese of Apamea extended to the Syrian coast between the river Thrascaia, northern boundary of the diocese of Latakia, and the Orontes, Charon, II, p 234.

person to have the sentence reversed by the pope.[1]   Cahen has
suggested that Aimery may have imposed this ban on his suffragans because he feared that his own election would once again be
called in question.[2]   It seems more probable that he feared that
the matter of Tyre might be raised at the synod, and that his
suffragan might be coerced into recognising the archbishop of
Tyre and the patriarch of Jerusalem.   In 1149 this was a more
serious problem than it had been in the days of Bernard of
Valence, for if Gibelet, Tripoli and Tortosa were restored to the
archbishop of Tyre the patriarch of Antioch would be left with
only three suffragan bishops and one titular archbishop.
Throughout his reign Aimery refused to relinquish control over
the dioceses of the county of Tripoli, which was a matter of acute
grievance to William of Tyre.[3]

When Raymond of Poitiers was killed, Aimery was left in virtual
command of Antioch. Raymond's widow, Constance, was princess
in her own right and had a young son, Bohemond III, who would
one day succeed her, but the armies of Nur-ad-Din posed a
threat to what was left of the principality which made it seem
impractical to leave the government in the hands of a woman and
Baldwin III of Jerusalem intervened and gave the patriarch the
powers of regent.[4]   Aimery proved a capable ruler in this time of
crisis and even paid the army from his own treasure.[5]

A churchman could not, however, be an effective military
leader: he might accompany his troops into battle, but he usually
took no part in the fighting, and a military leader was clearly what
was needed in Antioch at this time. The obvious solution was that
the princess Constance should remarry, and accordingly in 1152
Baldwin III held a council at Tripoli to which he summoned
Constance and the barons of Antioch, together with the patriarch
and his suffragans.   The chief item to be discussed was the remarriage of Constance, and the council was also attended by
Baldwin's mother, queen Melisende, and her sister, Hodierna,
countess of Tripoli, both aunts of the princess Constance, presumably in the hope that they would be able to make their niece see
reason.   Constance rejected all the highly-suitable prospective
husbands who were suggested for her, and William of Tyre
blamed the patriarch for her stubbornness, accusing him of

    1. Anonymous continuator of Sigebert of Gembloux, 'Historia Pontificalis', c 36,
MGH SS, XX, pp 540–1.
    2. Cahen, *Syrie*, p 505.
    3. WT, XIV, 14, *RHC Occ*, I, pp 626–7.
    4. MS, XVII, 10, vol III, p 290; Bar Hebraeus, *The Chronography*, ed and trans
E.A. Wallis Budge, 2 vols, Oxford 1932, I, p 275.
    5. WT, XVII, 10, *RHC Occ*, I, p 775.

wishing to retain sole power in his own hands.[1] This is hypothetical, and does not take into account the fact that the princess
might have had a will of her own; certainly few of the women in
her family willingly acquiesced in letting other people make
decisions for them.

It is a matter of fact that a year later Constance married a man
of whom her aunts might not have approved, Reynald of Châtillon, a knight of not very distinguished birth, who had accompanied Louis VII on the second crusade, stayed on in Syria and
served as a mercenary.[2] In making this marriage she was
certainly not influenced by the patriarch, who was at no pains to
conceal his disapproval of it. Reynald thus became prince of
Antioch, and Aimery's secular rule, which had lasted for four
years, came to an end. It was not likely that the two would work
harmoniously together, but the form which their quarrel took
startled Frankish Syria and was viewed with mild surprise even
in Constantinople. The cause was predictable: the prince needed
money to run his government, the patriarch was known to be rich,
but he refused to subsidise Reynald. Reynald's reaction was
extravagant even judged by the standards of a more flamboyant
age. The prince had the patriarch beaten, he was then stripped,
and his wounds were covered with honey, and he was stood on the
tower of the citadel of Antioch, a prey to the insects which infest
a Syrian summer. Public opinion was much shocked by this
unedifying quarrel. King Baldwin III sent a delegation of bishops
to Antioch to mediate peace, and Reynald's penitence was as
colourful as his anger had been. He set the patriarch free,
restored all his goods to him, and walked beside him through the
streets of Antioch holding the bridle of the patriarch's mare.
Nevertheless, Aimery refused to stay in Antioch and returned to
Jerusalem with king Baldwin's envoys. These events took place
probably in 1154.[3]

Aimery stayed in Jerusalem for some years. The opportunity
for him to return to Antioch was provided, ironically in view of
his earlier attitude towards John Comnenus, by renewed Byzantine intervention in north Syria. Reynald of Châtillon was the
immediate cause of this, for in 1156 he had raided the rich
Byzantine island of Cyprus. The Byzantine historian Cinnamus

1. *Ibid.*, XVII, 18, p 790; Mayer, 'Queen Melisende', *DOP*, 26, 1972, p 160;
Hamilton, in Baker, *Medieval Women*, p 154, n 59.

2. WT, XVII, 21, 26, *RHC Occ*, I, pp 796, 802; B. Hamilton, 'The elephant of
Christ: Reynald of Châtillon', *SCH*, 15, 1978, pp 97–8.

3. WT, XVIII, 1, *RHC Occ*, I, pp 816–17; John Cinnamus, *Epitome rerum ab
Ioanne et Alexio (sic) Comnenis gestarum*, IV, 18, ed A. Meineke, *CSHB*, Bonn 1836,
pp 181–3.

reports that when it was known in Jerusalem that the emperor
Manuel was coming to Syria with an army Aimery wrote to him,
offering to capture prince Reynald and hand him over to the
emperor, to which Manuel is alleged to have replied that he
wished to be victorious in a fair fight and not through fraud.[1]
This simple story may mask a more complicated diplomatic
exchange, for the patriarch, who must have feared that Manuel
would restore an Orthodox patriarch in Antioch, may have offered
to secure the submission of Reynald in return for being left in
control of the city himself, and Manuel may not have wished to
commit himself so explicitly.

Baldwin III of Jerusalem went to Antioch to meet the emperor
and Aimery accompanied him and presided at the liturgy on
Easter day 1159 when Manuel came to give thanks for a successful campaign at Antioch cathedral.[2] Manuel did not try to impose
a Greek patriarch on Antioch at this stage, perhaps he had learned
from his father's experience. He had forced an humiliating submission on Reynald of Châtillon and was welcomed by most of
the Franks, including Baldwin III, as a defender against the growing power of Nur-ad-Din. He may have been anxious not to
disturb the Frankish alliance by interfering with the religious
settlement at Antioch. When the emperor left Syria later that
year Aimery remained in Antioch: he did so with the tacit approval of the emperor who was the acknowledged overlord of the
principality and therefore had nothing to fear from prince
Reynald. Nor did the two men have to work together for very
long, for in the autumn of 1161 Reynald was captured by Nur-ad-
Din's forces and imprisoned at Aleppo.[3]

Prince Bohemond III was still only twelve, but the princess
Constance was older and more self-assured than she had been in
1149 and assumed control of the government herself. Her position was also much stronger because in 1161 the emperor Manuel
married her daughter Maria as his second wife. The barons of
Antioch throughout the twelfth century showed a deep-rooted
dislike of being ruled by a woman, and they found an ally in the
patriarch, who no doubt resented the fact that he had not been
asked to act as regent. The barons wished to invest Bohemond
III with power and, when Constance appealed against them to
Manuel, her opponents, led by the patriarch, summoned the

1. He was in Jerusalem in 1158 and solemnised the marriage of Baldwin III and
Theodora Comnena, WT, XVIII, 22, RHC Occ, I, p 858; Cinnamus, loc.cit.

2. Cinnamus, IV, 21A, pp 187–8.

3. WT, XVIII, 28, RHC Occ, I, pp 868–9; Kamal-ad-Din, 'History of Aleppo', trans
E. Blochet, ROL, 3, 1895, p 533. Concerning the date of this, Hamilton, 'Reynald of
Châtillon', SCH, 15, 1978, p 98, n 13.

Armenian prince Thoros to their aid. Manuel was too committed to affairs in the Balkans to send any help, so Constance was removed from power in 1163 and Bohemond recognised as prince.[1] Since the young prince owed his power to the patriarch and was inexperienced in the arts of government, it seemed that Aimery had regained the position of *eminence grise* in the principality which he had held after the death of Raymond of Poitiers.

In 1164 the confederate armies of Frankish north Syria were defeated by Nur-ad-Din and Bohemond III was among the many eminent Franks who were taken prisoner. There was nothing to prevent Nur-ad-Din from following up his victory by launching an attack on Antioch itself. Aimery took charge of the government and wrote to Louis VII of France, whom he had met on the second crusade, to ask for his help.[2] No help came from the west, but the expected Muslim attack did not come either. Nur-ad-Din, it seemed, still feared Byzantine reprisals if he attacked Antioch and in 1165 he released Bohemond on parole on condition that he paid a large ransom. The young prince went to Constantinople to ask Manuel, his brother-in-law, for financial aid, which Manuel gave him on condition that an Orthodox patriarch was restored in Antioch. So Bohemond returned later that year with the titular patriarch, Athanasius III.[3]

The significance of this appointment for relations between the Latin church and the Orthodox will be discussed more fully in a later chapter:[4] what concerns the present argument is the reaction of Aimery of Limoges. Although expelled from his cathedral, Aimery did not go to live in Jerusalem as he might have been expected to do. He anathematized those Franks at Antioch who recognised his rival and went to live in the castle of Qusair, a few miles south of Antioch.[5] This virtually impregnable fortress had been captured (or perhaps recaptured) from the Muslims by king Fulk while he was *bailli* of Antioch in 1134:[6] he may have handed it over to Bernard of Valence. Certainly it had come into the possession of the patriarchs of Antioch by 1165. Aimery was restored to power not by any change of policy on the part of Bohemond III but by a fortuitous circumstance. In 1170 there was a severe earthquake, which damaged the walls of Antioch and

---

1. MS, XVIII, 10, vol III, p 324.
2. *PL*, 201, 1403–7.
3. MS, XVIII, 11, vol III, p 326.
4. See chapter 7 below.
5. MS, XVIII, 11, vol III, p 326; R. Dussaud, *Topographie historique de la Syrie antique et médiévale*, Paris 1927, p 429.
6. MS, XVI, 5, vol III, p 234.

the sanctuary of the cathedral, and among the injured was the Orthodox patriarch, Athanasius. Prince Bohemond and his advisers interpreted this calamity as a sign of God's anger with them for the way in which they had slighted the Latin patriarch and, dressed in sackcloth, Bohemond rode to Qusair to beg Aimery to return. Aimery agreed to do so only if his injured rival were first carried out of the city. Athanasius subsequently died of his wounds, the cathedral was rebuilt, and Aimery once again ruled over the church of Antioch.[1]

Aimery did not find it any easier to work harmoniously with Bohemond III than he had with the princess Constance or with Reynald of Châtillon. The occasion of the dispute between them was the repudiation by Bohemond of his Byzantine wife, Theodora, in 1181 and his remarriage to a certain Sibyl. Although Aimery viewed the pro-Byzantine policies of the princes of Antioch with disfavour, he was staunch in his defence of the principles of canon law and excommunicated the prince and the priest who had performed the second marriage. The dispute then escalated, for Bohemond confiscated church property and arrested the clergy who resisted him. The patriarch and his household took refuge in 'a certain *municipium* of the church', probably the castle of Qusair, and the lord of al-Marqab defied the prince and offered asylum to other church leaders in his castle. The patriarch then placed the principality under an interdict. Although its formal causes were dissimilar, this quarrel bore a striking resemblance to that between Aimery and Reynald of Châtillon a quarter of a century before and the underlying reasons for the animosity between the prince and the patriarch were probably identical. The prince of Antioch in both cases was in desperate need of money, for he had lost much territory, yet his defence costs remained high: the church of Antioch had great wealth, but the patriarch refused to place it at the disposal of the state. In both cases the dispute was settled in the same way: intervention by the Franks of Jerusalem who feared that a civil war in Antioch would weaken all the Frankish states in the east. An imposing delegation of noblemen and clergy from the kingdom of Jerusalem came to the north and held a conference at Latakia with the prince and the patriarch. Among the delegates was Reynald of Châtillon, now lord of Oultrejourdain, who was Bohemond III's stepfather, and who alone of those present had practical experience of the tensions that could develop between a prince of Antioch and this particular patriarch. A compromise solution was effected: Bohemond III restored church property and released the clergy,

---

1. *Ibid.*, XIX, 6, p 339.

and in return Aimery lifted the interdict. It was, however, resolved that the prince should remain excommunicate until his matrimonial position had been regularised.[1] Although Bohemond never put away his second wife, he and Aimery thereafter worked in harmony, for Aimery had vindicated the independence of the church of Antioch from secular control.

Aimery did not put the interests of the church above those of the state, even though he was unwilling to allow secular rulers to dictate how the church spent its money. Throughout his reign the power of the military orders grew in his patriarchate. This was not without problems for the secular church, since these orders were exempt from the jurisdiction of bishops and attracted money away from the secular clergy, a point which will be discussed at more length in a later chapter. Aimery, who saw that the military orders were essential for the defence of Frankish lands in north Syria, never raised any objection to their being granted wide jurisdiction.   In 1152 the bishop of Tortosa asked the Knights Templar to take charge of the defence of Tortosa, which they agreed to do provided that they were granted wide powers of ecclesiastical patronage in the diocese. Aimery, as patriarch and metropolitan of the see of Tortosa, must have given his assent to this arrangement even though it considerably diminished the powers of the secular church.[2]   As the years passed and the threat of Muslim aggression became greater Aimery even encouraged the growth of the power of the orders. •It was at his suggestion in 1180 that Bohemond offered to the order of St James of the Sword the fief of Bikisrail, which was then in Muslim hands, if they could reconquer it within a year.[3] This grant was not taken up, but it reflects the patriarch's awareness of the defence needs of the principality.   In 1186 Aimery advised Bohemond to allow Bertrand le Mazoir to sell his fief of al-Marqab to the knights of St John.   This comprised the cathedral city and most of the diocese of Valania and was therefore not without future problems for the Latin patriarchate. Yet Bertrand declared that he could not defend the principal castle of al-Marqab, 'so necessary to the Christian cause, because of the great expense involved and because of the nearness of the enemy', and Aimery therefore encouraged Bohemond to allow this fief to be transferred to the Hospital which was in a position to provide for its defence.[4] The patriarch's

1. *Ibid.*, XXI, 2, p 389; WT, XXII, 6–7, *RHC Occ*, I, pp 1071–5.
2. J. Riley-Smith, 'The Templars and the castle of Tortosa in Syria: an unknown document concerning the acquisition of the fortress', *EHR*, 84, 1969, pp 284–8.
3. A.F. Aguado de Cordova, A.A. Aleman de Rosales, I.L. Agurleta, eds, *Bullarium Equestris Ordinis S. Iacobi de Spatha*, Madrid 1719, pp 22–3.
4. *CGOH*, no 783.

direct contribution to the defence of Antioch consisted in reducing the number of canonries in the cathedral by a third and using the prebends to pay for the refortification of the castle of Qusair.[1]

Aimery was still in office when Saladin defeated the Christian army at Hattin in 1187 and overran the kingdom of Jerusalem. Although he was by now an old man, he showed no lack of decisiveness, for he sent a delegation to the west, led by the bishop of Jabala, asking king Henry II of England to come to the help of the Franks in Syria.[2]   This was one of the missions which prepared the west for the preaching of the third crusade, but in 1188, before the crusade arrived, Saladin campaigned in the north. He met with little resistance: apart from a few isolated fortresses only the city of Tripoli, the castle of Tortosa, al-Marqab, where the bishop of Valania was living, the city of Antioch and the patriarch's own fortress of Qusair withstood him.[3] The third crusade neutralised the danger of a renewed attack by Saladin and Antioch and those strongholds which remained in Christian hands in north Syria were included in the terms of peace which Richard I negotiated with the sultan in 1192.[4] But the church of Antioch had suffered a grievous loss: the dioceses of Latakia, Jabala and Gibelet were in Muslim hands, while those of Tortosa and Valania were virtually controlled by the military orders, so that the patriarch had little authority in either of them. In accordance with his earlier policy when the sees of Edessa had been lost, Aimery made no attempt to appoint titular bishops to the sees which Saladin had conquered after their last bishops died.[5]

The decline of the Latin church of Antioch which characterised Aimery's long reign was, however, reversed in the province of Cilicia. This was under Byzantine rule, wholly or in part, from 1137–73, during which time there were no Latin bishops there. Nor did the situation immediately improve for the Latins when the Armenian prince Mleh led a revolt against the Byzantines in 1172–3 and drove out their garrisons, for he was anti-Frankish and ruled with the support of Nur-ad-Din. But in 1175 he was overthrown by his brother, Roupen III, in whose reign a *rapprochement* took place with the Franks of Antioch.[6] Mleh had

---

1. Pressutti, no 3497.
2. *PL*, 201, 1407–8; *Chronicle of the reigns of Henry II and Richard I*, ed Stubbs, II, p 38.
3. Cahen, *Syrie*, pp 428–34.
4. S. Painter, 'The Third Crusade: Richard the Lionhearted and Philip Augustus', in Setton, II, p 85.
5. Gibelet was recovered in 1197 and bishops restored there, but no bishops are recorded in Jabala between 1188 and 1260, or in Latakia between 1187 and 1254. See chapter 9 below.
6. Der Nersessian in Setton, II, pp 636–43.

presumably expelled the Orthodox bishops, but Roupen allowed Latin bishops to return to their sees. By 1178 there was once again a Latin archbishop at Tarsus[1] and during the 1180s when, as a result of the growing threat posed by Saladin, Armenian relations with the Frankish church became far more cordial, the full Latin hierarchy in Cilicia was restored. Thus in 1186, when Bohemond III enfeoffed the Hospital with al-Marqab, his charter was dated by his chancellor, the archbishop of Tarsus, and witnessed by the archbishop of Mamistra.[2]

Yet even when this development has been taken into consideration it remains true that the church of Antioch was greatly diminished by the end of Aimery's long pontificate. He had jurisdiction over only six suffragans, the archbishops of Tarsus and Mamistra, the titular archbishop of Apamea, and the bishops of Valania, Tortosa and Tripoli. The hopes which had existed when Aimery first became patriarch of restoring Antioch to the extent and dignity which it had enjoyed before the Arab conquests had proved sadly illusory.

During his long tenure of the patriarchate Aimery became throughout the western world the best known religious leader in Frankish Syria. William of Tyre's strictures on his lack of learning do not seem to be borne out by his correspondence with the Pisan theologian, Hugh Etherianus, who sent him a copy of his treatise on the procession of the Holy Spirit, written against the views of the Orthodox, which Aimery welcomed, asking in return for more of Hugh's works.[3] Aimery also corresponded with Louis VII of France and Henry II of England. Despite his intransigent attitude towards the Orthodox, who threatened his authority in Antioch, he showed great sympathy and sensitivity in dealing with other groups of eastern Christians, a theme which will be discussed at more length later in this work. He was undoubtedly an ambitious man and as a result of this his relations with the princes of Antioch throughout most of his reign were stormy and flamboyant, but his ability was commensurate with his ambition, as he showed when, after the death of Raymond of Poitiers in 1149, and the capture of Bohemond III in 1164, he took control of the secular, as well as the spiritual, government of Antioch in times of grave crisis, and proved himself to be extremely competent as a ruler. Although successive princes resented his wealth and he resisted forcefully the attempts which they made to gain control of it, he was not averse from spending it in ways which he

1. MS, XX, 7, vol III, p 377.
2. *CGOH*, no 783.
3. E. Martène, U. Durand, eds, *Thesaurus novus Anecdotorum*, 5 vols, Paris 1717, I, 479–81.

considered were conducive to the public good. In 1149 he paid the garrison of Antioch himself because the treasury was empty[1] and when there was a drought in north Syria in 1178 he spent money lavishly to relieve the sufferings of the poor.[2] He ruled the church of Antioch for fifty-three years and, if he was above the canonical age of thirty when he was consecrated, he must have lived into his middle eighties. In twelfth-century Syria, where a man in his late sixties was accounted extremely old,[3] Aimery must have been regarded with much the same kind of awe which attaches to an active centenarian in our own society. He died at his castle of Qusair in 1193 and was buried in the cathedral of Antioch.[4]

In Christian tradition the patriarch of Antioch took precedence over his brother of Jerusalem: his see had enjoyed patriarchal status for longer and his jurisdiction was more extensive. The patriarch of Antioch was in theory the head of the church throughout Asia, whereas the patriarchate of Jerusalem covered only a very small area. During the twelfth century the positions were reversed. In practice the patriarch of Jerusalem was treated as the most important Latin prelate in the east, even though his brother of Antioch may have continued to enjoy an honorary precedence, for example at church councils. This was partly a result of the veneration in which the crusaders held the church of Jerusalem, but it was also a distinction grounded in fact. For although the patriarchs of Antioch attempted to establish once again the traditional hierarchy of their church in the territories under Frankish rule, and in so doing gained the admiration of the native Christian population,[5] their success was at best partial and in most cases ephemeral. Their control was only fitfully recognised in Cilicia; their jurisdiction in Edessa and the northern lands

1. WT, XVII, 10, *RHC Occ*, I, p 775.
2. MS, XX, 6, vol III, p 375.
3. E.g. Ali-el-Herewy in 1173 met a Frankish knight, whom he calls Biran, who had been present at Hebron in 1119 when the graves of the patriarchs were discovered. He told Ali that he was thirteen at the time, and had therefore been born in 1106 and was sixty-seven when Ali met him. Ali describes him as 'well known among the Franks because of . . . his great age'. P. Riant, Invention de la sépulture des Patriarches Abraham, Isaac et Jacob à Hébron, le 25 juin 1119', *AOL*, II, pp 413–14.
4. The date of Aimery's death is attested by his contemporary, Michael the Syrian, XXI, 8, vol III, p 412. Although the western redaction of the Old French continuation of William of Tyre names Aimery as alive in 1194, *RHC Occ*, II, p 209, while the 'Chronique de Terre Sainte', c 54, *Gestes*, p 15, places his death in 1196, both ignore the existence of Aimery's successor, Ralph II (1194–6). Cahen is surely right in suggesting that those passages in the continuator of William of Tyre and in the 'Chronique' refer to Ralph II, *Syrie*, pp 508–9.
5. St Nerses of Lampron, 'On the Institutions of the Church', *RHC Arm*, I, pp 576–81.

of Antioch came to an end in 1151; their authority in the coastal sees of Tripoli was disputed throughout the century, albeit unsuccessfully, by the archbishops of Tyre and the patriarchs of Jerusalem; the Muslims conquered the diocese of Rafaniyah in 1137, that of Artah in 1148, and the metropolitan see of Apamea in 1149. The Latin patriarchs of Antioch only enjoyed undisputed authority throughout this period in the three coastal sees of Latakia, Jabala and Valania. The first two of these were conquered by Saladin in 1188, while the third virtually ceased to be controlled by the patriarch and came directly under the authority of the knights of St John. In view of this it is scarcely surprising that the western church in general regarded the Latin patriarchs of Antioch as of less consequence than their brothers of Jerusalem.

3. THE ESTABLISHMENT OF A LATIN CHURCH AT JERUSALEM

When the Latin clergy established their rule in the church of Jerusalem in 1099 they found there, just as their colleagues did at Antioch, a list of Orthodox sees in the patriarchate, dating, it would seem, from before the Arab conquest. This recorded the four metropolitan sees of Caesarea Maritima, with nineteen suffragans; Scythopolis with eight; Rabba Moabitis with twelve and Bosra with thirty-four, as well as the twenty-five *syncelloi*, bishops who were immediately subject to the patriarch.[1] There is no contemporary list of Orthodox bishoprics in the southern patriarchate at the time of the first crusade, but all available evidence suggests that the reality was very different from the archaic precedents which the list recorded.[2] In Jerusalem as at Antioch the Franks had to create a new Latin church to take the place of an Orthodox church which at the time of the conquest was largely a paper construct. But as at Antioch they preserved where possible the Orthodox diocesan divisions, except that they amalgamated some of the smaller sees to form larger bishoprics after the western European pattern.

The Franks had, of course, to conquer the territories of the patriarchate before they could undertake the work of church organisation. They gained control of most of the inland regions of Judaea, Samaria and Galilee in the first year of their settlement, but the coastal cities, in which the wealth of the region was concentrated, proved more difficult to subdue. Yet by 1110, with the help of the Italian communes, the Franks had captured all of them except Ascalon and Tyre, and by the time Baldwin I died in 1118 the kingdom of Jerusalem had virtually attained the boundaries which, with minor variations, it was to preserve until 1187. This contained all the lands of the patriarchate of Jerusalem, with the exception of the province of Bosra which always remained in Muslim control. It might therefore have

1. Tobler, Molinier, I, pp 339—43. The province of Bosra was also claimed by Antioch, *ibid.*, p 333, but was never in Frankish control.

2. The Orthodox sees of Palestine recorded in the tenth-century Byzantine list, Charon, II, p 233, are all in the Orthodox patriarchate of Antioch: those of Acre, Tyre, Sidon and Beirut. There is no list of comparable date for the Orthodox patriarchate of Jerusalem.

been expected that the Latin church in the kingdom would have been fully organised at a relatively early date. Yet when the council of Nablus met in 1120 the patriarch was attended by only four Latin bishops who made up the total Latin episcopate of the kingdom.[1]

This delay in establishing the Latin hierarchy is chiefly explicable in terms of the stormy history of the patriarchate in the first two decades of the twelfth century. Unlike his colleague of Antioch, whose jurisdiction extended over the lands of three Frankish princes and who was unlikely to be on bad terms with all of them simultaneously, the patriarch of Jerusalem had jurisdiction only over the kingdom, and it was therefore correspondingly more important that there should be harmonious relations between the patriarch and the lay ruler. This proved difficult to achieve at Jerusalem.

Daimbert of Pisa, who appeared to be ideally suited by training and character to rule the church of Jerusalem, proved to have one fatal flaw: formed in the spirit of the Hildebrandine reformers, he regarded the *sacerdotium* as the true source of authority. At Christmas 1099, immediately after his enthronement, both Godfrey of Bouillon and Bohemond did homage to him for their lands.[2] In Bohemond's case this was a practical solution of the vexed question of the oath which he had sworn to Alexius Comnenus, by which he had undertaken to restore to the emperor the former lands of Byzantium which he gained from the Turks; for by receiving investiture of Antioch at the hands of the legate he became a vassal of the pope, and in the eyes of his own vassals this would validate his position at Antioch. Such a ceremonial investiture at the hands of the church was not necessarily damaging to the interests of secular rulers as the Norman princes of south Italy had conclusively shown since 1059 in their dealings with the papacy. According to William of Tyre Daimbert also had concrete temporal ambitions and demanded the cession of the cities of Jerusalem and Jaffa, and Godfrey, who was dependent on the help of the Pisan fleet and the goodwill of the holy see, in part gave way to these demands. On Candlemas day 1100 he granted a quarter of Jaffa to the patriarch and on Easter day he granted him the whole of Jerusalem, on condition that Godfrey should continue to enjoy the revenues of both cities until he had conquered others of equal importance, but that should he die without a legitimate heir both cities should devolve on the patriarch. The authority on which William of Tyre, it would seem, based this

1. WT, XII, 13, *RHC Occ*, I, pp 531–2.
2. Fulcher of Chartres, III, 34, s 16, ed Hagenmeyer, pp 741–2.

account, is a letter of Daimbert's, which some scholars have considered a forgery, with the result that the authenticity of the entire account is in some doubt.[1]

In any case, even if the account is true, the agreements between Godfrey and Daimbert were in the nature of academic exercises. Godfrey was a comparatively young man who could be expected to rule for a long time and the rights of his heirs were safeguarded by the terms of the agreements. But whatever the truth of this matter, his unforeseen death on 18 July 1100 certainly provoked a crisis in which the patriarch took a leading part. Daimbert, in conjunction it would seem with Tancred, sought to gain control of the state, but the Lorraine garrison of Jerusalem refused to hand the city over to him and sent an embassy to Godfrey's brother, Baldwin, count of Edessa, asking him to come and take over the government.[2] Daimbert in his turn wrote to Bohemond urging him to prevent Baldwin from coming south, by force if necessary. The Lorraine embassy was successful and Baldwin accepted their offer, whereas the messenger of Daimbert was detained by the Provençal garrison of Latakia who feared lest the patriarch's action should lead to a civil war among the Franks. But in any case Bohemond could not have intervened in the south because, shortly afterwards, he was taken prisoner by the Danishmendid Turks.[3]

Daimbert's behaviour had been criminally irresponsible, for he had sought to unleash civil war in lands which were only very insecurely held by the Franks. The arrival in Jerusalem of a prince against whom he was known to have conspired was not calculated to promote concord between church and state in the new reign. Baldwin of Boulogne, who had been trained for the church, and who possessed a measure of literacy and detachment unusual in the secular rulers of his age,[4] was not the kind of man who would wilfully provoke a conflict which he was not sure of winning. His position in relation to Daimbert was strengthened by the presence of a new papal legate who reached the east that autumn.

This was Maurice, cardinal bishop of Porto, appointed by Paschal II, who arrived at Latakia with a Genoese fleet in

1. WT, IX, 16, *RHC Occ*, I, pp 388–9. Daimbert's letter, *ibid.*, X, 4, pp 405–6; cf. *RR*, I, p 4, no 32.

2. WT, X, 3, *RHC Occ*, I, pp 403–4, says this was done at the instigation of Arnulf; Albert of Aix, VII, 30, *RHC Occ*, IV, p 524, ascribes it to Warner of Grey; Hagenmeyer, *Chronologie*, pp 305–6, no 489.

3. Albert of Aix, VII, 27, 30, *RHC Occ*, IV, pp 524–7.

4. R. Hill, *Gesta Francorum*, introduction, p xiv.

September 1100.[1] The pope does not seem to have doubted the suitability of Daimbert's appointment as patriarch,[2] but to have wished to exercise some measure of control over affairs in Franish Syria. Baldwin met the legate on his journey south and discussed his plans with him: he therefore knew that he had the support of the pope's representative in the policies he intended to pursue, and Daimbert, who was aware of this, was unable to oppose the new ruler.[3]

When Baldwin reached Jerusalem he took no action against Daimbert, but was publicly reconciled to him: he knew that he could afford to wait for the most opportune time to deal with the patriarch. He was crowned king of Jerusalem at Bethlehem on Christmay day 1100, but he did no homage to the church for his lands. However, he did subsequently receive confirmation of his title from pope Paschal II.[4]

When the legate came south with the Genoese fleet in the spring of 1100, Baldwin accused Daimbert of treason, but the patriarch succeeded in buying a respite for himself by giving the king a large bribe.[5] This suited Baldwin well. He was perpetually in need of money and he would be able to find a fresh opportunity for bringing Daimbert to trial. In the following winter the patriarch made the tactical error of embezzling part of a benefaction sent to him by duke Roger of Apulia for the defence of the kingdom. He was tried at a council at which cardinal Maurice presided, was charged with a variety of crimes including treason, and was deposed.[6] He sought refuge with Tancred, regent of Antioch, who, like the patriarch, was hostile to Baldwin I, an enmity which dated from their rivalry during the Cilician campaign of 1097.[7] Cardinal Maurice died in the winter of 1101–2, and the church of Jerusalem remained without a head. Baldwin I probably thought that no patriarch should be appointed without

1. Appointed in May 1100, *CICO*, I, p 798, no 384; Albert of Aix, VI, 46–7, *RHC Occ*, IV, pp 538–9, attributes his appointment to a complaint made to Paschal II by Baldwin I against Daimbert. Baldwin was not king in May 1100, but Godfrey could have lodged a complaint about Daimbert then. Date of Maurice's arrival in Syria, Hagenmeyer, *Chronologie*, pp 319–20, no 502.

2. Paschal II to the consuls of Pisa, *PL*, 163, 44, no 23.

3. Hagenmeyer, *Chronologie*, pp 322–3, no 506.

4. Fulcher of Chartres, II, 6, s 1, ed Hagenmeyer, pp 384–5. In 1128 Honorius II stated that Paschal II had conferred a crown on Baldwin I, de Rozière, pp 17–18, no 15. This must have been a retrospective confirmation by the pope of Baldwin's coronation since there was not time for envoys to be exchanged with Rome between Baldwin's accession and Christmas 1100.

5. Albert of Aix, VII, 48–9, 51, *RHC Occ*, IV, pp 538–40.

6. *Ibid.*, VII, 58–9, 61–2, pp 545–8.

7. *Ibid.*, VII, 63, p 548; Runciman, *Crusades*, I, pp 195–212.

reference to the pope, otherwise Daimbert might contest his deposition. While the see was still vacant in 1102 Baldwin, hard-pressed by the Fatimids of Egypt, appealed to Tancred for military aid. Tancred agreed to this request only on condition that Daimbert should be restored to power. Although this was not to the king's liking he had no alternative but to accept the condition, but he was aided by the arrival in Syria of a new papal legate. This was cardinal Robert of Paris whom the king won over to his side. Daimbert was enthroned in Jerusalem once again in accordance with Baldwin's promise, but immediately afterwards he was tried by the legate and found guilty and was therefore deposed for a second time and once again retired to Antioch.[1]

With the assent of the cardinal a new patriarch was chosen in 1102. He was Evremar, a priest who came from the same village as Arnulf,[2] and who was a complete contrast to both Arnulf and Daimbert. Albert of Aix describes him as:

> a clerk who was well-esteemed; he was most generous and good-natured in giving alms to the poor; he was devout and had a good reputation.[3]

He appears to have been responsible for appointing his compatriot, Arnulf, as archdeacon of Jerusalem, which was a sensible way of placating a man with an arguable claim to the patriarchate.[4]

Daimbert could not be bought off in a similar way. A former metropolitan archbishop and patriarch, he was not willing to spend the rest of his life as an honoured pensioner of the princes of Antioch. When Bohemond I, having been released from captivity, returned to the west in 1104 to seek help against the Byzantine emperor, Daimbert accompanied him and pleaded his case before Paschal II.[5] Evremar's position was therefore called in question from the second year of his pontificate, but neither he nor Baldwin sent representatives to Rome to defend his election, and in 1107 the case went to Daimbert by default, and Paschal II reinstated him as patriarch. He was travelling to take up his appointment when he died at Messina on 16 June.[6]

1. Albert of Aix, IX, 14, 16–17, *RHC Occ*, IV, pp 599–600.

2. 'Versus de viris illustribus dioecesis Tarvanensis', Martène, Durand, *Vet. SS.*, V, 539.

3. Albert of Aix, IX, 17, *RHC Occ*, IV, p 600.

4. In 1100 he was 'praelatus Templi Domini', Albert of Aix, VII, 30, p 526. He is first named as archdeacon in 1102 at the council which elected Evremar, *ibid.*, IX, 14, p 599. Evremar had presumably agreed to this appointment: he needed an archdeacon he could work with and had known Arnulf from youth.

5. R.B. Yewdale, *Bohemond I, Prince of Antioch*, Princeton 1924, pp 102, 106; WT, XI, 1, *RHC Occ*, I, p 451.

6. *Ibid.*, XI, 4, pp 456–7.

When the pope's decision became known in Jerusalem, but before the news of Daimbert's death had been received there, Evremar went to Rome to plead his own case before the pope. Evremar was preferable in king Baldwin's eyes to the imperious Daimbert, but the king was not entirely satisfied with him. Although Evremar was a devout man of upright character, these were not the qualities which were most needed in a patriarch at that time: he lacked those skills in the arts of government and diplomacy which would enable him in moments of crisis to make decisions in the king's name and to help in the work of administration. When Baldwin learned that Daimbert was dead, he too sent envoys to the pope, led by archdeacon Arnulf, demanding Evremar's deposition.[1] Pope Paschal was scandalized and with reason: Evremar came armed with letters from the king, the clergy of Jerusalem and the canons of the Holy Sepulchre, asking the pope to confirm him in office; shortly afterwards Arnulf reached Rome with letters from the king, the clergy of Jerusalem and the canons of the Holy Sepulchre, asking the pope to depose Evremar. The pope, unable to decide between these conflicting stories, appointed a legate to visit Syria and make a decision about the dispute in his name.[2]

The legate he chose was Gibelin, archbishop of Arles, who presided at a church council at Jerusalem in 1108 at which it was decided that Evremar's election had been invalid because Daimbert had been deposed through undue royal pressure. Baldwin I must have connived at this decision, which was unexceptionable in canon law, and which cost the king nothing, since there was no longer any danger that Daimbert would be restored. The true reason for Evremar's deposition is almost certainly the one mentioned by Paschal II, that in a letter to the pope Baldwin had described Evremar as 'virtually useless'.[3] No stain attached to Evremar's character and he was translated to the archbishopric of Caesarea which had just fallen vacant, 'on account of his great piety and remarkable innocence of life'.[4] Gibelin of Arles was elected patriarch in his place.[5]

This proved to be a wise choice. At the time of his election Gibelin was an elderly man and had considerable experience in church administration. He seems to have viewed with some

1. Fulcher of Chartres, II, 37, s 1, ed Hagenmeyer, pp 512—14; Albert of Aix, X, 58, *RHC Occ*, IV, p 658, states that Paschal II confirmed Evremar in office but that Baldwin I refused to accept him. This differs from the account given by Paschal himself.

2. de Rozière, pp 8—11, no 10, of 4 December 1107.

3. 'tamquam inutilem', de Rozière, p 8.

4. WT, XI, 4, *RHC Occ*, I, p 457.

5. *Idem*; Albert of Aix, X, 58, *RHC Occ*, IV, p 659.

reluctance a translation from the ordered archdiocese of Arles to the unruly patriarchate of Jerusalem.[1]   His misgivings were not without foundation: the church of Jerusalem had been virtually without a head since the city had come under Frankish rule; the king, who had secured the deposition of two patriarchs in eight years, was clearly not an easy man to work with; and two other former holders of the patriarchate were present in the kingdom, either of whom might conspire to bring about Gibelin's downfall.

The new patriarch was fortunate in enjoying the full confidence of the pope, who confirmed his election[2] and allowed him to retain full legatine powers.[3]   In this he was unique among the patriarchs in the first kingdom of Jerusalem.   He disarmed his two potential rivals by a judicious use of magnanimity.   By translating Evremar to Caesarea he made him the patriarch's second-in-command, since Caesarea was the only metropolitan see in the church of Jerusalem at that time.   Arnulf was potentially a more dangerous opponent: he was more eloquent than Evremar and more subtle.   He was not promoted from the post of archdeacon, but was won over by Gibelin who treated him as his chief adviser, and who, when he drew up his will, could describe Arnulf as 'my dearest friend and son'.[4]   Arnulf was associated with Gibelin in all his major acts and this sensible policy worked well since it enabled Gibelin to harness the considerable administrative gifts of Arnulf in a constructive way.

Gibelin was the first patriarch of Jerusalem whose rule was not disputed and he was able to take in hand the much-needed work of ordering the Latin church in the kingdom.   When he came to power there were only two suffragan bishops in the entire patriarchate.   The bishopric of Lydda-Ramla had been set up in 1099 and Gibelin was probably responsible for the appointment of a successor to Robert of Rouen in that see. The second Latin bishop, Roger, is first mentioned towards the end of Gibelin's reign: he held office for thirty-five years and was a man of real ability.[5]   The only Latin diocese to be founded between 1099 and 1108 was that of Caesarea. This city had been a metropolitan see in Orthodox times and Baldwin I appointed a Latin archbishop there when he captured it in 1101.[6]   This

1. *GC*, I, pp 557–8.

2. *Ibid.*, I, p 558.

3. Gibelin styled himself 'Apostolicae sedis legatus' at the end of his reign in 1112, *CGOH*, vol II, p 899, no 4.

4. de Rozière, p 79, no 42.

5. Robert of Rouen is last mentioned in 1103, Albert of Aix, IX, 16, *RHC Occ*, IV, p 599.   Bishop Roger is first mentioned in 1112, *CGOH*, no 28.   The reference to bishop R. of Lydda in 1108, Kohler, pp 112–13, no 1, might relate to either bishop.

6. Tobler, Molinier, I, p 339; WT, X, 16, *RHC Occ*, I, p 423.

occurred during Daimbert's pontificate and presumably with his assent. Gibelin's appointment of Evremar to this see proved eminently satisfactory.[1]

Gibelin's immediate concern was to make proper provision for the service of the holy places. Baldwin I had a special devotion to the church of the Holy Nativity at Bethlehem, in which he had been crowned, and wished to make it a cathedral. This was contrary to Orthodox tradition, for Bethlehem had previously only been a shrine church.[2] When the king sought papal permission to make Bethlehem a Latin bishopric Paschal II delegated this matter to the legate, Gibelin.[3] On reaching Jerusalem Gibelin found that the king had already secured the appointment of Aschetinus, cantor of Bethlehem, to the see of Ascalon, but, since that city was in Muslim hands, he was, in effect, a titular bishop, even though part of his diocese may have been under Frankish control. The legate therefore decided, in consultation with the king and the clergy of Jerusalem, to translate Aschetinus to be first Latin bishop of Bethlehem and to make Ascalon subject to Bethlehem 'parochiali iure'. Mayer has argued that the new see was set up in 1108[4] although the arrangements about its endowments were not completed until 1109—10.[5]

The canonical relationship between Ascalon and Bethlehem remained a theoretical matter until the Franks captured Ascalon in 1153. The most important mosque there was then consecrated as the cathedral church of St Paul[6] and the patriarch Fulcher of Jerusalem appointed a canon of the Holy Sepulchre, Absalom, as Latin bishop. Bishop Gerald of Bethlehem appealed to Rome against this settlement and won his case. The church of Ascalon remained subject to that of Bethlehem and bishop Absalom was deposed.[7] But the memory of the episcopal status of Ascalon was very tenacious. The anonymous author of 'Les pelerinages por aler en Iherusalem', which dates from the reign of Frederick II,

1. See below, chapter 5.
2. It is not listed among the Orthodox dioceses of Jerusalem, Tobler, Molinier, I, pp 339—43.
3. This matter was raised in Rome by Arnulf during negotiations about the deposition of Evremar, WT, XI, 12, RHC Occ, I, p 473.
4. H.E. Mayer, 'Die Gründung der Bistümer Askalon und Bethlehem', Bistümer, Klöster und Stifte im Königreich Jerusalem, Stuttgart 1977, pp 44—80. Aschetinus is first mentioned as bishop in a document of 1109, Kohler, pp 113—14, no 2.
5. WT, XI, 12, RHC Occ, I, pp 472—4.
6. 'Eracles', XVII, 30, RHC Occ, I, p 812.
7. WT, XVII, 30, RHC Occ, I, pp 812—13. Absalom remained a bishop without a see. He is last recorded in 1169, de Rozière, pp 129, 305, nos 63, 167. Mayer, 'Die zweite Gründung des Bistums Askalon und die Ausbildung der Doppelgrafschaft Jaffa-Askalon', Bistümer, pp 112—71.

comments on this fact:

> soloit on appeler l'evesque de Bethléem evesque d'Escalone; mès por
> la dignité du lieu de Bethléem fu translaté l'evesque d'Escalonie au
> saint leu de Bethléem; et encores i est li siéges de l'avesq[ue] en l'yglise
> de monseignor saint Poul . . . [1]

The other important holy place, Nazareth, was captured by
prince Tancred in 1099 and in the following year he founded a
Benedictine monastery on Mount Tabor, the site of the Transfiguration.[2] No attempt was made to set up a diocesan organisation in Galilee and perhaps for that reason in 1103 Paschal II
granted abbot Gerald of Tabor archiepiscopal powers throughout
the principality.[3] The abbot of Tabor was thus in the position
of being virtually immune from any ecclesiastical authority save
that of the pope and no bishop had been appointed to serve the
church of Nazareth. Gibelin of Arles was responsible for bringing
Galilee within the organisation of the secular church. The first
Latin bishop of Nazareth is recorded in a document of 1109 when
his see had presumably been newly established.[4] There was no
conflict with tradition in setting up a Latin diocese here. There
had been a bishop at Nazareth in Orthodox times who had been a
syncellos, or immediate suffragan, of the patriarch.[5] The Latins
did not appoint *syncelloi*, for there was no analogue to them in
the western church, and both at Jerusalem and Antioch the
patriarchs' suffragans were restricted to those regions in which
the patriarchs exercised metropolitan jurisdiction and were not
taken from other provinces. However, in Orthodox times the
metropolitan see of Galilee had been at Scythopolis (known later
as Bethsan), which in the twelfth century was almost deserted.[6]
No attempt was made to revive this archdiocese in the period of
Frankish rule and at first the bishop of Nazareth remained
directly subject to the patriarch. The bishop of Nazareth enjoyed
episcopal jurisdiction throughout Galilee, and the power of the
abbot of Tabor was rescinded. Gibelin, indeed, in his capacity as
legate, carefully delimited the powers of the new abbot of Tabor.
He was made immediately subject to the patriarch, who reserved
to himself the right to enthrone the abbot, ordain priests in the
community and consecrate chapels there. In minor matters, such
as the consecration of the holy oils, the community was subject to

1. 'Les pelerinages por aler en Iherusalem', 4, Michelant, Raynaud, p 92.
2. The foundation was made in Godfrey's reign, Paoli, pp 200–1, no 156.
3. Pflugck-Harttung, II, pp 180–2, no 218.
4. Kohler, pp 113–14, no 2.
5. Tobler, Molinier, I, p 343; cf. *ibid.*, p 339.
6. WT, XXII, 16, *RHC Occ*, I, p 1093.

the bishop of Nazareth as diocesan. Gibelin thus incorporated Galilee into the framework of the Latin church of Jerusalem.[1]

Gibelin also tried to make provision for the appointment of Latin bishops in the important coastal cities of the kingdom. Acre had been in Frankish control since 1104 but no attempt had been made to found a diocese there despite its importance. When, however, in 1110 Baldwin I captured Beirut and Sidon this matter could no longer be ignored. As all these cities formed part of the province of Tyre, which was traditionally subject to the patriarch of Antioch, Gibelin sought a ruling from the pope on this matter and, as has been seen in the last chapter, on receiving a favourable reply, nominated a bishop of Beirut in conjunction with the king.[2] But because of the objections lodged in Rome by the patriarch of Antioch this scheme could not be put into execution: the bishop of Beirut was not consecrated and bishops were not nominated to Sidon and Acre. There matters rested at the time of Gibelin's death. It is nevertheless true to say that the final form of the ecclesiastical settlement in the province of Tyre owed its shape to him, since the compromise which was finally adopted was that which he had worked out in conjunction with Paschal II.

Gibelin was not simply an ecclesiastical administrator but also took an active part in secular affairs. Despite his age he made the long journey to Antioch in 1110 with the royal host as bearer of its standard, the relic of the True Cross, and he took part in the campaign that followed, against Maudud, the militant atabeg of Mosul.[3] He died in Lent 1112.[4] His brief reign had left the church of Jerusalem far stronger and better organised than it had been at his accession and he had shown that co-operation between king and patriarch was not only possible but also valuable to the state.

He was succeeded by Arnulf, an election made without reference to the pope, but carried out, as Arnulf later himself described it, 'by king, clergy and people'.[5] It seems likely that he was appointed immediately after Gibelin's death so that he could

1. *CGOH*, vol II, p 899, no 4, presumably issued because a new abbot had been appointed. Archbishop-abbot Gerald is not mentioned after 1103. He should, perhaps, be identified with the cross-bearer at Ramla in 1101, and with archbishop Gerhard, sent as an envoy to Alexius I in 1102, Albert of Aix, VII, 66, VIII, 47, *RHC Occ*, IV, pp 550, 584.

2. *PL*, 163, 289—90, no 324; *CGOH*, vol II, p 899, no 4. Fedalto, *Chiesa Latina*, II, p 56, names Arnald as first bishop of Beirut in 1111, citing de Rozière, pp 192—4, no 98, but this refers to Arnald as 'episcopus Biterrensis', that is, bishop of Béziers.

3. Albert of Aix, XI, 40, *RHC Occ*, IV, pp 682—3.

4. Röhricht, 'Syria Sacra', *Zeitschrift des deutschen Palästinavereins*, 10, 1887, p 7, n 4.

5. de Rozière, p 46, no 25.

preside over the Holy Week liturgy in Jerusalem for the benefit of
the many pilgrims who came to the city with the spring sailings
from the west.[1]   He was an obvious choice: he had been archdeacon for nine years and so was fully trained in the work of
church administration, and he had proved in Gibelin's reign that
he could work well with the king. The passing years had not made
him any less controversial a figure. In a conventional way he was a
man of considerable piety.   On the day of his election he freed
the Hospital of St John from the payment of tithe in his diocese;[2]
he had a devotion to the Blessed Virgin and gave benefactions to
the community of Josaphat to enable them to rebuild their church
which was the chief Marian shrine in the patriarchate;[3]   and he
made the secular canons of the Holy Sepulchre accept the rule of
the Austin canons in accordance with Gibelin's dying wishes and
made financial arrangements for their support which were honoured throughout the years of the first kingdom.[4]

He proved a valuable adviser to the king in secular affairs also
from the beginning of his reign.   Almost immediately after
Arnulf's election Byzantine ambassadors came to Jerusalem to ask
Baldwin to help Alexius I to restore imperial rule in Antioch.
Baldwin intended to refuse this request, but Arnulf advised him to
do so during a solemn ceremony of crown-wearing. This provided
the king with a symbolic context in which to assert the sover-
eignty of the kingdom of Jerusalem and one which the Byzantine
envoys would understand.[5]   Arnulf was also instrumental in
arranging the marriage of Baldwin with Adelaide, dowager
countess of Sicily, whose dowry temporarily relieved the penury
of the kingdom.   Baldwin had an estranged Armenian wife who
was living in Constantinople, but Arnulf, who must have been
aware of this, was willing to disregard the fact in the wider interests of the kingdom.[6]   Arnulf also had personal courage. When
Maudud of Mosul invaded Galilee in 1113 Arnulf accompanied
the king on his unsuccessful campaign against him, as bearer of the
True Cross.[7]

1. Easter day 1112 fell on 21 April. The first dated document of the reign comes
from 20 June 1112, *CGOH*, no 28.
2. *Ibid.*, no 25. This is dated only by the year.
3. Delaborde, pp 21–2, no 1. In 1115 he persuaded Roger of Lydda to endow
Josaphat, Kohler, pp 117–18, no 7.
4. de Rozière, pp 44–7, no 25; cf. WT, XI, 15, *RHC Occ*, I, p 479, who makes
disparaging comments.
5. Albert of Aix, XII, 7, *RHC Occ*, IV, p 693. H.E. Mayer, 'Das Pontifikale von
Tyrus und die Krönung der lateinischen Könige von Jerusalem', *DOP*, 21, 1967, p 169.
6. WT, XI, 21, *RHC Occ*, I, pp 487–9; Hamilton in Baker, ed, *Medieval Women*,
pp 145–7.
7. Fulcher of Chartres, II, 49, s 5, ed Hagenmeyer, p 569.

The new patriarch, though able and in some respects devout, was not without his critics. Among them was Evremar, archbishop of Caesarea, whose deposition as patriarch he had helped to secure.[1] Arnulf was also unpopular because he promoted the interests of his own family and used the wealth of the church to do so. He arranged a marriage for his niece, Emma, to Eustace Garnier, lord of Caesarea and Sidon, and gave her Jericho, which belonged to the church of Jerusalem, as a dowry.[2] He was also still accused of keeping mistresses.[3]   But the most damaging charge which he had to face was that he had knowingly solemnised a bigamous marriage for the king.

His opponents complained to the pope about the irregularity of his birth and of his life and added that he had been forced on the electors by royal fiat. In 1115 Paschal II sent the bishop of Orange as his legate to Syria to investigate these charges. Arnulf was found guilty and was deposed, but he immediately went to Rome in person to appeal against this sentence. He was accompanied by an imposing delegation, consisting of the bishop of Bethlehem, the abbot of Josaphat, the prior of Mount Sion and two canons of the Holy Sepulchre, all of whom swore that no force had been used by the king in Arnulf's election and begged the pope to reinstate him. Paschal II allowed Arnulf to clear himself on oath of the charges brought against him, and granted him a dispensation in regard to his defect of birth. In 1116 he returned to Jerusalem to take up his duties as patriarch once again.[4] The pope, however, was not willing to overlook Baldwin I's irregular marriage and Arnulf's reinstatement seems to have been conditional on his persuading the king to put away his wife, a purpose he achieved at Easter 1117 when, with Baldwin's consent, his marriage to Adelaide was annulled by a church synod at which Arnulf presided and the queen was packed off to Sicily.[5]

---

1. de Rozière, pp 11—13, no 11.

2. WT, XI, 15, *RHC Occ*, I, p 479. Niece may be a euphemism for daughter, but throughout this work, unless there is evidence to the contrary, the words niece and nephew in the sources will be taken in their plain sense. To treat all the nieces and nephews of the clergy as sons and daughters in disguise shows scant respect for historical evidence and implies that clergy families were unusual in having no collateral branches.

3. Named by Paschal II, de Rozière, p 13, no 11.

4. WT, XI, 26, *RHC Occ*, I, p 499; Fulcher of Chartres, II, 54, s 8, ed Hagenmeyer, pp 590—1; de Rozière, pp 11—13, no 11 (dated 1117 by its editor, but written in 1116, *RR*, I, p 19, no 83).

5. Albert of Aix, XII, 24, *RHC Occ*, IV, p 704; Hamilton in Baker, ed, *Medieval Women*, pp 146—7.

On this occasion Arnulf sacrificed the interests of the kingdom to save his own office. Without his promptings Baldwin would probably never have repudiated Adelaide, and by doing so he alienated the Norman rulers of Sicily who were the nearest western power to Frankish Syria. For, as William of Tyre commented half a century later, the Sicilian Normans, alone of all the rulers of the west, had never sent help to Jerusalem.[1]

Arnulf did not reign for long after this. On Palm Sunday 1118, as he was leading the procession from the Mount of Olives towards the Golden Gate, the patriarch was met by a cortège bearing the body of Baldwin I who had died while returning from a campaign against Egypt. Arnulf was already an elderly man, he must at this time have been about sixty-three, and the shock of the king's death affected him profoundly. He gave his assent to the popular demand that the throne should pass to the late king's cousin, Baldwin of Le Bourg, count of Edessa, who was visiting Jerusalem at the time, and a short while after this he died.[2] Arnulf was clearly a man of ability, and had been on good terms with the king, but no further measures had been taken in his reign for the development of the Latin church in the kingdom because, except in his final year, he did not enjoy the confidence of the pope and most of his reign was spent with the threat of deposition hanging over him.

Baldwin II was therefore free at the beginning of his reign to make the choice of a new patriarch. He nominated Warmund who came from Picquigny in the diocese of Amiens.[3] Nothing is known about his earlier career: Baldwin may have sent to the west for him, or he may already have been in his service at Edessa. No difficulty was made about the appointment either by the clergy of Jerusalem or by the holy see, and pope Calixtus II sent the new patriarch a *pallium*.[4] Warmund proved a useful coadjutor to the king who was a stranger in the country and who until 1129 had no close male kin with whom he could share the responsibility of government.

In 1120 Baldwin and Warmund jointly summoned a council of clergy and barons to Nablus to discuss the state of emergency brought about by the occurrence of earthquakes, plagues of locusts, and consequently famine in the kingdom. They interpreted these disasters as signs of God's anger and drew up twenty-five canons dealing with a wide spectrum of church law and

1. WT, XII, 29, *RHC Occ*, I, p 506.
2. Albert of Aix, XII, 29–30, *RHC Occ*, IV, pp 708–9.
3. WT, XII, 6, *RHC Occ*, I, p 519; Albert of Aix, XII, 30, *RHC Occ*, IV, p 710.
4. de Rozière, pp 14–15, no 13.

public morality. These ranged from rulings about the payment of
tithe to regulations about marriage and sexual morality, and also
included regulations about treatment of regular clergy who
apostatised, and the penalties attaching to bringing accusations at
law which could not be substantiated.[1] The canons of the council
of Nablus formed a body of canon law specifically designed to
meet the needs of Frankish society in the Holy Land. The degree
of co-operation between church and state which led to their enactment augured well for unity among Frankish settlers in the
kingdom of Jerusalem in the face of common problems, a unity
which had been little in evidence since 1099.

That the king's choice of Warmund had been well made was
shown in 1124. Baldwin II had sought the help of Venice to
capture Tyre, the only port in the north of the kingdom still in
Muslim hands, but when the Venetian fleet reached Acre in the
autumn of 1123 the king was a Muslim prisoner in north Syria.
Warmund therefore negotiated a treaty with the Venetians in
the king's name, granting them extensive privileges in return for
their help, and guaranteed that Baldwin would ratify it when he
was released.[2] Tyre was captured with Venetian help and after
the king had been ransomed he substantially confirmed the
treaty.[3] During the royal captivity the patriarch had acted as
head of state.

Warmund seems to have had a greater taste for military affairs
than was common in a churchman. At the beginning of his reign
he accompanied the king on a campaign against Damascus,[4] and
his last illness developed when he was besieging the fortress of
Belhacem, near Sidon, which was in the hands of bandits, probably Muslims.[5] He was later remembered as the first protector of
the knights Templar, founded in 1119 by Hugh of Payens to
guard pilgrim routes in the kingdom.[6]

Warmund seems, nevertheless, to have been more interested in
the conduct of temporal affairs than in his religious duties. An
anecdote preserved by an anonymous canon of Hebron gives some
indication of the patriarch's lack of central interest in ecclesiastical
affairs. Soon after Warmund came to power the Austin canons at
Hebron were excited by a quasi-archaeological excavation under
their church which revealed what they supposed to be the bones

1. WT, XII, 13, *RHC Occ*, I, pp 531–2; Mansi, XXI, 263–6.
2. WT, XII, 25, *RHC Occ*, I, pp 550–3; TT, I, pp 79–89, no 40.
3. *Ibid.*, I, pp 90–4, no 41.
4. Fulcher of Chartres, III, 4, s 2, ed Hagenmeyer, p 625.
5. WT, XIII, 25, *RHC Occ*, I, p 594.
6. *Ibid.*, XII, 7, pp 520–21; D'Albon, *Cartulaire général de l'Ordre du Temple,
1119?–1150*, I, Paris 1913, p 99, no 141, charter of William of St. Omer of 1137.

of the patriarchs, Abraham, Isaac and Jacob. The community was anxious that the patriarch should preside over the solemn translation of these relics into the priory church, but

> the prior went to Jerusalem to tell the patriarch Warmund about the discovery and to invite him to come to Hebron for the translation of the relics. Warmund, full of benevolence, several times promised to come, but did not keep his word.[1]

This leisurely attitude towards ecclesiastical duties meant that for much of Warmund's reign little progress was made in church organisation. About 1122 Warmund consecrated a certain Odo as archbishop of Tyre while the city was still in Muslim hands, which was a necessary pre-condition for appointing bishops to the other coastal dioceses of the kingdom.[2] Odo died before the city was conquered in 1124[3] and no steps were taken to appoint a successor for the next three years, during which time Tyre and its daughter churches were administered — according to William of Tyre, not very well administered — by the patriarch or his officials.[4] Finally, in about 1127, Warmund consecrated William, who was an Englishman and prior of the Holy Sepulchre, as archbishop. He went to Rome against the patriarch's wishes to receive his *pallium* from the pope. There was no precedent in the Frankish east for a metropolitan acting in this way although the two patriarchs regularly received their *pallia* from Rome. Archbishop William's intention in doing so does not seem to have been to circumvent the authority of the patriarch of Jerusalem, but to obtain papal support for the recognition of his full rights as metropolitan. Warmund had acted in accordance with the ruling of Paschal II in consecrating the metropolitan of Tyre, but a corollary of this action was that only those parts of the province of Tyre which came within the political boundaries of the kingdom of Jerusalem would be under the archbishop's jurisdiction: the northern sees would remain subject to the patriarch of Antioch. Such a solution was not acceptable to the archbishop of Tyre, any more than it was to the patriarch of Antioch, and William obtained a mandate from Honorius II which, while recognising the jurisdiction of the patriarch of Jerusalem over the province of Tyre, ordered all the suffragans of Tyre, even those in the patriarchate of Antioch, to give canonical obedience to their new metropolitan. The pope sent Gilles, cardinal bishop of Tusculum, as his legate to Syria to see that

1. Riant, 'Invention de la sépulture des patriarches', *AOL*, II, p 418.
2. Fulcher of Chartres, III, 11, s 1, ed Hagenmeyer, pp 646—7.
3. WT, XIII, 13, *RHC Occ*, I, p 575.
4. *Ibid.*, XIV, 14, p 626.

these orders were obeyed, but his mission had no effect as far as the patriarchate of Antioch was concerned, as has been seen in the preceding chapter.[1] The acceptance by the pope of the subjection of the archbishop of Tyre and his suffragans in the kingdom of Jerusalem to the authority of the southern patriarch was a major victory for Warmund, since it ensured that the church and kingdom of Jerusalem should be coterminous. But in Warmund's reign no suffragan sees of Tyre were set up in the kingdom of Jerusalem: the organisation of the Latin church there was still far from complete.

The only other work of any consequence in the organisation of the secular church which took place under Warmund was that Nazareth was raised to an archbishopric. This occurred between the death of the first bishop, Bernard, at some time after 1125, and the appointment of his successor, William, in March 1128.[2] The new archbishop thus became metropolitan of Galilee, but the Franks remained conscious that they were making an innovation in the Orthodox tradition and, writing in the reign of Baldwin IV, William of Tyre thought an explanation was in order:

> Scythopolis is the capital of Palestina Tertia . . . It is also called Bethsan. Nowadays Nazareth, which is situated in the same diocese, enjoys its prerogative.[3]

Warmund's abilities were those of a statesman and a military leader rather than those of a churchman. But he guided the kingdom, and with it the Latin church, through one of the most critical periods of its history, that of the king's captivity at the hands of Nur-ad-Daulah Balik in 1123—4. He died on 27 July 1128.[4]

The ideal successor happened to be visiting the Holy Land at this time. This was Stephen, abbot of St John *de valle* at Chartres, who had come on pilgrimage and was waiting for a sailing when Warmund died. He had all the necessary qualifications: he was well-educated; he had been trained as a knight and had been

---

1. *Ibid.*, XIII, 23, pp 591—3.

2. Bishop Bernard is last mentioned in 1125, *CGOH*, no 71. His successor, William, was made an archbishop after his appointment, Delaborde, pp 56—8, no 44. This had happened by 1129; de Rozière, pp 138—9, no 67, of 1129 names him bishop; *ibid.*, pp 81-3, no 44, of March 1129, names his archbishop (on the dating of this document, Hamilton in Baker, ed, *Medieval Women*, p 148, n 37). His promotion therefore occurred in the early months of 1129.

3. WT, XXII, 16, *RHC Occ*, I, p 1093.

4. His year of death is given by Orderic Vitalis, XII, 48, vol VI, p 388; WT, XIII, 25, *RHC Occ*, I, p 595. The day and month are given by a calendar of the Holy Sepulchre, now in the Bibliotheca Angelica, Rome, F. Wormald in H. Buchthal, *Miniature Painting in the Latin Kingdom of Jerusalem*, Oxford 1957, p 116.

viscount of Chartres before he entered the religious life; he was an experienced administrator, a man of moral integrity, and, for good measure, a kinsman of the king. He was elected without any dissent.[1]

At first he and the king co-operated well.[2] A new diocese was set up at Sebastia, as a suffragan see of Caesarea, to serve the province of Samaria.[3] This had been an Orthodox bishopric[4] but in the twelfth century it was far less important as a town than Nablus, the administrative capital of the region. The pilgrim Theoderich, who visited Sebastia in about 1170, comments that 'its great ruins give it the appearance of a city'.[5] But although few people lived there it was revered as the place of St John the Baptist's burial, and it was therefore considered more fitting that this important shrine should be served by a Latin bishop rather than any of the other eighteen dioceses which had been suffragan sees of Caesarea in the Orthodox period. The patriarch Stephen was also responsible for the organisation of the knights Templar, who were granted recognition as a religious order by Honorius II in 1128.[6]

Yet relations between Baldwin II and his new patriarch were soured by Stephen's demand that the king should surrender the entire city of Jaffa to the Holy Sepulchre and should also agree to hand over Jerusalem as well once Ascalon had been captured. There is a similarity between this demand and the claims which Daimbert is alleged to have made but which duke Godfrey only accepted in part. Baldwin II was so angered by this that ill-feeling between the two men persisted for the rest of Stephen's reign. The patriarch Stephen was a gifted man from whose rule the church of Jerusalem, though perhaps not the kingdom, would have benefitted, but he held office for less than two years, dying in 1130, his quarrel with Baldwin still unresolved.[7]

The last patriarch whom Baldwin II appointed was a man whom he already knew well, William, prior of the Holy Sepulchre. He came from Flanders, had been a canon of the Holy Sepulchre since

1. WT, XIII, 25, *RHC Occ*, I, pp 594–5; Orderic Vitalis, XII, 48, vol VI, p 388.
2. At his request Baldwin II freed pilgrims from the payment of various onerous dues in the port of Acre, de Rozière, pp 85–6, no 46.
3. Baldwin, bishop of Sebastia, first mentioned 1129, *ibid.*, pp 81–3, no 44. See n 2 p. 67 above.
4. Tobler, Molinier, I, p 342.
5. *Theoderich's description of the Holy Places, circa 1172 A.D.*, trans A. Stewart, *PPTS*, 1891, pp 62–3.
6. WT, XII, 7, *RHC Occ*, I, pp 520–21; 'instituta est eis regula et habitus assignatus . . . de mandato domini Honorii papae et domini Stephani Hierosolymitani patriarchae'.
7. WT, XIII, 25, *RHC Occ*, I, pp 594–5; cf. *ibid.*, IX, 16, pp 388–9.

at least 1117[1] and during Stephen's reign he became prior.[2] William of Tyre, who may have known him, described him as 'a handsome man, not particularly well-educated, but of good moral character'.[3] Unlike Stephen, William was not centrally interested in political power. This does not mean that he was devoid of political sense, or incapable of taking action in temporal affairs if the need arose. Thus in 1134 when Hugh II of Le Puiset, queen Melisende's cousin, being accused of treason, retired to his fief of Jaffa and allied with the Muslims of Ascalon, the patriarch averted civil war by obtaining lenient terms for the rebels.[4] Mayer has argued that there was more at stake in this revolt than William of Tyre, our chief source, makes apparent, and I agree with him about this, although I have some reservations about certain points of his argument which I have stated elsewhere.[5] Baldwin II had been succeeded in 1131 by his eldest daughter, Melisende, and her husband, Fulk of Anjou, but in the early years of his reign Fulk excluded Melisende from power, which deprived her of patronage. This was resented by the native nobility, led by Hugh of Le Puiset, and, although his rebellion failed, it had, as the patriarch's intervention showed, the full support of the church. The church's adhesion to the queen's cause seems to have been the decisive factor in persuading Fulk to admit Melisende to an equal share of power. It is indicative of William's general lack of interest in secular affairs that he made no attempt to capitalise on Melisende's favour in order to increase his own power either after her reconciliation with Fulk in 1136, or when, as queen-regnant, with the minor Baldwin III, she became all-powerful in the kingdom in 1143. Similarly, although William had little interest in military matters, he could be decisive in a crisis. Thus when king Fulk was besieged at Montferrand in 1137 the patriarch raised troops and marched to his assistance.[6]

But much of his energy was devoted as patriarch to placing the affairs of the Holy Sepulchre on a firm footing. He mediated in property disputes which involved the canons;[7] he obtained

1. de Rozière, p 12, no 11.
2. *Ibid.*, pp 18–22, no 16.
3. WT, XIII, 26, *RHC Occ*, I, p 598.
4. *Ibid.*, XIV, 15–18, pp 627–33; on the date of Hugh's revolt, Mayer, 'Queen Melisende',*DOP*, 26, 1972, pp 104–6.
5. Hamilton in Baker, ed,*Medieval Women*, pp 150–51.
6. Orderic Vitalis, XIII, 33, vol VI, pp 496–502, where the patriarch is wrongly called Ralph.
7. de Rozière, pp 77–9, no 41, pp 80–1, no 43, pp 146–8, no 73, pp 219–20, no 117; *CGOH*, nos 139, 140; E. Rey, 'Chartes de l'Abbaye du Mont-Sion', *MSAF*, ser 5, 8, 1887, p 47.

privileges for the church from Raymond II of Tripoli;[1] he secured
control of property at Antioch belonging to the church;[2] and he
obtained a detailed confirmation of the lands and privileges of the
Sepulchre from the pope.[3]   Indeed, in the early years of his reign
much of his time was spent dealing with routine business relating
to the Holy Sepulchre which could equally well have been trans-
acted by the prior.[4]

But William was also concerned about the wider areas of his
responsibility.   In the early years of his reign suffragan bishops
were at last appointed for Tyre: Baldwin, who had been bishop-
elect of Beirut since 1112, was consecrated by 1133 and by the
same year a Latin bishop had been consecrated for Sidon as well.[5]
The first Latin bishop of Acre is mentioned in a charter of 1135.[6]
These foundations were made in the life-time of archbishop
William of Tyre, himself a former prior of the Sepulchre and
therefore well-known to the patriarch. His successor, Fulcher, had
been abbot of a house of canons regular at Angoulême and had
resigned his office after the disputed papal election of 1130
because he supported Innocent II, while the local bishop supported Anacletus II. Fulcher subsequently came to Jerusalem, where
Innocent II was recognised, and became a canon of the Holy
Sepulchre. Not unnaturally, when the see of Tyre fell vacant in
1134–5, this distinguished canon was nominated to the office
with the assent of the patriarch, who consecrated him.

Fulcher had considerable independence of mind. Against the
wishes of the patriarch he went to Rome, officially to receive a
pallium, but also, as later events made plain, to seek a reversal of
the pragmatic settlement which had been reached about the province of Tyre, whereby the northern suffragans remained directly
subject to the patriarch of Antioch. As he had faced exile rather
than admit the authority of a rival pope Fulcher was assured of a
friendly reception from Innocent II. In July 1138 the pope ruled
that, until the dispute with Antioch had been finally settled,
Fulcher should remain subject to the patriarch of Jerusalem,[7] but
he gave Tyre the dignity of ranking first among the metropolitan
sees of Jerusalem, a position which in Orthodox times that see had

1. de Rozière, pp 184–7, 190–2, nos 93–4, 97.
2. *Ibid.*, pp 172–8, no 89.
3. *Ibid.*, pp 74–6, no 39.
4. *Ibid.*, pp 206–7, no 106 (1132); pp 199–200, no 101 (1136–45); Archives de
l'Ordre de Malte, division I, i, 34(b); Delaville le Roulx, *Les Archives, la Bibliothèque et
le Trésor·de l'Ordre de St Jean de Jérusalem à Malte, BEFAR,* 32, Paris 1883, pp 73–4,
no 5 (1137); de Rozière, pp 164–5, no 84, pp 168–9, no 87 (1138).
5. *CGOH,* no 100.
6. *Ibid.*, no 112.
7. de Rozière, pp 4–6, nos 5–7; cf. *RR*, I, p 44, nos 175, 178.

held in the patriarchate of Antioch.[1]

Fulcher found when he returned to Syria that the patriarch had in his absence assumed direct control over the province of Tyre and its suffragans, presumably because he considered that the archbishop had displayed a total disregard of patriarchal authority in dealing with the holy see directly, and that this threatened his own position. Fulcher complained to the pope about this and received full support from Innocent II who ordered the patriarch to restore the archbishop to his full rights and threatened that if this were not done he would remove the province of Tyre from the jurisdiction of the patriarch of Jerusalem and make it immediately dependent on the holy see.[2] Innocent also absolved the bishops of Gibelet, Tripoli and Tortosa from their oath of obedience to the patriarch of Antioch, and ordered them to obey the archbishop of Tyre.[3] Although the pope's injunctions had no effect at Antioch, Fulcher's position in the church of Jerusalem had been vindicated. He now ranked second after the patriarch himself and his position was further improved in 1140 when the Franks captured Banyas, the ancient Caesarea Philippi, and a Latin diocese was established there as a suffragan see of Tyre.[4] Like Sidon, Beirut and Acre, Banyas had once been an Orthodox see.[5]

Tyre with its four suffragan sees was the most important metropolitan see in the patriarchate of Jerusalem, not only in order of precedence, but also in practical terms, for none of the other metropolitans ever had so large a number of subordinates. Nevertheless, its authority had diminished since the Orthodox period when it had ranked as the premier metropolitan see of the east and was known as the *protothronos*.[6] The province had, for political reasons, been cut in half and the archbishops were never able to regain control over the three northern sees which had once been subject to Tyre. William of Tyre deplored this when he became archbishop and blamed the papacy for it:

> the Roman church may not improperly be blamed for this evil legacy, for while it does not enjoin obedience to the church of Jerusalem [on the northern sees of Tyre] it has allowed us to be cut off from the church of Antioch without any reason. If our rights were restored, like obedient sons, we should be prepared to obey either master without question or obstruction.[7]

1. WT, XIV, 11, 12, *RHC Occ*, I, pp 621–4.
2. *Ibid.*, XIV, 11, pp 622–3.
3. *Ibid.*, XIV, 13, pp 624–5.
4. *Ibid.*, XV, 11, pp 674, 676.
5. Tobler, Molinier, I, p 332.
6. WT, XIV, 12, *RHC Occ*, I, p 623.
7. *Ibid.*, XIV, 14, p 627.

Towards the end of William's reign as patriarch a new Latin diocese was founded at Tiberias.[1]   This was a suffragan see of Nazareth and had once been an Orthodox bishopric,[2] but the city was chosen less for any religious associations than because it was the capital of the principality of Galilee.   Thus by the end of William's reign the ecclesiastical organisation of the northern and central areas of the kingdom had been completed.

William was a painstaking administrator, not openly ambitious for the church as his predecessor had been, but willingly patiently to consolidate and enforce the many little rights that it already possessed.   In this way he resembled the early Capetian kings of France in their policies.   He was also a peacemaker: much of his time was spent settling disputes between religious bodies in the kingdom.   He has some claim to be regarded as the real founder of the Latin church of Jerusalem: certainly by the time of his death it was better organised and more harmoniously run than it had previously been.   He was, in many ways, an ideal patriarch, capable in secular affairs if circumstances required him to be, but not politically motivated and therefore able to work harmoniously with the crown.   He died after a reign of fifteen years on 27 September 1145.[3]

The unusual situation existed in the kingdom at that time of joint rule by a mother and her son.   King Fulk had died in 1143. His widow, Melisende, was not regent, but queen-regnant jointly with her son, Baldwin III, whom she did not associate with her in power when he came of age in 1145.   It must therefore have been the queen who nominated Fulcher of Tyre as the new patriarch.[4]   He was the natural choice, a man of wide experience who held the second most important church office in the kingdom.   The only factor which might have told against him was his age.   William of Tyre describes him as 'almost a centenarian' in 1155,[5] but this expression must not be taken too literally since in that year he successfully made the return voyage by sea to Rome, which would scarcely have been within the physical capacity of so old a man.   Nevertheless his contemporaries thought of him as old and he was probably about seventy at the time of his election.

1. The first bishop, Elias, is mentioned in 1144, de Rozière, pp 65—8, no 34, and may have been appointed a few years earlier: he appears in de Rozière, pp 156—8, no 79, which on internal evidence dates from 1139—46. H.E. Mayer, 'Die Anfänge des Bistums Tiberias', in *Bistümer*, pp 81—97.
2. Tobler, Molinier, I, p 343.
3. WT, XVI, 17, *RHC Occ*, I, p 733.
4. He was not elected until 25 January 1146. The reason for the delay is not known, but it cannot have arisen from a desire for papal ratification since communication between Rome and Syria was not normal in the winter months.
5. WT, XVIII, 6, *RHC Occ*, I, p 827.

But if Melisende had hoped that this aged prelate would be subservient to her she must soon have been disillusioned. The first task which had to be undertaken in the new pontificate was that of filling the vacant see of Tyre. Melisende nominated her chancellor, Ralph, who, according to William of Tyre, though very well educated was also very worldly. The patriarch, however, joined with the chapter of Tyre in objecting to this candidate and appealed to Rome against his appointment. The queen invested Ralph with the temporalities of the see, which he administered for four years,[1] but he could not be consecrated while his nomination was *sub judice*. Pope Eugenius III finally upheld the patriarch's objection, and Fulcher's own candidate, Peter, prior of the Holy Sepulchre, was enthroned as archbishop of Tyre in 1151.[2]

Despite this disagreement Fulcher approved of Melisende's rule. When Baldwin III, who considered that he had been excluded from power by his mother, demanded that the patriarch should perform a crown-wearing ceremony for him alone in the Holy Sepulchre on Easter day 1152, Fulcher refused to act unless Melisende were also present. Since this would have frustrated the king's intention Baldwin was forced to devise a secular ceremony of crown-wearing.[3] As I have argued elsewhere, although the patriarch's influence was not sufficiently strong to make the queen victorious in the civil war which developed between her and Baldwin, it was nevertheless decisive in assuring that she obtained generous terms in defeat.[4] Fulcher, who had antagonised Melisende when she was powerful because of his obstinate stand about the see of Tyre, became her ally at the point when she lost effective authority and must thereby have incurred the displeasure of Baldwin III. This probably explains why, by comparison with other patriarchs of Jerusalem, Fulcher took almost no part in public life throughout most of his reign except when protocol demanded that he be present, as at the council of Acre in 1148 at which the campaign of the second crusade was planned.[5]

Fulcher was a staunch defender of the rights of his church and

1. *Ibid.*, XVI, 17, pp 733—4. Ralph was still elect of Tyre in 1150, A. de Marsy, 'Fragment d'un cartulaire de l'Ordre de Saint-Lazare en Terre Sainte', *AOL*, II, p 128, no 7.

2. He is first recorded as archbishop in May 1151, *ibid.*, pp 129—30, no 9; Amalric, the new prior of the Sepulchre, is first named in May of that year, de Rozière, pp 159—61, no 81.

3. WT, XVII, 13, *RHC Occ*, I, p 781. Mayer, 'Das Pontifikale von Tyrus', *DOP*, 21, 1967, pp 167—8.

4. Hamilton in Baker, ed, *Medieval Women*, pp 152—4. For a full account of the war, Mayer, 'Queen Melisende', *DOP*, 26, 1972, pp 164—70.

5. WT, XVII, 1, *RHC Occ*, I, p 758.

this brought him into conflict with the Hospital of St John. The new romanesque basilica of the Holy Sepulchre was completed during his reign and consecrated on 15 July 1149, the fiftieth anniversary of the crusader conquest of Jerusalem. The patriarch was naturally not best pleased when the Hospitallers began to erect buildings at their Jerusalem headquarters, just across the road from his cathedral, which were more costly and more lofty than those of the church of the Resurrection. In 1154 Anastasius IV gave formal recognition to the possession by the Hospitallers of privileges which made them an exempt order,[1] and they were accused of using this immunity to disregard excommunications and interdicts which Latin bishops in the Holy Land imposed and were also said to be refusing to pay tithes to those bishops for their lands. As a result the ill-feeling between the patriarch and the Hospital escalated. When the patriarch preached in his cathedral the Hospitallers rang their bells so loudly that he could not be heard and on one occasion there was a fight between the supporters of the two sides in the church of the Holy Sepulchre itself.[2]

The patriarch decided to make a direct appeal to the pope, apparently hoping that he would rescind the privileges of the Hospitallers. In 1154 Fulcher went to Italy, taking with him two-thirds of the episcopate of the kingdom.[3] They arrived at a time when the new English pope, Hadrian IV, was attempting to break the power of the Norman kings of Sicily in conjunction with the Byzantine emperor Manuel.[4] However just some of the patriarch's grievances may have been, it was not a propitious time to ask the pope to antagonise an international religious order which held considerable property in the Norman kingdom. Moreover, the sequel suggests that justice was not entirely on Fulcher's side, for it was almost certainly after this visit that he sent an encyclical letter to all the daughter-houses of the Holy Sepulchre ordering them to restore property belonging to the Hospital of St John which they held unjustly.[5] The pope refused categorically to side with Fulcher and he and his clergy had to return to the Holy Land in 1156 having spent a good deal of money to no purpose.[6]

1. In the bull *Christianae fidei religio*, *CGOH*, no 226. See chapter 4 below.
2. WT, XVIII, 3, *RHC Occ*, I, pp 820−22.
3. *Ibid.*, XVIII, 6, pp 826−7.
4. Lamma, *Comneni e Staufer*, I, pp 149−242.
5. de Rozière, pp 326−8, no 183; *CGOH*, no 176.
6. WT, XVIII, 8, *RHC Occ*, I, pp 826−30. They were at the papal court in November−December 1155, *Annali Genovesi di Caffaro e de' suoi continuatori*, ed L.T. Belgrano, C. Imperiale di Sant' Angelo, 5 vols, Rome 1890−1929, I, 43; *RR*, I, p 80, no 312; cf. Riley-Smith, *Knights*, pp 399−400.

The patriarch found that an unedifying breach of discipline had occurred during his absence. On Ascension day the prior of the Holy Sepulchre had led the canons in procession to the church of the Mount of Olives to sing Mass there. The community of that church had refused to recognise the right of the prior of the Sepulchre to deputise for the patriarch, had turned the procession away, and the prior of the Mount of Olives had sung the Mass himself. Fulcher was not the kind of man to overlook such a public insult to his church and representative. He convoked a synod of all the bishops of the kingdom, together with the heads of all the religious houses in Jerusalem, at which sentence was given that in the absence of the patriarch the prior of the Holy Sepulchre had the right to deputise for him at all the station Masses on great feasts. The unfortunate prior and canons of the Mount of Olives were forced to do penance by walking barefoot through the city from their own house to the Holy Sepulchre.[1]

To the end of his life Fulcher remained adamant about what he considered to be questions of principle. In 1157 he refused his assent to the marriage of the king's brother, Amalric, to Agnes of Courtenay, daughter of Joscelin II of Edessa, on grounds of consanguinity. The couple were third cousins and only had a great-great-grandfather in common, and it would not have been difficult to obtain a dispensation, but Fulcher did not suggest this. They subsequently married despite his disapproval, but may have waited until after his death which occurred later in that same year.[2]

It must have been with some relief that the king learned of the death of this inflexible prelate on 20 November 1157.[3] He had spent most of his reign in fierce litigation with people who were admitted by their contemporaries to have been ornaments of Christian society, like the devout queen Melisende and the saintly grand master of the Hospital, Raymond of Puy. It is difficult not to think that some of these tensions could have been avoided if the patriarch had been willing to compromise about matters which were not, in most cases, questions of religious principle, but simply of ecclesiastical discipline.

Baldwin III seems to have taken no part in the appointment of a new patriarch. William of Tyre alleges that the election was manipulated by the king's aunt, Sibyl, countess of Flanders, who

1. de Rozière, pp 136–8, no 66.
2. WT, XIX, 4, *RHC Occ*, I, pp 888–9. Date of marriage in Robert of Torigni, 'Chronicle', in *Chronicles of the Reigns of Stephen, Henry II and Richard I*, ed, R. Howlett, London 1889, *RS*, 82 (I–IV), IV, p 194; cf. Hamilton in Baker, ed, *Medieval Women*, p 159.
3. WT, XVIII, 19, *RHC Occ*, I, p 851.

had taken the veil at the convent of Bethany, and an unnamed sister of queen Melisende, presumably Yveta, the abbess of that house. The Old French version of William of Tyre names Melisende herself as one of the principal agents in the election and this seems more plausible since the king might have delegated the conduct of church affairs to his mother.[1]   The royal ladies appointed Amalric, a Frenchman from Nesle in the diocese of Noyon, who had been prior of the Holy Sepulchre since 1151.[2] Although an appeal was lodged against his election by the archbishop of Caesarea and the bishop of Bethlehem, Hadrian IV ruled in his favour and sent him a *pallium*.[3]

Soon after he was confirmed in office there was a disputed papal election in 1159. Alexander III sent a legate to the Holy Land and a council was held at Nazareth which was attended by the patriarch and the bishops, and the king and the principal lay lords, to decide whether to acknowledge Alexander. The bishops were divided between his claims and those of his rival, Victor IV, and, fearing that a religious schism might cause a dangerous division in the state, Baldwin III persuaded the council to remain neutral in the conflict.[4]   It is significant that this decision was made by the king rather than the patriarch: it is impossible to conceive of the patriarch Fulcher allowing the king to take such a decision for him but Amalric of Nesle does not seem to have had a very forceful personality.   Later that year the clergy of Jerusalem unanimously agreed to recognise Alexander.[5]   This decision was never reversed during the long years of schism which followed.

In 1163 Baldwin III died childless. The barons, whose spokesman was the patriarch, refused to accept his brother Amalric as king unless his marriage with Agnes of Courtenay, which the patriarch Fulcher had refused to sanction, were annulled. Amalric accepted this condition, provided that the children whom Agnes had borne him were legitimised, and the patriarch performed the annulment.[6] Whatever the reasons for this divorce may have been, it was a humiliating condition to impose on the new king and the

---

1. *Ibid.*, XVIII, 20, p 854 (with Old French translation).

2. de Rozière, pp 159—61, no 81; pp 211—13, no 110; p 242, no 130; pp 247—9, no 134; pp 326—8, no 183; *CGOH*, no 176.

3. WT, XVIII, 20, *RHC Occ*, I, p 854. Papal confirmation had not been received by September 1158 when the exiled patriarch of Antioch solemnised the marriage of Baldwin III and Theodora Comnena, *ibid.*, XVIII, 22, p 858.

4. *Ibid.*, XVIII, 29, pp 870—71.

5. *PL*, 200, 1362—3; *RR*, I, p 93, no 357.

6. WT, XIX, 4, *RHC Occ*, I, pp 889—90; 'Eracles', XXIII, 3, *RHC Occ*, II, p 5; Ernoul, p 17; Hamilton in Baker, ed, *Medieval Women*, pp 159—60.

patriarch must have been held in part responsible for it by king Amalric. For even had Amalric of Nesle only been acting as a mouthpiece of the baronage, he acquiesced in their decision, which, since it was a matter of canon law, he alone had the power to obstruct.

The king made no attempt to secure the patriarch's deposition but was content for most purposes to ignore him. In ecclesiastical matters they appeared to work together harmoniously. In 1168 the ecclesiastical organisation of the kingdom was completed by the foundation of two new dioceses. One was at Petra, which had been the third metropolitan see of Jerusalem in Orthodox times.[1] A Latin archbishop, Guerricus, a canon of the *Templum Domini* at Jerusalem, was appointed to this office by Amalric of Nesle, and his see was fixed in the castle of Kerak of Moab.[2] The other diocese was founded at Hebron as a suffragan see of Jerusalem. Its first bishop was Rainald, a nephew of the patriarch Fulcher.[3] Hebron, the shrine of the three patriarchs, Abraham, Isaac and Jacob, was an important pilgrimage centre for the peoples of the three religions of the kingdom, Christians, Jews and Muslims, and it had been served by a priory of Austin canons since the reign of Baldwin I.[4] They became the new cathedral chapter. But, unlike all the other sees in the kingdom except Bethlehem, Hebron had not been an Orthodox diocese.[5]

Both these sees seem to have owned their foundation to the initiative of the king rather than to that of the patriarch. Both Hebron and the lands beyond Jordan had been in Frankish hands since the early years of the settlement but for most of that time they had had little strategic importance. This situation changed radically in Amalric's reign when he and Nur-ad-Din, ruler of Damascus and Aleppo, were both striving to gain control of the weakened Fatimid caliphate of Egypt. In the wars which followed, Hebron and Oultrejourdain acquired great strategic importance and the appointment of Latin bishops in both regions, nominated by the king and acting as his representatives there, seems to have been part of Amalric's plan for the defence of the southern regions of his kingdom, on a par with his settlement and fortification of the coastal city of Darum to the south of Gaza.[6]

1. WT, XX, 3, *RHC Occ*, I, p 944. Mayer, 'Der kirchliche Neugliederungsversuch von 1168', *Bistümer*, pp 172–96.
2. James of Vitry, *HO*, p 95.
3. WT, XX, 3, *RHC Occ*, I, p 944.
4. First mentioned 1112, *CGOH*, nos 25, 28.
5. 'sed tempore Graecorum prioratus fuerat', WT, XX, 3, *RHC Occ*, I, p 944.
6. *Ibid.*, XX, 19, p 975. M.W. Baldwin, 'The Latin States under Baldwin III and Amalric, 1143–1174', in Setton, I, pp 549–58.

In 1169 a proposal was made by the king and patriarch to restore a bishop to the former Orthodox see of Jaffa. The canons of the Holy Sepulchre, who had ecclesiastical control of this city, appealed to Rome against this proposal on the grounds that it would cause them financial hardship, but Alexander III upheld the patriarch's right to restore the see on condition that the canons should receive adequate compensation. Nothing came of this plan, nor was it ever revived.[1]

Although Amalric of Nesle did not oppose the setting up of new bishoprics at Hebron and Petra the scheme does not appear to have been entirely to his liking. Those areas had formerly been directly under the jurisdiction of the patriarchs of Jerusalem and consequently he lost revenue when they were transferred from him. He asked the pope to confirm to him other Orthodox dioceses to which no bishops had been appointed and which he controlled, and Alexander III did so, specifying Jericho, Nablus and Darum.[2] This ruling may have safeguarded the patriarch's remaining revenues, but to make good the losses which he had suffered he tried to annexe some of the traditional revenues of the canons of the Holy Sepulchre. The chapter of the Sepulchre complained to the pope about this and he reprimanded the patriarch who soon afterwards issued a detailed confirmation for the canons of their property rights and financial privileges.[3] The only other complaint made against Amalric on this score was lodged by the abbot of Josaphat, who alleged that the patriarch and canons of the Sepulchre had demanded to be fed by the monks of Josaphat when they came to sing the station Mass there on the feast of the Assumption. Alexander III decreed that this was contrary to the privileges of Josaphat and must not occur again since it had led to quarrelling, scandal and even violent death.[4]

King Amalric died in 1174 and was succeeded by his son, the leper king, Baldwin IV. It was unfortunate for the patriarch that the young king's mother, Agnes of Courtenay, became very influential in the new reign[5] since she can have had little liking for the man who had debarred her from becoming queen. By this time Amalric of Nesle was growing old. He did not attend the third Lateran council in 1179, perhaps because he could not face the long sea voyage.[6] He died on 6 October 1180.[7] William of

1. de Rozière, pp 291–2, no 162; *RR*, I, p 121, no 461.
2. de Rozière, pp 319–22, no 180.
3. *Ibid.*, pp 283–5, nos 157–8, pp 301–5, no 167; *RR*, I, p 115, nos 441–2.
4. Kohler, pp 141–2, no 31.
5. Hamilton in Baker, ed, *Medieval Women*, pp 163–70.
6. WT, XXI, 26, *RHC Occ*, I, p 1049.
7. *Ibid.*, XXII, 4, p 1068.

Tyre, who knew him well, and was, indeed, consecrated by him, had a low opinion of him. He describes him as 'reasonably well educated, but bereft of intelligence and virtually useless'.[1]

It must be admitted that his judgment has some force. Amalric was quite competent as an ecclesiastical administrator, which was what he was trained to be. Most of the acts of his long reign relate to the conveyancing of church property and the settlement of law-suits relating to church lands.[2] It may not have been entirely his fault that as a result of arranging the annulment of Amalric's marriage with Agnes of Courtenay the patriarch was out of favour at court for most of his reign. That he was so is not in question: he was only once asked to witness a royal charter, and that was by queen Melisende who had appointed him.[3] It was, perhaps, a matter of temperament that the patriarch showed no interest in military affairs. Although the kingdom was almost constantly at war throughout his pontificate it is never recorded that he accompanied the royal army into battle as bearer of the True Cross. His only contribution to the political life of the kingdom was to write an encyclical to the west after the defeat of the north Syrian armies at Harim in 1164 offering indulgences to those who would come to the defence of the Franks in the east.[4] In 1169 he volunteered to go to the west in person to help recruit aid, but his ship was wrecked as he was leaving Syria and, although he escaped, he was replaced as envoy by the archbishop of Tyre.[5] Amalric clearly did not possess those qualities of leadership of which the hard-pressed kingdom stood so much in need, particularly in the years which followed king Amalric's death. Nor did he evince any qualities of great personal piety which might have made him a respected religious leader in a society torn by faction: he gave no alms except for his own requiem,[6] and, so far as is known, did not even institute any special prayers for the kingdom in its peril, as, for example, on the eve of the battle of Montgisart. No other Latin patriarch had ruled for so long: no other had made so little contribution to the life of the kingdom and of the church.

His successor, Heraclius, the last Latin patriarch to rule in the first kingdom, is perhaps a less controversial figure than he should

1. *Ibid.*, XVIII, 20, p 854.
2. de Rozière, pp 115–17, no 58, pp 131–5, nos 64–5, p 140, no 68, pp 150–2, no 75, pp 231–2, no 127, pp 249–50, no 135, pp 322–5, no 181; *CGOH*, nos 376, 422; Delaville Le Roulx, *Archives*, pp 97–9, no 19, pp 107–8, no 25, pp 124–5, no 37; Delaborde, pp 82–3, no 35.
3. Delaborde, pp 81–2, no 34.
4. P. Riant, 'Six lettres relatives aux croisades', *AOL*, I, pp 286–7, no 2; *RR*, I, p 107, no 410.
5. WT, XX, 12, *RHC Occ*, I, pp 960–1.
6. de Rozière, pp 305–7, no 168.

be. Posterity has accepted, on the whole uncritically, the portrait of him given in the chronicle attributed to Ernoul and in the Old French continuations of William of Tyre. These sources derive their information largely from the political opponents of the Courtenays and the Lusignans and depict Guy of Lusignan and his supporters, among whom was the patriarch, in a consistently unflattering way. Moreover, because the sources were written after the defeat of Hattin, their writers held Guy and his party responsible for the loss of the kingdom. Such accounts must be treated with caution.

According to Ernoul Heraclius was born in the Auvergne and came to Jerusalem after he had been priested.[1] He was archdeacon of Jerusalem from 1169—75[2] and archbishop of Caesarea from 1175—80.[3] According to some of the Old French sources he had been the lover of Agnes of Courtenay and owed his promotion to her.[4] It is impossible to determine whether there is any truth in the accusation that Heraclius and Agnes were lovers, but it seems certain that she had no part in his appointment to Caesarea, since this occurred in 1175 when Raymond III of Tripoli was regent for Baldwin IV and when Agnes had no influence at court.[5]

When Amalric of Nesle died Heraclius was chosen to succeed him within ten days. William of Tyre reports this without comment.[6] The Old French chronicles state that the canons of the Holy Sepulchre nominated both Heraclius and William of Tyre and that Baldwin IV, on the advice of Agnes of Courtenay, chose the former. They also add that this was done against the advice of William of Tyre who tried to persuade them to choose an independent candidate from western Europe.[7] Agnes, as the king's mother, probably did have a decisive voice in this appointment just as queen Melisende had had in that of Amalric of Nesle. The naïve account in the Old French sources, moreover, reflects the deep political division in the kingdom. The leper king's health was deteriorating in 1180: the heir to the throne was his sister Sibyl who had recently married Guy of Lusignan, but her succession was opposed by the king's cousin, Raymond III of

1. Ernoul, p 82.
2. His predecessor, Ralph, is last mentioned in 1160, de Rozière, pp 115—17, 133—5, nos 58, 65. Heraclius is named in *ibid.*, pp 301—5, no 167 (1169), pp 322—5, no 181 (1171); *CGOH*, no 422 (1171); Delaville Le Roulx, *Archives*, pp 124—5, no 37 (1175).
3. WT, XXI, 10, *RHC Occ*, I, p 1021.
4. Ernoul, p 82; MS G of 'Eracles', *RHC Occ*, II, p 58, n 19.
5. Hamilton in Baker, ed, *Medieval Women*, p 164.
6. WT, XXII, 4, *RHC Occ*, I, p 1068.
7. Ernoul, pp 83—4; 'Eracles', XXIII, 38, *RHC Occ*, II, p 59.

Tripoli. William of Tyre, as is clear from his *History*, was a firm supporter of Raymond, and, since the Courtenays and the Lusignans would not give the headship of the church to a known supporter of their chief rival, they chose Heraclius as the alternative candidate. The choice of Heraclius is explicable in terms of politics alone: there is no need to presume that Agnes was motivated by a desire to advance the career of her former lover.

In some ways Heraclius was more like Arnulf than any other twelfth-century patriarch of Jerusalem. Ernoul's account of the patriarch's keeping a mistress is probably true, since it is very circumstantial and not just vague gossip. She was called Pascha de Riveri and was the wife of a merchant at Nablus. She openly set up house with Heraclius, to whom she bore children, and was popularly known as *madame la patriarchesse*.[1] But a more serious criticism of Heraclius derives from his alleged treatment of William of Tyre. The Old French sources relate that William appealed to the pope against Heraclius's appointment, and that the patriarch, fearing that he would be deposed, sent to Rome his physician who poisoned the archbishop of Tyre.[2] This story must be treated with some reserve. William of Tyre's presence in the kingdom is securely attested in a series of charters which he dated as royal chancellor between March 1181 and March 1183[3] so that he can only have gone to Rome after that date. Hiestand has shown that he died in Rome on 29 September 1186: his successor, Joscius, was in office by October of that year.[4] The Old French sources may reflect a true tradition when they state that William died in Rome while appealing to the pope against the patriarch, but the grounds of his appeal may have been connected with the metropolitan rights of the see of Tyre, a subject about which William, like most of his predecessors, had strong feelings, rather than with the validity of the patriarch's election which he had accepted without demur for more than three years. It was a

1. Ernoul, pp 86—7.
2. *Ibid.*, pp 84—6; 'Eracles', variant reading, *RHC Occ*, II, pp 59—60.
3. 10 September 1181, Delaville Le Roulx, *Archives*, pp 149—51, nos 57—8; 13 November 1181, Strehlke, p 13, no 13; 6 February 1182, *CGOH*, no 625; 24 February 1182, Strehlke, pp 13—14, no 14; 1 March 1182, *CGOH*, vol II, p 909, no 20; 27 April 1182, Strehlke, pp 14—15, no 15; 14 November 1182, *CGOH*, no 645; 19 March 1183, Strehlke, pp 15—16, nos 16—17.
4. Joscius, Strehlke, pp 19—21, nos 21—3, of 21 October 1186. *CGOH*, no 819 of 17 October 1186 names William as archbishop of Tyre. This is known only in a précis contained in an eighteenth-century calendar, and it seems probable that the original did not give the bishop's name but the copyist added it and inferred, wrongly, that William of Tyre was still alive then. Cf. Runciman, *Crusades*, II, pp 425—6, n 1. R. Hiestand, 'Zum Leben und Laufbahn Wilhelms von Tyrus', *Deutsches Archiv für Erforschung des Mittelalters*, 34, 1978, pp 345—80, specially p 369.

standard reaction of twelfth-century writers to suppose that
unexpected deaths were the result of poison, but there seems as
little reason to suppose that Heraclius plotted the death of William
of Tyre as there does to accept the accusation that Baldwin II
procured the death of the patriarch Stephen, although it was
widely believed at the time that he had done so.[1]

Whatever his moral failings may have been, Heraclius was
willing to take the initiative in the political life of the kingdom
and in this regard he must have been a welcome change from
Amalric of Nesle. He led the delegation from Jerusalem which
mediated peace between Bohemond III of Antioch and the patriarch Aimery of Limoges in 1181 and was responsible for persuading Raymond III of Tripoli to join the negotiators, for although
Raymond was at enmity with the court of Jerusalem he was
trusted by Bohemond, who, in the patriarch's opinion, would
listen to his advice. The success of this mission, which averted a
civil war in north Syria, was due in part at least to the initiative
of Heraclius.[2] He also tried to act as peacemaker in the southern
kingdom when the king quarrelled with his brother-in-law, Guy of
Lusignan, in 1183. Guy had been acting as regent, and Baldwin
IV not merely deprived him of that position, but also wished the
patriarch to annul Guy's marriage to Sibyl. This exclusion of the
heir-presumptive led to a threat of civil war between the king and
Guy. Heraclius had no wish to abet this: not only did he take no
action about instituting nullity proceedings, he also persuaded the
grand masters of the Temple and the Hospital to join him in an
appeal to the king in the High Court to be reconciled with Guy
and when this failed all three petitioners angrily left the council
chamber.[3]

Later in 1184 a mission was sent to the west to ask for military
aid against the rising power of Saladin. This was led by Heraclius
and both grand masters and conferred successively with pope
Lucius III, Frederick Barbarossa, Philip Augustus and Henry II of
England.[4] Heraclius was the first Latin patriarch of Jerusalem to
lead a deputation of this kind: he was clearly an effective
preacher, for when he described the plight of the Holy Land to
the English court the king and his barons were reduced to

1. WT, XIII, 25, *RHC Occ*, I, p 595.
2. *Ibid.*, XXII, 6—7, pp 1071—5.
3. *Ibid.*, XXII, 29, XXIII, 1, pp 1127—8, 1133; 'Eracles', XXIII, 1, *RHC Occ*, II,
pp 1—3.
4. Arnold of Torroja, grand master of the Temple, died in the west, letter of Lucius
III to Henry II of England, *PL*, 201, 1312—13, no 182. R.C. Smail, 'The international
status of the Latin Kingdom of Jerusalem, 1150—1192', in P.M. Holt, ed, *The Eastern
Mediterranean Lands in the period of the Crusades*, Warminster 1977, pp 26—7.

tears.[1] Although it had no immediate result this mission undoubtedly helped to prepare the way for the immense response which later came to the preaching of the third crusade.

By the time Heraclius returned to Palestine the leper king had died, leaving a strange will. He designated his nephew, Baldwin V, as his heir, but stipulated that if the boy died while still a minor the barons of the kingdom were to ask the pope and the rulers of western Europe to judge between the claims of Baldwin IV's sisters, the two princesses, Sibyl and Isabel. As is well known, when Baldwin V died in 1186 Heraclius was responsible for ignoring Baldwin IV's will and crowning Sibyl and her husband, Guy of Lusignan. Although he was subsequently much criticised for this the majority of tenants-in-chief of the crown were willing to abide by his decision at the time. Sibyl was the lawful heir to the throne, as Reynald of Châtillon is alleged to have stated at the time: 'ce est li plus apareissanz et li plus dreis heirs dou roiaume'. His testimony is the more impressive, because Raymond of Tripoli's candidate for the crown, Humphrey of Toron, husband of Sibyl's sister Isabel, was Reynald's stepson.[2]

Heraclius was later accused of cowardice for not accompanying the royal army on the Hattin campaign in 1187[3] but he may have been placed in charge of the defence of Jerusalem in the king's absence. He certainly assumed responsibility there after the Christian defeat, persuading Balian of Ibelin to take charge of its defences, and stripping silver from the edicule of the Holy Sepulchre to mint money with which to pay the garrison when Saladin besieged the city, thus preventing desertions to the Muslims.[4] When the city surrendered to the sultan and 11,000 poor people were unable to pay their ransom Heraclius and Balian offered themselves as hostages to the sultan so that the poor could go free until their ransom money had been raised, but Saladin refused these terms.[5] Although he was allowed to leave Jerusalem, and presumably accompanied the queen to Tripoli,[6] Heraclius did not choose to go on living in safety there but joined

1. Roger of Wendover, *Chronica*, ed H.G. Hewlett, *RS*, 84 (I–III), London 1886–9, I, pp 134–5.

2. Ernoul, pp 130–9; 'Eracles', XXIII, 17–21, *RHC Occ*, II, pp 26–33, Reynald of Châtillon's speech, *ibid.*, p 28.

3. Ernoul, p 156; 'Eracles', XXIII, 29, p 46.

4. *Ibid.*, XXIII, 46, p 70; Ernoul, p 176. Imad ad-Din al-Isfahani, *La Conquête de la Syrie et de la Palestine par Saladin*, trans H. Massé, Paris 1972, p 49, accuses the patriarch of removing this silver for his personal use when Jerusalem was evacuated.

5. 'Salahedin dist que ce ne feroit il mie, XI mile homes por II', 'Eracles', XXIII, 62, *RHC Occ*, II, p 98.

6. He went with Guy of Lusignan from Tripoli to Tyre in 1189, Roger of Houedene, vol III, p 20.

Guy of Lusignan in his attack on Acre in 1189. He died at the siege in the summer of 1190, a victim of the epidemic which was ravaging the crusader camp.[1]

Because Heraclius crowned Guy of Lusignan, and because Guy led the army of the kingdom to defeat at Hattin, Heraclius's name was blackened by his contemporaries and their verdict has been accepted, perhaps too uncritically, by later writers. His moral character was not above reproach, but he showed real ability as a diplomat, a capacity for taking action in the interests of the kingdom in times of crisis, and qualities of loyalty towards his friends, which have never received adequate recognition.

By the time of Heraclius's death the entire kingdom of Jerusalem, with the exception of Tyre, was in Muslim control, and his successors had to rebuild the Latin church just as Guy of Lusignan's successors had to rebuild the Frankish kingdom. But until 1187 the restored patriarchate of Jerusalem had possessed a far greater degree of stability than the sister-patriarchate of Antioch. The only southern diocese which was lost to the Muslims before Hattin was Banyas, which Nur-ad-Din captured in 1164.[2] The bishop, who was absent when this happened, continued to hold the title until his death in 1170[3] but no attempt was made thereafter to appoint a titular bishop to the see.

The Latin patriarchate of Jerusalem was modelled very closely on the Orthodox pattern. All the provinces of the Orthodox patriarchate were restored with the exception of that of Bosra, and part of Tyre was annexed to Jerusalem from Antioch. The thirteen Frankish dioceses which were finally set up were, it is true, few by comparison with the 102 Orthodox dioceses which they replaced, but the ecclesiastical establishment of the kingdom was, nevertheless, large when judged by contemporary western European standards. There were, for example, only sixteen dioceses in the far larger Angevin kingdom of England.[4] In choosing locations for their sees from the multiplicity of possible places which had had bishops in the Orthodox period the Franks were guided by two considerations. Some sees were sited in places of military or administrative importance, like those of Tiberias and Kerak of Moab, while others were situated at pilgrimage centres, like Sebastia and Hebron. The very nomenclature which

---

1. *Itinerarium Peregrinorum et Gesta Regis Ricardi*, I, 42, ed W. Stubbs, London 1864, *RS*, 38, p 93.
2. WT, XIX, 10, *RHC Occ*, I, p 899–900.
3. He died in Paris while on a mission to the French court, *ibid*., XX, 12, pp 960–1.
4. Canterbury, York, London, Winchester, Rochester, Chichester, Salisbury, Bath and Wells, Exeter, Worcester, Hereford, Coventry-Lichfield, Ely, Norwich, Lincoln, Durham.

the Franks used for some of their bishoprics, St George (Lydda-Ramla), St John (Sebastia), St Abraham (Hebron), reflects their preoccupation with the cult centres which they had restored to Christian control.

The Latin church of Jerusalem was organised in a state which had reasonably stable frontiers throughout most of this period, but its growth was slow. Until 1127 there were only five Latin bishops in the kingdom including the patriarch. The major organisation of the church was carried out in the pontificate of the patriarch William and after his death in 1145 only two new sees were created, those of Hebron and Petra, both for military rather than ecclesiastical reasons. But although the establishment of dioceses was a slow process the jurisdiction of the patriarchs of Jerusalem was recognised throughout the kingdom all through this period. The only challenge to their authority came from the archbishops of Tyre and this was fitful and unsuccessful. It is the stability of the church of Jerusalem which contrasts most markedly with the fluctuating fortunes of the church of Antioch during this period and which caused Jerusalem to be considered in practice, if not in theory, as the more important of the two by the papacy and the western church in general.

4. LATIN PARISH ORGANISATION

Although the Franks attempted to create a coherent system of bishoprics throughout the areas they governed, no parallel attempt was made to produce a uniform network of Latin parishes. Bishoprics formed part of the Frankish pattern of government, whereas parishes reflected the Frankish pattern of settlement, which was very uneven. The Franks were a ruling minority: Benvenisti has estimated that at the height of their power in the twelfth century there were about 140,000 Franks in the kingdom of Jerusalem, who formed about a fifth of the entire population.[1] Statistics for the northern states are less easy to determine, but it is probable that the proportion of Franks in Tripoli and Antioch was comparable, but that they were less numerous in the county of Edessa.[2] Of course, all these settlers did not arrive with the first crusade, but came to Syria gradually in the course of the twelfth century, and the Latin parish system grew accordingly.

The earliest western settlers lived almost exclusively in towns, although a high proportion of them must have been peasants before they came to the east. Town life was attractive: the towns of Syria had better amenities than the villages, and they were more secure, which was particularly important in the early years of the settlement when Frankish control over large areas of their states was very tenuous. There was room for more settlers in the towns of Syria, for the Franks in their first flush of triumphalism either slaughtered the Muslim inhabitants, as at Antioch in 1098, Jerusalem in 1099 and Caesarea in 1101, or expelled them, as at Arsuf in 1101 and Acre in 1104.[3] These intolerant measures sometimes created a population vacuum which it proved difficult to fill. Baldwin I, for example, brought Bedouin from beyond Jordan to live in Jerusalem, but the evidence suggests that throughout the twelfth century the population of the holy city was smaller than it had been before the first crusade.[4]

1. M. Benvenisti, *The Crusaders in the Holy Land*, Jerusalem 1972, pp 18, 215.
2. The northern states are not so well documented, nor have the settlement patterns there been so thoroughly surveyed as those in the kingdom of Jerusalem.
3. Hagenmeyer, *Chronologie*, pp 149—51, no 265 (Antioch); pp 250—3, nos 405—7 (Jerusalem); Fulcher of Chartres, II, 8, s 3 (Arsuf); II, 9, ss 5—8 (Caesarea), ed Hagenmeyer, pp 397—8, 402—4; Albert of Aix, IX, 29, *RHC Occ*, IV, pp 606—7 (Acre).
4. WT, XI, 27, *RHC Occ*, I, p 501; J. Prawer, 'The settlement of the Latins in Jerusalem', *Speculum*, 27, 1952, pp 490—503.

The Franks did not form the only element in the population of the towns which they settled. The native Christians were left undisturbed. The Franks made no attempt to force the separated eastern churches, such as the Jacobites and the Armenians, into union with Rome, but granted them virtual religious autonomy. No attempt was made therefore to integrate the churches belonging to those communions into the Latin parish system. In the case of the Orthodox, although their clergy were made subject to the canonical authority of Latin bishops and they formed part of a single communion with western Catholics, no attempt was made to latinise their worship.[1]   They preserved their own traditional forms of worship and ceremonial, and therefore their churches, in which the liturgy was celebrated in Greek or Syriac, were not suitable for the devotional needs of Latin-rite Christians, so that new Latin churches had to be founded for the Frankish population. It is true that in certain shrine churches, of which the Holy Sepulchre was the most notable example, the liturgy was celebrated in both the Orthodox and the Latin rites,[2] but such instances were exceptional and resulted from the need to cater for pilgrims of different rites.   The normal practice in towns was to have separate churches for Latins and for Orthodox.

In rural areas the situation may sometimes have been different. Certainly Latins and Orthodox shared the church of St George outside Tiberias, which belonged to the Benedictines of Josaphat who owned the estate on which it was built.[3]   But although this may not have been unparalleled, such sharing of churches was probably rare, for, as will be seen later in this chapter, rural churches of the Latin rite were uncommon, and they could only be shared with Orthodox when they were situated in areas where the peasantry was Orthodox. The number of places where both these conditions obtained — the existence of a church of the Latin rite and an Orthodox peasantry — was probably not very great.

In the twelfth century every town with a Frankish population usually had a single parish church of the Latin rite. This was not necessarily the only Latin place of worship in the town, but the only one which possessed *ius parochiale*: that is to say that the parish church alone exercised cure of souls. In practical terms this meant that baptisms had to take place in the parish church,[4] as

1. For the Orthodox see chapter 7 below; for the separated churches see chapter 8 below.
2. Theoderich, *Description of the Holy Places*, p 15.
3. Delaborde, pp 87–8, no 40.
4. When St Demetrius, Acre, was deprived of parish status this was symbolised by the destruction of its font, TT, III, p 33, no 343.

did churchings and the solemnisation of marriages. Easter confessions, which seem to have been common in the Frankish east even before the fourth Lateran council made them obligatory,[1] were normally heard by the parish priest, and he alone had the right to visit the sick and dying and administer the last sacraments to them. The dead had to be buried in the cemetery of the parish church.[2]

In cities where a Latin bishopric was established the cathedral was, in the twelfth century, usually the only Latin parish church. This was true even in Jerusalem, where the only Latin church with *ius parochiale* was the Holy Sepulchre. Such towns were, of course, exceptional, but in all the cities where the Franks settled the provision of a parish church of Latin rite seems to have been regarded as essential from the beginning. Tancred endowed a Latin church at Tiberias immediately after he conquered the city in the winter of 1099;[3] at Jaffa the church of St Peter was set aside for Latin Christians in the very early days of the kingdom;[4] and at Tyre the former Orthodox cathedral of St Mary's was given to the canons of the Holy Sepulchre after the Frankish conquest of 1124 and before an archbishop had been appointed to the see.[5] As the Frankish population grew in the twelfth century it was sometimes necessary to found new churches to cater for their needs. Thus in 1168 the patriarch Amalric of Nesle confirmed to the canons of the Holy Sepulchre the church of St Nicholas in the *faubourg* of Jaffa and conferred full parish status on it:[6] the parish church of St Peter in the old city could obviously no longer cope with the increase in population.

After the third crusade there is evidence that new Latin parishes were created in some of the Frankish cities: certainly there were multiple parishes at Acre by 1200 and at Antioch by 1227.[7] This development may, in the first instance, have arisen in response to the growth of the Latin-rite population of those

1. An agreement of 1175 between the bishop of Acre and the Hospital comments: 'si quis parrochianus Acconensis ecclesie quadrigesimali tempore . . . ut mos est, peccata sua confiteri voluerit . . . ', *CGOH*, no 471.

2. For typical definitions of parish rights in twelfth-century Syria, de Rozière, pp 287—90, nos 160—1.

3. WT, IX, 13, *RHC Occ*, I, p 384.

4. Arnulf gave it to the canons of the Sepulchre, de Rozière, pp 15—17, no 14.

5. It is listed in Honorius II's confirmation of 1128, de Rozière, p 19, no 16, and was confirmed by archbishop William of Tyre in 1129, *ibid.*, pp 138—9, no 67. Mayer, 'Die Marienkirche im Tyrus und die Anfänge des dortigen Erzbistums', *Bistümer*, pp 98—111.

6. de Rozière, pp 289—90, no 161.

7. Müller, pp 82—3, no 52 (Acre); Riant, *Etudes sur l'histoire de l'Eglise de Bethléem*, 2 vols, Genoa 1889, Paris 1896, I, p 145, no 11 (Antioch).

cities brought about by an influx of refugees from former Frankish lands which passed under Muslim control in 1187.

The growth of cities and the establishment of new parishes to meet the needs of a rising urban population was a phenomenon found throughout much of western Europe in the twelfth and thirteenth centuries and in no way a problem unique to the Frankish east. The chief difference between the parish organisation of the church in Frankish Syria and that found in western Europe lay in its rural distribution. By the time of the first crusade, except in some regions recently reconquered from the Saracens, like Sicily and parts of central Spain, and mission countries like Scandinavia, the entire rural population was Latin Christian, and most villages of any size had a parish church. Since the west was, for all its urban growth, still predominantly a rural society, the majority of parishes there were in country districts. It is here that the chief distinction between the west and the Latin east is to be found.

In the Syrian countryside the Franks dispossessed the Muslim landowners and took over their position. This meant that they came to form the bulk of the landowning class, since before the first crusade the only Christian landowners in those regions had been the native Christian churches and monasteries, together with some Armenian lords in what later became the Frankish states of Antioch and Edessa. The Franks, initially at least, made no attempt to dispossess Christian landlords. Because of the absence of detailed evidence it is impossible to tell what proportion of the peasantry in territories occupied by the Franks had become Muslim by 1098. Some were certainly still Christians,[1] but in some areas the peasants were predominantly Muslim.[2] The Franks, of course, made no attempt to displace the native Christians, but they did not expel the Muslims either, as they had done with their co-religionists in some of the cities, for they were aware of the need to preserve a native labour-force.

The role of the Latin church in rural Syria can only be understood in the context of the economic system which the Frankish landlords introduced. The tenurial system in the Crusader States differed from that in operation in much of western Europe at that time in that the Frankish landlords did not customarily own demesne land. The peasantry, native Christian or Muslim, were tied to the land and in law had the status of western serfs, but

1. For example, the *Suriani* in the *casalia* of Ramatha, Bethelegel, Aithara, Calandria and Belferage listed in a diploma of Baldwin III, who have Christian names, de Rozière, pp 107–10, no 55.

2. Ibn Jubair in 1184 stated that the villages between Toron and Acre were predominantly Muslim; *The Travels*, trans R.J.C. Broadhurst, London 1952, pp 316–17.

they paid rent to their lords (some percentage of their produce and some fixed dues) and were not normally required to perform labour services.[1]

One consequence of this was that Frankish lords did not usually live in native villages. They either lived in cities, or, in cases where the lordship was remote from a city, in castles, which were, in effect, artificial Frankish towns. The remains of some fortified Frankish manor-houses dating from the twelfth century have been found in the kingdom of Jerusalem, which may imply that the evidence of the written sources needs to be modified and that some Frankish lords did live in the country and administer their estates directly.[2] But this is not the only possible inference. It is arguable that these manor-houses were administrative centres, built in the Frankish style, but used by the lords' officials for collecting their share of the produce, which was frequently paid in kind, and analogous, therefore, to the fortified villages found in some lordships which served the same purpose.

The isolated Frankish manor house and the fortified administrative centre were exceptions to the general rule: most villages did not have any Frankish inhabitants. Consequently there was no call to build a Latin church in such places. For if the village was Christian it would already have an eastern-rite church, and if it was Muslim it would not need a church at all. Muslims were allowed the free practice of their faith in the countryside, though they were required to pay a tax to their rulers (as were the Jews).[3] This was a reversal of the practice which had obtained before the first crusade when non-Muslims had been taxed, and it was a practice which was also employed in the twelfth-century kingdom of Sicily.[4] There was, therefore, every incentive to western landlords to leave well alone and not to try to convert their Muslim tenants by founding churches in their villages since, if they succeeded, they would lose revenue. The only Latin churches which were built in the native villages of Frankish Syria, therefore, were situated in administrative centres for the use of the lords' officials, and they were not very numerous.[5]

1. J. Riley-Smith, 'The domain in the countryside', *The Feudal Nobility and the Kingdom of Jerusalem, 1174–1277*, London 1973, pp 40–61.

2. Benvenisti, *Crusaders in the Holy Land*, pp 233–45.

3. Papal confirmations of the rights of religious houses in Syria often contain the clause: 'Redditus vero qui de rusticorum infidelium censu vestro monasterio constituti sunt, vel in futuro, prestante Deo, conferentur, vobis integros manere censemus', e.g. Paschal II for Josaphat, Delaborde, pp 22–3, no 2.

4. F. Chalandon, *Histoire de la domination normande en Italie et en Sicile*, 2 vols, Paris 1907, II, pp 690–3.

5. For example, the church 'cum iure parrochiali' in the royal *casale* of St Gilles, de Rozière, pp 258–60, no 142. There is no complete list of Latin rural churches in Syria.

Frankish landlords were naturally anxious to develop fully the agricultural potential of their lands. Since there was no surplus native labour force they encouraged Franks to settle in villages, offering them advantageous terms. The earliest of these foundations were at al-Bira on the Jerusalem-Nablus road, and al-Qubaibah on the Jerusalem-Jaffa road, founded around 1120 by the canons of the Holy Sepulchre, and known to the Franks respectively as Magna Mahomeria and Parva Mahomeria. This example was later imitated by the crown. Baldwin III in 1153 founded the village of Castel Imbert (Akhziv) to the north of Acre, and his brother, Amalric, in 1168 made a similar foundation at Darum to the south of Gaza. There are only about ten such settlements known throughout the whole period of Frankish rule, and all of them were in the kingdom of Jerusalem.[1] Their inhabitants were exclusively Frankish, and churches of the Latin rite were built to serve them. Some of these were quite large. The pilgrim Theoderich gives an enthusiastic description of the church of St Mary at Magna Mahomeria, outside which stood 'a great cross of hewn stone, raised upon seven steps, which . . . are ascended by pilgrims, who from thence behold . . . the Tower of David'.[2]

The church of Latin Syria was, therefore, unusually circumstanced in the twelfth century. It had, in the south at least, by the third quarter of that century, a reasonable establishment of bishops and cathedral clergy, but there were comparatively few urban parishes and rural parishes were even rarer and existed for the benefit of a ruling Frankish minority. There are no lists of Latin parishes in Syria comparable to the lists of Latin dioceses which were so carefully copied in the Frankish east and at Rome. Evidence about parishes comes either from accounts of disputes between the ordinary and churches outside the diocesan structure which claimed parochial status, or from casual references in the definition of property boundaries in deeds of conveyance, or from confirmations of the lands of cathedral chapters. Considered together these sources reveal a uniform pattern throughout the Frankish states and suggest that the number of parishes in any Latin diocese was comparatively small.

All parish clergy were subject to the diocesan bishop who had certain well-defined rights, grounded in western canon law. Parish priests owed him canonical obedience: they had to attend diocesan synods; they were required to enforce interdicts and

1. J. Prawer, 'Colonisation Activities in the Latin Kingdom of Jerusalem', *Revue belge de philologie et d'histoire*, 29, 1951, pp 1063–1118.
2. Theoderich, *Description of the Holy Places*, p 60.

excommunications which the bishop promulgated; the diocesan bishop alone had the right to consecrate altars and chapels in their parishes; he alone could ordain clergy to serve those parishes; the holy oils, used in baptism and extreme unction, had to be obtained from the bishop, who blessed them in his cathedral church on Holy Thursday; and the diocesan reserved the right to confirm candidates whom the parish priest presented to him. In addition, of course, the bishop was entitled to a share of the tithe and the fees of the parish clergy.[1] The relation between the bishop and his parish clergy was an orderly one, but the situation in Latin Syria was complicated by the existence of other Latin clergy who were either only partially subject to the bishop or completely exempt from his jurisdiction.

Like their colleagues in the west the nobility of Frankish Syria employed domestic chaplains. This was true not only of heads of state[2] but also of feudal lords whose chaplains, in addition to their religious duties, also carried out the work of chancellor for their patrons.[3] Viscounts, who were deputies of the crown or of great lords in the work of government, also sometimes employed domestic chaplains who acted as notaries.[4] Chaplains officiated in the chapels of castles and if there was more than one castle in a lordship a lord might employ several of them.[5]

Most information about chaplains in Frankish Syria comes from documents which they wrote or witnessed, but the letters of appointment issued by Baldwin IV to his chaplain in the royal castle of Jaffa have been preserved among the charters of Josaphat. This source relates that the appointment was in the king's gift and that the king paid the stipend, and it also records that the chaplain exercised full parochial rights within the castle. The privilege is witnessed by the dean of Jaffa, representative of the Holy Sepulchre to whom the city parish of Jaffa belonged.[6] There is every reason to suppose that similar conditions governed the appointment of other royal chaplains and it is reasonable to infer that the chaplains of lesser lords enjoyed comparable powers,

1. A typical statement of the bishop's rights occurs in a privilege of Bernard of Lydda, de Rozière, pp 322–5, no 181. Confirmation is mentioned only once in such definitions: bishop Theobald's privilege for the Pisan church of Acre, Müller, pp 82–3, no 52.

2. For example, three served the palace of Antioch in Raymond of Poitiers's reign, de Rozière, pp 169–78, nos 88- 9.

3. E.g. Baldwin, lord of Marash, *CGOH*, no 313; Reynald of Châtillon, lord of Oultrejourdain, *ibid.*, no 521.

4. E.g. Roland, viscount of Tripoli, *ibid.*, no 482.

5. In 1160 Hugh and Balian of Ibelin between them had four chaplains, de Rozière, pp 133–5, no 65.

6. Delaborde, pp 85–6, no 38.

since in most other respects lordships mirrored the organisation of the royal court.[1] Technically, no doubt, the chaplains owed canonical obedience to the diocesan bishop and, although this may have been in large measure nominal, they probably did not constitute a serious threat to his authority. But as they enjoyed parochial powers within their castles it follows that castles were exempt from the authority of ordinary parish clergy. Since, with very few exceptions, all the important towns of the Frankish east contained castles, the power of the Latin parish clergy in the cities must have been correspondingly diminished.

Many castles were, of course, situated in rural areas, and *faubourgs* often sprang up around them which contained a proportion of Frankish settlers. In such cases it was normal practice to build a separate church for the *faubourg* rather than to allow the people who lived there to assist at Mass in the castle chapel. Thus the church of St Mary was founded in the *faubourg* of Crac des Chevaliers,[2] while the church in the *faubourg* of Kerak of Moab became after 1168 the pro-cathedral of the archbishop of Petra.[3] Practical considerations may in part have dictated this kind of arrangement, since the chapels of secular lords, at least, were sometimes not very large, but the clergy of the *faubourg* churches seem, in most cases, to have been appointed by the bishop, not by the castellan, and this restricted the powers of royal and noble chaplains.

In addition to the secular clergy there were also, from the earliest days of Frankish rule, communities of regular clergy in the Latin east. It is not the purpose of this study to examine the monastic life of Outremer, but some consideration of the amount of church patronage which these communities exercised there is essential. The first crusade was launched under the auspices of the reformed papacy. The Austin canons were a principal instrument in the attempts which the reformers made to extend their ideals to cathedrals and collegiate churches[4] and they naturally came to occupy an influential position in the Latin church in Syria.

The most important shrine in Syria was the church of the Holy Sepulchre, which was administered by Latin canons from the beginning of Frankish rule, but which became a house of Austin canons only in 1114.[5] Through the generosity of successive patriarchs they came to exercise considerable patronage in the

1. J. Prawer, *The Latin Kingdom of Jerusalem*, London 1972, pp 126—58.
2. Delaville Le Roulx, 'Inventaire', no 26.
3. James of Vitry, *HO*, p 95.
4. J.C. Dickinson, *The Origins of the Austin Canons and their Introduction into England*, London 1950, pp 26—58.
5. de Rozière, pp 44—7, no 25.

diocese of Jerusalem. This included the city of Jaffa, a gift of the patriarch Arnulf, where the canons appointed a dean to represent them; the shrine of St Lazarus at Bethany, also the gift of Arnulf, which they exchanged in 1138 for the estates of Thecua so that queen Melisende could found the convent of Bethany; and the shrine of Quarantene, the traditional site of Christ's temptation in the wilderness, which was a gift of the patriarch William.[1] The canons of the Sepulchre naturally had the gift of livings in the Frankish villages which they established,[2] and in addition they were given a parish church in the *faubourg* of Nablus in 1168[3] and in 1175 they bought from the Mount Tabor monastery the parish church of St Gilles, an important royal administrative centre situated between Jerusalem and Nablus.[4] Because they were a cathedral chapter of regular clergy there was no conflict between the canons of the Sepulchre and the authority of the patriarch in the diocese of Jerusalem.

The Holy Sepulchre owned extensive lands throughout the Frankish east[5] but its ecclesiastical patronage in other dioceses there was very restricted. In the patriarchate of Antioch the canons owned only a priory on Mount Pilgrim and the rural church of St George, both the gifts of the devout Raymond IV of Tripoli.[6] In the patriarchate of Jerusalem they only owned two urban churches in other dioceses, one at Acre and one at Tyre;[7] and only four rural churches, two in the archdiocese of Caesarea,[8] one near Acre,[9] and the village church of Bethel in the diocese of Lydda.[10] In addition they received outline planning permission in 1171 from the bishop of Lydda to build five other rural parish churches in his diocese, but there is no evidence that this was ever taken up.[11] This forms a great contrast to the extent of patronage which the canons of the Sepulchre enjoyed in western Europe at the same time: sixty-one churches and monasteries in Italy, France and Spain are listed as belonging to them in the very detailed confirmation of their property issued by

---

1. *Ibid.*, p 47, no 25 (gift of Jaffa and St Lazarus); pp 123–4, no 61, (appointment of dean of Jaffa); pp 50–2, no 27 (gift of Quarantene); pp 60–5, no 33 (exchange of Thecua).
2. Listed in Celestine III's bull of 1195, *ibid.*, p 235, no 128.
3. *Ibid.*, pp 287–9, no 160: this church was 'in novo burgo', p 279, no 156.
4. *Ibid.*, pp 258–60, no 142.
5. Confirmation of Alexander III, *ibid.*, pp 296–300, no 166.
6. *Ibid.*, pp 180–3, no 91.
7. *Ibid.*, pp 145–6, no 72 (Acre); p 19, no 16 (Tyre); Mayer, *Bistümer*, pp 98–111.
8. de Rozière, p 19, no 16, pp 279–80, no 156.
9. *Ibid.*, pp 145–6, no 72.
10. *Ibid.*, pp. 131–5, nos 64–5.
11. *Ibid.*, pp 322–5, no 181.

pope Eugenius III in 1146.[1]

The restriction of their patronage in Syria must have been part of a deliberate policy implemented by the Latin bishops. For although a bishop could require canonical obedience from chaplains appointed by the canons of the Sepulchre to parishes in his diocese,[2] this was, perhaps, less easy to enforce, since, should any conflict arise between the canons and the bishop, the patriarch, and in the last resort the pope as well, might be expected to take the part of the canons. There was no similar problem in western Europe since parishes were far more numerous there.

Parallel situations existed in regard to the two other great shrine churches of Nazareth and Bethlehem. Both were cathedrals, and both had chapters of Austin canons.[3] Although the early charters of Bethlehem relating to property in Syria have not been preserved, there is a very full record of the community's property in Gregory IX's bull of confirmation issued in 1227. Bethlehem owned much land in the Frankish east, but only had four churches there: St Mary's on Mount Pilgrim, St Mary's at Gibelet, St Martin's at Tyre and an unnamed church in Jaffa. In western Europe, by contrast, the canons of Bethlehem owned sixty-six churches.[4] The archives of the church of Nazareth have not been preserved so there is no complete list of its property, but it is known that it possessed sixteen churches in south Italy in 1172,[5] whereas it is not known to have owned any churches in Syria outside the diocese of Nazareth itself, except for one church in Acre which is first recorded as its property in 1256.[6] It therefore seems reasonable to infer that, as in the case of the Holy Sepulchre, Latin bishops in Syria were unwilling to accord church patronage in their dioceses to the holy places of Bethlehem and Nazareth, so highly regarded by popes, patriarchs and kings, for fear that this would prejudice their rights as diocesan.[7]

The Latin bishops showed an equal reserve in their dealings with the communities of monks and of canons who served the shrine churches of Jerusalem. The oldest of these foundations was the Benedictine abbey of Sta Maria Latina which had been founded in

1. *Ibid.*, pp 36–41, no 23.

2. *Ibid.*, pp 323–4, no 181.

3. A prior of Bethlehem is first mentioned in 1106, *ibid.*, pp 181–3, no 91; the canons of Nazareth are first mentioned in 1109, Kohler, pp 114–15, no 3.

4. Riant, *Bethléem*, I, pp 140–7, no 11.

5. S. Santerano, ed, *Il Codice diplomatico Barlettano*, Barletta 1924, I, pp 18–20, no 5.

6. Bourel de la Roncière, no 1300.

7. The cathedrals of Tripoli and Hebron also had chapters of Austin canons, but neither of them owned very much property outside their own dioceses and they were not, therefore, much of a problem to other bishops.

the mid-eleventh century as a centre for Latin pilgrims visiting the holy places. Annexed to it was a hospital which in the reign of Baldwin I evolved into the order of St John of Jerusalem, and a small convent, which grew in importance in the twelfth century and became known as Ste Marie la Grande.[1] The Benedictines also administered the shrine of Our Lady of Josaphat, which was founded soon after 1099.[2] The chapel of this house stood on what was believed to have been the site of the Assumption of the Blessed Virgin and, since Marian devotion was widespread throughout the western church in the twelfth century, this house enjoyed a particular eminence. The church of Mount Sion, scene of the Last Supper and the Descent of the Holy Spirit, was served by a community of Austin canons, as were the church of the Ascension on the Mount of Olives, and the *Templum Domini*, the mosque better known as the Dome of the Rock, which the Franks had converted into a church.[3]

None of these churches had parochial jurisdiction, but they had liturgical importance and the patriarch celebrated Mass in them on the appropriate feasts.[4] In addition, the laity could, of course, assist at Mass in them whenever they wished, and the additional Latin services which these communities provided were probably of value to the canons of the Holy Sepulchre, who alone had parochial rights in Jerusalem, when dealing with the large influx of pilgrims who came to the city from the west each Eastertide. The communities received numerous benefactions throughout the Frankish east and in western Europe as well and, in addition, they were granted special privileges by the holy see. One of the earliest examples of this is the privilege granted to Latina by Paschal II in 1112:

1. WT, I, 10, XVIII, 5, *RHC Occ*, I, pp 30–31, 824–6.

2. Foundation attributed to duke Godfrey, WT, IX, 9, pp 376–7; Mayer, 'Zur Geschichte des Klosters S. Maria im Tal Josaphat. A. Die Gründung', in *Bistümer*, pp 258–86. There was a Latin community there in c 1103, *Saewulf's pilgrimage to Jerusalem and the Holy Land*, trans W.R. Brownlow, *PPTS*, 1892, p 18.

3. Alexander III attributed Sion's foundation to duke Godfrey, Rey, 'Chartes du Mont-Sion', *MSAF*, ser 5, 8, p 39. The earliest other evidence for the community is from 1112, de Rozière, pp 11–13, no 11; Mayer, 'Aus der Geschichte des Sionsstiftes', *Bistümer*, pp 230–42. The foundation of *Templum Domini* was also attributed to duke Godfrey, WT, IX, 9, *RHC Occ*, I, pp 376–7; earliest evidence of canons there from 1112, *CGOH*, no 25; Mayer, 'Zur Frühgeschichte des Templum Domini in Jerusalem', *Bistümer*, pp 222–9. The archives of the Mount of Olives have not been preserved, and nothing is known about the extent of its ecclesiastical patronage.

4. On Candlemas at the *Templum Domini*, on Ascension day at the Mount of Olives, on Pentecost at Mount Sion, on the Assumption at Josaphat, de Rozière, p 138, no 66.

We decree that the cemetery in the cloister of that monastery, or of those churches which belong to it, shall be completely free, so that no impediment shall exist for those who express a wish to be buried there, in writing, or on their death-beds, provided that they are not excommunicate.[1]

The pope gave a similar privilege to the community of Josaphat in the following year.[2]   In 1155 Hadrian IV greatly increased the immunities of Josaphat.   The house and its dependencies were made immune from excommunication and interdict at the hands of diocesan bishops throughout the kingdoms of Sicily and Jerusalem; in the Sicilian kingdom at least the daughter-houses of Josaphat were given the right to obtain the holy oils from any bishop of their choice, not just from the ordinary, and were freed from episcopal visitation and from the payment to the bishop of all occasional dues.   The mother-house in Jerusalem may have attempted to claim equal privileges.[3]   Pope Alexander III granted even wider immunities to the canons of Mount Sion in 1178 for, in addition to those already accorded to Josaphat, the canons might have altars and chapels consecrated and clergy ordained to serve them by any Catholic bishop in place of the diocesan.[4]   No doubt the canons of the Mount of Olives and those of the *Templum Domini* received similar privileges, but they are not so well documented.

Since these privileges applied not merely to the shrine churches of Jerusalem but also to any chapels which their communities might own elsewhere they posed a serious threat to the authority of Latin bishops. Chapels belonging to these communities did not, without special licence from the bishop, enjoy parochial rights, so that baptisms, churchings and marriages might not be performed in them, and the fees for those services were not, therefore, taken away from the parish clergy.   But there was no way of preventing lay people from attending Mass in these chapels and making offerings to their clergy which might otherwise have been given to the parish church.   The right of laymen to choose to be buried in the cemeteries of monastic chapels was one which the secular Latin clergy of Syria found particularly alarming, since dying men frequently made bequests to the churches in which they were to be buried.   When Alexander III confirmed this privilege to Latina he tried to protect the interests of the parish clergy by inserting

1. W. Holtzmann, 'Papst-Kaiser-und Normannenurkunden aus Unteritalien', *QFIAB*, 35, 1955, p 52, no 1.
2. Delaborde, pp 22–3, no 2.
3. *Ibid.*, pp 76–7, no 31.
4. Rey, 'Chartes du Mont-Sion', *MSAF*, ser 5, 8, pp 48–9.

the clause 'saving the rights of those parish churches from which these bodies are removed'.[1]   This enacted that the parish clergy should still receive the customary burial fees even if their parishioners chose to be interred elsewhere, but it did not, of course, prevent those parishioners from making pious bequests to the clergy who served the monastic chapels. This was of no great consequence in western Europe where the entire population was Catholic and the amount of money likely to be diverted away from the parish churches was in most cases comparatively small, but it mattered a good deal in the east where the Franks were in a minority.

Consequently, although the great shrine churches of Jerusalem received extensive endowments throughout the Latin east they had comparatively few priories or chapels there, whereas in western Europe, where they did not pose the same threat to diocesan authority, their ecclesiastical patronage was quite considerable. The community of Latina had two churches at Latakia, a church at Mount Pilgrim, Tripoli, a church at Gibelet, churches at Jaffa, Acre and Beirut, and the shrine of St Stephen outside the walls of Jerusalem.[2]   Latina also acquired a ruined church, 'known as al-Shbuba', at Antioch which they leased in 1113 to an Orthodox priest, Karman ibn Abraqili, who undertook to rebuild it.[3]   Our Lady of Josaphat, certainly the most popular and also the best documented church in the Frankish states, fared little better. It had one priory at Sichar, near Nazareth, a hospital in Tiberias and a church outside that town;[4] a church at Ligio in the archdiocese of Nazareth;[5] another in the main square at Haifa;[6] a church on the slopes of Mount Carmel;[7] a church outside Sidon;[8] a chapel at Saffuriyah;[9] a church at Jaffa;[10] a rural chapel in the diocese of Lydda[11] and another in the archdiocese of Caesarea;[12] an oratory at Antioch;[13] and a church at Ascalon

1. Holtzmann, *op. cit.*, *QFIAB*, 35, p 58, no 2.
2. *Ibid.*, pp 56–9, no 2.   J. Richard, 'Le chartrier de Sainte-Marie-Latine et l'établissement de Raymond de Saint-Gilles à Mont Pèlerin', *Mélanges d'histoire du Moyen Age dediés à la mémoire de Louis Halphen*, Paris 1951, p 610.
3. S. Cusa, *I diplomi greci ed arabi di Sicilia*, I(ii), pp 645–8. I am indebted to Professor J. Riley-Smith for drawing my attention to this Arabic source and for lending me his translation of it.
4. Kohler, pp 150–1, no 43, pp 113–14, no 2; Delaborde, pp 36–7, no 11.
5. *Ibid.*, pp 35–6, no 9.
6. *Ibid.*, p 34, no 8.
7. *Ibid.*, p 30, no 6.
8. Kohler, p 124, no 14.
9. Delaborde, p 65, no 28.
10. Kohler, p 142, no 32.
11. Delaborde, pp 49–50, no 20.
12. *Ibid.*, p 65, no 28.
13. Kohler, pp 172–3, no 64.

whose possession was disputed by the chapter of Bethlehem.[1] This amounted to thirteen churches scattered through three states, whereas in Norman south Italy Josaphat owned thirty-three churches by the middle of the twelfth century.[2] The canons of Mount Sion were in a similar position. The detailed confirmation of their property issued in 1178 by Alexander III lists only three churches in Syria (St Leonard and St Romanus at Acre and St Leonard at Tyre), compared with thirteen in western Europe.[3] Nothing is known about any property which the *Templum Domini* may have owned in western Europe, but in the early years of the kingdom the canons acquired ecclesiastical control of the city of Nablus, which was part of the patriarchal see of Jerusalem,[4] and were represented there by a dean just as the canons of the Holy Sepulchre were at Jaffa.[5] Apart from this, the confirmation of their property issued by king Amalric in 1166 lists only three churches: St Julian's, Tyre, St Andrew's near Acre, and the 'domus S. Iohannis', now known as Ain Karim, in Judaea.[6] The Mount of Olives is the most poorly documented of all the Jerusalem monasteries and nothing is known about any churches which it may have administered.

Many of these churches were acquired by the religious communities in the early days of Frankish settlement when secular clergy were in short supply and when bishops seem to have welcomed the assistance of monks and canons regular in the work of administering their often very large dioceses. But as the secular church became better organised such grants grew rarer, and even the limited patronage which the religious communities did enjoy was challenged by the diocesan authorities. For example, Bernard, the first Latin bishop of Nazareth, granted the parish church in the *casale* of Ligio in his diocese to the community of Josaphat.[7] His successor, archbishop Robert, was not satisfied with this arrangement because this parish was virtually exempt from his jurisdiction. He appointed a chaplain of his own to the church, ostensibly to say Mass there for the soul of William of Bures, late prince of Galilee, but he then gave the chaplain full rights as parish priest and inhibited the monks from exercising

1. *Ibid.*, pp 143–4, no 34.
2. Delaborde, pp 72–8, no 31.
3. Rey, *op. cit.*, *MSAF*, ser 5, 8, pp 37–53.
4. James of Vitry, *HO*, c 58, p 98.
5. de Rozière, pp 287–9, no 160.
6. F. Chalandon, 'Un diplôme inédit d'Amaury I, roi de Jérusalem, en faveur de l'abbaye du Temple-Notre-Seigneur', *ROL*, 8, 1900–1, pp 311–17. St Andrew's 'extra muros . . . Accon' is not to be confused with the more famous church with the same dedication inside the walls.
7. Delaborde, pp 35–6, no 9.

cure of souls. This proved difficult to enforce, since the monks continued to celebrate Mass in the church, and the Franks of Ligio assisted at these Masses. Matters came to a head one day when a priest of Josaphat was saying Mass and was attacked by a clerk in the household of the bishop's chaplain, who attempted to knock him down and had to be forcibly restrained by the congregation. This unedifying scene led to a prolonged period of litigation between the archbishop of Nazareth and the abbot of Josaphat which was only settled in 1161 when archbishop Letard of Nazareth recognised the right of Josaphat to administer this parish but enforced his own right to receive canonical obedience from the chaplains who served it.[1]

This was not an isolated case. Bishop Bernard of Nazareth in the first year of his reign in 1109 had given the monks of Josaphat the church of St George's outside Tiberias.[2] This city then formed part of the diocese of Nazareth, and the bishop probably welcomed monastic assistance in administering his very large see. But from 1144 Tiberias itself became a diocese,[3] and the privileges and immunities of the Josaphat community continued to grow. A virtually exempt monastic church so near the cathedral of Tiberias was bound to be a source of discord and in 1178 the archbishop of Nazareth as metropolitan, assisted by the bishop of Acre, drew up a concordat between the bishop of Tiberias and the community of Josaphat. From this it is clear that Josaphat had ignored episcopal authority and drawn parishioners away from the cathedral parish. The concordat enacted that the monks of St George's should not admit parishioners of Tiberias, who had been excommunicated or placed under an interdict by the bishop, to divine worship; nor should they baptise children of the Latin rite, church women, or solemnise marriages; St George's cemetery should be reserved for the use of the brethren, their servants, and Syrian Christians; and the monks should further acknowledge the bishop's authority by certain financial payments.[4]

The three great Benedictine convents of Jerusalem did not, so far as is known, have any chapels in their gift. St Anne's and Ste Marie la Grande at Jerusalem seem only to have possessed the chapels which formed part of the mother-houses, and even the great convent of Bethany which, as William of Tyre relates, queen Melisende endowed richly 'so that it should not be esteemed inferior in temporal goods to any house of men or women religious',[5]

1. *Ibid.*, pp 56–8, no 24, pp 58–9, no 25, p 64, no 28, pp 82–3, no 35.
2. Kohler, pp 113–14, no 2.
3. See p 72, n 4 above.
4. Delaborde, pp 87–8, no 40.
5. WT, XV, 26, *RHC Occ*, I, p 699.

only owned one church, that of St John the Evangelist in Jerusalem,[1] apart from the shrine of St Lazarus which formed part of
the mother-house.

The only other important early monastic foundation in the
southern kingdom was the Benedictine monastery of Mount Tabor
which is quite well-documented since its archives later passed to
the knights of St John.[2] It owned some churches in the archdiocese of Nazareth, presumably in villages which belonged to the
monks, and these rights probably dated from the early years of
the foundation when its abbot had enjoyed episcopal authority
in Galilee.[3] The community also had a priory church at Palmaria,
near Haifa,[4] and the patriarch William of Jerusalem granted them
the parish church of St Gilles, a rural administrative centre in his
diocese, which they sold to the canons of the Holy Sepulchre in
1175 'because the place is very distant and extremely expensive
to maintain'.[5] The other important area of Latin monastic settlement in the east was at Antioch and in the Black Mountain nearby, but this is poorly documented in the twelfth century and it is
not known whether any of these houses controlled chapels or
parishes in Syria.[6]

The Frankish east was, of course, affected by the development
of new monastic orders in western Europe during the twelfth
century. In 1131 at the council of Rheims Innocent II commissioned a group of the newly-founded Premonstratensian canons
to preach to the pagans in the Holy Land.[7] Two foundations
were subsequently made there, that of SS. Joseph and Habacuc
near Ramla and that of St Samuel's Mountjoy, on the outskirts
of Jerusalem.[8] In view of their evangelical mission it might have
been expected that the canons would found a number of rural
churches as centres for converting the Muslim peasantry. This did
not happen: the canons of St Habacuc are only known to have
built a single chapel, at Bethel, which they ceded to the Holy

1. Ernoul, p 206.

2. See below, chapter 11.

3. Archbishop Henry of Nazareth renounced his rights as metropolitan over the
Mount Tabor monastery and its churches in 1263 after they had been granted to the
knights of St John, CGOH, no 3054.

4. Ibid., vol II, p 908, no 19.

5. Ibid., vol II, p 907; de Rozière, pp 258–60, no 142.

6. The most important Latin monasteries at Antioch were St Paul's and St George's
(a house of Austin canons).

7. N. Backmund, Monasticon Praemonstratense, 3 vols, Straubing 1949–56, I, pp
397–9.

8. Ibid., p 404; St Bernard of Clairvaux, 'Epistolae', nos 253, 355, PL, 182, 453–4,
557–8; R. Van Waefelghem, ed, L'Obituaire de l'Abbaye de Prémontré, Louvain 1913,
p 75, records the death of the first abbot of St Samuel's.

Sepulchre in 1160,[1] while in the very detailed confirmation of the property of St Samuel's issued by Baldwin V in 1185 only two churches are listed: St John the Evangelist at Nablus, the gift of queen Melisende, and St Longinus at Jerusalem, endowed by king Amalric.[2]   It is significant that both these chapels were in cities and that both were the gift of rulers. It would seem, therefore, that the interests of the Frankish baronage, who wished to keep a contented Muslim labour force, and those of Frankish bishops, who were averse from allowing religious orders to found exempt churches in their dioceses, combined to frustrate the purpose for which the Premonstratensian houses had been founded.

The Cistercians came to the east in 1157, when they founded the monastery of Belmont in the mountains to the south-east of Tripoli.[3]   Twelve years later Belmont founded a daughter-house at St John in nemore, a shrine of St John the Baptist in the environs of Jerusalem.[4]   A third Cistercian monastery, Salvatio, a daughter of Morimond, was founded in the kingdom of Jerusalem in 1163, but its location is unknown.[5] It is not known that any of these houses administered chapels elsewhere in the Frankish east and this is consonant with the world-renouncing character of the white monks in their early years.

Yet despite the attempts of bishops to restrict the growth of monastic patronage in Frankish Syria, there were few towns of any consequence which did not have at least one monastic chapel in the twelfth century either in the city itself or very near it. These were found at Antioch, Latakia, Tripoli, Gibelet, Beirut, Sidon, Tyre, Acre, Haifa, Jaffa, Tiberias, Nablus, and, of course, in large numbers in Jerusalem itself. Some cities, notably Tyre, Acre and Tripoli, contained four or more monastic chapels, and the provision of these additional places of worship for the Frankish population must considerably have diminished the authority of the parish clergy.

1. de Rozière, pp 131–5, nos 64–5.

2. H.E. Mayer, 'Sankt Samuel auf dem Freudenberge und sein besitz nach einem unbekannten diplom König Balduins V', QFIAB, 44, 1964, pp 35–71 (text of diploma, pp 68–71).

3. Hamilton, 'The Cistercians in the Crusade States', in M.E. Pennington, ed, One Yet Two. Monastic Tradition East and West, Cistercian Studies, 29, Kalamazoo 1976, pp 404–6.

4. L. Janauschek, Originum Cisterciensium, one volume, Vienna 1877, I, p 158, no 405. In the article cited in n 3 I stated that the location of this house was unknown and I would now retract that opinion. Richard, Le Comté de Tripoli, p 61, suggests a location in the county of Tripoli, but this is not tenable.

5. Hamilton, op. cit., n 3 above, pp 405–7. The two Cistercian abbots sent in 1186 by the barons at Nablus to forbid the coronation of the countess of Jaffa, Ernoul, pp 131–2, were presumably those of Salvatio and St John in nemore.

In the coastal cities of the three maritime states, Antioch, Tripoli and Jerusalem, there were a number of churches of the Latin rite belonging to Italian merchant communities. The Frankish princes of Syria never had adequate navies of their own and these cities were captured chiefly with the help of the three great Italian naval powers, Genoa, Pisa and Venice, which, in return for their assistance, were granted extensive commercial privileges in Syria and quarters in certain cities. The earliest grant of this kind was that made by Bohemond I to the Genoese in 1098 when he granted them a quarter in Antioch which included the church of St John.[1] The Genoese community of Antioch worshipped there and the commune appointed the clergy, but the priests were subject to the authority of the patriarch of Antioch.[2] Although prince Tancred offered the Genoese a church at Latakia and churches in other ports in his dominions in 1101 there is no evidence that the commune ever took up this offer in the twelfth century,[3] nor do the full archives of the republic record that it owned any churches before 1187 in the county of Tripoli or the kingdom of Jerusalem.

The Pisans were granted the church of St Nicholas at Latakia by Tancred in 1108[4] but are not known to have had any other churches in the principality or in the neighbouring county of Tripoli. In the kingdom of Jerusalem, although Amalric, count of Jaffa, granted them the right to build a church at Jaffa in 1157 they do not seem to have availed themselves of this permission, probably because Jaffa was not a very satisfactory port.[5] It was not until 1168 that Amalric, who had then become king, granted them a quarter in Acre in return for their help against Egypt, and they did subsequently build the church of St Peter there, and at some time before 1187 a hospital and chapel of the Holy Spirit as well.[6]

The republic of Venice was granted a church at Acre as early as 1111.[7] In 1123 the patriarch Warmund granted the Venetians very extensive privileges in the kingdom to secure their help in the assault on Tyre, and these were subsequently ratified by Baldwin II:

1. Hagenmeyer, *Kreuzzugsbriefe*, pp 155—6, no 13.
2. Imperiale, I, pp 16—18, no 12.
3. The Genoese had a church at Mamistra in 1201, *ibid.*, III, p 190, no 75, but it seems unlikely that it dated from the time of prince Tancred.
4. Müller, p 3, no 1.
5. *Ibid.*, p 8, no 6.
6. *Ibid.*, p 14, no 11, pp 82—3, no 52, pp 94—5, no 63.
7. TT, I, p 75, no 34.

> In all places within the lordship of the king and of his successors and in all the cities of his barons the Venetians shall have a church, a whole street, a square, a bath and an oven, and shall own them in perpetuity by hereditary right, without paying any kind of due, as though they were the king's own property.[1]

The Venetians only took very sparing advantage of these sweeping grants. They had churches dedicated to St Mark at Acre and Tyre by 1165,[2] but none, it would seem, anywhere else in the kingdom, and none at all in the northern states. After the third crusade the republic claimed, as the holy see judged rightly, that their church at Tyre had possessed full parochial rights from its foundation.[3] But this may simply reflect the greater power wielded by Venice in the kingdom after the third crusade and is better considered in a later chapter together with similar claims made by the other Italian maritime powers.

The evidence therefore suggests that the ecclesiastical powers of the Italian communes in the Frankish states of Syria were not commensurate with the powers of commercial privilege and secular jurisdiction which they enjoyed before 1187. There is no evidence, except in the case of the Venetian churches of Tyre and Acre,[4] that any of their churches had the status of parishes and this is borne out by the fact that there is no record in the archives of any of the three republics of a dispute between their chaplains in Syria and the local Latin bishops in the period before 1187, whereas such disputes were numerous in the thirteenth century. In the twelfth century it would appear that the Italian churches existed to serve the spiritual needs of their own nationals without prejudice to the rights and financial dues of the local parish clergy. They must therefore have been a help to the Latin bishops in dealing with the pastoral care of the large numbers of Latin-rite Christians who came to live in the ports of Frankish Syria, but they did not constitute a threat to the position of the secular church.

The other important element in the religious organisation of Frankish Syria at this time was provided by the military orders. The knights of St John evolved from the hospital attached to the

---

1. *Ibid.*, I, p 85, no 40.
2. *Ibid.*, I, p 145, no 60.
3. *Ibid.*, I, pp 281–6, no 87, pp 424–6, no 108.
4. The Venetian *bailli* in Syria in 1243 recorded of Tyre: 'Meminerint cuncti, quod habemus in nostro tercierio ecclesiam S. Marci, que in captione terre primitus fuit fundata a Venecia . . . que est libera et nulli iurisdictioni supposita, habendo ius parrochiale . . . et omnia sacramenta ecclesiastica faciendi, ut aliqua cathedralis ecclesia facere potest'. *Ibid.*, II, p 362, no 299.

monastery of Latina at Jerusalem which antedated the first crusade. It naturally attracted benefactions from all over the Catholic world after Jerusalem had been liberated, and in 1113 Paschal II made it independent of the abbot of Latina so that the master of the Hospital became the head of an international order directly subject to the holy see.[1] The order was only later militarised, in imitation, it was believed in the thirteenth century, of the order of the Temple, founded as a military order in Baldwin II's reign with its headquarters in Jerusalem.[2]

The earliest record of the ecclesiastical patronage enjoyed by the order of the Hospital in Syria is the confirmation issued by Calixtus II in 1119 of gifts made to it by bishops of Tripoli. These comprised the church of St John on Mount Pilgrim, the churches in the fief of William Rostagne, and the church of Arqah.[3] In 1131 or earlier the Hospital also acquired a hospital and the church of St Romanus at Tell Bashir in western Edessa, gift of count Joscelin I.[4] At the time these grants were made the Hospital was a charitable institution, little different in character from the religious communities of the great shrine churches of Jerusalem.

The first sign that its character was changing came in 1136 when king Fulk granted the Hospital the castle of Bethgibelin guarding the approach road from Hebron to Ascalon.[5] Like any other castellan the master of the Hospital must have had the right to nominate the castle chaplain, but there is no evidence that he had any other ecclesiastical rights there. But in 1137 the order was granted the right to establish churches in deserted territory and later to build villages near the Saracen frontiers, provided that there were no other religious communities nearby.[6] They availed themselves of this privilege, though probably not until after the fall of Ascalon in 1153, by founding a Frankish village at Bethgibelin, and the church there must have been in their gift.[7] At this stage there was no conflict between the Hospital and the Latin bishops. In 1141 the patriarch and canons of the Holy Sepulchre allowed the Hospital to keep part of the tithe of their lands at Abu Ghosh (which the Franks identified with Emmaus) to maintain churches and chaplains there.[8] Whether

1. Riley-Smith, *Knights*, pp 32—43.
2. *Ibid.*, pp 52—9; James of Vitry, *HO*, c 65, p 110.
3. *CGOH*, no 48.
4. *Ibid.*, no 104.
5. WT, XIV, 22, *RHC Occ*, I, pp 638—9; *CGOH*, no 116; Riley-Smith, *Knights*, p 52.
6. *CGOH*, no 122; Riley-Smith, *Knights*, p 435.
7. The settlement was made while Raymond of Puy (†1160) was grand master, *CGOH*, no 399.
8. *Ibid.*, no 140; de Rozière, pp 219—20, no 117.

they built several churches there is not known, but they certainly built one, which the Marquis de Vogüé bought in 1873 and which was later restored to the Catholic cult.[1]

As the twelfth century progressed and the Franks became more threatened by their Muslim neighbours, increasingly extensive powers were granted to the Hospital, which acquired what amounted to palatinate lordships in frontier areas. The first of these grants was made in 1144 by Raymond II of Tripoli, who gave the Hospital the fief of Crac des Chevaliers and also the city of Rafaniyah and the castle of Montferrand if they could be re-captured from the Muslims.[2]   It seems likely that the knights of St John enjoyed full ecclesiastical as well as secular jurisdiction in this area from the beginning, since these lands formed part of the diocese of Rafaniyah, which was vacant after about 1139.[3]

The order was able to discharge ecclesiastical duties without reference to the diocesan authorities because it had its own priest brethren.   Anastasius IV in his bull *Christianae Fidei Religio* of 1154 gave official recognition to the clerical privileges of the order, but this, as Riley-Smith points out, was probably merely endorsing long established practices: this bull virtually exempted the chaplains of the order from the authority of diocesan bishops and made them responsible to the chapter of the order and the pope alone.[4]   Such privileges could, of course, be exercised in all the churches which the order administered, and this was one reason which led the patriarch of Jerusalem, who had the support of most of his suffragans, to seek to have the privileges of the order annulled by the pope in 1155.[5]   In this he was unsuccessful and, however unacceptable the power of the Hospital may have been to the secular church, political necessity made its growth inevitable.   The Hospital made an increasingly important contribution to the army of the kingdom of Jerusalem and the defence of border regions in the northern states and both barons and rulers made demands on its aid.[6]

Thus in 1157 Humphrey II of Toron granted the order the castle of Chastelneuf and half the city of Banyas in northern Galilee menaced by Nur-ad-Din of Damascus.   This must have diminished the power of the bishop of Banyas, although that was a short-lived problem since the city was captured by Nur-ad-Din in

1. Benvenisti, *Crusaders in the Holy Land*, pp 347–51.
2. *CGOH*, no 144. For date see above, p 23, n 7.
3. See chapter 12 below.
4. Riley-Smith, *Knights*, pp 233–4, 377.
5. WT, XVIII, 3, 6–8, *RHC Occ*, I, pp 820–2, 826–30.
6. R.C. Smail, *Crusading Warfare, 1097–1193*, Cambridge 1956, *passim*.

1164.[1] In 1168 Bohemond III of Antioch granted the Hospital the fief of Apamea on conditions similar to those offered by Raymond II at Crac des Chevaliers.[2] This must have diminished what was left of the authority of the archbishop of Apamea. Eighteen years later, in 1186, Bohemond III allowed the fief of al-Marqab to be sold to the Hospital and since this was virtually co-extensive with the diocese of Valania the order acquired virtual control of that bishopric.[3] In the kingdom of Jerusalem the Hospital acquired by purchase the castle and fief of Belvoir in 1168 which must have diminished the powers of the bishop of Tiberias.[4]

As the property of this exempt order increased, disputes became more common between the Hospital and the bishops. The hierarchy could do little about fiefs which the Hospital controlled, but they were anxious to restrict the growth of Hospitaller jurisdiction in cities. By the reign of Alexander III the Hospital had a church at Jaffa. The prior of the Holy Sepulchre, to whom the parish of Jaffa belonged, complained to the pope that the Hospital chaplain had refused to observe an interdict which the canons had laid on the city. The pope found in the canons' favour and refused permission to the Hospital to build a second church there.[5] In 1175 a settlement was reached between the bishop of Acre and the Hospital chapel in the city by the terms of which the rights of the Hospitallers were considerably restricted. Women should be churched at the cathedral, not in the Hospital chapel; Hospitaller chaplains should not normally hear Easter confessions, which should be made to the parish clergy; burials might only take place in the Hospital cemetery with the consent of the bishop; the last rites might only be administered by the brethren to sick pilgrims staying in their house and to *confratres* of the order; the holy oils must be received from the bishop, who reserved the right to ordain priests to serve the Hospital chapel.[6] In the following year a dispute between the Hospital and the archbishop of Apamea was brought before the patriarch of Antioch and a papal legate. This concerned two estates in the lordship of Saone over which the archbishop and the Hospital both claimed jurisdiction: it was agreed that the archbishop should have one estate and the Hospital the other, but the

1. *CGOH*, no 258.
2. *Ibid.*, no 391.
3. *Ibid.*, no 783.
4. *Ibid.*, no 398.
5. de Rozière, pp 286–7, no 159, written between 1166 when the addressee, Peter, became prior (*ibid.*, pp 276–8, no 155) and Alexander III's death in 1181.
6. *CGOH*, no 471.

archbishop ceded all his diocesan rights in the Hospital's estate to the order.[1] As these cases show, the Hospital was not always able to exercise in practice the extensive theoretical powers of exemption which it undoubtedly possessed.

The knights Templar obtained the full privileges of an exempt order from Innocent II in the bull *Omne Datum Optimum* issued in 1139.[2] In time they came to exercise considerable ecclesiastical patronage. The city of Tortosa was devastated by Nur-ad-Din and in 1152 its bishop asked the Templars to take charge of its defence in order to protect Tortosa cathedral which was an important Marian shrine.[3] Only the terms of the ecclesiastical settlement are relevant here. The Templars were to have control of the castle chapel at Tortosa, but all other churches in the city and the port were to remain in the hands of the bishop. Throughout the rest of the diocese the Templars were to hold 'free and absolutely' all churches, and to have full parochial rights in them, except in five named places, one of which, Maraclea, was specifically reserved to the bishop. The Templars were also granted all the castle chapels in the diocese except those which were already in the hands of the Hospital. Since the Templars had their own priest brethren, who were exempt from the jurisdiction of the ordinary, they could, under the terms of this settlement, fill all the cures in the diocese of Tortosa and withdraw them from episcopal obedience.[4]

The Templars may have exercised similar rights at Gaza. This frontier fortress was rebuilt by Baldwin III in 1150 and entrusted to them 'in perpetuity, together with all the surrounding regions',[5] but no details are known about the ecclesiastical settlement there. The order also acquired the castle of Baghras and other fortresses in the Amanus march on the north-western frontier of the principality of Antioch;[6] the castles of Chastel Blanc and Arima in the county of Tripoli;[7] and those of Safad in Galilee and Ahamant in Oultrejourdain in the kingdom of Jerusalem.[8] The chapels in all of these must have been served by priest brethren who were exempt from the authority of local bishops, but it is not known

1. *Ibid.*, no 474.
2. R. Hiestand, *Papsturkunden für Templer und Johanniter*, Göttingen 1972, pp 204–10, no 3.
3. *Burchard of Mount Sion, A.D. 1280*, trans A. Stewart, *PPTS*, London 1896, p 20.
4. Riley-Smith, 'Templars and the castle of Tortosa', *EHR*, 84, 1969, pp 278–88.
5. WT, XVII, 12, *RHC Occ*, I, p 778.
6. J. Riley-Smith, 'The Templars and the Teutonic Knights in Cilician Armenia', in T.S.R. Boase, ed, *The Cilician Kingdom of Armenia*, Edinburgh 1978, pp 92–7.
7. W. Müller-Wiener, *Castles of the Crusaders*, London 1966, pp 51–3.
8. Strehlke, pp 5–6, no 4 (Safad); P. Deschamps, *La défense du royaume de Jérusalem*, Paris 1939, pp 38, 48 (Ahamant).

whether the order controlled other churches in those areas. As their headquarters the Templars owned the former mosque of Al-Aqsar in Jerusalem. They had a chapel there from the reign of Baldwin II, but the pilgrim Theoderich described in 1170 how 'they are laying the foundations of a new church of wonderful size and workmanship . . . by the side of the great court'.[1] This church was, of course, exempt from the jurisdiction of the patriarch of Jerusalem.

There is no evidence of disputes between bishops and Templars in the twelfth century. This may merely be a result of the fact that the archives of the Temple have never been found, but such evidence as there is suggests that good relations existed between them and the Latin episcopate. They came to Tortosa at the bishop's request; Gaza, though technically part of the archdiocese of Jerusalem, had been deserted before the Templars took it over. They were not, therefore, depriving the patriarch of control over churches, but were building churches where there had been none before. The chapels in their castles served by priests of the order were in no very different case from the chapels of secular lords, over whose chaplains bishops had only a tenuous control.

Indeed, the position of the Templars in the twelfth century was very different from that of the Hospitallers, although the two orders came to resemble one another and in the following century both posed an equal threat to the authority of the secular church. The Templars were founded as a military order and received their privileges of exemption within eleven years of their foundation. Bishops who gave them churches were therefore aware from the start of the disadvantages which this might entail. The Hospital was at first a charitable institution and became militarised and acquired privileges only gradually. As a result of this churches were given to the Hospital in its early years which were later able to claim exemption from episcopal jurisdiction.

There were other minor military orders which had houses in Syria in the twelfth century, but they did not rival the Templars and Hospitallers in the extent of their wealth or the number of their privileges. The Brethren of St Lazarus, who cared for lepers, were founded probably in the reign of king Fulk. They had their own chaplains[2] but only owned two churches, the mother-house, situated just outside the north wall of Jerusalem, and a hospital and chapel at Tiberias.[3] In the reign of Baldwin IV the Spanish order of St Mary's, Mountjoy, established its headquarters,

1. Theoderich, *Description of the Holy Places*, pp 31–2.
2. de Marsy, 'Cartulaire de Saint-Lazare', *AOL*, II, p 127, no 6.
3. *Ibid.*, pp 132–3, no 13.

including a church, next to the abbey of St Samuel's, Mountjoy. Alexander III granted to the master of this order in 1180:

> that the house of Mountjoy at Jerusalem and the church which you have begun to build there, together with any oratories which you shall build in desert places, that is to say places at least a mile distant from cities, castles and villages, shall be under the authority of nobody except the Roman pontiff.[1]

The loss of Jerusalem seven years later terminated the work of this order in the Holy Land: probably the Latin episcopate was not entirely displeased by this.

The overall picture which emerges of the Latin Church in Syria in the twelfth century reveals that the parish structure was inchoate by comparison with the diocesan structure. This was particularly true of the rural areas. Churches of the Latin rite were founded in all major castles and their *faubourgs*, in most important rural administrative centres, even if only a handful of Franks lived there, and in the few Frankish villages which were established. It must always be borne in mind that only a fraction of the twelfth-century archive material for Latin Syria has survived and that it is therefore possible that the Franks built other churches of which we have no written record. Archaeological excavation has revealed some of these, but such evidence is difficult to evaluate unless there is corroborative epigraphic material because native Christians living under Frankish rule learned to build in western styles. The discovery of the remains of a church built in the western style does not necessarily imply that it was of Latin rite.[2]

Conversely there are written records of a great many rural settlements in the Frankish east which had no Latin church. The implication is that in many, probably the majority, of the villages which they controlled the Franks made no attempt to introduce a western parish system. It would have been expensive to build a church and to maintain a priest who would have had to be a Frank, and therefore a free man, and who would have needed an income commensurate with his social status. There was no place in Frankish Syria, as there was in much of western Europe in the twelfth century, for a Latin parish priest who was of servile origin. In any case, even had money been available, a parish priest would have had no function. If Franks did not live in the village, and they did not live in most villages, the priest would have had no cure of souls, and if he had attempted to impose the Latin rite on

---

1. J. Delaville Le Roulx, 'L'Ordre de Mountjoye', *ROL*, I, 1893, pp 51–4.
2. E.g. the chapel of St Phocas at Amyun, south of Tripoli, a romanesque building, designed and decorated by eastern-rite Christians, P. Deschamps, *Terre Sainte romane*, Paris 1964, pp 237–8.

native Christians, or to convert Muslims, he would have risked antagonising the labour-force and this would have spelled economic ruin for the Franks. Rural parishes were therefore exceptional.

In addition to the parishes in town and country which formed an integral part of the diocesan organisation there were also churches and chapels belonging to religious communities, to the military orders, and in certain coastal cities to the Italian communes. In the early days of Frankish settlement when bishops were few and church organisation slight, the Latin hierarchy seems to have welcomed the cooperation of these institutions which provided useful spiritual services for the Frankish population at no expense to the secular church, and which were able to supply trained priests of whom there was a shortage. But as the church became more highly organised, and as the religious and military orders became more privileged, disputes between the two became common and bishops grew reluctant to allow churches to be controlled by religious.

Yet although bishops suffered a loss of revenue through the privileges of the orders their authority does not seem to have been seriously impaired by them before 1187. For even the greatest orders, like the Templars and the Hospitallers, were usually willing to reach some compromise with the bishops in case of dispute, whereby they waived some of their rights of exemption.[1] The power of the Templars in the diocese of Tortosa may appear to contradict this, but the powers of the knights in ecclesiastical matters probably look greater on paper than they were in fact. It is doubtful whether there had ever been many rural parishes in the diocese before 1152, except in castles, over which, even before that time, the bishop would have had very little control, whereas the bishop retained full control over his cathedral city and over Maraclea, the only other important town in the diocese, and these were the places where most of the Latin clergy of the diocese would have been concentrated.

The Latin church in twelfth-century Syria was an unusual institution. Bishops had few subordinate clergy: these were found mainly in the towns, but a few were in outlying and randomly-disposed rural parishes. Some parishes, both in town and country, were run by chaplains appointed by monasteries or by the military orders and their relations with the bishops were a matter of contention. In cities there was usually only a single parish in the twelfth century, but there were often also a large number of

---

1. This kind of compromise was not peculiar to the Frankish east. For compromise of this kind between the Templars and Aragonese bishops, A, Forey, *The Templars in the Corona de Aragón*, London 1973, pp 174 *seq.*

chapels and oratories of the Latin rite which did not form part of the diocesan organisation but which, as is clear from the regularity of complaints which bishops made about them, attracted a large number of worshippers. Thus, though cure of souls may technically have been in the hands of the diocesan clergy, in practice it was frequently exercised by the chaplains of the religious houses and the military orders. One consequence of this was that bishops had few subordinate clergy and less scope for pastoral work than their colleagues in the west.

5. THE SENIOR LATIN CLERGY IN THE TWELFTH CENTURY

Many of the lesser diocesan clergy of Latin Syria are known by name, but in most cases that is all that is known about them. Chaplains, parish priests, members of cathedral chapters appear as charter witnesses, but they do not come alive as people. There are, of course, exceptions to this general rule. Ansellus, cantor of the Holy Sepulchre in the reign of Baldwin I, sent a relic of the True Cross to the canons of Notre Dame, Paris. His accompanying letter was preserved because it authenticated the relic, and it affords a glimpse of the character of a man who would otherwise be simply a name:

> Although it is now twenty-four years since I left your church, in which I grew up and received my education, yet . . . you are always in my thoughts. I always talk to pilgrims who come out here each year and who know you . . . and ask them what you are doing and how you all are. And I often dream that I am back with you, taking part in the processions on great feasts and singing the night office.[1]

Evidence of this kind is rare as far as the lesser clergy are concerned, but more is known about the senior clergy, the priors and deans of cathedral chapters, the archdeacons, and, of course, the bishops, archbishops and patriarchs. The patriarchs have already been considered in some detail in the preceding chapters, and this chapter will deal with the bishops and archbishops, who are the best documented group of clergy in Frankish Syria.

One hundred and five Latin bishops are known to have held office there between 1098 and 1187, and detailed information exists about thirty-eight of them, or just over a third of the total. The rest are known only in a formal sense: they are mentioned in official documents, or their presence is recorded at church synods, but nothing is known about their earlier careers or about their personalities.

When the Franks first settled in Syria their choice of men to fill the bishoprics that they set up was limited to those who had accompanied them on the crusade. Few of these men had received adequate training for the positions which they were called upon to

1. *GC*, VII, 44, 'Instrumenta Ecclesiae Parisiensis', no LIII.

occupy, and there was the additional hazard that there were no experienced administrators in their dioceses who could give them guidance, or to whom they could delegate routine business, as there would have been had they been appointed to western European sees. They were in the position of missionary bishops who had to build up an entire church organisation in their dioceses, but with this difference, that they had not been trained to accept that kind of responsibility.

All the first generation of Latin bishops in Syria seem to have been either simple priests or chaplains to noble households before they came on crusade. It is an illustration, perhaps, of the truth of Toynbee's theory of challenge and response, that most of them proved efficient at coping with the responsibilities which were entrusted to them. Peter of Narbonne, the first Latin bishop to be appointed in the east, was one of the Provençal priests who accompanied the army of Raymond IV of Toulouse, but he ruled the archdiocese of Apamea effectively for over twenty years[1] and left behind him a reputation for integrity of character which was remembered long after his death.[2]

Not all choices proved equally successful. It has already been seen how Evremar, priest of Chocques, was found to lack the qualities of leadership and authority which were needed in a patriarch of Jerusalem. Evremar himself was very conscious of his own shortcomings. Soon after his election as patriarch he wrote to his former bishop, Lambert of Arras:

> Therefore, dearest friend, trusting in your goodwill, I beseech you, if you will, to help me to lighten the weight of responsibility which you know has been thrust upon me, in accordance with the Apostle's teaching: 'Bear ye one another's burdens'.[3]

Yet although he lacked the abilities which were needed in the head of the Latin church of Jerusalem, Evremar proved himself to be quite adequate for the post of archbishop of Caesarea to which he was translated in 1108. He held the see for twenty-one years and no complaints were ever made about his conduct in that office. As might have been expected he took little part in public life as long as Baldwin I lived, for he cannot have been on very cordial terms either with the king or with the two successive

---

1. He was at the *Ager Sanguinis* in 1119, WT, XII, 10, *RHC Occ*, I, p 526, and may be the unnamed archbishop of Apamea captured by the emir Balik in 1123, Gibb, *Damascus Chronicle*, pp 168–9.

2. 'vir honestae conversationis et valde religiosus', WT, VII, 8, *RHC Occ*, I, p 288.

3. *PL*, 162, 677, no 77.

patriarchs, Gibelin and Arnulf, who had secured his deposition.[1] But by the time Baldwin II came to the throne Evremar had become one of the senior churchmen in the kingdom and his services were in much more demand both by the king and the patriarch Warmund. In 1119 Evremar accompanied the king on a campaign to Antioch as bearer of the True Cross after the death of prince Roger on the *Ager Sanguinis*.[2] He attended the council of Nablus in 1120[3] and helped to negotiate the treaties with the Venetians about their help in attacking Tyre;[4] Honorius II appointed him a judge-delegate in a dispute between the Hospital and the church of Tripoli,[5] and he was involved by both king and patriarch in the routine administration of the church and kingdom.[6]

As the years passed his family in western Europe began to regard with a certain awe this survivor of the first crusade who held high office in the church of Jerusalem. One of his nephews, a monk of St Amand, wrote tentatively to him to ask for a gift of relics. In his concern to impress with his learning the uncle whom he had never met, he was led into making the infelicitous request that:

> the ointment upon the head, that ran down unto the beard, even unto Aaron's beard, and went down to the skirts of his clothing, through your blessing, with its pious unction, may water the dryness of my heart.[7]

Evremar died in 1129[8] a respected member of the Latin hierarchy, devout, charitable to pious foundations,[9] competent in the administration of his see, and well esteemed by the leaders of church and state. He was one of the last survivors of the first generation of Latin bishops in Syria who were largely self-taught in the execution of their duties.[10]

Once the Latin church had been established in the east facilities existed for training clergy. Each cathedral had a chapter of canons

---

1. Ernoul, p 3, says he officiated at Baldwin I's funeral. Little reliance can be placed on this late source which is contradicted by Albert of Aix, XII, 29, *RHC Occ*, IV, p 709.
2. Fulcher of Chartres, III, 4, s 2, ed Hagenmeyer, pp 645—6.
3. WT, XII, 13, *RHC Occ*, I, pp 531—2.
4. TT, I, pp 79—94, nos 40—41.
5. *CGOH*, no 72.
6. Delaborde, pp 37—8, no 12; de Rozière, pp 83—5, no 45.
7. Martène, Durand, *Thes. Nov.*, I, 351—2.
8. His successor was 'electus' in October 1129, Kohler, pp 125—7, no 17.
9. *CGOH*, no 29; Kohler, pp 124—5, nos 14, 15; de Rozière, pp 142—3, no 70.
10. Bernard of Valence, patriarch of Antioch, outlived him, as did Baldwin, bishop-elect of Beirut, who had come on the first crusade, 'Versus de viris illustribus dioecesis Tarvanensis', Martène, Durand, *Vet. SS.*, V, 540.

which varied in size between six and eighteen according to the wealth and importance of the see.[1]   The chapters of Jerusalem, Bethlehem, Nazareth, Hebron and Tripoli were communities of Austin canons, but in the other cathedrals the canons were secular clergy and did not live in community. At the head of each chapter was a prior in the case of the Austin canons, or a dean in the case of secular clergy. Other less important administrative or liturgical offices, such as those of treasurer, almoner and cantor were allocated to members of the chapter. A canon with any ability therefore had a reasonable opportunity of being trained in the work of church administration which would prove of great help to him if he were later appointed to a bishopric.

In addition, each bishop was assisted in the administration of his diocese by an archdeacon who was responsible principally for the judicial business of the see. However large dioceses were in the Frankish east, and in the early years of the twelfth century some of them, like Edessa, Tripoli and Jerusalem itself, were very large indeed, they were never subdivided into a number of archdeaconries as was common practice in large western European dioceses like Toulouse. This reflects, of course, the comparatively small numbers of Latin Christians who were settled in these large areas, but who were the only people who came under the archdeacon's jurisdiction. Indeed, it proved possible for William of Tyre, albeit for a short space of time, to hold the archdeaconries of Tyre and Nazareth in plurality.[2]   Archdeacons, whose time was spent performing legal and administrative work, were obviously well equipped to be bishops. The same was true of the chancellors who were employed by the patriarchs of Jerusalem and Antioch, and also by the archbishops of Tyre, though not, it would seem, by any other bishops in the east.

Indeed, a career in church administration came to be regarded as a recommendation in any candidate for a bishopric once the Latin church had become firmly established. The previous careers of twenty-eight bishops who held office in the sixty years before 1187 are known. Of these, seven had been priors or deans of cathedral chapters,[3] seven had been archdeacons[4] and three had

1. Antioch had eighteen, Pressutti, no 3497; Tripoli, twelve, *ibid.*, no 6135; Nazareth only six in the thirteenth century, Berger, no 5538.

2. *CGOH*, no 468.

3. John, bishop of Acre; Aimery of Limoges, patriarch of Antioch; Letard II, archbishop of Nazareth; William I, archbishop of Tyre; William I, patriarch of Jerusalem; Amalric of Nesle, patriarch of Jerusalem; Peter, archbishop of Tyre.

4. Frederick, bishop of Acre, former archdeacon of St Lambert, Liège; William, bishop of Acre; Adam, bishop of Banyas, former archdeacon of Acre; Odo, bishop of Beirut; Heraclius, archbishop of Caesarea; William II, archbishop of Tyre, former archdeacon of Tyre and Nazareth; Arnulf, patriarch of Jerusalem.

been chancellors of the patriarch of Jerusalem.[1]   It was not enough to have been an administrator in any diocese: bishops were normally chosen from among the deans and priors of those cathedrals which owned a great deal of land and who therefore had wide experience in administration.   Of the seven bishops in this category no fewer than four had been priors of the Holy Sepulchre, which was one of the greatest landowning bodies in the Frankish east,[2] one had been prior of Nazareth, which also had a good deal of property to administer, including lands in western Europe,[3] and one had been dean of the patriarchal church of Antioch.[4]   The only exception to this general rule was John, prior of Acre cathedral, who became the first Latin bishop of Acre, but this was an unusual case as he had probably been exercising delegated authority in the Acre region on behalf of the archbishop of Tyre before the see was set up.[5]

The same kind of pattern is discernible in the promotion of archdeacons to bishoprics: most had either been archdeacons of Jerusalem or of Tyre.[6]   The archdeacon of Jerusalem's importance is self-evident, but the archdeacon of Tyre had more work than his colleagues in the other metropolitan sees because Tyre had four suffragans, whereas none of the other metropolitans in the Frankish period had more than one.   Archbishop Frederick of Tyre had been archdeacon of Liège before he came to Syria and this was probably a fact which told in his favour, but the only Syrian archdeacon of a lesser see who was promoted to the episcopate was Adam of Acre, consecrated first Latin bishop of Banyas in 1140.[7]   Banyas, though strategically important, was not a very large or eminent diocese and in any case Acre was, even in the twelfth century, one of the largest cities in the kingdom of Jerusalem and had a high proportion of Latin Christians in its population, so that archdeacon Adam must have had a fairly wide experience in administration.

It was possible to combine a career in the church with service in the royal administration.   This was the case with Ralph, the chancellor of queen Melisende and Baldwin III, who was

1. Baldwin II, archbishop of Caesarea, chancellor of the patriarch William I; Ernesius, archbishop of Caesarea, chancellor of the patriarch William I and of the patriarch Fulcher; Aimery, archbishop of Caesarea, chancellor of the patriarch Amalric.

2. William I of Tyre; Peter of Tyre; William I of Jerusalem; Amalric of Jerusalem.

3. Letard II of Nazareth.

4. Aimery of Limoges, patriarch of Antioch.

5. He had been prior since 1129, de Rozière, pp 138–9, no 67.

6. Former archdeacons of Jerusalem: Patriarchs Arnulf and Heraclius, (archbishop of Caesarea before he became patriarch).   Former archdeacons of Tyre: William, bishop of Acre; Odo, bishop of Beirut; William II, archbishop of Tyre.

7. WT, XV, 11, *RHC Occ*, I, pp 675–6.

unsuccessfully nominated to the see of Tyre in 1146 but who became bishop of Bethlehem in 1156,[1] an appointment which his enemies said he owed to the fact that the pope at that time was Hadrian IV, who was an Englishman like Ralph himself.[2] While holding this office Ralph continued to act as chancellor of the kingdom until his death in 1174[3] and the phrase in which William of Tyre sums up his character, 'he was indeed a well-educated man but a very worldly one', probably describes him very accurately.[4]

The appointment of a chancellor of a kingdom to a bishopric was standard practice in many western European states at this time, for it was a way of making financial provision for an important officer of state at no expense to the crown. A similar policy was followed in regard to Ralph's successor as chancellor, William of Tyre. His career structure had been different from that of Ralph. He was appointed archdeacon of Tyre in 1167 when the holder of that office, archdeacon William, was appointed bishop of Acre.[5]   Then in 1170 he became tutor to the young prince Baldwin, son of Amalric.[6]   In 1174 he succeeded Ralph of Bethlehem as chancellor and continued to be archdeacon,[7] then when the archdiocese of Tyre fell vacant he was consecrated to that see in 1175,[8] but continued to act as chancellor until 1183.[9]

In the principality of Antioch a similar policy was adopted. John, the chancellor of Antioch, was also archdeacon of Antioch and was appointed bishop of Tripoli in 1183 although he relinquished his office as chancellor soon afterwards.[10] His bishopric seems to have been intended as a reward for services already rendered, and clearly he could not continue to act as chancellor while living in another state. But the chancellorship of Antioch was then given to archbishop Albert of Tarsus,[11] who, like William of Tyre, while holding a secular and an ecclesiastical office concurrently, at least had the advantage of having been trained in church administration.   Bishop Ralph of Bethlehem, who came to a bishopric

1. 'Elect' of Bethlehem by 7 June 1156, *CGOH*, no 244.
2. *Ibid.*, XVI, 17, pp 733–4.
3. His last recorded act as chancellor is dated 18 April 1174, *CGOH*, no 643. WT, XX, 30, *RHC Occ*, I, p 999.
4. *Ibid.*, XVI, 17, p 733.
5. *Ibid.*, XX, 1, p 943.
6. *Ibid.*, XXI, 1, pp 1004–5.
7. *Ibid.*, XXI, 5, p 1012.
8. *Ibid.*, XXI, 9, p 1020.
9. His last recorded acts as chancellor date from 19 March 1183, Strehlke, pp 15–16, nos 16–17.
10. In May 1183 he dated a charter of Bohemond III as chancellor of Antioch and bishop of Tripoli, *CGOH*, vol II, p 911, no 23. By 1184 he had relinquished the chancellorship, *CGOH*, no 676.
11. *CGOH*, nos 782–3, of 1186.

after training in a secular career, was, as far as is known, unique in the twelfth-century Latin church in Syria.

Some very senior offices in the church were filled by translating bishops from less important sees. This occurred most frequently in the case of patriarchs. Two of the three Latin patriarchs of Antioch in the twelfth century were translated from other sees: Bernard of Valence from Artah, and Ralph of Domfront from Mamistra.[1] In the case of Jerusalem, apart from the two exceptional appointments of Daimbert and Gibelin, both of whom had previously held episcopal office in western Europe, two Latin bishops in Syria were translated to the patriarchate: Fulcher, archbishop of Tyre, and Heraclius, archbishop of Caesarea. No bishops were translated to metropolitan sees, except in the case of Tyre where this happened twice: both archbishop Frederick (1164—74) and archbishop Joscius (c 1186— c 1201) had previously been bishops of Acre.[2] But Tyre was the only metropolitan see in Latin Syria of sufficient consequence to justify the translation of bishops from other sees.

On the whole men who had been trained as ecclesiastical administrators made very competent bishops. An excellent example of this is Peter of Barcelona who succeeded William as prior of the Holy Sepulchre when the latter became patriarch of Jerusalem in 1130.[3] He held this office for twenty-one years, and at the beginning received considerable assistance from the patriarch in the conduct of business.[4] Peter proved to be a patient and remarkably competent administrator who succeeded in placing the financial resources of the Holy Sepulchre on a firm footing by discovering exactly what the property rights of the canons were and securing their legal enforcement,[5] by settling disputes about property in which the canons were involved,[6] and by obtaining detailed confirmation of their lands and privileges from Frankish rulers and from the holy see.[7] The cartulary of the Holy Sepulchre bears witness to his labours, for almost a fifth of the documents it contains were drawn up during his term of office.[8]

1. WT, VI, 23, XIV, 10, RHC Occ, I, pp 274—5, 619—20.
2. Ibid., XIX, 6, pp 892—3; Joscius's appointment to Acre, ibid., XX, 25, p 990; first mentioned as archbishop of Tyre in 1186, Strehlke, pp 19—21, nos 21—3.
3. WT, XVI, 17, RHC Occ, I, p 734.
4. See p 70, n 4, above.
5. de Rozière, pp 166—7, no 86, pp 172—83, nos 89—91.
6. Ibid., pp 56—60, no 32, pp 156—8, no 79, CGOH, no 140.
7. de Rozière, pp 169—72, no 88, pp 184—7, nos 93—4, pp 190—2, no 97, pp 22—7, nos 17—18, pp 29—32, no 20, pp 36—41, no 23.
8. The cartulary contains 185 documents, 37 of which date from Peter's reign: ibid., nos 5—7, 17—20, 22—4, 26—8, 31—4, 40—41, 72—4, 79—80, 82—3, 89—90, 97, 101—2, 104, 107, 109, 111, 117, 120.

In 1151 he was appointed archbishop of Tyre, an office which he held for thirteen years.[1] As the second most important prelate in the kingdom he had an important role to play in secular affairs. He was frequently in attendance at court[2] and he occasionally accompanied the king on campaign.[3] As he was one of the senior churchmen in the realm the king paid attention to what he said: it seems to have been on his advice that Jerusalem recognised Alexander III as pope.[4] He had independence of judgment and, when the imperious patriarch Fulcher condemned the prior and canons of the Mount of Olives to do public penance, Peter persuaded two of his suffragans, the bishops of Banyas and Beirut, to join with him in accompanying the canons as they walked barefoot through Jerusalem, which was an effective way of dissociating himself from the severity of the patriarch's sentence.[5] Despite his inevitable involvement in affairs of state he was considered an exemplary archbishop of Tyre. The 'Eracles' describes him as 'douz et piteus vers povres gens' and he is the only one of his predecessors for whom William of Tyre has unqualified praise:

> He was a man of remarkable innocence and gentleness of character. He feared God and abhorred evil, and his memory will be held blessed by God and by men ... He was a nobleman by birth, but he was even more noble in his spiritual life. Volumes could be written about his life and character.[6]

Very occasionally a member of a cathedral chapter would be promoted to a bishopric without holding any important administrative office before. Thus in 1172 Joscius, canon of Acre, was appointed bishop of that see.[7] The recommendation of this relatively obscure candidate was presumably made by the metropolitan, archbishop Frederick of Tyre, and it proved a very shrewd choice, for Joscius had a gift for diplomacy which led him to be entrusted with the delicate mission of trying to negotiate a marriage between the princess Sibyl, sister of Baldwin the leper and heir to the throne, and the duke of Burgundy in 1178–9.[8] Since his value to the kingdom in general, and not simply to the church, was evident, he was translated to Tyre when that see fell vacant on the

---

1. WT, XVI, 17, *RHC Occ*, I, p 734.

2. Delaborde, pp 69–70, no 29; *CGOH*, nos 225, 258; de Rozière, pp 102–7, no 54; Strehlke, pp 3–5, no 5.

3. WT, XVII, 21, XVIII, 21, *RHC Occ*, I, pp 827, 856.

4. *Ibid.*, XVIII, 29, pp 870–1. Cf. Amalric of Nesle's letter to Alexander III, *PL*, 200, 1362–3.

5. de Rozière, pp 136–8, no 66.

6. WT, XVI, 17, *RHC Occ*, I, p 734 ('Eracles' printed on the same page).

7. *Ibid.*, XX, 25, p 990.

8. *Ibid.*, XXI, 26, p 1049.

death of archbishop William in 1186.[1]   But his greatest service to
the kingdom was performed after the battle of Hattin, when he
sailed to the west in a ship with a black sail to inform the kings of
Europe of the loss of the Holy Land.   His activities there were
extensive: he informed the king of Sicily and the pope, and
travelled to France where he mediated peace between Henry II of
England and Philip II of France and persuaded both of them to
take the cross at Gisors in 1188.[2]   After his return to Syria he
became chancellor of the restored kingdom under Henry of
Troyes[3] and Aimery of Lusignan[4] until his death around 1201.[5]

Only two other instances are known of bishops who circum-
vented the normal *cursus honorum* of the Latin church and were
drawn from the ranks of the secular clergy. One dates from the
very early years of the settlement when men of talent were probably few: this was Anschetinus, cantor of Bethlehem, who became
first Latin bishop of that see and held the office for fifteen years.[6]
The other was Odo, precentor of the church of Tyre, who had
been a member of the chapter since 1163[7] and who was appointed
bishop of Sidon in 1176, presumably at the suggestion of archbishop William.[8]   He died during the siege of Acre by Guy of
Lusignan in 1190.[9]

It is noticeable that very few of the bishops in Syria came from
religious communities, except for those Austin canons who had
been members of cathedral chapters. Fulcher, archbishop of Tyre
and later patriarch of Jerusalem, had been trained in a house of
canons regular in western Europe, but his was an unusual case

1. Strehlke, pp 19—21, nos 21—3. See p 81, n 4, above.
2. 'Eracles', XXIV, 5, 8, *RHC Occ*, II, pp 111—12, 115; *Itinerarium Regis Ricardi*, I,
17, II, 3, pp 31—2, 140—1; *Chronicle of the Reigns of Henry II and Richard I*, ed
Stubbs, vol II, pp 29—30.
3. Imperiale, III, pp 87—9, 112—15, nos 28, 40; Strehlke, pp 24—7, nos 28—32;
CGOH, nos 954, 972; Müller, pp 65—6, no 40; Kohler, p 164, no 53.
4. *CGOH*, no 1032; Strehlke, pp 28—31, nos 35—6, 38; Kohler, pp 166—7, no 57.
5. Died before 30 May 1202, TT, I, pp 424—6, no 108.
6. WT, XI, 12, *RHC Occ*, I, pp 472—4. Even he had previously been titular bishop
of Ascalon.
7. de Rozière, pp 230—1, no 126.
8. WT, XXI, 11, *RHC Occ*, I, p 1023.
9. Roger of Houedene, vol III, p 87. Fedalto, *Chiesa Latina*, II, p 206, accepts the
evidence of Delaville Le Roulx, *Archives*, p 151, no 58, of 10 September 1181 (which
names 'Reinaldus Sydonensis episcopus'), and lists the bishops of Sidon as Odo I (1175),
Reinald (1181), Odo II (1187). The 1181 document exists in another copy, *ibid.*, pp
149—50, no 57, where the bishop of Sidon is not mentioned, but at the same point in
the list of witnesses the name 'Reynaldus Sydonensis dominus' appears. It would seem
that the term *episcopus* in the first document is a scribal error, and that bishop Odo
reigned from 1175—90. Had he died before 1181 it might be expected that William of
Tyre would mention the fact, since he is meticulous in recording the deaths of his own
suffragans.

because he owed his appointment to his distinguished career in France before he came to Jerusalem.[1]   The same is true of Frederick, bishop of Acre and later archbishop of Tyre, who was, it is true, an Austin canon of the *Templum Domini* before he was elected to Acre, but who, like Fulcher, owed his appointment to the training which he had received in western Europe.[2]   In both cases the fact that these men were canons regular was almost fortuitous in determining their choice as bishops.   The only bishop who is known to have been a canon regular and nothing more before his appointment is Guerricus, the first Latin archbishop of Petra.[3]

Black monks were even more uncommon on the Syrian bench. The patriarch Stephen of Jerusalem was a Benedictine, but he was appointed patriarch because he was of the blood royal.[4] Aimery, archbishop of Caesarea (1180—97) and patriarch of Jerusalem (1197—1202), was always known as 'the monk', but he owed his appointment to the see of Caesarea to the fact that he had been chancellor of the patriarch Amalric of Nesle.[5]   It is not known where he had been professed: he is never associated with any of the Latin monasteries of Syria, but he was a Florentine by birth[6] and it is possible, therefore, that he had formerly been a member of an Italian community before he came to the Holy Land.

But throughout the whole of the twelfth century only two monks were chosen to be bishops in Syria who had no other recommendation than that they were trained monastic administrators.   One was Albert, abbot of St Erard at Marseilles, whom Raymond IV of Toulouse nominated as first Latin bishop of Tripoli.[7]   This was in the early days of the settlement when trained clergy were difficult to find in Syria, and the count brought this abbot from overseas to take charge of the Latin church in his newly-founded state. The other monastic bishop was Bernard, abbot of Mount Tabor, who was appointed to Lydda in 1168.[8]   He was nominated by king Amalric and proved a most effective choice. Despite his monastic training he was prepared

1. WT, XIV, 11, *RHC Occ*, I, pp 621—2.

2. *Ibid.*, XXI, 4, p 1010; Alberic of Trois Fontaines, 'Chronica', *MGH SS*, XXIII, p 853.

3. WT, XX, 3, *RHC Occ*, I, p 944.

4. *Ibid.*, XIII, 25, pp 594—5.

5. Chancellor, 1171—80: *CGOH*, no 422; Delaborde, pp 124—5, no 37; de Rozière, pp 305—7, 322—5, nos 168, 181.

6. Monachus of Florence, bishop of Acre, 'De Recuperatione Ptolemaide Liber', ed Stubbs, in Roger of Houedene, vol III, pp cv—cxxxvi.

7. William of Malmesbury, *Gesta Regum*, IV, 388, vol II, p 458.

8. WT, XX, 12, *RHC Occ*, I, p 959.

if the need arose to take part in campaigning,[1] and when the patriarch Heraclius went to the west in 1184 he appointed Bernard as his vicar in Jerusalem, a post which he discharged with efficiency, recruiting pilgrim knights to join the royal army as volunteers in order to relieve Kerak of Moab to which Saladin had laid siege.[2] He held office for twenty-two years and died at the siege of Acre in 1190.[3]

A high proportion of the bishops came from overseas. This was true of all the patriarchs of Jerusalem and Antioch who held office before 1187. There were thirteen of them altogether and none of them had been born in Syria. The same was true of many of the archbishops and bishops as well, although many of them, like many of the patriarchs, had received their training in the Syrian church before they were promoted. The bench of bishops was made up of men of a wide variety of races. Most of them were, of course, French, just as was the majority of the Frankish population of Syria, but some of them, like William I of Tyre and Ralph of Bethlehem, were English;[4] some, like Peter of Tyre, were Aragonese;[5] some, like Aimery of Caesarea, were Italians;[6] and there were men from Lorraine, like Frederick of Tyre;[7] and from Flanders, like William, patriarch of Jerusalem.[8] The one important group of western Europeans not represented were the Germans. Germans do not seem to have been very popular in the predominantly French Crusader States before the foundation of the Teutonic order after the third crusade. The reason for this would seem to have been less a display of French chauvinism than a language barrier. No comparable impediment to conversation existed between the French and other romance speakers, while even the English spoke French of a kind, at least, if they were sufficiently well-born. The difficulty experience by German speakers in the Frankish east is remarked upon by the pilgrim, John of Würzburg, who in the reign of king Amalric found at Jerusalem

a hospice and a church which has been newly built in honour of St Mary, and which is called the house of the Germans, upon which hardly any men who speak any other language bestow any benefactions.[9]

1. *Ibid.*, XX, 19, p 974.
2. B. de Brousillon, 'La charte d'André II de Vitré et le siège de Karak en 1184', *BHCTH*, 1899, pp 50–3.
3. Roger of Houedene, vol III, p 87.
4. WT, XIII, 23, XVI, 17, *RHC Occ*, I, pp 591–2, 733.
5. *Ibid.*, XVI, 17, p 734.
6. See n 6 p 122 above.
7. WT, XIX, 6, *RHC Occ*, I, pp 892–3.
8. *Ibid.*, XIII, 26, p 598.
9. *Description of the Holy Land by John of Würzburg, A.D. 1160–1170*, trans C.W. Wilson, *PPTS*, 1890, p 46.

There were, of course, some bishops who were drawn from the native Frankish population of Syria: William of Tyre is the most eminent example of this.[1] Nevertheless, it is a sufficiently remarkable fact that, at a time when the majority of bishops and abbots throughout the western church were of aristocratic birth, none of the ruling families of Jerusalem, Antioch, Tripoli or Edessa, and none of the great baronial families in any of those states, are known to have given a son to the church in the whole of the twelfth century. This is in marked contrast to their treatment of daughters. King Baldwin II's daughter, Yveta, was professed as a nun at St Anne's, Jerusalem, and later became abbess of the convent of Bethany,[2] and Stephanie, the daughter of count Joscelin I of Edessa, became abbess of Ste Marie la Grande, Jerusalem.[3]

There were good reasons why the aristocracy of Frankish Syria, unlike their peers in western Europe, did not consider the church a suitable career for their younger sons. In the first place Frankish Syria suffered from a constant shortage of knights, and this removed social and economic pressures from younger sons to seek a career in the church, because they could always find employment in the pursuit of arms. Secondly, the absence in the Frankish states of any great feudal fiefs of the church[4] made an ecclesiastical career for their sons seem less attractive to the nobility there than to noblemen in the west.

Nevertheless, it would be misleading to suppose that the Frankish nobility took no interest in church appointments. They may not have given their sons to the church but they certainly imported from western Europe kinsmen who were already in orders and sought to benefice them. King Baldwin II appointed two of his kinsmen to important church offices: Stephen to be patriarch of Jerusalem and Gelduin to be abbot of Our Lady of Josaphat.[5] The baronage behaved in a similar way: Peter Armoin, castellan of Antioch, for example, brought his nephew Aimery from Normandy and secured his appointment as dean of Antioch.[6]

There is very little evidence of nepotism among the clergy themselves. Ernesius, the nephew of the patriarch William of Jerusalem, became chancellor of the diocese in his uncle's lifetime and continued to hold that office in the reign of the patriarch

---

1. WT, XIX, 4, *RHC Occ*, I, p 889. R.C. Schwinges, *Kreuzzugsideologie und Toleranz. Studien zu Wilhelm von Tyrus*, Stuttgart 1977, pp 19—35.

2. de Rozière, pp 60—5, no 33.

3. WT, XIX, 4, *RHC Occ*, I, p 889.

4. See chapter 6 below.

5. WT, XIII, 25, *RHC Occ*, I, pp 594—5; Delaborde, pp 33—5, no 8.

6. WT, XV, 18, p 688.

Fulcher, until he was appointed archbishop of Caesarea around 1160.[1] The only other twelfth-century instance of a bishop's kinsman attaining high office is Rainald, nephew of the patriarch Fulcher. He became first Latin bishop of Hebron in 1168, eleven years after his uncle's death: it is not known what his earlier career had been or whether it had been materially advanced by his uncle's influence.[2]

The evidence suggests, therefore, that many of the senior clergy in the Crusader States in the twelfth century were recruited initially from western Europe; and that these men were members of noble families who had kinsmen or acquaintances in the Frankish east whom they supposed would be able to promote the interests of their younger sons whom they had destined for the church. When such men came to the east they usually first became members of cathedral chapters and the successful ones among them subsequently attained more important positions.

Frederick, William of Tyre's predecessor as archbishop, is an example of a churchman with this kind of career structure. He was the son of Albert de Rupe, and nephew of count Godfrey of Namur, and entered the church and became archdeacon of St Lambert's at Liège.[3] He then came to Jerusalem and was professed as an Austin canon at the *Templum Domini*.[4] A nobleman of this kind with experience in church administration was a suitable candidate for a bishopric, and when the see of Acre fell vacant, at some time between 1148 and 1153, he was appointed to it.[5] Frederick took no great interest in the administration of his see and probably delegated the routine work to his archdeacon and the dean of Acre. The only part which he took in ecclesiastical administration was to witness documents issued either by the king or the patriarch for religious communities.[6] His gifts were those of a secular administrator rather than those of a churchman. He took part with the royal army in the siege of Ascalon in 1153,[7] and in 1154—5 went to Antioch, together with Ralph, Baldwin III's chancellor, as a representative of the high court of Jerusalem to mediate peace between price Reynald and the patriarch

1. Nephew and chancellor of the patriarch William, *CGOH*, no 150; chancellor of the patriarch Fulcher, de Marsy, 'Saint Lazare', *AOL*, II, p 127, no 6, p 129, no 8; de Rozière, pp 77—9, no 41; Delaborde, pp 60—1, no 26.

2. WT, XX, 3, *RHC Occ*, I, p 944.

3. Alberic of Trois Fontaines, 'Chronica', *MGH SS*, XXIII, p 853.

4. WT, XXI, 4, *RHC Occ*, I, p 1010.

5. His predecessor, bishop Rorgo, is last mentioned in 1148, WT, XVII, 1, p 759. Frederick is first mentioned in 1153, *ibid.*, XVII, 21, pp 795—6.

6. Müller, p 8, no 6; Strehlke, pp 3—5, no 3; Delaborde, pp 82—3, no 35; de Rozière, pp 102—7, no 54; *CGOH*, nos 224—5, 258.

7. WT, XVII, 21, *RHC Occ*, I, pp 795—6.

Aimery of Limoges, a mission which he accomplished successfully.[1] When Amalric of Nesle's election as patriarch of Jerusalem
was contested by some of the bishops in 1157, Frederick represented the patriarch and the crown of Jerusalem at Rome and
obtained confirmation of the election from pope Hadrian IV.[2]
Frederick was an adviser to both Baldwin III[3] and his brother,
Amalric, count of Jaffa.[4] After Amalric had become king, and
while Amalric of Nesle was patriarch, Frederick was translated to
the metropolitan church of Tyre when that see fell vacant in
1164.[5]

Since king Amalric was on cool terms with the patriarch of
Jerusalem[6] Frederick of Tyre, as the senior metropolitan, became
the king's chief episcopal adviser.[7] He enjoyed warfare and in
1167 brought forces to Egypt by sea to aid the king in his attack
on Alexandria, but contracted dysentery and was forced to return
home.[8] After Saladin's occupation of Egypt in 1169 Frederick
led an embassy to the west, accompanied by his suffragan, the
bishop of Banyas, who was virtually an auxiliary of the church of
Tyre, since his diocese was in Muslim hands. Frederick stayed
in the west for two years trying, without success, to raise help
for the threatened Frankish states in Syria and only returned to
Jerusalem in 1171.[9] He died soon after king Amalric, in October
1174, and was buried in the *Templum Domini.*[10] William of Tyre,
who had been his archdeacon, describes him as

> a nobleman who came from Lorraine. He was extremely tall, and
> although he was not very well-educated he took great pleasure in
> warfare.[11]

Latin bishops in the twelfth century were chosen by lay rulers
throughout the Frankish east and it was normal practice for those
rulers to take the advice of other bishops in the province about the

1. *Ibid.*, XVIII, 1, pp 816–17.
2. *Ibid.*, XVIII, 20, p 854.
3. *CGOH*, nos 224–5, 258.
4. Müller, p 8, no 6.
5. WT, XIX, 6, *RHC Occ*, I, pp 892–3.
6. See chapter 3 above.
7. *CGOH*, no 402; Müller, pp 11, 14, nos 9, 11; de Marsy, 'Saint Lazare', *AOL*, II,
p 140, no 22; Chalandon, 'Un diplôme inédit', *ROL*, 8, 1900–1, pp 311–17; J. Delaville
Le Roulx, 'Chartes de Terre Sainte', *ROL*, 11, 1905–8, pp 183–4, no 2.
8. WT, XIX, 28, *RHC Occ*, I, p 932.
9. *Ibid.*, XX, 12, 25, pp 960–1, 988. Alexander III's crusader encyclical, *PL*, 200,
599–601, no 626.
10. Röhricht, 'Syria Sacra', p 17, n 6, places his death in 1173. This is incorrect,
since he died in the same year and month as Miles of Plancy, who was assassinated in
October 1174, WT, XXI, 4, *RHC Occ*, I, p 1010.
11. *Ibid.*, XIX, 6, pp 892–3.

choice of candidates. The election was formally in the hands of cathedral chapters, but Mayer has argued that for much of the century kings had stalls in the Holy Sepulchre and in some other cathedrals in the kingdom and thus had a canonical right to be present at elections.[1] It was possible for the canons to appeal to the pope against a royal nominee and in such a case the bishop-elect could not be consecrated until he had received papal approval, although he could in the interim be invested with the temporalities of the see. There is only one instance in which a successful appeal was lodged against a royal candidate: that was in 1146 when the chancellor, Ralph, was nominated to the see of Tyre. This was a highly unusual appointment since Ralph had not held any church office before his election and no other candidate for a bishopric in the Frankish east during the twelfth century is known to have been in an analogous position. Moreover, the crown was unfortunate on that occasion because it was opposed by the patriarch Fulcher who was an unusually obstinate man. Otherwise, popes always found in favour of royal candidates even if the grounds of an appeal were strong and had wide support among the native clergy, as was the case with the appeal against Arnulf in Paschal II's reign.[2]

Except as a court of appeal the papacy took no part in the appointment of bishops in Frankish Syria before 1187, although it was essential to obtain the assent of the pope to secure the deposition of a bishop after he had been consecrated. The holy see reserved the right to confirm the appointment of patriarchs, who received *pallia* from the pope as a sign that they were in communion with the Roman see, but the only other prelates in the east who received parallel recognition were the archbishops of Tyre and this came about as a result of their own initiative, not that of the papacy. Papal surveillance of the Latin church in Syria was exercised through legates, who were sent to the east at irregular intervals. In the twelfth century no patriarch of Jerusalem or Antioch enjoyed legatine powers with the sole exception of Gibelin of Arles.[3]

The Latin bench of bishops therefore reflected in its composition the preferences of the kings of Jerusalem, the princes of Antioch and the counts of Edessa and Tripoli. What these rulers wanted were men who were not simply qualified to carry out religious duties, or even to perform the tasks of diocesan

---

1. Mayer, 'Das Pontifikale von Tyrus', *DOP*, 21, 1967, pp 185–7.
2. Fulcher of Chartres, II, 54, s 8, ed Hagenmeyer, pp 590–91; de Rozière, pp 11–13, no 11 (Arnulf); WT, XVI, 17, *RHC Occ*, I, pp 733–4 (Ralph of Tyre).
3. *CGOH*, vol II, p 899, no 4.

administration: those functions could, after all, be delegated to subordinate clergy; but bishops who, as members of the feudal establishment, could take a full share in the performance of secular duties. Such men as Frederick of Tyre were ideally suited by temperament and upbringing to fulfil such a role.

In the early days of the settlement, when bishops were few and dioceses were huge, all the bishops must have spent some reasonable part of their time doing strictly ecclesiastical work. They had to organise the church: to set up parishes, train clergy, define the property rights of the church and its sources of income, and inaugurate an extensive programme of church building. As more dioceses were created, and as the institutions of the church became well-established in Syria, these activities took up less time and could at need be delegated to trained subordinates.

Compared with their colleagues in western Europe the bishops of Frankish Syria had much less ecclesiastical business to deal with. In the first place their sees were, on the whole, far smaller than most western sees. They also had far fewer clergy in their charge than any western bishop, and they were not encumbered with the administration of large feudal fiefs as many western bishops were. How, then, were they employed?

The patriarchs of Jerusalem had a heavy round of liturgical duties. Like the popes in Rome they were expected to celebrate the station Masses on the principal church feasts at the great shrine churches of Jerusalem, but, unlike the popes, they had no cardinals to whom they could delegate this work.[1] Some other bishops, whose cathedrals were shrine churches, may also have been expected to preside at the liturgy for the benefit of pilgrims: cathedrals which had this status were those of Bethlehem, Nazareth, Hebron, Lydda, Sebastia and Tortosa, but such work was seasonal since there were few pilgrims around in the winter months. But most bishops, unless they were exceptionally devout, need have spent little time performing liturgical duties and much of the work of administration could have been delegated by them.

James of Vitry, who was bishop of Acre in the early thirteenth century, gave an account of a typical day in his life when writing to friends in Paris:

I have arranged my day in the following way . . . Having celebrated Mass at dawn, I hear confessions until midday, and then, having with great difficulty forced down some food — for I have lost my appetite

1. If the see was vacant the senior-ranking metropolitan could deputise: Baldwin of Caesarea celebrated the Ash Wednesday liturgy at Mount Sion in 1108, Albert of Aix, X, 27, *RHC Occ*, IV, p 644. If the patriarch was absent the prior of the Holy Sepulchre could deputise, de Rozière, pp 136–8, no 66, pp 233–8, no 128.

... since I came overseas — I visit the sick in the city until the hour of nones or vespers. After this I hear cases relating to widows and orphans and other people ... with the result that I have no pleasant time left for reading, except at Mass or mattins, or when I can hide myself away for some brief space of time. I have kept the quiet time of night for prayer and recollection.[1]

James was both devout and conscientious in discharging his pastoral duties in which, as he makes clear, he spent much of his day. Plainly he had very little administrative work since he could deal with judicial business in the early evening. Yet he was bishop of one of the greatest cities in the Frankish east. It is difficult to escape the conclusion that many bishops of lesser sees, if they were willing to delegate pastoral work, could have lived in a very leisured way.

Many bishops took a leading part in military affairs. Any bishop might find himself called upon to take charge of the defence of his city if the lay lord happened to be away. Robert of Rouen, first Latin bishop of Lydda, held one of the few ecclesiastical lordships in the Frankish east and had to protect his flock in the cathedral when the Fatimid army launched an unexpected attack on the kingdom in 1102.[2] Archbishop Hugh of Edessa had to take charge of the defence of that city when it was attacked by Zengi of Mosul in 1144 while count Joscelin II was absent. He was later criticised for not being willing to spend his treasure in hiring sergeants to defend the walls, but, if this is true, he paid a heavy penalty for his parsimony, being trampled to death among the press of people trying to gain entry to the citadel after Muslim forces had breached the outer defences of the city.[3]

In the kingdom of Jerusalem a bishop normally had to accompany the royal army on campaign, since its standard was the relic of the True Cross and it was considered unseemly for a lesser cleric to have charge of an instrument of the Passion. This task was normally performed by the patriarch, although this was not invariable practice, and neither Amalric of Nesle nor Heraclius is ever recorded as being present on a campaign.[4] In their absence any bishop could perform this function, as archbishop Peter of Tyre did on Baldwin III's campaign against Nur-ad-Din in 1158, or Albert, bishop of Bethlehem, at the battle of Montgisart in 1178.[5]

---

1. James of Vitry, *Lettres*, ed R.B.C. Huygens, Leiden 1960, p 90, no 2.
2. Fulcher of Chartres, II, 15, s 3, pp 426–7.
3. WT, XVI, 5, *RHC Occ*, I, pp 711–12.
4. Heraclius was present at Saffuriyah when the royal host mustered there in 1182, but took no part in the subsequent campaign. *Ibid.*, XXII, 15, p 1092.
5. *Ibid.*, XVIII, 21, XXI, 22, pp 856, 1042.

The majority of bishops did not owe knight service to the crown, but some of them did owe a number of sergeants. Smail has argued, convincingly in my opinion, that the sergeants were foot-soldiers and that therefore they were used chiefly for defensive purposes when the states were invaded, but were not suitable for use on offensive campaigns when speed and surprise were important.[1] This would certainly explain the presence of a large number of bishops on campaigns which occurred inside the Frankish states, of which the best documented example is the siege of Ascalon in 1153, for on such occasions they were presumably expected to muster their sergeants and lead them to the royal host.[2]

But some bishops clearly enjoyed warfare and accompanied armies into battle on occasions when they were not obliged to do so. This remained true throughout the twelfth century in both the northern and the southern states: Baldwin of Caesarea and Gerard, abbot-archbishop of Tabor, both took part in the first battle of Ramla in 1101;[3] the archbishops Peter of Apamea and Roger of Tarsus accompanied the confederate forces of the Franks on campaign against Maudud of Mosul in 1110;[4] Ralph of Bethlehem and Bernard of Lydda helped king Amalric repel an attack which Saladin made on Darum in 1170.[5] Such examples could be multiplied, but it is more difficult to determine what part bishops played in such campaigns.

By western canon law priests and bishops were forbidden to shed blood, so they were presumably not expected to fight.[6] The fact that Bernard, patriarch of Antioch, went on the campaign against Harran in 1104 riding on a mule, suggests that he took no part in the fighting, but was present to encourage the Christian knights and to give them absolution before the battle.[7] It may have been generally the case that bishops did not fight, but they could be involved in considerable physical danger on the battlefield, perhaps greater danger than the knights if they were not armed. Archbishop Benedict of Edessa was captured by the Muslims at that same battle of Harran, and only rescued because prince Tancred saw what had happened and made a spirited foray to save him.[8] In 1132 bishop Gerard of Tripoli was captured in

1. Smail, *Crusading Warfare*, pp 90−2.
2. WT, XVII, 21, *RHC Occ*, I, pp 795−6.
3. Albert of Aix, VII, 66, *RHC Occ*, IV, p 550; see above p 61, n 1.
4. Albert of Aix, XI, 40, pp 682−3.
5. WT, XX, 19, *RHC Occ*, I, p 974.
6. This rule was not always observed. The Byzantine world was greatly shocked by Latin priests who fought, Anna Comnena, *Alexiad*, X, 8, ed Leib, II, p 218. This instance may be a piece of propaganda but it is not unparalleled.
7. Ralph of Caen, c 150, *RHC Occ*, III, p 711.
8. *Ibid.*, cc 148−9, p 710.

battle and had to be ransomed, but this proved quite cheap because he had not been identified by the enemy: this implies that he was wearing no distinctive dress and perhaps wore armour and looked like a knight.[1] Capture was not the only danger a bishop ran: Ralph of Bethlehem lost all his baggage and was severely wounded in 1165 while campaigning against Shirkuh in Egypt;[2] bishop Rufinus of Acre was killed at the battle of Hattin;[3] and bishop Ralph II of Bethlehem was executed by Saladin, with whom he was trying to negotiate the surrender of the citadel of Jaffa in 1192, when a relief force arrived unexpectedly and the garrison went back on its word to deliver the fortress to the sultan.[4] Except when circumstances left no other choice open to him, for example if the Saracens attacked a city in which the bishop was the senior ranking feudal nobleman, a bishop was not bound to take any part in military affairs. Amalric of Nesle never did so during the twenty-three years that he was patriarch, and it is not known that William of Tyre ever took part in a campaign while he was archbishop.

In Jerusalem, though not it would seem in the northern states, bishops took their place among the king's advisers and attended meetings of the high court. This body had a dual function: it was a feudal court, dealing with the business of the king's vassals, and when it met in that capacity only the bishop of Lydda and the archbishop of Nazareth attended since they were the only bishops in the kingdom who held feudal fiefs of the crown.[5] But the high court was also the supreme advisory body in the kingdom, and the patriarch and some of the bishops were usually in attendance when it met in that capacity to decide questions of peace and war, royal marriages, alliances with the Italian cities, or questions affecting the royal succession. In addition, the king sometimes acted with the advice of the bishops in making strictly feudal arrangements which would affect the structure of power in the kingdom: thus the archbishop of Tyre and the bishop of Acre, together with the bishop of Latakia as a member of the delegation of the count of Tripoli, were present at the court in 1161 when Baldwin III arranged for Philip of Milly to exchange with the crown his lands at Nablus for the great fief of Oultrejourdain.[6] Through attendance at such meetings a bishop

1. WT, XIV, 23, RHC Occ, I, p 640.
2. Ibid., XIX, 25, p 927.
3. Itinerarium Regis Ricardi, I, 5, p 15. Ralph of Coggeshall, Chronicon Anglicanum, ed J. Stevenson, RS, 66, London 1875, p 21.
4. Western redaction of 'Eracles', RHC Occ, II, pp 194, 196.
5. See chapter 6 below.
6. Strehlke, pp 3—5, no 3.

could develop considerable expertise in the work of secular government if he had the right temperament: the patriarch Warmund, as a result of such training, was able to act as virtual regent of the kingdom while Baldwin II was a prisoner of war in the years 1122—4.[1]

Despite their close association in the work of government bishops were very seldom appointed to any of the chief offices of state. The matter of bishops who were also chancellors has already been discussed, but such appointments were exceptional. The work which bishops were most frequently called upon to perform by the secular administration was to act as ambassadors. They were ideally suited to such a role since they had status by virtue of their office and they were trained in the art of public speaking; moreover, it was easier in a state constantly at war to be temporarily without the services of a bishop than without those of a great lord. Even at the very beginning of the settlement bishops performed functions of this kind: Robert of Rouen, bishop of Lydda, led the delegation sent by the garrison of Jerusalem to ask Baldwin of Edessa to take over his brother's rule.[2] However, while bishops were few they could not so easily be spared and the negotiations for the marriage of Adelaide of Sicily to Baldwin I in 1112, for example, though inspired by the patriarch Arnulf, were conducted by laymen.[3] Bishops first began to be used on diplomatic missions as a matter of course towards the end of Baldwin II's reign, by which time there were more of them. Thus in 1128 archbishop William I of Tyre and bishop Roger of Lydda visited Rome to consult with pope Honorius II about the affairs of the Holy Land and also to arrange the marriage of the king's eldest daughter, Melisende, to Fulk V, count of Anjou.[4]

Thereafter they were regularly used on diplomatic missions. When the Franks wished to negotiate with John Comnenus in 1142 king Fulk sent Anselm, bishop of Bethlehem, as his envoy to the imperial camp in Cilicia,[5] while the bishop of Jabala had the unenviable task of conveying to the emperor the refusal of the barons of Antioch to hand over their city to him.[6] Archbishop Attard of Nazareth was one of the ambassadors sent by Baldwin III to Constantinople in 1157 to arrange a marriage alliance with the emperor Manuel,[7] and archbishop Ernesius of

1. See chapter 3 above.
2. Albert of Aix, VII, 30, *RHC Occ*, IV, p 526.
3. WT, XI, 21, *RHC Occ*, I, pp 487—9.
4. de Rozière, pp 17—18, no 15; *RR*, I, p 122, no 30.
5. WT, XV, 21, *RHC Occ*, I, pp 691—2.
6. Otto of Freising, *Chronica*, VII, 28, pp 354—5.
7. WT, XVIII, 16, 22, *RHC Occ*, I, pp 846, 857.

Caesarea was charged with the lengthy negotiations at the Byzantine court, lasting two years, which led to the marriage of king Amalric of Jerusalem and Manuel's great-niece, Maria.[1] When Amalric visited Constantinople in person in 1171, bishop William of Acre was a member of his suite and was sent by the king on a diplomatic mission to Italy in the course of which he was murdered by a mentally unbalanced member of his own household.[2] In the winter of 1178–9 bishop Joscius of Acre was instructed, while staying in Italy in readiness to attend the third Lateran council which had been called for March 1179, to visit France in order to arrange a marriage between the princess Sibyl of Jerusalem and the duke of Burgundy.[3]

Bishops were also used in attempts which were from time to time made by the Frankish rulers of the east to promote a new crusade. An imposing delegation of this kind, consisting of the patriarch of Jerusalem, the archbishop of Caesarea and the bishop of Acre, was shipwrecked off the Syrian coast in 1169, an experience which caused the prelates to lose their nerve for further sea-travel. Their place was taken by Frederick, archbishop of Tyre, and the bishop of Banyas.[4] In 1184–5 the patriarch Heraclius and the grand masters of the Temple and Hospital conducted a similar mission in the west,[5] while the disaster of Hattin led to the sending of two missions, one from the kingdom of Jerusalem led by the archbishop of Tyre, the other from the principality of Antioch, led by the bishops of Jabala and Valania.[6]

Bishops were also used to mediate peace inside the Frankish states. Frederick, bishop of Acre, accompanied Ralph, Baldwin III's chancellor, to Antioch to arbitrate in the dispute between Reynald of Châtillon and the patriarch Aimery;[7] and a quarter of a century later the patriarch of Jerusalem, the archbishop of Caesarea and the bishop of Bethlehem formed part of the delegation sent to mediate between the same patriarch of Antioch and prince Bohemond III.[8] In May 1187 Joscius, archbishop of Tyre, was among the envoys sent by Guy of Lusignan to persuade Raymond III of Tripoli to recognise the king in the face of the threat posed by Saladin.[9]

1. *Ibid.*, XX, 1, p 942.
2. *Ibid.*, XX, 22, 25, pp 981, 989–90.
3. *Ibid.*, XXI, 26, p 1049.
4. *Ibid.*, XX, 12, 25, pp 960–1, 988.
5. *PL*, 201, 1312–13, no 182.
6. 'Eracles', XXIV, 5, *RHC Occ*, II, pp 111–12; *Chronicle of the Reigns of Henry II and Richard I*, ed Stubbs, II, pp 36–8.
7. WT, XVIII, 1, *RHC Occ*, I, pp 816–17.
8. *Ibid.*, XXII, 7, pp 1073–5.
9. Ernoul, p 143; 'Eracles', XXIII, 29, *RHC Occ*, II, p 44.

Indeed, the only embassies in which bishops played no part were those sent by the Frankish leaders to Muslim princes, although members of the military orders sometimes represented the Franks on such occasions.[1] The importance of bishops as diplomats should not be underestimated. In the twelfth century no western power, except, perhaps, the holy see with its system of legates, had any accredited ambassadors, so that there were no men trained in the arts of diplomacy available to rulers. Yet the exercise of such arts was particularly important to the Franks in the east whose position was very vulnerable and who depended for their survival on the support which they received from their Christian neighbours in Byzantium and the west.

The average level of education among the Latin bishops of Syria was not very high. Some educated clergy accompanied the first crusade, like Arnulf of Chocques, and some came to settle in the east in the years that followed, like Arnulf's pupil, Ralph of Caen, and Achard of Arrouaise, who became prior of the *Templum Domini*,[2] but there were never enough of them at any one time to bring about a flourishing of Latin learning in the Crusader States. Schools for training clergy were attached to some Latin cathedrals,[3] but there were no centres of scholarship in the Latin east to rival the great cathedral schools of western Europe. At a time when the west was experiencing the great intellectual awakening commonly called the twelfth-century renaissance Frankish Syria was an academic backwater. Consequently the kind of clergy who were attracted there from the west were not on the whole men with strong intellectual interests. It is, perhaps, significant in this connection, that the best educated Syrian bishop in this period, William of Tyre, was born in the east and went to the west to be educated, before returning to a career in the church of Jerusalem.[4] It was possible that native Franks would develop intellectual interests, but less likely that westerners with such interests would come to Syria. The situation was not unlike that which obtained in the later western colonial settlements of Australia and New Zealand in the nineteenth century. This is not to say that the episcopate of Latin Syria was composed entirely of the semi-literate, apart

1. E.g. the Templar Geoffrey who was part of Amalric's embassy to the Fatimid caliph in 1167, WT, XIX, 17—19, *RHC Occ*, I, pp 908—13.

2. M. de Vogüé, 'Achard d'Arrouaise, poème sur le *Templum Domini*', *AOL*, I, pp 562—79.

3. There was a *magister scholasticus* at the Holy Sepulchre by 1103, de Rozière, p 72, no 36.

4. R.B.C. Huygens, 'Guillaume de Tyr étudiant. Un chapître (XIX, 12) de son "Histoire" retrouvé', *Latomus*, XXI, 1962, pp 811—29; Schwinges, *Kreuzzugsideologie und Toleranz*.

from William of Tyre. Aimery of Caesarea, for example, wrote Latin verse, but his surviving poem, *De recuperatione Ptolemaide*, does not stand comparison with the work of the Archpoet, as the following couplet, in which the archbishop of Caesarea bemoans his sufferings during the siege of Acre, will show:

Esse mallet quilibet sine aqua rasus
Quam pati, quot passus sum, tot adversus casus.[1]

It is a very far cry from *Aestuans intrinsecus*, though the metre is the same.

It would be misleading to give the impression that the Latin bishops of Syria were all worldly men, even though the greater part of their time was spent in secular affairs or ecclesiastical administration. Their piety, it is true, was of a practical rather than a contemplative kind, but they were appointed because they were considered to have qualities which suited them to take an active part in affairs of state, and although intense interior piety is not of its nature incompatible with administrative ability the combination is a very unusual one. The Latin bishops showed a great concern for the maintenance and due performance of the liturgy in the holy places entrusted to their care, and there were a great many of these.[2] But they also showed a desire to perform the corporal acts of mercy which occupy a central place in the practice of the Christian life, feeding the hungry, caring for the poor and the sick, and the range of their charitable activities excited the admiration of leaders of eastern Christian churches among whom they lived.[3]

No twelfth-century bishop in Frankish Syria was translated to any see in the western church, though one archdeacon, John of Tyre, did become cardinal of S. Martino *ai Monti*.[4] Few of the bishops, or even the patriarchs, were known outside the Crusader States, with the exception of William of Tyre through his writings, and Aimery of Limoges, perhaps, on account of his longevity. As a group they were more like an earlier generation of western bishops than their twelfth-century western colleagues: those bishops of the pre-crusading period, who had not been very much influenced by the principles of Gregorian reform and who lived before the new spiritual and intellectual forces which dominated western Europe in the twelfth century had come into being. The

1. Roger of Houedene, vol III, p cxi.
2. See below chapter 14; B. Hamilton, 'Rebuilding Zion : the Holy Places of Jerusalem in the twelfth century', *SCH*, 14, 1977, pp 105–16.
3. St Nerses of Lampron, 'Letter to Leo II', *RHC Arm*, I, pp 599–600; MS, XX, 6, vol III, p 375.
4. WT, XVI, 17, *RHC Occ*, I, p 733.

Latin bishops of Syria were content, on the whole, to work in harmony with secular princes and to take a large share in affairs of state as well as in those of the church. Their piety, though sometimes deep, was of a practical rather than a devotional kind, and they were not much given to speculative thought. At the time of the first crusade there were still many bishops of a similar kind in the west, although even by then changes were beginning to be felt in the choice of bishops, but by the time of the third crusade the bishops of Syria appeared to belong to an older order of society by comparison with their brethren in western Europe.

6. THE SOURCES OF INCOME OF THE LATIN CHURCH IN THE TWELFTH CENTURY

The establishment of a Latin church in Syria posed economic problems for the Frankish authorities. In theory the Franks were simply substituting Latin for Greek bishops in the Orthodox patriarchates, and had this been merely a matter of appointing new personnel to existing sees, as it was in the Byzantine empire after the Latin conquest of 1204, there would have been no economic difficulties since the endowments of those sees could have been transferred to new incumbents. But in many cases the Latins were creating a new church on an archaic model and were appointing to sees which had had no Orthodox bishop for centuries. New sources of income therefore had to be found to support the Latin ecclesiastical establishment, and various methods were used to provide them.

One solution was to give the newly appointed bishops rights of territorial lordship. This was done in the case of the two earliest appointments. When Peter of Narbonne was made bishop of Albara in 1098 Raymond of Toulouse 'immediately gave him half the city and the surrounding region'.[1] Similarly, when Robert of Rouen was appointed to the bishopric of Lydda in 1099 the crusader leaders gave him the two cities of Lydda and Ramla and the surrounding territory.[2] This was not a practice which commended itself to Frankish rulers once their states had been set up. The bishop of Lydda could not be deprived of the lordship he already held, but his powers were reduced. By 1120 a lay lord of Ramla had been appointed, an event which may have occurred after the death of the first bishop,[3] and thereafter the bishop only had lordship over Lydda and a small area round it for which he owed the service of ten knights to the crown.[4] The only other ecclesiastical lordship to be established in the kingdom of Jerusalem was that of Nazareth, set up in 1109, whose bishop owed the king the service of six knights.[5] There would seem to have been no ecclesiastical lordships at all in the counties of

---

1. Raymond of Anguilers, ed Hill and Hill, p 92; WT, VII, 8, *RHC Occ*, I, p 288.
2. *Ibid.*, VII, 22, p 313.
3. *Ibid.*, XII, 13, p 532.
4. John of Ibelin, 'Livre', c 271, *RHC Lois*, I, p 422.
5. *Ibid.*, p 423.

Tripoli or Edessa. In the principality of Antioch, apart from the archbishop of Apamea, who presumably continued to enjoy territorial lordship over half of Albara even after his see had been translated,[1] only the patriarch is known to have had temporal jurisdiction: he ruled the castle of Qusair and the lands around it.[2] It is also possible that the bishops of Artah may have exercised lordship over their cathedral city: certainly no lay lords of this strategically important town are mentioned in any of the sources, which suggests that it may have been an ecclesiastical lordship.

Another way of providing income for the Latin clergy was to transfer Orthodox endowments to them. This could only be done in the case of bishoprics since parish churches and monasteries remained in Orthodox control together with any property they owned.[3]   At Antioch the Latin patriarch simply took over the endowments of the see from his Orthodox predecessor.   In Jerusalem the situation was slightly more complicated, because the Orthodox patriarch and his canons had been living in exile for eight years before the Franks captured the city, so that the property of the church of Jerusalem had to be identified before the Latin patriarch could be given possession of it. The twenty-one *casalia* assigned to the Holy Sepulchre by duke Godfrey may have been part of the traditional lands of the church, although this is not specified in later confirmations of the Sepulchre's pro-perty.[4]   In Frankish times the patriarch also exercised jurisdiction over the quarter of the city in which the Holy Sepulchre was situated.   This was not a figurative quarter, but almost exactly a quarter of the whole city area, in which the patriarch was lord, and the Franks believed that they were perpetuating a tradition which dated from 1063, when the Orthodox patriarch had been given this grant of jurisdiction by the Fatimid caliph of Egypt.[5]

It was not always easy for Latin bishops to gain control of Orthodox property even when it could be identified and even when the areas in which it was situated were in Frankish control. Prior Peter of the Holy Sepulchre, who was a very painstaking administrator, found records dating from the Orthodox period in the archives, which showed that the Sepulchre had once owned property at Antioch. He raised this matter with king Fulk while he was *bailli* of Antioch during the minority of the princess Constance, and in 1135 the king in the high court of Antioch issued a general confirmation of the property which the Holy

1. See chapter 2 above.
2. The patriarch's jurisdiction at Qusair, Auvray, no 4471.
3. See chapter 7 below.
4. de Rozière, pp 54–5, no 29.
5. WT, IX, 17–18, *RHC Occ*, I, pp 389–93.

Sepulchre had held there 'in the time of the Greeks'.[1]   This did
not result in more than a paper vindication of the Sepulchre's
rights: the canons were not granted corporal possession of their
property, and when, in 1139, the new prince of Antioch,
Raymond of Poitiers, came on pilgrimage to Jerusalem the patriarch William and prior Peter raised the matter again.   He was
co-operative and in 1140 the prior and some of the canons went
to Antioch to plead their case.   They arrived on 1 February, but
matters were delayed by a dispute with the Benedictines of St
Paul's about a garden and some land which the monks had been
given by the former patriarch, Bernard of Valence, but which the
canons claimed was part of their property.   The case was debated
at length by the high court, and the prior of the Sepulchre, who
was anxious to return to Jerusalem to keep Easter, on one
occasion even sought out the unfortunate prince Raymond while
he was on campaign to demand a judgment.   The matter was only
finally settled when the prior found four Orthodox witnesses of
mature age, presumably men who were old enough to remember
Antioch before 1098, who affirmed that the property had indeed
belonged to the Holy Sepulchre in Orthodox times, and judgment
was finally given in favour of the canons on 19 April.[2]   They
also received a confirmation of other property there, which dated
from the Orthodox period: this consisted of two water-mills, one
of which was completely derelict, one vineyard, one shop, and
six houses, one of which had no tenant.[3]   The prior had to arrange
for this property to be leased and for a canon to live at Antioch to
receive the dues owing to the chapter there.[4]   The properties were
not very considerable and would not have produced very much
revenue, and the money derived from them would almost certainly
have been taken up by the expense of maintaining a canon permanently in Antioch to administer them.   When the costs of the
lawsuit, the travelling expenses of the prior and the canons and
their living expenses at Antioch have been taken into account, the
Holy Sepulchre probably ended up by making an overall financial
loss in recovering this property.

It seems probable, though no details are known about this,
that the Latin sees in coastal cities in which there had been Orthodox bishops before the Frankish conquest took over the lands of
the Orthodox churches.   Nineteen bishoprics are named in the
tenth-century Byzantine list, dividing the Syrian coast between

1. de Rozière, pp 166–7, no 86.
2. *Ibid.*, pp 172–8, no 89.
3. *Ibid.*, pp 169–72, no 88.
4. *Ibid.*, pp 178–80, no 90.

them from Acre to Tarsus.[1]   Of these Acre, Tyre, Sidon, Beirut, and Gibelet each became the seat of a Latin bishopric and the Orthodox see of Sarepta was merged with the Latin see of Sidon. The three Orthodox bishoprics of Orthosias, Arqah and Tripoli came to form the Latin see of Tripoli; and the Orthodox sees of Antarados, Arados and Maraclea were formed into the Latin see of Tortosa.[2]   The Orthodox bishopric of Valania became a Latin see, but the bishopric of Apaltos did not, and was, perhaps, merged with the neighbouring Orthodox see of Jabala to form the Latin diocese of that name; Latakia and Apamea were both Orthodox sees which became Latin sees; the see of Seleucia, of which the Black Mountain of Antioch formed part, together with its many monasteries, did not survive as an independent bishopric and was probably placed directly under the control of the Latin patriarch of Antioch. The Latins preserved the two Orthodox sees of Tarsus and Mamistra in Cilicia, but the Orthodox see of Adana was suppressed, and perhaps merged with Tarsus.[3]   Yet in the Orthodox period, given the small size of the majority of these sees, it is unlikely that any could have been particularly well endowed with property that the Franks could sequester for the use of the Latin church, even assuming that these sees all still had bishops at the time of the Frankish conquest and so retained their properties. The number of sees was reduced by amalgamation, but other sources of income would have been needed to keep the Frankish bishops in a style commensurate with their dignity in a feudal society.

Some Latin sees were established in places where there had been no Orthodox bishop for centuries, so that there were no existing endowments which could be used. In such cases dioceses had to be newly endowed by Frankish princes. Bethlehem is a case in point. In the Orthodox period this had merely been a shrine church: it is not known whether it had possessed lands of its own then, or whether it had had to rely on the support of the Orthodox hierarchy of Jerusalem and the offerings of pilgrims. No mention is made in the foundation charter of the Latin diocese, preserved by William of Tyre, of possessions dating from Orthodox times, but Baldwin I gave the bishop the city of Bethlehem itself, an estate nearby, and four other *casalia*, one at Nablus, one at Acre, and two in the area of Ascalon.[4]

1. Charon, II, pp 233—4.
2. WT, XIV, 14, *RHC Occ*, I, p 626.
3. There is no information about the relation between Orthodox and Latin sees in the rest of north Syria comparable to that given by William of Tyre for the province of Tyre.
4. WT, XI, 12, *RHC Occ*, I, pp 472—4.

The church of the Holy Nativity was a great shrine, and it attracted benefactions from the Frankish settlers in Syria. The earliest confirmation of its property which is known is that issued in 1227 by pope Gregory IX at a time when Frederick II was about to go on crusade and there was a hope that the house might recover some of its lost lands. Since many of the places named in this bull had been in Saracen hands since 1187 it must be supposed that the church of Bethlehem had acquired them before that date. In addition to Bethlehem city itself, the bull lists twenty-seven *casalia* belonging to the cathedral (together with other less important pieces of land), situated in the dioceses of Bethlehem, Hebron, Jerusalem, Lydda, Caesarea, Nazareth, Tiberias, Tripoli and Antioch. In addition the church owned one or more houses and other property in the cities of Ascalon, Jerusalem, Jaffa, Acre, Nablus, Tiberias, Tyre and Antioch.[1] If the rents of these properties had been regularly collected the church of Bethlehem must have been modestly well-endowed with property in the Frankish east before the battle of Hattin, though the extent of its landed wealth there should not be over-estimated because part of it must have been absorbed in the costs of administration. Nor is it possible to tell from the confirmation whether the canons of Bethlehem had obtained all these lands by gift, or whether they had bought some of them with money received from other sources.

The church of Jerusalem is very well documented, for its cartulary survives containing 185 items, all but a small fraction of which relate to the property of the Holy Sepulchre before 1187.[2] It owned a great deal of property in the Frankish east, but a close examination of the evidence shows that very little of this was the gift of Frankish benefactors. Leaving aside its ecclesiastical patronage which has already been discussed in chapter four, the major properties which the canons of the Sepulchre received as gifts from the faithful were these: the twenty-one *casalia* near Jerusalem given by duke Godfrey;[3] the lands given as compensation by Baldwin I when Bethlehem was made an independent bishopric;[4] the four *casalia* attached to St Lazarus at Bethany, which the canons exchanged at the wish of queen Melisende in 1138 for the estate of Thecua;[5] the *casale* of Capharmelech near Nablus, given by Baldwin II to be quit of the payment of 1,000

---

1. Riant, *Eglise de Bethléem*, I, pp 140–7, no 9.
2. The only documents dating from after 1187 are, de Rozière, nos 145, 151, 154, 174, 176–9.
3. *Ibid.*, pp 54–5, no 29.
4. *Ibid.*, pp 15–17, no 14.
5. *Ibid.*, p 49, no 26, pp 60–5, no 33.

measures of wheat a year from the royal estates of Nablus that
had been granted to the canons by his predecessor;[1] four *casalia*
in the diocese of Lydda given by bishop Roger;[2] one *casale* at
Tyre, the gift of Baldwin II;[3] another in the diocese of Caesarea,
and rights in half of a second one there;[4] two *casalia* in Galilee;[5]
one at Ascalon, given by count Amalric after the city had been
captured in 1153;[6] seven *casalia* in the county of Tripoli;[7] and
one other *casale* near Lydda, though it is not known whether
this was acquired by gift or purchase.[8] In addition they owned
houses in Jerusalem and a house at Acre.[9]

Not all these gifts were of equal value. A *casale* was only a
source of immediate profit if it had a labour force, otherwise it
was only a potential asset. Some *casalia* which were given to the
Sepulchre were deserted when the canons acquired them. Magna
Mahomeria is a case in point: it was one of the twenty-one *casalia*
granted by duke Godfrey, but the canons only made it profitable
when they induced Frankish settlers to live there and work the
land some twenty years later.[10] Moreover, even those which had
a work-force were not of equal size and their lands were not
equally productive. Thus when the canons wished to commute
the annual pension of 150 besants which they paid to the knights
Templar to a permanent gift of land of the same value, they
transferred to the order two of the *casalia* they had received from
duke Godfrey, together with an adjacent *gastina*.[11] It may be
doubted whether any very significant part of the income of the
Holy Sepulchre was derived from these properties acquired by
gift. Those in the neighbourhood of Jerusalem may have been of
some profit to them, though this was not, on the whole, very rich
agricultural land, but it may be suspected that in other parts of
the kingdom the revenues of their scattered estates were largely
eroded by the costs of administration. The estates in the county
of Tripoli were administered by a priory of the Jerusalem house,
established by the devout count Raymond IV of Toulouse on

1. *Ibid.*, p 55, no 29, pp 80–1, no 43.
2. *Ibid.*, p 49, no 26.
3. *Ibid.*, pp 56–7, no 30.
4. *Ibid.*, p 16, no 19, pp 98–9, no 53.
5. *Ibid.*, pp 148–50, no 74.
6. *Ibid.*, pp 115–17, no 58.
7. *Ibid.*, pp 180–3, no 91, pp 190–4, nos 97–8.
8. The *casale* mentioned *ibid.*, pp 251–2, no 136, of 1160 is not one of the four given by bishop Roger, *ibid.*, p 49, no 26.
9. *Ibid.*, pp 58–60, no 32, pp 29–32, no 20.
10. Magna Mahomeria had formerly been called Birra (al-Bira), *ibid.*, p 263, no 144. It was one of the twenty-one *casalia* given by duke Godfrey, *ibid.*, p 55, no 29. In 1128 it was described as 'castrum Maome cum ecclesia', *ibid.*, p 19, no 16.
11. *Ibid.*, p 262, no 144, pp 150–2, no 75.

Mount Pilgrim, and the profit which the mother-house derived from this benefaction can have been only nominal.[1]

If the benefactions received by the greatest shrine churches in the kingdom, the Holy Sepulchre and the church of the Holy Nativity, were modest, it may be supposed that other cathedrals, which were not cult centres, fared even less well. Even the cathedral of Nazareth, which was an important holy place, is not known to have owned any property in the east outside its own diocese. Thus when Nur-ad-Din of Damascus occupied some of its estates to the east of the sea of Galilee in king Amalric's reign the canons were forced to appeal to the pope for help and Alexander III wrote an encyclical to the faithful of France asking them to give generously to the canons who had come to the west to raise funds for their church.[2] The situation of other cathedrals would seem to have been similar: such lands as they had were situated in their own dioceses and do not seem to have been numerous.

The holy places also attracted the munificence of the faithful all over western Europe. This is true of the great cathedral shrines of Jerusalem, Bethlehem and Nazareth, though it would not appear that the lesser cathedral shrines of Lydda, Hebron or Sebastia received any western property. The shrine of Our Lady of Tortosa, the only cathedral shrine in the patriarchate of Antioch, owned land in the west in the thirteenth century, but there is no evidence of this in the twelfth.[3] Detailed papal confirmations exist of the western properties of the Holy Sepulchre in the twelfth century;[4] Gregory IX listed the properties held in the west by the church of Bethlehem in 1227, and information survives about how some of them had been acquired in the course of the twelfth century;[5] and although there is no analogous confirmation of the western lands of the church of Nazareth, it is known to have owned much land in southern Italy before 1187.[6]

The precise value of these lands to the communities which received them is less easy to determine. The problem of administration is of cardinal importance here. There were two possible

1. *Ibid.*, pp 180–3, no 91, pp 190–2, no 97.
2. *PL*, 200, 757–8, no 831. Nazareth owned property in Acre in the thirteenth century, but there is no evidence that it did so in the twelfth.
3. Guiraud, no 1019.
4. de Rozière, pp 15–17, no 14 (Calixtus II); pp 18–22, no 16 (Honorius II); pp 22–7, nos 17–18 (Innocent II); pp 29–32, no 20, pp 74–6, no 39 (Celestine II); pp 36–41, no 23 (Eugenius III); pp 278–82, no 156, pp 296–300, no 166 (Alexander III).
5. Riant, *Eglise de Bethléem*, I, pp 131–3.
6. F. Nitti di Vito, ed, *Le pergamene di Barletta, Archivio Capitolare, (987–1285). Il Codice Diplomatico Barese*, 8, 1914, pp 123–4, 155–6, 170, 178–9; Santerano, *Codice diplomatico Barlettano*, I, pp 18–20.

ways of dealing with this: if the mother-house obtained control of a church or a chapel in the west, and, as has been seen in chapter four this was frequently the case, then the incumbent could act as administrator for the properties of the community in that area. If the properties were extensive enough, or if they included, as they sometimes did, the gift of an abbey, then a priory of the mother-house in Syria could be set up to administer the lands of the shrine in that region. Isolated properties can have had only a theoretical value, since the costs of collecting rents from them would have outweighed any possible profits. The Holy Sepulchre in particular received gifts of this kind from devout pilgrims like Bertold, who in 1142 gave them a reversionary interest in all his property at Kendorf in Swabia.[1] Such outlying properties could, of course, be sold, but that would have involved the canons in heavy expenses, through sending a representative to Europe and paying the legal costs of conveyancing the property. While wishing to keep their legal title to such lands by having them registered in any general confirmation of property, the canons did not derive any direct profit from some of the lands which are listed in lengthy papal bulls concerning their estates in western Europe.

The Holy Sepulchre, the church of Bethlehem, and to a lesser extent the church of Nazareth, became the mother-houses of congregations of canons regular with priories situated in the west. This undoubtedly gave them prestige and certain fringe benefits. Their representatives in the west could organise the collection of alms for the mother-house at no additional cost; if the brethren travelled in the west they could be entertained at priories and clergy-houses belonging to the congregation; the gift that the papacy made to the Holy Sepulchre of the church of St Giles at Rome, at which the canons or their representatives could stay when they visited the curia on business, must have been of value in that way.[2] The European priories also, of course, provided places of refuge to which the clergy of the mother-houses could retire if they were driven from Syria. Yet it is important not to exaggerate the wealth which these Syrian communities derived from their extensive western properties. Some of the revenues of those lands were absorbed in the costs of local administration, while the transfer of money or of produce to the mother-houses in Syria could be adversely affected by local conditions such as bad harvests, the sometimes restrictive policies of local rulers, outbreaks of war, and the hazards of sea travel.

Had land been the only source of income enjoyed by the Latin

1. de Rozière, pp 162–3, no 83.
2. *Ibid.*, pp 76–7, no 40, pp 272–3, no 150.

clergy in Syria many of them would have been seriously impoverished, since in most cases their revenues would not have been commensurate with their expenses. They had, however, a more important source of income, the tithe. This was a church tax which was theoretically payable on all sources of income. It could be levied on trade and industry, and was sometimes imposed on such revenues in Frankish Syria. For example, in 1193 the Hospital agreed to pay tithe on dues from the market and the dye-works at al-Marqab to the bishop of Valania,[1] and tithes were quite commonly paid on the profits of water-mills.[2] But in the Latin east as in western Europe such tithes seem never to have been imposed systematically and it would appear that they became less common during the thirteenth century, perhaps because of the difficulties involved in evaluating revenues of that kind.[3]

The constant and principal source of tithe was agricultural produce. The landlord was responsible for its payment, and it was levied on his share of the crops at harvest time but not normally on the share of the peasants who worked his land. There are isolated examples of attempts made by the Latin clergy to levy tithe on the native peasantry as well as on the landlords,[4] but such cases seem to have been exceptional. The free Frankish peasantry of newly-founded villages, who held their land in burgage tenure, were, of course, required to pay tithe,[5] and Frankish burgesses in towns were also subject to the payment of tithe for agricultural products which they grew in market-gardens, orchards and vineyards.

Before the fourth Lateran council tithe was levied only on lands which belonged to Latin Christians, for there was no tradition of a tax of this kind in any of the eastern churches. In the kingdom of Jerusalem the only lands of any consequence which were exempt from tithe were those owned by native Christian religious communities, and although these were fairly numerous in Judaea they were less common in other parts of the kingdom. In the northern states there were considerable estates in some areas in the ownership of noblemen of eastern rite, chiefly Armenians, as well as the property which belonged to the various eastern churches. A great deal of land at Edessa must have been owned by Armenians in the

1. *CGOH*, no 941.
2. E.g. *ibid.*, no 664.
3. G. Lepointe, 'Dîme', *DDC*, IV, 1232–3.
4. E.g. in 1112 archbishop Evremar of Caesarea granted the Hospital freedom from payment of tithe on all their property in his diocese, 'tam de casalibus, tam de villanis, sive de omnibus ceteris rebus', *CGOH*, no 29.
5. de Rozière, pp 238–41, no 129.

early years of Frankish rule there, and the same must have been true of Cilicia during the years when it formed part of the principality of Antioch.

The agricultural tithe was particularly valuable in Frankish Syria where there were two harvests a year.[1] Constable has pointed out that in the Latin east tithes were not impropriated to lay lords, as they were in much of the west, and rightly sees in this the influence of the papal reform movement on the first generation of Frankish settlers.[2]   In the early period, nevertheless, princes did sometimes grant the tithe of certain estates as money fiefs to knights for reasons of defence: Tancred did so in regard to some of the estates of the Mount Tabor monastery and no doubt the practice was quite common at that time.[3]   It was, however, seen as an emergency measure, not as a permanent pattern.   Some lay lords were reluctant to pay tithe; but their objections were not upheld.   Guy, lord of Bethsan, for example, was forced to restore the tithes of two *casalia* to the Tabor community in 1152 by judgment of a papal legate.[4]

But in theory tithe was payable to the diocesan bishop on all land owned by Franks. A bishop did not, of course, receive tithe on land which his church owned which was situated in another diocese. Thus when queen Melisende arranged that the patriarch and the canons of the Holy Sepulchre should exchange their lands at Bethany for those of Thecua they did not receive the tithe of Thecua but had to pay tithe for those lands to the bishop of Bethlehem in whose diocese they were situated.[5]

Religious communities often enjoyed a limited exemption from the payment of tithe. This was expressed by the Roman curia in the formula:

> We forbid tithe to be exacted from you by the officials of a bishop or bishops, or by anybody else, in respect of those lands which you work with your own hands, or which are cultivated at your own expense, or in respect of the foodstuffs of your animals.[6]

Few of the aristocratic communities of the twelfth century, with the exception perhaps of the early Cistercians and Premonstraten-

---

1. Both harvests were tithed. Balian, constable of Jaffa, gave the first tithe of certain lands to the bishop of Lydda and the second tithe to the hospital of Nablus, *CGOH*, nos 59, 354.

2. G. Constable, *Monastic Tithes, from their Origin to the Twelfth Century*, Cambridge 1964, p 85, n 2.

3. Paoli, pp 200—1, no 156.

4. *CGOH*, vol II, p 903, no 11.

5. The tithe of Thecua heads the list of Bethlehem's property in Gregory IX's confirmation of 1227, Riant, *Eglise de Bethléem*, I, p 141, no 11.

6. E.g. Alexander III for the Holy Sepulchre, de Rozière, p 281, no 156.

ians, worked their lands themselves, beyond, perhaps doing a little ritual weeding out of respect for the injunctions of the Rule, but this general privilege freed them from payment of tithe on the produce of their demesne lands. The exemption also normally extended to any priories which the mother-house might have, but even the most liberal interpretation of such a privilege could not cover all the property owned by a rich community like Josaphat.

Bishops could, of course, free communities from the payment of tithe. Exemptions of that kind come mostly from the early days of Frankish settlement, when the monasteries had not become great landowners and when the few Latin bishops that there were ruled large dioceses and were less concerned about the loss of tithe. The patriarch Arnulf in 1112 freed the Hospital from the payment of all tithe on all lands which it owned in his diocese and bishop Bernard of Nazareth granted them a similar privilege in his diocese in 1125.[1] The monastery of Latina was freed from the payment of all tithe on its property in the diocese of Lydda.[2] It was also possible for bishops to make charitable grants of tithe to religious communities, and there are numerous examples of this: the patriarch Gibelin of Jerusalem, for example, gave to the *Templum Domini* 1,000 besants of the tithe which he received from the lands beyond Jordan which then formed part of his diocese.[3]

Tithe was paid to support the Latin hierarchy, but the situation became complex if a religious community built a parish church on its lands and maintained a chaplain there at its own expense and not at that of the diocese, or if a cathedral chapter such as the Holy Sepulchre did the same on land which it owned in another diocese. The question then naturally arose of whether the bishop was entitled to the whole tithe of that land when he was not responsible for the maintenance of the church fabric or of the parish clergy. The canons of the *Templum Domini* received the greater part of the tithe of Nablus which, though part of the diocese of Jerusalem, was under their ecclesiastical control. Such powers were exceptional and dated from the early days of the kingdom.[4] A more normal type of arrangement was that which the canons of the Holy Sepulchre reached with the Mount Tabor monastery concerning the lands of St Gilles in the diocese of Jerusalem, where the Tabor community had a parish church. The monks of Tabor were granted half the tithe of St Gilles itself and

1. *CGOH*, nos 25, 71.
2. Holtzmann, *op. cit.*, *QFIAB*, 35, 1955, pp 56–9, no 2.
3. Chalandon, *op. cit.*, *ROL*, 8, 1900–1, p 315.
4. *Ibid.*, pp 313–14; see above chapter 3.

of two adjacent *casalia* which they owned and all the tithe of the three vineyards they had there, but the remaining tithe was reserved to the Sepulchre.[1]

Modifications of this fairly simple arrangement were innumerable. Bishop Roger of Lydda, when making a grant of four *casalia* in his diocese to the Holy Sepulchre in 1136, retained the full tithe of two of them but freed the other two from payment except for half the tithe of the grain harvest.[2] In 1141 the Holy Sepulchre granted to the Hospital of St John, which owned Emmaus and other adjacent *casalia* in the diocese of Jerusalem and had a parish church there, half the tithe of wheat, oil, wine, beans, lentils, peas and chick-peas, together with all the tithe of other products, for the support of their clergy.[3] In 1122 Balian, constable of Jaffa, presumably by prior arrangement with the bishop of Lydda, granted the tithe of the winter harvest on his lands in that diocese to the hospital of Nablus, reserving to the bishop the more considerable tithe of the summer harvest.[4]

It is noticeable that as the twelfth century progressed and the number of Latin bishops increased, as did the extent of the properties owned by religious communities, complete grants of exemption from tithe became almost unknown, although partial exemptions were still granted. Thus as late as 1170 bishop Amalric of Sidon freed the monks of Josaphat from payment of half the tithe on all their lands in his diocese.[5] Occasionally the inducement of freedom from tithe could be used to bring litigation to a satisfactory conclusion. Thus John, the first Latin bishop of Acre, freed the Hospital of St John from the payment of tithe on all their lands in his diocese on condition that they abandoned the embarrassing lawsuit which they had brought against him for building the west door of his new cathedral of the Holy Cross on their property.[6]

In all dioceses, therefore, there were some properties, of varying extent and number, which were owned by religious communities and which paid either no tithe or only partial tithe, but these were few in comparison with the lands which paid the full tithe to the bishop. The real threat to the episcopal tithe did not come from the monasteries but from the military orders when, from about the middle of the twelfth century, they began to acquire extensive fiefs. The earliest of these grants, that of Crac des Chevaliers and

1. de Rozière, pp 77–9, no 41.
2. *Ibid.*, pp 146–8, no 73.
3. *Ibid.*, pp 219–20, no 117.
4. *CGOH*, nos 59, 354.
5. Delaborde, pp 84–5, no 37.
6. *CGOH*, no 112.

the surrounding lands which Raymond II of Tripoli granted to the Hospital in 1144, did not create a problem in regard to tithe, since these lands formed part of the diocese of Rafaniyah, which no longer had a bishop.[1] Pope Alexander IV later granted the Hospitallers the right to all the tithe of that fief provided that all the parish churches there were held by them.[2]

A more typical case is that of Tortosa, where the castle was given to the knights Templar in 1152 at the bishop's request. The bishop granted the knights half the tithe of the entire diocese, including, it would appear, that of the city of Tortosa itself, but reserved to the sole use of the diocese all the tithe of Maraclea and to the sole use of the knights all the tithe of Chastel Blanc.[3] The only other diocese which came virtually under the control of a military order in this period was Valania, granted to the knights of St John in 1186,[4] but the implications of that settlement are better considered in the second half of this work. The bishop of Valania had certainly already in 1163 granted the Templars the right to collect half the tithe on lands which they owned in his diocese.[5] Other bishops were less accommodating, and William of Tyre reports that the non-payment of tithe by the Hospital of St John was one of the major causes of complaint which the patriarch of Jerusalem and his suffragans made against the order to the pope in 1155.[6] In the twelfth century the growth in power of the military orders must have been an anxiety chiefly in the patriarchate of Antioch. In that of Jerusalem they held no great lordships except for Gaza, Safad and Belvoir and, although their property was extensive, it cannot have equalled or exceeded that over which the local bishop had undisputed right to tithe in any of the dioceses of the kingdom of Jerusalem.

Although tithes were doubtless sometimes paid in kind they were often commuted for a fixed money payment. The community of Josaphat agreed in 1178 to pay ten besants a year in lieu of tithe to the bishop of Tiberias for the lands attached to the church of St George at Tiberias;[7] in 1181 the knights of St John undertook to pay the archbishop of Petra forty besants a year for the tithe owed by their property in his archdiocese, but agreed that half tithes should be payable in addition on any new property which they acquired there;[8] while the monks of Josaphat

1. *Ibid.*, no 144.
2. Delaville Le Roulx, 'Inventaire', no 71.
3. Riley-Smith, *op. cit., EHR*, 84, 1969, pp 284–8.
4. *CGOH*, no 783.
5. Paoli, pp 40–1, no 39.
6. WT, XVIII, 3, *RHC Occ*, I, p 820.
7. Delaborde, pp 87–8, no 40.
8. N.b. They refused to pay tithe on hay, *CGOH*, no 610.

complained to the pope that in 1144 they had been coerced into making an agreement with the archbishop of Nazareth whereby they paid a gold mark a year in lieu of tithe for their *casale* at Ligio.[1] It was doubtless more convenient for a bishop to receive a money payment than a payment in kind, since the produce in the latter case would have had to be collected and sold and part of the profit would thereby have been eaten up in the costs of administration.

Apart from the landed endowments of sees, and tithes, some churches at least had other sources of income. Latin parish churches are very poorly documented, but some of them had lands which were the property of the parish priest: Bohemond III of Antioch, for example, gave a *casale* to the priests of St George's church outside Jabala in 1186.[2] All parish clergy received certain dues from their parishioners. Fees for baptisms formed an important part of the income of parish clergy, but there was no danger that they would be alienated by chapels belonging to religious houses as only parish churches had fonts.[3] The churching of women, however, could be performed in any chapel, and parish clergy were anxious to restrict the rights of chaplains of religious houses to conduct churchings because this entailed a serious diminution of parish income.[4] Marriage fees, on the other hand, seem to have been considered of little importance, probably because, unless property was involved, few people bothered to have their common law marriages blessed in church.[5] Burial fees, on the contrary, made up a substantial part of parish income since burial was a luxury which no Christian, however lukewarm in the practice of his faith, could afford to forgo.

All churches received some offerings from their congregations and placed special reliance on pious bequests made by dying parishioners.[6] But the offerings made in the great shrine churches were particularly valuable. Those in the church of the Holy

---

1. Delaborde, pp 56—8, no 24.
2. Delaville Le Roulx, 'Inventaire', no 159.
3. See n 1, p 88 above.
4. E.g. In the concordat between the bishop of Acre and the Hospital of St John of 1175, in which the rights of the Hospital to exercise cure of souls are delimited, no mention is made of baptism, but an article is devoted to churching, *CGOH*, no 471.
5. E.g. The patriarch Amalric did not include it among the normal ministrations of the parish clergy of the Holy Sepulchre, Nablus, or St Nicholas, Jaffa, de Rozière, pp 287—90, nos 160—61.
6. The concordat between the bishop of Acre and the Hospital in 1175 enacts: 'The chaplains of the Hospital are bound by order of the Master to warn any sick persons they visit, whether inside their house or outside it, to be mindful of the church of the Holy Cross [Acre cathedral] when they make bequests'. The bishop gave a similar undertaking to the Hospital on behalf of his clergy, *CGOH*, no 471.

Sepulchre were so great that the patriarch Arnulf had to arrange
for their just division between the patriarch and the canons. They
should divide between them the offerings made at the Lord's
Sepulchre, but the canons should retain the offerings made to the
relic of the True Cross, except on Good Friday, or when offerings
were made to the Cross when it was carried on campaign by the
patriarch, on both of which occasions the patriarch should keep
the money.[1]

In addition the Holy Sepulchre also possessed a monopoly of
the ovens of Jerusalem, except for one which belonged to the
Hospital and another which was owned by the monastery of
Latina.[2] This must have proved a useful source of regular income
since the baking of bread was a routine activity and there were
twenty-five ovens belonging to the Sepulchre from which they
could collect dues.[3]

One final source of income which some Latin bishops optimist-
ically claimed was the Melchizedek tithe, that is, a tithe of the
booty captured in war by Christian princes fighting the Saracens.
This claim was based on the account in Genesis of how Abraham
offered to Melchizedek, priest of the most high God, a tithe of
all the spoil which he had taken from Tidal, King of the Nations,
and his allies.[4] The bishop of Jabala explained this to Otto of
Freising when they met at the papal court in 1145, for the bishop
had come on behalf of the patriarch of Antioch partly to complain
that Raymond of Poitiers did not observe this godly custom.[5]
That some custom of this kind was generally held to obtain seems
clear from the grant which Maurice, lord of Montréal, made to the
Hospital of St John in 1152: 'a tenth of all the goods and of all
the money which I shall gain from the Saracens, or receive from
them, whether in times of truce, or of war'.[6] It is impossible to
determine how general such payments were.

From these various sources of income bishops had to meet a
whole range of expenditure. First there was the maintenance of
the bishop himself and of his household. A Latin bishop was a
great lord and his household was sizable. As part of a settlement
of a dispute, the archbishop of Nazareth once demanded hospit-
ality for himself and his household from the community of
Josaphat for a day each year when he visited Jerusalem. The
archbishop specified that his retinue would consist of twenty men

1. de Rozière, p 46, no 25.
2. Ibid., pp 55–6, no 29.
3. Ibid., pp 329–31, no 185.
4. Genesis, XIV, 20.
5. Otto of Freising, 'Chronica', VII, 33, pp 364–5.
6. CGOH, no 207.

who must be fed, together with their horses.[1] The canons of the
cathedral church had to be assigned prebends, unless they were
canons regular and lived in community.   This could be a heavy
expense: when Evremar became patriarch of Jerusalem in 1103
and the Holy Sepulchre was still served by secular canons he fixed
their prebends at 150 besants each a year, specifying that additional
sums of 150 besants should be paid to the cantor, the succentor
and the head of the cathedral school, and an additional 100
besants a year to the treasurer and the sub-dean.[2] If this is a fair
index of the size of prebends in other twelfth-century cathedrals
in Syria, then the cost of supporting, for example, the eighteen
canons of Antioch must have been in excess of 3,000 besants a
year.[3] In addition, most Latin bishops had to build new cathedrals, either because there was no Orthodox cathedral in existence,
or because they did not consider it large enough, for the Orthodox tended, after the Iconoclast period, to build very small
churches.[4] One of the few cathedrals which the Franks did not
attempt to rebuild was that of St Peter's at Antioch.   In addition
a bishop had to pay the expenses of his parish clergy, and to build
Latin parish churches where these were needed.   Since, in most
cases, Orthodox churches remained in the hands of the native
Christian community, virtually all Latin parish churches had to be
purpose-built.

In addition to these routine ecclesiastical expenses bishops also
had certain secular obligations to meet. Although only the bishops
of Lydda and the archbishops of Nazareth in the patriarchate of
Jerusalem owed knight-service to the crown (and there is no
parallel information about the military obligations of the Latin
church of Antioch), all the bishops of the kingdom of Jerusalem,
with the exception of the archbishop of Petra and the bishops of
Beirut and Banyas, were required to supply sergeants to the royal
armies.   The patriarch of Jerusalem and the canons of the Holy
Sepulchre each had to furnish the crown with 500 sergeants, while
the other bishops between them had to contribute a further thou-
sand sergeants: the quota varied from 200 in the case of Bethlehem to fifty in that of Hebron.   Together the bishops provided
almost two-fifths of the total force of sergeants in the kingdom
and this obligation must have placed a heavy charge on the

1. Delaborde, pp 56—8, no 24.
2. de Rozière, pp 71—2, no 36.
3. Honorius III stated that there had been eighteen canons there in the twelfth
century, Pressutti, no 3497.
4. A. Grabar, *Byzantium. Byzantine Art in the Middle Ages*, London, 1966, pp
74—80.

financial resources of the Latin church.[1]   In addition, bishops performed regular charitable works on which some proportion of diocesan income was spent.[2]

The wealth of dioceses in the Frankish East was very unevenly distributed. In the early years of the settlement, when there were few bishops, the patriarchs of Jerusalem administered dioceses to which neither a bishop nor a metropolitan had been appointed. Thus Acre, Sidon and Beirut came under the patriarch's jurisdiction when they were without bishops and before an archbishop of Tyre had been appointed,whereas Tiberias was administered by the archbishop of Nazareth, as metropolitan of Galilee, before it had a bishop of its own. No doubt a similar system obtained at Antioch, which is less well documented. Since the Franks ruled almost as much territory by 1120 as they did at any subsequent time, and their lands were subject to the payment of tithe, the few bishops who were appointed then enjoyed larger revenues than any of their more numerous successors after the sees had been subdivided. It is a truism, though one which it is necessary to make, that dioceses were by no means equal in terms of agricultural wealth from which the tithe was derived. The most fertile regions of the kingdom were the coastal plain, the valley of Jezreel, which stretched from Mount Carmel into Samaria, and the lands to the east of the Jordan, extending from the area south of Damascus down to Moab. The tithe of dioceses like Acre, Caesarea, Tiberias and Nazareth was, as a result, more valuable than that of Hebron, Bethlehem and the diocese of Jerusalem itself, much of which consisted of the fairly barren lands of Judaea. The other factor which must be taken into consideration is the extent to which different dioceses were vulnerable to Muslim attack. Few of them were totally immune from raiding, but some were more regularly devastated than others. The lands of Lydda and Bethlehem were particularly vulnerable to attack by the garrison of Ascalon as long as that city remained in Muslim hands. After 1154, when Nur-ad-Din became ruler of Damascus, the lands of Banyas, Tiberias and Nazareth beyond the Jordan were also open to raiding; while the great archdiocese of Edessa can rarely have enjoyed a year of peace uninterrupted by raiding through all the period of Frankish occupation. This helps to explain why the Latin church, although it enjoyed undisputed

1. John of Ibelin, 'Livre', c 272, *RHC Lois*, I, pp 426—7. The number of sergeants owed by bishops was as follows: Bethlehem, 200; Lydda, 200; Acre, 150; Tyre, 150; Nazareth, 150; Sebastia, 100; Tiberias, 100; Caesarea, 50; Sidon; 50, Hebron, 50. Smail, *Crusading Warfare*, pp 90—2.
2. St Nerses of Lampron, 'Letter to Leo II', *RHC Arm*, I, p 600; MS, XX, 6, vol III, p 375.

title to tithe, which seems on the whole to have been conscientiously paid by Frankish landowners, and although it had few subordinate clergy to maintain, was not unusually rich. Quite frequently part of the tithe must have been lost as a result of enemy raids, and in some areas the tithe cannot have been very considerable because the land was not economically productive.

Nevertheless, great dioceses did have considerable wealth. The patriarchs of Antioch were reputed to have been very rich throughout the twelfth century and this was a major cause of friction between Aimery of Limoges and both Reynald of Châtillon and Bohemond III.[1] This is a surprising fact, for the lands of Antioch were repeatedly devastated by warfare throughout the century and many of them were lost from 1144 onwards. But the patriarchs had comparatively few expenses beyond those of maintaining their own household and the cathedral clergy, and could continue to collect the revenues of their estates and the tithe on all lands in their diocese still in Frankish control, whereas the princes had heavy defence commitments to meet from diminishing resources for, as the lands of the principality grew fewer, so they must have come to rely increasingly on the services of mercenary troops.

The best documented cathedral in twelfth-century Syria is the Holy Sepulchre, and its cartulary reveals how from the reign of Baldwin III the canons began to accumulate reserves of money which could be invested in property. They managed their property very well in ways which allowed them to accumulate money for investment. One example of this is the kind of payment of annuities which they arranged with some house owners in Jerusalem, who were either childless or only had daughters, and were worried about providing for themselves in old age. An example of this is the agreement made by a widow called Mabel in 1132. She owned an orchard and a house in Jerusalem, and gave the canons the outright possession of the orchard and the reversionary interest in her house in return for their undertaking to make substantial repairs to the orchard wall and the cistern. Furthermore, they paid her 170 besants and undertook to provide her with food from their kitchen for the rest of her life. Mabel was very specific about what she wanted: a loaf of bread a day, half a litre of wine, and a cooked meal, which on Sundays and great feast days should be a meat meal, or, at least, the food which was

---

1. Although money is not said to have been the chief cause of either quarrel, both princes despoiled the church after the trouble had begun, WT, XVIII, 1, XXII, 6–7, *RHC Occ*, I, pp 816–17, 1071–5.

served to the canons themselves.[1]   This is only one example of
several similar transactions,[2] and the canons ended up owning
houses in Jerusalem which they leased for rents which totalled
161 besants a year.[3]

The canons were equally careful in the management of their
rural property. They built up the free Frankish villages of Parva
and Magna Mahomeria on waste land which belonged to the house.
This system proved profitable and was extended to other properties belonging to the community: in 1160, for example, they gave
land at Ramla which they owned to Frankish burgesses in return
for a quarter of the grain and vegetables which they produced
each year and a fifth part of the wine and olives, together with
the customary payment of tithe: but the land on which the
tenants' houses were to be built was rent-free.[4]

The money which the canons saved by careful management of
their assets was available for investment. Initially their purchases
were modest: a vineyard at Jerusalem in 1129 which cost 140
besants;[5] a house in that city in 1135 at the price of 200 besants;[6]
two shops there in 1155 costing 170 besants;[7] land near Caesarea
and freedom from the payment of tolls in that city, bought from
the lord in 1166 for 400 besants.[8] But as the century wore on
the canons became richer and were able to buy on a larger scale.
Thus in 1155 they bought three *casalia* belonging to Hugh of
Ibelin for 7,000 besants;[9] and five years later bought a further
two estates from him for the sum of 3,000 besants. On the
second occasion, if not the first, Hugh needed the money to pay
ransom, and although all these estates formed part of his feudal
fief no difficulty was created by the crown about their transfer to
the church.[10]   In 1161 John Gothmann, another royal vassal,
being similarly placed, sold to the canons four *casalia* belonging to
his fief for the sum of 1,400 besants.[11]   A few years later the
Sepulchre bought three *gastine*, which had been bequeathed to the
Orthodox abbey of St Sabas by queen Melisende, for 480 besants,
with which the abbot proposed to buy a more compact estate
from the king.[12] In 1175 the canons bought out the rights of the

1. de Rozière, pp 206–7, no 106.
2. *Ibid.*, pp 199–200, no 101, pp 203–5, no 104.
3. *Ibid.*, pp 329–31, no 185.
4. *Ibid.*, pp 251–2, no 136.
5. *Ibid.*, pp 155–6, no 78.
6. *Ibid.*, pp 161–2, no 82.
7. *Ibid.*, p 209, no 108.
8. *Ibid.*, pp 276–8, no 155.
9. *Ibid.*, pp 124–7, no 62, pp 117–20, no 59, pp 110–13, no 56, pp 92–3, no 50.
10. *Ibid.*, pp 113–15, no 57, pp 120–23, no 60, pp 128–30, no 63.
11. *Ibid.*, pp 195–9, nos 99–100.
12. *Ibid.*, p 256, no 140.

abbey of Tabor in the *casale* of St Gilles, which was in the diocese
of Jerusalem. The monks of Tabor ceded to them the parish
church, other properties which they owned there, and their right
to half the tithe in the village itself and in two neighbouring
casalia, for 2,000 besants.[1]   The abbot of Tabor was probably
willing to sell at this time because his lands in Galilee were being
raided by the forces of Saladin and he was glad to have money
instead of this distant *casale* which was difficult for him to
administer, but which would cause no parallel problem for the
Holy Sepulchre.[2]

The priory of the Sepulchre on Mount Pilgrim at Tripoli seems
to have pursued a similar policy. It certainly exported some of the
olive oil produced in its estates, since in 1140—1 Raymond II of
Tripoli freed it from the payment of dues on this and other
unspecified commodities which were shipped from the port of
Tripoli.[3]   There, as in the mother-house, the profits of the
community were invested in real estate: the prior of the Sepulchre
at Tripoli bought some houses in that city in 1143 for eighty-
one besants.[4]

If other cathedrals were better documented, no doubt a parallel
pattern of administration would emerge, at least in some dioceses.
The patriarch Aimery of Limoges certainly proved himself able,
on occasion, to drive a hard business bargain. A case came before
his court in 1185 concerning three water-mills on the Orontes
belonging to the knights of St John who had leased them to the
master of the Hospital of St Peter attached to Antioch cathedral.
The mills had been badly damaged by the winter floods, and
neither the Hospital of St Peter as tenant nor the Hospital of St
John as owner was willing to accept liability for the repairs. The
patriarch therefore arranged a settlement whereby the Hospital of
St Peter surrendered its lease to the Hospital of St John in return
for a donation of 300 besants to be spent on new property with
which to support its charitable work, while the Hospital of St
John would still be required to pay tithe on the mills. If this is at
all typical of Aimery's handling of the business affairs of the
church of Antioch it is not to be wondered at that in the course of
his long patriarchate he amassed a large fortune.[5]

---

1. *Ibid.*, pp 258—60, no 142 (gives price as 1,000 besants); *CGOH*, vol II, p 907,
(gives the price as 2,000 besants).
2. He stated that he was selling because the community were 'pergravati, remotione
loci et magnitudine expensarum'.
3. de Rozière, pp 184—7, nos 93—4. See Appendix.
4. *Ibid.*, pp 187—9, no 95.
5. *CGOH*, no 665.

Not all bishops were equally careful of the property of their sees. Ralph of Bethlehem, for example, in 1163 mortgaged an estate belonging to his see at Acre and some houses in the city to the merchants of Marseilles for the curiously precise sum of 1,211 besants.[1] William of Tyre in his obituary notice of Ralph describes him as 'a generous and very open-handed man',[2] and with his secular training he seems to have had the quality of liberality which was esteemed a virtue by the nobility of his age, rather than the parsimonious attachment to property rights which characterised those of his colleagues who had been trained as church administrators.

Indeed, since much of what is known about the twelfth-century bishops of Latin Syria is derived from property deeds, which were thoughtfully brought back to western Europe in the late thirteenth century in the hope that one day a new crusade might recover the Holy Land for the Latin church, it is difficult not to form the impression that a great deal of their time was spent conveyancing land, or bringing actions against laymen or other clergy who had infringed their property rights. Although this is only partially true, bishops and their officials undoubtedly were very careful to safeguard the property rights of their churches. They were, of course, trained to be so, but, as it has been the intention to show in this chapter, they also had cause to be so. The churches of the Frankish east, although some of them were theoretically very richly endowed, were not wealthy: they did not possess great territorial lordships like some of the sees of western Europe; their landed endowments in Syria were comparatively few, and those which some churches owned in the west were not consistently of great profit to them. The bishops were supported chiefly by tithe, but in almost all the dioceses agricultural land was vulnerable to enemy raiding and the revenues of a church would fluctuate accordingly. Moreover, Syria differed from most of western Europe in that its economic wealth was not derived chiefly from land, but from trade, and the church did not systematically tithe the wealth of cities. It was only by careful management of their revenues that the Syrian bishops were able to build up financial reserves, and this bred in them a reluctance to exempt religious orders from the payment of tithe and also involved them in a good deal of litigation about comparatively minor rights.

It is true that the church, which had a system of taxation in the form of the tithe which was imposed throughout all the Frankish

1. E. G. Rey, *Recherches géographiques et historiques sur la domination des Latins en Orient*, Paris 1877, pp 21–22.

2. WT, XX, 30, *RHC Occ*, I, p 999.

states and which the secular governments lacked, was in a position to buy up the lands of impoverished noblemen who needed ready money, particularly to pay ransom. Nevertheless, the lands which the secular church acquired in this way were not considerable: real financial resources were in the hands of the two military orders, who were rich enough to buy out whole fiefs rather than a few villages, which was all that even the Holy Sepulchre could rise to. Had the states lasted longer the process of mortmain would scarcely have worked to the advantage of the bishops and cathedral chapters, but to that of the Temple and the Hospital who had begun to acquire palatinate jurisdiction in large areas of the northern states even before the battle of Hattin. The conquests of Saladin, however, totally changed the economic structure of the Frankish east.

7. RELATIONS WITH THE ORTHODOX, 1098–1187

The members of the first crusade experienced a considerable culture-shock when they reached Syria and found themselves surrounded by a multiplicity of Christian confessions, with all of which they were unfamiliar. They instinctively classed all eastern-rite Christians as heretics because they appeared so different from western Catholics,[1] but this sweeping view was never endorsed by the papacy or by the Latin hierarchy of Syria. The western church made a formal distinction between separated eastern Christians, who were not in communion with Rome, and the Orthodox, who were members of the Catholic church of which the western church formed a part. That is why it was Orthodox sees which the Latins took over, not Jacobite or Armenian ones, and Orthodox traditions which they sought to perpetuate in their form of church organisation. This attitude is reflected by William of Tyre who, when he speaks of the substitution of a Latin patriarch of Antioch for the Orthodox John IV, says that the former resigned his see 'realising that a Greek could not rule over Latins effectively enough',[2] not because he was schismatic, which he clearly was not.

Before considering the consequences for the Orthodox community in Syria of this Latin policy, some clarification is needed about references in the source material to the Orthodox, for there is a problem of nomenclature. When western writers speak of Greeks there is no problem since this term invariably means Orthodox. The use of the term Syrian (*Surianus*) is more ambiguous. It certainly always means Christian, one who used Syriac as his liturgical language. Now this term can be applied to Jacobites, in whose church Syriac was the sole liturgical language. However, Syrians cannot simply be equated with Jacobites, since there was a linguistic division within the Orthodox patriarchates of Jerusalem and Antioch. Educated men, from whom the episcopate was almost exclusively chosen in the pre-crusading period, spoke Greek, and were either citizens of the Byzantine empire or drawn from the Greek-speaking families of Syrian cities. Naturally they celebrated the liturgy in Greek. Communities of Orthodox

1. Letter of princes to Urban II, Hagenmeyer, *Kreuzzugsbriefe*, p 164, no 16.
2. WT, VI, 23, *RHC Occ*, I, p 274.

peasants and urban artisans, on the other hand, spoke Arabic, and used Syriac as their liturgical language since, although this was no longer commonly spoken, it had been the common speech before the Arab invasions.[1] Syrians are frequently mentioned in twelfth-century documents from the kingdom of Jerusalem, and, as Every has argued, the majority of these must have been Orthodox.[2] Theoretically they could have been Jacobites, but the very full consecration-lists of the Jacobite patriarchs of this period show that there were almost no Jacobite bishops in the southern kingdom, which suggests that there were few Jacobite congregations there.[3] Moreover, Latin writers, when speaking of Jacobites in the kingdom of Jerusalem, usually call them this (*Jacobini*) even in casual references made to them in, for example, boundary definitions.[4] It is clear from the writings of James of Vitry that the Syrians living under Frankish rule in the kingdom of Acre were Orthodox,[5] and Old French sources of the later thirteenth century sometimes spell this out by speaking of 'Suriens de la loi de Grece'.[6] It would therefore appear that when Frankish writers in the kingdom of Jerusalem speak of Greeks they mean Orthodox who used Greek as their liturgical language, and when they speak of Syrians they mean Orthodox who used Syriac as their liturgical language. Benjamin of Tudela, the Jewish rabbi who visited the Holy Land in the reign of king Amalric, was sufficiently influenced by Frankish usage to describe the Sinai community as Syrians, since this was the term most commonly used by the Franks when speaking of the Orthodox.[7] In the patriarchate of Antioch, where Syrian-speaking Jacobites were numerous,[8] the term Syrian was on the whole avoided and the Orthodox were described as Greeks, irrespective of the language they used for worship, in order to avoid ambiguity.[9] Jacobite writers are much clearer on this subject: they use the term Orthodox to describe

---

1. Western writers of the twelfth and thirteenth centuries refer to Syriac as Chaldaean.
2. G. Every, 'Syrian Christians in Palestine in the Middle Ages', *ECQ*, 6, 1945–6, pp 363–72.
3. Chabot's edition of Michael the Syrian, MS, vol III, pp 476–82. There was a Jacobite bishop at Jerusalem throughout this period and one at Acre in the thirteenth century.
4. E.g. Delaville Le Roulx, 'Inventaire', no 367.
5. He distinguished between *Iacobitae* and *Suriani*, stating that the *Suriani* of Acre recognised that they owed him canonical obedience. *Lettres*, pp 83–5, no 2.
6. E.g. the so-called Templar of Tyre, cc 271, 480, *Gestes*, pp 151, 238.
7. Benjamin of Tudela, *Itinerary*, ed and trans M.N. Adler, London 1907, p 77.
8. This is evident from the number of bishops of north Syrian sees recorded in the twelfth-century consecration lists, MS, vol III, pp 476–82.
9. In 1183 Bohemond III gave serfs whom he described variously as Greeks, Armenians and Jews to the Hospital, *CGOH*, no 648. Since the rural population of Antioch was Arabic-speaking, the Greek serfs can have been Greek only in religion. In the kingdom of Jerusalem they would have been called Syrians.

their own community and speak of the Orthodox Greeks and Syrians as Chalcedonians.[1]

Orthodox communities were found in almost all the coastal cities of the Frankish states and in some inland cities, notably Jerusalem, Antioch and Edessa.[2]   In addition some villages were inhabited by Orthodox peasantry: these were more common in the kingdom of Jerusalem than in the northern states. There was also quite a large Orthodox population in the lands beyond Jordan which later became the fief of Montréal.[3]

The Franks initially expelled Orthodox bishops from their sees and with them the Orthodox clergy who administered the cathedrals.[4]   In Jerusalem this policy was applied to the Holy Sepulchre, which was the cathedral church: but it was more than a cathedral, it was also one of the principal shrines of the entire Christian world, and before the first crusade, while the administration had been in Orthodox hands, Christians of all confessions had been admitted to celebrate their liturgy there. The Franks put a stop to this: in 1099 they expelled all eastern-rite Christians, including the Orthodox, and reserved the cathedral exclusively for the use of Latin clergy.[5]   Although Matthew of Edessa, when expressing his indignation about this, speaks of the exclusion of eastern Christians from shrines in the plural,[6] this must be understood in the sense that the Latins did not admit other confessions to the shrine churches of Jerusalem which they restored. It is clear from the unanimous testimony of early western pilgrims that, except for the Holy Sepulchre, all the shrine churches of Jerusalem were in ruins in 1099 and probably had been so since the time of the caliph Hakim.[7]   At the Holy Sepulchre the Franks were merely implementing the same policy as they applied in all other Latin cathedrals: they did not initially contemplate sharing places of worship with Christians of other rites.

In other respects the Orthodox enjoyed virtual religious freedom under Frankish rule. They did not, however, enjoy equality at law with the Franks. From the beginning the Franks granted to all native Christians, Orthodox or separated, the right to have their

1. E.g. MS, XVI, 2, vol III, pp 225–6.
2. Under Frankish rule they worshipped in the Holy Wisdom, Segal, *Edessa*, p 238.
3. Albert of Aix, X, 31, *RHC Occ*, IV, pp 64–5; WT, XI, 27, *RHC Occ*, I, p 501.
4. MS, XV, 9, vol III, p 191.
5. Raymond of Aguilers, ed Hill and Hill, p 154.
6. Matthew of Edessa, c 21, *RHC Arm*, I, pp 54–5.
7. 'nothing has been left habitable by the Saracens . . . in all . . . the holy places outside the walls . . . of Jerusalem', *Saewulf's pilgrimage*, p 22 (c 1103); Albert of Aix, VI, 25, *RHC Occ*, IV, pp 480–81, asserts that inside Jerusalem only the Sepulchre and Sta Maria Latina had been left to the Christians in 1099; Hamilton, *SCH*, 14, 1977, pp 105–16.

own courts, to administer their traditional laws and customs, presided over by a member of their own community.[1]   Cases involving native Christians and Franks must, of course, always have been judged by the Frankish courts. This system of native courts based on confessional divisions within the native Christian community was taken over by the Franks from their Muslim predecessors, since this was the traditional Muslim method of governing religious minorities. It ensured that the native Christians enjoyed their traditional way of life, and Frankish customs only impinged on them in an indirect way inasmuch as they became involved in litigation with the Franks.

Membership of the Frankish courts, the courts of burgesses, the seigneurial courts and the high courts of the Frankish states, was reserved to Franks alone, and these were the bodies which exercised effective power in the Latin east. A Frank was, by definition, a Catholic of the Latin rite, and eastern-rite Christians, whether they were Orthodox or not, were debarred from membership of those courts. This had an important corollary: in the kingdom of Jerusalem at least an eastern-rite Christian could not be the holder of a fief. As a result, as Riley-Smith has shown, some of the indigenous population were received into the Latin church and became, for all legal purposes, Franks.[2]   Some of these converts were certainly Muslims, but there may also have been eastern-rite Christians among them.

This lack of legal equality was a result of the nature of Frankish primary settlement. The Franks came as conquerors: whatever their legal status in western Europe had been they were all treated as free men in Syria. Racially, however, they were of very diverse origins and the only factor which they all had in common was membership of the Latin church, and so that membership was used in law to define a Frank. The Orthodox were in an ambiguous position since legally, like other eastern-rite Christians, they were second-class citizens, whereas in the eyes of the Latin church they were members of the one, holy, catholic church to which the Franks also belonged. The only way in which an Orthodox could acquire legal equality with a Frank would have been to become a Christian of the Latin rite, and although this may not have been technically impossible, it was probably more difficult for an Orthodox to achieve than for any other kind of eastern-rite Christian, simply because he already was a member of the same church as the Latins. This may well have given the Orthodox

---

1. John of Ibelin, 'Livre', c 4, *RHC Lois*, I, p 26; J. Riley-Smith, 'Some lesser officials in Latin Syria', *EHR*, 87, 1972, pp 2—9.
2. Riley-Smith, *Feudal Nobility*, pp 10—11.

a justified social grievance inasmuch as they had been placed in a position of social and legal inequality from which there was little prospect of escape.   The Frankish settlers would have found nothing incongruous in the double standard of inferior legal status and equal spiritual status under which the Orthodox lived, for almost the entire population of western Europe belonged to the Latin church, but serfs, who made up a large part of it, did not enjoy legal equality with free men, although they did possess equal spiritual rights with them.

Among the native Christians of Syria the Orthodox stood in a special ecclesiastical relation to the Franks in that they alone were placed under the authority of Latin bishops.   This had no effect on the practice of their faith, except in the technical sense that their clergy owed canonical obedience to the Latin hierarchy and therefore implicitly to the pope.   In the twelfth century there is no evidence that recognition of the papal primacy was ever explicitly required of the Orthodox clergy of Syria, and the parish clergy may not have found it burdensome to accept the rule of Latin bishops, for, as Runciman has justly observed, the majority of the Orthodox parish clergy were Arabic-speaking and used the Syriac liturgy, and Greek bishops would have been just as alien to them as Latins.[1]

The Orthodox, of course, kept their own churches.   At Jerusalem they had the church of St Chariton where the liturgy was celebrated in Syriac,[2] for there was a large community of Arabic-speaking Orthodox in the city, whom Baldwin I had persuaded to come there from the lands beyond Jordan to help make up for the decline in population produced by the crusader massacre of 1099.[3]   At Antioch the Orthodox had the church of St Mary's,[4] while at Edessa they seem to have used the old cathedral of the Holy Wisdom, although they had no bishop of their own.[5]   The Orthodox liturgy was celebrated in Greek or Syriac according to the needs of the congregation and the traditional rites were used. More remarkably, no attempt was made to force the Orthodox to conform to Latin usage or doctrine at those points where their own practice and faith diverged from the norms of the western church.   James of Vitry, Latin bishop of Acre from 1216–29, noted with some horror that the Orthodox in his diocese, who technically recognised him as their diocesan, had married priests and deacons, that they celebrated the Eucharist with leavened

1. Runciman, *Eastern Schism*, p 103.
2. John of Würzburg, p 48.
3. WT, XI, 27, *RHC Occ*, I, p 501; Prawer, *Speculum*, 27, 1952, pp 490–503.
4. de Rozière, pp 172–8, no 89.
5. Segal, *Edessa*, p 238.

bread, that their priests confirmed infants as part of the rite of baptism, whereas the western church customarily reserved confirmation to a bishop, and that they omitted the *Filioque* from the Nicene creed.[1] The Orthodox under Latin rule had not suddenly reverted to these traditions in the early thirteenth century in order to dissociate themselves from the Latin church which had launched the fourth crusade: rather, they had never been asked to relinquish them when they first came under Latin obedience in the late eleventh century.

In chapter five it has been argued that the Latin bishops of the twelfth century were not, on the whole, a speculative group of men. It is true that William of Tyre and Aimery of Limoges, patriarch of Antioch, did know a good deal about the theology of the eastern churches, but they were exceptional in this. A language barrier separated most of the Latin clergy from Orthodox public worship. Few of them knew Greek, it would seem: certainly it was thought worthy of comment if any of them could speak that language.[2] It seems safe to assume that none of them knew Syriac, which was even then virtually a dead language. Most Latin bishops would therefore probably not have been aware of divergences in the expression of belief by their Orthodox clergy even if they attended their churches. Certainly when Manuel Comnenus paid Greek craftsmen to embellish the church of the Holy Nativity at Bethlehem with mosaics depicting, among other things, the seven general councils of the church, the Greek inscription describing the work of the first council of Constantinople in 381 formulated belief in the procession of the Holy Spirit without the addition of the *Filioque*.[3] This concession to Orthodox faith is all the more striking in that it is found in a Latin cathedral, not in a church reserved for Orthodox worship, and was executed at a time when this doctrine was the subject of fierce and often acrimonious debate between western and Byzantine theologians.[4] Attempts to alert the bishops of Latin Syria to the errors of Orthodox teaching were made by western theologians like Hugh Etherianus, who sent a copy of his treatise on the dual procession

---

1. James of Vitry, *HO*, c 75, pp 139—44.

2. Geoffrey, abbot of the *Templum Domini*, was used as an envoy by king Fulk to John II Comnenus in 1142, and by Baldwin III to Manuel I Comnenus in 1159, because he could speak Greek, WT, XV, 21, XVIII, 24, *RHC Occ*, I, pp 691—2, 861. His use on both occasions suggests that none of the bishops of the kingdom knew Greek at all well.

3. H. Stern, 'Les représentations des Conciles dans l'Eglise de la Nativité à Bethléem', *Byzantion*, XI, 1936, pp 101—54, XIII, 1938, pp 415—59. The text of the 381 Council, *ibid.*, XIII, p 421, cf. p 437.

4. E.g. the debate between Anselm of Havelberg and Basil of Ochrida, Runciman, *Eastern Schism*, p 54.

of the Holy Spirit to the patriarch Aimery of Antioch.[1] Aimery, as will be seen later, had little reason to favour the Orthodox, and was, moreover, interested in theology, and he asked Hugh to send him copies of his other polemical works,[2] but his reaction was unusual. On the whole such controversies held little interest for the Latin episcopate in Syria. Certainly the worldly bishop Ralph of Bethlehem, in whose reign the council mosaics were erected, seems to have taken a very tolerant view of differences in the formulation of Trinitarian doctrine.

As was true of so many other aspects of life in Frankish Syria, Latin relations with the Orthodox were shaped by attitudes which had been commonly held in the western church at the time of the initial settlement. Although even in the late eleventh century trained theologians could become heated about almost any subject, there was, nevertheless, a wide consensus of opinion in the Latin church that unity was more important than uniformity, and that diversity was permissible in many matters, including the marriage of the clergy, the kind of bread to be used at the Eucharist, and even the retention or omission of the *Filioque* from the creed.[3] A wise use of discretionary powers in such matters had enabled the holy see to effect the transfer of the Greek population of Calabria and Sicily from the obedience of Constantinople to that of Rome with the minimum of disturbance, and this may well have influenced the Latin clergy of Syria in their dealings with the Orthodox in the early years of the twelfth century.[4] During that century, for a variety of reasons not germane to the present discussion, relations between the western church and the patriarchate of Constantinople became increasingly acrimonious, and on both sides the hierarchies took up entrenched positions about matters of doctrine and usage which had earlier been considered open to a variety of interpretations. These theological developments made little impact on the bishops of Frankish Syria who continued to implement their traditional policies in regard to the Orthodox, although these became increasingly out of step with the official policies of the Roman church.

In the Orthodox world monasteries occupied an even more

1. Martène, Durand, *Nov. Thes.*, I, 479.

2. *Ibid.*, I, 480–1.

3. Exemplified in the discussions between Latins and Greeks at the council of Bari in 1098, Hefèle, Leclercq, V (I), pp 459–60; B. Leib, *Rome, Kiev et Byzance à la fin du XIe siècle*, Paris 1924, pp 287–96.

4. E. Jordan, 'La politique ecclésiastique de Roger I et les origines de la légation sicilienne', *Le Moyen Age*, ser 2, 24, 1922, pp 237–73; 25, 1923, pp 32–65; L.T. White, *Latin Monasticism in Norman Sicily*, Cambridge, Mass. 1938, pp 38–46; Leib, *Rome, Kiev*, pp 122–42.

important place than they did in the medieval western church:
the majority of bishops had been trained as monks; monasteries
were the principal centres of theological scholarship and, as
centres of prayer, were focuses for the spiritual life of Orthodox
lay-people. The Franks made no changes in the Orthodox monastic establishment of Syria: the communities, though required to
acknowledge the canonical authority of Latin bishops, were in all
other ways left undisturbed. They retained possession of their
lands, which owed no tithe to the Latin church, and their abbots
enjoyed an equality of social status with Latin abbots. The
Russian abbot Daniel, who came on pilgrimage to the Holy Land
in the reign of Baldwin I, has left a description of the monastic
life of the southern kingdom as it was in the early days of Frankish settlement. He based himself at the Orthodox priory of St
Sabas in Jerusalem, near the Tower of David, and was shown
round the holy places by an elderly member of the community.[1]
In the Jordan valley Daniel found three Orthodox communities:
that of St John the Baptist at the site of the Lord's baptism;
that of Our Lady of Kalamonia, at the point where the Jordan
enters the Dead Sea, which possessed a miraculous icon of the
Virgin and was served by twenty monks; and a few miles away
the monastery of St John Chrysostom, which was fortified and
reputed to possess many lands.[2] South of Jerusalem, in the
Judaean wilderness, Daniel visited St Sabas, the mother-house
of the priory in which he was lodging, and the greatest Orthodox
monastery in the kingdom. Like all visitors up to the present day
he was impressed by its dramatic and austere situation. Quite
near to it he found another Orthodox house, that of St
Theodosius,[3] and just south of Bethlehem was the Orthodox
monastery of St Chariton.[4]

Over seventy years later, shortly before the end of the first
kingdom, another Orthodox pilgrim to the Holy Land left a full
account of his travels. This was John Phocas, who had once
served in the armies of the emperor Manuel, and subsequently
became a monk at Patmos.[5] He found that, so far from being
adversely affected by almost a century of Latin domination, the
Orthodox monastic establishment in the Holy Land had increased.
At St Sabas he found forty monks 'of whom six converse directly

1. *The Pilgrimage of the Russian Abbot Daniel in the Holy Land*, trans C.W. Wilson,
PPTS, 1888, p 3.
2. *Ibid.*, pp 27–8, 30–1.
3. *Ibid.*, pp 33, 35–6.
4. *Ibid.*, p 48.
5. *The Pilgrimage of John Phocas to the Holy Land in the year 1185 A.D.*, trans
A. Stewart, *PPTS*, 1889, pp iv, 29.

with God';[1] like Daniel, Phocas visited the nearby monastery of
St Theodosius, but he also found a community living in a fortified
monastery at St Euthymius, a site which Daniel had remarked
upon as being in ruins.[2]   Phocas penetrated to a monastery in the
wilderness of Judaea which abbot Daniel had not reached, that of
Choziba, but he admits that

> it was with some difficulty that I climbed into and out of this monas-
> tery, both because of the precipitous nature of the place and the over-
> powering heat of the sun.[3]

In the Jordan valley Phocas found that the monastery of St
John the Baptist had been ruined by an earthquake, but had been
restored at the expense of the emperor Manuel.[4]   He, like Daniel,
visited the monastery of Kalamonia and its sacred icon, and went
on to that of St John Chrysostom where he met a Georgian
hermit, whom he had previously encountered living on the coast
of Asia Minor, near Attalia, while he was on active service in the
Byzantine army.[5]   More Orthodox monasteries had sprung up in
the area of Bethlehem since abbot Daniel's visit for, in addition to
that of St Chariton, Phocas speaks of the Abbot's monastery two
miles outside Bethlehem, and also the monastery of St Elias,
between Jerusalem and Bethlehem, which had been damaged, like
that of St John the Baptist, in an earthquake and rebuilt through
the munificence of the emperor Manuel.[6]
When Phocas travelled to Galilee he visited Mount Tabor. In
Daniel's time there had only been a Latin community there,
founded by prince Tancred,[7] but by 1185 a Greek community
had been established as well.   Phocas found this arrangement
entirely proper: on Mount Tabor 'are two monasteries, wherein
Christians who are vowed to the same life invoke the mercy of
God in hymns of various tongues'.[8]   Among the other sites of
Tabor shown to visitors was the cave of Melchizedek, where
local tradition claimed the priest-king had met Abraham returning
from his victory over the invading kings.   Phocas, however, was
not told, or if he was he did not believe it, the story which Daniel
heard from his guides, that

1. *Ibid.*, pp 23—4.
2. *Ibid.*, pp 24—5; cf. Daniel, pp 35—6.
3. Phocas, p 25.
4. *Ibid.*, p 27.
5. *Ibid.*, p 29.   The translator is in error in rendering 'Iberian' 'Spaniard': in a
Byzantine source it means Georgian.
6. *Ibid.*, pp 30—1.
7. Daniel, p 67.
8. Phocas, pp 13—14.

the holy Melchizedek often comes there to perform the liturgy. All the faithful who live upon the mountain . . . certified the truth of this to me.[1]

The German pilgrim, Theoderich, identified the community who served the chapel of the Tree of the Cross outside Jerusalem as Syrian Orthodox. Both Phocas and Daniel, who were better informed about the differences within the Orthodox church, recognised them as Georgians.[2] It was an understandable mistake for a western pilgrim, who had no knowledge of eastern languages, to make, for the Georgian church was, indeed, Orthodox, though it had its own catholicus, and used its own vernacular language in the liturgy.[3]

All the Orthodox monasteries which have been mentioned so far were situated outside cities, and all of them were communities of monks, understandably so, since they were vulnerable to enemy attack. There was, however, a community of Orthodox nuns inside the walls of Jerusalem.[4]

The other great concentration of Orthodox monasteries in Syria, as of Latin monasteries, was in the Black Mountain of Antioch. The Franks behaved in the same tolerant way to these communities as they did to those in the south. Orderic Vitalis reports that Bohemond confirmed the Orthodox in their possessions, and only placed Latin monks in charge of those houses which had been ruined before the Frankish conquest.[5] The great monastery of St Symeon's certainly remained in Orthodox control throughout this period, despite all the political disturbances between the princes of Antioch and the Byzantine empire.[6] There may have been Orthodox monasteries in other parts of the principality, but it is impossible to tell of what rite some monasteries were since there are only casual references to them in descriptions of property.[7]

The greatest of all the Orthodox monasteries of the Frankish East was Mount Sinai, founded by Justinian,[8] and the see of an

1. Daniel, p 69.
2. Theoderich, p 56; Phocas, p 30; Daniel, pp 50—1 ('Iberians' has been wrongly translated again here, cf. note 5, p 167 above; see also, 'Vie et pèlerinage de Daniel, hégoumène russe, 1106—1107', trans B. de Khitrowo, *Itinéraires russes en Orient, Publications de la Société de l'Orient Latin, Série géographique*, 5, Geneva 1889, I (I), p 50).
3. R. Janin, 'Géorgie', *DTC*, VI (I), 1239—89.
4. *CGOH*, no 376; Delaville Le Roulx, *Archives*, pp 139—40, no 49.
5. Orderic Vitalis, X, 12, vol V, p 278.
6. MS, XVIII, 10, vol III, p 325.
7. E.g. those mentioned in *CGOH*, no 783.
8. G.H. Forsyth, K. Weitzmann, *The Monastery of Saint Catherine at Mount Sinai: the church and fortress of Justinian*, Ann Arbor, 1965.

archbishop. The Franks regarded this house with considerable respect, an attitude reflected in the handbook for pilgrims which goes under the name of Fetellus, and which was probably written in the reign of king Fulk:

> So religious are the monks and hermits . . . so illustrious their reputation, that from the confines of Ethiopia to the utmost bounds of the Persians they are venerated by every eastern people . . . They have their cells in Egypt and in Persia, around the Red Sea and in Arabia . . . They are held in such reverence that no-one presumes to offend them in anything . . . Around the mountain they dwell, each in his own cell, living not in common, but of common property.[1]

Sinai was, in the early years of Frankish settlement, a kind of no-man's land between the kingdom of Jerusalem and the Fatimids of Egypt. Its abbot did not, however, share the confidence of 'Fetellus' about the invulnerability of his property, for when king Baldwin I made an expedition to Aqaba in 1115 and expressed a wish to visit the community, the abbot sent messengers to him begging him not to come for fear that the Egyptians would take reprisals against the monks.[2] But as the Franks consolidated their power in the lands beyond Jordan, and as the Fatimid empire grew weaker, Sinai was drawn within the Frankish orbit, although it never, perhaps, strictly became part of their dominions. Certainly Franks began to visit the community. Thus when Maurice, lord of Craon, went on pilgrimage to the Holy Land in around 1169 he was given a relic of St Catherine of Alexandria by Philip of Milly, grand master of the Templars. In his letters of authentication Philip described how, before his profession, when he had been lord of Montréal, he had gone on pilgrimage to Sinai and had persuaded the abbot to open St Catherine's reliquary and give him a relic.[3]

Sinai was not the only Orthodox shrine to be held in veneration by the Franks. The monastery of Our Lady of Sardenay near Damascus, which was always in Muslim hands, was highly regarded, and guidebooks for the use of pilgrims regularly recommended a detour to it.[4]

In the kingdom of Jerusalem in the twelfth century the Orthodox enjoyed a privileged position: they were not simply tolerated as members of a subject race who happened to be in communion with the Latin church. Their good standing was partly the result

1. *Fetellus, circa 1130 A.D.*, trans J.R. Macpherson, *PPTS*, 1892, pp 16–17.
2. Albert of Aix, XII, 21, *RHC Occ*, IV, p 703.
3. B. de Broussillon, *La Maison de Craon, 1050–1480*, 2 vols, Paris 1893, I, p 101, no 138. I am indebted to my colleague, Dr M.C.E. Jones, for this reference.
4. E.g. *Les pèlerinages por aler en Iherusalem*, c 21, ed Michelant, Raynaud, p 103.

of Baldwin I's perceiving their value. His awareness of this was prompted by a seemingly trivial event in 1101. At Easter a large crowd of pilgrims of all confessions had gathered in Jerusalem to assist at the liturgy, the climax of which was the ceremony of the New Fire. Some version of this, the lighting of the paschal candle, formed an integral part of the Easter liturgy throughout the Christian world, symbolising the Lord's Resurrection, but in Jerusalem, where the Resurrection had taken place, the fire was not kindled with tinder and flint, but lighted spontaneously in the Holy Sepulchre itself.[1] At Eastertide 1101 the fire did not light, and its failure to do so was taken as a grave sign of God's displeasure and produced much the same effect on the crowds as the failure of the blood of S. Gennaro to liquefy on the appropriate day would have on the population of modern Naples. The eastern Christians were probably correct in their diagnosis that the miracle would not occur because they had been expelled by the Latins from the Holy Sepulchre. Calling a temporary truce to their deep doctrinal divisions, the members of the eastern religious communities in Jerusalem conducted solemn processions through the streets, imploring the mercy of God, and their intercession proved efficacious, for, after a long delay, the miracle duly occurred.[2]

This lesson was not lost on king Baldwin. Pilgrims came to Jerusalem from all over the Christian east, from the Byzantine empire, the principalities of Russia, the Caucasus and, of course, from the Muslim world. They brought money to Jerusalem, which was badly needed, since the city was economically viable only as a pilgrimage centre, and they brought information about what was happening in neighbouring lands, which was politically valuable to the crown. The kingdom could not afford to sacrifice these assets by too rigidly insisting that the Holy Sepulchre should be in Latin hands. Thereafter the Orthodox were readmitted, at least for the Easter ceremonies, and there was no further problem about the New Fire. Thus when abbot Daniel was in Jerusalem at Easter, Baldwin I invited him and the abbot of St Sabas to form part of the royal suite at the Easter liturgy.[3]

It is possible that from king Baldwin's reign Orthodox clergy were readmitted to the Holy Sepulchre on a permanent basis. The evidence that they had been dates from a much later period, and we only know what the arrangements were after the new Latin

1. H. Leclercq, 'Pâques', *DACL*, XIII(ii), 1559–71.

2. Fulcher of Chartres, II, 8, s 2. This passage occurs only in one manuscript of Fulcher. Hagenmeyer considered it interpolated and printed it separately, pp 831–7; cf. pp 395–6, n 5. Matthew of Edessa, c 21, *RHC Arm*, I, pp 54–5.

3. Daniel, pp 76–80.

cathedral had been completed in 1149. The Latins retained the Byzantine cathedral, a *rotunda* built over the shrine of the Sepulchre itself, but made an opening in the wall at the east end to give access to the new cathedral which they had built. The patriarch's throne behind the Latin high altar thus faced towards the shrine of the *anastasis* itself.[1]   Theoderich, who came to Jerusalem after this work had been completed, describes how

> before the door of the choir is an altar of no small size which . . . is used only by the Syrians in their services when the daily Latin services are over.[2]

In other words the Orthodox were not hidden away in a side chapel, but had a large altar in a prominent part of the church at which the Orthodox liturgy was celebrated daily. In addition, they also had a chapel of the Holy Cross on the north side of the church in which their relic of the Cross was venerated.[3]   In king Amalric's reign the Orthodox clergy who served the Holy Sepulchre had the status of canons, although, of course, they were quite distinct from the Latin chapter, and were at least five in number.[4]

The Orthodox also had an altar of their own in the chief Marian shrine of Jerusalem, the church of Our Lady of Josaphat.[5] None of the separated eastern churches were allowed to celebrate the liturgy in any Latin shrine: this privilege was reserved to the Orthodox who alone recognised the authority of the Latin church.

Part of the esteem in which the Franks held them must have been due to the fact that a high proportion of the queens of Jerusalem were Orthodox in faith. Morphia of Melitene, the wife of Baldwin II, was an Orthodox Christian, although of Armenian birth,[6] and some of her religious attitudes influenced her daughter, queen Melisende, who bequeathed estates to the Orthodox monks of St Sabas to pray for the repose of her soul.[7]   Both Melisende's sons, Baldwin III and Amalric, married Byzantine Greek wives, so that throughout the period from 1118–87 there were influential women in the kingdom, either queens or dowager queens, who were sympathetic towards the Orthodox and who might have been expected to promote their interests.

---

1. C. Couäsnon, *The Church of the Holy Sepulchre in Jerusalem*, London 1974, pp 57–62; Hamilton, *SCH*, 14, 1977, pp 105–7.
2. Theoderich, p 15.
3. *Ibid.*, p 16.
4. *CGOH*, no 443.
5. Theoderich, p 38.
6. WT, X, 24, *RHC Occ*, I, p 437.
7. de Rozière, p 256, no 140.

In the patriarchate of Antioch the situation of the Orthodox was very different. Their parish clergy and their monastic establishment, as has been seen, were allowed religious freedom under Latin bishops, and no attempt was made to interfere with their rites and usages, but they enjoyed no special privileges. There were no Orthodox canons of Antioch cathedral, nor were Orthodox abbots held in particular esteem by the Norman princes. In part this was fortuitous: the early Norman princes and princesses of Antioch all married western Christians so that there were no influential Orthodox members of the Norman court. This, it is true, changed in the reign of Bohemond III, whose sister, Maria, married the Byzantine emperor Manuel in 1161, and who himself later married a Byzantine princess, Theodora. But this pro-Byzantine phase in the history of Antioch was as brief as it was untypical: Bohemond repudiated his wife in 1181, and his sister was murdered in Constantinople by the order of Andronicus I after he seized the imperial throne in 1182.[1]

The normal state of relations between Antioch and Byzantium was one of war, punctuated by periods of uneasy truce. The view of all the Comnenian emperors was that the Norman principality of Antioch should not exist: under the terms of the oath which the crusader leaders had sworn to Alexius I in 1097 the city should have been restored to the Byzantine empire. This had an important consequence for the Frankish religious settlement in that the Byzantine court and church refused to accept the latinisation of the church of Antioch. When John IV returned to Constantinople and abdicated as patriarch of Antioch in October 1100, making it clear that he had been expelled from his see by the Franks,[2] the Byzantines refused to accept his Latin successor, Bernard of Valence, as lawful patriarch, and appointed a titular Greek patriarch to the see.[3] There was a practical reason for this, though it was probably not the dominant one in the minds of Byzantine churchmen. The area of north Syria under Frankish rule was not coterminous with the area under the ecclesiastical jurisdiction of the Orthodox patriarch of Antioch. There were Orthodox bishops in the twelfth century in Aleppo and Damascus, both of which remained permanently in Muslim hands. Even if these prelates had been willing to acknowledge a Latin patriarch in Antioch as their canonical superior, it is extremely doubtful whether the Muslim authorities, who were at war with

---

1. WT, XXII, 6–7, *RHC Occ*, I, pp 1071–5; C.M. Brand, *Byzantium confronts the West, 1180–1204*, Cambridge, Mass. 1968, pp 45–7.
2. Benechewitch, *Catalogus Codicum*, p 279.
3. John V. Grumel, *Chronologie*, p 448.

the Franks, would have allowed this, whereas they would have had no objection to their recognising a titular head in distant Constantinople. Reasons of pastoral concern might, therefore, have dictated this policy, but in fact the dominant reasons were political.

Ever since Bohemond had refused to hand over Antioch to Alexius's envoys in 1099 the Byzantines had made sporadic war on the Normans there, and it was this that led Bohemond to seek the support of pope Paschal II in launching a crusade against the Byzantine empire. This gained wide support, and in 1107 Bohemond attacked the Adriatic coast of the empire but was decisively defeated by the emperor in the following year, and forced to sign the humiliating peace of Devol by which he undertook to do liege homage to Alexius for his eastern lands.[1] The terms of the ecclesiastical settlement which Bohemond pledged himself to implement at Antioch were these:

> . . . the patriarch of Antioch shall not any more be one of our race, but a man whom your majesties shall promote and choose from the clergy of the great church of Constantinople. Such is the man who will hold the see of Antioch and exercise all the functions of a bishop . . . in accordance with the privileges of that see.[2]

Bohemond never returned to Syria, but retired to his lands in south Italy where he died in 1111, while regents continued to rule Antioch until his son, Bohemond II, came of age in 1126. Although the peace of Devol was never implemented, future Byzantine emperors treated it as a blueprint for the kind of settlement they wished to impose in north Syria.

It is not known when the new titular patriarch of Antioch, John V, was appointed. He is first recorded in 1117 as present at a synod in Constantinople at which the writings of Eustratius of Nicaea were condemned.[3] But it seems probable, in view of Alexius's declared intentions, that he had been elected immediately after John IV's abdication, so that when, as the emperor intended should happen, Antioch should once again come under Greek rule, he might be restored there.

John V died in about 1134 and his place was taken by the patriarch Luke.[4] There seemed a real prospect that he might be restored, for in 1136 John Comnenus took his army to south-

---

1. Yewdale, *Bohemond I*, pp 115–31.
2. Anna Comnena, *Alexiad*, XIII, 12, s 20, ed Leib, vol III, p 134.
3. Grumel, *Regestes*, no 1003.
4. V. Grumel, 'Les patriarches grecs d'Antioche du nom de Jean (XIe et XIIe siècles)', *EO*, 32, 1933, pp 279–99; 'Notes pour l'*Oriens Christianus*', *EO*, 33, 1934, pp 54–5.

east Asia Minor with the declared intention of recovering Antioch.[1]
In 1136—7 he subdued Cilicia, where Armenian princes had made
themselves independent of Latin rule, and expelled the Latin archbishops of Tarsus and Mamistra from their sees, replacing them
with Orthodox ones.[2]   He then went to Antioch where prince
Raymond did homage to him on the advice of king Fulk.[3]   The
Latin patriarch, Ralph of Domfront, feeling that his position was
threatened, appealed to the pope for help, and this provoked the
quarrel between him and the prince which ended in Ralph's
deposition.[4]   Ibn al-Qalanisi, observing these events from
Damascus, is quite explicit about the reason for the quarrel:

> A report was received that the lord of Antioch had arrested the Frank-
> ish patriarch there and had plundered his house. The reason for this
> was said to be that the king of the Greeks, when peace was established
> between him and Raymond, lord of Antioch, had stipulated as one of
> the conditions of peace that he should set up in Antioch a patriarch
> for the Greeks, as had been the custom of old but had lapsed in later
> years.[5]

In fact the threat to the Latin patriarch never materialised. John
was forced by the situation in western Europe to return to Constantinople in 1138, before he had placed a Byzantine garrison in
Antioch, and, although he returned to Syria in 1142 and demanded the surrender of the city, he met with a refusal and died early
in the following year before he had been able to mount a siege.
His death, of course, led to the withdrawal of his forces.[6]

So the patriarch Luke died in about 1156 without setting foot
in Antioch.   His successor, Soterichus Panteugenus, soon after
his election, had the misfortune to take the wrong side in a
controversy about eucharistic sacrifice and, although he abjured
his errors, the synod of Constantinople declared him unworthy
of episcopal consecration in May 1157.[7]

He was succeeded by Athanasius III, whose prospects of being
recognised in Antioch at first seemed very good.   For in 1158
Manuel Comnenus invaded Cilicia and not only subdued rebellious
Armenian princes there, but also forced Reynald of Châtillon,
prince of Antioch, who had sacked the rich Byzantine island of
Cyprus, to make an humiliating act of public penance, to do

1. Cinnamus, I, 7, ed Meineke, p 16.
2. Odo of Deuil, *De Profectione Ludovici VII*, p 68.
3. Orderic Vitalis, XIII, 34, vol VI, pp 506—8.
4. See chapter 2 above.
5. Gibb, *Damascus Chronicle*, p 245.
6. Hussey, 'Byzantium and the Crusades', in Setton, II, pp 133—4.
7. Grumel, *Regestes*, nos 1041, 1043.

homage to the emperor for his lands, and to agree to the restoration of a Greek patriarch at Antioch.[1] All the Franks in Syria were frightened at this time of the growing power of Nur-ad-Din, ruler of Edessa, Aleppo and Damascus, and with differing degrees of enthusiasm welcomed the prospect of Byzantine military protection. King Baldwin III of Jerusalem, who had married Manuel's niece, came to Antioch to pay his respects to the emperor and to consult with him, and Manuel was able to enter the city in a solemn triumph on Easter day 1159.[2] The emperor did not at this stage raise the question of an Orthodox patriarch in Antioch: he had received *de facto* recognition of his overlordship throughout the Frankish east, which contrasted markedly with the hostile reception accorded to his father twenty years before. He seems to have realised that this could be placed in jeopardy if he disturbed the religious susceptibilities of the Franks, and also that by imposing an Orthodox patriarch on them he might antagonise the pope who was the linchpin in his western alliance against Frederick Barbarossa.[3] After a brief campaign against Nur-ad-Din, Manuel returned to his capital in 1159, where Athanasius of Antioch remained. He was still there two years later, when Manuel married Maria of Antioch, and assisted at the solemnity.[4]

The emperor had not reversed the policy of his father and grandfather, who had sought to restore the Orthodox patriarch to Antioch, but was merely waiting for a suitable occasion to do so. This presented itself a few years later. In 1164 the confederate armies of the Christian rulers of north Syria were decisively defeated by Nur-ad-Din at the battle of Harim, and prince Bohemond III of Antioch was taken prisoner. King Amalric, fully occupied in preventing Nur-ad-Din's forces from gaining control of Egypt, was unable to intervene in the north, and nothing stood in the way of Nur-ad-Din's launching a direct attack on Antioch itself except his fear of antagonising the Byzantine empire. Nur-ad-Din did not attack, and, indeed, released Bohemond III on condition that he paid a large ransom. Bohemond therefore went to Constantinople to ask the emperor, who was his overlord and his brother-in-law, to give him the ransom money, which Manuel agreed to do on condition that the Orthodox patriarch was restored.[5] Bohemond and his advisers had no alternative but to accept these terms since,

1. Cinnamus, IV, 20, ed Meineke, pp 185–6.

2. *Ibid.*, IV, 21A, pp 187–8.

3. Manuel was only able to campaign in Syria because pope Hadrian IV had arranged peace between Sicily and Byzantium to meet the threat of Barbarossa in 1158, Lamma, *Comneni e Staufer*, I, pp 243–311.

4. Cinnamus, V, 4, ed Meineke, p 211.

5. MS, XVIII, 11, vol III, p 326.

had they refused them, Manuel could have withdrawn his protection from the principality and Nur-ad-Din would no longer have had any reason to hold back from attacking it.   Consequently, when Bohemond returned to Antioch in 1165, he brought the patriarch Athanasius with him and he was enthroned in St Peter's cathedral.   The Latin patriarch, Aimery of Limoges, did not, however, abdicate, but retired to his fortress of Qusair, anathematising the Franks who recognised his rival, and he stayed there throughout Athanasius's reign.[1]

There matters rested for five years, until in 1170 there was a severe earthquake, which damaged the walls of Antioch and destroyed the sanctuary of the cathedral.   Prince Bohemond interpreted this as a sign of God's displeasure, and led a deputation of the Franks to Qusair to ask the pardon of the patriarch Aimery and to beg him to return to the city. He agreed to do so only if the patriarch Athanasius first left, but any fears that he may have had that his rival would attempt to oppose him proved unfounded, for Athanasius had been mortally wounded in the earthquake and died soon after.[2]   Thenceforward, Aimery was in undisputed control of the church of Antioch.

Athanasius's restoration is very poorly documented: Latin Christian writers ignore the whole episode. William of Tyre, who was living in the kingdom of Jerusalem and writing his great history at the time, makes no reference to it. This reticence is understandable, for the restoration was the greatest humiliation which the Latin church in Syria suffered in the twelfth century. The silence of Byzantine writers is less explicable: as J.M. Hussey has said, the restoration of Athanasius was the crowning achievement of Manuel's Syrian policy,[3] yet the Byzantine historians ignore it. Our only source for these events is the Syriac historian, Michael the Syrian, Jacobite patriarch of Antioch, who was not only a contemporary writer, but also visited Antioch during the time of Athanasius's rule.[4]   Michael was interested in what was happening at Antioch, because he was on good terms with the Latins, but had a profound distrust of the Orthodox who were far less tolerant of the Monophysite Jacobites than the Franks were. It is also significant that the pope made no protest about this invasion of the rights of the Latin church. The conduct of Alexander III in this regard is very different from that of Innocent II when faced with the possible restoration of a Greek patriarch in Antioch by

---

1. Michael the Syrian visited him there in 1168, *ibid.*, XIX, 3, vol III, p 332.
2. *Ibid.*, XIX, 6, vol III, p 339.
3. Hussey in Setton, II, p 140.
4. MS, XIX, 3, vol III, p 332.

John Comnenus. But Alexander's relations with the Byzantine empire were very different from those of Innocent II: for Alexander was engaged in a struggle with the western emperor, Frederick Barbarossa, who refused to recognise him as pope, and Alexander relied heavily on the subsidies which Manuel Comnenus paid to the Italian communes, who were his allies in his struggle to prevent Barbarossa from gaining control of north and central Italy.[1] Alexander III was, therefore, in no position to protest about what was happening at Antioch. It must, however, be assumed that during his tenure of office Athanasius III was recognised as canonical head of the church of Antioch by the Latin as well as by the Orthodox clergy of his patriarchate, and that Aimery of Limoges, while not officially deposed, was stripped of effective power. Certainly there is no evidence to suggest that the patriarchs exercised some kind of *condominium*, a solution which would have been acceptable to neither of them. On the other hand, there is no evidence that Athanasius attempted to disturb the religious settlement by replacing Latin bishops by Orthodox ones, or even that he displaced the Latin canons from Antioch cathedral. The chief practical change which his pontificate produced was the establishment of close links between Antioch and the patriarchate of Constantinople, which had been broken since the abdication of John IV: in the spring of 1166 Athanasius attended a church synod in Constantinople, for example.[2] But his reign did not produce any substantial reduction of Latin power in the church of Antioch, such as the Orthodox world might reasonably have hoped for, and perhaps this is why Byzantine writers fail to mention the whole episode.

The experiment was not repeated. It is difficult to understand why this was. Nur-ad-Din was more powerful than he had been before, since his lieutenant Saladin had gained control of Egypt in 1169: the Syrian Franks therefore were as dependent as they had ever been on Byzantine aid, and in 1171 king Amalric of Jerusalem had gone to Constantinople in person to ask the emperor for help.[3] Nor had the situation in the west changed substantially, for the pope and the Byzantine emperor were still allies in the war against Barbarossa.[4] It seems unlikely, therefore, that had Manuel chosen to do so he could not have forced the Franks of Antioch to accept another Orthodox patriarch as successor to Athanasius. It seems possible that Manuel's decision was not unconnected with

1. Lamma, *Comneni e Staufer*, II, pp 75–159.
2. Grumel, *Regestes*, no 1059.
3. WT, XX, 22–4, *RHC Occ*, I, pp 980–7.
4. Lamma, *op. cit.*, II, pp 239–53.

the appointment of a new patriarch of Constantinople, Michael III of Anchialus, in 1170. For Michael was far more hostile to the Latin church than any of his twelfth-century predecessors had been, and responded to papal overtures about church unity, which included, of course, a recognition of the Roman primacy, by saying that it would be preferable to live under Muslim rule than to be subject to the spiritual authority of the Latins.[1] Such a man was likely to press for the complete restoration of an Orthodox hierarchy at Antioch, not simply for the recognition of an Orthodox patriarch there, and Manuel may have judged that this would create widespread disaffection among the Franks and threaten the political hegemony which he had achieved in Latin Syria. Certainly the new titular patriarch, Cyril II, spent all his reign in Constantinople.[2]

The last titular patriarch to be appointed in this period was the distinguished canon lawyer, Theodore Balsamon.[3] By his time Orthodox theological attitudes towards the Latins were hardening, at least in the patriarchate of Constantinople, and in 1190 Theodore, who had been consulted by the Orthodox patriarch of Alexandria about the lawfulness of administering the sacraments to Frankish prisoners of war in Egypt, replied that the Latins should not be admitted to the sacraments of the Orthodox church until they had abjured their errors.[4] A man who held such extreme opinions could not have been admitted to the exercise of patriarchal powers by the Franks of Antioch, since he would not have been willing to work in harmony with the Latin bishops.

The position of the Orthodox hierarchy in Antioch in the twelfth century is therefore clear. The Franks expelled Orthodox bishops from their sees and substituted Latin prelates who had full canonical authority over the Orthodox clergy. The Orthodox priests and monks retained full religious freedom under Latin obedience, but did not hold a particularly privileged position in the state. The Byzantine government refused to accept the latinisation of the church of Antioch and appointed titular patriarchs who lived for the most part in Constantinople, apart from the brief period when Athanasius III was restored to power in Antioch. But the intervention of the Byzantine emperors in the affairs of north Syria, their restitution of Orthodox metropolitans to the sees of Cilicia, which formed part of the patriarchate of

---

1. Cited by Runciman, *Eastern Schism*, p 139, from the text of C. Loparev, 'On the unionism of the Emperor Manuel Comnenus', *Vizantiskii Vremennik*, 14, 1917, pp 344–57 (in Russian), which I have not seen.
2. V. Grumel, 'Notes pour l'*Oriens Christianus*', *EO*, 33, 1934, pp 53–4.
3. Grumel, *Chronologie*, p 448.
4. Theodore Balsamon, *Responsa ad Interrogationes Marci*, *PG*, 138, 967.

Antioch, and their official recognition of the titular patriarchs kept alive in the Orthodox community under Frankish rule a sense of its own identity. This prevented the achievement of any symbiosis between the Latins and the Orthodox, beyond the technical union which political circumstances forced upon them, and was to lead to open schism in the church there in the thirteenth century.

The situation in the patriarchate of Jerusalem was different. The Byzantines did not regard the kingdom of Jerusalem as rightfully part of their empire and never questioned the legitimacy of the Latin kings, even though, ideally, they welcomed recognition by them of Byzantine suzerainty, a situation which obtained in the reign of the emperor Manuel.[1] The Byzantine attitude to the ecclesiastical settlement in the southern patriarchate was therefore not determined in any way, as it was at Antioch, by political factors. Moreover, Frankish rule in the patriarchate of Jerusalem was virtually coextensive with the effective limits of Orthodox ecclesiastical jurisdiction. There were no outlying Orthodox dioceses there which remained under Muslim control, and were thereby prevented from acknowledging the authority of the Latin patriarch, as there were at Antioch. Pastoral considerations did not, therefore, enter into Orthodox attitudes towards the Latin hierarchy there.

Initially the church authorities in Constantinople seem to have taken no action when, after the death of the Orthodox patriarch of Jerusalem, Symeon II, in 1099, the Franks appointed Latin patriarchs. In 1107–8 an Orthodox bishop called John came to Constantinople and informed the holy synod that he had been bishop of Tyre, but had left his see because of Muslim persecution and had gone to Jerusalem where the Orthodox community had elected him as their patriarch. The synod ratified his appointment. Grumel has argued that John VIII's election as patriarch should be dated to the period before the first crusade, when Symeon II had taken refuge in Cyprus and the Orthodox of Jerusalem were left without an effective leader.[2] This seems implausible, for before 1099 Tyre was under Fatimid rule, and the Fatimids were well disposed towards their Christian subjects and to the Byzantine empire, whereas the Artukid Turks in Jerusalem persecuted their Orthodox subjects and had driven Symeon into exile: if, for local reasons, John had been expelled by the Fatimids from the see of Tyre, he would not have taken

1. J.L. Lamonte, 'To what extent was the Byzantine Empire the suzerain of the Crusading States?', *Byzantion*, 7, 1932.

2. Grumel, *Regestes*, no 986.

refuge in Jerusalem.

The situation makes much more sense if it is placed after the first crusade, when the see of Jerusalem was in any case vacant. The Fatimid governors of the coastal cities, at war with the Franks of Jerusalem, might well have viewed their native Christian subjects as a potential fifth column and have persecuted them, in which case it would have been natural for an Orthodox bishop to take refuge in Frankish territory.[1] If this were so, John's election can only have taken place with the agreement of the Frankish authorities and there may have been an element of misunderstanding in the whole situation. The Latin patriarch might well have welcomed an Orthodox coadjutor who could, under his authority, undertake the supervision of the Orthodox communities in his charge; whereas John may have considered that he was lawful Orthodox patriarch and needed the ratification of the oecumenical patriarch to regularise his position.

Nothing more is known about John VIII, but the position of his successor, the patriarch Sabas, is very similar. In 1117—18 he came to Constantinople and explained to the synod that he had been archbishop of Caesarea in Palestine and had been translated to the patriarchate of Jerusalem. He clearly intended to stay in Byzantium, for the synod gave him the revenues of the see of Maronea in Thrace to support him.[2] This suggests that he too, like John VIII, had been placed in charge of the Orthodox communities of Palestine by the Latin authorities, but that he had disagreed with them and gone into exile.

After that time the Byzantine authorities appointed a series of titular patriarchs to the see of Jerusalem, who, like the Orthodox patriarchs of Antioch, lived in Constantinople. They were Nicholas (c 1122— c 1156);[3] John IX (1157);[4] Nicephorus II (c 1166— c 1173);[5] Leontius II (1174—5 — 1184—5); and Dositheus I (appointed before 1187).[6] No attempt was made by the Byzantine government to secure their enthronement at Jerusalem, and the reason for their appointment seems to have been simply one of ecclesiastical convenience. In the Orthodox tradition supreme authority in the church was vested in the pentarchy of patriarchs, but in the twelfth century, because of tensions with the western church, the concurrence of the Roman pontiff was no longer

---

1. As the Orthodox bishop of Aleppo fled to Antioch in 1124 to escape anti-Christian rioting, *Anon. 1234*, 'HC', c 291, pp 69—70.

2. Grumel, *Regestes*, no 1004.

3. Grumel, *Chronologie*, p 448; *Regestes*, no 1038.

4. *Ibid.*, nos 1041, 1043.

5. *Ibid.*, no 1059.

6. Choniates, *De Isaacio Angelo*, ed Van Dieten, I, p 406.

normally sought in reaching decisions. However, since two of the four eastern patriarchates were in Latin hands, only the Orthodox patriarch of Alexandria could be expected to support the patriarch of Constantinople in reaching decisions which affected the whole Orthodox world. There was, therefore, a certain advantage in appointing Orthodox patriarchs to the sees of Jerusalem and Antioch, who lived permanently in Constantinople and who could give weight to the decisions of the holy synod of the Byzantine patriarchate. This did mean, of course, that the Byzantine church did not recognise the canonical authority of the Latin patriarchs of Jerusalem, but it also meant that the question of restoring the Orthodox patriarch to effective power at Jerusalem was not considered to be of primary importance. Nevertheless, the Orthodox living under Latin rule in the kingdom of Jerusalem were aware of the existence of the titular patriarch in Constantinople, and this coloured their attitude towards the ecclesiastical settlement which the Frankish rulers had imposed on them.

If, as the evidence suggests, the Franks in the reign of Baldwin I had allowed the Orthodox of Jerusalem to choose a bishop of their own, this can only have been done on the assumption that he was a coadjutor of the Latin patriarch, who alone possessed canonical authority. The Orthodox may have understood this differently and considered that they, like the other eastern-rite Christians in the kingdom, were being granted religious autonomy under Frankish rule, for, as will be seen in the next chapter, the separated eastern churches all had their own bishops and effectively owed no obedience to the Latin hierarchy. If this were the case, then the patriarch Sabas's departure to Constantinople in 1117–18 would have been occasioned by his unwillingness to accept subordination to the Latin patriarch.

The traditional western view on the subject of what would now be called uniate clergy was expressed in canon IX of the fourth Lateran council in 1215, 'Concerning different rites in the same faith':

> in many regions there are, within the same city and diocese, people of different races, speaking different languages, who hold the same faith with a diversity of rites and customs . . . Now we altogether forbid the appointment of several bishops in one and the same city or diocese, for it is a monstrous thing that one body should have several heads. But if urgent necessity demands it . . . the bishop of such a place shall with due care appoint a catholic bishop, chosen from among those people, as his vicar over them, who in all things shall be obedient and subject to him.[1]

1. *CICO*, II, pp 483–4.

This left the Latin patriarchs of Jerusalem with three alternatives. They could, like the patriarchs of Antioch, assume direct control over the Orthodox themselves and appoint no Orthodox bishops; they could leave some sees in the sole control of Orthodox bishops who acknowledged the authority of the Latin patriarch; or they could appoint coadjutors, who had no territorial jurisdiction, but assisted the Latin bishops in administering the Orthodox communities.

They chose a mixture of the second and third alternatives. The only Orthodox prelate whom the Franks recognised as a full diocesan bishop was the archbishop of Sinai. No Franks lived in his diocese, which extended over the Sinai peninsula, so this created no social problem about an Orthodox having rule over Latins, and, in any case, Frankish control over Sinai was tenuous and ephemeral. But in official ecclesiastical lists the Orthodox archbishop of Sinai appeared as a suffragan of the Latin metropolitan archbishop of Petra.[1]

At some time in the twelfth century the Latin church of Jerusalem adopted the practice of appointing Orthodox coadjutors. When cardinal Pelagius drew up his constitution for the Latin church of Cyprus in 1222, by the terms of which an Orthodox coadjutor was appointed in each of the Latin sees, he stated:

> the four Greek bishops who, with our assent . . . shall always hold office in Cyprus, shall be obedient to the Roman church and to the Latin archbishop and bishops, according to the custom of the kingdom of Jerusalem.[2]

But Pelagius makes it clear that the Orthodox bishops are an administrative convenience. They have no territorial jurisdiction:

> all Greek priests and deacons shall owe canonical obedience to the Latin archbishop and bishops . . . just as in the kingdom of Jerusalem Greek priests and deacons obeyed . . . Latin bishops from the time when the Latin clergy and laity first obtained lordship there.[3]

That there were Orthodox coadjutors in the kingdom of Jerusalem at the time when Pelagius wrote is clear from the works of James of Vitry,[4] but evidence about their existence in the first kingdom is scanty. Jobert, grand master of the Hospital of St John (1172–7), granted the monastery of St George at Beersheba,

---

1. List of the suffragan sees of Jerusalem, James of Vitry, *HO*, c 56, p 95.
2. L. de Mas Latrie, *Histoire de l'Ile de Chypre* . . . , 3 vols, Paris, 1852–61, III, p 622.
3. *Ibid.*, III, p 620.
4. 'Habent enim proprios episcopos Graecos', *HO*, c 75, p 139. He specifies that there was an Orthodox bishop in Acre and an Orthodox archbishop in Sidon, *Lettres*, pp 85, 92, no 2.

which belonged to his order, to Meletus the Syrian, 'archbishop of all the Syrians and Greeks living in the area of Jabin and Gaza'. Archbishop Meletus was a *confrater* of the Hospital, and it was enacted that after his death the monastery should revert to the order and be used to provide alms for the poor, for the repose of the souls of Meletus himself, of the benefactors of the monastery, and of Manuel Comnenus, 'most holy emperor of the Romans at Constantinople, *semper augustus*', who, it may be supposed, had agreed to finance the rebuilding of the house which was in ruins.[1] Meletus was clearly a coadjutor of the Latin hierarchy, probably of the patriarch himself in this most southerly part of his diocese. It is also possible that Paul of Antioch, Orthodox bishop of Sidon, held office in Manuel's reign, but the evidence about this is uncertain since it hinges on the interpretation of certain passages in his writings.[2] There may also have been an Orthodox bishop of Lydda in the first kingdom. The 'Syrian archbishop' of that see came to greet Richard I in 1192, and although it is possible that he had only been appointed in the years following Hattin, this seems unlikely because the Orthodox patriarch had not been readmitted to Jerusalem by Saladin at that time, so that no major reorganisation of the Orthodox hierarchy could have been carried out.[3]

It is noteworthy that all the Orthodox bishops who may have held office in the Frankish kingdom were Syrians. Meletus, despite his Greek name, is called a Syrian, as is the unnamed bishop of Lydda, while Paul of Antioch wrote in Arabic, not in Greek. This was a complete reversal of the custom of the pre-crusade period by which the Orthodox episcopate had been made up of Byzantine Greeks, separated by language and culture from the communities over which they ruled. The elevation of native Syrians to the episcopate, from which they had previously been excluded, may have done much to reconcile the Orthodox in the kingdom of Jerusalem to a union with the Latin church in which final authority was exercised by Latin bishops.

Mayer has argued that the appointment of Orthodox bishops in the Latin patriarchate of Jerusalem was a consequence of the alliance with the emperor Manuel, forged by Baldwin III and continued by king Amalric.[4] This may be so, but it is equally possible that some arrangement of this kind existed from the

---

1. *CGOH*, no 443.
2. P. Khoury, ed and trans, *Paul d'Antioche, évêque melkite de Sidon (XIIe s.)*, Beirut 1965.
3. *Itinerarium Regis Ricardi*, V, 53, p 376. See chapter 12 below.
4. Mayer, *Crusades*, pp 124–5.

earliest days of the kingdom. It was not particularly in Manuel's interests that there should be Orthodox bishops in the kingdom of Jerusalem who acknowledged the Latin patriarch rather than the Orthodox patriarch who lived in Constantinople, and it therefore seems more probable that this solution was devised by the Latin hierarchy themselves as a means of administering the large Orthodox community in their charge.

Whatever their origin, the function of Orthodox bishops in the kingdom of Jerusalem was not analogous to that of the Orthodox episcopate in Lusignan Cyprus. In Cyprus almost the entire native population was Orthodox and there had been a full Orthodox hierarchy there at the time of the Latin conquest.[1] In Jerusalem the Orthodox were only found in certain areas, and in many parts of the patriarchate there had been no Orthodox bishops at the time of the first crusade. The Latins are not likely to have appointed Orthodox bishops either in places where there were no Orthodox congregations, or in those where there had been no Orthodox sees before, so that almost certainly there was not an Orthodox coadjutor in every Latin see. The details of Orthodox organisation in the Latin patriarchate of Jerusalem are not known, but it is clear that such a system was in operation by the second half of the twelfth century, and it may have existed in some form from the beginning.

Although the Byzantines did not attempt to disturb the ecclesiastical settlement in Jerusalem, in the reigns of Baldwin III and Amalric the emperor Manuel succeeded in reasserting his traditional role as protector of Orthodox Christians there. His liberality was not restricted to rebuilding Orthodox monasteries, for, as has been noted above, he paid for the church of the Holy Nativity at Bethlehem to be redecorated and also had mosaic decorations executed in the shrine of the Holy Sepulchre,[2] although both churches were in Latin hands. The Latin bishop of Bethlehem, as John Phocas noticed, was duly grateful for the benefaction and hung Manuel's portrait in the sanctuary of his church.[3] Byzantine intervention in the patriarchate of Jerusalem was not, therefore, divisive in the way that it was at Antioch.

Superficially, relations between the Franks and their Orthodox subjects in the kingdom of Jerusalem appeared to be good. From an early period they had been able to take united religious action when that seemed appropriate. Fulcher of Chartres records how,

---

1. An archbishop and thirteen suffragans, J. Hackett, *A History of the Orthodox Church of Cyprus*, London 1901, pp 303–28.
2. Phocas, p 19.
3. *Ibid.*, p 31.

when Baldwin II was a prisoner of war in 1123 and the Fatimids launched an attack on Jaffa, the Latins, Greeks and Syrians of Jerusalem joined together and held religious processions in the streets to ask for God's aid.[1] According to the Armenian scholar, St Nerses of Lampron, in the Latin cathedrals of Jerusalem and Antioch the gospel was sung first in Greek and then in Latin, as a sign of the unity of faith in diversity of language which existed in the universal church,[2] although the patriarchal sees of Syria may, of course, simply have been imitating the traditional usage of the solemn papal Masses in Rome.

Yet relations between the Franks and their Orthodox subjects were not as harmonious as they appeared to be on the surface. Had the Latin patriarch of Jerusalem, Amalric of Nesle, visited the Mount Sinai monastery accompanied by a Greek interpreter and assisted at the divine liturgy he would have been given pause for thought, for the brethren prayed

> For the safety and peace . . . of our holy father Nicephorus, patriarch of Jerusalem, and of his companions, the three great, holy, oecumenical, orthodox patriarchs, Luke of Constantinople, Sophronius of Alexandria and Athanasius of Antioch . . . [3]

There was a fundamental divergence of attitude here. In the view of the Latin hierarchy Sinai was a suffragan see of the Latin archbishop of Petra, whereas the Greek archbishop of Sinai and his brethren regarded themselves as members of the Orthodox communion and prayed, not for the Latin patriarch of Jerusalem, but for the titular Orthodox patriarch living in Constantinople; moreover, they prayed for the patriarch of Constantinople but did not commemorate the pope at all. It would appear from this that, in so far as Greeks held office in the church of Jerusalem, they did not give inward assent to the authority of Latin bishops, even though they were prepared to grant those bishops *de facto* recognition. Some hint of this feeling is conveyed by the story which Michael the Syrian tells, about how the Greeks of Jerusalem refused to attend the legatine synod convoked by Alberic of Ostia in 1141 at which doctrinal differences between Latins and Armenians and Jacobites were to be discussed, on the grounds that the Byzantine emperor was not present.[4] This story may not be literally true, since it was written from hearsay, and Michael was hostile to the Orthodox, but it accurately reflects the attitude

1. Fulcher of Chartres, III, 18, s 2, ed Hagenmeyer, p 665.
2. St Nerses of Lampron, 'Letter to Leo II', *RHC Arm*, I, p 596.
3. From a diptych written for the Sinai community around 1166, ed F.E. Brightman, C.E. Hammond, *Liturgies Eastern and Western*, I, Oxford 1896, p 501.
4. MS, XVI, 10, vol III, p 256.

which the Greek clergy among the Orthodox did hold. Their cultural links were entirely Byzantine, and they were aware of the growing hostility in the Byzantine church towards the Roman see, while, on a practical level, they had had the monopoly of high offices in the patriarchate of Jerusalem before the first crusade and had been deprived of most of them by the Franks. However well the Franks treated them, it was only natural that they should bear some resentment.

The mass of the Orthodox in the church of Jerusalem were Syrians who had seldom been bishops before the Franks came. It was probably a matter of indifference to them whether they prayed for the Latin patriarch of Jerusalem or the Orthodox claimant to that see. Nevertheless, they too experienced difficulties in identifying with the Latins, although for rather different reasons from their Greek brethren. The Syrian Christians spoke Arabic and, despite the difference of faith, shared strong cultural links with the Muslim world. These links did not remain theoretical after the Frankish conquest: Cahen has drawn attention to the case of Abu-l-Khayr, the son of a Christian physician, whose father became a monk at Jerusalem in the reign of king Amalric. Abu-l-Khayr taught Baldwin the leper to ride, but he also took a message from his father, a noted astrologer, to Saladin, assuring him that he would conquer Jerusalem. When Saladin did so, he not unnaturally increased the salaries of this family of Christian physicians.[1]   The Franks found such attitudes incomprehensible: to them all Muslims were enemies of the faith, and, indeed, they stood to lose everything if the Muslims conquered their territory.   But the Syrian Orthodox could see a great deal of difference between the barbarous Artukid Turks, from whose rule they had initially welcomed the crusaders as liberators, and the tolerant, civilised Aiyubids. They knew that they had little to lose if Saladin conquered the kingdom of Jerusalem, since they could see that, in the best tradition of early Islam, he treated his other Christian subjects well and in some ways had a greater understanding of them, though not of their faith, than had the alien Franks, who were members of the same church.

Thus when Saladin laid siege to Jerusalem in 1187 part of the Orthodox community plotted to open the gates of the city to him.[2]   This came as a great shock to the Franks, for the Orthodox community had hailed them as deliverers when they had first

1. C. Cahen, 'Indigènes et Croisés', Syria, 15, 1934, pp 351–60.
2. See the passage from an Arab history of the patriarchs of Alexandria cited in translation, RHC Occ, II, p 85, note a.

come there ninety years before,[1] and they had always treated the Orthodox well and assumed that this cordiality was reciprocated.

It could not be alleged in Jerusalem, as it could at Antioch, that Byzantine political intervention had preserved among the Orthodox community an awareness of their corporate identity. The Latin hierarchy in Jerusalem had made every effort to achieve a true union in a single church with the Orthodox faithful and they had failed, not because of differences in doctrine or usage, of which they were remarkably tolerant, but because of cultural differences which they were powerless to change. The Frankish legal system reinforced those differences and created a justified resentment among the Orthodox. An Orthodox Christian might only enjoy legal equality with the Franks if he became a Christian of the Latin rite. This was probably very difficult to achieve, since, unlike Muslims and separated eastern Christians, the Orthodox could not be received as converts into a church to which they already belonged. But even if this technical difficulty could be overcome it served only to emphasise the division between the Orthodox and the Franks, since the Orthodox could achieve equality only by renouncing their cultural heritage and by becoming assimilated to the Frankish ruling class. The cultural gulf between the Latin rulers and the mass of their Orthodox subjects proved unbridgeable.

1. Albert of Aix, V, 44, *RHC Occ*, IV, pp 461–2.

8. RELATIONS WITH THE SEPARATED EASTERN CHURCHES, 1098–1187

Although the Orthodox formed a majority among the native Christians in the kingdom of Jerusalem, they were a minority in the northern states, except in the coastal cities and in Antioch. Most of the native Christians of Antioch, Edessa and Tripoli belonged to churches which had become estranged from the Catholic church in east and west centuries before the first crusade.   The two confessions with the greatest number of adherents were the Jacobites and the Armenians.   The Latin clergy knew that members of these churches, and of other eastern churches with fewer members in their states, differed from the western church in matters of faith, not merely in rites and ceremonies, and that they therefore could not be considered members of the Catholic church.

In Antioch and Edessa, where Jacobites and Armenians formed an important section of the indigenous population, they were granted complete religious autonomy.   They owed political obedience to Frankish princes but they were not subject in any way to the authority of Latin bishops. This raised no administrative or legal problems, for the Jacobite patriarch and the Armenian catholicus lived in north Syria and could be approached by the Frankish rulers about any matters which might arise in connection with their communities. Since these religious leaders also exercised authority over the numerous members of their respective churches who lived under Muslim rule, the Latin princes were anxious to gain their support, and for that reason they treated their Armenian and Jacobite subjects with great tolerance.

The situation in the kingdom of Jerusalem was different: only small groups of Armenians and Jacobites lived there in some of the cities, and both confessions had bishops in Jerusalem. But the heads of these churches, who lived far away, could not easily be consulted about problems which arose in relation to their communities, and for this reason, it would seem, the Latins placed the Armenian and Jacobite congregations under the authority of the Latin patriarch of Jerusalem. John of Ibelin states that in the first kingdom the archbishops of the Armenians and the Jacobites in Jerusalem had both been reckoned among the suffragans of the

Latin patriarch.[1] He is, admittedly, a late source, but overall the
information which he gives about the institutions of the first kingdom is accurate and there is no reason to doubt the validity of
his evidence on this point. Nevertheless, the authority of the
Latin patriarch in regard to Armenians and Jacobites in the kingdom seems in practice to have been a legal technicality rather than
a religious reality. There is no instance, as will be shown later in
this chapter, of the effective exercise of such powers by the
patriarchs in the twelfth century: new Armenian and Jacobite
bishops were appointed by the catholicus and the Jacobite patriarch of Antioch respectively; when they took office there is no
evidence that they were required to take an oath of obedience to
the Latin patriarch, or to give him any profession of orthodox
belief; nor is there any instance of a Latin patriarch's intervening
in the internal administration of those churches. This suggests
that the legal enactment may date from an early period in the
history of the kingdom, when the Franks were still unfamiliar
with the problems posed by a diversity of confessions in one state
and adopted a pragmatic solution which in practice was not
enforced. The immunity from Latin control which the Jacobites
and Armenians enjoyed may well date from the reign of Baldwin
II, who had ruled Edessa for almost twenty years before coming
to Jerusalem, and was used to a settlement whereby the separated
eastern churches were treated as autonomous. In practice the
Armenians and Jacobites enjoyed virtual religious autonomy in
the first kingdom, even though technically they were subject to
the Latin patriarch.

Separated eastern Christians under Frankish rule were, like the
Orthodox, freed from the payment of the religious tax which the
Muslims had levied on them and, in so far as they were landowning, they were not required to pay tithe to the Latin church. They
kept their own cathedrals, churches and monasteries and their
church lands, and were allowed complete freedom in the practice
of their faith. The Franks did not try to coerce them into accepting Catholic definitions of faith, nor was any pressure put on them
to acknowledge the primacy of the Roman see. This policy differed so radically from that of the Byzantines, who had ruled much
of north Syria before the Seljuk invasions which had taken place
less than thirty years before the first crusade, that the bishops of
the separated churches viewed Frankish tolerance with astonish-
ment as well as with pleasure. Michael the Syrian, Jacobite
patriarch of Antioch, described how

---

1. John of Ibelin, 'Livre', c 261, *RHC Lois*, I, p 416.

> The Franks . . . who occupied Antioch and Jerusalem had . . . bishops
> in their states, and the bishops of our church lived among them without
> being persecuted . . .   The Franks never raised any difficulty about
> matters of doctrine, or tried to formulate it in one way only for
> Christians of differing race and language, but they accepted as a Christ-
> ian anybody who venerated the cross, without further examination.[1]

The Jacobites, over whom Michael ruled, were Syrian Monophysites who rejected the definition of the divine and human
natures of Christ formulated by the council of Chalcedon in 451.
They took their name from Jacob Baradaeus who, in the reign of
Justinian, had organised the Monophysites of Syria as a separate
church from that of the Orthodox, and their patriarchs claimed
to be the rightful successors of Severus whom Justin I had deposed
from Antioch in 518 on account of his Monophysitism. In the
Jacobite hierarchy Jerusalem was a metropólitan see of Antioch,
since the patriarchate of Jerusalem had only been established at
Chalcedon, which the Jacobites did not recognise. They formed
part of a single Monophysite communion with the Coptic church
of Egypt, organised under the Coptic patriarch of Alexandria,
which was very influential in the crusader period, since it had
many adherents in Egypt and its patriarch had ecclesiastical jurisdiction also over the Christian kingdoms of Nubia and Ethiopia.
The only distinction between the Jacobites and the Copts was in
the liturgical languages they used: the Jacobites worshipped in
Syriac and the Copts in Coptic.[2]

Although there was a Jacobite community in Jerusalem, and
others in some of the coastal cities of Palestine and the county of
Tripoli, the greatest numbers of Jacobites were found in north
Syria, in Antioch and Edessa, and in the Muslim lands to the east
and north of the Frankish states. In the twelfth century their
patriarch had some thirty-five suffragans under his jurisdiction,
many of whom lived under Muslim rule.[3]   The Jacobite urban
communities consisted of professional men, such as doctors,
traders, and artisans; most of the rural Jacobites were peasants.
They had lived under Muslim rule for centuries, with the consequence that there were no great landowners among them apart
from the abbots of some of the important monasteries, which
owned extensive estates.

---

1. MS, XVI, 1, vol III, p 222.
2. Brief surveys of Coptic and Jacobite history and belief in M. Jugie, 'Monophysite.
(Eglise Copte)', DTC, X (II), 2251–2306; I. Ziadé, 'Syrienne. (Eglise)', ibid., XIV (II),
3017–88.
3. This is the average of the consecration lists of Athanasius VII (1090–1129),
Athanasius VIII (1138–66) and Michael I (1167–99), ed Chabot, MS, vol III, pp
476–82.

The Franks in the northern states on the whole were on very good terms with them. They were united in their dislike of the Byzantines, whom the Franks regarded as political adversaries and the Jacobites as dangerous heretics; and the Jacobites witnessed the expulsion of Byzantine Greek bishops and their replacement by Latins with considerable satisfaction.[1] Although no doubt there was some intermarriage between Frankish burgesses and Jacobite townspeople, the Frankish nobility could not take Jacobite wives since there were no Jacobite families of equal social class. This might have proved divisive, but on the whole it helped in the maintenance of friendly relations between the new rulers and their Jacobite subjects since Jacobite laymen had no lands which the Franks considered worth expropriating.

The Jacobite patriarch was, however, very influential, since his authority was recognised in the lands of all the Muslim rulers of north Syria. It was therefore politically advantageous to the Franks to be on good terms with him, and, if possible, to persuade him to live in their territory. When the Franks first settled in Antioch the patriarch was Athanasius VII, who had been elected in 1090. He experienced no difficulty with the new Frankish rulers until, at some time in the regency of Roger of Antioch (1112–19), he excommunicated the Jacobite archbishop of Edessa. The archbishop complained to the Frankish rulers about the way in which he had been treated and they, no doubt, were anxious to settle religious differences among their Christian subjects as speedily as possible, so the patriarch Athanasius was summoned to attend a synod in Antioch cathedral at which the Latin patriarch, Bernard of Valence, presided. The Latin bishops and the Jacobites, who spoke Arabic, had no common language, so discussions had to be conducted through an interpreter. This led to misunderstandings, for when the patriarch Athanasius was asked why he refused to absolve the archbishop of Edessa and replied 'because of the injury he has done me', the interpreter translated this 'because of the money he owes me'. The Latin bishops were scandalised, supposing that this was evidence of simony, and placed the patriarch under house-arrest in one of the Jacobite churches of the city. Athanasius appealed to prince Roger and by making a judicious gift to him secured his release. The prince, it is said, reprimanded the Latin patriarch: 'It is not your business to judge Syrian Christians: you do not have authority in such matters'.[2] Certainly this was the only occasion in the twelfth century when an ecclesiastical case involving separated

1. *Ibid*., XVI, 2, vol III, pp 225–6.
2. *Ibid*., XV, 13, vol III, pp 207–10.

eastern Christians is known to have come before the Latin church courts.

Prince Roger had every right to be annoyed with the patriarch Bernard who by his ill-judged intervention had disturbed the position which the prince was trying to build up of being protector of the eastern Christian churches, a role which would give him some measure of influence in the lands of his Muslim enemies. But the harm had been done, and, despite his prompt release of Athanasius, the Jacobite patriarch felt that he had received an affront, withdrew to Diyar-Bakr in Muslim territory and placed the church of Edessa under an interdict.[1] He stayed at Diyar-Bakr for about ten years and only left because of a dispute with the Muslim governor. Athanasius had excommunicated a Jacobite layman in the city who was one of the governor's friends, and refused to absolve him even when the governor came in person to his monastery to beg him to do so. The governor therefore gave orders that he was not to be allowed to leave the monastery. Athanasius seems to have been a man of litigious and inflexible temperament, in some ways similar to the patriarch Fulcher of Jerusalem, who did not hesitate to antagonise secular rulers in what he considered was a righteous cause. Having fallen out with his Muslim protector he appealed to count Joscelin I of Edessa for help, which was given willingly since the Franks wished to be seen as the defenders of the Jacobite church against Islamic oppression. Joscelin threatened to make war on Diyar-Bakr unless Athanasius were released: the governor gave way, and in 1129 the patriarch went to live in the Jacobite monastery of Bar Sauma in the county of Edessa, where shortly afterwards he died, having ruled the Jacobite church for almost forty years.[2]

The synod which elected his successor met in Frankish territory at Kesoun and the man they chose was abbot of Dovair, a Jacobite monastery near Antioch. Count Joscelin not only offered his protection to the new patriarch, John XII, but also allowed him to be consecrated and enthroned in the Frankish church of Tell Bashir, a ceremony attended by the count of Edessa and his court. After his election the interdict on Edessa was at last lifted and the Jacobite churches were open once more. John worked in harmony with the Frankish rulers, spent much of his reign in their territory, and died in his own former monastery near Antioch in 1137.[3]

1. *Ibid.*, XV, 14, vol III, pp 212–13.
2. *Ibid.*, XVI, 3, vol III, p 228.
3. *Ibid.*, XVI, 4, 8, vol III, pp 231, 247.

It was not always possible for the Franks to assert control over the affairs of the Jacobite church, for it was large and many of its bishops lived under Muslim rule and preferred to have a patriarch who was acceptable to the Muslim authorities. Thus John XII's successor was enthroned at Diyar-Bakr chiefly through the influence of the eastern bishops living in Muslim states, and the governor of the city gave a great feast to the members of the synod, evidently wishing to vie with the Franks as a protector of Jacobites. The new patriarch, Athanasius VIII, was not, therefore, particularly friendly with the Franks, and count Joscelin II of Edessa took exception to the fact that he did not make a formal visit to the county immediately after his election.[1]   Athanasius succeeded in placating the count by agreeing to the translation of Basil, bishop of Kesoun, to the metropolitan see of Edessa when it fell vacant, at the count's request.[2]

Joscelin's judgment of character appeared to be justified when Zengi of Mosul attacked Edessa during the count's absence in 1144, for archbishop Basil, together with the Armenian bishop of the city, assisted archbishop Hugh in organising the defence.[3] When the city fell Basil was taken prisoner, and Zengi upbraided him with not handing over the city to the Muslims. Basil had the wit to reply that the atabeg should be pleased, since he had not broken the oath which he had sworn to the Franks and might therefore be expected to keep any oath which he swore to Zengi. Zengi was amused and restored him to power, but his luck did not hold good for long.[4]   When Joscelin II made an abortive attempt to retake the city in 1146 Basil sided with him and fled to western Edessa when the Muslims were victorious; but count Joscelin had not forgiven him for collaborating with Zengi in 1144 and imprisoned him for three years.[5]   This, though a political arrest, not an act of religious persecution, was quite at variance with normal Frankish treatment of Jacobite bishops, but it caused less resentment in the Jacobite community than a later act of Joscelin's. The count was in a difficult position: his territory was reduced to western Edessa and he was hard-pressed to defend it from neighbouring Muslim powers. His great need was money with which to hire troops, and in 1148 he sacked the great Jacobite monastery of Bar Sauma and held the relics of the saint to ransom.[6]   This can have done little to allay the anti-Frankish

1. *Ibid.*, XVI, 9, 10, vol III, pp 250–2, 256.
2. *Ibid.*, XVII, 1, vol III, pp 259–60.
3. *Anon 1234*, 'HC', c 411, p 90.
4. MS, XVII, 2, vol III, p 262.
5. *Ibid.*, XVII, 5, 6, vol III, pp 271, 277.
6. *Ibid.*, XVII, 9, 11, vol III, pp 283–7, 293.

sympathies of the patriarch Athanasius and, indeed, there was little political inducement for him to value a Frankish alliance. In 1151 western Edessa was overrun by the Muslims, and the armies of Nur-ad-Din, Zengi's son, defeated and slew prince Raymond of Antioch in 1149, and overran his lands east of the Orontes and most of the northern lands of the principality as well. In the space of seven years Frankish power in north Syria had been reduced to the control of the Amanus mountains and a narrow strip of coast west of the river Orontes.[1]   The greater part of the Jacobite church was once again under Muslim rule.

There were not many Jacobites in the kingdom of Jerusalem, but the Frankish rulers considered them very important because of their links with the Coptic church of Egypt, for the Fatimids of Egypt were, in the early years of the kingdom, its most powerful enemies.   The Jacobites had a cathedral at Jerusalem dedicated to St Mary Magdalen[2] and owned two estates near the Dead Sea. When the first crusade was known to be approaching Jerusalem the Jacobite community, under their archbishop Cyril, withdrew to Egypt: perhaps, like other Christian groups in the city, they had been expelled by the Fatimid governor so that they could not act in collusion with the crusade.[3]   The Franks, when they took over the city, gave the Jacobite estates as a fief to a knight called Geoffrey, but he was subsequently captured in battle by the Fatimids and imprisoned in Egypt. When Cyril died, at some time after 1103, the patriarch Athanasius VII consecrated a new archbishop for Jerusalem, Ignatius I, and lodged a complaint with Baldwin I that the estates of his church in Jerusalem had been confiscated.   Baldwin I restored them, and the new archbishop re-established the Jacobite community in Jerusalem, where he built a hospice for Jacobite pilgrims adjoining the cathedral. He also fortified the estates of the community, which were open to Muslim raiders, and established a priory of the Jerusalem monastery to administer them.[4]   Ignatius died in 1125, and the patriarch appointed as successor Ignatius II, who came from northern Syria.   His reign passed peacefully until, in 1137, Geoffrey, the Frankish knight to whom the Jacobite estates had originally been given, was released from prison by the Egyptian authorities. He returned to Jerusalem and was greeted with great acclaim as one of the few surviving comrades of Godfrey of Bouillon.   Not unnaturally he demanded his estates back, but queen Melisende

1. Cahen, *Syrie*, pp 368—89.
2. John of Würzburg, p 48.
3. Albert of Aix, V, 44, *RHC Occ*, IV, p 462.
4. Muslim raiding parties from Ascalon harried Judaea until the approach roads were blocked in king Fulk's reign, *ibid.*, XII, 33, pp 712—13.

intervened, and a compromise was reached whereby the Jacobites kept the estates but paid compensation to Geoffrey. This story, which has all the appearance of a popular romance, is recorded in the colophons of Jacobite breviaries written in 1138.[1] It is evidence of the importance in which the Jacobites were held by the crown of Jerusalem, for although queen Melisende, daughter of an Orthodox mother, may have had some sympathy with eastern-rite Christians, this factor was probably less decisive than the goodwill of the Jacobite community who had such strong links with Fatimid Egypt.

The Jacobites were not readmitted to the Holy Sepulchre: that was a privilege reserved among eastern-rite Christians to the Orthodox. They were allowed to have a chapel at the entrance to the new Latin cathedral but with access only from the outside of the church.[2] This was a compromise which absolved the Latins from any charge that they had admitted heretics to serve the shrine, while enabling Jacobite pilgrims to attend their own liturgy within the precincts of the Sepulchre. Queen Melisende's benevolence towards the Jacobite community was reciprocated by the patriarch, for when Ignatius II died, soon after the judgment, Athanasius VIII allowed Ignatius III, a member of the Jacobite community of Jerusalem, to succeed him.[3] The new Jacobite archbishop was, it would appear, a royal choice whom the patriarch confirmed, and he worked harmoniously with the Frankish rulers.

Whereas it was to the advantage of the small Jacobite community in Jerusalem to be on good terms with the Franks, it might have been supposed that once Frankish power had declined in north Syria there would have been no inducement for the Jacobite patriarchs to seek their friendship. Athanasius VIII, indeed, made no attempt to do so in his reign of almost thirty years, but when he died in 1166[4] the synod chose as his successor Michael, the abbot of the Bar Sauma monastery, which by that time, of course, was in Muslim territory. He is better known as Michael the Syrian, a distinguished historian, and the Jacobite equivalent of William of Tyre, whose contemporary he was. Michael did not live in Frankish territory: that would probably have caused too many pastoral difficulties, but fixed his see at Mardin.[5]

1. Paris, Bibliothèque Nationale, *Syrien* 51, f 117v, Bibliothèque de Lyons, *Syriaque* 1, f 3 v, ed J.P.P. Martin, 'Les premiers princes croisés et les Syriens jacobites de Jérusalem', *Journal Asiatique*, ser 8, 12, 1888, pp 471–90; 13, 1889, pp 33–79.
2. 'Eracles', Rothelin MS, c 4, *RHC Occ*, II, p 494.
3. MS, XVI, 9, vol III, p 252.
4. *Ibid.*, XVIII, 11, vol III, p 327.
5. *Ibid.*, XIX, 2, vol III, pp 329–31.

Nevertheless, he was very well disposed towards the Franks and towards the Latin church, and the Muslim authorities made no difficulties about his visiting his flock in Frankish territory whenever he wished.

In 1168 he made a pilgrimage to Jerusalem, where he presided over the Holy Week ceremonies in the Jacobite cathedral and was well received by the Latin patriarch, Amalric of Nesle.[1] His visit could scarcely have been better timed, and no doubt that is why Michael chose to go there when he did, for king Amalric had just gained the ascendancy in Egypt, the Fatimid vizir was tributary to him, and a Frankish resident had been established in Cairo.[2] A visit of the Jacobite patriarch of Antioch to the Frankish capital might have helped to commend king Amalric to the Copts of Egypt, who were an influential minority in the country.[3]

On leaving Jerusalem Michael went to Antioch where, it will be remembered, the Orthodox patriarch, Athanasius III, had been enthroned three years previously. Michael pointedly ignored the Orthodox patriarch and made an official visit instead to the evicted Latin patriarch, Aimery of Limoges, in his castle of Qusair. This assured him of a welcome there. But he was also well-received in the city of Antioch by the Frankish rulers and it was later claimed that he had been enthroned in St Peter's chair of Antioch, the first Monophysite to enjoy this honour since the deposition of Severus in 518.[4] There is every reason to believe this statement, although it is uncorroborated. The Latin patriarch was in no position to authorise such a thing, and the Orthodox patriarch would surely never have initiated it, but there was good reason for Bohemond III to insist upon it. Nur-ad-Din, ruler of Edessa, Aleppo and Damascus, was striving to gain control of Egypt, and if he were successful he would pose a severe threat to the continued existence of all the Frankish states in Syria. In 1168 Amalric was in the ascendant in the struggle for Egypt, but his continued success was as important to the Franks of Antioch as it was to those of Jerusalem. Therefore Bohemond III's reasons for treating the head of the Jacobite church with every courtesy were the same as those of king Amalric.[5]

1. *Ibid.*, XIX, 3, vol III, p 332.
2. M.W. Baldwin, 'The Latin States under Baldwin III and Amalric I', in Setton, I, pp 552–5.
3. I. Hrbek, 'Egypt, Nubia and the Eastern Desert', *Cambridge History of Africa*, III, p 23.
4. *Anon. 1234*, 'HE', p 230. Michael, perhaps from modesty, does not say this of himself, MS, XIX, 3, vol III, p 332.
5. Nur-ad-Din's power was not in doubt. He had destroyed the confederate Christian armies of north Syria in 1164 and only the fear of Byzantine intervention deterred him from attacking the city of Antioch.

Michael stayed in Antioch for almost a year and kept Easter with the Jacobite community there in 1169.[1] During this time he became involved in discussions with the Orthodox about matters of faith. The emperor Manuel was anxious to restore unity between the Orthodox church and the separated churches of north Syria, and had, some years earlier, initiated a correspondence on this with the Armenian church. If, while an Orthodox patriarch ruled over the church of Antioch, the Armenians and Jacobites could be persuaded to enter into communion with the Orthodox, the emperor's position as protector of all the Christians living in north Syria would greatly enhance his political power in that area, among the Muslims as well as the Franks. Michael entered into correspondence with Manuel about this while he was staying at Antioch, and subsequently sent representatives to the meetings held between the Orthodox and the Armenians in 1170 and 1172 at which the emperor was represented by the theologian Theorianus. On the second occasion Michael's envoy was his pupil, Theodore Bar Wahboun, who is said by Jacobite writers to have been so well-versed in Greek philosophy that he succeeded in demolishing the philosophical arguments which Theorianus had advanced in support of Orthodox doctrine, so that the imperial representative lost his temper and exclaimed: 'What have the teachings of the heathen Aristotle to do with us?' The Jacobites, unlike some of the Armenians, were drawn no closer to Constantinople as a result of these discussions, and, although Manuel wrote to Michael asking him to come to the imperial capital and discuss plans for union in person, the patriarch refused and sent a stiff, formal answer:

> We greatly desire . . . union with all those who do not deviate from the faith of the fathers and, like Athanasius and Cyril, we confess one nature in the incarnate Word.[2]

This marked the effective end of negotiations.

Michael's oecumenical sympathies lay primarily with the Latins. In 1178 he visited Antioch again: Aimery of Limoges was once more in power and he invited Michael to attend the third Lateran council, which had been summoned to meet in Rome in the following Lent. So far as is known the Jacobite patriarch was the only eastern-rite church leader from the Crusader States to receive such an invitation. He declined to be represented there, but when he discovered that the Cathar heresy was one of the

1. MS, XIX, 3, vol III, p 332.
2. Bar Hebraeus, *Chronicon Ecclesiasticum*, ed with Latin trans J.B. Abbeloos, T.J. Lamy, 2 vols, Louvain 1872–7, 550–60.

items on the council's agenda he wrote a treatise setting out the teachings of the fathers on this subject for the consideration of the council.[1]   It is a matter of regret that this text has never been discovered. It is, perhaps, a sign of Michael's great regard for the Franks that when the Jacobite archbishop of Jerusalem, Ignatius III, died in 1185 after holding the see for forty-five years, Michael appointed his own brother, Athanasius, to succeed him.[2]

Michael's last years were clouded by the intrigues of his former pupil, Theodore Bar Wahboun. Theodore was a learned man, who spoke Greek, Armenian, Syriac and Arabic,[3] and was both eloquent and persuasive. He was also extremely ambitious and sought to displace Michael as head of the Jacobite church. Having been excommunicated by the patriarch, he went to Jerusalem shortly after 1185, where he approached the Latin patriarch, Heraclius, and promised that he would secure the reunion of the Jacobite church with Rome if he were recognised as lawful patriarch. He was naturally opposed by Michael's brother, archbishop Athanasius, and, it would seem, successfully, in so far as he did not secure control of the Jacobite cathedral there. After Saladin's conquest Bar Wahboun left the city (his extreme pro-Frankish policies would have had little appeal to the sultan) and went to north Syria where he opened negotiations with the Armenian authorities, promising them too that he would, if recognised as patriarch, promote unity between their church and his. Leo II of Cilicia had him proclaimed as patriarch, but nothing came of this scheme since Bar Wahboun died shortly afterwards, an event which the Jacobites ascribed to the intervention of St Bar Sauma.[4]

Michael was still patriarch when Saladin overran the greater part of Frankish territory. His brother Athanasius left Jerusalem, perhaps being required to do so by the sultan on account of his Frankish sympathies, and retired to north Syria where Michael appointed him his vicar in the city of Antioch, a post which he held until his death in 1192–3.[5] The goodwill which the Jacobite patriarch felt for the Franks was not based solely on a desire for their protection, for it persisted until the end of his life and it was clear by then that they were not able to adopt an offensive policy towards Islam.

This goodwill was rooted rather in experience. The Franks and the Jacobites were willing to extend a limited *de facto* recognition to each other's churches without seeking to establish full religious

1. MS, XX, 7, vol III, pp 377–8.
2. *Ibid.*, XXI, 3, vol III, p 394.
3. Bar Hebraeus, *Chron. Ecc.*, 582–4.
4. MS, XXI, 1, vol III, pp 386–7.
5. *Ibid.*, XXI, 7, 8, vol III, pp 409, 411–12.

unity. Thus, when Edessa was placed under an interdict by Athanasius VII and the Jacobite churches of the city remained closed for years, the Jacobites had their children baptised by Latin priests and the Latin clergy raised no difficulty about this.[1] Later, in 1134, when north Syria was attacked by a plague of locusts, the relics of the Jacobite saint, Bar Sauma, were brought to Edessa and venerated in the Latin cathedral by a mixed congregation of Franks and Jacobites.[2]   In 1156 a Frankish nobleman at Antioch built a new Jacobite church in the city, whose consecration was attended not only by the leaders of the Jacobite community but also by members of the Frankish court;[3] and when count Joscelin II of Edessa was dying in prison at Aleppo in 1159 he received the last rites from the Jacobite bishop of the city.[4]

Neither the Jacobites nor the Latins took any of these expressions of mutual esteem as implying that their two churches were in full communion. Indeed, the question of church unity was only raised on one occasion in the twelfth century, when Alberic, bishop of Ostia, invited the Jacobite archbishop of Jerusalem to attend a legatine synod at which the Armenians were also represented. Archbishop Ignatius produced a written profession of faith, which the synod examined and, according to Michael the Syrian, who is our only source for this, but not an unprejudiced one, pronounced completely orthodox.[5] No attempt was made to follow up these negotiations by trying to procure the submission of the Jacobite church to Rome, perhaps because the Frankish authorities had the sense to realise that the Jacobite patriarch, living under Muslim rule, would not be free to accept such terms even had he wished to do so. The wisdom of the tolerant policy of non-intervention which the Frankish rulers and the Latin bishops in Syria adopted towards the Jacobites was proved after 1187 when the Jacobites continued to show sympathy towards the Franks even though they were on the losing side.

Frankish relations with the other large group of separated Christians, the Armenians, were more complex. The Armenians had originally lived in Great Armenia[6] in the Caucasus, where they had had independent kingdoms. They had been converted to

1. *Ibid.*, XV, 14, vol III, pp 212–13.
2. *Ibid.*, XVI, 6, vol III, pp 238–9; Bar Hebraeus, *Chronography*, I, pp 257–8.
3. MS, XVII, 13, vol III, pp 303–4.
4. *Ibid.*, XVII, 11, vol III, p 295.
5. *Ibid.*, XVI, 10, vol III, pp 255–6.
6. I wish to thank Mr Edward Gulbekian for explaining that the correct translation of *Meds Hayq* is Great Armenia, not Greater Armenia, as is often used by western scholars.

Christianity in the early fourth century and had subsequently adopted a vernacular liturgy. The head of their church was styled the catholicus, and this office had, with rare exceptions, remained in the control of members of the family of St Gregory the Illuminator, apostle of Armenia, until the time of the crusades. Like the Copts and the Jacobites, the Armenians did not accept the authority of the council of Chalcedon at which they had not been represented, and for that reason they were often considered Monophysites, although they have never been in full communion with any of the Monophysite churches; but they were not in communion with the Orthodox either, and they formed a separate church with their own hierarchy, liturgy and canon law.[1]

Armenian colonies had long been settled in many of the cities of the Byzantine empire, but, as a result first of the Byzantine annexation of the Armenian kingdoms in the early eleventh century and subsequently of the Seljuk invasions of Great Armenia, there was a large-scale Armenian immigration from the fatherland to south-east Asia Minor and to north Syria in the period preceding the first crusade. Armenian princes were able to take advantage of the political chaos there, much as the crusaders were later to do, in order to establish independent Armenian states. The crusaders indeed received great help from these independent Christian rulers, of whom the most notable were Oshin of Lampron, who ruled in the western Taurus, Constantine the Roupenid, who ruled in the eastern Taurus, Gabriel of Melitene, Kogh Vasil, lord of Raban, and Thoros of Edessa, since they controlled the passes through the Taurus and Anti-Taurus mountains which guarded the approach roads to Antioch.[2] The catholicus of Armenia, Gregory II Vahram, had accompanied the princes into exile after the Seljuk invasions but had no fixed see.[3]

It was, perhaps, inevitable that the Franks should have sought to gain control of territory from the Armenian princes. At first they were highly successful in this: Baldwin of Boulogne took over the government of Edessa from the unpopular Armenian ruler, Thoros, in 1098;[4] the Norman princes of Antioch annexed the coastal plain of Cilicia, even though the Turks had been driven out with Armenian help;[5] and in 1115 Baldwin II of

1. M. Ormanian, *The Church of Armenia*, London 1955.

2. Der Nersessian, in Setton, II, pp 630—5.

3. The sultan Alp Arslan took Ani, traditional see of the Armenian catholicus, in 1065, the year of Gregory II's election.

4. Hagenmeyer, *Chronologie*, pp 137, 139—40, nos 246—7, 249, lists the sources.

5. Oshin of Lampron helped Tancred capture Adana, Ralph of Caen, cc 39—40, *RHC Occ*, III, pp 634—6. Runciman, *Crusades*, I, pp 199—200.

Edessa annexed Raban.[1]   The Franks did not attempt to drive the Armenian princes from their mountain strongholds in the Taurus, however, and in 1132 Leo I, the Roupenid, seized the province of Cilicia from the Franks, thereby creating what was later to become the Cilician Kingdom, sometimes called Lesser Armenia. Frankish rapacity for territory was bitterly resented by the Armenians, as is clear from the writings of Matthew of Edessa and from the funeral oration preached by the Armenian Basil over Baldwin, count of Marash.[2]

Despite this, relations between the Frankish rulers and Latin bishops and the Armenian church were on the whole good. Large numbers of Armenians lived in the Frankish territories of north Syria and Armenian communities were also found in some of the cities of the southern kingdom, including Jerusalem, where the Armenians had an archbishop. Unlike the Jacobites, the Armenians made no claim to the patriarchal throne of Antioch, although they had a bishop for members of their communion in that city, who lived in an Armenian monastery in the Black Mountain.[3] There were sound political reasons why the Frankish government should have treated the Armenian church well, for the catholicus was head of a large diaspora, much of which still lived in Great Armenia and in regions of north Syria under Muslim rule, but part of which lived in the Byzantine empire with which the princes of Antioch were intermittently at war. The goodwill of the head of the Armenian church was therefore potentially an asset in Frankish diplomacy. But another, quite different, factor which conditioned Frankish attitudes to the Armenian church was that the Armenians were the only native Christians in Syria who possessed a nobility with whom the Frankish aristocracy could intermarry. Such marriages were frequent, and by the middle of the twelfth century there were few noble families in Antioch and Edessa who did not have some Armenian blood,[4] and who, therefore, while remaining Latin Christians themselves, did not feel some measure of sympathy and respect for the Armenian church.

The Armenians, like other Christian subjects of the Franks, were granted religious freedom under their own hierarchy. In Jerusalem they had their own cathedral of St James, with an attached hospice, and although they, like the Jacobites, were not

---

1. *Ibid.*, II, pp 129–30.
2. Matthew of Edessa, *RHC Arm*, I, pp 117–18; Basil, 'Funeral Oration for Baldwin, count of Marash and Kesoun', *ibid.*, I, pp 204–22.
3. He lived in the monastery of the Jesuéens, *ibid.*, I, p 112, n 2.
4. W.H. Rüdt-Collenberg, *The Rupenides, Hethumides and Lusignans: the structure of the Armeno-Cilician dynasties*, Paris 1963.

readmitted to the church of the Holy Sepulchre by the Latins, they were allowed a chapel in the courtyard of the new Latin basilica.[1]   The Franks not merely tolerated the Armenians, they also acted as benefactors of their church, and when Basil I of Ani, the coadjutor of the aged catholicus Gregory, visited Edessa in 1103 count Baldwin II gave considerable endowments to him for the use of his church.[2]   Indeed, the only example in the twelfth century of Frankish ill-treatment of an Armenian church-man occurred in 1108 when Baldwin of Edessa arrested the Armenian archbishop of the city on a charge of treason and threatened to blind him. This was a political, not an ecclesiastical quarrel, and in any case the threat was not carried out because the Armenian community of Edessa paid the count a large indemnity to secure the archbishop's release.[3]

The goodwill which existed between Franks and Armenian churchmen was by no means one-sided. The Armenian church had a great reverence for the see of Rome, for they believed that St Gregory the Illuminator had made a pact with St Sylvester of Rome, thus creating a special bond between their two churches.[4] This sentiment remained strong in the twelfth century. When the catholicus, St Nerses the Gracious, wrote an *Elegy on the Fall of Edessa*, he addressed the Roman Church in these words:

> O Rome, magnificent and revered mother of cities; see of the great St Peter, chief of the Apostles; church which cannot be moved, built on the rock of Cephas, against which the gates of hell will never prevail . . . [5]

On a practical level the Armenian clergy were prepared to co-operate fully with the Frankish rulers. The Armenian bishops of Antioch and Marash accompanied Bohemond on his campaign against the Danishmendids who were attacking Melitene in 1100, and both lost their lives in the ensuing battle;[6] and the Armenian archbishop of Edessa gave his full support to the Franks when Zengi attacked the city in 1144.[7] It might be argued with some

---

1. The cathedral was built in the twelfth century with the help of craftsmen trained in the western tradition. It is recorded c 1170 by John of Würzburg, p 45. K. Hintlian, *History of the Armenians in the Holy Land*, Jerusalem 1976, pp 51–6; T.S.R. Boase, 'Ecclesiastical Art in the Crusader States in Palestine and Syria', in Setton, IV, pp 94–5. Theoderich, p 21, notes the Armenian chapel near Calvary.

2. Matthew of Edessa, *RHC Arm*, I, pp 70–71.

3. *Ibid.*, p 88.

4. E.g. Guiragos of Kantzag, 'History of Armenia', with French trans, *RHC Arm*, I, p 417.   F. Tournebize, *Histoire politique et religieuse de l'Arménie depuis les origines des Arméniens jusqu'à la mort de leur dernier roi*, Paris 1910, pp 54–6.

5. *RHC Arm*, I, p 228.

6. Matthew of Edessa, *RHC Arm*, I, p 52.

7. *Anon. 1234*, 'HC', cc 411, 432, pp 90, 110.

truth that in both these instances the Armenians were motivated in some part by self-interest, but the same cannot be said of the fact that the Armenian authorities allowed Latin bishops to retain their sees after they conquered Cilicia from the Franks in 1132.[1] Despite political acrimony there was no ill-will between Armenian and Latin churchmen.

At the beginning of the reign of the catholicus Gregory III in 1113, David, bishop of Agthamar, set himself up as rival catholicus and received a considerable following in the province of Vaspurakan, but Gregory's authority remained paramount throughout the rest of the Armenian church and the schism did not seriously weaken his position.[2] The Franks made no attempt to bring the Armenians into communion with the Latin church until 1141, when Alberic, cardinal of Ostia and papal legate in Syria, convoked a synod at Jerusalem which was attended by the catholicus, Gregory III. Different accounts of why he was present are given in the sources. According to Michael the Syrian, the Orthodox of Antioch had accused the Jacobites and Armenians of heresy when the legate visited the city, and he had therefore summoned them to the synod at which Jacobite orthodoxy was vindicated but that of the Armenians left in doubt.[3] Michael, however, is a prejudiced source in regard to Armenian affairs, since the Armenian church had recognised his rival, Bar Wahboun, as Jacobite patriarch, and he tends to represent them in an unfavourable light. According to Armenian writers, of whom the earliest is Samuel of Ani, Gregory happened to be in Jerusalem when the synod was held and was invited to attend as a matter of courtesy.[4] It seems possible, however, that John Comnenus's annexation of Cilicia in 1137 and his threat to the independence of Latin Antioch had led the Armenians and the Franks to seek a *rapprochement.*

The legate could have been quite well informed about Armenian beliefs because of the correspondence between pope Gregory VII and the catholicus Gregory II which existed in the papal registers. In 1080 Gregory II had sent the priest John to the papal court to ask Gregory VII's help in dealing with an Armenian named Macharus who had been condemned for heresy by the Armenian church and had sought refuge in south Italy. Pope Gregory was willing to co-operate in this matter; he also examined the priest

1. They were only evicted when John Comnenus campaigned there. Odo of Deuil, *De Profectione Ludovici VII*, p 68.

2. Tournebize, *op. cit.*, pp 235–6.

3. MS, XVI, 10, vol III, pp 255–6.

4. Samuel of Ani, 'Chronography', extracts with French trans, *RHC Arm*, I, pp 449–50; Sempad the Constable, 'Chronicle of the Kingdom of Little Armenia', with French trans, *ibid.*, I, p 618; Guiragos of Kantzag, *ibid.*, I, pp 417–18.

John and found that his opinions were orthodox, but he had grave reservations about the general orthodoxy of the Armenian church. In his reply to the catholicus he reported that he had heard that the Armenians did not receive the fourth general council of the church; that they recited the phrase 'who was crucified for us' in the *Trisagion*; that they venerated the heresiarch Dionysius as a saint; that they substituted butter for balsam in the holy oils and celebrated Mass with an unmixed chalice. The pope asked the catholicus to send him a written profession of faith and to reform the faith and practice of his church in those points in which it differed from Catholic orthodoxy, if, as he had been informed, it did.[1]   So far as is known the catholicus did not reply to this letter, but issues of this kind must have been in the mind of the pope's legate at the synod of 1141.

Reports about the outcome of the synod are as divergent as the reasons given for the Armenian presence at it. Samuel of Ani reports that the catholicus made a profession of faith which the Latins accepted as orthodox;[2] whereas Michael the Syrian relates that when asked whether they had any mental reservations about the written profession they had submitted the Armenians refused to answer, thus indicating that they were concealing the truth about their beliefs.[3]   Perhaps the most trustworthy evidence is that of William of Tyre, who must have seen the *acta* of the synod: he relates that the catholicus promised to amend many of the matters in which his church differed from Catholic norms.[4]

The conference was, whatever its outcome, clearly most amicable. Guiragos of Kantzag, a thirteenth-century Armenian writer, described it as a renewal of the pact between SS. Gregory and Sylvester; while William of Tyre speaks of the catholicus as 'a distinguished theologian'.[5]   No pressure was put on the Armenians by the Latin church after this time to implement any changes in discipline or doctrine, or to enter into communion with the Roman see.   The Armenians, however, looked on Rome as a possible ally against the Orthodox bishops who had been established in Cilicia by the Byzantine government in 1137.   In 1145 the catholicus sent envoys to pope Eugenius III asking him to arbitrate between the Armenians and the Orthodox about the correct way of celebrating the Eucharist and the date at which Christmas should be kept.   The pope received them courteously and invited them to attend a papal high Mass to see for themselves

1. Caspar, *Das Register Gregors VII*, VII, 28, VIII, 1, vol II, pp 509–14.
2. Samuel of Ani, *RHC Arm*, I, p 450.
3. MS, XVI, 10, vol III, p 256.
4. WT, XV, 19, *RHC Occ*, I, p 687.
5. Guiragos of Kantzag, *RHC Arm*, I, p 418; WT, XV, 19, *RHC Occ*, I, p 687.

how the liturgy should be performed.[1]

Gregory III, while being on cordial terms with the Latin church, had no wish to be subordinate to the Latins or the Orthodox. He had no permanent see, but about 1150 he obtained the gift of the castle of Hromgla on the upper Euphrates from Beatrice, wife of count Joscelin of Edessa who was a Muslim prisoner at the time.[2] Although this area passed under Muslim rule a year later, Hromgla remained the headquarters of the catholici for the rest of the crusading period, presumably because it afforded them a greater measure of independence than they would have enjoyed had they lived under the protection of an Armenian prince.

Gregory III ruled the Armenian church for fifty-three years and died in 1166. During the reign of his successor, St Nerses IV, the Gracious (1166–73), and the early years of the next catholicus, Gregory IV (1173–93), the Roupenid princes evicted Byzantine garrisons from Cilicia and definitively ended Byzantine rule there.[3]   From 1172/3 until 1375 Cilicia was an independent Armenian state. Yet it was in this period of political hostility that union was almost achieved between the Armenian church and the Orthodox church. This was due to the initiative of the emperor Manuel, the effects of which on the Jacobite community have already been noted. Manuel entered into negotiation with St Nerses about this soon after his elevation, and conferences were subsequently held between the Byzantines and the Armenians. At the second of these in 1172 the Byzantine negotiator, Theorianus, submitted a nine-point plan of reform for the Armenian church, which St Nerses undertook to place before the synod of his church, but he died in 1173 before it had been convened. His successor and nephew, Gregory IV, continued the negotiations, and in 1179 the synod of Hromgla, under his presidency, asserted the adhesion of the Armenian church to Chalcedonian orthodoxy. Manuel Comnenus, who had been the principal Byzantine proponent of this scheme for unity, died in 1180 before the decisions of the synod of Hromgla had been considered by the Byzantine church, and further negotiations were suspended because of the political unrest which occurred in the empire in the next few years.[4] Had Manuel's plan succeeded, the Latin church, at least in north Syria, would have found itself very isolated from the bulk of the native Christian subjects, and this was, no doubt, part of

1. Otto of Freising, 'Chronica', VII, 32, pp 360–3. Otto wrongly supposed that the Armenians used leavened bread at Mass like the Greeks.
2. Sempad the Constable, *RHC Arm*, I, p 618; Guiragos of Kantzag, *ibid.*, I, p 415.
3. Der Nersessian, in Setton, II, pp 642–3.
4. P. Tekeyan, 'Controverses Christologiques en Arméno-Cilicie dans la seconde moitié du XIIe siècle (1165–98)', *OCA*, 124, 1939, pp 14–42.

Manuel's intention.

The collapse of Byzantine military power following the death of Manuel marked the effective end of Byzantine political intervention in north Syria, but the growing power of Saladin posed an equal threat to the continued existence both of the Frankish and of the Armenian states. It was clear to all the Christian rulers of Syria that military aid could only come from western Europe, and it seems probable that Roupen III of Cilicia urged the catholicus to form closer links with Rome. In 1184 Gregory IV sent an Armenian bishop to pope Lucius III with a profession of faith. This has not been preserved, but the pope's answer is known in the Armenian translation made by St Nerses of Lampron. The pope sent the catholicus a *pallium* and a copy of the *Rituale Romanum*, which St Nerses also translated.[1] The pope evidently understood the catholicus's letter to be an act of submission to the Roman see, and his conferring of the *pallium* on Gregory shows that he was recognising that the Armenian church had come into full communion with Rome, while the gift of the *Rituale* was intended to enable the Armenians to correct their usages in conformity with Catholic practice.

One immediate consequence of these negotiations was that Lucius III ordered the Armenian clergy of the diocese of Valania, who had no bishop of their own, to obey the Latin bishop, and placed them on an equal footing with the Orthodox in that diocese. This instruction was repeated by pope Urban III (1185–7) and again in 1225 by Honorius III.[2] This represented a change from earlier papal policy: those Armenian congregations could now properly be placed under the authority of a Latin bishop since it was assumed that they had entered into union with the Catholic church.

It seems doubtful in the light of subsequent events, which may more conveniently be considered in a later chapter, whether the Armenian hierarchy themselves understood the negotiations with Lucius III in the same way as the pope did. The Armenians customarily used flamboyant language when speaking of the Roman see, but by their embassy to pope Lucius they had probably intended no more than a renewal of the pact between St Gregory and St Sylvester. The conquests of Saladin, which followed very soon after this exchange, diverted the attention of both sides from the question of church unity to the more urgent matter of political survival.

Contacts between the Armenians and the Franks in the twelfth

---

1. *CICO*, I, pp 811–13, no 395; cf. Hamilton, *ECR*, 10, 1978, p 69.
2. *CICO*, III, pp 178–80, no 132.

century had led to a growth of mutual esteem for each other's religious traditions. The favourable impression which the catholicus Gregory III made on the Franks has already been noted, and St Nerses of Lampron is eloquent about the virtues of the Latin church, though not uncritical of it. Writing about the institutions of the church in 1177 he said of the Latins:

> We cannot compete at all with their piety, their charitable works, their zealous regard for canon law, the regularity with which they publicly celebrate the Divine Office.[1]

This mutual respect formed a good basis for the growth of true religious unity, but it was an experience which only a fraction of the Armenian hierarchy shared, since the majority of bishops and abbots continued to live in Great Armenia under Muslim rule and had no contact with the Latin church at all. Yet their assent was essential before any valid union could be entered into with the Latin church.

Jacobites and Armenians were found in the greatest numbers in Antioch and Edessa. The principal native Christian group in the county of Tripoli were the Maronites. The Maronites appear to take their name from the monastery of St Maro near Apamea, which had originally been their spiritual centre, and to have become separated from the Orthodox church by adopting the doctrine of Monotheletism in the seventh century, which was condemned as heretical by the sixth general council of Constantinople in 680. As a result of the Qarmatian invasions of the early tenth century they had been displaced from their original homes and had come to live in the Lebanon mountains.[2] William of Tyre estimates their numbers at some 40,000 and says that in the twelfth century they were to be found in the Latin bishoprics of Gibelet and Tripoli.[3] They were not in communion with any other Christian confession, but were organised under their own patriarch and bishops.

The Maronites came down from their mountains in 1099 and consulted with the leaders of the first crusade about the best route to take on their march to the south.[4] The Franks always liked them for, unlike the Orthodox and the Jacobites who had never been allowed to bear arms under Muslim rule, the Maronites had always retained a measure of independence, not unlike that of the Christians of Montenegro in the Ottoman empire. William of Tyre

1. *RHC Arm*, I, p 574.
2. P. Dib, 'Maronites', *DTC*, X (I), 1–142; C. Frazee, 'The Maronite Middle Ages', *ECR*, 10, 1978, pp 88–100.
3. WT, XXII, 8, *RHC Occ*, I, p 1076.
4. *Ibid.*, VII, 21, p 310.

describes them as 'fine warriors, who proved most useful to our
men in the major battles which they regularly had with the
enemy'.[1]   Like all native Christians the Maronites were granted
religious autonomy by the Franks under their own patriarch and,
although they were not admitted to the Holy Sepulchre, they had
a chapel for the use of pilgrims in Jerusalem.[2]

About 1181 Aimery of Limoges, Latin patriarch of Antioch,
persuaded the Maronite community to enter into full religious
union with Rome.[3]   It is not known how these negotiations were
conducted, or, indeed, why they were initiated. It is possible that
the threat of Saladin drew the Maronites closer to the Latins just
as it had the Armenians. William of Tyre relates that they abjured
their error, by which he presumably means Monotheletism, and
'were prepared to receive and reverently to observe the traditions
of the Roman church'.   The Maronites thus became the first
uniate church, preserving their own rites, ceremonies and canon
law in so far as these were compatible with Catholic tradition,
living under the authority of their own patriarch and bishops without the intervention of the Latin hierarchy, and having no other
religious superior but the pope.   Owing to the political upheavals
which occurred in Lebanon a few years after this settlement had
been reached, its full details were not worked out until the early
thirteenth century, but the Maronite union was a vindication of
Frankish tolerance, for, without any pressure, the Franks had
succeeded in reconciling to the Roman church a considerable
group of eastern Christians who had been living in complete
isolation from other Christian communities for five centuries.
As Salibi has shown, the union did not at this stage command
the support of all Maronites, and a substantial group, particularly
among those living in the Lebanon mountains, remained hostile
to it.[4]

In Jerusalem there were many other confessions which owned
churches and chapels.   The Latin kings granted religious toleration to them all, but this was like extending official recognition
to an ecclesiastical diplomatic corps, since most of these groups
had few or no adherents in the rest of the Frankish east and were
present merely to cater for the needs of pilgrims of their own faith
who visited the holy places.   The German traveller, John of

1. *Ibid.*, XXII, 8, p 1077.
2. John of Würzburg, p 69.
3. WT, XXII, 8, *RHC Occ*, I, pp 1076–7; R.W. Crawford, 'William of Tyre and the
Maronites', *Speculum*, 30, 1955, pp 222–8. The evidence for an earlier union c 1140 is
tenuous, K.S. Salibi, 'The Maronite Church in the Middle Ages and its Union with
Rome', *Oriens Christianus*, 42, 1958, p 94.
4. For opposition to the union, *ibid.*, p 95.

Würzburg, who visited Jerusalem in king Amalric's reign, states that among those who had churches there were Egyptian Copts, *Capheturici*,[1] Nestorians, and Indian Christians.[2]

Except in liturgy the Egyptian Copts did not differ from the Jacobites, and any members of those confessions who lived elsewhere in the Crusader States would have been subject to the authority of Jacobite bishops.[3]   Their chapel in Jerusalem must have existed by courtesy of the Jacobite archbishop to perform the liturgy in a familiar tongue for pilgrims from the Fatimid empire.   The Indian Christians to whom John of Würzburg refers were representatives of the church of the Malabar, some-times called St Thomas's Christians, who in the twelfth century recognised the authority of the Nestorian patriarch.[4]   The Nestorian church was quite separate from any of the other eastern-rite communities. Its original members had refused to accept the authority of the third general council of Ephesus in 431 and had mostly gone to live in the Persian empire, where they had as their head the patriarch of Seleucia-Ctesiphon. Like the Jacobites they had a Syriac liturgy, but the similarity ended there: the two confessions were bitterly divided on Christological issues and viewed each other with grave mistrust. The Nestorian church had survived the Islamic invasions and had grown to be the greatest Christian communion in Asia, with dioceses in Mesopotamia, Persia, central Asia, India and even China.[5]

Apart from their representatives in Jerusalem, the Nestorians appear to have had few adherents in the Frankish states in the twelfth century, although Burchard of Mount Sion, writing in the later thirteenth century, reports that there were Nestorians in the city of Tripoli and the Lebanon.[6]   They may have been there a hundred years earlier, but it is possible that they came there as a result of the major shifts of population brought about in the near east as a result of the Mongol invasions. The Franks took little interest in the Nestorians, perhaps rather less than was advisable

---

1. Not, as their position in the list might suggest, Ethiopians. A.D.V. den Brincken, *Die 'Nationes Christianorum Orientalium' im Verständnis der lateinischen Historio-graphie*, Cologne, Vienna 1973, pp 349–50, concludes that all that can be said of them with certainty is that they were neither Ethiopians nor Chalcedonians.

2. John of Würzburg, p 69.

3. See n 2, p 190 above.

4. E. Tisserant, *Eastern Christianity in India*, London 1957, pp 11–18.

5. E. Tisserant, E. Amann, 'Nestorius. 2. L'Eglise Nestorienne', *DTC*, XI (I), 157 *seq*.

6. Burchard of Mount Sion, pp 16, 26. James of Vitry found some Nestorians at Acre in 1216, *Lettres*, p 85, no 2. Oliver of Paderborn reports them at Antioch c 1221, 'Historia Damiatina', c 66, ed H. Hoogeweg, *Die Schriften des Kölner Domscholasters späteren Bischofs von Paderborn und Kardinalbischofs von S. Sabina, Oliverus, Biblio-thek des literarischen Vereins in Stuttgart*, vol 202, Tübingen 1894, p 266.

given the very influential position which that confession occupied in the lands of eastern Islam. Occasional pieces of news, probably relayed by Nestorian merchants trading with the Frankish states of north Syria, would attract the attention of the Franks. The Latin bishop of Jabala, for example, told the German historian, Otto of Freising, whom he met at the papal court in 1145, about the activities of Prester John in Persia, an account which seems to be based on rumours of the invasion of the Islamic lands beyond the Oxus by the Kara-Khitai, a people who had Nestorian Christians among their subjects.[1] But beyond satisfying their curiosity about what was happening in the unknown world of further Asia, the Franks seem to have made no use of the diplomatic opportunities which contact with the great Nestorian church of Asia afforded them.

The Frankish rulers were principally concerned to find a *modus vivendi* with their native Christian subjects who made up a substantial part of the rural labour-force in some parts of their dominions, and formed an important part of the urban population in almost all of their states.   Whereas their relations with the Orthodox were far from satisfactory, they were, on the whole, on good terms with the members of the separated eastern churches. This was also true of the Latin clergy. Some of the Latin bishops in the twelfth century were not well instructed in the finer points of Christological definition which divided the separated eastern churches from Catholic unity, but this was by no means true of all of them.   William of Tyre clearly knew a good deal about the beliefs of eastern Christians, and the same was true of Aimery of Limoges, despite William's comments about his general ignorance. Such men were, however, anxious to avoid theological controversy which might weaken the Frankish states, although they were more than willing to discuss plans for church unity which, conversely, would strengthen both those states and the Catholic church.   They therefore accepted that the separated eastern churches should enjoy virtual religious autonomy, and, in the case of the Latin patriarchs of Jerusalem, they did not seek to enforce the jurisdictional powers over eastern Christians which the laws of the kingdom had conferred on them. By this course of action they created an atmosphere in which it was possible for a mutual esteem, the necessary foundation for true religious unity, to develop.   They were rewarded by the praise of the Armenian theologian, St Nerses of Lampron, the friendship of the Jacobite

1. Otto of Freising, 'Chronica', VII, 33, pp 365—7. On the invasion of the Kara-Khitai, Abu-l-Fida, 'Annals', 536 A.H., *RHC Or*, I, p 25.

scholar and patriarch, Michael the Syrian, and the entry of a substantial part of the Maronite community into full union with the western church.

9. THE LATIN CHURCH OF ANTIOCH AFTER 1187

Having conquered most of the kingdom of Jerusalem as a result of his victory at Hattin in 1187, Saladin turned his attention to the northern states in the following year. He was largely victorious, but failed to take the city of Tripoli, Tortosa, where the Templars held out in the citadel, the Hospitaller fortress of al-Marqab above the city of Valania, Antioch itself and the region round about, and some fortresses inland, notably Crac des Chevaliers and the patriarch of Antioch's fortress of Qusair.[1] He did not even attack the Cilician state. He never returned to the north, and the continued independence of those areas was guaranteed by the terms of the treaty which the sultan made with king Richard of England in 1192.[2] Saladin died in March 1193 and his great empire was divided among the many princes of his family, the Aiyubids, who at first were too faction-torn to constitute any threat to the surviving Frankish territories. Subsequently, under the hegemony of the sultans of Egypt, the Aiyubid princes of Syria were for the most part content to live at peace with their Frankish neighbours, a peace only broken by the arrival of new crusades from the west intent on restoring Frankish control of the holy places.[3]

As a result of Saladin's conquests the Latin patriarchate of Antioch was cut in half. Antioch itself remained Frankish, and there continued to be Latin archbishops in the neighbouring Armenian state of Cilicia, but Jabala and Latakia were ruled by the Aiyubid prince of Aleppo, and communications with the bishoprics of Valania, Tortosa and Tripoli were only possible by sea. Moreover, for some years after the peace of 1192 the Muslims also controlled Gibelet, Beirut and Sidon, thus dividing the Franks of Tripoli from those of Acre. The problems which this created should not be exaggerated: the Aiyubids were quite well disposed towards their Frankish neighbours, and in 1223, for example, the Latin archbishop of Apamea was able to live in the Muslim-held city of Latakia,[4] which, admittedly, had a western merchant

1. Cahen, *Syrie*, pp 428–31.
2. Painter in Setton, II, p 85.
3. H.A.R. Gibb, 'The Aiyubids', *ibid.*, pp 693–714.
4. Honorius III permitted the archbishop of Apamea to celebrate Mass in his chapel at Latakia, Pressutti, no 4425.

colony.[1]

Political changes also came to north Syria in the late twelfth century. Raymond III, count of Tripoli, died without heirs in the autumn of 1187, and his county passed to the princes of Antioch: in the first instance Bohemond III's younger son, also called Bohemond, took over the government there.[2] The other important change was that Richard I annexed the Byzantine island of Cyprus in 1191 and it subsequently passed to the rule of Guy of Lusignan, former king of Jerusalem, and after his death to his brother Aimery and his descendants.[3] In Aimery's reign a Latin hierarchy was established there, with an archbishop at Nicosia, and suffragans at Limassol, Famagusta and Paphos, but they were not made subject to the patriarch of Antioch and remained, as the Orthodox church of the island had previously been, an independent church, except that the Latin archbishop recognised the canonical authority of the pope.[4] Naturally the Latin kings and bishops of Cyprus became involved to some extent in the affairs of the Frankish states and churches of Syria.

During the initial period of crisis following the battle of Hattin the church of Antioch was still presided over by Aimery of Limoges. Following the policy he had first adopted forty years earlier when Zengi and Nur-ad-Din had annexed many Frankish lands in the north, he made no attempt to appoint titular bishops to the sees which Saladin had conquered. Jabala, Latakia and Gibelet were left vacant.[5] At the end of his reign he was therefore reduced to six suffragans: the archbishops of Tarsus and Mamistra, living under Armenian rule; the archbishop of Apamea, who was virtually a coadjutor of the see of Antioch since he had no cathedral of his own, even though part of his lands may have remained in Frankish control; and the three bishops of Valania, Tortosa and Tripoli.

When Aimery died in 1193 the canons of Antioch, acting, it is to be supposed, on the orders of Bohemond III, chose one of their number, an elderly canon, as the patriarch Ralph II.[6] He only reigned for three years, but during that time one event of importance took place, the erection of a commune in Antioch. This occurred in 1193 when Leo II of Cilicia, having invited Bohemond III to a colloquy, arrested him. The people of Antioch, fearing

1. TT, II, pp 62–6, no 185.
2. Richard, *Comté de Tripoli*, p 8.
3. E.C. Furber, 'The Kingdom of Cyprus, 1191–1291', in Setton, II, pp 599–604.
4. Mas Latrie, *Chypre*, III, pp 599–606.
5. Lists of incumbents in Fedalto, *Chiesa Latina*, II, pp 59, 125, 137.
6. MS, XXI, 8, vol III, p 412. Cahen, *Syrie*, p 508, n 23 suggests that he may be Ranulphus, canon of Antioch in 1185, *CGOH*, no 665.

that the Armenians would attempt to take over the city, formed a commune under the guidance of the patriarch to take charge of its defence.[1]   Henry of Troyes, ruler of the southern kingdom, intervened, secured the release of Bohemond, and arranged a peace whereby Bohemond's heir, Raymond, married Alice, niece and heiress of Leo II.[2]   This should have had the effect of uniting the two Christian states of north Syria under a single ruler after Bohemond and Leo were dead, which would immeasurably have strengthened the power of the Armenians and the Franks. The commune of Antioch was not dissolved once the crisis was ended, and it caused difficulties to the Latin church in so far as, following Byzantine custom with which the Orthodox section of the population was familiar, the commune claimed the right to tax the clergy and to try them for civil and criminal offences in its courts, which was contrary to western canon law.[3]

When Ralph died Bohemond III appointed Peter of Angoulême as his successor.[4]   Peter had been archdeacon of Tripoli and had been appointed chancellor by Guy of Lusignan when he came to join queen Sibyl in Tripoli after his release by Saladin in 1189.[5] Peter and bishop Aimery of Tripoli accompanied Guy to the siege of Acre, and when Aimery died there Guy secured Peter's appointment to the bishopric of Tripoli, in which capacity he continued to act as chancellor.[6]   When Guy was offered Cyprus, which the Templars, to whom Richard I had given it, wished to sell, Peter succeeded in raising the purchase price as a loan from the merchants of Tripoli.[7]   When Guy went to Cyprus in 1192 Peter, of course, ceased to be his chancellor, and returned to Tripoli where he spent the next four years as bishop under the young count Bohemond. Nothing is known about his relations with the count, but there are suggestions that they were not smooth. When a disagreement arose in 1194 between the bishop and the commune of Pisa, the count intervened in the commune's favour, and, as Peter explained to Innocent III, he thought it necessary when he became patriarch to make an immediate appointment to the vacant see of Tripoli because had there been any delay Bohemond would have despoiled the temporalities of the church.[8]

1. 'Eracles', western redaction, *RHC Occ*, II, p 209, where the patriarch is said to be Aimery of Limoges, but see above, p 50, n 4; Cahen, *Syrie*, pp 508, 584.
2. Cahen, *ibid.*, pp 585–6.
3. Innocent III, 'Reg', I, no 512, *PL*, 214, 474.
4. 'Chronique de Terre Sainte', c 54, *ann.* 1196, *Gestes*, p 15, states wrongly that he succeeded Aimery of Limoges.
5. Müller, pp 36–9, nos 31–2.
6. Aimery's death: Roger of Houedene, vol III, p 122. Peter, bishop of Tripoli and chancellor: *CGOH*, no 917 (1192); Strehlke, pp 23–4, no 27 (1192).
7. Western redaction of 'Eracles', *RHC Occ*, II, p 187.
8. Müller, p 65, no 39; Innocent III, 'Reg.', I, no 502, *PL*, 214, 462–4.

In 1196 Peter was by far the most experienced senior church-man in the patriarchate of Antioch and the obvious choice to succeed Ralph II. He approached his new office with vigour. The bishop of Valania, whose see had been devastated by Saladin, lived throughout the rest of the period of Frankish rule in the Hospital-ler castle of al-Marqab.[1]   The bishop appointed in Ralph II's reign was a Hospitaller, and therefore subject by reason of his vows to the order. Almost certainly at the new patriarch's suggestion, the bishop received a ruling from pope Celestine III that this situation would not prejudice the independence of future holders of this see.[2]   In 1197 the Franks recovered control of Gibelet and immediately a new Latin bishop was appointed there.[3]   Peter also reopened in Rome the moribund dispute over the rights of the church of Antioch in the province of Tyre, and even added, for good measure, that Antioch claimed to control the archdiocese of Petra as well. In the situation in which the Latin east found itself after the third crusade, this question had taken on a new relev-ance, since unlike almost all other provinces of the Latin church, that of Tyre was almost completely in Christian hands. Naturally enough the complaint produced no results, for had it done so the patriarch of Jerusalem would have lost the greater part of his jurisdiction.[4]

This appeal was heard by Innocent III who became pope in 1198. His zeal for the rights of the universal church matched that of Peter for those of his own patriarchate, and the support of a vigorous minded pope could have done much to strengthen what remained of the Latin church of Antioch. But papal surveillance had its disadvantages. Within two months of his consecration the pope wrote to complain that Peter had translated the archbishop-elect of Apamea to the see of Tripoli, thereby diminishing his dignity, and contravening canon law which reserved such trans-lations to the holy see, and he suspended Peter from exercising his normal patriarchal right to confirm bishops in office.[5]   Peter succeeded in giving the pope a satisfactory explanation and was restored to his full powers very quickly,[6] but Innocent's action was typical of the closer supervision which the Roman see from that time began to exercise over the Latin churches of Syria and for which there was no twelfth-century precedent. The patriarch

1. Buchard of Mount Sion, pp 20–21.
2. *CGOH*, no 999.
3. Innocent III, 'Reg.', I, no 516, *PL*, 214, 476.
4. *Ibid.*, 'Reg.', I, 505, *PL*, 214, 466–7; cf. 'Reg.', IX, nos 52, 253, *PL*, 215, 363–4, 1083.
5. *Ibid.*, 'Reg.', I, no 50, *PL*, 214, 45–6.
6. *Ibid.*, 'Reg.', I, nos 502–3, *PL*, 214, 462–4.

also had to obtain a special dispensation from making regular *ad limina* visits, a burden which had been imposed on none of his predecessors.[1] It was this kind of papal intervention which made Peter's role so difficult during the war of the Antiochene succession.

In 1197 prince Raymond of Antioch, eldest son of Bohemond III and husband of the heiress of Cilicia, died, leaving an infant son, Raymond-Roupen. In the following year Leo II of Cilicia, the child's great-uncle, was crowned king by the chancellor of the western emperor, Henry VI, and secured the union of the Armenian church with Rome in the presence of the papal legate, Conrad of Mainz. The religious aspects of this policy will be dealt with in a later chapter,[2] but the political consequence was that the pope gave his full support to this illustrious convert to Catholic unity. One immediate result was that the legate persuaded Bohemond III to make the barons of Antioch swear to recognise Raymond-Roupen as his successor.[3] This was sound political sense, since it would have in time secured the union of Antioch and Cilicia, but this policy had powerful enemies. One was Bohemond III's younger son, Bohemond, count of Tripoli, who did not wish to be excluded from the succession in the interests of the king of Armenia, who would be regent for Raymond-Roupen in the event of the elder Bohemond's death. Another was the order of the Temple, which was in dispute with Leo II about the possession of the castle of Baghras. Saladin had seized it from them in 1188, and after the withdrawal of his garrison it had been occupied by Leo II who refused to return it to the Templars because it commanded the main approach road from Cilicia to Antioch.[4] The commune of Antioch was also opposed to Raymond-Roupen's claims, since it had been expressly founded to prevent the Armenians from gaining control of the city.

The very multiplicity of parties left room for diplomatic manoeuvre on the part of the patriarch, and Peter of Angoulême was experienced in secular affairs, but his hands were tied by the pope. He could not reach an understanding with the commune, since Innocent III had ordered him to withdraw Latin clergy in the city from its jurisdiction, and this had caused hostility between commune and patriarch.[5] He was bound to support the Armenians in the case of the succession, since the pope's primary wish was to

1. *Ibid.*, 'Reg.', IX, no 53, *PL*, 215, 864.
2. See chapter 13 below.
3. Boase, ed, *The Cilician Kingdom*, p 19.
4. J. Riley-Smith, 'The Templars and the Teutonic Knights in Cilician Armenia', *ibid.*, pp 92–101.
5. Innocent III, 'Reg.', I, no 512, *PL*, 214, 474.

preserve the union, and this necessarily earned him the hostility of the Templars. When Bohemond III died in 1201 and Bohemond IV seized power with the support of the commune, the patriarch was therefore placed in the invidious position of leading a faction which was hostile to the new prince, and his only natural allies were the knights of St John who were rivals of the Templars.[1]

War broke out between Antioch and Cilicia, but Bohemond IV retained control of the city largely because he had the support of az-Zahir of Aleppo, who had no wish to see a strong, united, Christian state in north Syria.[2] Peter was not allowed to try to negotiate a settlement himself, for Innocent III sent a stream of legates to Antioch, who not only proved ineffective, but one of whom, Peter of S. Marcello, even sided with the Templars, excommunicated Leo II and placed his kingdom under an interdict, which had no effect on Cilicia, but which seemed to deprive Peter of Angoulême of papal support in his stand for the claims of Raymond-Roupen.[3]

Peter nevertheless sustained his authority in this difficult situation until Peter of S. Marcello came to Antioch again in the winter of 1205—6. A dispute broke out between them about the appointment of a new archdeacon and two canons of Antioch. The previous archdeacon with two canons had gone to Rome, and it was presumed that they had been drowned at sea, as they never reached their destination. The patriarch, on learning of this, nominated his nephew to the vacant archdeaconry, but sent him to Rome to obtain a dispensation from the pope because he was below the canonical age. Peter of S. Marcello refused to accept this, claiming that as the benefices had not been filled within six months of falling vacant their collation had devolved to the holy see, whose representative he was. He therefore nominated candidates to all three vacant benefices, and, when the patriarch refused to institute them, excommunicated him and suspended him from the exercise of all canonical powers. The commune of Antioch, which was largely Orthodox, seized this opportunity to proclaim an Orthodox patriarch, Symeon II, with the connivance of Bohemond IV. The legate and the patriarch were both appalled by this and hastily made their peace, and Peter of Angoulême was restored to office,[4] but the damage had been done. For although

1. *Ibid.*, 'Reg.', VIII, no 125, *PL*, 215, 698.
2. Cahen, *Syrie*, pp 600—608.
3. Legates: cardinal Soffred of Sta Prassede, cardinal Peter of S. Marcello, the abbots of Locedio and Mount Tabor with two lay associates, Innocent III, 'Reg.', VIII, nos 1—2, 119, *PL*, 215, 555—9, 687—92.
4. *Ibid.*, 'Reg.', X, no 186, *PL*, 215, 1278—82.

the patriarch placed the city under an interdict this proved ineffective, since his opponents, Latin as well as Orthodox, recognised his rival.[1]

As a result of his quarrel with the legate Peter was deprived of religious authority in the city of Antioch, though he continued to act as head of the Latin church in the patriarchate.[2] Bohemond IV now felt strong enough to take action against the patriarch who had always opposed his rule, and sought to provoke Peter into open rebellion by arresting two of his nephews.[3] The patriarch responded by trying to procure an uprising in Antioch in favour of Raymond-Roupen, but failed to capture the citadel, and was arrested by the prince,[4] though not before he had deposited the treasures of the church in the safe-keeping of the knights of St John.[5] He was imprisoned in the citadel of Antioch and, according to one rumour, was subjected to the singularly unpleasant torture of death through thirst.[6] This probably occurred early in 1208, since news of his death had reached the pope by July of that year.[7]

Peter of Angoulême had real abilities as a secular and ecclesiastical administrator, but, largely through the intervention of Innocent III, he was placed in a position where he could not use them. In fairness to the pope it should be said that his overriding concern was to preserve the union between the Roman and Armenian churches, but this policy left Peter no opportunity to use his diplomatic gifts in a situation which required flexibility. Consequently his reign witnessed not only the unedifying spectacle of a Frankish prince fighting against an Armenian king in communion with the holy see, while allied with a son of Saladin, but also the development of a schism between the Latins and the Orthodox in the patriarchate of Antioch which was never subsequently healed.

1208 was a disturbing year for Innocent III. On 14 January Peter of Castelnau, his legate in Languedoc, was assassinated, as the pope supposed with the collusion of count Raymond VI of Toulouse, and in July he received news that the Latin patriarch of Antioch had been murdered by count Bohemond IV. The first of these murders led the pope to preach the crusade against

1. *Ibid.*, 'Reg.', XI, no 9, *PL*, 215, 1345.
2. Kohler, pp 172–3, no 64, of May 1207.
3. Innocent III, 'Reg.', X, no 214, *PL*, 215, 1321–3.
4. Cahen, *Syrie*, p 613.
5. *CGOH*, no 1336.
6. 'Eracles', XXXI, 3, *RHC Occ*, II, p 314.
7. Innocent III, 'Reg.', XI, no 110, *PL*, 215, 1428–9.

the count of Toulouse,[1] but he could not take similar measures against the prince of Antioch who was officially defending part of the Latin east against the infidel. Instead, he wrote to the patriarch of Jerusalem, St Albert, ordering him to excommunicate Bohemond until he gave satisfaction for Peter of Angoulême's death, and to supervise the election of a new patriarch of Antioch.[2]

All earlier patriarchs of Antioch, with the exception of Ralph of Domfront, had been appointed by the prince. Bohemond IV was clearly in no position to use his traditional powers of appointment, and it seems probable that Innocent III himself suggested the new candidate. The election was canonically carried out by the chapter of Antioch under the patriarch of Jerusalem's supervision, although the dean and two of the canons, who had taken refuge in the castle of Qusair, refused to leave its safety and acknowledged their concurrence by letter.[3] Like so many of the men whom Innocent entrusted with high office, the new patriarch was a Cistercian monk, Peter of Ivrea.[4] Alberic of Trois Fontaines confused him with another Cistercian, Peter, abbot of Locedio,[5] and many modern writers have accepted his evidence.[6] While it is true that Peter of Locedio visited north Syria in 1205,[7] he should not be identified with Peter, patriarch of Antioch, who had been a monk of La Ferté before he became bishop of Ivrea.[8] When he was nominated to Ivrea in 1205–6 Peter was reluctant to accept the charge and before he was consecrated left his see and retired to a hermitage. Innocent III wrote a sympathetic letter to him, in which he wrestled with the exegetical problem of why Christ's words to Mary of Bethany, type of the contemplative life, should not be taken literally; but he ordered Peter under obedience to resume his episcopal duties.[9]

It was this monk, with a strong desire for the eremitical life, whom Innocent III used in the service of the secular church as Gregory VII had once used St Peter Damian. Superficially Peter

1. M. Roquebert, L'Epopée Cathare, 2 vols, Toulouse 1970–7, I. *1198–1212: L'Invasion*, pp 200–231.

2. Innocent III, 'Reg.', XI, no 110, *PL*, 215, 1428–9.

3. *Ibid.*, 'Reg.' XII, no 38, *PL*, 216, 46–8.

4. *Ibid.*, 'Reg.', XII, no 8, *PL*, 216, 18–19.

5. 'Chronica', *MGH SS*, XXIII, p. 892.

6. Cahen, *Syrie*, p 616; M. Hardwicke, 'The Crusader States, 1192–1243', in Setton, II, p 536.

7. Innocent III, 'Reg.', VIII, nos 1–2, *PL*, 215, 555–9.

8. Innocent III wrote to Peter when he was bishop of Ivrea and mentioned his election 'abbatia de Firmitate, ad quam fueras evocatus, dimissa', 'Reg.', IX, no 172, *PL*, 215, 1005.

9. Innocent III, 'Reg.', IX, no 172, *PL*, 215, 1004–8.

of Ivrea did not seem to be at all suited to deal with the problems of faction-torn Antioch, but he was to prove a wise choice. The fact that, unlike his predecesor, he had received his training as a bishop in western Europe, and was therefore used to working in co-operation with the papacy, which was engaged in centralising the administration of the church, was a help to him, because he naturally expected to refer controversial matters to Rome. More-over, when Peter II was appointed, Innocent III was about to launch the Albigensian crusade, and this led him to keep trained personnel of the curia in Europe, and to delegate Syrian business to Albert, patriarch of Jerusalem, who had legatine powers.[1] This proved advantageous to Peter of Ivrea, since Albert of Jeru-salem was well informed about the situation in Antioch, whereas the legates with whom Peter of Angoulême had had to work had often been poorly informed about local issues and had made wrong judgments.

The pope invested Peter II with the *pallium* himself,[2] and the new patriarch arrived at Antioch in October 1209 when he was granted possession of the movable treasures of the church which the Hospitallers had been guarding.[3] Innocent III had ordered Bohemond IV to seize the patriarch of all the temporalities of his see,[4] and the prince seems to have made no difficulty about this, probably because he was anxious that the pope should support him in his quarrel with the king of Cilicia. It would seem that Peter II had few dealings with the prince, since Bohemond appointed his eldest son, Raymond, his *bailli* at Antioch, probably when the boy came of age in 1210.[5]

The war of the Antiochene succession was still raging when Peter reached Antioch, but the pope's commitment to the Armen-ian cause, which had been one of the principal stumbling-blocks facing Peter of Angoulême, had begun to weaken. This was partly the result of pressure brought to bear on the holy see by the Templars, who threatened to withdraw from Syria altogether unless Baghras were restored to them.[6] When Peter II tried to mediate, Leo II not only refused to submit to his judgment, but also confiscated all the property of the Templars in Cilicia, and when the pope learned of this in 1211 he ordered the patriarch publicly to excommunicate Leo.[7] While not helping to end the

1. *Ibid.*, 'Reg.', XI, no 108, *PL*, 215, 1427.
2. *Ibid.*, 'Reg.', XII, no 8, *PL*, 216, 18–19.
3. *CGOH*, no 1336.
4. Innocent III, 'Reg.', XII, no 39, *PL*, 216, 48.
5. Cahen, *Syrie*, p 620.
6. Innocent III, 'Reg.', XII, no 45, *PL*, 216, 54–6.
7. *Ibid.*, 'Reg.', XIV, no 64, *PL*, 216, 430–1.

war, this papal reversal of policy made Peter II's position in
Antioch far easier, since he was now aligned with the chief communities in the city, the prince, the Templars and the commune.
This did not lead to good feelings between the patriarch and the
king of Cilicia, and in 1211 Innocent III took the unprecedented
step of writing to ask the prince of Aleppo, az-Zahir, to take the
patriarch of Antioch under his protection.[1] Since the Aleppo
alliance was the chief means which Bohemond IV had used to
block Armenian occupation of Antioch, this was good political
sense.

The patriarch was able to use his new position at Antioch to
secure the expulsion of the Orthodox patriarch, Symeon II,[2]
and was henceforth undisputed head of the church of Antioch.
He also tried to mediate peace between Leo II and the commune,
but the king broke the truce. Leo ravaged the lands of Antioch,
and took hostile action against the Latin church. When the
archbishop-elect of Tarsus died in 1212, he expelled the Latin
canons and claimed their endowments which he distributed as
military fiefs. He also gave asylum to the exiled Orthodox
patriarch of Antioch, who was thus able to continue to direct his
Orthodox flock from the safety of the Cilician kingdom, which
impeded the healing of the schism.[3]

The whole situation in north Syria changed in 1213. Leo II,
whom the pope had threatened with a military blockade, restored
the estates of the Templars in Cilicia, though not the castle of
Baghras, as a goodwill gesture, and the excommunication against
him was lifted.[4] This was a necessary condition if any peaceful
solution to the problems of north Syria was to be found. Then
at the end of the year the young prince Raymond of Antioch was
killed in Tortosa cathedral by members of the sect of the
Assassins, who had recently returned to Sunnite orthodoxy and
therefore perpetrated their religious murders on Christians rather
than, as hitherto, on Muslims.[5] This led to the absence of a
resident ruler in Antioch, since Bohemond IV lived chiefly in
Tripoli; it also led to war between Bohemond and the Assassins,
which weakened his alliance with az-Zahir of Aleppo, who was to
some measure involved on the Assassins' side. az-Zahir's friendship for the Franks was placed under a further strain by the
news that a new crusade was being arranged in the west.[6]

1. *Ibid.*, 'Reg.', XIV, no 69, *PL*, 216, 434.
2. See chapter 12 below.
3. Innocent III, 'Reg.', XVI, no 2, *PL*, 216, 784–6.
4. *Ibid.*, 'Reg.', XVI, 7, *PL*, 216, 792–3.
5. M.G.S. Hodgson, *The Order of Assassins*, The Hague, 1955, pp 217–20.
6. A new crusade was placed on the agenda of the fourth Lateran council, invita-
tions to which were sent out in 1213.

The weakness of Bohemond IV led to a reversal of policy at Antioch, where a group of noblemen, led by the seneschal, invited Leo II to instal Raymond-Roupen who had now come of age.[1] This occurred in the early part of 1215.[2] The patriarch is not known to have been privy to this plot, but he was not opposed to it: he used it to restore peace to north Syria and to strengthen the powers of the church of Antioch. The castle of Baghras was restored to the Templars, thus bringing to an end the feud between them and the king;[3] Latin archbishops were restored to the Cilician sees of Tarsus and Mamistra;[4] and Raymond-Roupen did homage to the patriarch for Antioch and was solemnly anointed by him.[5] Leo II was astute enough to realise that he would be in a far stronger position in regard to the pope if the principality were held by his great-nephew as a fief of the church. It is also probable that Leo withdrew his patronage from the Orthodox patriarch of Antioch at this point, and that Symeon II was forced to submit to the Latin patriarch, but he subsequently took refuge in the Byzantine empire.[6] The remainder of Peter II's reign was peaceful, and he co-operated well with the new prince.

Peter II did not wait until peace was fully established before trying to restore the fortunes of the church of Antioch, which had suffered in his predecessor's reign both as a result of prolonged war and because of the quarrel between Peter I and Bohemond. He leased some of the church lands, which had been laid waste in the fighting, in *emphyteusis*, so that they once more became financially productive;[7] and he increased the canonries of the cathedral from his own income.[8] In reorganising the finances of the church he ran into some opposition from Peter of Angoulême's nephews, who complained to the pope that the new patriarch had withheld from them certain revenues granted to them by their late uncle, including the sum of 1,000 besants set aside to finance their studies. Innocent III was not entirely

---

1. 'Chronique de Terre Sainte', c 74, *Gestes*, p 19; 'ATS', *AOL*, II, p 436; Marino Sanudo, 'Liber Secretorum Fidelium Crucis', bk III, pt XI, c 5, ed J. Bongars, *Gesta Dei per Francos*, 2 vols, Hanover 1611, II, p 206, places this event in 1216; 'Eracles', XXXI, 7, *RHC Occ*, II, p 318, ascribes a reign of four years to Raymond-Roupen, which would place his accession in 1215.
    2. He was in power by April 1215; *CGOH*, nos 1441–2.
    3. Riley-Smith, *op. cit.*, in Boase, *Cilician Armenia*, p 107, who accepts Cahen's dating of these events to 1216; Cahen, *Syrie*, pp 622–3.
    4. *CGOH*, no 1441.
    5. O. Raynaldus, *Annales Ecclesiastici . . .* , vols 13–21, Colonia Agrippina, 1694–1727, 13, p 133, quotes a letter of Leo II wrongly attributed to 1205. For the correct date, Cahen, *Syrie*, p 621.
    6. See below, p 315, n 3.
    7. Innocent III, 'Reg.', XIV, 71, *PL*, 216, 435.
    8. *Ibid.*, 'Reg.', XIV, 70, *PL*, 216, 434–5.

sympathetic to this plea, for he ordered Peter II to investigate the complaint himself.[1]

Peter's career as an ecclesiastical administrator was marked by a strong desire for peace. Whereas Peter I had tried to gain jurisdiction over the province of Tyre, Peter II granted prebends to the archbishop of Tyre on account of his poverty until the fief of Toron could be recovered.[2] Similarly, when the see of Valania fell vacant in 1215, and the chapter elected Odo, archdeacon of Beirut, and questioned the right of the master of the Hospital of al-Marqab to veto their choice, the patriarch ruled that the master should have the same powers in his fief over episcopal elections as the king of Jerusalem and the prince of Antioch had in their dominions. As a result the master accepted the candidate whom the chapter presented to him, and a lengthy and useless quarrel was avoided.[3]

Despite his involvement in ecclesiastical and political administration, Peter II never lost his desire for the contemplative life. He later explained:

> When the holy see strictly ordered us to take up the burden of ruling the holy church of Antioch . . . we talked with the pope informally about one matter, namely that, as we were growing old, it grieved us to be separated in distant lands from the society of the Cistercian order in which we had lived since boyhood, and we ended up by asking that if any abbey in the Black Mountain wished to be incorporated in the Cistercian order, we should be empowered to grant their request . . . [4]

Peter found a monastery which was willing to accept the Cistercian rule, that of St Mary *de Jubino*,[5] which became a daughterhouse of his own community of La Ferté in 1214,[6] and where Peter was able to stay in the autumn of that year.[7]

When the fourth Lateran council met in November 1215, Peter was too ill to attend and sent the bishop of Tortosa to represent him:[8] he died in the spring of 1217.[9] The confidence which

1. *Ibid.*, 'Reg.', XV, no 181, *PL*, 216, 697–8.
2. Pressutti, no 1141.
3. *CGOH*, no 1432.
4. Letter transcribed in Gregory IX's registers, Auvray, no 3468.
5. J. Richard, 'L'abbaye cistercienne de Jubin et le prieuré Saint-Blaise de Nicosie', *Epeteris tou Kentrou Epistemonikon Ereunon*, 3, Nicosia, 1969–70, pp 63–74; Hamilton in Pennington, ed, *One Yet Two*, pp 409–10.
6. J-M. Canivez, *Statuta Capitulorum Generalium Ordinis Cisterciensis*, 6 vols, Louvain, 1933–, I, p 415, no 56, II, p 172, no 18.
7. Auvray, nos 3468, 3469. The community was inaugurated on 22 March 1214, Janauschek, *Originum Cisterciensium*, I, p 217, no 564.
8. Alberic of Trois Fontaines, 'Chronica', *MGH SS*, XXIII, p 903.
9. The pope had been informed of his death and had considered the succession by August 1217, Pressutti, no 760.

Innocent III had reposed in this contemplative bishop had not been misplaced. Peter of Ivrea had helped to restore political peace to a society which was faction-torn; he had secured the outward obedience at least of both Latins and Orthodox in his patriarchate to the authority of a single patriarch; he had reconstituted the temporalities of his see, and, whenever the opportunity presented itself, he had worked for ecclesiastical peace. But perhaps his most notable achievement was to bring white monks to the Black Mountain of Antioch in the middle of the war of the Antiochene succession. It might indeed have been said of him as it had been of Sidonius Apollinaris more than seven centuries before that 'he lived tranquil amid the swelling seas of the world'.[1]

The see of Antioch remained vacant for two years. The chapter requested the appointment of Pelagius, cardinal-bishop of Porto, a well-known and controversial figure in the near east.[2] This request was made, presumably, at the wish of Raymond-Roupen, and the attraction of this candidate for the young prince is evident, since Honorius III had nominated Pelagius legate in command of the fifth crusade, the vanguard of which reached Syria in 1217.[3] The request was refused and in August 1219 Honorius himself appointed a new patriarch, Peter of Capua, papal subdeacon, doctor of theology in the schools of Paris and 'a man greatly esteemed for his knowledge, character and reputation'.[4] Peter was never consecrated for this see, for Honorius rapidly promoted him to be a cardinal, and in December 1219 wrote to the chapter of Antioch that he had consecrated his own vice-chancellor, Rainier, as their new patriarch.[5]

The political situation in north Syria had changed dramatically since the death of Peter II. Prince Raymond-Roupen had quarrelled with Leo II of Cilicia, and, deprived of Armenian support, was driven from Antioch in the spring of 1219 by the supporters of Bohemond IV, but before he left he placed the citadel in the hands of the Hospitallers. He then went to Egypt where the fifth crusade was besieging Damietta, to seek the support of the legate, cardinal Pelagius, whose candidacy to the episcopal throne of Antioch he had supported. At this juncture Leo II of Cilicia died, leaving his infant daughter Isabel as his heir, and Raymond-

1. 'Vivit ... mundi inter tumidas quietus undas', *AA SS, Aug.*, IV, 620.

2. Pressutti, no 760. J.P. Donovan, *Pelagius and the Fifth Crusade*, Philadelphia 1950, pp 1–24.

3. Pelagius did not join the crusaders until September 1218, T. Van Cleve, 'The Fifth Crusade', Setton, II, p 402.

4. Pressutti, no 2031.

5. *Ibid.*, no 2285.

Roupen persuaded the legate to support his cause in both states. Raymond-Roupen went to Cilicia with the legate's blessing to contest the kingship, and succeeded in establishing himself in Tarsus with the help of the Hospitallers,[1] but Bohemond IV had meanwhile expelled the Hospitallers from the citadel of Antioch, and was excommunicated by the legate for his treatment of that order, and for usurping the rights of Raymond-Roupen.[2]

This was the situation which the new patriarch inherited. The prince of Antioch was once again excommunicate and Cilicia, which came under the ecclesiastical jurisdiction of Antioch, was riven by civil war. In addition, the church had been without a head for almost three years. During that time the pope had collated to vacant bishoprics, and had appointed Geoffrey, archdeacon of Tours, to the see of Tripoli.[3] The appointment of bishops who had received their training in the western church to the Latin sees of north Syria thus continued. It was a process which had begun with the nomination of Peter II as patriarch.

The new patriarch, learning perhaps from the fate of Peter of Angoulême, took no direct part in the politics of Antioch, but he could not help but be involved with them indirectly. In 1221 Raymond-Roupen was captured, and subsequently murdered, by the regent of Cilicia, Constantine of Lampron.[4] Since he was childless, and since no other Cilician prince had any claim to the throne of Antioch, the long war of succession was finally at an end. At this point it might have been expected that Bohemond IV would have been reconciled to the church. Indeed, Honorius III wrote urging Pelagius to treat prince Bohemond with care, since the loss of Antioch would do more harm to the church than the loss of many Damiettas,[5] but Pelagius did not have the temperament for a graceful compromise, and the prince of Antioch remained excommunicate throughout the reign of the new patriarch.

Rainier experienced problems in his dealings with prince Bohemond, who was presumably very short of money and confiscated church property, or encouraged his vassals to do so. Pope Honorius had to order the patriarch to forbid the prince to impose financial burdens on the monks of St Symeon's,[6] and a

1. Cahen, *Syrie*, pp 630–2.
2. *CGOH*, nos 1824, 1837, 1955.
3. Alberic of Trois Fontaines, 'Chronica', *MGH SS*, XXIII, pp 892–3, dates his consecration some years after 1211. He is presumably the bishop of Tripoli consecrated in 1217, Pressutti, no 956, and should not be confused with bishop G. of Tripoli mentioned in documents of 1204, 1209, *CGOH*, nos 1198, 1336.
4. 'Chronique de Terre Sainte', c 79, *Gestes*, p 20.
5. Pressutti, no 3495.
6. *Ibid*., no 5061.

year later he empowered the archbishop of Caesarea and the bishop of Acre to compel secular rulers to restore to the patriarch his
full rights of jurisdiction in his diocese.[1] Bohemond was not able
to gain control of the patriarchal fief of Qusair, since Rainier
entrusted this to his nephew, Philip.[2] But it was probably a shortage of money which made the patriarch once again raise the
subject of jurisdiction over the province of Tyre, an appeal which
led to a counter-claim by the archbishop of Tyre to the three
sees of the county of Tripoli: Honorius III very sensibly ruled that
further discussion about this was unprofitable while the Holy
Land was still mostly in the hands of the infidel.[3]

The patriarch's position was made more difficult by fresh
troubles in Cilicia. After the death of Raymond-Roupen peace
was cemented between Antioch and Cilicia by the marriage of
Bohemond's son, Philip, to the infant queen Isabel, but the regent
of Cilicia, Constantine of Lampron, was opposed to the Frankish
alliance and in 1224 put Philip in prison, where he died a year
later. This led to a renewal of hostilities between Antioch and
Cilicia,[4] but it also led to the expulsion of the Latin hierarchy
from Cilicia by the regent when he seized power,[5] and probably to
the readmission there of the exiled Orthodox patriarch of Antioch.
Certainly by 1225 the schism between Orthodox and Latins in the
church of Antioch had reopened, and some Orthodox clergy were
refusing obedience to the Latin patriarch.[6]

This was the situation when Rainier died in September 1225.[7]
The prince was excommunicate and was despoiling the lands of
the church; the Orthodox population was refusing canonical
obedience to the Latin patriarch; one of the few remaining provinces of the church of Antioch, that of Tarsus, had been lost;
while even the bishop of Tortosa had complained to the pope that
the Templars had broken their convention of 1152 and were
usurping his rights in his cathedral city.[8] The responsibility for
this lamentable state of affairs cannot be placed entirely on
Rainier. Although he does not seem to have been a very dynamic
personality much of his trouble sprang from the quarrel between

1. *Ibid.*, nos 5568, 5572.
2. *Ibid.*, no 5560.
3. *Ibid.*, nos 4091, 4320.
4. Cahen, *Syrie*, pp 631—5.
5. Pressutti, no 5222.
6. *CICO*, III, pp 186—7, no 141.
7. Pressutti, no 5658. Presumably he died while visiting Rome, for Honorius wrote
on 25 September to say that the patriarch had died on 16 September and news could
not have reached him from Syria so quickly.
8. Pressutti, no 5266.

cardinal Pelagius and Bohemond IV, which rendered co-operation between prince and patriarch impossible, but which it was not within Rainier's power to heal.

Pope Honorius III suggested to the canons of Antioch that they should elect in Rainier's place the former chancellor of prince Raymond-Roupen,[1] but although Bohemond IV was excommunicate and therefore had no part in the election, such an appointment would have made relations between the prince and the church even more contentious, and perhaps for that reason the chapter did not act on the pope's suggestion. During the vacancy the archbishop of Tarsus, chief metropolitan of Antioch, in exile from his own diocese, administered the patriarchate.[2]

No decision about a new patriarch had been reached when Gregory IX became pope in 1227, and, as the appointment had devolved to the holy see, the pope nominated Albert of Rizzato, bishop-elect of Brixen, and gave him full legatine powers in his patriarchate.[3] The problems of his church proved largely intractable. The province of Cilicia could not be restored for reasons totally outside Albert's control. In 1226 the regent of Cilicia secured the marriage of the widowed queen Isabel to his young son Hetoum.[4] Unlike the Roupenids, the Hetoumids were not pro-western, and during much of the rest of the century the union with Rome, though not formally repudiated, was virtually in abeyance,[5] and although the kings were prepared to have diplomatic dealings with the papacy[6] they were not willing to readmit the archbishops of Tarsus and Mamistra to their sees. The archbishopric of Tarsus was consequently allowed to lapse for many years at some time after 1233, when the exiled archbishop died.[7] That of Mamistra was retained rather longer since the titular archbishop was useful as a deputy for the patriarch.[8] It also proved impossible to heal the schism with the Orthodox in the patriarchate for reasons which will be discussed in a later chapter.

Bohemond IV finally made his peace with the Hospital and was reconciled to the church at Tripoli in 1232 through the mediation of Gerold, patriarch of Jerusalem.[9] He died in the following year

1. *Ibid.*, no 5659.
2. *Ibid.*, no 6026.
3. Auvray, nos 342–3.
4. Sempad the Constable, *RHC Arm*, I, p 648.
5. See chapter 13 below.
6. 'Links of friendship were strengthened with the pope of Rome', Sempad the Constable (*sub anno* 1226), *RHC Arm*, I, p 648.
7. An archbishop of Tarsus is mentioned in 1233, Auvray, no 1101. There is no record of a successor until 1292, Langlois, no 6401.
8. There is no break in the succession to this see until 1259.
9. *CGOH*, no 2000; Auvray, no 1223.

and was succeeded by his son, Bohemond V. The change of ruler
did little to ease relations between church and state in Antioch.
Albert, standing on precedent, required the prince to do homage
to him for the principality and met with a refusal. This was the
beginning of a stormy relationship between them. The prince
later arrested some of the patriarch's officials, including the
castellan of Qusair, because, if we may believe pope Gregory IX,
he had ordered the murderer of a priest to be hanged.[1] Further
complaints reached Rome from the patriarch about the prince's
violation of the temporalities of his see.[2]

Yet although he was empowered by the pope to excommunicate Bohemond V, Albert did not do so. He even tried to find
conciliatory solutions to some of the disputes which existed
between the prince and the knights of St John; a legacy of his
father's long-standing quarrel with that order. For example, the
fief of Maraclea had been granted to the knights by Bohemond III
in 1198, but they had subsequently restored it to him on condition that it should revert to them at his death. This condition
had never been fulfilled, and the order appealed to the pope about
it after the death of Bohemond IV. The judge-delegate appointed
by Gregory IX was the bishop of Valania who, since he lived in
the Hospital's castle of al-Marqab, might not have been considered
impartial. Bohemond V certainly refused to accept his judgment
in favour of the Hospital and the matter was referred back to
Rome. The case was finally heard by the patriarch Albert in his
capacity as legate in 1241. He ruled that as the heir of the fief
was under age a *bailli* should be appointed for him by the prince,
who should administer the fief on the prince's behalf. When the
heir came of age he should decide whether he wanted the prince
or the order to be his lord, but in the meantime the prince should
pay a fixed composition to the order. In other words no final
decision was reached, but both parties were satisfied.[3] By such
means as this Albert avoided in so far as was possible a confrontation with the prince of the kind which had proved so costly to
his predecessors.

The patriarch's relations with his clergy were not without
difficulties. These sprang from the fact that the revenues of the
church of Antioch were no longer fully adequate to support its
establishment, and at root this was the same reason which caused
the quarrels between successive patriarchs and princes, since the
latter sought to augment their inadequate finances at the expense

1. *Ibid.*, nos 4471–2.
2. *Ibid.*, no 4473.
3. *CGOH*, nos 2094, 2280; Riley-Smith, *Knights*, pp 452–3.

of the church. The patriarch had a long dispute with the Cistercian monks of Jubin about the payment of tithe and other matters of jurisdiction, which he won.[1] In 1237 he deprived archdeacon Aimery of Tripoli, nephew of a former bishop of that see,[2] of his office and his canonry and awarded them to his own chancellor, Hubert. Aimery appealed to the pope, who upheld the patriarch's right to appoint to the archdeaconry, but ruled that Aimery should either be given back his prebend or receive compensation.[3] The significance of this dispute is that the patriarch controlled very little ecclesiastical patronage and so the church of Tripoli was a temptation to him because it was one of the richest of the northern dioceses remaining in Frankish hands.

A change had come over the hierarchy of Antioch as a result of papal intervention, which had made itself felt by Albert's reign. Bishop Vassal of Gibelet, a devout man, who, although his see was very poor,[4] encouraged the Cistercians to make a new foundation there in 1233,[5] died during Albert's reign. It is not known how his successor was appointed, although Albert must have confirmed him in office; perhaps he was a nominee of the Embriaci who were lords of the city. A complaint was made about the new bishop to Innocent IV in 1243, who appointed judges-delegate to investigate the charges. In his instruction to them the pope wrote:

> Our reverend brother, the bishop of Gibelet, who has never received a proper education, who has not read Donatus or so much as opened a volume of Cato, and cannot express himself in writing, not considering that life without learning is a living death . . . is called a bishop to no purpose.[6]

Such a judgment would have excluded from the bench many of the bishops described by William of Tyre, but the Syrian church in the thirteenth century was no longer remote from the life of the western church in general as it had been a hundred years earlier, because papal intervention, and the appointment of patriarchs who had received their training in the west, exposed it to all the influences which were at work in the Latin church in Europe.

Albert of Rizzato was a gifted diplomat, and it was in that field that he achieved his greatest successes. From 1232–4 he was

1. Hamilton in Pennington, ed, *One Yet Two*, pp 416–17, see chapter 11 below.
2. That is of bishop Geoffrey, once archdeacon of Tours, see note 3, p 225 above.
3. Auvray, no 3639.
4. James of Vitry, *Lettres*, p 93, visited Gibelet in 1216 and described the bishop, perhaps bishop Vassal, as 'pauperrimus sed liberalis et humilis'.
5. E. Petit, 'Chartes de l'abbaye cistercienne de Saint-Serge de Giblet en Syrie', *MSAF*, ser 5, 8, 1887, pp 23–30; Hamilton in Pennington, ed, *One Yet Two*, pp 414–15.
6. Berger, no 57.

much occupied in the affairs of the kingdom of Jerusalem where a war had broken out between the emperor Frederick II and the native baronage, led by the Ibelin family and supported by the commune of Acre. Pope Gregory IX, who had initially excommunicated Frederick, had become reconciled with him in 1230 and was therefore anxious that his claim to the throne of Jerusalem should be recognised in Syria.[1] He used Albert as his intermediary in these negotiations and, with the help of the grand master of the Teutonic order, Hermann of Salza, Albert succeeded in arranging a peace between the two factions, though it did not prove enduring.[2] Gregory IX clearly thought highly of his ability, and in 1235 employed him in Italy on a variety of missions: to investigate charges made against the council of Piacenza of sheltering heretics; to relax the interdict which had been laid on Cremona; and to confer with the rectors of the Lombard League about negotiations with the emperor Frederick.[3]

At the end of Gregory IX's reign the Mongols, who for the past thirty years had been consolidating their power in eastern and central Asia, launched their attack on the Christian world, conquering Kievan Russia, and laying waste large areas of Catholic Europe in Poland, Hungary and Silesia. They also moved closer to the Franks in the east: since 1231 they had ruled in Azerbaijan, but in 1243 one of their armies attacked Asia Minor and made the Seljuk sultan tributary.[4] The Franks in the east knew of this mysterious people chiefly from reports which had reached them from the west of the devastation that they had caused there, and the patriarch Albert was bothered by this new threat to the entire Christian world. The emperor Frederick was at that time engaged in a fierce struggle with the papacy, and as a result Christian Europe was unprepared to make concerted resistance to a new Mongol attack should there be one or to send help to their fellow Christians in the east. Albert was on good terms with the emperor, whose interests he had tried to promote in Jerusalem, and was also a valued servant of the pope. When the new pope, Innocent IV, called the council of Lyons for 1245, Albert went to Europe in the previous winter and visited the imperial court where he tried to produce a settlement which would be acceptable to the papacy.[5] In the event he failed, and

---

1. T. Van Cleve, *The Emperor Frederick II of Hohenstaufen*, Oxford 1972, pp 222–33; Auvray, nos 836–8.
2. *Ibid.*, no 1841.
3. *Ibid.*, nos 2603, 2777, 2780.
4. J.J. Saunders, *The History of the Mongol Conquests*, London 1971, pp 73–89.
5. Van Cleve, *Frederick II*, p 479.

this was his last diplomatic undertaking since he died while attending the council.[1]

Albert of Rizzato's talents were largely wasted in the dying church of Antioch whose problems had become virtually intractable. Yet the dignity of his office was so great that there was no see to which he could be translated which would not have been disparaging, except the holy see itself. He was the most cosmopolitan of the Latin patriarchs of Antioch and could move as easily in the western church as in his own patriarchate, but he had far less power than his twelfth-century predecessors, for by his reign the chair of St Peter of Antioch had become largely an empty honour.

There is some confusion about Albert's successor. The see of Antioch remained vacant for almost two years after his death, but by July 1247 Innocent IV had appointed a new patriarch, who was granted legatine powers in October of that year.[2] This appointment coincided with the launching of St Louis's crusade, and there was a real hope that Christian fortunes might at last be reversed in Syria. The king reached Cyprus in the autumn of 1248, and it is possible that the patriarch accompanied him, for he was certainly present in Acre at that time, where he offended the patriarch of Jerusalem by using his legatine powers to take precedence on liturgical occasions: the pope reprimanded him, reminding him that his legateship was confined to his own patriarchate of Antioch.[3] The patriarch was still in Syria in 1252 when Bohemond V of Antioch died: his widow, Lucia of Segni, wished to assume the regency, but she was unpopular, and St Louis, who had stayed in Syria after the defeat of his crusade in Egypt in 1250, arranged that her young son, Bohemond VI, should assume power, even though he was a minor. The pope approved of this decision and ordered the patriarch of Antioch and the bishop of Tripoli to enforce it.[4] In 1253 Innocent IV ordered that part of the legacy which the patriarch Gerold of Jerusalem had, before his death, deposited with the Templars, should be paid to the patriarch of Antioch.[5]

All the information about this patriarch between his election and 1253 comes from the papal registers, and, as was customary in the curia, the name of the patriarch is not recorded. In 1254 the Old French continuator of William of Tyre and the 'Annales de

1. Berger, no 2026.
2. *Ibid.*, nos 3075, 3299, 3300.
3. *Ibid.*, no 4225.
4. *Ibid.*, no 6070.
5. *Ibid.*, no 6432.

Terre Sainte' both record the arrival of the patriarch Opizo of Antioch in Syria.[1]   There is no doubt that this was Opizo dei Fieschi, nephew of pope Innocent IV.   Cahen has conclusively shown that the assertion by some earlier writers that Albert was succeeded at Antioch by patriarchs called Elias and Christian was based on a misunderstanding of the sources, and has argued that Opizo was appointed patriarch in 1247, and that the references to his arrival in 1254 relate to his return to Syria from Rome, where he had been to make the *ad limina* visit.[2]   This does seem to be the correct explanation.   It is inconceivable, given the fullness of the papal registers for Innocent IV's reign, that the see of Antioch was held from 1247–53 by an unnamed patriarch who was succeeded in 1254 by Opizo, without the death of the former and the appointment of the latter being mentioned in any papal document.   Moreover, practical considerations favour the same interpretation.   The pope presumably wished to honour his nephew or he would not have resorted to nepotism at all.   The see of Antioch was, after Rome and Constantinople, the third greatest see in the Latin church, and in 1247, when a new crusade was being planned, there was a possibility that it might once again become great in a temporal as well as an ecclesiastical sense; whereas in 1254 it was one of the poorest and most vulnerable sees in Christendom.   It does indeed seem highly probable that Opizo had returned to Rome in 1253 and told his uncle of the true state of affairs at Antioch, for thereafter the pope was very concerned to make proper financial provision for his nephew. In addition to the bequest of the patriarch Gerold to which reference has already been made, the pope granted Opizo the legacy of the bishop of Norwich, which was to be spent on travelling expenses, presumably to enable him to return to Syria in due state.[3]   At the same time Innocent assigned the administration and revenues of the archbishopric of Nicosia to Opizo on account of the poverty of his see.   Since Hugh of Fagiano was, and remained, archbishop of Nicosia, it is difficult to know whether this letter reflects more than a papal decision to translate Hugh, which was never put into effect.[4]   Later that year the pope wrote to the Cistercian abbot of Jubin ordering him to reserve the first bishopric which fell vacant in the church of Antioch or that of Cyprus for the benefit of the patriarch and Innocent also granted

    1. 'ATS', *AOL*, II, p 446; 'Eracles', XXXIV, 2, *RHC Occ*, II, p 441.
    2. Cahen, *Syrie*, pp 662–4.
    3. Berger, no 7398.
    4. *Ibid.*, nos 7393–6. L. de Mas Latrie, 'Histoire des archevêques latins de l'Ile de Chypre', *AOL*, II, p 234.

Opizo a tithe of clerical income for three years from the churches of Antioch and Cyprus to enable him to strengthen the fortifications of his castle of Qusair.[1]

When the patriarch Robert of Jerusalem died in 1254 the canons of the Holy Sepulchre, perhaps acting on a suggestion of Innocent IV, nominated Opizo of Antioch as his successor. But, before his candidacy had received the papal assent, Innocent IV died, and his successor, Alexander IV, refused to agree to it.[2] Pope Alexander did make adequate financial provision for Opizo, however, by appointing him administrator of the see of Limassol in Cyprus when its bishop was translated to Vicenza in 1256.[3]

New bishops from western Europe were appointed to other dioceses in the patriarchate in this reign. When the bishop of Tripoli died in 1248–9[4] the pope, with the assent of his nephew, nominated his legate in Lombardy, Gregory of Montelongo, to the see.[5] Gregory was probably never consecrated, and may never have gone to Syria, but he was clearly a man of some ability and in 1251 was appointed to the important patriarchal see of Aquileia. His place as bishop of Tripoli was taken by another Italian, also called Opizo.[6] A more unusual appointment was that of friar Augustine of Nottingham to Latakia in 1254. He was the brother of William of Nottingham, provincial minister of the Franciscans in England, and was the first mendicant who is known to have held a see in the patriarchate of Antioch. He accompanied Opizo to Syria when he returned from Rome in 1254.[7] His appointment is also significant in that his see was in Muslim hands, and had been without a bishop since the time of Aimery of Limoges: he was therefore a titular bishop, and must have acted chiefly as an assistant to Opizo. Not unconnected with this new appointment may be the fact that the two other titular bishoprics in the province were allowed to lapse at about this time. There is no record of any archbishop of Apamea in Opizo's reign, the last recorded act of archbishop Peter II being in 1244.[8] Similarly the see of

---

1. Berger, no 7873. Innocent IV's enactment about tithe is recorded in a letter of Alexander IV, Bourel de la Ronciére, no 1087.

2. *Ibid.*, no 317.

3. *Ibid.*, no 1175.

4. His death is recorded in February 1249, Berger, no 4364.

5. *Ibid.*, no 4367.

6. Ughelli, V, 92, of 29 November 1252, records Gregory's translation. His successor was in office a year later, Berger, no 6070, and was called Opizo, *ibid.*, no 7910.

7. *Ibid.*, nos 7397, 7399. W.R. Thomson, *Friars in the Cathedral. The First Franciscan Bishops, 1226–61*, Toronto, 1975, pp 202–3.

8. Peter II of Apamea vidimated a document in 1244, G. Schlumberger, F. Chalandon, A. Blanchet, *Sigillographie de l'Orient Latin*, Paris 1943, p 99, no 73.

Mamistra was left unfilled when the archbishop died at some time after 1259.[1] Apart from his Franciscan assistant, Opizo in the late 1250s therefore only had four suffragans: those of Gibelet, Tripoli, Tortosa and Valania, and the last of those sees was virtually controlled by the knights of St John.

Unlike his immediate predecessors Opizo lived peaceably with the prince of Antioch: the young Bohemond VI does not seem to have taken very much interest in the affairs of Antioch city, but to have lived in the county of Tripoli. Nor was there any further hostility between the Franks and the Armenians, for St Louis, before he left the east in 1254, had arranged a marriage between Bohemond VI and Sibyl, daughter of king Hetoum I.[2] This was to have unforeseen consequences for the Latin patriarchate of Antioch. King Hetoum was on friendly terms with the Mongols, who had become overlords of his enemies, the Seljuks of Iconium, in 1243, and in 1254 he had visited the Mongol court and made his submission to the great khan Mongke.[3] When the Mongol armies under the command of Mongke's brother, Hulagu, launched their attack on the Abbasid empire in 1258, and advanced against the Aiyubid princes of Syria in the winter of 1259—60, king Hetoum persuaded his son-in-law, Bohemond VI, to make an alliance with them. The Mongols wanted Christian allies in their war against Islam, for an influential group among the Mongol confederacy were Nestorians, and this included princesses of the ruling house. The Mongols had already, in effect, made alliances with the king of Cilicia and the Byzantine emperor of Nicaea,[4] although, of course, their terminology did not admit of allies, merely of subjects of the great khan, vice-regent of Heaven.

Bohemond made his submission, and this proved beneficial to him. Not merely did the Mongols refrain from attacking his territories, but they also recognised his suzerainty over the lands west of the Orontes which had been lost to Antioch since the time of Saladin, and Bohemond was subsequently able to recover the coastal cities of Jabala and Latakia, together with parts of the Orontes valley. He accompanied the Mongol general Kitbogha when he attacked Damascus in the spring of 1260, and was granted one of the mosques of the city for use as a church of the Latin

---

1. Last recorded in Bourel de la Roncière, no 2960.
2. Runciman, *Crusades*, III, p 278.
3. Der Nersessian in Setton, II, pp 652—3.
4. William of Rubruck found envoys of John III Vatatzes at the court of the great khan Mongke in 1253, W.W. Rockhill, *The Journey of William of Rubruck to the Eastern Parts of the World, 1253—5, Hakluyt Society*, ser 2, 4, London 1900, pp 169—70.

rite.[1] The Mongols felt no animosity towards the Latin church, but because they were allied with Byzantium they insisted that an Orthodox patriarch should be restored in Antioch, not, it would seem, as sole patriarch, but as head of the Orthodox community.[2]

Opizo certainly must have remained effective head of the Latin church there and have been responsible for the re-establishment of Latin bishops in the lands south of Antioch which had reverted to Frankish rule. A Dominican was appointed to the long-vacant see of Jabala,[3] and by 1265 another Dominican, Peter of S. Hilario, had been made bishop of Latakia,[4] which was no longer, as earlier in Opizo's reign, a titular see.[5] But at some time in the early 1260s Opizo returned to the west. It would appear that he was still in Antioch in 1263 when pope Urban IV ordered him to provide the Dominican, William of Fréjus, whom the pope had consecrated as a missionary bishop, to some titular see 'in Arabia, or Media or Armenia';[6] but the patriarch had certainly left the east by 1264, when Bartholomew, archdeacon of Antioch, was acting as his vicar.[7] By 1265 he is known to have been in Italy where pope Clement IV employed him in a great deal of papal business.[8]

For all its superficial attractions Bohemond VI's alliance with the Mongols did not work out well. The barons of the southern kingdom would not endorse this policy and adopted an attitude of benevolent neutrality towards the Mamluk sultan of Egypt when he wished to move troops through their territory to check the Mongol advance. The pope's legate, Thomas, bishop of Bethlehem, excommunicated all Latin Christians who made their submission to the Mongols, and had no reason to modify this judgment when the Mamluks defeated the Mongol armies at Ain Jalut in Galilee in September 1260 and subsequently drove them back beyond the Euphrates.[9] Bohemond VI thus found himself

1. Cahen, *Syrie*, pp 703–12; Templar of Tyre, c 303, *Gestes*, pp 161–2.
2. H-F. Delaborde, 'Lettre des Chrétiens de Terre Sainte à Charles d'Anjou (22 avril 1260)', *ROL*, 2, 1894, pp 211–15.
3. Letters of Clement IV, Martène, Durand, *Thes. Nov.*, II, 505, nos 402–3. Both Röhricht, 'Syria Sacra', p 27, n 23, and Fedalto, *Chiesa Latina*, II, p 125, assume that 'frere Raoul evesque de Gibel' (*CGOH*, no 3045 of 1262) is bishop of Jabala. He could equally well be the bishop of Gibelet.
4. Potthast, nos 19354–5.
5. The date of death of Augustine, appointed bishop of Latakia in 1254, is not known, Thomson, *Friars in the Cathedral*, pp 202–3. He might have lived to be restored to his cathedral.
6. Guiraud, no 338.
7. Delaborde, pp 117–19, no 57.
8. Jordan, nos 926, 945, 955, 962, 978, 986, 989, 1035, 1076, 1094, 1133, 1136, 1198, 1235, 1278, 1387.
9. For the consequences of Ain Jalut see Saunders, *Mongol Conquests*, pp 154–6.

excommunicated as so many of his predecessors had been, and the Franks in Syria were surrounded by the power of the Mamluk sultans, who took over the former Aiyubid lands of Syria which they had conquered from the Mongols. Not unnaturally they were particularly hostile to those Christians, like the prince of Antioch and the king of Cilicia, who had been Mongol allies, although they took little direct action against them until after the death of the Mongol ilkhan of Persia, Hulagu, in 1265.

Bohemond's excommunication proved an embarrassment to the new bishop of Tripoli. Bishop Opizo had died at about the time of the Mongol invasion, and had been replaced by the Roman nobleman, Paul, brother of the countess Lucia of Segni, prince Bohemond's mother.[1] This appointment indicates that even in the thirteenth century, when the papacy scrutinised episcopal appointments in Syria very closely, it was possible for secular rulers to secure the confirmation of their own nominees, but this happened only at Tripoli in the second half of the thirteenth century since there were no resident rulers at either Antioch or the southern capital of Acre during most of that time. Bishop Paul was a Franciscan, another indication of the growing influence of the mendicant orders in the Latin church in Syria, which reflected a parallel growth throughout the western church at the same time.[2] He approached pope Urban IV about how to deal with his excommunicate nephew, and the pope allowed him a fairly wide measure of discretion as Bohemond's case was still *sub judice* by the Roman see.[3] A renewed quarrel between the prince of Antioch and the church was thus avoided. Probably because he was excommunicated the prince was allowed no share in the appointment to the see of Tortosa which fell vacant in 1263, to which the pope himself nominated his chaplain, William, also a Franciscan.[4]

In 1266 the Mamluk sultan Baybars gave orders for an attack to be made on the Frankish coastal cities of Syria, although the main object of his campaign that year was the kingdom of Cilicia.[5] This incursion appears to have caused irreparable damage to the district of Jabala, for in 1267 pope Clement IV translated the bishop of Jabala to Potenza 'so that he may no longer be oppressed by unbearable poverty'.[6] He was never replaced, and the city

---

1. Opizo is last mentioned in July 1259, Delaville Le Roulx, 'Inventaire', no 315. Paul is first mentioned in October 1261, Guiraud, no 10. His relationship to Bohemond VI, *ibid.*, no 292.
2. G. Golubovich, *Biblioteca bio-bibliografica della Terra Santa e dell'Oriente francescano*, 5 vols, Quaracchi presso Firenze, 1906—27, I, pp 253—4.
3. Guiraud, no 292.
4. *Ibid.*, nos 219, 1019.
5. M.M. Ziada, 'The Mamluk Sultans to 1293', in Setton, II, pp 748—9.
6. Martène, Durand, *Thes. Nov.*, II, p 505, no 402.

itself passed out of Frankish control soon after.

In 1268 Baybars took Antioch itself and sacked it.[1]   Opizo was still in the west and no longer had any inducement to return. He was still drawing the revenues of the see of Limassol and continued to do so until 1280[2] when, it would appear, he was appointed administrator of the south Italian see of Trani.[3]   His castle of Qusair, which was extremely well fortified, continued to resist the Mamluks for some years, but finally fell to them in 1275.[4]   Thereafter, the only revenues which could accrue to Opizo in the Levant were those which belonged to him as dues from his suffragans. It would appear that his vicar, Bartholomew, archdeacon of Antioch, escaped the Mamluk sack. When the see of Tortosa fell vacant in 1272 a Bartholomew, a native of Antioch, was appointed to it and continued to act as the patriarch's vicar.[5] It would strain coincidence too far to suggest that he and archdeacon Bartholomew were different men, and it seems reasonable to infer that the patriarch nominated his vicar to the first diocese which fell vacant after the loss of Antioch.

The patriarchate of Antioch was now reduced to the five coastal cities of Gibelet, Tripoli, Tortosa, Valania and Latakia. Of these, Tripoli was by far the most important, but the ecclesiastical superior of the area was the patriarch's vicar, the bishop of Tortosa. This seems to have created no problems until prince Bohemond VI of Antioch died in 1275. His son, Bohemond VII, was a minor, and Bohemond VI's widow, the Armenian princess Sibyl, asked bishop Bartholomew of Tortosa to act as regent. Hugh III of Cyprus, king of Jerusalem, offered his assistance, but Bartholomew declined his help.[6] The presence of another bishop, with secular jurisdiction, in the city of Tripoli would probably have led to trouble with the diocesan, but such rivalry was exacerbated in this case by the fact that, as vicar of the patriarch, Bartholomew was able to outrank bishop Paul on an ecclesiastical level as well.

There were tensions in the county which the clash between the two bishops brought into the open. Bishop Paul had held the see of Tripoli for over fourteen years and had had the support in his early days of his sister, the countess Lucia. Many knights of Roman birth had entered the service of count Bohemond VI

1. Cahen, *Syrie*, p 716.
2. Gay-Vitte, no 635.
3. Ughelli, VII, 906, where he is wrongly called Othobonus.
4. Cahen, *Syrie*, p 717, n 17.
5. Bishop William is last mentioned in 1268, Delaville Le Roulx, 'Inventaire', no 347; a new bishop had been appointed by 1272, Guiraud-Cadier, no 363, identified as Bartholomew by Templar of Tyre, c 385, *Gestes*, p 202.
6. 'Eracles', XXXIV, 19, *RHC Occ*, II, p 466.

under the bishop's patronage and the native baronage objected
to this. They found a supporter in bishop Bartholomew, the
regent, and soon after he had come to power there were riots in
the city in which some of the Roman knights were killed, and the
bishop of Tripoli, who was a *confrater* of the Temple, found it
necessary to place himself and his goods under the protection of
that order.[1]   Matters were complicated in 1276 when the
Genoese lord of Gibelet married his son to a rich heiress to whom
the bishop of Tortosa had intended to marry one of his own
nephews: this led to war between Guy II Embriaco of Gibelet and
the young prince Bohemond.[2]   The rivalry between Bartholomew
of Tortosa and Paul of Tripoli continued, and by 1277 had
developed into an all-out war between the prince and his government, and the knights Templar who were protecting the bishop of
Tripoli.[3]   The bishop of Tripoli later complained to pope Nicholas
III that the prince had despoiled him of his goods and imprisoned
his servants; that when he had taken refuge with the Templars the
prince's followers had attacked the house; that when he had
excommunicated Bohemond VII and placed the city under an
interdict the prince had ignored the censures and had ill-treated
the clergy who obeyed them, and that he had finally ejected the
bishop from the Templar house and from his see.[4]

Although we do not have the count's story of what occurred,
matters had certainly reached so critical a point by the autumn
of 1278 that Roger of San Severino, *bailli* of the kingdom of
Jerusalem for Charles of Anjou, and Nicholas Lorgne, grand
master of the knights of St John, came to Tripoli to mediate
peace between the prince and the bishop.[5] It must be supposed
that Bartholomew of Tortosa was partly to blame for this trouble:
it was almost certainly he who, by virtue of his superior ecclesiastical authority, absolved the prince from observing the bishop of
Tripoli's interdict, and he was cited to appear in Rome in person
to answer the charges which the bishop of Tripoli had made
against him.[6]   Bishop Paul of Tripoli subsequently went to Rome
in 1279 to appeal to the pope in person. Nicholas III took a very
strong line with Bohemond VII, threatening to refuse to lift his
excommunication unless he redressed the grievances of the bishop
of Tripoli, and to unleash the force of the military orders against
him if he failed to do so.[7]   This was rhetoric, given the state of

1. *Ibid.*, XXXIV, 21, pp 468—9; Gay-Vitte, no 520.
2. Templar of Tyre, cc 391—3, *Gestes*, pp 204—5.
3. 'Eracles', XXXIV, 36, *RHC Occ*, II, p 481.
4. Gay-Vitte, no 520.
5. *CGOH*, no 3673.
6. Gay-Vitte, no 104.
7. *Ibid.*, no 520.

Christian power in Syria, and Bohemond VII must have known this. Whether he ever fully restored the property of the church of Tripoli is not known, but bishop Paul never returned to his see. He had property in the Papal States,[1] and he spent the rest of his life in Italy, sometimes acting as a papal legate, as when he helped to arrange the marriage between Rudolph of Habsburg and a daughter of Charles of Anjou.[2] He nominated a canon of Tripoli, Peter Orlando of Valmoton, to act as his vicar in the diocese.[3] Bishop Bartholomew of Tortosa, who in 1278 had been summoned to appear in Rome within eight months to answer the charges against him, finally appeared at the papal court in 1285. By that time bishop Paul was dead, and so was pope Nicholas, and the new pope, Martin IV, ordered the case to be dropped.[4] But when Bohemond VII died childless in 1287, and his mother suggested that bishop Bartholomew should once again be regent, this time for her daughter Lucia who had married a Sicilian nobleman and was living in south Italy, the barons of Tripoli unanimously refused her request.[5] Bartholomew's rule had been too turbulent for them to wish for it to be repeated.

Paul of Segni proved to be the last Latin bishop to rule in Tripoli. When he died pope Martin IV reserved the collation of the see to the papacy, and his successor, Honorius IV, designated the papal chaplain, Cinthius de Pinea of Rome, but, in 1286, before he had been consecrated, he was translated to the vacant archbishopric of Capua.[6] In his place the pope nominated a Benedictine abbot, Bernard of Montmajour in the diocese of Arles, but he did not immediately go to Syria.[7] In 1288 he was appointed administrator of the Romagna, pending the appointment of a new rector, and in the following year he was commissioned by the pope to mediate peace between the patriarch of Aquileia and the doge of Venice.[8] Since the death of bishop Paul the Latin patriarchate of Antioch had been steadily declining. The Mamluk sultan Kalavun captured the Hospitaller fortress of al-Marqab, all that remained of the diocese of Valania, in 1285. In 1287 Latakia was captured by him, and if there was still a Latin bishop of that see[9] he was killed or expelled at that time. In 1289 the

1. Guiraud, no 10.
2. Gay-Vitte, no 765; cf. nos 766–7, 772–5, 797–8, 801, 804, 831–2, 860.
3. Mas Latrie, *Chypre*, III, p 662.
4. Olivier-Martin, no 556.
5. Templar of Tyre, c 467, *Gestes*, p 231.
6. Prou, nos 231, 502.
7. *Ibid.*, nos 544, 674.
8. Langlois, nos 6966, 1334.
9. The last recorded bishop is Peter of S. Hilario who resigned for reasons of health in 1272, Eubel, I, p 292, note.

sultan's troops took Tripoli, and overran the rest of the county; the only place to remain in Christian hands was Gibelet which Peter of Embriaco held as a fief of the Mamluks for several more years.[1]   After this time the only part of the patriarchate of Antioch which was still in Frankish hands was the Templar fortress of Tortosa, where bishop Bartholomew had his see.

With the possible exception of the bishop of Latakia, all the Latin bishops were either absent from their sees when the Mamluks captured them, or they succeeded in escaping. Gerard, the last bishop of Valania, who was a Hospitaller, took refuge in Acre, and in 1289 was assigned by the abbot of Mount Sion income from the European property of that community: 120 *livres* of Paris to be paid annually at Acre from the revenues of St Samson's, Orleans, together with administration of the priory of St Samson's, Douai.[2]

Bishop Hugh of Gibelet, a Franciscan, although he could have stayed in his see under Muslim suzerainty, did not do so, but came to the court of king Edward I of England in 1289, where he stayed for two years. During his time there he met a member of the community of Lanercost on the Scottish border to whom he gave a graphic account of the Muslim sack of Tripoli which became incorporated in the chronicle of that house.[3] Bishop Bernard of Tripoli finally went to Syria after the fall of his see, as commander of a fleet of papal galleys which reached Acre in 1290.[4] He survived the fall of that city in 1291, and was given the administration of the see of Famagusta in Cyprus.[5] Later that year he was sent to England as an envoy from pope Nicholas IV, who ordered the English clergy to subscribe two silver marks a day for his upkeep.[6] Pope Boniface VIII later made him administrator of the abbey of Monte Cassino (Bernard was unique among the bishops of the patriarchate of Antioch in being a Benedictine monk), and he died in 1296.[7]

Tortosa was one of the last fortresses in Syria to remain in Frankish hands. The Templars evacuated it on 3 August 1291 and bishop Bartholomew left with them. A year later he was living at Tarsus in Cilicia, the only part of the former Latin dominions which was still in Christian hands under its Armenian kings. Pope

1. Runciman, *Crusades*, III, pp 395—407.
2. *RR*, I, pp 386—7, nos 1483—4.
3. *The Chronicle of Lanercost, 1272—1346*, trans H. Maxwell, Glasgow 1913, pp 61—7.
4. Langlois, nos 2252, 2258, 2269, 4387—8, 4389.
5. *Ibid.*, no 5968.
6. *Ibid.*, no 7632.
7. Thomas-Faucon-Digard, no 608.

Nicholas IV wrote to him there on 5 January, sending him a dispensation for the daughters of Julian, lord of Sidon, who were legitimised despite the fact that their parents had been related within the prohibited degrees. The letter was also addressed to the Latin archbishop of Tarsus.[1] This see, which had remained vacant for sixty years, was revived at this juncture, chiefly for the benefit of Frankish refugees from Outremer who had entered the service of the Cilician crown, but partly because, in the face of the Mamluk threat, the Armenian church was once again willing to strengthen its links with the Roman see. In the fourteenth century Tarsus remained the sole diocese of the Latin patriarchate of Antioch.

When Frankish rule in Syria finally ended the patriarch Opizo of Antioch was still alive. He had not been to the east for a quarter of a century, and he seems to have been something of an embarrassment to the western church, for he ranked as fourth most important prelate in the entire Christian world, yet he had no see and no revenue save what he could draw from the administration of the relatively minor bishopric of Trani. Pope Nicholas IV rectified this by making him administrator of the archdiocese of Genoa in 1288.[2] Three years later his income was further increased: the pope made him administrator of the priory of S. Maria de Taro at Genoa, and ordered the Cistercian order and the Premonstratensian order to pay him a pension of 400 *livres* of Tours each, annually and for life.[3] He died a year later, having held the patriarchal office for forty-five years, the last Latin patriarch of Antioch who had ruled in the east.

The Latin church of Antioch never recovered from the territorial losses inflicted on it by Saladin. Its history in the years after 1187 is dominated by quarrels between churchmen and princes about the possession of lands and revenues, enlivened only occasionally by the disputes which both parties had on the same subject with the military orders. Church leaders like Peter of Angoulême and Bartholomew of Tortosa who had a strong drive to political power, and who, had they held office at a time when the lands of the patriarchate were more extensive, might have made a positive contribution to its defence and government, were diminished by the constricted area within which they had to work. Their concerns can only appear petty.

Yet despite the tedious litigation which occupies so large a place in the sources relating to thirteenth-century Antioch, the

---

1. Langlois, no 6401.
2. *Ibid.*, no 142.
3. *Ibid.*, nos 5979–82, 5985–6.

church there was drawn into the mainstream of European life in a way in which before 1187 it had not been. Many of the bishops who held power had been trained in western Europe: the standard of clerical education was far higher than it had previously been, and some of the men whom the popes appointed were eminent on an international, not merely on a local level. The patriarch Albert of Rizzato was an outstanding example of this, but so, in a different way, was his saintly predecessor, Peter of Ivrea, whose qualities of contemplative piety and practical competence would have earned him respect and high office in any part of the church. Moreover, in the second half of the thirteenth century a majority of the surviving Latin bishoprics in Antioch were held by Dominicans and Franciscans, trained in the ideals of orders which had been founded in response to the needs of contemporary society, and thus better able to give pastoral care to the Franks in their charge. The thirteenth-century church of Antioch had many faults, not least an obsessive care about its temporalities, which the presence of mendicant bishops did nothing to lessen, and which made it a source of discord in Frankish states which were in desperate need of unity; yet to the end it remained a living church, open to new influences from the west, and one whose bishops, whatever their failings, stayed with their flocks so long as their dioceses remained in Christian hands.

10. THE LATIN CHURCH OF JERUSALEM AFTER 1187

Before the third crusade reached Syria the prospects of the Latin church of Jerusalem looked very bleak. Tyre was the only part of the old kingdom which had survived the conquests of Saladin, and the remaining Christian forces were vainly attempting to lay siege to Muslim-held Acre, while themselves being besieged by the armies of Saladin. With the exception of the bishop of Sebastia, whose fate is unknown,[1] and of the archbishop of Tyre, who was touring the west raising support for the new crusade,[2] all the Latin bishops of the kingdom, led by the patriarch Heraclius, gathered in the camp at Acre. Bishop Rufinus of Acre had been killed at the battle of Hattin,[3] but a successor was chosen in the camp as an expression of confidence in the Christian certainty of victory, so that when the city did fall a Latin bishop could once more be enthroned there.

Conditions of life in the camp at Acre between the mounting of the siege in the autumn of 1189 and the arrival of the main French and English armies in the spring of 1191 were very harsh. Plague broke out and carried off queen Sibyl and her children, and this may have accounted for the high death-rate among the bishops too. During this period the patriarch died, and so did the archbishops of Nazareth and Petra, the bishops of Beirut, Hebron, Lydda, Sidon and Tiberias, together with the newly-elected bishop of Acre.[4] Later, during the course of the campaign of Richard I, the bishop of Bethlehem fell into Saladin's hands and died in a Muslim prison.[5] The only Latin prelate to live right through the siege was Aimery, archbishop of Caesarea, and the only other survivor from the episcopate of the old kingdom was archbishop Joscius of Tyre, who returned to Syria with the third crusade.

By his treaty with Saladin in 1192 which ended the war, Richard I of England secured for the Franks a narrow strip of coastal territory, extending from Jaffa to Tyre, which included condominium with the Muslims over Lydda and Ramla. Only three

---

1. Bishop Ralph is last recorded in May 1187, Ernoul, p 148.
2. *Itinerarium Regis Ricardi*, I, 17, II, 3, pp 31–2, 140–1; 'Eracles', XXXIV, 5, 8, *RHC Occ*, II, pp 111–12, 115.
3. Ralph of Coggeshall, p 21.
4. Roger of Houedene, III, p 87.
5. 'Eracles', western redaction, *RHC Occ*, II, pp 194, 196.

of the thirteen cathedral cities of the Latin patriarchate remained
in Frankish hands: Tyre, Caesarea and Acre. The first two had
archbishops who had survived the wars, and on 17 August 1191
the canons of Acre elected a new bishop.[1] This was Theobald,
former prior of Nazareth cathedral,[2] who is first recorded as a
canon there in 1174.[3] His appointment presented no canonical
problem, since he was a suffragan of the archbishop of Tyre.

The secular government of the new state passed to Henry of
Troyes, a nephew of Richard I of England, who in 1192 had
married Isabel, the daughter of king Amalric and the only surviving member of the old royal family of Jerusalem. Although Isabel
was styled queen, her husband did not take the royal title, probably because he deferred his coronation in the hope that it might
take place in Jerusalem if that city were recaptured. It was
important for administrative reasons that a new patriarch should
be chosen to have charge of the Latin church, but it was also
important for reasons of Christian morale. Neither the Franks in
the east nor the western Church ever admitted that the settlement
of 1192 was permanent: they wished to regain the lands of the
kingdom as it had existed before Hattin and, above all, to restore
Christian control of the holy places. Failure to appoint a new
patriarch would be tantamount to admitting that they had no
immediate hopes of achieving these ambitions. Nevertheless, the
patriarchal office remained vacant for some years.

A western redaction of the 'Eracles' relates that the canons of
the Holy Sepulchre elected archbishop Aimery of Caesarea as new
patriarch without reference to Henry of Troyes and that the count
was very angry when he learned of this and imprisoned them.
Archbishop Joscius of Tyre acted as mediator, and persuaded the
count to avoid a confrontation with the pope by accepting the
nomination, and to make his peace with the new patriarch by
knighting his nephew, Gratian, and giving him a valuable fief.
The canons of the Sepulchre sent envoys to Rome to tell the pope
what they had done and Celestine III confirmed their appointment
and sent back a *pallium* for the new patriarch.[4] These events are
usually placed in 1194, but there is no warrant for this in the text,
and it seems likely that they occupied several years, while the
pope heard the procurators of the canons and also those of Henry
of Troyes, who based his objection on the fact that the method
of election was contrary to the traditional privileges of the rulers

1. *Chronicle of the Reigns of Henry II and Richard I*, ed Stubbs, II, p 189.
2. Innocent III, 'Reg.', I, no 517, *PL*, 214, 476−7.
3. *CGOH*, vol II, p 906, no 16; cf. Delaborde, pp 87−8, no 40, of 1178.
4. *RHC Occ*, II, pp 203−5.

of Jerusalem.[1]   The judgment went against Henry, and although later rulers were, of course, able to influence patriarchal elections, they had to work through the machinery of the Roman curia, whereas their twelfth-century predecessors had chosen candidates at will, and the papacy had not been consulted unless an appeal against the royal choice were lodged at Rome by the canonical electors.

Aimery first appears in office in October 1197, very shortly before Henry of Troyes fell to his death from a gallery in the palace of Acre.[2]   A few months later queen Isabel married Aimery of Lusignan, king of Cyprus, and the ceremony was performed in Cyprus by the archbishop of Tyre, although the patriarch subsequently crowned the royal couple.   Aimery was not altogether happy about this marriage, and was reprimanded by Innocent III for disparaging its validity.[3]   His reasons are not known: perhaps he considered that Isabel was not free to remarry, since her first husband, Humphrey IV of Toron, from whom she had been forcibly separated in 1190, was still alive.[4]   This interpretation would accord with the fact that after Humphrey died in 1198[5] Aimery's relations with the king and queen were quite amicable.

Once the new patriarch had been appointed it became possible to take in hand the reorganisation of the Latin church, notably the filling of vacant benefices. Joscius remained archbishop of Tyre and chancellor of the kingdom under Aimery of Lusignan. In 1197, partly with the help of the vanguard of the crusade which the western emperor, Henry VI, was intending to launch, the coastal region between Tyre and Beirut, the northern frontier of the old kingdom, was recovered by the Franks. The city of Beirut came completely into Frankish hands, and a condominium over the ruined city of Sidon was initially arranged with the Aiyubids, who then ceded their remaining rights to the Franks in 1204.[6]   Bishops were appointed to the sees of Beirut and Sidon within a year,[7] and thus Joscius of Tyre restored the full number of suffragans which he had had before 1187.

Aimery consecrated a Frenchman, Peter of Limoges, to his former see of Caesarea. Nothing is known about his origins, but he

1. The date of 1194 is given in the most recent list: Fedalto, *Chiesa Latina*, II, p 134.

2. A privilege issued by Henry of Troyes on 19 October 1197, Müller, p 73, no 45.

3. Innocent III, 'Reg.', I, no 518, *PL*, 214, 477–8.

4. Hamilton in Baker, ed, *Medieval Women*, pp 172–3.

5. Roger of Houedene, IV, p 78.   Innocent III later called the annulment of Isabel's marriage to Humphrey in question, 'Reg.', XVI, 11, *PL*, 216, 980–81.

6. E.N. Johnson, 'The Crusades of Frederick Barbarossa and Henry VI', in Setton, II, p 111; Hardwicke, *ibid.*, p 532.

7. Innocent III, 'Reg.', I, nos 73, 516, *PL*, 214, 64–5, 476.

must have been a comparatively young man since he held that office for thirty-eight years.[1] The patriarch fixed his own see in Acre, which was the new royal capital, as it had formerly been the commercial capital, of the Frankish kingdom. He did not lack money, since the Holy Sepulchre possessed extensive lands all over the west, as well as some property in the area of Palestine which remained under Frankish control. The patriarch also had direct ecclesiastical control over the city of Jaffa,[2] but he did not live there, for it had become a frontier city and was remote from the new centre of government. His establishment of his pro-cathedral in Acre, which had a bishop of its own and which was part of the ecclesiastical province of Tyre, was not without problems, not least because the patriarch's presence attracted there other exiled bishops and religious communities. Consideration of this is best deferred to a later chapter.[3]

The problem of the organisation of the Latin church in the kingdom of Acre was a complex one, since the new political boundaries did not, in most cases, coincide with the former diocesan boundaries. The pragmatic solution adopted by Aimery, which was continued by his successors until the middle of the thirteenth century, was this: if a former Latin diocese remained partly in Frankish hands so that its lands provided an adequate source of revenue a Latin bishop should be appointed to it, even though his cathedral city was in Muslim territory; while in the case of those sees which were entirely controlled by Muslims bishops should continue to be appointed if the diocese owned enough property elsewhere to pay for the upkeep of the bishop, his household and his officials. Only in cases where the diocese was in Muslim hands and had no adequate endowments elsewhere was a see allowed to lapse completely.

Thus a new bishop was appointed to Lydda, even though the cathedral of St George had been wrecked by Saladin[4] and the co-cathedral at Ramla was in territory partly controlled by Muslims, because a large part of the diocese was in Frankish hands. He was employed by Innocent III in western Europe to enlist support for the new crusade which the pope was organising.[5] New bishops were also appointed to Tiberias and Sebastia, for although both cathedrals were deep in Muslim territory it is possible that some of the western parts of these dioceses remained in Frankish hands. In 1198 the new bishop of Tiberias brought a lawsuit against the

1. Kohler, p 167, no 58, of 1199.
2. See chapter 3 above.
3. See chapter 11 below.
4. Baha ed-Din, *Life of Saladin*, trans C.R. Conder, London 1897, p 300.
5. Innocent III, 'Reg.', I, nos 328, 343, *PL*, 214, 293–4, 317–18.

Templars to gain possession of 1,300 besants and other valuables which his predecessor had deposited with them, while the new bishop of Sebastia took a leading part in the patriarchal election which followed Aimery's death.[1]

It was essential to appoint new bishops to Bethlehem and Nazareth since these holy places were an important focus for the piety of western Europe. Although all their lands were in Saracen territory, both churches possessed extensive property in western Europe which would yield revenues to support a bishop and canons, and new incumbents had been appointed for both sees by 1196, perhaps through the direct intervention of the pope, since the appointment of the patriarch seems still to have been *sub judice* at that time.[2]

No attempt was made to appoint strictly titular bishops, who had neither dioceses nor other sources of revenue, and for that reason no effort was made to find new bishops for Petra or Hebron.[3] By the time of Aimery's death in 1202[4] the Latin church of Jerusalem had been reconstituted, with a patriarch, three archbishops, in Tyre, Nazareth and Caesarea, and seven bishops, in Acre, Beirut, Bethlehem, Lydda, Sidon, Sebastia and Tiberias. The hierarchy was once again as large as it had been in the reign of king Fulk, although the bishops exercised jurisdiction in only a small fraction of the territory of the old kingdom. This meant in practice that the ecclesiastical establishment was far in excess of the needs of the Frankish population and a considerable drain on the economic resources of the kingdom of Acre, but when the new church was set up nobody in Syria supposed that the loss of territory was anything but temporary.

Indeed, the early thirteenth century was a period of intense crusading zeal. Between the capture of Jerusalem in 1099 and its loss in 1187 only two major crusades had come to the east; that of 1101 which came to grief in Asia Minor, and the second crusade of 1148. In the sixty years following the battle of Hattin, no fewer than eight crusades were launched to recover the holy places:[5] not all of them reached their destination, and some

---

1. *Ibid.*, 'Reg.', II, no 257, *PL*, 214, 816–18. R. Hiestand, H.E. Mayer, 'Die Nachfolge des Patriarchen Monachus von Jerusalem', *Basler Zeitschrift für Geschichte und Altertumskunde*, 74, 1974, p 128.

2. Pflugck-Harttung, II, p 400, no 457.

3. Hebron was left vacant until the reign of Innocent IV. An archbishop of Petra is mentioned only once after 1190, in 1238, Auvray, no 4504. Nothing else is known about him.

4. Last recorded May 1202, TT, I, pp 424–6, no 108; his successor is first mentioned in August 1203, Innocent III, 'Reg.', VI, no 129, *PL*, 215, 141–5.

5. The third crusade; the crusade of Henry VI; the fourth crusade; the fifth crusade; the crusade of Frederick II; the crusade of Theobald of Navarre; the crusade of Richard of Cornwall; the first crusade of St Louis.

proved to be exercises in diplomacy rather than in war against the infidel, but from the point of view of the Franks in the kingdom of Acre this sustained interest in the holy places shown by the Christians of the west must have created the expectation that it was only a matter of time until the old kingdom was restored to its former frontiers.

Indeed, when the patriarch Aimery and his colleagues arranged for the appointment of what proved to be a superfluity of bishops they did so in the sure expectation of western aid. The emperor Henry VI organised a crusade whose vanguard reached the Holy Land in 1197, but this enterprise was halted by his death.[1] When Innocent III became pope in the following year one of his first concerns was to launch a new crusade which assembled at Venice in 1202. The church of Jerusalem took a lively interest in this: the bishop of Lydda had helped to preach the crusade, and bishop Peter of Bethlehem and John, the new bishop-elect of Acre, attached themselves to the staff of the crusader army.[2] The pope sent cardinal Soffred of Sta Prassede to Syria to make arrangements for the arrival of the crusade.

At some time in 1202 the patriarch Aimery died. Hiestand and Mayer have published an important new set of evidence about the appointment of his successor. This relates how the electors, unable to reach any agreement, delegated the choice of a candidate to the archbishop of Tyre, who nominated Peter of Limoges, archbishop of Caesarea. Since archbishop Joscius of Tyre had predeceased the patriarch[3] this must refer to his successor, Clarembaud of Broies (or Brie), who had recently come to Syria from France,[4] and who may have been asked to arbitrate because, as a newcomer, he was thought to be impartial. The pope refused to ratify the election and, it is to be assumed, delegated the matter to his legate, cardinal Soffred. The cardinal quashed Peter of Limoges's appointment and was himself chosen as new patriarch, at some time before May 1203.[5] Before he became patriarch he quarrelled with the new archbishop of Tyre, who had been consecrated without his permission, but this altercation was probably not unconnected with the legate's decision about Clarembaud's

1. Johnson in Setton, II, pp 116–22.
2. Alberic of Trois Fontaines, 'Chronica', *MGH SS*, XXIII, p 880.
3. Last known act, October 1200, Strehlke, pp 30–1, no 38; he died before May 1202, TT, I, pp 424–6, no 108.
4. Innocent III, 'Reg.', VI, no 131, *PL*, 215, 147–8, which relates to Clarembaud's consecration at a time when Soffred was still legate but before he had been elected patriarch.
5. *CGOH*, no 1176. Hiestand and Mayer, *op. cit.*, *Basler Zeitschrift*, 74, 1974, pp 109–30, specially p 128.

choice of patriarch.[1]

By the summer of 1203 it was evident in Syria that the fourth crusade was not intending to come there directly, but to make a diversion to Constantinople, officially to restore a pro-Latin pretender. The patriarchate of Jerusalem then seemed less attractive to Soffred than his office of cardinal, for the possibility of the holy city's being recaptured had become more remote. He therefore sought to resign his see. Innocent III wrote him an eloquent letter, begging him to reconsider his decision, and sent him a *pallium* at the hands of a new legate, Peter of S. Marcello.[2] The pope's pleas were of no avail: not only did Soffred resign his see, but when news reached the Holy Land of the crusader capture and sack of Constantinople in 1204 and the subsequent dismemberment by the crusaders of the Byzantine empire, both Soffred and his fellow legate, cardinal Peter, left Syria and went to Constantinople. There Peter dispensed the crusaders from their vows to liberate the Holy Sepulchre, and thus effectively brought the crusade to an end and ensured that no help would reach the Franks of Syria. Byzantium and its spoils acted like a magnet to the impoverished Franks in Syria and churchmen were not above taking part in this scramble for temporal goods. The new archbishop of Tyre left his see and went to Constantinople,[3] while the bishops of Acre and Bethlehem stayed with the crusaders instead of returning to their dioceses. They were among the electors of the first Latin emperor of the east, Baldwin,[4] and the bishop of Bethlehem was killed at the battle of Adrianople in 1205 when the Frankish army suffered a crushing defeat at the hand of the Bulgars.[5]

The Franks of Syria were neglected while all this excitement was happening in Frankish Greece, and their situation was dangerous. In the north the war of the Antiochene succession was in progress, while in the south king Aimery of Jerusalem died on 1 April 1205, and queen Isabel shortly after,[6] and the heir to the throne was queen Maria, daughter of Isabel and Conrad of Montferrat, who was fourteen years old. Pope Innocent saw that a new patriarch was needed for the church of Jerusalem, whose authority would be respected in the kingdom during the regency which must follow. He therefore secured the translation of

1. Innocent III, 'Reg.', VI, no 131, *PL*, 215, pp 147–8.
2. *Ibid.*, 'Reg.', VI, no 129, *PL*, 215, 141–5.
3. *Ibid.*, 'Reg.', VIII, no 136, *PL*, 215, 699–702.
4. Alberic of Trois Fontaines, 'Chronica', *MGH SS*, XXIII, p 884.
5. Geoffrey of Villehardouin, *La conquête de Constantinople*, s 361, ed E. Faral, 2 vols, Paris, 1938–9, II, p 170.
6. The exact date of Isabel's death is not known.

Albert, bishop of Vercelli.[1] Albert had had a good education in theology and canon law, and had been trained as an Austin canon. He had held the see of Vercelli for twenty years and had a great deal of experience as a diplomat, having acted as mediator between pope Clement III and the emperor Frederick Barbarossa and having been a trusted adviser of Barbarossa's son, Henry VI. Innocent III had employed him in 1199 to restore peace between Parma and Piacenza.[2] He was the most distinguished churchman to occupy the patriarchal throne of Jerusalem since the deposition of Daimbert of Pisa a century before and the pope granted him full legatine powers for four years and, when that period ended, he renewed them.[3]

Albert discouraged the proliferation of sees in his patriarchate which had been inaugurated by his predecessor. When he reached the east in 1206 there had been no effective patriarch of Jerusalem for three years and some sees had fallen vacant. There is no evidence that new incumbents were appointed to the sees of Lydda, Beirut, Sebastia, or Tiberias during his reign.[4] The see of Tiberias, indeed, remained vacant until 1241 when it was once again in Christian hands. If the establishment of bishops was indeed reduced, and if this impression is not merely caused by an absence of source material about those dioceses in this period, it was an eminently sensible move. The fourth crusade had been no help to Syria, in 1208 the Albigensian crusade began to be preached against Languedoc, and it must have been clear to Albert that no aid would reach him from the west. An establishment of a patriarch and six bishops was more than adequate for the needs of the kingdom of Acre, and less of an economic drain on its resources than the larger episcopate set up under Aimery had been.

The bishop of Bethlehem is never recorded as present in Syria in Albert's reign and it seems probable that he lived in the dependencies of his church in the west.[5] Of the remaining five bishops, Peter of Caesarea and Clarembaud of Tyre were already in office when Albert was appointed. The other three were nominated during his reign: Walter of Florence, who became bishop of Acre around 1208,[6], Robert, archbishop of Nazareth

1. Innocent III, 'Reg.', VIII, no 136, PL, 215, 699–702; Hiestand and Mayer, op. cit., loc. cit., pp 128–30.

2. P. Marie-Joseph, 'Albert de Verceil', DHGE, I, 1564–7.

3. Innocent III, 'Reg.', VIII, nos 101–3, 169–73, PL, 215, 669–70, 751–3.

4. There are no records of bishops of Lydda 1199–1223; of Tiberias, 1200–41; of Beirut 1200–21; of Sebastia, 1203–53.

5. Riant, Eglise de Bethléem, I, p 25, argues that the see was vacant from 1205–11.

6. Eracles, XXX, 13, RHC Occ, II, p 306.

from about 1210,[1] and Ralph of Merencourt who became bishop of Sidon around 1210.[2]

Albert's gifts as a diplomat were much needed in the Frankish east when he arrived there, for the northern Christian states had been thrown into confusion by the war of the Antiochene succession, while the throne of Acre was held by a minor, Maria, and the ruler of Cyprus, Hugh I of Lusignan, was also under age. The role of Albert of Jerusalem in the affairs of Antioch, where he excommunicated Bohemond IV for the murder of the patriarch Peter of Angoulême and arranged the election of a new patriarch, has already been examined in the previous chapter. At the pope's request arrangements were made for the marriage of Hugh I of Cyprus to Alice, daughter of Isabel of Jerusalem and Henry of Troyes, and the marriage contract was drawn up at the end of 1207 by the archbishop of Tyre.[3]

The most important matter to settle was the marriage of Maria, queen of Jerusalem. The patriarch presided over a council in 1208 at which it was decided to send envoys to Philip Augustus to ask him to choose a suitable husband for the queen, and one of the ambassadors who was sent was bishop Walter of Acre.[4] These negotiations proved slow, and before a reply was received the truce with Egypt expired: the sultan al-Adil offered to renew it, but his terms were rejected by the patriarch and bishops, who had the support of the grand master of the Templars, and their wishes prevailed against those of the regent of Acre, John of Ibelin, the barons of the kingdom and the masters of the knights of St John and of the Teutonic knights, which is an index of the power of the new patriarch in temporal as well as ecclesiastical affairs.[5]

Philip Augustus finally designated John of Brienne as husband for the young queen. He came to Syria in the autumn of 1210 and Albert of Jerusalem immediately performed the marriage and subsequently crowned the royal couple at Tyre.[6] John was well-born, related to the royal house of Sicily,[7] and proved an effective ruler. He appointed Ralph of Merencourt, bishop of Sidon, as his chancellor.[8] John had no roots in the kingdom and only held the

1. He may be the unnamed archbishop of 1196—9; Pflugck-Harttung, II, p 400, no 457: Innocent III, 'Reg.', I, no 567, PL, 214, 521—3.
2. 'Eracles', XXXI, 1, RHC Occ, II, p 311.
3. Martène, Durand, Thes. Nov., I, 806—7.
4. 'Eracles', XXX, 12, 13, RHC Occ, II, pp 305—6.
5. Ibid., XXX, 16, p 309.
6. Ibid., XXXI, 1, p 311.
7. In 1200 his brother Walter had married Alberia, daughter of king Tancred of Sicily. See genealogy in Van Cleve, Frederick II, p 43.
8. Delaborde, pp 95—6, no 46.

crown in his wife's right; when Maria died in 1212 having given
birth to an infant daughter, Isabel, the king's position was called
in question by some of the nobility. He sent his chancellor to the
pope to inform him of the problems this caused him[1] and Innocent III ordered the patriarch to rally support for the king and
his infant daughter, a task which Albert seems to have carried out
effectively, since John's rule was not subsequently challenged.[2]

It is difficult to avoid the impression that Albert, as patriarch
and papal legate, was a more important person in Acre than the
king in the early years of the new reign. The pope certainly found
him an invaluable support and used him on business outside the
kingdom. In addition to being required to mediate in the war of
the Antiochene succession,[3] Albert was also used to restore peace
between Hugh I of Cyprus and the former *bailli*, Walter of
Montbéliard,[4] and to scrutinise the election of the new archbishop of Nicosia, which he quashed.[5] In 1213 the pope wrote
to invite him to the forthcoming Lateran council, and to ask him
to undertake the delicate mission of arranging the visit of a papal
nuncio to the court of the sultan of Egypt in order to request
him to restore Frankish territory in Syria peacefully.[6]

Albert of Jerusalem was more than a diplomat and a statesman.
He was asked by St Brocard, the prior of a group of hermits living
on Mount Carmel, to draw up a rule for his followers, and the
work which he composed in sixteen chapters, distinguished by its
great emphasis on austerity, became the primitive rule of the
Carmelite order, which was later ratified by pope Honorius III.[7]
Albert's cult was later established among the Carmelites, although
it was never extended to the universal church.[8]   He is the only
Latin bishop in the crusader states who has been raised to the
altars, and he may justly be considered as one of the great
monastic legislators of the western church. The career of this
able and devout man was brought to a sudden end when he was
assassinated during a procession in Acre on Holy Cross day 1214
by a clerk who considered that he had been unjustly deposed from
office by the patriarch.[9]

1. Innocent III, 'Reg.', XV, 211, *PL*, 216, 738—9.
2. *Ibid.*, 'Reg.', XV, no 210, *PL*, 216, 738.
3. See chapter 9 above.
4. Innocent III, 'Reg.', XIV, no 104, *PL*, 216, 466.
5. *Ibid.*, 'Reg.', XIV, 134, XV, 204, *PL*, 216, 494, 733—4.
6. *Ibid.*, 'Reg.', XVI, 36, *PL*, 216, 830—1.
7. B. Zimmermann, *Monumenta Historica Carmelitana*, I, Lirinae 1905, pp 12—17;
D. Knowles, *From Pachomius to Ignatius*, Oxford 1966, pp 55—6.
8. *AA SS, Apr.*, I, 769—77.
9. 'Chronique de Terre Sainte', c 71, *Gestes*, p 18; 'ATS', *AOL*, II, p 436.

The nomination of a successor was effectively in the hands of the crown, and John of Brienne designated his chancellor, Ralph of Merencourt, bishop of Sidon, who was consecrated patriarch by Innocent III during the fourth Lateran council.[1] The see of Tyre fell vacant at about this time, and a member of a Frankish family in Syria, Simon of Maugastel, was appointed archbishop before 1216.[2] These nominations to some extent reversed the trend, which had been growing since the death of the patriarch Aimery, to choose as bishops in the kingdom of Acre men who came direct from the west. But the change was only partial: when the see of Acre fell vacant Innocent III secured the appointment of James of Vitry, who was consecrated on 31 July 1216.[3] James had been trained in the cathedral schools of Paris and was a noted preacher, zealous for the crusading movement, who had preached the Albigensian crusade in northern France in 1211.[4] He came to the east immediately after his appointment[5] for the fifth crusade had been launched at the fourth Lateran council and he was eager to prepare the Franks in Syria for its arrival.

The new crusade was greeted with enthusiasm by the leaders of the Frankish church there. It was a quarter of a century since the third crusade had dispersed, and the new movement presented the first real opportunity to the Latin church of regaining the lands which it had lost at Hattin. The vanguard of the army arrived in Syria in the autumn of 1217. The patriarch Ralph carried the Cross when the host set out to campaign in Galilee that autumn, and he accompanied the crusaders when they went to strengthen the defences of Caesarea in the following Lent.[6] Reynier, bishop of Bethlehem, who is said to have been a Cistercian,[7] came out to Syria with the crusade, and he, together with the bishop of Acre and the archbishop of Nicosia, went with the patriarch as part of the army which laid siege to Damietta in June 1218.[8] The bishop of Acre and the patriarch remained there

---

1. 'Eracles', XXXI, 8, *RHC Occ*, II, p 319.
2. Clarembaud is presumably the archbishop mentioned in 1214, TT, II, pp 174–5, no 240; Simon was in office by 1217, 'Eracles', XXXI, 10, *RHC Occ*, II, p 323, and is probably the archbishop referred to in Pressutti, nos 16, 18, 23 of 1216. No archbishop of Tyre was present at Lateran IV, which suggests that the see was then vacant.
3. James of Vitry, *Lettres*, p 74, no 1.
4. Peter des Vaux-de-Cernay, *Histoire Albigeoise*, c 285, trans P. Guébin, H. Maisonneuve, Paris 1951, pp 115–16; P. Funk, *Jakob von Vitry, Leben und Werke*, Berlin 1909.
5. He reached Acre on 4 November 1216, *Lettres*, p 83, no 2.
6. *Ibid.*, p 99, no 2; Oliver of Paderborn, 'Historia Damiatina', cc 2–3, 5, ed Hoogeweg, pp 163–7, 168–9.
7. He was not at the council of Acre in 1217, 'Eracles', XXXI, 10, *RHC Occ*, II, p 323, but joined the army at Damietta in 1218, Pressutti, no 1580. Riant, *Eglise de Bethléem*, I, p 25, suggests that he may have been a Cistercian.
8. Oliver of Paderborn, 'Historia Damiatina', c 10, ed Hoogeweg, pp 175–6.

throughout most of the campaign. They did not take part in the fighting, but gave spiritual support to the Christian forces: during the attack on the chain tower of Damietta, for example, the patriarch lay prone on the ground imploring divine aid.[1]   When al-Kamil, the sultan of Egypt, offered the crusaders the cession of all their former territory in Jerusalem with the exception of the lands beyond Jordan if they would evacuate Egypt, the patriarch supported the legate, cardinal Pelagius, in his rejection of those terms, although this was against the wishes of the king and of most of the native baronage, and he must have felt justified in this decision when Damietta fell to the crusade a few weeks later.[2]

It is apparent that a change had taken place in the crusading ideal from the reaction of the bishop of Acre to the fall of the city.   His immediate concern was to baptise the little children who had survived the rigours of the siege,[3] a practice which he had already adopted after the Tabor campaign of 1217, when he bought captive Muslim children from the crusaders, baptised them and placed them in convents to be reared in the Christian faith.[4] To modern sensibilities the rearing of one's enemies' children in an alien faith may appear a crude and insensitive form of idealism, but it marked a great change from the indiscriminate slaughter of all unbelievers, irrespective of age, which had characterised the first crusade. Within a generation western Europe would produce religious leaders who would be more concerned to convert the infidel than to kill him, and this profound change in religious outlook was already prefigured by the appearance in the crusader camp at Damietta of St Francis of Assisi, who was admitted to an audience by the sultan and attempted to persuade him, it is true to no purpose, of the truth of the Christian revelation.[5]

When Damietta fell it must have seemed to Latin churchmen that the crusade was going to be successful, and it was probably at this time that appointments began to be made to vacant sees. When Ralph of Merencourt had been translated to Jerusalem the see of Sidon had been left vacant and its administration placed in the hands of the archbishop of Tyre, a situation which lasted until at least 1218.[6]   But by 1221 a new bishop of Sidon had been appointed, and in that same year a new bishop of Beirut is

1. *Ibid.*, c 13, p 183.
2. James of Vitry, *Lettres*, pp 124–5, no 6.
3. Oliver of Paderborn, *op. cit.*, c 33, ed Hoogeweg, p 229.
4. *Ibid.*, c 3, p 167; James of Vitry, *Lettres*, p 128, no 6.
5. *Ibid.*, pp 132–3 (see Huygens's note on this passage, p 132); Golubovich, *Terra Santa . . . Francescana*, I, pp 1–104.
6. Pressutti, nos 18, 1094.

also mentioned.[1]   Two years later there is evidence of a bishop of Lydda once again, although he was allowed to keep his prebend in the north-west Spanish cathedral of Orense because of the poverty of his see.[2]

In fact, the fall of Damietta marked the zenith of crusading fortunes.   In 1220 al-Muazzam, the sultan's brother, and ruler of Damascus, attacked the remaining Frankish territory in Palestine, and the Latin clergy there, led by the archbishops of Caesarea and Nazareth, the bishop of Bethlehem and the heads of the great religious houses, addressed an appeal for help to Philip Augustus of France.[3]   In the following year the crusade itself was defeated while attempting to advance on Cairo and was forced to sue for peace, which the sultan granted on condition that Damietta was handed over to him and the army evacuated from Egypt.   James of Vitry was one of the leaders who negotiated this peace, and together with the king was one of the hostages taken by the sultan to ensure that the terms of the treaty were carried out.[4]

As a result the Latin church of Acre found itself in a worse position after the crusade than it had been in before.   The number of sees had increased to nine[5] whereas the amount of territory which the Franks controlled had not increased at all. The bishop of Bethlehem returned once more to the west and lived on the properties of his see in Italy.[6]   This was a personal and not a corporate solution: the Franks of Syria needed powerful western allies who could secure the restoration of their former territory.   For this reason at the end of 1222 the patriarch Ralph accompanied John of Brienne and the grand master of the Hospitallers to Verona to discuss the possibility of a marriage between the western emperor Frederick II, who had recently become a widower, and Isabel, daughter of king John, and heiress of the kingdom of Jerusalem.[7]   Frederick, as emperor and king of Sicily, was the most powerful ruler in western Europe

---

1. *Ibid.*, no 3498.
2. *Ibid.*, no 4197; J. Riley-Smith, 'Latin Titular bishops in Palestine and Syria, 1137–1291', *Catholic Historical Review*, 64, 1978, pp 8–9.
3. Delaborde, Appendix, pp 123–5.
4. Ernoul, pp 444, 446; Roger of Wendover, III, pp 263–5, cites a letter from the grand master of the Temple to the preceptor of England about the treaty with the sultan, which states that 'the bishop of Acre, the chancellor', was in Damietta when the treaty was made and was opposed to the surrender of the city. James of Vitry was not at Damietta then, nor was he chancellor of the kingdom, so it would appear either that the grand master named the wrong bishop, or that his text was incorrectly transcribed by the chronicler, or by a later copyist.
5. Jerusalem, Tyre, Caesarea, Nazareth, Bethlehem, Lydda, Beirut, Sidon and Acre.
6. Riant, *Eglise de Bethléem*, I, p 135, no 8.
7. Oliver of Paderborn, 'Historia Damiatina', c 89, ed Hoogeweg, p 280; 'Chronique de Terre Sainte', c 80, *Gestes*, p 20. The meeting was finally held at Ferentino in March 1223.

and was known to be interested in the crusade, since he had taken the cross at Aix in 1215 when the fifth crusade was first preached and had contributed some troops to it.[1]   Although the negotiations went well, some of the Frankish bishops in Syria felt discouraged by the failure of the fifth crusade and the anomalies presented by a Latin church in exile from the holy places, and in 1224 Honorius III had to write to James of Vitry urging him to persevere in his charge and not to resign his see.[2]

Ralph of Merencourt returned to Syria in 1223[3] and died in the course of the following year.[4]   If the account in the 'Eracles' is to be believed he crowned Isabel as queen of Jerusalem at Tyre. If so this must have happened some time before her marriage to Frederick II which did not occur until the autumn of 1225. The archbishop of Capua came to Syria then as the emperor's representative and married the young queen as proxy for his master, and Isabel set sail for Italy, accompanied by the senior Latin prelate in Syria, Simon of Maugastel, archbishop of Tyre.[5]

With the heiress of the kingdom married to the western emperor the prosperous future of the Franks in Syria seemed assured.   Frederick II, however, disconcerted both his father-in-law and public opinion in general by asserting that, as Isabel had come of age, her father's regency was at an end and that he, and not John of Brienne, was lawful king of Jerusalem.[6]   The consequences of this must have been obvious at the time: Frederick, it is true, was committed to leading a crusade to the east, but it could not reasonably be expected that he would live there permanently when his chief dominions were in western Europe. He could delegate the government of Jerusalem to a son of his marriage with Isabel, but it would be many years before such a child would come of age to assume those responsibilities, and there would therefore be a long period of regencies for an absentee king. If John of Brienne had been left in power that period would have been considerably lessened. This was not only a political problem or a constitutional one, for the absence of a resident king at Acre had a profound effect on the evolution of the Latin church in Syria during the remaining years of Frankish rule there.

1. T. Van Cleve, 'The Crusade of Frederick II', in Setton, II, pp 429–38.
2. James of Vitry, *Lettres*, pp 154–5; Pressutti, no 4839.
3. Philip of Novara, c 107, *Gestes*, p 30.
4. *Ibid.*, c 109, p 30; 'ATS', *AOL*, II, p 438; Pressutti, no 5219.
5. Huillard-Bréholles, II, pp 921–4; 'Eracles', XXXII, 20, *RHC Occ*, II, pp 357–8; Philip of Novara, c 116, *Gestes*, p 33, places Isabel's coronation after Ralph of Merencourt's death. If this is true, the ceremony must have been performed by Simon of Maugastel, archbishop of Tyre.
6. Van Cleve, in Setton, II, pp 442–4.

An experienced bishop was chosen to be the new patriarch of Jerusalem, Gerold of Lausanne, bishop of Valence and formerly abbot of Cluny.[1] He waited in the west until the new crusade was ready to set out, and in his absence Peter, archbishop of Caesarea, took charge of the affairs of the Latin church in Palestine.[2] Although the archbishop of Tyre was the senior metropolitan in the patriarchate, there is no evidence that Simon of Maugastel ever returned to Syria after escorting queen Isabel to Italy, and in 1229 he was translated to the Latin patriarchate of Constantinople.[3] This was the first occasion on which a Syrian Latin bishop had been translated to an office elsewhere in the church and showed that stricter papal control over the church in Syria did not work entirely to the disadvantage of the native clergy.

Frederick II had given a solemn undertaking to Honorius III that he would lead his crusade to the Holy Land not later than the feast of the Assumption 1227, but, pleading that illness made him unfit to travel on that date, he sent the advance guard of his army ahead, together with the new patriarch.[4] The bishops of Syria were hopeful of the emperor's success, and bishop Reynier of Bethlehem obtained from the new pope, Gregory IX, a detailed confirmation of the lands of his see, many of which were under Saracen rule.[5] James of Vitry, bishop of Acre, who might have been expected to give his enthusiastic support to this crusade, returned to the west at about this time and in 1228 resigned his see: he was appointed cardinal-bishop of Tusculum in the following year.[6] Clearly a change was taking place in the Latin church of Jerusalem which in the space of a year could provide a new patriarch of Constantinople and a cardinal-bishop for the universal church. James's place at Acre was taken by John of Pruvino, dean of Paris, who was consecrated in Rome by the pope and who reached Syria in about 1230.[7]

By the time bishop John reached Acre the situation in Syria had changed radically. Pope Gregory IX had excommunicated Frederick II in 1227 for failing to fulfil his obligations as a crusader, supposing that the emperor was using the deferred crusade to neutralise papal opposition to his Italian political policies.[8]

1. Appointed by May 1225, Pressutti, nos 5473–4, where the editor has wrongly added the patriarch's name as Matthew.
2. *Ibid.*, nos 5568, 5572, 5808.
3. Auvray, no 328.
4. 'Eracles', XXXII, 23, *RHC Occ*, II, p 364; Philip of Novara, c 121, *Gestes*, p 35; cf. Van Cleve in Setton, II, pp 440–6.
5. Riant, *Eglise de Bethléem*, I, pp 140–7, no 11.
6. Alberic of Trois Fontaines, 'Chronica', *MGH SS*, XXIII, p 923.
7. *Idem.* Auvray, no 491.
8. Van Cleve in Setton, II, pp 446–7.

When Frederick finally did come to Syria in 1228 it was as an excommunicate, and this posed problems for the patriarch, the Latin hierarchy and the military orders. The patriarch and the archbishops of Caesarea and Nazareth were present with the vanguard of his army, but refused to serve under his command.[1] In the event this proved an academic point, since the crusade was bloodless and the emperor achieved the restoration of Jerusalem, Bethlehem and Nazareth to the Franks, with thin corridors of land connecting them to the main coastal territory of Acre, together with the lands around the ruined city of Sidon, by negotiation with the sultan al-Kamil of Egypt.[2]   Although the treaty seemed to have obtained what the Christian world most wanted, the church and the military orders were far from satisfied with it, with the exception of the Teutonic knights who gave the emperor their full support.   The patriarch wrote to the pope deploring that he and the bishops had not been represented at the negotiations and complaining about the deficiencies of the settlement.   The Muslims had been allowed to keep the Temple area in Jerusalem and openly to practise their faith there: the sound of muezzins summoning the Islamic faithful to prayer was certainly not consonant with the crusading ideal that Jerusalem should be purified as a sacred Christian city, and the knights Templar were particularly offended that their traditional headquarters were to remain in infidel hands.   Further, the emperor had not secured the return of any church lands in the neighbourhood of the three holy cities and therefore the economic plight of the great Latin shrine churches had not been relieved.   The ruler of Damascus had not ratified the treaty and there was no guarantee that he would observe it, nor did the patriarch have any confidence that once the emperor had withdrawn his army the sultan of Egypt would honour the commitments which he had entered upon.[3]

What should have been an occasion for rejoicing in Frankish Syria, the restoration of the holy places to Christian control after forty years, therefore became a matter of contention. Frederick II took possession of Jerusalem on 17 March 1229 and, as Mayer has persuasively argued, ceremonially wore the imperial crown there on the following day.   But on the day after that the archbishop of Caesarea came to Jerusalem and, acting on the

---

1. For the part played on this crusade by the bishops of the kingdom of Acre, Roger of Wendover II, p 351; 'Eracles', XXXIII, 5, *RHC Occ*, II, p 370.

2. Huillard-Bréholles, III, pp 86—99; Roger of Wendover, II, pp 365—9; Van Cleve in Setton, II, pp 455—6.

3. Huillard-Bréholles, III, pp 86—90, 102—8: two letters sent by the patriarch Gerold to the pope; cf. western redaction of 'Eracles', *RHC Occ*, II, p 375.

patriarch's orders, placed the city under an interdict, so that the crusaders who had accompanied Frederick were unable to assist at Mass in the holy places.[1]   When the emperor returned to Acre he found that, in contravention of the treaty he had made with the sultan, the patriarch was raising mercenaries to defend the kingdom.   This disregard of royal authority could not be tolerated by any ruler and Frederick expelled both the patriarch and the knights Templar, who were confederate with him, from Acre. Gerold promptly wrote an encyclical to all the faithful of the west complaining about this treatment.[2]   This civil war was brought to an end when news reached Frederick that a papal army, led by his father-in-law, John of Brienne, had invaded the kingdom of Sicily, and he left with his troops for the west on 1 May 1229.[3]

His departure did not end friction in the east.   His followers quarrelled with the native baronage, led by John of Ibelin, and there was open civil war in the kingdom until 1233, after which power was virtually divided between the imperialists, who held Tyre and the city of Jerusalem, and the native baronage who controlled the rest of the country.[4]   The patriarch's position in this situation was not at all an easy one, not least because Frederick II made his peace with the pope in 1230 and was thenceforth recognised by Gregory IX as lawful king of Jerusalem, until, that is, he quarrelled with the holy see again.[5]   Gerold and Peter of Caesarea, together with the grand masters of the Temple and the Hospital, did attempt to mediate peace between the two factions during the civil war, but they met with no success.[6]   The emperor was persuaded that the patriarch was his enemy, as indeed, experience had shown him to be, and in 1232 prevailed on the pope to recall Gerold to Rome.[7]   It would not appear that the patriarch obeyed this summons for over a year,[8] but when he finally reached Rome in 1233 he was detained there for four years.[9]

Gerold returned to Syria in 1237 with his full legatine powers restored.[10]   His presence there was much needed, for Peter of

---

1. Auvray no 308; Mayer, 'Das Pontifikale von Tyrus', *DOP*, 21, 1967, pp 200—10.
2. Huillard-Bréholles, III, pp 135—40.
3. Van Cleve, *Frederick II*, pp 208—13, 227—8.
4. Runciman, *Crusades*, III, pp 194—222.
5. Auvray, no 836; Van Cleve, *Frederick II*, pp 230—33.
6. 'Eracles', XXXIII, 28, *RHC Occ*, II, p 394.
7. Auvray, nos 815, 823, 840.
8. He was still at Acre on 30 September 1233, Mas Latrie, *Chypre*, III, pp 636—7; *RR*, I, p 273, no 1045.
9. Auvray, no 6181, undated, would seem to refer to this period when Gerold was in the west.
10. *Ibid.*, no 3522.

Caesarea had just died after reigning for thirty-eight years, and Hugh of Nazareth had also died after a reign of seventeen years.[1] None of the other Latin bishops had their breadth of experience, with the possible exception of Reynier of Bethlehem who also died at about that time;[2] bishop John of Acre had died after a reign of only two years and had been replaced around 1231 by another Frenchman, Ralph of Tournai;[3] after the brief pontificate of archbishop Hugh of Tyre (1231—4) his place had been taken by Peter of Sargines, who is first mentioned in that office in 1236;[4] Geoffrey Ardel, the new bishop of Sidon, had been appointed in 1236 and was not yet consecrated;[5] while the bishop of Lydda had been in the Holy Land for less than ten years.[6]

After Gerold's return the vacant sees were soon filled. This was done without reference to the emperor, since his authority was not recognised in most of the kingdom. A certain Bertrand, whose earlier career is unknown, was appointed to Caesarea;[7] Henry, bishop of Paphos in Cyprus, was nominated to Nazareth by the patriarch and the pope confirmed this;[8] but when Gerold attempted to quash the election of the dean of Antioch as bishop of Bethlehem which the canons of Bethlehem made, they appealed to the pope on the grounds that their church was subject to the holy see alone, and the pope appointed judges-delegate to investigate the appointment.[9] Clearly the powers of patronage exercised by the patriarch had grown greater during the virtual interregnum in royal authority which had occurred since 1229, and appointments were now entirely in the hands either of the patriarch or of the pope. They were never restored to lay control.

Although it would appear that the chapters of Nazareth and Bethlehem returned to their cathedrals now that they were once more in Frankish hands, Gerold did not restore his see to Jerusalem, but continued to live in Acre. There was a good practical

1. 'ATS', *AOL*, II, p 439.
2. A bishop of Bethlehem died in 1237—8, Auvray, no 4291. This may have been Reynier, but this is not certain, since the name of the bishop of Bethlehem is not given in documents from the years 1227—38 relating to that see.
3. Alberic of Trois Fontaines, 'Chronica', *MGH SS*, XXIII, p 923.
4. Archbishop Hugh, *CGOH*, nos 2002, 2058; Aurvray, no 3294 may relate to archbishop Peter, but this is not certain as the archbishop's name is not given.
5. J.L. Lamonte, 'A Register of the Cartulary of the Cathedral of Sancta Sophia of Nicosia', *Byzantion*, 5, 1929—30, p 497; Auvray, no 3597.
6. 'Electus' in 1225, Pressutti, no 5696: this was bishop Ralph, who reigned till 1244. 'A. episcopo Liddensi' mentioned in a charter of 1233, Mas Latrie, *Chypre*, III, p 637, would seem to be a copyist's error for 'R. episcopo Liddensi'.
7. Auvray, no 4291; Strehlke, pp 68—9, no 86.
8. Auvray, no 4753.
9. *Ibid.*, no 4699.

reason for this, since the walls of Jerusalem had been dismantled by al-Muazzam during the fifth crusade and were never restored during the reoccupation under Frederick II. It is doubtful whether the patriarch could have afforded to undertake this considerable work of fortification, although he did improve the defences of Jaffa, which came under his jurisdiction.[1] But he also objected to the terms of the treaty of 1229 in principle, not simply because they had been made by an excommunicate emperor: it was not fitting, in his view, that the holy city should be shared with the votaries of a false religion. He therefore appointed the dean of Jaffa and the abbot of the Mount of Olives as his vicars in Jerusalem, but so far as is known he did not visit the city himself.[2]

The truce which Frederick II had negotiated with al-Kamil expired in 1239, and a new crusade came to Syria in that autumn led by Theobald of Navarre, a nephew of Henry of Troyes. Gerold, together with the new archbishop of Tyre and the bishop of Acre, accompanied the crusading army in an attack on Egyptian-held territory in southern Palestine, but it was defeated near Gaza.[3] This was Gerold's last known public act: he died later that winter[4] and left a fortune estimated at more than 16,000 besants which he deposited with the Templars for the defence of the Holy Land.[5] Before his appointment as patriarch Gerold had already proved himself to be a man of considerable administrative ability, but he had no opportunity to use these gifts in Syria which throughout his reign was racked by civil war. Had he been willing to accept the restoration of Jerusalem on the terms which Frederick II negotiated, it is possible that he might have succeeded in making the city an administrative centre of the church in the kingdom and in persuading the communities of the shrine churches, in exile at Acre, to return there in force. But because of his sincerely held religious views, which could be labelled bigoted, but which would have been axiomatic in all Latin Christians a generation earlier, the recovery of the holy city remained largely a wasted opportunity in terms of the rehabilitation of the church as it had existed in the first kingdom.

1. 'ATS', *AOL*, II, p 438; Philip of Novara, c 157, *Gestes*, p 77.
2. de Rozière, p 317, no 178.
3. 'Eracles', Rothelin MS, c 22, *RHC Occ*, II, p 531.
4. 'ATS', *AOL*, II, p 440, places his death in 1238, and if this is true the reservations expressed by the editor of the Rothelin MS about his presence at Gaza in 1239 are well founded. The pope wrote to him in March 1239 (Auvray, no 4753), but might not have learned of his death at the time of writing had it occurred in the previous winter. Alberic of Trois Fontaines, 'Chronica', *MGH SS*, XXIII, p 947, places Gerold's death in 1239. His successor was appointed in May 1240.
5. Berger, no 6432; Bourel de la Roncière, no 1492.

After a bad start to the new crusade, in which even Jerusalem was temporarily lost to the lord of Kerak, Theobald of Navarre succeeded in recovering the lands of Galilee west of the Jordan, together with full control over the coastal regions of Sidon and Beirut, by negotiation with the ruler of Damascus. He also initiated discussions with the sultan of Egypt about the restoration of lands in the south of the kingdom before he left for the west in the autumn of 1240.[1] While Theobald was in Syria a new patriarch was appointed. The canons of the Holy Sepulchre, acting perhaps on Theobald's suggestion, had asked for James of Vitry, but he died in the winter of 1239–40 and Gregory IX nominated Robert, bishop of Nantes.[2] Robert had formerly been a bishop in Apulia, but had been expelled from his see because of his opposition to Frederick II and had been translated to Nantes in 1236.[3] His appointment to Jerusalem, which Frederick II claimed to rule, reflected the renewed hostility which had developed between pope and emperor and which had led to Frederick's second excommunication in 1239.[4] Robert did not immediately come to the east, but appointed Peter of Sargines, archbishop of Tyre, as his vicar there.[5]

A few weeks after Theobald's departure a new crusade reached the Holy Land led by Richard of Cornwall, brother of Henry III of England, and brother-in-law of the emperor Frederick who ordered his officials in the east to co-operate with him. Richard completed the negotiations with Egypt which Theobald had initiated and in 1241 concluded a treaty with the sultan whereby Jerusalem, Bethlehem, Ascalon and the region round Gaza were restored to the Christians.[6] By the time he left for the west later that year most of the first kingdom had been recovered by the Franks, with the exception of Samaria, Hebron and the lands beyond Jordan. At this time the diocese of Tiberias was revived, as the cathedral was once again in Christian hands, and the office was given to Geoffrey, chancellor of the patriarch of Antioch.[7]

Before the new patriarch reached Syria a fundamental constitutional change occurred. Frederick II held the crown of Jerusalem by virtue of his marriage to the queen, but Isabel II had

---

1. S. Painter, 'The Crusade of Theobald of Champagne and Richard of Cornwall', in Setton, II, pp 472–81.
2. Auvray, no 5179.
3. L. de Mas Latrie, 'Les patriarches latins de Jérusalem', *ROL*, I, 1893, p 23.
4. Van Cleve, *Frederick II*, pp 427–41.
5. TT, II, p 355, no 299.
6. Painter in Setton, II, pp 481–5.
7. 'Jofreyessit de Tabie et Chancellier d'Antioch', *CGOH*, no 2280, rightly interpreted by Röhricht, 'Syria Sacra', p 30, n 26, as 'Jofrey eslit de Tabarie . . .'.

died in 1228 after giving birth to a son, Conrad. In the view of the lawyers of the kingdom Frederick was, after his wife's death, only regent for his son, who in 1243 came of age according to the custom of the kingdom. Frederick did not dispute this interpretation, and his son sent Thomas, count of Aquino, as his *bailli* to receive the homage of the Jerusalem baronage. This they refused to give on the grounds that the young king must first come in person before he had the right to appoint a *bailli*, and, while not contesting his theoretical claims to the crown, they appointed as regent the senior member of the blood royal in Syria, Alice, queen of Cyprus, the eldest surviving child of queen Isabel I. Alice did not exercise power directly, but delegated it to *baillis* chosen from the baronial party, and for the next quarter of a century this pattern of government obtained in Syria: regents who ruled in the name of absent Hohenstaufen kings, while delegating their authority to baronial *baillis*. One consequence of this was that the *baillis* did not attempt to exercise patronage in church affairs, and that therefore the church became independent of secular control. The appointment of Alice as regent coincided with the expulsion by the baronage of Frederick II's garrison from Tyre. The civil war in the kingdom was at an end, and the barons were now in undisputed control.[1]

Robert of Nantes came to Syria in 1244.[2] He seems seriously to have intended to restore his see to Jerusalem, and Innocent IV had attempted to raise money to repair the fortifications of the city.[3] One of the first acts of the new patriarch was to make a pilgrimage there[4] but very soon after this the kingdom was attacked by Khorezmian warbands. These troops, whose lands had been overrun by the Mongols, had, since the death of their last shah in 1231, been causing havoc in north Syria: in 1244 they had accepted an invitation from the sultan of Cairo to enter his service, and it was on their journey to Egypt that they sacked Tiberias and on 23 August 1244 captured Jerusalem, where they laid waste the churches and slaughtered the Christian population.[5] They were not attempting to capture territory, but Jerusalem passed under Egyptian control once more and was never recovered by the Franks.

1. Riley-Smith, *Feudal Nobility*, pp 209–12.
2. 'ATS', *AOL*, II, p 441.
3. Berger, no 53.
4. Letter of the grand master of the Hospital in Matthew Paris, *Chronica Maiora*, ed H.R. Luard, *RS*, 57 (I–VII), London 1872–83, IV, p 308.
5. 'Eracles', XXXIII, 54, Rothelin MS, c 41, *RHC Occ*, II, pp 428, 563–4; Matthew Paris, IV, pp 300–305, 307–11, 337–45.

The threat of the Khorezmians drew together the Franks and the Aiyubid prince of Damascus, both of whom stood to lose if Egypt grew too strong. The Franks mustered the largest army which they had put into the field since Hattin, and this was joined by the patriarch and many of the bishops. The confederate army of Jerusalem and Damascus was routed by the Egyptians outside Gaza on 18 October 1244, and the archbishop of Tyre and the bishop of Lydda were among those missing, presumed dead, in the battle. The patriarch escaped and with the Frankish survivors took refuge in Ascalon.[1] Robert of Nantes was the most important single person in the kingdom and he took the lead in trying to organise a relief operation. He and the senior clergy drafted an encyclical letter to the rulers of the west asking for help, and bishop Galerand of Beirut was much praised for sailing to the west in the winter to convey this message.[2] He was present at the council of Lyons, summoned by Innocent IV in 1245, and that winter he travelled to England in the hope of enlisting the support of Henry III.[3] But the only western ruler to take the cross was Louis IX of France.

Before St Louis's crusade reached the east the sultan as-Salih of Egypt recaptured the eastern areas of Frankish-held Galilee and the city of Ascalon in 1247. This raised a problem for the bishop of Tiberias who lost most of his diocese, and Robert of Nantes attempted to solve it by nominating him administrator of the vacant see of Sidon, but the canons of Sidon refused to accept his intervention and nominated their own archdeacon, Peter, a decision which the pope upheld.[4] At the time the problem did not seem too serious because it was hoped that St Louis would recover lost territory.

The chief ecclesiastical difficulty which the patriarch faced during the years of waiting concerned the see of Bethlehem. The bishop-elect of this see, John the Roman, a nominee of Gregory IX,[5] had lost possession of his diocese after the fall of Jerusalem in 1244 and had attempted to raise money by selling off all the property of his church in Syria. In 1245 he was translated to Paphos in Cyprus and the pope nominated in his place Godfrey de

---

1. 'Eracles', XXXIII, 56, Rothelin MS, c 41, *RHC Occ*, II, pp 429–31, 564; Templar of Tyre, c 252, *Gestes*, pp 145–6; Matthew Paris, IV, pp 341–2, 310–11.
2. Western redaction of 'Eracles', Rothelin MS, c 41, *RHC Occ*, II, pp 435, 565.
3. Matthew Paris, IV, pp 431, 433–4, 488–9; P. Riant, 'Indulgences octroyées par Galérand, évêque de Béryte, ambassadeur de Terre Sainte en Angleterre', *AOL*, I, pp 404–5.
4. Berger, no 3286; cf. *ibid.*, no 49.
5. Gregory IX had quashed the election of 1238, Auvray, no 4699, and had presumably appointed the new bishop-elect.

Prefectis, a Roman nobleman, who had been cantor of the church of Tripoli, although it would not appear that he had resided in the east. He naturally wished to recover the property of his see, and much of the patriarch's time was occupied in instituting lawsuits to that end.[1] Godfrey de Prefectis was an unusual appointment in that he was not consecrated until ten years after his nomination: normally the Latin bishops in Syria in the thirteenth century were required to take orders as soon as possible.[2] He did not come to the east for some years, being employed as papal legate in Scotland in 1247,[3] but he was in Syria by 1253.[4]

Although St Louis was known to be preparing a crusade, Robert of Nantes wished also to persuade the English to take part and with this in view he sent a phial of the Holy Blood to Henry III. This was solemnly translated to the abbey of Westminster in 1247, and the presence of this relic in England may have contributed to the belief that St Joseph of Arimathea had brought the Holy Grail to this country, but the English proved resistant to the idea of another crusade.[5]

St Louis, however, reached Cyprus in 1248, and in the following year attacked Egypt and captured Damietta. Robert of Nantes accompanied the king on this campaign, and was with the army when it was defeated at Mansurah in 1250, and was taken into captivity with the king.[6] As is well-known, St Louis succeeded in negotiating the release of his army in return for the surrender of Damietta and the payment of a large ransom, and he then stayed in the east for a further four years, and was effective in healing the feuds which had divided Frankish society there during Frederick II's reign, and in arranging truces both with the Aiyubid princes of north Syria and with the new Mamluk dynasty which had come to power in Egypt.[7]

His presence certainly had a good effect on the morale of the Latin church. Archbishop Henry of Nazareth, for example, decided to restore the proper performance of the Christian cult in his cathedral, and drew up a new constitution for his church, which he submitted to the pope for approval. There should be a prior and six canons to serve the cathedral, who should live under

1. Berger, nos 837, 956–7.
2. Bourel de la Roncière, no 756.
3. Matthew Paris, IV, p 602.
4. Strehlke, pp 81–2, no 102. He may have been in Syria by 1252, *ibid.*, p 81, no 101.
5. Matthew Paris, IV, pp 640–44.
6. Templar of Tyre, c 264, *Gestes*, p 148; 'Eracles', XXXIV, 1, Rothelin MS, c 66, *RHC Occ*, II, pp 438, 615; John of Joinville, *Histoire de Saint Louis*, ed N. de Wailly, Paris 1868, cc 36, 71, pp 59, 128–9.
7. J.R. Strayer, 'The Crusades of Louis IX', in Setton, II, pp 503–8.

the rule of St Augustine, and the archdeacon of Nazareth should be a secular priest.[1]   In the twelfth century Nazareth had been the least regarded of the holy places, but the loss of Jerusalem and Bethlehem had given it prestige as the only major dominical shrine in the Holy Land which still belonged to the Franks, and the due observance of the Latin cult there became correspondingly more important.

Although St Louis never claimed the royal title in Jerusalem, which belonged to Conrad IV, claimant of the western empire, he was the effective ruler of all Latin Syria during his years in the east. He even had some measure of control over church patronage, which no secular ruler had enjoyed since the time of John of Brienne.   It is not known whether he had any part in the appointment of Nicholas Larcat, papal chamberlain and non-resident cantor of Tripoli, to the archdiocese of Tyre in 1251,[2] but he certainly nominated the new archbishop when Nicholas died in 1253. This was the Breton, Gilles, whom St Louis had nominated bishop of Damietta when the Franks captured the city in 1249, and who, since the failure of the crusade, had been without a see.[3]

It seems more doubtful whether St Louis had any hand in the revival of sees which had long been vacant. This seems to have been part of a deliberate policy inaugurated by pope Innocent IV. In 1252 the pope's register records the existence of a bishop of Banyas, a see which had been vacant for eighty years. This seems to have been a titular appointment, for the bishop lived in Italy, and two years later was translated to the bishopric of La Grasse in the province of Embrun.[4]   It was a different matter in the case of Hebron, a see which had been vacant since Hattin, for a certain Bartholomew, a Cistercian monk from Fossa Nova, was consecrated as bishop and came to the east, where in 1252 he inaugurated proceedings against the Teutonic order relating to property which they held in Acre which had belonged to his diocese before the third crusade.[5]   Similarly in 1253 the pope ordered the patriarch to induct Hugh of Nissun, a kinsman of the grand master of the Temple, to the administration of the long-vacant see of Sebastia which had never been in Frankish hands in the thirteenth century.[6]   The patriarch appears to have delayed inducting Hugh, although he was made a canon of the Holy Sepulchre, for in 1256

    1. Berger, no 5538.
    2. 'Eracles', XXXIV, 2, RHC Occ, II, p 441 (the only source in which he is called Peter Larcat): 'ATS', AOL, II, p 445; Berger, no 5048.
    3. 'Eracles', XXXIV, 2, RHC Occ, II, p 441; 'ATS', AOL, II, p 445; Berger, nos 7902–3; cf. RR, I, p 265, no 1012.
    4. Berger, nos 6038, 7255.
    5. Strehlke, pp 81, 82–4, nos 101, 104.
    6. Berger, nos 6350, 6490.

Alexander IV informed the clergy and people of Sebastia that Hugh had been invested with the administration of the see in Rome, and was allowed to hold a canonry of the Sepulchre in plurality.[1]

St Louis left Syria in April 1254, and on 8 June of that year the patriarch died.[2] His reign had witnessed the final loss by the Christians of Jerusalem and Bethlehem, and the hopes raised by St Louis's crusade had proved illusory. Robert had shown by his conduct in the years between the defeat of Gaza and the arrival of the French king that the patriarch had now become the natural leader of the kingdom in the absence of a resident king. In ecclesiastical affairs, however, he was subordinate to the pope, and papal intervention, though essential to the continued life of the kingdom and often beneficial to the church in that it secured the appointment of more able men to the episcopate than the native clergy could have provided, sometimes had deleterious effects. Certainly this was true in the pontificate of Innocent IV who revived long-lost sees, for by the time of Robert's death all the bishoprics of the kingdom which had existed before 1187 had been restored, with the exception of the archdiocese of Petra. Although Banyas seems to have been a titular see the others were not: their incumbents came to Syria and proved a drain on the resources of church and kingdom, for in the little territory which remained to the Franks an ecclesiastical establishment of a patriarch, three archbishops and eight bishops was far in excess of requirements.

The canons of the Holy Sepulchre tactfully petitioned Rome for the translation of pope Innocent IV's nephew, Opizo, patriarch of Antioch, to the see of Jerusalem, but by the time their request reached the curia Innocent IV was dead and Alexander IV had become pope. He declined the request and nominated instead James Pantaleon, one of the few men of poor birth to rise to a position of prominence in the thirteenth century outside the mendicant orders. James had been archdeacon of Liège and, since 1252, bishop of Verdun, and was appointed patriarch of Jerusalem in April 1255.[3] The appointment of a western bishop entailed some delay before he could reach the east and take up his duties: the pope ordered the archbishop of Tyre and the bishop of Lydda to administer the temporalities of the see until the new patriarch

1. Bourel de la Roncière, nos 1151–3.

2. 'Eracles', XXXIV, 2, RHC Occ, II, p 441; 'ATS', AOL, II, p 446.

3. Bourel de la Roncière, no 317. G. Sievert, 'Das Vorleben des Papstes Urban IV', Römische Quartalschrift für christliche Altertumskunde und für Kirchengeschichte, 10, 1896, pp 451–505.

arrived,[1] and James nominated archbishop Joscelin of Caesarea as his vicar.[2]

The patriarch was given legatine powers in his province, which extended also to the military orders,[3] and he reached Acre in June 1256.[4]   A few weeks later the new bishop of Acre also arrived in Syria: he was Florence, a former canon of Laon, who had been consecrated in Rome.[5]   Some tension developed between the patriarch and the bishop, both of whom were living in Acre, for the pope found it necessary in 1257 to inhibit the bishop of Acre from excommunicating the patriarch or his household.[6]   The archbishop of Nazareth also came to live in Acre at this time,[7] for although much of his see was still in Christian hands, including his cathedral, conditions there were very unsettled.[8]

Acre was not very peaceful at this time either. In 1256 the war of St Sabas broke out as a result of a boundary dispute between Venetian and Genoese merchants.   The patriarch favoured the Venetians[9] and so, after 1257, did the Pisan colony, and when in 1258 the high court of Jerusalem also gave its support to Venice the Genoese were driven from the city and had to take refuge in Tyre, but this did not happen until after large parts of Acre had been laid waste.[10]   Yet at this unpromising time archbishop Gilles of Tyre founded a hospital in Acre for his Breton compatriots, a sign that the energies of Latin churchmen were not entirely taken up with political activities.[11]   It was also at this time that a bishop of Beirut resigned his see to enter the Cistercian order: by 1260 he had become abbot of Belmont in the county of Tripoli.[12]

The disastrous civil strife produced by the war of St Sabas was overshadowed by the news which reached the Franks of the Mongol advance into the lands of the Abbasid caliph which began in the same year, 1256. The armies of Hulagu khan sacked

---

1. Bourel de la Roncière, no 305.
2. *CGOH*, no 2732.
3. Bourel de la Roncière, nos 992, 1264.
4. 'Eracles', XXXIV, 3, *RHC Occ*, II, p 442; 'ATS', *AOL*, II, pp 446–7.
5. Bourel de la Roncière, no 125.
6. *Ibid.*, no 1775.
7. *Ibid.*, no 1300.
8. *CGOH*, no 2934.
9. 'Eracles', XXXIV, 4, *RHC Occ*, II, p 445.
10. Runciman, *Crusades*, III, pp 282–6.
11. Bourel de la Roncière, no 1274; J. Delaville Le Roulx, 'Titres de l'Hôpital des Bretons à Acre', *ROL*, 1, 1893, pp 423–33. The archbishop had bought the land before the war started, but persisted with his project during it.
12. Delaborde, pp 106–7, no 51.

Baghdad in 1258 and were expected to advance into Syria.[1] This news alarmed the holy see, whose knowledge of the Mongols was based chiefly on the destructive raids into eastern Europe which their armies had made in 1240–2, and on the alarming reports of Mongol military strength subsequently brought to the west by papal envoys who had visited the court of the great khans.[2] As their dealings with the Byzantine rulers of Trebizond and Nicaea, the king of Cilician Armenia and the prince of Antioch showed, the Mongols were anxious at this time to have Christian allies in their war against Islam: they were tolerant of Christianity, and many Nestorians held positions of authority in their empire. It was unfortunate that the term 'alliance' did not exist in the official Mongol vocabulary, and that they could speak only of 'submission' to the great khan, since this antagonised Frankish opinion in the kingdom of Acre and caused the papacy to regard the Mongols as enemies.[3] In order to prepare the Franks of Syria for dealing with this threat, pope Alexander IV appointed a legate *a latere* to Acre, who was also empowered to deal with the warring Italian communes there. This was Thomas Agni of Lentino, who had been Dominican prior of Naples, and who had professed St Thomas Aquinas.[4] The pope appointed him bishop of Bethlehem, which it was within his rights to do because the papacy had claimed since the reign of Gregory IX that the church of Bethlehem was an immediate dependency of the holy see.[5] Thomas thus became the first mendicant to hold episcopal office in the church of Jerusalem. His appointment nevertheless raised difficulties for the patriarch: as legate *a latere* Thomas outranked the patriarch, whereas in the tradition of Syria the bishopric of Bethlehem was a suffragan see of Jerusalem. The 'Eracles' describes how James Pantaleon, 'scorning that he who should have been his subordinate came with legatine powers as his superior, went from Syria to the court of Rome'. The official reason for the patriarch's departure was that he wished to appeal against the pope's decision to suppress the convent of Bethany, which was immediately subject to his authority, and to transfer its many endowments to the knights of St John.[6] But this was clearly

1. Saunders, *Mongol Conquests*, pp 108–12.

2. Rockhill, trans, *The Journey of William of Rubruck*.

3. The text of Goyuk khan's letter to Innocent IV demanding the pope's submission is given (in English translation) in C. Dawson, gen ed, *The Mongol Mission*, London 1955, pp 85–6; cf. A. van den Wyngaert, *Sinica Franciscana*, Quaracchi, Firenze 1929, I, pp 134, 142–3.

4. Mas Latrie, 'Patriarches Latins', *ROL*, I, 1893, p 25.

5. Auvray, no 4699.

6. 'Eracles', XXXIII, 3–4, *RHC Occ*, II, pp 444–6; *CGOH*, no 2925 (Alexander IV's transfer of the convent of Bethany to the Hospital).

only a pretext, since the normal course would have been for the patriarch to appoint deputies to plead this case.

The patriarch was therefore absent from the kingdom when the Mongol armies advanced into Syria in the early months of 1260, and the decisive authority there was Thomas of Bethlehem. He sent an appeal for help to Charles of Anjou, brother of St Louis, which was signed by the archbishops of Tyre, Caesarea and Nazareth, as well as by the archbishop of Nicosia, head of the Latin church in Cyprus.[1] Thomas further excommunicated all Latin Christians who had made their submission to the Mongols or given them aid.[2] His was probably the decisive voice in the high court when the Mongol question was debated and the decision was reached to remain neutral in the war between the Mongols and the Mamluks but to allow Egyptian troops to pass through Frankish territory. This enabled the Mamluks to move their army with speed and to secure the decisive defeat of Mongol forces at Ain Jalut in Galilee on 3 September 1260, as a result of which the Mongols were driven back beyond the Euphrates.[3] The long-term consequences of this victory for the Franks of Syria were disastrous, since the Mamluks took over the lands of the Aiyubid princes in north Syria, and the Franks were completely hemmed in by the Egyptians, who could, therefore, evict them from the Syrian littoral whenever they chose.

But in these years of crisis when there was no effective lay ruler in Acre, the legate, Thomas of Bethlehem, was in practice the dominant force in the kingdom. After the Mongol threat had receded in 1261 he, together with the other Latin clergy, attempted to mediate peace between the Venetians and the Genoese in Acre, and although he was not entirely successful and war between the Italian communes continued to disturb the Levant for some years, yet he did bring about an end of open warfare in Acre itself.[4]

James Pantaleon never returned to Acre. He was still in the west when Alexander IV died in May 1261, and on 29 August he was chosen as pope by the conclave and took the name of Urban IV.[5] The new pope was in the unique position of knowing from experience what the needs of the kingdom of Jerusalem were and having the power to deal with them. He worked with deliberation: it was not until November 1262 that he translated bishop Florence

1. Delaborde, 'Lettre . . . à Charles d'Anjou', *ROL*, 2, 1894, pp 211–15.
2. Guiraud, no 292.
3. Runciman, *Crusades*, III, pp 311–14.
4. TT, III, pp 39–44, no 346.
5. Templar of Tyre, c 312, *Gestes*, p 166; 'Eracles', XXXIV, 4, *RHC Occ*, II, pp 445–6.

of Acre to be archbishop of Arles,[1] and he then nominated William, bishop of Agen, as the new patriarch of Jerusalem and gave him the administration of the see of Acre until Jerusalem could be recovered from the infidel.[2] This was eminently good sense: as the pope was aware, the only part of the diocese of Jerusalem which remained in Christian hands was the city of Jaffa, and the patriarch was in an anomalous position while he lived in the city of Acre, which had its own bishop, and which was the richest diocese in the thirteenth-century kingdom.

William was an experienced administrator who had held the see of Agen for sixteen years.[3] In the interval between his appointment and his arrival in the east the bishop of Hebron and the archdeacon of Acre were entrusted with the administration of his two sees.[4] In May 1263 William came to Rome to confer with the pope about the state of the Holy Land and was granted legatine powers not only in his own province, but also in what remained of the patriarchate of Antioch, in the Armenian kingdom of Cilicia and in Cyprus.[5] This was possible because the Latin patriarch of Antioch was intending to leave Syria[6] and it placed the new patriarch of Jerusalem in a stronger position than that which any of his predecessors had held: that of sole papal representative in Frankish Syria.

Urban IV also realised that the greatest practical need of Frankish Syria was money to meet the costs of defence, and in 1263 he levied a tax of one hundredth on the incomes of the French clergy for five years, which he deputed Gilles, archbishop of Tyre, and John of Valence, lord of Haifa, to collect.[7] Gilles was chosen because he had been appointed by St Louis and could be expected to enjoy the full support of the French crown in this work. The pope also took thought for some of his other former suffragans in the Holy Land. William, bishop of Lydda, was translated to the new patriarch's former see of Agen,[8] and John of Troyes was appointed as his successor.[9] Hugh of Nissun, bishop of Sebastia, whose see was in Saracen hands, was made prior of the Holy Sepulchre, but was allowed to remain administrator of the see of Sebastia.[10] One of Urban's first concerns was to ensure that the

---

1. Guiraud, no 165.
2. *Ibid.*, no 168.
3. Eubel, vol I, p 77.
4. Guiraud, no 191.
5. *Ibid.*, no 241.
6. See chapter 9 above.
7. Guiraud, nos 373–96; Martène, Durand, *Nov. Thes.*, II, pp 7–9, nos 5–6; pp 47–9, nos 19–20; p 81, no 54.
8. Guiraud, no 236.
9. *Ibid.*, no 1555; Templar of Tyre, c 364, *Gestes*, p 190.
10. Guiraud, no 264.

Catholic cult was properly observed in the church of Nazareth, the most important holy place in Christian control. Within a few weeks of his elevation to the papacy he instructed the cardinal of Tusculum to create four new canons of Nazareth and to appoint a prior, since the church of Nazareth 'abounds in temporal goods but has collapsed as a spiritual centre'.[1] Clearly the reforms instituted by archbishop Henry in 1252 had been of short duration.

While the patriarch William remained in the west real power in the church of Jerusalem was exercised by Thomas of Bethlehem, the legate.[2] But Urban IV had no intention of making his successor submit to the humiliation which he had suffered of having a suffragan who outranked him, and he recalled Thomas to the west in September 1263, shortly before William arrived to take up his duties.[3] Urban bore no outward resentment towards bishop Thomas, who had proved himself a capable man, but appointed him his vicar in the city of Rome and entrusted to him the preaching of the crusade against Manfred of Sicily.[4]

When Urban IV died after a brief reign of three years and was succeeded by Clement IV in October 1264 no change occurred in papal policy towards the church of Jerusalem. William of Agen retained his full legatine powers, and Thomas of Bethlehem was kept in Europe and, after the victory of Charles of Anjou over Manfred of Sicily in 1266, was translated to the archbishopric of Cosenza in 1267.[5] As new bishop of Bethlehem the pope appointed another Dominican, his penitentiary, Gaillard, but he also was at first retained in the west to perform curial duties.[6] Pope Clement also renewed the grant of clerical hundredths in the kingdom of France for the defence of Outremer,[7] and made new arrangements for its collection when Gilles of Tyre died in France in April 1266.[8] There was some confusion about the appointment of his successor to the see of Tyre. The pope wished to translate the bishop of Le Mans,[9] but the canons of Tyre elected the archdeacon of Tyre and the patriarch of Jerusalem confirmed their candidate; the pope quashed this appointment, and instead

1. *Ibid.*, no 45, cf. no 1508.
2. *Ibid.*, no 191 (bis).
3. 'Eracles', XXXIV, 4, *RHC Occ*, II, p 447; Templar of Tyre, c 320, *Gestes*, p 168; 'ATS', *AOL*, II, p 451.
4. Guiraud, nos 753, 778.
5. Jordan, no 511, of 18 August 1267.
6. *Ibid.*, nos 524, 1292.
7. Martène, Durand, *Nov. Thes.*, II, pp 126–7, no 52.
8. Jordan, nos 1499, 1505. Gilles's epitaph is in Delaville Le Roulx, 'L'Hôpital des Bretons', *ROL*, 1, 1893, p 425, n16.
9. Jordan, no 386.

nominated the Dominican bishop of Sidon, John of St Maxentius.[1]

But although the patriarch William's powers of patronage in his church may have been curtailed by papal intervention there is no doubt that he was the real authority in the kingdom of Acre and indeed throughout Frankish Syria. Thus in 1267 when a Catalan knight escaped from an Egyptian prison and came to Acre with news of an impending Egyptian attack he was immediately brought before the patriarch rather than before the *bailli* of the kingdom.[2] Similarly, it was the patriarch rather than the lay authorities who wrote to Theobald of Navarre on behalf of Hugh of Brienne to explain why he had been unable to return to France to claim the fief of his recently deceased elder brother.[3] Moreover, it was William, not the archbishop of Nicosia, who crowned Hugh III of Cyprus on Christmas day 1267, for he was carrying out a visitation of the island as legate when the throne fell vacant.[4]

A strong authority was necessary in the Frankish east because of the threat posed by Baybars, Mamluk sultan of Egypt, who was hostile towards Christians because of the support which many of the Christian minorities of Mesopotamia and Syria had given to the Mongols in their wars against the Muslim powers. In 1263 he sacked the basilica of Nazareth, bringing the Latin cult there to an end. In 1265 he captured and razed to the ground the cities of Caesarea, Arsuf and Haifa; in 1266 he captured the fortresses of Safad and Toron and gained control of upper Galilee; in 1268 he captured Lydda, Jaffa and the fortress of Belfort; and in 1271 he took Montfort, headquarters of the Teutonic knights and the last inland fortress in the kingdom of Acre to remain in Christian control.[5] It seemed possible that he would eliminate Frankish power in Syria completely, but he did not attempt to follow up these victories, since a new crusade was known to be assembling. In 1267 St Louis had once again taken the cross, and his brother, Charles of Anjou, king of Sicily, and the lord Edward, heir to the throne of England, had given their adhesion to the project.[6]

But before this crusade set out a constitutional problem arose in the kingdom of Acre. The execution of Frederick II's grandson, Conradin, in 1268, left the throne of Jerusalem vacant, since he was the last surviving descendant of Frederick II and queen Isabel

1. *Ibid.*, no 522.
2. Templar of Tyre, c 351, *Gestes*, p 185.
3. Martène, Durand, *Nov. Thes.*, I, pp 1013—14.
4. 'Eracles', XXXIV, 10, *RHC Occ*, II, p 456; Templar of Tyre, c 355, *Gestes*, p 187.
5. 'ATS', *AOL*, II, p 451 (Nazareth); Runciman, *Crusades*, III, pp 318—34.
6. Strayer in Setton, II, pp 508—11.

II. The possible claimants for the crown were Hugh III, king of Cyprus, and Mary of Antioch, both of whom were descended from queen Isabel I. The patriarch gave his adhesion to king Hugh, who, on his orders, was crowned king of Jerusalem at Tyre in 1269 by the bishop of Lydda, despite the fact that the lady Mary had already lodged an appeal to the pope against his succession.[1] Hugh was the first king of Jerusalem to be resident in the east for forty-four years, which meant that nobody in authority could remember a time when there had been a king there. The restoration of a monarch was bound to raise many practical problems among a nobility which had been used to freedom from royal control for so long, and in giving his support to Hugh rather than to the lady Mary the patriarch was acting in a disinterested way, since the presence of a king would undoubtedly diminish his own power in temporal affairs. Yet it was a course of action which the peril of the kingdom made necessary, since what Acre needed above all was a strong military leader and somebody who could co-ordinate Frankish resistance to the Mamluks, which the king of Jerusalem and Cyprus must have seemed capable of doing.

William of Agen died in April 1270[2] before St Louis's crusade had set out. The kingdom of Acre had greatly diminished in size during his reign, since, apart from the castle of Athlit, which remained in the hands of the Templars, it was now restricted to a coastal strip extending from Mount Carmel to Beirut, and was even smaller than it had been at the end of the third crusade. Yet despite this the ecclesiastical establishment remained high. The patriarch of Jerusalem, it is true, now administered the see of Acre, but there were also archbishops not only of Tyre, which was still in Christian hands, but of Caesarea, which the Muslims ruled, and also of Nazareth, where a successor named Guy was appointed to archbishop Henry who died in 1268 after a reign of thirty years.[3] There were also bishops of Lydda and Tiberias, although both sees were outside Frankish control, and even the bishop of Bethlehem returned to the east, perhaps in the hope that the new crusade would restore him to his diocese.[4] Bishop Peter of

1. Guiraud-Cadier, no 103; Riley-Smith, *Feudal Nobility*, pp 220–3.

2. 'ATS', *AOL*, II, p 454 (11 April); 'Eracles', XXXIV, 13, *RHC Occ*, II, p 458 (21 April).

3. *Ibid.*, XXXIV, 11, p 457. His successor, Guy, is first mentioned in 1271, *CGOH*, no 3414. Archbishop Lociaumes of Caesarea died in 1267, 'Eracles', XXXIV, 9, p 445; his successor, Matthew, was still in office in 1280, Mas Latrie, *Documents Nouveaux servant de preuves à l'histoire . . . de Chypre*, Paris 1882, pp 348–9, no 6.

4. John of Lydda reigned until 1271, *CGOH*, no 3422; Eustorgius of Tiberias until 1273, 'Eracles', XXXIV, 17, *RHC Occ*, II, p 464; Gaillard of Bethlehem was at Acre in 1271, *CGOH*, no 3422, and had, perhaps, come there in the previous year.

Hebron had succeeded in finding a source of income by granting property at Antioch which belonged to his church to the knights of St John in return for an annual pension, and when he died in 1267 the pope ordered the patriarch of Jerusalem to appoint a successor and a Dominican was duly inducted.[1]   The only see in the patriarchate which was allowed to lapse was Sebastia, after the death of Hugh of Nissun.[2]   Only four sees remained in Christian hands, Tyre, Acre, Sidon and Beirut, yet the establishment consisted of the patriarch, three archbishops and six bishops, but the hope remained that the new crusade would once more restore Frankish power over the former kingdom of Jerusalem.

William of Agen had governed the church of Jerusalem during the most testing period of its history since the battle of Hattin. He had been aided by the co-operation of pope Urban IV who had ensured, by granting him the administration of the church of Acre, that he had adequate revenues and, by giving him full legatine powers, had made him effective papal representative in the east.   William had restored the monarchy in Jerusalem, believing this to be in the best interests of the kingdom, but by that time the state of Acre had effectively become a theocracy, since its survival depended on the continued support in manpower and money which the holy see alone could co-ordinate.

When William died the papacy had been vacant since the death of Clement IV in November 1268. While there was no pope no new patriarch of Jerusalem could be appointed and, it is to be supposed at the instance of king Hugh, canon Raymond of Nicosia was appointed to administer the see.[3]   The only help which came to the Franks of Syria from the west was an Aragonese force which reached Acre in the winter of 1269–70 but achieved little. St Louis's crusade, from which so much had been expected, was diverted to Tunis and had to be abandoned as a result of an outbreak of plague in the French camp which carried off the king himself in August 1270.[4]   In the following spring the English crusaders under the lord Edward did reach Palestine, and with them came Theobald Visconti, archdeacon of Liège. Theobald was staying in Acre when he was elected pope, which brought to an end the longest vacancy in the history of the holy see, and he returned to Rome where he was enthroned in March

---

1. Jordan, no 460.   Godfrey, O.P., was appointed to Hebron in 1268, 'Eracles', XXXIV, 11, *RHC Occ*, II, p 457. On the finances of the bishopric see chapter 11 below.
2. Hugh, prior of the Holy Sepulchre, died c 1268, Jordan, no 639.
3. *CGOH*, nos 3414, 3422.
4. Strayer, in Setton, II, pp 511–18.

1272.[1] Before he left Syria he must have consulted king Hugh about the appointment of a new patriarch, for the man he designated was Thomas of Lentino, former bishop of Bethlehem: Thomas alone among the bishops of western Europe had first-hand knowledge of the Frankish east and had shown himself a capable administrator while he was legate there. He reached Syria in October 1272, shortly after the departure of Edward of England, who had negotiated a truce with the sultan of Egypt.[2]

Thomas therefore came to a kingdom which was at peace and, indeed, no further Frankish territory was lost in the kingdom of Acre until the final assault was made in 1291. Gregory X continued the policy which Urban IV had initiated and granted the new patriarch the administration of the see of Acre and full legatine powers in Jerusalem, north Syria, Cilicia and Cyprus, and these were extended by subsequent popes to his successors as long as the kingdom lasted.[3] In Thomas's reign, and perhaps under the influence of king Hugh, the promotion of local church-men to vacant bishoprics, which had been rare in the middle years of the century, became comparatively common again. The new archbishop of Tyre, the Dominican, Bonacursus de Gloire, had been born in the Holy Land;[4] the dean of Sidon, Adam of Romery, was appointed bishop of that city in 1274;[5] and two successive bishops of Tiberias were chosen from the local clergy: in 1273 William of Salonica, who had been archdeacon of Lydda since 1260,[6] and on his death in the following year, William le Velus, cantor of Lydda and chancellor of Cilicia.[7]

Despite the failure of St Louis's crusade the Franks had not lost hope of recovering their lost lands, since one of the first acts of the new pope, Gregory X, was to summon the council of Lyons to discuss plans for a new crusade.[8] The council, which met in 1274, failed in its purpose[9] and the situation of the Franks of Acre deteriorated when in 1276 king Hugh declared that he found

1. 'Eracles', XXXIV, 25, *RHC Occ*, II, p 471.

2. Guiraud-Cadier, no 8; 'ATS', *AOL*, II, p 456; 'Eracles', XXXIV, 15, *RHC Occ*, II, p 462; F.M. Powicke, *King Henry III and the Lord Edward*, 2, vols, Oxford 1947, pp 597—617.

3. Guiraud-Cadier, nos 9—10.

4. 'Eracles', XXXIV, 15, *RHC Occ*, II, p 462; J. Echard, J. Quetif, *Scriptores Ordinis Praedicatorum*, 2 vols, Paris 1719—21, I, p 159.

5. 'Eracles', XXXIV, 19, *RHC Occ*, II, p 466.

6. *Ibid.*, XXXIV, 17, p 464; Kohler, pp 183—5, no 77.

7. 'Eracles', XXXIV, 19, *RHC Occ*, II, p 466.

8. P.A. Throop, *Criticism of the Crusade*, Amsterdam 1940, pp 12—212, discusses Gregory's preparations for the crusade and the discouraging replies he received to his preliminary inquiries.

9. *Ibid.*, pp 262—82.

the kingdom ungovernable and retired to Cyprus. Thomas of Lentino took charge of the situation and secured the appointment of Balian of Ibelin as *bailli*.[1] But a year later matters changed when the lady Mary, rival claimant to the throne of Jerusalem, completed the lengthy transactions by which she sold her rights to the throne to Charles of Anjou, king of Sicily.[2] His representative, Roger of S. Severino, reached Acre in 1277 and gained control of the citadel despite the opposition of some members of the baronial party. This change of government was, on the whole, beneficial to Frankish Syria, for Sicily was the nearest great western power to the Holy Land, her ruler was on friendly terms with the Mamluk sultan of Egypt, and his rule afforded the best protection for which the Franks could hope in the absence of a new crusade.

This was the situation when Thomas died in September 1277.[3] The canons of the Holy Sepulchre, probably acting on orders from Charles of Anjou, asked for the translation of the archbishop of Naples to Jerusalem, but pope Nicholas III refused this request and instead nominated John of Vercelli, general of the Dominican order.[4] The latter, however, refused to accept the charge and so there was another long vacancy in the patriarchate at the end of which a Frenchman, Elias, bishop of Périgueux, was appointed in May 1279.[5] During the interval the archbishop of Tyre acted as vicar of the patriarch.[6]

No patriarch since the death of Amalric of Nesle a century before made so little impression on the church and state of Jerusalem as Elias. During his reign there seems to have been a slight reduction in the ecclesiastical establishment in that no new archbishop was appointed to Caesarea after the death of archbishop Matthew, which occurred around 1280.[7] Moreover, the new bishop of Bethlehem, Hugh, former bishop of Troia, whom the pope, manifestly acting under Angevin influence, translated in 1279,[8] spent most of his reign in Italy, only visiting the Holy Land briefly in 1283.[9] This was merely common sense, since

1. 'ATS', *AOL*, II, p 456; 'Eracles', XXXIV, 28–9, *RHC Occ*, II, pp 474–5.
2. *RR*, I, p 366, no 1411.
3. 'Eracles', XXXIV, 33, *RHC Occ*, II, p 478.
4. Gay-Vitte, no 53.
5. *Ibid.*, nos 309, 529, 567.
6. 'Eracles', XXXIV, 33, *RHC Occ*, II, p 478.
7. Matthew is last mentioned in October 1280, Mas Latrie, *Documents Nouveaux*, pp 348–9, no 6.
8. Gay-Vitte, no 575.
9. He was at Acre in that year, G. von Pettenegg, *Die Urkunden des deutsch-Ordens-Centralarchives zu Wien in Regestenform*, Prague, Leipzig 1887, I, pp 159–60, no 618.

Bethlehem possessed few lands in Syria at this time but had extensive properties in western Europe from which the bishop drew his revenues.

Elias was entrusted by pope Honorius IV with large sums of money to be spent on the defence of Syria, part of it the legacy of pope Hadrian V, and part the product of a papal tax levied in Tripoli and Cyprus.[1] He returned to the west, probably to confer with the pope, and may have been there in 1286 when Angevin rule in Acre came to an end. The power of Charles of Anjou had been diminished since the Sicilian Vespers of 1282 which had brought Peter of Aragon to power in the island of Sicily,[2] and after Charles's death in 1285 there was a party in Acre which opened negotiations with the young king Henry II of Cyprus who had the best claim to the crown of Jerusalem. He gained general acceptance, the Angevin garrison evacuated Acre, and on the feast of the Assumption 1286 the young king Henry was crowned at Tyre by archbishop Bonacursus. The patriarch took no part either in the negotiations or in the coronation, which suggests that he was not in Syria at the time.[3] Certainly he was in Rome a year later, and it would seem that he died there in the winter of 1287–8.[4]

Pope Nicholas IV nominated his penitentiary, the Dominican, Nicholas of Hanapes, as new patriarch, and granted him more extensive privileges than any of his predecessors had enjoyed, including that of nominating to all vacant benefices in the area of his legation whose collation had devolved upon the holy see.[5] Despite the fact that there was once again a king in Acre, the patriarch's political power was considerable, for Henry of Lusignan also had the kingdom of Cyprus to govern and spent comparatively little time on the mainland. Thus when the pope organised a fleet of galleys to be sent to Acre their military commanders were placed under the authority of the patriarch.[6] Nicholas's reign was short, for the Mamluks launched their final assault on the kingdom in 1291. According to one source the patriarch took a decisive part in directing military operations at the siege of Acre, in the view of the chronicler in an ill-conceived way.[7] If not literally true, this passage has a symbolic truth, for it

1. Prou, nos 183–4.
2. S. Runciman, *The Sicilian Vespers*, Cambridge 1958.
3. Templar of Tyre, c 439, *Gestes*, p 220; 'ATS', *AOL*, II, p 458; Mas Latrie, *Chypre*, III, pp 671–3.
4. Martène, Durand, *Nov. Thes.*, I, pp 1230–1. He died before 30 April 1288, Langois, no 85.
5. Langlois, nos 85–95, 219, 2100.
6. *Ibid.*, no 4385.
7. *Chronicle of Lanercost*, trans Maxwell, p 80.

had been the patriarchs who had embodied authority in the Frankish east during much of the thirteenth century. When the city of Acre fell Nicholas escaped to the harbour but was drowned while trying to board a Venetian ship, not, it would seem, without some hint of foul play, since his treasure-chest had already been taken on board.[1]   Within a few months the remaining cities of the kingdom were in Mamluk possession: the kingdom of Jerusalem had come to an end and with it an organised Latin church in Syria.[2]

To the very end the Franks maintained a full complement of resident bishops in Syria. It is true that bishops and archdeacons of Banyas, who appear in documents in the years 1272–8, may have been titular clergy, even if they were sometimes called upon to deal with business relating to the Frankish east,[3] but they were exceptional. When the see of Nazareth fell vacant in 1288, although the archdiocese of Nazareth had been in Saracen hands for almost a quarter of a century, Nicholas IV nominated a new archbishop, a Templar, William of St John. He could have lived in western Europe, where his church owned much property, but he was resident in the Holy Land and an effective archbishop, for the pope sent him a *pallium* and arranged for his consecration. William, it would appear, died in June 1290, and was succeeded by archbishop Peter who lived in Acre for as long as the city was held by the Franks.[4]   In 1291 there were a patriarch, two archbishops and five bishops in the small area which remained in Christian control, not counting the bishop of Bethlehem who was living in the west.[5]   Some of these bishops, more fortunate than the patriarch, escaped to the west at the Mamluk conquest. The archbishop of Tyre and the bishop of Lydda were still alive in 1295,[6] the last bishop of Bethlehem to visit Acre while it was in Christian hands lived until the turn of the century,[7] while

1. Templar of Tyre, c 503, *Gestes*, p 254.

2. Runciman, *Crusades*, III, pp 421–3.

3. Guiraud-Cadier, no 103; Gay-Vitte, nos 107, 116, refer to archdeacons of Banyas.

4. Langlois, nos 165–9, 175–7. J. Prawer, 'A Crusader Tomb of 1290 from Acre and the last Archbishops of Nazareth', *Israel Exploration Journal*, 24, 1974, pp 241–51.

5. Archbishops of Tyre and Nazareth; bishops of Beirut, Sidon, Lydda, and perhaps also of Hebron and Tiberias. William le Velus, bishop of Tiberias, is last mentioned in 1283, Pettenegg, *op. cit.*, I, pp 159–60, no 618; *RR*, I, pp 308–9, nos 1449, 1451. Bishop Godfrey of Hebron is last mentioned in 1286, Mas Latrie, *Chypre*, III, p 671. Both may still have been alive in 1291. Bishop Hugh of Bethlehem was employed in Italy collecting the papal tithe for the war against Peter of Aragon, Prou, nos 12, 36, 60, 130, 180, 193, 266, and cf. 729.

6. Thomas-Faucon-Digard, no 357; Schlumberger, Chalandon, Blanchet, *Sigillographie*, p 114 (bishop Andrew of Lydda).

7. *Ibid.*, p 110. Hugh is last mentioned in 1299, Riant, *Eglise de Bethléem*, II, pp 22–53.

archbishop Peter of Nazareth escaped to Padua where he remained until his death in about 1326.[1] Yet although titular patriarchs of Jerusalem continued to be appointed by the holy see, the Latin church in Syria had effectively come to an end in 1291.

The bishops of the Latin church of Jerusalem in the thirteenth century were more often recruited from the west than their twelfth-century predecessors had been, and this reflects a greater degree of papal intervention in the affairs of the Latin church in Syria. The degree of western influence should not be exaggerated: the background of forty of the bishops in the patriarchate of Jerusalem who held office between 1192 and 1291 is known, and twenty-five of these came directly from the west to episcopal office in Syria; but the remaining fifteen, almost 40% of the sample, were men who had been trained in Syria as their twelfth-century predecessors had been. It is, perhaps, significant that only two of the Syrian-trained group became patriarchs.[2]

As a result of greater western influence a wider range of talent was found on the Jerusalem bench in the thirteenth century than had been present in the twelfth. Some of the Latin bishops were men of unusual ability, and this is shown by the offices which they attained in the universal church. The church of Jerusalem in the thirteenth century provided Catholic Christendom with a pope, a Latin patriarch of Constantinople, a cardinal-bishop of Tusculum, an archbishop of Arles, an archbishop of Cosenza and a bishop of Agen.[3] A century before it would not have been possible to find men of this calibre in such numbers on the Syrian bench. Moreover, the thirteenth-century bishops were, on the whole, better educated than twelfth-century bishops had been. James of Vitry's scholarship may have been no greater than that of William of Tyre, but he was no longer an isolated example of a learned bishop as William had been. Gaillard, bishop of Bethlehem, for example, had been lector in the Dominican houses of Narbonne and Agen before he came to the Holy Land.[4]

As a result the church of Jerusalem was no longer a backwater in relation to the universal church as it had in some measure been earlier. Latin Syria through its bishops felt the impact of the complex revival of scholarship, jurisprudence and literature

---

1. Prawer, op. cit., Israel Exploration Journal, 24, 1974, pp 248–9.
2. Aimery the Monk and Ralph of Merencourt.
3. James Pantaleon, patriarch of Jerusalem, became pope Urban IV; Simon of Maugastel, archbishop of Tyre, became Latin patriarch of Constantinople; James of Vitry, bishop of Acre, became cardinal bishop of Tusculum; Florence, bishop of Acre, became archbishop of Arles; Thomas Agni, bishop of Bethlehem, became archbishop of Cosenza; William, bishop of Lydda, became bishop of Agen.
4. Schlumberger, Chalandon, Blanchet, Sigillographie, p 108.

commonly called the twelfth-century renaissance. Many of the bishops in the second half of the thirteenth century were Dominicans, and through their activity the spirituality of the newly-founded mendicant orders became part of the heritage of Latin Christians in Syria also. Not all western influences were equally benign, and one of the last instructions which the patriarch Nicholas of Hanapes received from pope Nicholas IV was to set up the Inquisition in the Frankish east.[1]

The majority of bishops in the patriarchate of Jerusalem in the thirteenth century lived in the Holy Land at a time when non-residence was becoming more common in the western church. Moreover, virtually all of them had been consecrated, although in many cases they had almost no spiritual responsibilities because their sees were in Saracen hands. Many of them were men of genuine ability who were condemned by the circumstances of their ministry to spend their lives in relative inactivity. The chief reason for the presence of so many bishops in so comparatively small an area seems to have been talismanic. Until the failure of the second council of Lyons in 1274 to launch a new crusade, it was a plank of papal policy that the Holy Land could be recovered from the infidel. Failure to appoint as many bishops as possible, even in some cases to sees which were entirely in enemy hands and which had no endowments in western Europe, would have seemed a tacit admission that the hope of recovering the lands of the first kingdom had been abandoned. Nevertheless, the presence of so many supernumerary clergy in Frankish territory did place a severe strain on the slender economic resources of the kingdom of Acre.

---

1. Langlois, no 2095.

11. THE ECONOMIC PROBLEMS OF THE LATIN CHURCH IN THE THIRTEENTH CENTURY

Although the Franks recovered some lost territory in the course of the thirteenth century, they never ruled such extensive lands as they had in the twelfth. The annexation of Cyprus by Richard I did little to compensate for this loss as far as the Latin church in Syria was concerned, for the Lusignan kings of Cyprus had to maintain a dual Greek and Latin hierarchy and had little land to spare for the needs of the churches of Jerusalem and Antioch. It might be supposed that the economic plight of the church of Antioch was more severe than that of Jerusalem at this time, since the northern states were never aided by any of the numerous crusades of the thirteenth century and, before the Mongol invasions of 1260, did not regain any of the territory which they had lost in 1188.[1] This, however, was not the case.

Unlike the Holy Sepulchre, the church of St Peter at Antioch had no western endowments which it could use to supplement its revenues. Yet the patriarch of Antioch was more fortunate than his brother of Jerusalem in that his see, and with it many of the estates of his church, remained in Christian hands after 1187. As has been seen, no attempt was made to appoint bishops to suffragan sees which had fallen into enemy hands, nor were there any exiled monastic communities to provide for at Antioch, since the Black Mountain, the principal monastic centre in the patriarchate, remained in Christian control until the Mamluk conquest of 1268. The states of Antioch and Tripoli had merely to provide for a diminished Latin hierarchy from the economic resources which remained in their control and until the middle of the thirteenth century this does not seem to have posed any insuperable problem.

Indeed, in the early years of the century the patriarch of Antioch seems to have remained quite rich. The treasures of the cathedral church were considerable, as can be seen from the inventory which the Hospital drew up in 1209 for Peter II, when he became patriarch, of the goods in their custody.[2] Moreover, the church still owned considerable lands in the area round the

---

1. See chapter 9 above.
2. *CGOH*, no 1336.

city and, although these had been devastated in the war of the Antiochene succession, the patriarch's title to them was not disputed, and Peter II was able to restore their productivity by leasing some of them in *emphyteusis*.[1]   By the end of Peter's reign the financial affairs of the see seem to have been restored to a sound basis, since he was able from his own revenues to endow two new canonries in the cathedral, bringing the total number of canons there to twenty,[2] and to give financial aid to the impoverished archbishop of Tyre.[3]

It is possible that Peter II was over-confident about the wealth of his see. Certainly pope Honorius III ordered his successor to reduce the number of canons to sixteen,[4] while in 1233 the patriarch Albert took the Cistercian abbot of Jubin in the Black Mountain to law for refusing to pay tithe. Albert argued that the Cistercians had forged the title-deeds of their house in order to claim exemption from patriarchal jurisdiction to which they were not entitled, and the papal judge-delegate found in his favour and entered copies of the authentic foundation charters of Jubin in the papal registers to show that the abbey was subject to the patriarch and did owe tithe to him.[5]   Since the costs of this litigation, which lasted for four years, must have been high, this suggests that the patriarch's income was becoming diminished by this time, and that he was anxious to secure additional sources of revenue.

Clearly by the middle of the thirteenth century the financial problems of Antioch were acute. Pope Innocent IV began to take action about this after his nephew, the patriarch Opizo, had made the *ad limina* visit in 1253. The pope ordered that the costs of his travelling expenses should be met in part from a legacy left for the needs of the Holy Land by the bishop of Norwich,[6] and further requested the Templars to pay him a third of the legacy which the late patriarch of Jerusalem, Gerold of Lausanne, had left for the defence of the Holy Land.[7]   In addition, the pope appointed Opizo to the administration of the archdiocese of Nicosia and, finding that he had been misinformed about the imminent resignation of its bishop, requested that Opizo be given the administration of the next see which should fall vacant

1. Innocent III, 'Reg.', XIV, no 71, *PL*, 216, 435.
2. *Ibid.*, 'Reg.', XIV, no 70, *PL*, 216, 435.
3. Pressutti, no 1141.
4. *Ibid.*, no 3497.
5. Auvray, nos 1011, 1887, 3466–9; Hamilton in Pennington, ed, *One Yet Two*, p 466.
6. Berger, no 7398.
7. *Ibid.*, no 6432.

in the provinces of Antioch or Cyprus.[1] That this was not simply
a matter of nepotism is clear from the fact that Innocent's successor, Alexander IV, who had no special reason to be benevolent
to the patriarch of Antioch, continued the same policy. Opizo
was made administrator of the see of Limassol in 1256[2] and was
allowed to levy a clerical tithe on the churches of Antioch and
Cyprus for three years to strengthen the fortifications of his
castle of Qusair, a tax from which only the Temple, the Hospital
and the Cistercians were exempt.[3] It was, however, difficult for
any pope to ensure that his orders were carried out. The Templars
proved reluctant to disburse the legacy of the patriarch Gerold
and, although this was estimated at 16,000 besants,[4] by 1256
Opizo of Antioch had only received 400 marks sterling, to be
shared with Bohemond V of Antioch for defence purposes.[5]
Similarly, the archbishop of Nicosia, richest of the Latin prelates
in Cyprus, refused to contribute towards the patriarch of
Antioch's tithe, and, although excommunicated by the official
collector, the archbishop of Mamistra, for refusing to comply
with papal instructions, he evaded both payment and censure by
appealing to Rome on a technicality of canon law.[6] By the time
of Alexander IV's death in 1259 the problems of the church of
Antioch were nearing their end. In Urban IV's reign the patriarch Opizo went to the west for good, and although financial
provision had to be made for him there, he ceased to be a
burden on the financial resources of Antioch itself. When the
city fell to the Mamluks in 1268, therefore, there was no longer
a problem about making provision for an exiled patriarch elsewhere in the province.[7]

The archbishops and bishops of the province were adequately
provided for. Nothing is known about the financing of the archdiocese of Apamea in the thirteenth century, but the archbishops
of Tarsus, who intermittently held office then, had revenues
derived from lands in Cilicia which were under Christian control:
when the Armenian kings were co-operative and allowed these
revenues to be drawn by Latin churchmen an archbishop and
canons were appointed, but when Cilician favour was withdrawn

---

1. *Ibid.*, nos 7393—6, 7873. Mas Latrie, 'Archevêques latins de Chypre', *AOL*, II,
p 234.
2. Bourel de la Roncière, nos 1175—6.
3. *Ibid.*, no 1087.
4. *Ibid.*, no 1492.
5. *Ibid.*, no 1086. They had also jointly received 320 marks from the Hospital.
6. *Ibid.*, no 2960.
7. Opizo administered successively the sees of Limassol, Trani and Genoa. See
chapter 9 above.

the see was left vacant.[1]   The archbishops of Mamistra drew part
of their revenue at least from lands controlled by Latin landlords:
by the thirteenth century these were in the hands of the knights
of St John, but the order paid tithe on them to the archbishops.[2]
Similarly, the order virtually controlled the see of Valania and was
responsible for the support of the bishop and canons who lived in
its castle of al-Marqab and to whom it paid tithe on certain lands.[3]

The church of Tortosa had been under the protection of the
Templars since 1152, but the bishops maintained their independence from the order throughout the thirteenth century.   In 1225
the bishop complained to the pope that the Templars were not
honouring their agreement, and presumably this matter was put
right, since there were no further complaints made to Rome on
that score.[4]   The bishops did not depend entirely on tithe for their
income: in 1215 they pledged an estate of their church to the
knights of St John for 1500 besants.[5]   Nevertheless, tithe must
have made up a substantial part of their revenues, and in 1251
the bishop claimed that the Hospitallers were not paying tithe on
certain properties belonging to his church.[6]   This appeal may
relate to Crac des Chevaliers and the estates of the Hospital
adjacent to it, which formed part of the long-vacant diocese of
Rafaniyah.   It is doubtful whether the Hospitallers had ever paid
tithe on these lands, and certainly they were specifically exempted from doing so by pope Alexander IV in 1255.[7]   Urban IV
reversed this decision by uniting the see of Rafaniyah to Tortosa
in 1263 so that the bishop of Tortosa could claim the tithe of this
land.[8]   This claim was substantiated by the bishop who in 1267
reached an agreement with the knights whereby they paid him
1,000 besants a year in lieu of tithe and an additional 1,500
besants in respect of arrears.[9]   Unlike any other church in north
Syria, Tortosa was a pilgrimage centre, because its cathedral was
a shrine of the Blessed Virgin, and therefore it attracted gifts from
the faithful, and had some property in western Europe at
Treviso.[10]   The bishop also tried to rationalise the finances of his
see by vesting the prebends in himself and paying annual salaries

1. The see had *redditus et casalia*, Innocent III, 'Reg.', XVI, no 2, *PL*, 216,
784–6.
2. Delaville Le Roulx, 'Inventaire', no 228; *CGOH*, no 2388.
3. *CGOH*, no 941.
4. Pressutti, no 5266.
5. Delaville Le Roulx, 'Inventaire', no 212.
6. Berger, no 5129.
7. Bourel de la Roncière, no 310.
8. Guiraud, no 1018.
9. *CGOH*, no 3282.
10. Guiraud, nos 1019–20.

to the canons in lieu of property endowments: Alexander IV allowed.this system to continue except in the case of the archdeacon who, he ruled, must be granted an independent prebend.[1] As a result of sound business sense on the part of its bishops, offerings made by the faithful at its shrine, and a willingness to take the military orders to law if they defaulted in the payment of tithe, the church of Tortosa was able to remain solvent during the thirteenth century.

The see of Gibelet in the south of the county of Tripoli, although very small, was also comparatively free from attack during most of the century. It cannot have been rich, but it was prosperous enough for bishop Vassal to found the Cistercian monastery of St Sergius there in 1233 and to free its lands from the payment of tithe.[2] The most important diocese in north Syria at this time after Antioch itself was Tripoli. The city was virtually the capital of Frankish north Syria after the death of Bohemond III in 1201 and it was also an important commercial centre. The entire diocese had remained in Christian hands, and the church possessed considerable landed property there as is apparent from casual references in boundary definitions, and from the fact that as late as 1278 Bohemond VII thought it worth his while to risk ecclesiastical censure by confiscating part of it.[3] The chief threat to the financial stability of the church came from the knights of St John, who had great power in the county of Tripoli. In 1198 Innocent III ordered them to restore the church of Nephin to the bishop,[4] and in 1259 the bishop brought a suit against them in the papal court concerning the payment of tithe: the Hospital was able to win this by producing an episcopal privilege of 1125 freeing them from the payment of tithe throughout the diocese,[5] although it would seem that this judgment was not uncontested, since in 1277 they did admit liability to the payment of some tithe on property in the diocese of Tripoli.[6]

The bishops kept their rights by a constant willingness to resort to litigation. This could prove expensive, however, since it cost a good deal to have a case judged in the papal courts. Both Innocent IV and Alexander IV gave permission to bishops of Tripoli to raise loans on the security of church property to defray the expenses of travelling to Rome,[7] but it sometimes proved

1. Bourel de la Roncière, no 1421.
2. Petit, 'Saint-Serge de Giblet', *MSAF*, ser 5, 8, 1887, pp 25–6.
3. Gay-Vitte, no 520.
4. Innocent III, 'Reg.', I, no 73, *PL*, 214, 64–5.
5. *CGOH*, no 2922; Delaville Le Roulx, 'Inventaire', no 315.
6. *Ibid.*, no 357.
7. Berger, no 2516; Bourel de la Roncière, no 2885.

easier to borrow money than to repay it. Thus in 1259 bishop Opizo of Tripoli was sued by the merchants of Florence, who had lent him 6,000 besants and demanded 4,000 besants in addition for the 'expenses' involved for failure to repay them in time. The curia, which judged this case, reduced what amounted to interest to 1,300 besants, but adjudged that it and the capital must be repaid in two instalments.[1]   Yet despite temporary embarrassments of this kind and the immunity of the lands of the Hospital from tithe, the see of Tripoli remained the richest in north Syria until the city fell in 1289.

When in 1260 Jabala and Latakia were once again restored to Frankish rule the Latin hierarchy was restored there also. This worked perfectly well at Latakia, which was an important port with a large population, and where a Frankish bishop remained until 1287.[2] Jabala was a different matter: the city was in ruins, and Frankish control over the hinterland may have been insecure, for in 1267 Clement IV was led to translate the bishop to the Italian see of Potenza because the revenues of Jabala were insufficient to support him.[3]

On the whole the church of Antioch after Hattin lived within its means. Bishops and canons were not maintained who were superfluous to the territorial requirements of the Franks, and the military orders, who were the principal landowners in the patriarchate, were obliged by the holy see to pay tithe and to contribute in this way to the support of the hierarchy.

The situation in the patriarchate of Jerusalem was quite different. The holy city itself and all the lands of the patriarch's own diocese, with the exception of the deanery of Jaffa, were lost to the Franks. The patriarch continued to have control over the former monastic communities of Jerusalem which were living on the coast in exile,[4] but this can have been of little more than nominal financial benefit to him, since they owed tithe on such lands as they still held to the bishops in whose dioceses they were situated. The canons of the Holy Sepulchre already owned a church in the city of Acre[5] and this became the headquarters of the patriarchate in exile.[6] The Holy Sepulchre, of course, owned considerable property throughout western Europe from which an income could be derived: it also owned lands in those parts of Syria which remained under Frankish control. In addition it

1. *Ibid.*, nos 2885–6.
2. See chapter 9 above.
3. Martène, Durand, *Nov. Thes.*, II, 505, no 402.
4. Pressutti, no 4319.
5. de Rozière, p 25, no 18.
6. 'Itinéraire de Londres à Jerusalem', Michelant, Raynaud, p 136.

received some new endowments in the thirteenth century: some of these were in the kingdom of Acre, but very few, since there was an acute shortage of land there;[1] it received some property in Cyprus;[2] and also some in Frankish Greece.[3]   The last, like the endowments given by the victors of the fourth crusade to other religious houses of Jerusalem, appear to have been in the nature of conscience money.   As the cardinal of St Susanna, papal legate to the Latin empire of Constantinople, explained to the abbot of Josaphat in 1206:

> The intention of all the Latins after God gave them the Roman empire was that the lands of the east might be helped through the establishment of that empire, and, as we think, they have continued to wish this.[4]

As in the case of the western European properties of the Holy Sepulchre and of other Latin religious houses in Syria, it is difficult to know whether benefactions of this kind were of any great profit, or whether the revenues which they produced were mostly absorbed in the costs of administration.

Tithe, which had formed a substantial part of the income of the Latin patriarchs before the battle of Hattin, cannot have contributed much to the treasury of their thirteenth-century successors, since it could only be levied in Jaffa.   Nevertheless, it may be symbolic of the straitened circumstances in which those prelates found themselves that on two occasions they thought it profitable to bring suits about tithe in the papal court: in 1196 against the knights Templar, who, it was admitted by the prosecution, were only required to pay half the tithe,[5] and in 1259 against the abbey of Josaphat, a case brought by the dean of Jaffa.[6]

It must be assumed that the patriarchs were able to support themselves from the properties they still owned in the east, and from such monies as they could obtain from their western properties, since the holy see did not find it necessary to give them financial aid in the crucial years before 1229.   The only instance of a concealed papal subvention was the license given to the patriarch Gerold in 1225 to hold the abbacy of St Margaret's, Campania, *in commendam*.[7]   From 1229—44, when Jerusalem itself was again in Christian hands, the patriarch must have derived

1. E.g. de Rozière, pp 268—9, no 145.
2. *Ibid.*, pp 314—17, nos 176—7.
3. *Ibid.*, p 2, no 2.
4. Kohler, pp 171—2, no 63.
5. de Rozière, pp 273—4, no 151.
6. Kohler, pp 182—3, nos 75—6.
7. Pressutti, no 5474.

some benefit from his share of the offerings which were made at the Sepulchre by Christian pilgrims. Certainly it is difficult to account in any other way for the large fortune which the patriarch Gerold bequeathed to the keeping at the knights Templar in 1239–40 for the defence of the Holy Land, for by the terms of Frederick II's treaty with al-Kamil virtually none of the former diocese of Jerusalem was restored, and only an insignificant part of the lands of the church.[1]

Although in 1243 pope Innocent IV ordered the abbot of Josaphat to give a subsidy to the new patriarch, Robert of Nantes, this was for his work as legate in Italy, for the patriarch did not come to Syria until the following year.[2] But after the definitive loss of Jerusalem in 1244 the holy see began to recognise that the patriarchs of Jerusalem needed some financial help. In 1253 the pope authorised the Templars to pay part of the patriarch Gerold's legacy to the new patriarch,[3] but it seems doubtful whether any money changed hands on that occasion, for three years later Alexander IV authorised the patriarch James to raise a loan of 150 oz of gold from the Hospital to defray the costs of coming to Rome to do business in the curia, and in the following year authorised him to receive 100 marks from the patriarch Gerold's legacy.[4]

Urban IV not merely increased the jurisdictional powers of his successor as patriarch, but also placed the financial affairs of the see of Jerusalem on a sounder basis. By uniting the sees of Jerusalem and Acre in a single administration the pope gave the patriarch a territorial base once more: he could receive the tithe of the diocese of Acre, and the ecclesiastical dues of the city, which was the largest in Syria. As will be shown later in this chapter this was a less munificent gift than it at first sight appeared, although it was a great improvement on the patriarch's former position. The conferment of the powers of legate throughout Syria, Cilicia and Cyprus on the patriarch was also not without financial advantages. Indeed, in April 1291 pope Nicholas IV wrote to complain about the 'great and unprecedented sum of money' which the patriarch of Jerusalem had tried to exact from the archbishop of Nicosia as a procuration for his work as legate in Cyprus, though the patriarch must have died before the arrival

---

1. Gerold complained about the settlement of 1229: 'sciendum quod patriarche extra civitatem [Hierusalem] non restituitur unus passus terre nec domui Sepulcri Dominici'. Huillard-Bréholles, III, p 105. Gerold's legacy was estimated at 16,000 besants, Bourel de la Roncière, no 1492.

2. Kohler, pp 180–81, no 72; 'ATS', *AOL*, II, p 441.

3. Berger, no 6432.

4. Bourel de la Roncière, nos 1096, 1937.

of the reprimand.[1]   Urban IV further increased the potential
financial powers of the patriarch by granting him direct control
over the daughter-houses of the Holy Sepulchre and of the convent of Bethany, which were exempted totally from the jurisdiction of ordinaries.[2]

As a result of these facilities the patriarch was able to sustain
the loss of Jaffa, the last remaining part of the patriarchal see, in
1268 with comparative equanimity.   It was only in the very last
years of the kingdom of Acre that financial problems again
became pressing for the patriarchs, for as Frankish territory was
diminished so was their property in Syria.   In 1288 Nicholas IV
licensed the patriarch to exchange property which his church
owned in England, from which, it may be presumed, it could draw
little profit, with property in Acre belonging to the Templars.[3]   In
the following year the pope allowed the patriarch to borrow 4,000
livres of Tours from the Holy Land tithe to meet expenses incurred by his church in the Roman curia;[4] and in 1290 he granted
him 2,000 *livres* of Tours for five years from the same source to
meet the expenses of his office.[5]   The patriarch was also encouraged to sell redundant churches in Acre, where land was at a
premium,[6] and the property of his church in Cyprus was freed
from the payment of tithe for five years.[7]   All these measures
suggest that in the last years of the kingdom the patriarch's
expenses were high, since he was carrying out much of the work
of secular government, whereas his income was diminishing.

The pattern of events in Tyre, the first metropolitan see in the
patriarchate, was somewhat different.   Tyre was the only city in
the kingdom which had never fallen into Saracen hands, but very
little of the rest of the diocese was controlled by the Christians
after Hattin.   Indeed, the relative poverty of its archbishops in
this period may be inferred from the fact that the pope found it
necessary to remind king Aimery in 1203 that he and his subjects
should pay tithe to the archbishop;[8] while the archbishop in 1218
had to be subsidised by being granted prebends in the churches
of Antioch and Tripoli,[9] although at the same time he held
the church of Sidon *in commendam*.[10]   Tyre was the only diocese

1. Mas Latrie, *Documents Nouveaux*, pp 349–51, no 7.
2. Guiraud, nos 44, 83, 210–11, 257.
3. Langlois, no 245.
4. *Ibid.*, no 1357.
5. *Ibid.*, no 2056.
6. St Demetrius and the house of the Penitents of Our Lord, *ibid.*, nos 2919, 3379.
7. *Ibid.*, no 2093.
8. Innocent III, 'Reg.', VI, nos 132–4, *PL*, 215, 148–9.
9. Pressutti, no 1141.
10. *Ibid.*, nos 18, 1094.

in the kingdom, apart from the shrine churches, which received any substantial new endowment in the period after Hattin: in 1197 Aimery of Cyprus gave the archbishop a *casale* in Cyprus which was later sold for 2,200 besants,[1] which must have helped to augment the revenues of the church.

The city of Tyre was, after Acre, the greatest in the kingdom, and also an important port. This had disadvantages for the archbishop, since all three great Italian communes had quarters there, and therefore had churches for their nationals. It is not known whether the Pisan church had parochial status,[2] but that which the Genoese built there after 1193 certainly had.[3] The greatest threat to the archbishop's jurisdiction came from the Venetians, who claimed a third part of the city by the terms of the treaty of 1124,[4] and who further claimed that their church was exempt from the jurisdiction of the bishop and was subject to the mother-church of St Mark's in Venice. Since the archbishop of Tyre's revenues in the early thirteenth century were largely derived from the city it is not to be wondered at that he contested this claim. The Venetians may, as they claimed, have enjoyed ecclesiastical immunity at Tyre from the beginning, and this may not have been disputed before 1187 because the archbishops had other adequate sources of revenue, but the point was certainly in dispute immediately after the battle of Hattin[5] and remained so until 1200 when Innocent III found in favour of the Venetians.[6] Six years later the Venetians complained that the papal ruling had been disregarded,[7] and in 1214 the case was once more reopened, and judgment was again given in favour of Venice in 1218.[8] The problem was not finally solved until 1247 when Innocent IV ruled that the Venetian church of Tyre was exempt from the archbishop's jurisdiction, and placed it under the special protection of the holy see, in recognition of which the church of St Mark's, Venice, should make an annual token payment to the holy see.[9] Two years later he instructed the archdeacon of Antioch to ensure that his wishes in regard to Tyre were being observed.[10]

1. Mas Latrie, *Chypre*, III, pp 606–7, 617.
2. Guy of Lusignan promised the Pisans that he would help them to gain freedom for their church in Tyre, but it is not known whether they succeeded in this aim, Müller, pp 36–8, no 31.
3. *PL*, 206, 913, no 55; Innocent III, 'Appendix ad Reg.', no 168, *PL*, 217, 215–16.
4. TT, I, pp 88, 92, nos 40–1.
5. Pflugck-Harttung, II, p 400, no 457, an act of Celestine III, which refers to litigation in the reign of Clement III (1188–91).
6. TT, I, pp 281–6, 424–6, nos 87, 108.
7. Innocent III, 'Reg.', IX, no 138, *PL*, 215, 966.
8. TT, II, pp 174–5, no 240; Pressutti, no 1294.
9. TT, II, pp 445–7, no 312.
10. *Ibid.*, II, pp 447–9, nos 313–14.

The archbishop of Tyre immediately complained to the pope about this settlement, and while not being willing to offend Venice, which was a powerful ally of the papacy in its war against the emperor Frederick, Innocent IV nevertheless ruled that St Mark's, Tyre, was not exempted from the payment of tithe on lands which it owned in the diocese, or from the payment of customary parochial dues to the bishop.[1] It did, however, enjoy full parochial rights: as the *bailli* of Venice in Syria reported to the senate in 1243, the priest-in-charge could perform all the sacraments 'which can be carried out in any cathedral church'.[2] To that extent the cathedral of Tyre lost money because of the Venetian immunity, since the Venetian colony, who formed an important part of the population of the city, paid church fees to their parish and not to the cathedral.

But the financial affairs of the church of Tyre became more stable after 1229 when Frederick II secured the restoration of most of the diocese including the fief of Toron. The archbishop was rich enough by 1261 to buy an estate for the church,[3] and the Venetian *bailli* reported in a casual reference in his inventory of Venetian property in Tyre in 1243 that the archbishop owned 2,040 olive trees.[4] The conquest of upper Galilee by Baybars must have once again reduced the wealth of Tyre, but there is no evidence that the church was ever so poor again in the remaining years before 1291 as it had been in the period between 1187 and 1229.

The archbishopric of Caesarea alone of the churches of the kingdom of Acre seems to have had few financial problems. The see and the most fertile part of the diocese remained in Frankish hands from the end of the third crusade until 1265, and although it was subject to intermittent raiding during those years the archbishop could still receive payment of tithe which formed the staple part of his income. Archbishop Peter of Limoges, indeed, was one of the very few prelates in the kingdom of Acre who felt rich enough, or who was generous enough, to be a patron of religious houses. He made a grant of tithe to Josaphat in 1199,[5] and at the end of his life granted a church to the knights of St Lazarus.[6] There is only one record of the archbishops of Caesarea receiving a supplement to their income, which was in 1246 when the pope allowed the archbishop not merely to retain a

1. Berger, no 4379.
2. TT, II, p 362, no 299.
3. Rey, *Recherches*, pp 40–1.
4. TT, II, p 384, no 299 (of 1243).
5. Kohler, p 167, no 58.
6. de Marsy, 'Saint-Lazare', *AOL*, II, p 154, no 37.

prebend at Antioch, where he had been a canon before his election, but also increased it by supplementary contributions from the abbeys of Antioch.[1] It is not known whether these payments were continued to his successors[2] or how the last archbishops were financed after the loss of Caesarea in 1265.

Nazareth, the third archbishopric in the patriarchate, had property in the west, but virtually none in the east after the loss of the archdiocese in 1187.[3] It is to be presumed that the archbishop and canons lived on their western revenues before the recovery of their see by Frederick II in 1229. This was a symbolic restoration, since very little of the diocese came into Christian hands at this time, and it was not until 1240 that the whole of the diocese was restored to Frankish control. Archbishop Henry (1238—68) was then able to place the finances of his see on a rational footing. It proved difficult for the canons of Nazareth to administer their estates: they were subject to attack, since they were situated in a frontier district, and they were worked by Muslim peasants who were not co-operative with their Frankish landlords.[4] The archbishop decided on a policy of leasing the property of his see to the knights of St John who had the necessary forces to defend these lands and who could also ensure that their peasants paid the customary dues. In 1255 he leased four *casalia* to the knights for ten years, in return for an annual payment of 1,300 besants in the first year, rising to 2,300 besants in the third and subsequent years when, it was hoped, they would have been restored to full productivity.[5] The arrangement evidently worked well, for in 1259 the terms of the contract were revised to cover a period of fifty years, at the slightly reduced annual payment of 2,000 besants.[6] In the same year the archbishop sold the entire lordship of Nazareth, consisting of nineteen *casalia*, to the knights in return for an annual payment of 14,000 besants.[7] Nazareth, it will be remembered, was one of two

1. Berger, nos 2026, 2028.
2. If Lociaumes, archbishop of Caesarea, whose death is recorded in 1267 ('Eracles', XXXIV, 9, *RHC Occ*, II, p 455), is identified with archbishop Joscelin (for Lociaumes is otherwise unknown), the payment cannot have been made to his successor, since Antioch fell in 1268.
3. There is no general confirmation extant of the lands of Nazareth. Except for the church in Acre, there is no reference in any document of the twelfth or thirteenth century to lands in Syria owned by the church of Nazareth outside its own archdiocese. Some Italian lands of the church are recorded in Nitti di Vito, ed, *Codice diplomatico Barese*, VIII, pp 210, 244–5, 337–8, 342–4, 346–7, 359–61, nos 164, 190, 267, 269–70, 273, 279–80.
4. *CGOH*, no 2934.
5. Delaville Le Roulx, *Archives*, pp 187–9, no 84; *CGOH*, no 2748.
6. *CGOH*, no 2934.
7. *Ibid.*, no 2936.

ecclesiastical lordships in the kingdom, and the consent of the
crown would normally have been needed for such a transaction,
but it was not obtained in this case, for king Conradin, though
recognised as formal ruler, had never received seisin of the realm.
The Hospital owned other estates in the diocese which did not
belong to the archbishop and they were obliged to reach an
agreement about the payment of tithe in such cases. The Hospital
agreed to pay half tithe in respect of wheat, wine, oil, hay and
vegetables for the fief of Belvoir, but no tithe on any other
commodity.[1]

However, when the Mount Tabor monastery was granted to the
Hospital by the holy see the archbishop of Nazareth renounced all
spiritual and temporal rights over it to the order, although it was
within his diocese, stating that its adequate defence was essential
to the well-being of his church.[2] This was true, and despite the
fact that the archbishop had sold the Hospital most of the lands
of his church already, there were other estates in the archdiocese
of Nazareth which belonged to other owners and from which he
could still draw tithe. Among these were the estates of Saffuriyah
and those of the *casale* Robert, which the Hospital owned,[3] and
the *casale* Anna, which belonged to the monks of Josaphat.[4]
Archbishop Henry even reopened the case of the *casalia* of Ligio
and Tannoch belonging to Josaphat, claiming the tithe of them,
a case which he lost in 1263 since the monks had privileges of
exemption which the holy see upheld.[5]

All the lands of Nazareth were lost in the late 1260s as a result
of the campaigns of the sultan Baybars, and, in accordance with
the terms of the agreements made with the Hospital, the revenues
of the archbishop ceased at that point, and the church of Nazareth
became once more, as it had been in the earlier part of the century,
dependent on the income derived from its possessions in western
Europe.   Nevertheless, for a brief period the archbishop and
canons had enjoyed a considerable income and had had almost no
expenses to meet. The basilica of Nazareth was not adequately
served by them,[6] they had delegated the administration of their
estates to the Hospitallers and were therefore free from the
expenses of estate management, and they had surrendered the

1. Delaville Le Roulx, 'Inventaire', no 318.
2. *CGOH*, no 3054.
3. Rey, *Recherches*, pp 36–8. The possession of the *casale* Robert was disputed
between the archbishop and the Hospital, Delaville Le Roulx, 'Inventaire', no 324. The
dispute continued until 1271, *CGOH*, nos 3051, 3414.
4. Delaborde, pp 107–9, no 52.
5. *Ibid.*, pp 112–16, nos 55–6; Kohler, pp 187–90, nos 79–80.
6. Guiraud, no 45.

lands of a lordship, given them in military tenure, in return for a fixed annual payment. It was thus possible, even in the disturbed conditions of life in thirteenth-century Palestine, for a particular church to derive profit from its lands if it was unscrupulous enough to fight for the preservation of its legal rights while evading its spiritual and temporal responsibilities.

Nazareth was, however, a unique example of ecclesiastical sharp practice, since in the case of other sees no opportunity existed for this pattern of behaviour. Bethlehem was in an analogous position to Nazareth, in that it had considerable property in the west, and also a little in Syria which was untouched by the conquests of Saladin, but it lost control of all the lands of its diocese after the battle of Hattin. As a result of the bishop's timely involvement with the fourth crusade his church obtained some share of the spoils of the Byzantine empire, and even had some claim to possession of the icon of the Hodegetria, which was disputed by the doge of Venice.[1] It was not always easy for the bishop to secure control over the property of his house in Europe, however, and in 1225 Honorius III remonstrated with the priors of daughter-houses of Bethlehem about their refusal to obey their bishop.[2]

The recovery of the cathedral for the bishop by Frederick II in 1229 must have helped to improve the finances of the church because of the offerings made there by pilgrims, although most of the diocese, and with it the principal estates of the church, remained in infidel hands. Richard of Cornwall's recovery of Ascalon, seat of the co-cathedral, and of the coastal region between it and Jaffa in 1241 brought the western part of the diocese once more briefly under the bishop's control, but this was lost again six years later.[3]

John the Roman, bishop-elect of Bethlehem in the early 1240s, seems to have attempted to do for his church what archbishop Henry was later to do so successfully for Nazareth: sell off its property in return for ready cash. This did not meet with the approval of the pope who, on appointing a new bishop in 1245, decreed that the acts of his predecessor were invalid and that the alienated property of the house must be recovered.[4] John the Roman seems to have made one principal tactical error, that of pledging the Hammer and Nail, instruments of the Passion, together with a reliquary containing the arm of the apostle

1. Riant, *Eglise de Bethléem*, I, p 141, no 11; Pressutti, no 5584.
2. *Ibid.*, no 5523.
3. The Aiyubids captured Ascalon in 1247, Gibb, in Setton, II, p 710.
4. Berger, nos 957, 1066, 2057.

Thomas, for a loan of 1,500 besants.[1] Since the chief aim of the crusading movement had been to restore the custody of the sacred relics, in which the Holy Land abounded, to Christian control, such an action was bound to scandalize the Catholic church and its head. It was, perhaps, in order to enable the church of Bethlehem to raise money to recover its lost property that Innocent IV empowered the brethren to take the unusual step of raising a general collection for their church throughout western Europe.[2]

It is clear from the confirmation of the lands of Bethlehem which Clement IV issued in 1266 that although the church had been given fresh endowments in western Europe during the thirteenth century it had received no new lands in the east.[3] As their eastern holdings diminished the clergy of Bethlehem became increasingly dependent on their western properties, and Thomas of Lentino, while bishop, obtained authority from the pope to exchange outlying properties of his see from which little profit could be derived with those of other religious houses which were more convenient to administer.[4]   The consequence of this economic dependence on the west was that as the kingdom of Acre declined the bishops of Bethlehem spent longer periods of time in western Europe: the last bishop before 1291 only paid one brief visit to Syria.[5]

Most of the sees in the patriarchate, unlike the three great shrine churches, had no possessions in the west with which to augment their incomes. Beirut city was continuously in Frankish hands after its recovery in 1197, but initially most of the diocese remained in Muslim control, and James of Vitry, who visited it in the winter of 1216–17, needed an armed escort to reach it.[6] However, it became more prosperous later in the century, part of its hinterland was recovered in 1229 and more in 1240, while the Ibelins, who were the lords of the city, developed the port of Beirut in the thirteenth century, which brought more money to the city.[7] The Venetians had a church there, but there is no evidence that it claimed exemption from the bishop.[8] There is slight evidence that by the second half of the century Beirut was regarded as one of the more stable dioceses in the kingdom: pope

1. *Ibid.*, no 1531; Rey, *Recherches*, p 27.
2. Berger, no 980.
3. Riant, *Eglise de Bethléem*, I, pp 147–54, no 12; cf. *ibid.*, pp 140–7, no 11 (Gregory IX's confirmation of 1227).
4. Jordan, no 32.
5. Bishop Hugh (1279–98) visited Acre in 1283: Pettenegg, *Die Urkunden des deutsch-Ordens-Centralarchives*, I, pp 159–60, no 618.
6. James of Vitry, *Lettres*, p 92, no 2.
7. TT, II, pp 230–2, no 261.
8. *Ibid.*, II, pp 423–5, 429–30, nos 305–6, 308.

Urban IV, who had first-hand knowledge of the state of affairs in the churches of Syria, provided a canon of Lydda to a prebend at Beirut in 1264.[1]

The neighbouring see of Sidon was in a less favoured position. Part of the district of Sidon was restored to Frankish rule by the treaty between Richard I and Saladin in 1192, but the city remained entirely Muslim. In 1197 the Aiyubids recognised a Frankish condominium over the city, but it was only restored completely to Frankish rule in 1229, and the entire district did not become Frankish until Theobald of Navarre's treaty in 1240.[2] Thereafter the district remained in Frankish control until 1291, although the city was sacked by the Mongols in 1260.[3] It will be seen from this that the control of the bishops over their diocese in the thirteenth century was very fluctuating. Part of it always remained in Christian hands, including, from the beginning, the city of Sarepta,[4] so that the bishop and clergy always had some source of income from tithe and other dues, but the bishops could not live in Sidon while it remained an open city under a joint Frankish–Muslim condominium.[5] When the full extent of the diocese was recovered in 1240 this led to a dispute with the neighbouring see of Beirut about the boundaries between them, which was referred to the curia.[6] The economic position of this see must always have been unstable.

The bishops of Lydda found themselves in a similar position. Part of their see always remained in Christian hands between 1192 and 1268, but their cathedral was right on the frontier and they lived at Acre in the church of St George throughout the thirteenth century.[7] The bishop received some financial help from the church of Acre,[8] but so long as part of his diocese remained in Christian hands he had a source of revenue, albeit a somewhat tenuous one.

Although the see of Tiberias was restored when that area came into Frankish hands again as a result of Theobald of Navarre's

1. Guiraud, no 1983.
2. Theobald's treaty secured the return to the Franks of the castle of Beaufort which commanded the approach roads to the coastal lands *via* the Litani valley.
3. Templar of Tyre, c 303, *Gestes*, p 162.
4. Sarepta was granted to Reginald Grenier by Saladin in October 1192, Hardwicke, in Setton, II, p 524.
5. Honorius III speaks of the see being in Saracen hands, Pressutti, no 18, as does James of Vitry, *Lettres*, p 92, no 2. It is doubtful whether the bishops ever returned there even after the whole diocese was restored to Christian control. The dean of Sidon was living in Acre in 1247, Berger, nos 3149–50.
6. *Ibid.*, nos 16, 2803.
7. B. Dichter, *The Orders and Churches of Crusader Acre*, Acre 1979, p 114.
8. Pressutti, no 5696.

crusade it did not prove very easy to collect church dues there. In 1243, only two years after the appointment of a bishop there, Innocent IV was suggesting to the patriarch of Jerusalem that the bishop should be translated because of the poverty of his see,[1] and, when that did not prove practical, the pope ordered the abbot of Josaphat to grant the bishop of Tiberias a subsidy.[2] No doubt the bishop faced problems similar to those of the archbishop of Nazareth: his diocese was on the frontier and subject to enemy raids, and his labour-force was composed almost entirely of Muslim peasants who would not willingly co-operate with their new Frankish landlords. The cathedral city was sacked by the Khorezmians in 1244[3] and the bishop retired to Acre.[4]   But bishops continued to be appointed to this see until the end of Frankish rule in Palestine, although after Baybars's conquest of Galilee they can have had little source of revenue, unless, as is possible, the boundaries of the see stretched into the coastal territory which the Franks continued to hold after 1270.

The see of Sebastia in Samaria, as has already been seen, never came into Frankish hands, and it was only possible to support a bishop of that diocese in the thirteenth century in a titular capacity, while he drew his revenues from other sources.[5] The case of the bishopric of Hebron was different in its outcome. This see was revived by pope Innocent IV in 1252 after being vacant for over sixty years. The diocese was never restored to Frankish control, but the pope ordered the bishop of Lydda and the bishop-elect of Bethlehem to make inquiries about the properties which had formerly belonged to the see with a view to recovering them for the bishop's use.[6]   Inevitably those properties which had remained in Frankish control had passed into other hands while the see was vacant. The first lawsuit which resulted from the inquiry initiated by the pope proved to be something of an anti-climax. The bishop of Hebron laid claim to certain houses at Montmusard, a suburb of Acre, which had passed into the hands of the Teutonic knights, and demanded an indemnity of 3,000 besants in respect of unpaid rents. The master of the order claimed that the Teutonic knights were exempt from any authority save the pope, and threatened to appeal to the papal

---

1. Berger, no 49.

2. Kohler, pp 180–81, no 72.

3. Matthew Paris, IV, p 338.

4. It is not known where the pro-cathedral of Tiberias was situated in the city, Dichter, *op. cit.*, p 75.

5. As canon, and later prior, of the Holy Sepulchre, Bourel de la Roncière, no 1153; Guiraud, no 260.

6. Strehlke, p 81, no 101.

court. Since this would have involved the bishop in considerable expense, which he could not hope to meet, he made a 'friendly' settlement with the order, by which they acknowledged that the houses in dispute belonged to his church and undertook to pay him an annual rent of seven besants for them.[1] The bishop later established his rights over the *casale* of Naharia near Antioch, which had come into the possession of the Hospitallers, who agreed to pay him a rent of 70 besants a year for it in 1265,[2] a source of income which must have come to an end in 1268 when Baybars conquered Antioch. The see of Hebron's finances continued to be conducted in a hand-to-mouth way: in 1273, at the request of the patriarch, the bishop sold his rights in two houses at Acre to the Hospitallers for 30 besants.[3] The bishop of Hebron and his officers must have lived in comparative poverty during the thirteenth century.

Potentially the richest of all the sees of the patriarchate of Jerusalem in the thirteenth century was Acre, though ecclesiastically its bishop was only a suffragan of the see of Tyre. The city was the capital of the kingdom of Jerusalem in exile, and the most important commercial centre on the Syrian coast. The diocese, which consisted of some of the best agricultural land in the kingdom, was continuously in Frankish control throughout the period, and the bishop should therefore have had no financial problems.

Yet as James of Vitry told his friends in Paris after he had come to take up his duties in 1216:

> I have discovered that Acre is like a monster, or a beast with nine heads, each one at odds with the other.[4]

This was no simple rhetorical figure of speech, for, as a result of the political circumstances of the kingdom in the years after Hattin, the city had become a place of competing ecclesiastical jurisdictions. The patriarch of Jerusalem fixed his see there, together with the canons of the Holy Sepulchre, and not unnaturally, he overshadowed the bishop of Acre as a focus of ecclesiastical authority. In addition, the communities which had served the great shrine churches of Jerusalem also went to live in Acre after the third crusade. These included the Austin canons of the *Templum Domini*, Mount Sion and the Mount of Olives, the Premonstratensian canons of St Samuel's, Mountjoy, the Benedictines of Our Lady of Josaphat and Sta Maria Latina, and

---

1. *Ibid.*, pp 82–4, no 104.
2. *CGOH*, no 3120; Delaville Le Roulx, 'Inventaire', no 339.
3. *CGOH*, no 3515.
4. *Lettres*, p 83, no 2.

the Benedictine nuns of St Anne's and of the convent of Bethany.[1] The military orders also had their headquarters there, not only the Templars and the knights of St John, but also the newly-founded Teutonic order.[2] The heads of the lesser military orders also lived at Acre: the knights of St Lazarus, and the English order of St Thomas of Canterbury, founded in 1190 by a member of the household of Ralph de Diceto, dean of London.[3] The Mount Tabor monastery also established itself in Acre while its mother-house was in enemy hands.[4]

Nor did the problem end there. The bishop of Lydda had his pro-cathedral in Acre throughout the thirteenth century, and the archbishops of Nazareth and the bishops of Bethlehem lived there for much of it.[5] The bishops of Tiberias came there in 1244,[6] and the bishops of Hebron after their see was re-established in 1252.[7] The three great Italian communes also had churches there: St Mark of the Venetians, St Lawrence of Genoa and St Peter of Pisa,[8] and during the thirteenth century the merchants of Amalfi, Ancona and Marseilles all built chapels there for their nationals.[9] In addition, new orders founded houses there, the Franciscans, the Poor Clares, the Dominicans, the Carmelites,[10] together with lesser orders like that of the Holy Spirit, the Redemptorists of the Holy Trinity, the order of Penitents of Jesus Christ, and the Convertites,[11] while there was even a convent of enclosed Cistercian nuns.[12]

All these religious houses, pro-cathedrals and military orders had chapels for the use of their own members, most of which were available to the general public as well. There were also secular churches, chapels and hospitals of the Latin rite, as well as churches of the eastern rite.[13] Acre is not a very large city, yet

---

1. Dichter, *op. cit.*, pp 26, 44, 62, 76–7, 84, 88.
2. *Ibid.*, pp 40, 47, 79. The Teutonic order was founded at Acre in 1198.
3. Dichter, *op. cit.*, pp 110, 117. Roger of Wendover, I, pp 178–9.
4. Dichter, *op. cit.*, pp 86–7.
5. *Ibid.*, pp 70, 94, 114.
6. *Ibid.*, p 75.
7. *Ibid.*, p 98.
8. *Ibid.*, pp 14–17, 32.
9. *Ibid.*, pp 22–3, 31.
10. *Ibid.*, pp 105–6, 88, 91; F.M. Abel, 'Le couvent des frères prêcheurs à Saint-Jean d'Acre', *Revue Biblique*, 43, 1934, pp 265–84; Bourel de la Roncière, no 3250 (Carmelite church).
11. Dichter, *op. cit.*, pp 35, 90, 115; *CGOH*, no 3105 (which mentions *sorores repentitae*).
12. Mas Latrie, *Documents Nouveaux*, pp 343–4, no 1; Hamilton in Pennington, ed, *One Yet Two*, pp 410–12.
13. E.g. Orthodox monasteries of St Margaret's (*CGOH*, no 2732) and St Sabas (Bourel de la Roncière, nos 390, 606); an Orthodox cathedral and a Jacobite cathedral (James of Vitry, *Lettres*, pp 83–5, no 2). The Jacobites' cathedral may have been St Mary Magdalen's (the dedication of their cathedral in Jerusalem): this was certainly an eastern-rite church, for it was served by married clergy (Strehlke, pp 33–4, no 41).

the most recent work has estimated that there were fifty-nine churches and chapels there in the thirteenth century.[1] This was not in itself an excessive number by the standards of many medieval cities of comparable size,[2] but what was unusual about Acre was that a large number of these churches were exempt from the authority of the bishop.

In the first place the patriarch and the canons of the Holy Sepulchre obviously could not be subordinate to the bishop in whose city they lived. Moreover, the patriarch retained jurisdiction over the monasteries and convents of Jerusalem in exile, together with the monastery of Tabor, even though their communities lived in Acre.[3] The other bishops who lived there also were autonomous in their own pro-cathedrals,[4] although neither they nor the patriarch possessed any parochial rights. The military orders were exempt even from the patriarch's jurisdiction and had no ecclesiastical superior but the pope. In practice such exemptions proved to be less absolute than they seemed on paper. Nothing is known about the relations between the bishops of Acre and the Templars, but the Hospital of St John was brought to acknowledge that the bishop had certain rights, though only after prolonged litigation. In 1200 bishop Theobald granted the Hospitallers the important privilege of a cemetery and a mortuary chapel outside Acre,[5] but this caused a considerable loss in burial fees to his church. James of Vitry, when bishop, contested the extent of the Hospital's exemption, and the dispute was settled by the legate, cardinal Pelagius of Albano, in 1221. He enacted that the Hospitallers should pay the bishop a half tithe on the vineyards that they owned; that they had the right to preach when they wished, though they might not summon the faithful to hear their sermons; that they might confer the last rites on any sick person in the city who had expressly wished to be buried in their cemetery, but not on any others; that they might bury any dead persons who were found in the streets of the city, and take the destitute sick of any parish into their hospital; and that their chaplains owed no financial

---

1. Dichter, *Orders and Churches*.

2. FitzStephen wrote of London in the reign of Henry II: 'there are in London and in its suburb thirteen great conventual churches, besides 126 lesser parish churches'. William FitzStephen 'Vita S. Thomae', ed J.C. Robertson, *Materials for the History of Thomas Becket, RS*, 67 (I–VII), London 1875–85, III, pp 2–3.

3. Pressutti, no 4319. Tabor had been made subject to the patriarch in 1112, *CGOH*, vol II, p 899, no 4.

4. Alexander IV's privilege for the archbishop of Nazareth, Bourel de la Roncière, no 1300.

5. *CGOH*, no 1113.

dues to the bishop.[1]   In 1228 the cardinal issued a new agreement, designed, it was alleged, to clarify some of the points in the
former document: among these was the provision that if the
Hospital had formerly paid tithe on land which it had subsequently converted into sugar plantations, it was equally bound to
pay tithe on its sugar-cane.[2]   Clearly the order had been indulging
in a primitive form of tax evasion.   Agreements were more easily
reached than enforced, and in 1238 the bishop of Acre complained to pope Gregory IX that the Hospital had defaulted in
payment of half tithes on certain property and had failed to
indemnify him in respect of burial dues, and asked for a payment
of 500 besants.[3]

In 1257 bishop Florence of Acre tried to regulate relations
between himself and the Teutonic knights, claiming that their
chaplain owed him manual obedience and a silver mark each year;
and that he should receive from them the tithe of the *casalia* of
the order in the diocese and of their mills in the city.   The master
lodged a counter-claim that he had paid 4,000 besants in tithe on
land which was exempt, which should be repaid by the bishop,
together with an indemnity of 30,000 besants for lands in
Chastiau dou rei which belonged to the order and which the
bishop held unlawfully.   The counter-claim seems to have been
largely directed to forcing the bishop to reach a settlement by
arbitration without recourse to the papal courts, which would
have been expensive, but which the order could more easily have
afforded than the church of Acre.   It was finally agreed that the
order should pay a silver mark a year to the bishop and grant him
a fifteenth on all the produce of its *casalia* in the diocese after
carriage charges had been deducted for marketing the goods, but
that the produce of its mills should be free from tithe.[4]

Bishops had similar battles with the Italian communes.   James
of Vitry claimed that the chaplains of Genoa, Pisa and Venice
acted as though they were exempt from his authority, refusing
to allow him to preach in their churches and failing to enforce
excommunications when he published them.[5]   No dispute is
known to have occurred between the bishops of Acre and the
Genoese clergy; and bishop Theobald reached an agreement
with the Pisans in 1200 which they seem to have honoured.   The
commune was to pay the bishop four besants a year in recognition of his authority, to receive the holy oils from him, and to

1. *Ibid.*, no 1718.
2. *Ibid.*, no 1911.
3. Auvray, no 4387.
4. Strehlke, pp 91–4, no 112.
5. *Lettres*, pp 85–6, no 2.

enforce interdicts and excommunications which he published. The territorial boundaries of the Pisan church were defined, and it was enacted that all Pisans living within that area should be freed from payment of dues to the church of Acre, whereas those who lived outside the Pisan parish, although they might receive the sacraments from the Pisan chaplains, were bound to pay half the dues to the bishop.[1] This privilege remained in force until 1247 when Innocent IV revoked it because the Pisans had supported Frederick II.[2]

The Venetians also enjoyed the rights of an exempt parish at Acre until these were called in question by James of Vitry. The matter was left unsettled when he resigned the see, and was re-opened by Gregory IX in 1235.[3] The case was still before the papal courts three years later when the pope ordered the Venetians to produce a privilege of exemption for St Mark's, Acre, within a year or to submit to the bishop's authority.[4] A final settlement was only reached in 1247 when Innocent IV confirmed that St Mark's was completely exempt from diocesan authority and was directly under the protection of the holy see.[5] There matters rested until 1260 when, as a result of territorial gains made by the Venetians during the war of St Sabas, the boundaries of their parish in Acre had to be redefined. In 1260 bishop Florence of Acre reached an agreement with the clergy of St Mark's whereby the city parish of St Demetrius was to lose its parochial status, to be incorporated in the parish of St Mark's, and to become a chapel in that parish. It was further enacted than no Venetian living outside the parish should be able to avail himself of the services of St Mark's without paying the customary dues to the bishop; that the clergy of St Mark's should pay the bishop rent for the property of St Demetrius; and that they should give obedience to him and pay him 50 besants a year in token of this. In other words, Venetian privileges were extended, but the bishop gained in return a measure of recognition which he had not received under the terms of the earlier settlement. The agreement needed ratification by the Venetian senate, and the bishop stipulated that if the senate refused its approval the Venetians should forfeit all their ecclesiastical rights in Acre.[6]

The majority of other churches in the city were not exempt from the bishop and did not have parochial status. Innocent IV

1. Müller, pp 82–3, no 52.
2. Berger, no 2801.
3. Auvray, no 2652.
4. *Ibid.*, no 4411.
5. TT, II, pp 445–7, no 312.
6. *Ibid.*, III, pp 31–8, nos 343–4.

did exempt the order of the Holy Spirit from the bishop,[1] but this was an unusual privilege and one that was not granted, for example, to the Breton hospital, even though it was founded by Gilles of Tyre who stood high in the regard of St Louis.[2] But most of these institutions also owned some land in the diocese, as did the exempt communities and the military orders, on which they sometimes paid no tithe, or only a reduced tithe: for example, the monastery of Josaphat owned six *casalia* in the diocese on which it paid no tithe.[3] Such exemptions considerably reduced the bishop's revenues.

The revenue from ecclesiastical dues in the city of Acre, which should have formed an important part of the church's income, was, as a result of the multiplicity of exempt jurisdictions, difficult to collect. Moreover, legacies, which formed a useful additional source of revenue to most churches, were diverted from the cathedral of the Holy Cross to the other many possible beneficiaries in the city. Take, for example, the will of the Genoese Saliba, drawn up in 1264, which, after bequests to the church of St Lawrence at Acre where he wished to be buried, continues:

> To the hospital of the Holy Spirit, three besants
> To the abbess Agnes and her sisters, fifty besants
> To the friars preacher, five besants
> To the friars minor, five besants
> To St Mary Magdalen, two besants
> To the Convertite sisters, two besants
> To the brethren of Carmel, five besants
> To the lepers of St Lazarus, six besants
> To the Hospital of St Anthony, three besants
> To Holy Trinity, three besants
> To St Bridget, two besants
> To the hospital of St Catherine, two besants
> To the church of St Mary of the Provençaux, two besants.[4]

A diversity of beneficiaries was not in the interests of the bishop's treasury, but Acre afforded more opportunity for diversifying pious bequests than most towns in the Frankish east.

When in 1262 the see of Acre was given *in commendam* to the patriarch, who also enjoyed full legatine powers, the financial situation was simplified. To begin with the financial jurisdictions of the two sees could be unified, and secondly it was less easy for the military orders and the Italian communes to break agreements with the patriarch and legate than with a simple bishop. The existing exemptions must have remained valid, but there is no

1. Berger, no 4758.
2. Bourel de la Roncière, no 1274.
3. Delaborde, p 101, no 49.
4. *CGOH*, no 3105.

evidence in the very full papal registers that there were any disputes over the payment of tithe or other dues in the diocese of Acre in the period of direct patriarchal rule there. Before that time, although there is no suggestion that the bishops of Acre were poor, their revenues cannot have been as extensive as the wealth of their see might imply, and a great deal of their energy and resources had to be spent in litigation with the military orders and the Italian communes, who possessed great power in the diocese, in order to enforce the rights of their church.

The financial problems of the patriarchate of Jerusalem in the thirteenth century were far greater than those of the sister-patriarchate of Antioch. The papacy can only indirectly be held responsible for this in so far as it resurrected some redundant sees in the middle of the century; before that time the local hierarchy had themselves perpetuated an establishment in excess of their needs in the false hope that the lands of the first kingdom would speedily be recovered by a new crusade. Although the papacy exercised a far greater degree of control over the Latin church in Syria in the thirteenth century than it had done before Hattin it did not recognise the extent of the financial problem. It is difficult to see how it could have realised this, since popes were asked to confirm the property of the Holy Sepulchre and of other Latin churches in Syria, which looked most impressive when set out in full. Since such confirmations always listed all the property to which a community had a juridical claim, whether it was in possession of it or not, and since the popes probably only had the most hazy notion about which places were still in Christian hands, they may justifiably have considered that any rumours which they heard about the poverty of the churches in Syria were greatly exaggerated. It was not until Innocent IV learned from his own nephew about the pitiable state of the church of Antioch that the holy see took any firm measures to alleviate the penury of that see, and it was equally not until James Pantaleon was translated from Jerusalem to the chair of St Peter in Rome that any attempt was made to rationalise the economic as well as the jurisdictional problems of the church of Jerusalem. The consequence of close papal control over episcopal appointments in thirteenth-century Syria, coupled with papal ignorance about the economic facts of ecclesiastical administration there, was that many able and learned men were tied to the Holy Land as bishops with insufficient income and with inadequate occupation.

It remains to consider what the consequences of this situation were for the lesser clergy. A greater degree of papal control certainly enabled some of them to obtain a better education than would have been possible a century earlier. In 1244, for example,

the pope gave permission for the treasurer of the church of
Tripoli to draw his prebend for the purpose of study overseas for
five years provided that he appointed a vicar to carry out his
work;[1] ten years later a similar permission was extended to a
canon of Acre.[2]

But a greater degree of papal control over lesser benefices
could and did work to the detriment of the Syrian churches. A
cursory glance at thirteenth-century papal registers suggests that
the holy see made extensive and indiscriminate use of its powers
of 'provision' to Latin benefices in Syria, but a closer examination
of the sources shows that such an impression is misleading. There
is only one case of papal provision in Syria in the reign of Innocent III, and that relates to a clerk of the church of Tripoli who
was provided to a canonry in that church. In the pontificates of
Honorius III and Gregory IX there are only three instances each
of such provisions:[3] the climax of this proces was reached in the
reign of Innocent IV, whose registers record twelve instances of
such appointments, although, from the evidence of complaints
reaching Rome, there were many more.[4] Alexander IV put a stop
to this procedure.[5] It was used four times by his successor, Urban
IV, but on all occasions in favour of clergy resident in the Holy
Land, and two of the appointments were to canonries of Valania:
since this see was controlled by the Hospital, the pope may have
envisaged these two provisions as a subsidy to the secular clergy
to be paid by that order.[6] There were no provisions made by
Clement IV and only three by Gregory X,[7] and thereafter the only
known instances are the holding by curial officials of the archdeaconry of Tripoli in the reign of Honorius IV,[8] although it is
possible that the archdeacons had been seconded to work in
Rome and allowed to retain their Syrian benefices. It is also
worth noting that the use of provisions was not made indiscrim-
inately: the bulk of the known cases relate to the church of
Tripoli, which was one of the most prosperous of the Latin
churches of Syria in that century.[9]

1. Berger, no 509.
2. *Ibid.*, no 8059.
3. Innocent III, 'Reg.', I, no 529, *PL*, 214, 482–3; Pressutti, nos 4107, 4129 (which
relate to a single provision), 5791, 6030; Auvray, nos 119, 433, 3270.
4. Berger, nos 837, 1079, 1749, 3075, 3138, 3209, 3662, 3667, 4042, 4354, 4394,
5048, 5390, 7744. See p 308, n 1, below.
5. Bourel de la Roncière, nos 216, 1750.
6. Guiraud, nos 931, 2467, 2478, 2640.
7. Guiraud-Cadier, nos 247, 433–4, 619.
8. Prou, nos 191, 237, 701.
9. Papal provisions recorded in the papal registers between 1198 and 1291 to the
Syrian church were awarded to the following sees in the numbers stated in brackets:
Tripoli (8): Antioch (3): Valania (3): Tyre (1): Acre (1): Lydda (1): Gibelet (1): the
abbey of Latina (1): to any vacant benefice (4).

Nevertheless, when all these factors have been considered, it remains true that the practice of provision had a deleterious effect on the life of the lesser clergy in Frankish Syria. A western clerk who was provided to a Syrian benefice was usually non-resident, and appointed a procurator to receive investiture of the office on his behalf, and then feed a vicar to perform his duties for him, and drew what remained of the stipend. Such a procedure inevitably set a bad example to those clergy who were in residence, who were tempted to follow suit and also fee vicars to carry out their duties for them. A further consequence of this was that the need for canons and other cathedral officials to take holy orders was removed, since they no longer had liturgical functions to perform. They could therefore receive an income from the church and enjoy the privileges of clerical status without being in major orders and suffering from the restrictions which, technically at least, these imposed. The vicars who were inadequately paid to perform the functions of the official clergy were often lax in their duties and ill-instructed in them.

This is not an imaginary reconstruction of what happened in Syria, but is confirmed by the highest ecclesiastical authority, that of the holy see. Papal provisions cannot be exclusively blamed for these evils, since the earliest complaints from Rome antedate the widespread use of this practice in the Syrian church, but there is no doubt that provisions aggravated and accelerated a practice which was already beginning to spring up independently. In 1229 Gregory IX complained that many of the canons of Antioch were not in residence;[1] nine years later he reprimanded the bishop of Acre because the Divine Office was neglected in his cathedral.[2] In 1256 Alexander IV discovered that there were not enough canons to ensure proper liturgical service at the Holy Sepulchre in Acre;[3] while the church of Nazareth proved an endemic problem. The archbishop admitted in 1252 that the shrine had not been properly served in living memory, although it had then been in Christian hands for a quarter of a century, and drew up a new constitution for it;[4] nine years later pope Urban IV instructed the cardinal bishop of Sabina to reconstitute the chapter of Nazareth and enforce the service of the basilica;[5] and a further constitution with a provision of residence in the pro-cathedral of Acre was enacted by Clement IV in 1267.[6]

1. Auvray, no 348.
2. *Ibid.*, no 4457.
3. Bourel de la Roncière, no 1077.
4. Berger, no 5538.
5. Guiraud, no 45.
6. Jordan, no 511.

More widespread evils were endemic in the churches of Jerusalem and Antioch. Pope Alexander IV related that in many
cases more canons had been appointed to cathedrals there than
there were prebends to support, and that the unedifying spectacle
had developed of five, or sometimes as many as ten, honorary
canons waiting for prebends to fall vacant. He attempted to solve
this by decreeing that in such cases only two of the unbeneficed
canons should retain their titular offices.[1] Pope Gregory X tried
to impose a more radical reform on the Latin church in Syria by
ordering the patriarch of Jerusalem to ensure that in all the
churches of his legation clergy were in residence and had also
received the grade of holy orders appropriate to their titular
office.[2] The fact that it was necessary to enact such a decree
shows how widely the rule must have been breached.

Certainly the operation of thirteenth-century canon law
allowed some very unpromising candidates to be beneficed. The
most unusual case in the papal registers is the dispensation granted
to a canon of Tripoli, Opizo de Strillaportis. Pope Nicholas IV
absolved him since

> being reduced to madness, he struck a certain priest, a member of his
> household, who was lying at the point of death, with an iron hammer
> and killed him, but now that he is restored to sanity [the pope]
> absolves him from excommunication, if by this act he has incurred it,
> and grants that he may hold those benefices which he has lawfully
> obtained, and dispenses him from any irregularity he may have com-
> mitted; provided that he does not exercise the ministry in the orders he
> has received, nor proceed to ordination as a priest.[3]

The number of beneficed clergy guilty of manslaughter (even if
they could plead diminished responsibility) in the thirteenth-
century Syrian church was probably small, but the overall picture
which emerges from a study of the sources is one of a general
collapse of morale among the lesser clergy there at that time. The
reasons for this are varied. The diminution of the number of sees
in the province of Antioch, and the growth in papal control which
led to the dominance of bishops appointed directly from western
Europe in both patriarchates, made the possibility of promotion
more remote to most of the cathedral clergy than it had been a
century before. The provision of non-resident clergy to benefices
in Syria by the popes set a bad example to the native clergy, which
proved difficult to eradicate. But in addition to these practical

---

1. Bourel de la Roncière, nos 324, 334.
2. Guiraud-Cadier, nos 15, 26.
3. Langlois, no 2647.

considerations there seems to have been a lack of zeal among the native clergy, engendered by the defeat at Hattin and intensified by the failure of subsequent crusades.

The lesser clergy in the first kingdom had conceived their duty in practical terms: to conduct the public worship of God according to the norms of the western church in those places 'where God was first acknowledged and held as Lord'. This will was lacking in their thirteenth-century successors, and although on the whole the bench of bishops was able and learned they had little support from their subordinates. James of Vitry, who went to the see of Acre with great zeal for the crusading ideal, complained about the people he described as scribes and pharisees, and it is clear from the context of his letter that he was talking about his clergy:

> Last and worse than all other kinds of men, and more hard-hearted and blind, I have found here scribes and pharisees, who . . . caring nothing about the salvation of souls, corrupt lay people by their speech and their example . . . [1]

A full Latin hierarchy had been preserved in the kingdom of Acre as a sign of hope that the Franks intended to regain their lost lands and to restore them to the worship of the Latin church. This aim, however, proved self-defeating, for the numerous clergy had too little employment to provide them with a practical incentive for carrying out their duties. Many of them had no lay congregations to whom to minister, and those who had could, with a quiet mind, leave that work to other bodies, like the mendicant orders, who had more of a taste for it. In most cases, the secular clergy had too little economic reward to act as a material incentive, since conscientious performance of duties would not lead to any improvement in their financial prospects. Only dedicated clergy will function efficiently if they lack both pastoral stimulus and material inducements and such men are rare in any age of the church. The attempt to preserve the zeal of the Franks in Syria by retaining a large ecclesiastical establishment therefore backfired, since a demoralised clergy was powerless to inspire fervour in the people among whom they lived.

1. *Lettres*, pp 86–7, no 2.

12. THE ORTHODOX SCHISMS AT JERUSALEM AND ANTIOCH

When news of Saladin's capture of Jerusalem reached Constantinople it must have seemed natural to the Byzantine emperor, Isaac II Angelus, to ask the sultan to restore an Orthodox patriarch in the holy city[1] and to revert to the position which had existed for centuries under Muslim rulers there before the Latin conquest. The Orthodox claimant at this time was living in the imperial capital. He was Dositheus, a man of Venetian parentage, who had been a monk of the monastery of Studius and had foretold Isaac II's accession, thereby becoming a close friend of the emperor's. At about the time of Isaac's *coup d'etat* the Orthodox patriarch of Jerusalem, Leontius II, had died,[2] and Isaac nominated Dositheus to that office. Saladin did not accede to the emperor's request, and Dositheus was therefore still living in Constantinople when the oecumenical patriarchate itself became vacant. Isaac II consulted the most distinguished Byzantine canon lawyer, Theodore Balsamon, about whether it was lawful to translate a patriarch from one see to another: as Theodore was himself titular patriarch of Antioch he not unnaturally supposed that the emperor was considering his own translation to Constantinople, and submitted an affirmative answer supported by an imposing range of canonical authorities. Armed with this authorisation, the emperor translated Dositheus of Jerusalem to the headship of the Byzantine church in 1189, but so great was the indignation among churchmen that Dositheus abdicated after only a few months.[3] Isaac was unwilling to accept this decision and caused him to be reinstated later that year. Meanwhile a new patriarch of Jerusalem was elected, Mark II Cataphlorus.[4] The problem remained that if Dositheus's elevation to Constantinople was contested, as it was, on the grounds that a patriarch could not be translated, then he, not Mark, was lawful patriarch of Jerusalem still. But Dositheus still enjoyed no support among the Byzantine senior clergy and in

---

1. F. Dölger, *Regesten der Kaiserurkunden des östromischen Reiches*, Berlin 1924, nos 1591, 1593.
2. Grumel, *Chronologie*, p 452, dates his death 14 June 1184—5.
3. Choniates, *De Isaacio Angelo*, II, 4, ed Van Dieten, I, pp 405—8.
4. Elected 1189—90, Grumel, *Chronologie*, p 452.

1191 he formally abdicated from the sees both of Constantinople and of Jerusalem.[1] This abdication proved to be final, and Mark was left undisputed patriarch of Jerusalem. In 1192 Isaac II sent an embassy to Saladin requesting that the Orthodox might be granted the Holy Sepulchre and the other churches of Jerusalem, which would have led to the restoration of the titular patriarch there. The sultan, however, refused this demand[2] and Mark therefore remained in Constantinople.[3]

The situation in Jerusalem after 1187 was a curious one. Saladin was on good terms with the Syrian Orthodox: they are alleged to have tried to aid him during the siege,[4] and they certainly expressed a wish to remain in Jerusalem after he captured it, since it was their home.[5] The sultan, it would seem, left them in charge of the Holy Sepulchre, where, apart from the Latins, they had been the only confession with altars during the years of Frankish rule.[6] When Hubert Walter, bishop of Salisbury, visited Jerusalem after the treaty had been concluded between Richard I and Saladin in 1192, he found the liturgy in the Holy Sepulchre celebrated in 'the barbarous Syrian rite' and asked the sultan to allow two Latin priests and two Latin deacons to officiate in the church, and to be supported, together with the Syrian clergy, by the offerings of pilgrims. He also asked for parallel concessions to be made at Bethlehem and Nazareth. Saladin magnanimously acceded to this request.[7] The Latins and Syrians were still willing to work together in Jerusalem at this time. Their fundamental unity had, indeed, been shown slightly earlier, while the war was still in progress, when the Syrian archbishop of Lydda, who lived under Saladin's rule, had come to greet king Richard on his march towards Jerusalem and had given him a fragment of the Syrian True Cross.[8]

There was, it would seem, no schism in the church of Jerusalem between Latins and Orthodox so long as there was no conflict about jurisdiction, but that would only last for as long as the rival Orthodox patriarch remained in Constantinople. Equally there could be no schism at Antioch, since the city had remained

1. Grumel, *Regestes*, no 1178; Choniates, *op. cit., loc. cit.*, n 3, p 310 above. For the dates of Dositheus's reign as patriarch of Constantinople, Brand, *Byzantium confronts the West*, p 342, n 63.

2. Baha ed-Din, *Life of Saladin*, pp 334–5.

3. He had a palace there, Brand, *op. cit.*, p 101.

4. *RHC Occ*, II, p 85, note a.

5. al-Isfahani, *Conquête de la Syrie*, p 50.

6. See chapter 7 above.

7. *Itinerarium Regis Ricardi*, VI, 34, p 438.

8. *Ibid.*, V, 53, p 376. Richard was also visited by the Orthodox abbot of St Elias, *ibid.*, V, 54, pp 377–8.

in Latin hands, Aimery of Limoges was still in power, and the
titular Orthodox patriarch, Theodore Balsamon, was safely in the
Byzantine capital, where he remained until his death, which
occurred sometime between 1195 and 1206.[1] An Orthodox
patriarch was restored at Jerusalem according to the Syrian
chronicler, Bar Hebraeus: he dates this event soon after 1187, but
as he was writing almost a century later this term cannot be
accepted in too precise a way.[2] The restoration may have taken
place after the patriarch Mark's death, which occurred after 1195;
anyway Mark's successor, Euthymius, certainly came to Palestine.
Whether he lived in Jerusalem is not known, but from the fact
that he died at the Sinai monastery in 1222 it is possible that he
made that his residence and appointed a Syrian as his vicar in
Jerusalem.[3] His successors in the see are shadowy figures, about
some of whom very little is known, but the evidence suggests that
they did live in Palestine, or at least at Sinai, for their presence is
never recorded at any meetings of the Byzantine synod, whereas
their twelfth-century predecessors had quite often attended such
meetings. Indeed, the signature of one of the eastern patriarchs
to a synodal decision gave it added authority, and it must therefore be presumed that in the thirteenth century the patriarchs of
Jerusalem were not available to attend such meetings.

The Orthodox patriarchs of Jerusalem had authority over
Orthodox, both Syrians and Greeks, living under Aiyubid rule
in Palestine, but for most of the century this did not bring them
into any conflict with the Franks. For there is no reason to
suppose that the Orthodox ever accepted the assigning of the
province of Tyre to the patriarchs of Jerusalem, which the Latins
had effected simply for political convenience. In the view of the
Orthodox hierarchy Tyre and its daughter-churches of Beirut,
Sidon, and Acre would come under the jurisdiction of the Orthodox patriarch of Antioch. This meant that only Jaffa, Caesarea
and such part of Lydda as was in Frankish hands came under the
theoretical jurisdiction of the Orthodox patriarch of Jerusalem in
the half-century after Hattin, and there seem to have been few
Orthodox living in those areas. James of Vitry relates that in the
early thirteenth century there was an Orthodox bishop of Acre
and an Orthodox archbishop of Tyre,[4] both of whom, had they
wished to acknowledge an Orthodox patriarch, would have

---

1. Theodore was present at a synod at Constantinople in 1195, Grumel, *Regestes*,
no 1184. By 1206 a new Orthodox patriarch had been elected at Antioch.

2. Bar Hebraeus, *Chronography*, I, p 327.

3. Mark is last recorded in 1195, Grumel, *Chronologie*, p 452.

4. *Lettres*, pp 85–92, no 2.

regarded themselves as suffragans of Antioch. What happened at Antioch was therefore of concern to all the Latin hierarchy in Frankish Syria.

But in the last decade of the twelfth century it must have seemed that nothing was going to happen at Antioch, for the Byzantine empire was no longer the great world power that it had been in the reign of the emperor Manuel and was not in a position to intervene militarily in north Syria and restore an Orthodox patriarch there by force. Indeed, the Byzantines had not attempted to intervene in their former province of Cyprus which had passed under Latin rule in the course of the third crusade. When the Orthodox archbishop of the island, Sophronius, died, the Greek bishops elected as his successor Isaiah, the exiled Orthodox archbishop of Lydda, without reference to Constantinople.[1] Although a Latin hierarchy was set up there in the reign of Aimery I, no attempt was at first made to interfere with the Orthodox, who preserved their full complement of bishops under the authority of the holy see.[2] This lenient treatment of the Orthodox church of Cyprus by the Latin kings therefore provided no cause for dissatisfaction among the Orthodox population of the near east, and the thirteenth century seemed to promise a continuance of the good relations between the Franks and their Orthodox subjects which had existed before Hattin.

The sack of Constantinople by the fourth crusade in 1204 and the consequent erection of a Latin empire in the European provinces of Byzantium, while doubtless shocking the Greek diaspora, did not in itself damage good relations between Latins and Orthodox in Syria or Cyprus. But it was while the Byzantine world was shaken by these events, and before the empire and the Byzantine church had set up their new headquarters in exile at Nicaea, that trouble broke out at Antioch. In 1206, in the middle of the war of the Antiochene succession, when a quarrel arose between the Latin patriarch, Peter of Angoulême, and the papal legate, Peter of S. Marcello, and the legate suspended the patriarch from his functions, prince Bohemond IV allowed his Orthodox subjects to elect a new patriarch. This election was carried out by the Syrians, and they chose a candidate from

---

1. Laurent, *Regestes*, no 1210. This happened in Aimery of Lusignan's reign, i.e. before 1205 (*ibid.*, p 12, n 6). He may have been exiled by the Aiyubids for his pro-Frankish sympathies.

2. Willebrand of Oldenburg, c 1211, cited Mas Latrie, *Chypre*, II, p 35, n 1; G. Hill, *History of Cyprus*, 4 vols, Cambridge 1940–52, II, p 47, n 3.

among themselves, Ibn Abu-Saibe, who took the title of Symeon II.[1] As Runciman has pointed out, since this happened when the Byzantine world was in confusion, the appointment could not be confirmed by the Byzantine emperor and patriarch,[2] and it is not known who consecrated the new patriarch of Antioch.

This was quite unlike the recognition of Athanasius III at Antioch, since that had happened under the auspices of a Byzantine emperor: Symeon II owed his elevation to a Latin prince who had quarrelled with the Latin patriarch. Moreover, when the Latin patriarch and the legate made their peace and the patriarch was able once again to exercise his functions, he placed the city under an interdict, whereupon the Orthodox clergy who recognised Symeon II ignored Peter of Angoulême's sanctions and admitted the Franks of Antioch, who were Latin Christians, to the liturgy in their churches.[3] There is no clear evidence whether there were already Orthodox suffragan bishops in the Latin patriarchate of Antioch before 1206 as there were in that of Jerusalem, but from the reign of Symeon onwards there were certainly Orthodox bishops there. It must therefore be assumed that either Orthodox bishops who were already there acknowledged the Orthodox patriarch once he had been enthroned, or that Symeon created new bishops to rule the Orthodox population under him.

Symeon would seem to have maintained his position in Antioch throughout the rest of Peter of Angoulême's stormy reign. The Latin patriarch never regained full ecclesiastical control of the city and spent the last few months of his life in prison, where he died of thirst in 1208.[4] Through his death he succeeded in achieving what he had been unable to encompass while alive, the submission of Bohemond IV to the church, for no Frankish prince could afford to antagonise the Roman see. St Albert of Jerusalem, the pope's legate, to whom Innocent III entrusted the task of restoring peace to the church of Antioch, excommunicated Symeon II and his followers, and the Orthodox patriarch was forced to seek refuge in the neighbouring Cilician kingdom. Leo II of Cilicia was the political rival of Bohemond IV for the throne of Antioch and it was natural that he should harbour political refugees from that principality. Symeon's flight occurred before 1213, and his influence over the Armenian king was such that when the Latin

1. Innocent III, 'Reg.', X, 186, *PL*, 215, 1278–82. The patriarch's Arab name is given in Vatican MS Arab, 79, f. 317, cited Karalevskij, 'Antioche', *DGHE*, III, col 617.
2. *Eastern Schism*, p 113, n 42.
3. Innocent III, 'Reg.', XI, 9, *PL*, 215, 1345.
4. See chapter 9 above.

archbishop of Tarsus died, Leo was persuaded to expel the Latin canons from the cathedral and to replace them by Greeks, though not, it would seem, by an Orthodox archbishop.   Possibly Symeon II ruled Antioch in exile from the Latin cathedral of Tarsus.[1]

In 1215 Leo II gained control of Antioch for his great-nephew, prince Raymond-Roupen.[2]   This involved making his peace with the Latin church, and the young prince did homage to the new Latin patriarch, Peter of Ivrea.   It would seem that Symeon II was also required at this time to make his submission to the Latin patriarch, for in 1217/18 he went to the Byzantine court in exile at Nicaea and there did penance, together with some of his bishops, for having entered into communion with the Roman church, after which he was restored to the communion of the Orthodox.[3]

Although there is no evidence that Symeon II ever returned to Antioch, the schism which had started there under his leadership persisted after he had left.   This was made possible by the growth in hostility between Orthodox and Latins.   In part this resulted from Frankish revulsion at the behaviour of their former Syrian Orthodox subjects in 1187, for they had been willing to make their peace with Saladin although the Franks had always treated them well and had regarded them as members of their own church. James of Vitry voiced the new Frankish attitudes when he claimed that the Syrians were useless at fighting and accused them of acting in collusion with the Saracens and of being willing to sell the secrets of the Christian powers to them.[4]   But there was also another factor which caused hostile relations between Latins and Orthodox in the thirteenth century, a growth on both sides of theological intolerance.   A high proportion of the Latin bishops of Syria in the thirteenth century had been trained in western Europe, and reflected in their thinking the greater desire for strict theological conformity with Roman standards of orthodoxy which inspired the papacy in its dealings with eastern-rite Christians from the pontificate of Innocent III.   Conversely, the Byzantine church, which had traditionally been regarded by the Orthodox of the three eastern patriarchates as the touchstone of Orthodoxy, was more bitterly hostile to the Latin church after the fourth crusade (especially because the Franks in Greece made inept attempts to latinise the Orthodox church there) than it had ever previously

1. Innocent III, 'Reg.', XVI, 2, PL, 216, 784—6.
2. See above, p 222, nn 1, 2.
3. Laurent, Regestes, no 1220.
4. James of Vitry, HO, c 75, pp 137—8.

been, and this attitude spread to the Orthodox of Syria and Cyprus living under Frankish rule.

James of Vitry, who came to Acre as Latin bishop in 1216, was immediately aware of what he regarded as signs of Orthodox deviations in faith and practice, but he was also aware of the suspicion with which the Orthodox in his diocese regarded the Latin church. He noted that they recited the Nicene creed without the addition of the *Filioque* clause, and that they denied the validity of the Latin Eucharist because it was celebrated with unleavened bread. They refused, he commented, to reverence the Blessed Sacrament when it was carried through the streets to the sick by Latin priests, and they washed down altars on which the Latin Mass had been said before they would use them for their own liturgy. They did not reserve the sacrament of confirmation to a bishop, but allowed simple priests to confirm babies as part of the rite of baptism. They had married priests, and refused to fast on Saturdays. They also had bishops of their own, one of whom was in James's own cathedral city,[1] and they refused to take any notice of excommunications or interdicts pronounced by the Latin hierarchy, saying among themselves, or so bishop James supposed, that the Latins were excommunicate already because of their heterodox theology. James adds

> They say they are obedient to the Latin bishops in whose dioceses they live, but they obey them superficially, in word but not in heart, through fear of secular lords.[2]

The picture which James of Vitry paints is one of two churches, nominally in communion, and outwardly professing obedience to the Latin hierarchy and through them to the pope, but in practice held together by fear of persecution by the secular arm. If any quarrel developed between a prince and the Latin church authorities, as had happened at Antioch in 1206, then the Orthodox would have no reason to be subservient to the Latin hierarchy any longer, since they attached no importance to the purely ecclesiastical sanctions which was all that the Latin bishops, unaided by secular support, could impose. Thirteenth-century Syria was to provide other examples to illustrate the truth of that supposition. Meanwhile the two sides seem to have acted with caution. The Latins, while demanding formal obedience from the Orthodox, and formal recognition of the papal primacy, did not attempt to force Latin usages on their Orthodox subjects, who continued to recite the creed in the Orthodox way, to celebrate Mass in leavened bread, and to delegate confirmation to simple priests,

1. *Lettres*, p 85, no 2.
2. *HO*, c 75, pp 139–44.

however little the Latins may have approved of such practices. On their side the Orthodox did not openly challenge Latin authority, and did not criticise publicly the errors of the Latin church in the matter of the azymes or in that of the dual procession of the Holy Spirit.

The fourth Lateran council of 1215 had imposed the obligation to pay tithe on all eastern-rite Christians, who had previously been exempt.[1] This was primarily intended to meet the situation in Frankish Greece and Cyprus where many landowners were Orthodox. Theoretically it should have been applied also to eastern-rite Christians in Latin Syria, but in practice this did not happen. Honorius III tried to enforce this ruling in the patriarchate of Antioch,[2] but local custom proved stronger. In 1238 Gregory IX asserted that he had received complaints that Latin Christians at Antioch were evading the payment of tithe by employing Greeks and Armenians to cultivate their lands, by deducting payment to them from the revenues, and by paying tithe only on what remained to them after such deductions had been made, since, by the custom of the principality, eastern-rite Christians did not pay tithe.[3] The Latin hierarchy on the whole seems to have acquiesced in the decision by the Frankish rulers that eastern-rite Christians should not pay tithe, despite the new ruling in canon law, provided that Frankish landlords did not try to manipulate this custom to evade the payment of tithe themselves.

But any goodwill which might have been generated either by this fiscal leniency, or by the general tolerance which Latin bishops showed towards variations in faith and usage on the part of the Orthodox, was dissipated by events in Cyprus. In 1222 cardinal Pelagius, papal legate in the Levant, in conjunction with the barons and the Latin bishops of Cyprus, drew up a new constitution for the church there. Part of this was concerned with relations between Latins and Orthodox: the Orthodox hierarchy was reduced from fourteen bishops to one archbishop and three bishops, each of whom was to be Orthodox suffragan in a Latin see, to owe obedience to a Latin bishop, and to be subject through him to the pope. Orthodox monasteries were likewise made subject to the authority of the Latin church.[4] This marked the effective end of Orthodox autonomy in the island, and the cardinal explained that he was merely following the custom which

1. Mas Latrie, *Chypre*, III, pp 643—4.
2. Pressutti, no 5567; *CICO*, III, p 186, no 140.
3. *Ibid.*, pp 324—5, no 247; Auvray, no 4474.
4. 'abbates et monachi, in sacerdotali vel diaconali ordine constituti, debent esse in omnibus spiritualibus obedientes archiepiscopo et episcopis latinis.' Clause 7.

had already been adopted in the kingdom of Jerusalem.[1]   The
cases of Jerusalem and Cyprus were not in the least analogous.
The Orthodox in the kingdom of Jerusalem had been a minority
religious group before the Franks came, living under Muslim rule,
and the bulk of the faithful had been Arabic-speaking Syrian
Christians, ruled over by Greek bishops appointed by the government of Byzantium; whereas the church of Cyprus had been autocephalous since the council of Ephesus in 431,[2] the entire population of the island was Orthodox in faith and Greek in speech and
had strong links with the Byzantine empire, of which Cyprus had
been a province until 1185.[3]   Thus whereas the Orthodox of
Jerusalem might regard subordination to a Latin hierarchy as
preferable to spiritual government by alien Greek bishops under
the temporal dominion of the infidel, the church of Cyprus could
only regard the Latin establishment as a grievous loss of autonomy,
while they could learn from Byzantium of the violation of conscience which was likely to follow upon such a process through
the imposition of Latin beliefs and usages on the Orthodox clergy
and people.

A delegation from Cyprus therefore came before the holy synod
of Constantinople at Nicaea in 1223 complaining that the Greek
archbishop had been driven from the island because he refused to
subscribe to the new constitution, and that the remaining bishops
had been forced to acknowledge Latin supremacy and to enter
into communion with the western church, and asking advice
about how to behave in such circumstances.   The synod's reply
was uncompromising: the Orthodox of Cyprus must withdraw
themselves from the ministrations of any clergy who had submitted to Rome.[4]   This injunction was renewed in 1229,[5] and
two years later thirteen Orthodox monks were executed in Cyprus
by the secular authorities for refusing to admit the authority of
the Latin church, and thus provided the Orthodox there with
martyrs for the faith.   It should be added that they had been
brought to trial by the archbishop of Nicosia in the first instance
because they impugned the validity of the Latin Mass, celebrated
in unleavened bread, rather than because they sought peacefully
to perpetuate their own traditions.[6]   Nevertheless, Cyprus was
effectively a part of Frankish Syria and knowledge of what

1. Mas Latrie, *Chypre*, III, pp 619–22.
2. Hefèle, Leclercq, II, pp 335–6.
3. At the end of Andronicus I's reign Cyprus was separated from the empire by
Isaac Ducas Comnenus, Brand, *Byzantium confronts the West*, pp 55, 330, n 63.
4. Laurent, *Regestes*, no 1234.
5. *Ibid.*, no 1250.
6. Hackett, *Orthodox Church of Cyprus*, pp 93–5; C. Sathas, *Bibliotheca Graeca
Medii Aevi*, 7 vols, Venice, Paris 1872–94, II, pp 20–39.

happened there could not be hidden from the Orthodox population in the other Frankish states. It may fairly be said that the conflict between Latins and Orthodox in Cyprus had a far greater effect in producing worse relations between the two confessions on the mainland than did Frankish activities in Greece after the fourth crusade.

There was, at this stage, no formal schism between Latins and Orthodox in the area under the control of the Latin patriarch of Jerusalem, but this was not so at Antioch. Antioch was nearer to Byzantine influence at Nicaea, and to the exiled patriarch Symeon, and in 1225 Honorius III found it necessary to instruct the Latin patriarch that Greek clergy in his diocese who refused to acknowledge his authority, but obeyed the Greek patriarch, were to be deprived of their benefices.[1]

In 1229 Frederick II recovered Jerusalem, Bethlehem and Nazareth for the Franks by treaty with the sultan of Egypt. These cities all formed part of the Orthodox patriarchate of Jerusalem, and, of course, came under the jurisdiction of the Latin patriarch once more. There is no evidence of any conflict between the two jurisdictions. One source accuses Frederick of protecting a Syrian bishop who had been schismatically ordained,[2] and, if this is true, it may refer to the vicar of the Greek Orthodox patriarch, head of the Syrian community in Jerusalem. As Runciman remarks, the whereabouts of the Orthodox patriarchs during the fifteen years of renewed Latin occupation of Jerusalem is a matter of conjecture,[3] but they need not have retreated very far from the city, since the Judaean wilderness, which remained under Aiyubid control, contained many Orthodox monasteries, such as St Sabas,[4] from which it would have been possible to conduct the affairs of the Orthodox church in the patriarchate.[5]

In this period of worsening relationships between Latins and Orthodox all over the Levant, cordial links were maintained between the papacy and the community of Mount Sinai, which had once formed part of the Latin patriarchate of Jerusalem. Simon, who became archbishop of Sinai in 1203, visited Crete while it was still part of the Byzantine empire and founded a priory there, receiving many gifts from the Greek landowners of the island.[6] The Venetians captured the island in 1207, and a

1. Pressutti, no 5570; *CICO*, III, pp 186–7, no 141.
2. Huillard-Bréholles, III, p 140, n 1.
3. Runciman, *Eastern Schism*, p 115.
4. See chapter 7 above.
5. For what is known about the Orthodox patriarchs of Jerusalem in the thirteenth century, G. Every, 'Syrian Christians in Jerusalem, 1183–1283',*ECQ*, 7, 1947, pp 46–54.
6. L. Cheikho, 'Les archevêques du Sinai', *Mélanges de la Faculté Orientale de l'Université Saint-Joseph, Beyrouth*, 2, 1907, pp 408–21.

Latin hierarchy was set up there in 1213.[1] The Latin archbishop confiscated some of the property of Sinai and imposed tithe on the rest of it, and archbishop Simon complained about this to the pope. Honorius III was most prompt in dealing sympathetically with this complaint: he took the Sinai community under his protection,[2] ordered the archbishop to restore the lands which he had seized, and asked the Venetian duke of Crete to ensure that this was done.[3] In 1223 he freed the property which Sinai had owned in Crete before 1215 from the payment of tithe, and granted the Sinai community in the island a special exemption from tithe on all fishponds, orchards and gardens which belonged to their house.[4] It was, of course, easier for the pope to issue instructions of this kind than to ensure that they were being observed, and in 1225–6 he had to repeat his orders because they had not been carried out.[5] Nevertheless, the pope's kindly dealings with the monks of Sinai, which were altruistic, since the community could not give any reciprocal help to the pope, illustrate the ambivalent attitude of the holy see towards the Orthodox at this time. The pope did not attempt to make his help conditional on the adoption by Sinai of Latin usages, or even on their explicit recognition of the Roman primacy: they were treated as fellow-Catholics for whom the pope had a proper paternal care. But an eirenical approach of this kind ran into difficulties in areas where there was a Latin hierarchy in existence, particularly one which had come into being as a result of Latin military conquest, since the Latin bishops refused to accept that their Orthodox colleagues could occupy a position of parity.

In Gregory IX's reign it was evident that relations between Latins and Orthodox were growing worse, and that they could only be put right if a better understanding were achieved between the holy see and the Byzantine patriarchate. For the Byzantine patriarchs of Nicaea were regarded as canonical heads of the church by those Orthodox of Frankish Greece who would not accept the Latin church; the Orthodox of Cyprus were stiffened in their resistance to Rome by the encouragement which they received from Nicaea; and the Orthodox patriarch of Antioch, who was the symbol of schism in the Latin churches of Syria, lived at the court of Nicaea. Accordingly, in 1231 the pope sent

---

1. Fedalto, 'La Chiesa Latina a Creta, 1204–1430', *Chiesa Latina*, I, pp 312–31; cf. II, pp 104–8.

2. Pressutti, no 709; *CICO*, III, pp 35–7, no 17.

3. G. Hofmann, 'Lettere pontificie edite ed inedite intorno ai monasteri del Monte Sinai', *OCP*, 17, 1951, pp 298–9.

4. Pressutti, no 4587.

5. Hofman, *op. cit.*, *OCP*, 17, 1951, pp 300–1.

five Franciscan friars to the Orthodox patriarch, Germanus II of Constantinople, to initiate discussions about church unity.[1] Since the pope officially recognised the Latin patriarch of Constantinople as head of the Byzantine church, this mission was in its way as revolutionary as United States' diplomatic recognition of the government of Peking was later to prove. The emissaries were well received, and their mission ended in the meeting of the council of Nymphaeum in 1234 at which they represented the pope. Discussions of the differences dividing the two churches, notably the matter of the azymes, reached no satisfactory conclusion. Matthew Paris gives a highly coloured account of how the patriarch of Antioch excommunicated the pope and the Roman curia for heresy. Even if this story is dismissed, or considered exaggerated, it remains true that he was one of the leading opponents of any degree of accommodation with the Roman church.[2]

That this patriarch was still Symeon II is clear from the request which Germanus II of Constantinople made to him shortly after the council for advice about granting patriarchal status to the Bulgarian archbishop of Trnovo. It also seems probable that it was Symeon who acted as intermediary between king Hetoum of Cilicia and the emperor John III Vatatzes and the patriarch Germanus about union between the Armenian and Orthodox churches in 1239. Certainly this was the work of a patriarch of Antioch and, although he is not named in the sources, it seems more likely that this was Symeon than that it was his Francophile successor.[3]

Throughout Symeon's long exile from Antioch after he made his submission to the Byzantine church in 1217—18 there continued to be some Orthodox clergy in the patriarchate who regarded him as their canonical superior. Since he had abjured the communion of the Latin church this was not a situation which the holy see could easily ignore. Honorius III's instruction of 1225, that any Orthodox priest in the Latin patriarchate of Antioch who failed to take an oath that he would not recognise Symeon should be deprived of his benefice, has already been considered.[4] This legislation led to no permanent solution

1. Laurent, *Regestes*, 1256—7; Auvray, nos 803—4; variant texts of letters from Germanus II, Matthew Paris, vol III, pp 448—60. Laurent, *loc. cit.*, discusses the textual problems.
2. Matthew Paris, vol III, pp 518—19; G. Golubovich, 'Disputatio Latinorum et Graecorum', *Archivum Franciscanum Historicum*, 12, 1919, pp 418—70; Laurent, *Regestes*, no 1267.
3. *Ibid.*, nos 1278, 1282, 1290.
4. See n 1, p 319 above.

of the problem. In 1238 Gregory IX gave more precise orders to the Latin patriarch: he was to instruct all his bishops to withdraw their licenses from Orthodox priests who had not taken an oath of obedience to the Roman church in the presence of their congregations and abjured all heresy, particularly that of stigmatizing the Latins as heretics because they celebrated the Mass with unleavened bread.[1]

In 1244 the Latins finally lost control of Jerusalem, which then returned to the sole jurisdiction of the Orthodox patriarch. In the same year the Latin patriarch of Antioch went to western Europe where a few months later he died. It was during his absence, or shortly after his death, that a new Orthodox patriarch, David, came to live in Antioch, which he can only have done with the consent of prince Bohemond V.[2] The new pope, Innocent IV, who had been elected in 1243, was anxious to restore religious unity in the near east, and initially delegated this work to the Dominicans of the province of *Terra Sancta*.[3] In 1246 he appointed his penitentiary, the Franciscan, Lorenzo of Orte, as his legate in Armenia, Turkey, Egypt, Cyprus, Greece, and to all the Greeks living in the patriarchates of Jerusalem and Antioch, as well as to Jacobites, Maronites and Nestorians. The pope said that he was sending him 'as an angel of peace'. His relations with the separated eastern Christians will be considered in the next chapter, but his special instructions in regard to the Orthodox of Jerusalem and Antioch are of interest here: 'that the Greeks of those regions, by whatever name they are known, be protected by papal authority, and that you do not allow them to be treated with violence, and that you do full justice to them in cases of injury caused to them by Latins'. The pope added that no Latin might claim rights of exemption from the legate's jurisdiction.[4] Innocent then wrote 'to our reverend brother the Greek patriarch of Antioch and his suffragans' commending Lorenzo to him.[5] This was the first time since the abdication of John IV in 1100 that the papacy had admitted that there was such a person as the Greek patriarch of Antioch.

Lorenzo met with success in Antioch where there was no Latin patriarch to oppose him in carrying out his work, but he met with difficulties in the kingdom of Acre, where Robert of Nantes was patriarch of Jerusalem. For Lorenzo inhibited the patriarch Robert from exercising jurisdiction over his Orthodox subjects

1. *CICO*, III, pp 310–11, no 230.
2. Grumel, *Chronologie*, p 448; Karalevskij, 'Antioche', *DHGE*, III, 618.
3. Berger, no 573; *CICO*, IV (I), pp 11–12, no 8.
4. *Ibid.*, p 73, no 31; Berger, no 3047.
5. *Ibid.*, no 3046; *CICO*, IV (I), pp 74–5, no 32.

and they withdrew their obedience from him. The reasons for the legate's actions are not known, since we have only a papal letter of protest on this subject, but it seems possible that the Orthodox patriarch of Antioch had claimed jurisdiction over Orthodox in the province of Tyre, and that Lorenzo was seeking to accede to this request. However, the patriarch of Jerusalem complained to the pope about the legate's behaviour, and Innocent IV overruled his decision in June 1247, stating that it had not been part of his purpose to diminish the authority of the Latin patriarchs in any way.[1] He further restricted the legate's originally very full powers by stating in August 1247 that his authority did not extend to judging Latin patriarchs, archbishops or bishops who were in conflict with Greeks, since such cases were reserved to the holy see, although he confirmed lesser judgments made by Lorenzo.[2] The legate had clearly offended the Latin hierarchy of Syria, who had complained about him to the pope.

It is not on record that the legate had any dealings with the Orthodox patriarch of Jerusalem, but his mission was an unqualified success in so far as it concerned the patriarch David of Antioch, who expressed a readiness to be reconciled with the pope. Innocent IV, however, in face of the manifest opposition of the Latin hierarchy, could not go ahead with what seems to have been his original plan for setting up an Orthodox uniate church at Antioch. He therefore ruled that if Orthodox clergy wished to enter into communion with the Roman church, those who had previously been subject to Latin bishops should remain subject to them, whereas those who had never taken any oath of obedience to the Latin hierarchy should be directly responsible to the pope alone, *nullo medio*. He urged the patriarch of Antioch, who enjoyed that freedom, together with such of his bishops as were in a similar position, to come to Rome to meet him, or at least to send proctors there, and added that he was willing to pay their expenses out of the papal treasury if that presented any difficulty.[3] Lorenzo's mission was terminated at this point, to judge from the silence of the papal registers after August 1247. Clearly the pope judged it a success, for in 1255 Lorenzo was made archbishop of Antivari, a see formerly held by John of Piano Carpini, the envoy whom Innocent had sent on the perilous mission to the Mongol great khan Goyuk in 1246.[4]

1. *Ibid.*, pp 78–9, no 35; Berger, no 2745.
2. *Ibid.*, nos 4052–3; *CICO*, IV (I), pp 81, 84, nos 37, 40.
3. *Ibid.*, pp 82–3, no 39; Berger, no 4051.
4. Eubel, vol I, p 92.

It is not known whether the patriarch David availed himself of the pope's terms and made his submission to the holy see and henceforth was independent of the Latin patriarch, though it might be supposed that this did happen since there are no more complaints about a Greek schism at Antioch in the rest of his reign. The pope's policy held indications of both hope and despair for the future of Latin—Orthodox relations in Syria: hope in that the Orthodox appeared to have no rooted objection to acknowledging the papal primacy provided that they were allowed to preserve their autonomy, and despair because the Latin clergy seemed unwilling to allow the Orthodox parity of jurisdiction with themselves.

In Cyprus Lorenzo went so far as to recall the Greek archbishop from exile before his mission was brought to an end. The pope followed this up by ordering his legate on St Louis's crusade, Odo, cardinal-bishop of Tusculum, to work out a solution there, and Odo made the archbishop and his Greek suffragans take an oath of obedience to the pope. The Orthodox bishops of Cyprus then petitioned the pope to restore their autonomy, and to free them from the jurisdiction of the Latin prelates in the island. Innocent IV did not refuse this request, but referred it to the cardinal for a final decision because he had knowledge of local conditions.[1]   Presumably the archbishop of Nicosia reacted in much the same way as the patriarch of Jerusalem had done to the prospect of losing control over his Orthodox subjects, for nothing came of these proposals. In 1260 Innocent's successor, Alexander IV, issued the *Constitutio Cypria* which enacted that there should be a Greek archbishop and three Greek bishops in the island, one in each Latin diocese, that they should be subordinate to the Latin hierarchy, but that the Orthodox clergy should have the right of choosing their bishops.[2]   This did not bring peace to the island, for in 1263 Urban IV complained to the *bailli* of Cyprus that Greek clergy who had promised obedience to the holy see were being boycotted by their congregations and were suffering harassment from them,[3] and in 1267 the patriarch of Jerusalem in his capacity as legate observed that some Greek clergy were not obedient to Latin bishops and that the Syrian Orthodox of Cyprus were refusing to pay tithe.[4]   Throughout the thirteenth century, therefore, the church of Cyprus presented to the Orthodox of mainland Syria an unedifying spectacle of division, which cannot have

---

1. Berger, no 4769.
2. Bourel de la Roncière, no 3186; Mansi, XXIII, 1037–46.
3. Mas Latrie, *Chypre*, III, pp 655–7.
4. *Ibid.*, III, pp 658–9.

helped attempts to achieve Latin–Orthodox symbiosis there.

An open breach occurred at Antioch in the reign of the patriarch David's successor, Euthymius. At some time before 1260 he quarrelled with the Latin patriarch, Opizo dei Fieschi, who excommunicated him, and he was driven from the city by prince Bohemond VI.[1] This marked the effective end to Innocent IV's policy of reconciliation. Euthymius was restored to power in an unexpected way. When Hulagu khan, at the head of the Mongol armies, received the submission of Bohemond in 1260, the only concession he demanded was the restoration of the Greek patriarch in Antioch. This did not involve the exclusion of the Latin patriarch, but it did effectively end his claim to be canonical head of the Orthodox as well as of the Latin community there. The intrusion of an Orthodox prelate in a Latin see through the intervention of a Mongol war-lord was predictably viewed with abhorrence by the Latin hierarchy in the kingdom of Acre, led by the papal legate, the bishop of Bethlehem, and they reported it to Charles of Anjou as a cardinal example of Mongol atrocities.[2] The motivation of Hulagu's demand is not known. He had no antipathy to the Latin church, and his lieutenant gave Bohemond VI and his Frankish troops a mosque at Damascus for use as a Latin church when they captured the city a few weeks later.[3] It can only be supposed that the Byzantine court, which was on friendly terms with the Mongols, had used diplomacy to secure this very conservative objective of the restoration of a Greek patriarch at Antioch.[4]

Euthymius did not stay in the city for long. Perhaps he was driven out when Bohemond VI wished to make his peace with the church after having been excommunicated for submitting to the Mongols.[5] It would appear that Euthymius took refuge in Cilicia around 1263,[6] but that shortly after this he quarrelled with the king, who planned to have him killed, but escaped because some

---

1. Grumel, *Chronologie*, p 448, dates Euthymius's accession to before 1258.
2. Delaborde, 'Lettre ... à Charles d'Anjou', *ROL*, 2, 1894, pp 211–15.
3. Templar of Tyre, c 303, *Gestes*, pp 161–2.
4. See chapter 9 above.
5. Guiraud, no 292.
6. George Pachymeres, *De Michaele et Andronico Palaeologis Libri Tredecim*, 'De Michaele', IV, 9, ed I. Becker, 2 vols, *CSHB*, Bonn 1835, I, p 271, states that the patriarch Arsenius of Constantinople censured Euthymius for communicating with the Armenians. This occurred before Arsenius's deposition in 1264. It could have happened during Euthymius's first or second exiles from Antioch, but the second was the more likely occasion of it, since he is known then to have sought refuge in Cilicia, but it is not known where he spent his first exile.

sailors took pity on him, a fact which he ascribed to the intercession of St. Nicholas of Myra.[1]   He then sought refuge in Constantinople which had been regained by the Byzantines in 1261.
He was certainly there by 1265, for in that year he formed part of
the escort of Maria Palaeologa when she went to Persia to marry
the ilkhan Abagha.[2]   In 1268 Antioch fell to the Mamluks, but
this did not enable Euthymius to return there since the city was
ruined in the sack, and he would seem to have remained in
Constantinople, where he died about 1274.[3]

In that year a general council of the church was held at Lyons
under the auspices of pope Gregory X, which was attended by
representatives of the Byzantine emperor, Michael VIII, and of
the patriarch of Constantinople, who were empowered to negotiate the union of the churches. This was formally achieved at a
session on 6 July 1274.[4]   The emperor had made a request concerning the Orthodox churches under Frankish rule, which is
remarkable for its moderate tone, but vague in its wording:

> Concerning the churches of Antioch, Cyprus and Jerusalem, let each
> bishop in his own church peacefully rule over his sheep, and let no
> Latin behave adversely towards a Greek nor a Greek towards a Latin,
> and let them divide the ecclesiastical revenues without dissension. And
> if there is a Latin bishop in any church and he dies, let another Latin
> be appointed; if there is a Greek and he dies, let him be replaced by a
> Greek; and let the same rules apply to the heads of religious houses.[5]

This could safely be acceded to by all those present at the council,
since it left unresolved the question of authority. Latins would
always be willing for an Orthodox bishop to have an Orthodox
successor, but they did not consider that this implied parity of
jurisdiction and, if it did not, then the provision about the allot-
ment of revenues would of necessity remain a dead letter, since
equal division would only be compatible with equality of
responsibility.

Despite very strong opposition among his subjects, Michael VIII
was firmly committed to the union of Lyons and it was therefore
important that he should nominate a patriarch to the vacant see of

---

1. *Ibid.*, VI, 1, vol I, p 429. Bar Hebraeus places this incident in 1272, *Chronography*, I, pp 449–50, but this would appear to be a mistake, since Euthymius fled from
Cilicia to Constantinople, and would not have returned to Cilicia again, and he is known
to have been at Constantinople by 1265.

2. *Ibid.*, I, p 445.

3. Pachymeres, 'De Michaele', VI, 5, vol I, p 437.

4. B. Roberg, *Die Union zwischen der griechischen und der lateinischen Kirche auf
dem II Konzil von Lyon (1274)*, Bonn 1964.

5. *CICO*, V (I), p 136, no 50.

Antioch who supported his policy.[1]   He sounded out Theodosius
of Villehardouin[2] and, finding that his views were satisfactory,
caused him to be elected in 1278.[3]   As his name implies the new
patriarch of Antioch belonged to the family of the Frankish
princes of Achaea who had conquered the Morea in the wake of
the fourth crusade.   But he was Orthodox in religion, and had
been a monk in one of the monasteries of the Black Mountain of
Antioch before the Mamluk conquest of 1268.[4]   His Frankish
descent made it more likely that he would favour closer links
with the western church, and soon after his elevation he wrote a
tract in support of the union in conjunction with his colleague,
the Orthodox patriarch of Alexandria.[5]   Alone of the four
eastern patriarchs, those of Alexandria had been on cordial terms
with Rome throughout the crusading period, for they alone had
never suffered any conflict of jurisdiction as a result of Frankish
occupation.[6]

Theodosius's appointment achieved the desired result in that
not merely did he give his assent to the union, but he was also
able to persuade Orthodox living under Frankish rule in Syria to
be reconciled with the Latin church.   The information about
this comes from an unpromising context, the letter of complaint
which pope Nicholas III wrote to prince Bohemond VII of
Tripoli—Antioch in 1279 in which he reprimanded him for the
way in which he had treated the church in his dominions. Among
other enormities which the prince had committed the pope noted
that:

> You do not allow certain Greeks, whom ancient error has led away
> from the obedience of the Roman church, to return to the unity and
> service of the holy see, as their leaders promised the Roman church
> they would do at the council of Lyons which has just been held; but
> you deprive them, and other clergy of different rites who are obedient
> to the Roman church, of their ecclesiastical freedom, irrespective of
> their clerical status and rank in the church, and cause them to be
> arrested and imprisoned.[7]

This refers to the prince's high-handed treatment of all clergy who
had obeyed the interdict which the Latin bishop had placed on

1. D.M. Nicol, 'The Byzantine reaction to the Second Council of Lyons, 1274',
SCH, 7, 1971, pp 113—46.
2. Pachymeres, 'De Michaele', VI, 5, vol I, p 437.
3. Laurent, *Regestes*, no 1438.
4. Pachymeres, 'De Michaele', V, 24, vol I, p 402.
5. Laurent, *Regestes*, no 1436.
6. Runciman, *Eastern Schism*, pp 115—16.
7. Gay-Vitte, no 520.

Tripoli, but the pope obviously feared that it would jeopardise the reconciliation of the Orthodox under their new pro-Latin patriarch. It is an indication that Theodosius's desire for unity had had some effect on his flock, although the pope does not suggest that all the Orthodox had been reconciled.

Theodosius was not able to exert his powers for reconciliation for very long. In 1282 the emperor Michael died and his son, Andronicus II, repudiated the union and deposed the patriarch of Constantinople who supported it.[1] Theodosius of Villehardouin resigned his see soon after this and went to live among the Franks on the Syrian coast.[2] His successor, Arsenius, was opposed to Rome, but had an equally short reign, for he offended the oecumenical patriarch by his delay in sending him a systatic letter,[3] and in 1286 was deposed on what was thought by some to be a trumped-up charge of having been in communion with the Armenians.[4]

When Henry II of Lusignan, king of Cyprus, was crowned king of Jerusalem in 1286 the Orthodox patriarchate of Antioch was once again vacant. It was perhaps this which prompted the Byzantine patriarch, Gregory II, to write to congratulate him on his accession and to ask him to treat his Orthodox subjects well.[5] Certainly such an action on the part of the Byzantine church was unprecedented in the two centuries of Frankish domination in Syria. Henry II was the most important single ruler in the Frankish east, but it was in Tripoli that the Orthodox bishops met to elect a new patriarch of Antioch in July 1287. They chose Cyril III, archbishop of Tyre, but this was a disputed election, since the Orthodox bishops of Cilicia chose Dionysius, bishop of Pompeiopolis. Effective power passed to Cyril, but he was not granted official recognition by Constantinople until 1296.[6] Even then he first had to give an assurance that he would not enter into communion with the Armenians if he went to live in Cilicia, for by that time all the former Frankish states were ruled by the Mamluks.[7]

1. Laurent, *Regestes*, no 1463; D.M. Nicol, *The Last Centuries of Byzantium, 1261–1453*, New York 1972, pp 99–113.
2. Pachymeres, 'De Andronico', I, 19, vol II, p 56.
3. Laurent, *Regestes*, no 1479.
4. *Ibid.*, no 1498; Pachymeres, 'De Andronico', II, 5, vol II, p 121.
5. Laurent, *Regestes*, no 1497.
6. V. Laurent, 'Le patriarche d'Antioche Cyrille II (1287–c 1308)', *Mélanges P. Peeters*, II, *Analecta Bollandiana*, 68, 1950, pp 310–17; Laurent, *Regestes*, no 1511; Grumel, *Chronologie*, p 448.
7. Pachymeres, 'De Andronico', II, 6, vol II, p 123; Laurent, *Regestes*, no 1568.

Burchard of Mount Sion, a German Dominican, who wrote the last of the pilgrim guides to the Holy Land to be produced in the period of Frankish rule, at some time between 1272 and 1284,[1] makes a distinction between the Syrian Orthodox living under Muslim rule and the Orthodox living in the Frankish cities on the coast. Of the former he says: 'they are Christians, but keep no faith with the Latins';[2] whereas he says of the latter:

> The Greeks are schismatics . . . save that a great part of them returned to the obedience of the church at a general council held by the lord pope Gregory X.[3]

Whether, after the abdication of Theodosius of Villehardouin, those who had returned to the Catholic fold remained there, is not known. It was, in any case, an academic problem, for within a few years Frankish rule in Syria, and with it the Latin hierarchy, had come to an end and there was no longer any conflict in jurisdiction between the Latin and the Orthodox hierarchies.

The symbiosis between Latin and Orthodox Christians which had been achieved in the twelfth century, at least in the patriarchate of Jerusalem, broke down in the years after 1187 for a variety of reasons. The Latins came to suspect the loyalty of the Orthodox, while theological intolerance grew on both sides. Latin bishops began to look askance at Orthodox faith and practice. They were reflecting papal attitudes about the need for eastern-rite Christians to conform to Roman standards of orthodoxy. On their side the Orthodox feared lest the purity of their faith should be contaminated by the heretical Latins. This attitude received every encouragement from the Byzantine church and court in exile at Nicaea, which were understandably very hostile to the Latin church. Latin behaviour towards the Orthodox population in Cyprus did little to assuage this antipathy.

On a practical level some accommodation was possible. The Latins allowed the Orthodox to have their own bishops and they did not require them to conform to Latin usages even in such controverted matters as the celebration of the Eucharist in leavened bread, nor did they even require them to recite the creed in the Latin form. Nevertheless, the Orthodox were expected to acknowledge the papal primacy and they were placed under the authority of Latin bishops. It was this last requirement which created schism between the two confessions. For although they

---

1. He knew of the fall of Crac des Chevaliers (1271), but not of the loss of al-Marqab (1285).
2. Burchard, p 103.
3. *Ibid.*, p 104.

were prepared to make great concessions to the Orthodox in the interests of preserving unity, the Latin hierarchy, as is plain from their reaction to Innocent IV's proposals about setting up uniate Orthodox churches independent of the Latin patriarchs, were not willing to treat the Orthodox on terms of parity.

The reasons for this were complex. Few Latin bishops, fighting to maintain their revenues against the encroachments of exempt religious communities and military orders and the reluctance of laymen to pay full tithe, would have welcomed Michael VIII's proposal that ecclesiastical revenues should be divided equally between Greeks and Latins, particularly at a time when, through loss of territory, their income was constantly decreasing; yet the erection of uniate churches would have involved some financial accommodation of that kind. Nevertheless, financial considerations might have been negotiable: certainly the willingness of Latin bishops to allow their Orthodox subjects not to pay tithe, despite the enactment of the fourth Lateran council that they should do so, suggests some readiness to compromise on that level.

The fundamental difficulty was a more subtle one, and less tractable in so far as it reflected attitudes which were largely unconscious. From the beginning the Franks, while treating the Orthodox as religious equals, had also considered them socially inferior: this was reflected in the law codes, in which Franks were privileged and were equated with Christians of the Latin rite. Only unusually enlightened rulers, like Baldwin I and queen Melisende, had not shared this prejudice. In a society where such attitudes prevailed it was unthinkable to consider granting the Orthodox full ecclesiastical parity. Burchard of Mount Sion gives a frank account of this attitude:

> The Greeks . . . honour and revere their bishops. I have heard one of their patriarchs say in my presence: 'We would willingly live in obedience to the church of Rome and reverence it; but I am surprised at my being ranked below the inferior clergy, such as archbishops, and bishops. Some archbishops and bishops wish to make me, a patriarch, kiss their feet and do them personal service, which I do not hold myself bound to do, albeit I would willingly do so for the pope, but for no-one else.'[1]

Members of the separated churches, Jacobites, Maronites and Armenians, had never had to compete with the Latins but had, from the beginning, been granted religious autonomy. Even in the twelfth century this had given the Orthodox some grounds for

1. *Idem.*

complaint, since a member of one of these other confessions who aspired to social and legal equality with the Franks could become a Latin Christian more easily than a member of the Orthodox community who was already in full communion with the Roman see; but when, in the thirteenth century, these various churches came into communion with Rome and preserved their autonomy under the pope, *nullo medio*, the Orthodox had a yet greater sense of grievance in that they were not accorded parity of treatment.

13. REUNION WITH SEPARATED EASTERN CHRISTIANS

James of Vitry in his *Historia Orientalis* records how the Maronites of the Lebanon had been brought into union with Rome by the patriarch Aimery of Limoges, who had persuaded them to renounce the Monothelete heresy. Despite the presence of a strong anti-uniate group among the Maronites, the bishop of Acre saw this *rapprochement* as a sign of hope for the extension of church unity among the separated eastern Christians: 'I believe', he wrote, 'that many of the heretics dwelling in the east, and many of the Saracens as well, might easily be converted to the Lord if they heard sound doctrine preached'.[1]

By the time this was written the Maronite union had been made more formal. Innocent III had ordered his legate in Syria, cardinal Peter of S. Marcello, to conduct a full inquiry into the position of the Maronites, and the cardinal had held discussions at Tripoli with the Maronite patriarch, Jeremias al-Amshiti, and two of his suffragans, in 1203. They had sworn obedience to the Roman pontiff, had renounced the Monothelete heresy, and had accepted Catholic teaching on the dual procession of the Holy Spirit. They had also agreed to reform their baptismal rite in accordance with western practice: henceforth they would use trine baptism with a single invocation of the Holy Trinity and would restrict the administration of confirmation to their bishops. They had also agreed to two minor reforms: that they would make the chrism from balsam and olive oil only, and that they would impose on their faithful the obligation of making confession once a year and receiving the Sacrament three times a year.

The Maronite patriarch attended the fourth Lateran council and when it was ended the pope issued a bull, *Quia divinae sapientiae*, setting forth the undertakings which the Maronites had made towards the Roman church and defining their position within it. The pope wished them to bring their rites into conformity with Catholic usage, but the points which he raised in this connection were all relatively minor ones: their bishops should use mitres and rings and pastoral staffs when officiating; the faithful should be summoned to worship with bells and not with semantras; and the

---

1. James of Vitry, *HO*, c 78, pp 151–3; *Lettres*, pp 96–7, no 2.

eucharistic vessels should be made from precious metals. In return the pope granted special privileges to the Maronites: their hierarchy should consist of a patriarch, two archbishops and three bishops. The patriarch should receive a *pallium* from the Latin patriarch of Antioch as a symbol of recognition by the pope of his jurisdiction over the Maronite church. Anybody who aassaulted a Maronite priest should be *ipso facto* excommunicated and the absolution of such offenders was reserved to the pope alone. Anybody who was excommunicated by the patriarch should be debarred from the sacraments and might only be absolved with the consent of the patriarch himself, unless *in articulo mortis*.[1]

The Maronite church was thus given uniate status. It retained its corporate identity and preserved its own rites and usages, with the minor changes required by the pope, and was ruled by its own hierarchy under the authority of the Maronite patriarch who was subject to the pope *nullo medio*. There was no question of Maronite bishops being subject to the Latin hierarchy of Syria. But throughout the period of Frankish rule a substantial body of Maronites remained hostile to the union. Some of the separatists may subsequently have been reconciled to Rome. In 1243, for example, pope Innocent IV confirmed the appointment which the Maronite patriarch had made of a new archbishop to the see of Aiole,[2] and papal intervention may have been necessary in this case, which is unique in the thirteenth-century papal registers, because this see had not entered into union with Rome before that time.

Relations between the uniate Maronites and Latin Christians remained very cordial. When James of Vitry was in Acre the Maronites had not yet conformed to the pope's injunctions about episcopal dress and the use of bells, but the bishop noted that in all other ways 'they observe the rites and usages of the Latins as a sign of their obedience to Rome'.[3] The papacy took a benevolent interest in the Maronites, and in 1246 Lorenzo of Orte was ordered by Innocent IV to visit them, and the pope wrote to the patriarch recommending the legate to him.[4] The uniate Maronites also had amicable relations with the Frankish counts of Tripoli: when Guy Embriaco, lord of Gibelet, was tried for treason at Nephin in 1283 the Maronite patriarch and two of his archbishops were among the clergy whom Bohemond VII requested to be present.[5]

1. *CICO*, II, pp 458—61.
2. Berger, no 58; on Maronite hostility to the union, Salibi, *op. cit.*, *Oriens Christianus*, 42, 1958, p 97.
3. James of Vitry, *HO*, c 78, p 153.
4. Berger, nos 3046—7; *CICO*, IV (I), pp 73—5, nos 31—2.
5. Mas Latrie, *Chypre*, III, pp 662—8.

Nevertheless, some Maronites remained implacably hostile to the union. In 1282 rival patriarchs were elected: Jeremias of Dimilsa, the uniate candidate, and his rival, Luke of Bharan, who was opposed to the union. Salibi considers that this schism may have weakened the county of Tripoli and hastened its fall in 1289.[1] Ironically, when the Mamluks overran the county they treated the Maronites, both uniate and anti-uniate, very savagely.[2] This had the effect of disposing the entire Maronite community in favour of the union with Rome, since they all came to look to western Christendom for protection against the harshness of Mamluk rule. For practical reasons contact between the Maronites and Rome was minimal in the century and a half following the Mamluk conquest, but the union was formally preserved. In 1439 the Maronite patriarch, John, was represented at the council of Florence by the prior of the Franciscans of Beirut, and received a *pallium* from pope Eugenius IV,[3] and, despite certain strains in the centuries which followed, the union has persisted to the present day.[4]

Relations between the Latin church and the Maronites were uncomplicated by political considerations, since the Maronites were a religious minority living under Latin rule. The same was not true of the Armenians, who had established an independent principality in Cilicia before the third crusade, and who, after the conquests of Saladin, had comparatively few adherents living under Frankish rule, although there were some Armenian communities in most of the main Frankish cities.[5] It will be remembered that pope Lucius III had sent a *pallium* to the catholicus of Armenia, Gregory IV, together with a copy of the *Rituale Romanum* in 1184, apparently under the misapprehension that the Armenian church had made its submission to the Roman see, whereas the catholicus seems to have considered his overture to Rome, which had led to this response, as no more than a renewal of the pact between SS. Gregory and Sylvester.[6] These negotiations were interrupted by Saladin's conquests, as a result of which Cilicia took on a new importance as the only large, independent,

1. Salibi, *op. cit.*, *Oriens Christianus*, 42, 1958, pp 97–8.

2. Salibi, 'The Maronites of Lebanon under Frankish and Mamluk rule (1099–1516)', *Arabica*, IV, 1957, pp 296–300; C. Frazee, 'The Maronite Middle Ages', *ECR*, 10, 1978, p 99.

3. Salibi, *op. cit.*, *Oriens Christianus*, 42, 1958, pp 97–8; J. Gill, *The Council of Florence*, Cambridge 1961, pp 335–6.

4. P. Dib, 'Maronites', *DTC*, X (I), 40–120.

5. E.g. at Acre, James of Vitry, *Lettres*, p 85, no 2; at Tripoli, Burchard of Mount Sion, p 16.

6. See above, chapter 8.

Christian state in north Syria, and pope Clement III wrote to Leo II, prince of Cilicia, and to the catholicus, asking them to facilitate the passage of Frederick Barbarossa's army.[1]

Barbarossa's crusade, as is well known, came to grief, and the third crusade did little to restore Christian power in north Syria, with the result that Cilicia remained very vulnerable to Muslim attacks and was anxious to secure the benefits of western support. It was this consideration which led Leo II in 1195 to send envoys to the western emperor, Henry VI, and to pope Celestine III, asking for a crown.[2] It was a belief widely held in the Christian near east that only a Roman emperor could make a prince into a king: since Leo wished to be crowned there were two possible sources of authority to which he could turn, Rome and Constantinople. He chose Rome because Constantinople traditionally claimed that Cilicia was a province of the empire and the Armenians had no wish to bring about the restoration of Byzantine rule there, but also because the western emperor, Henry VI, was known to be preparing a new crusade, and Leo wished to be a beneficiary of this help as a client king of the western empire. When news of his activities reached Constantinople the emperor Alexius III sent a crown to Leo and initiated discussions about church unity, but the Armenians put an end to these diplomatic overtures by stating two conditions which they knew would be unacceptable to the Byzantines: the subordination of the Orthodox patriarch of Antioch to the Armenian catholicus and the adoption by the Byzantine church of the Armenian tradition of celebrating the Eucharist in unleavened bread.[3]

Leo's requests were well received in the west, but they were made conditional on the Armenian church's accepting union with the Roman church. No doubt in the view of the pope this was merely regularising a position which had already been reached in the reign of pope Lucius III. A delegation reached Cilicia late in 1197 led by Conrad, bishop of Hildesheim, chancellor of the western empire and leader of the vanguard of Henry VI's crusade, who brought a crown for the Cilician prince, and Conrad, archbishop of Mainz, papal legate with the crusade, who was empowered to effect the union. Conrad of Mainz, on the pope's orders, insisted that the union should be proclaimed before the coronation took place. He laid down certain conditions: that the

1. Jaffé—Wattenbach—Löwenfeld, nos 16461–2. Clement III sent another copy of the *Rituale Romanum* to the catholicus, *ibid.*, no 16463.

2. John Dardel, 'Chronique d'Arménie', c 11, *RHC Arm*, II, p 9.

3. Sempad the Constable, *RHC Arm*, I, p 633; Tekeyan, 'Controverses Christologiques', *OCA*, 124, 1939, pp 59–65.

Armenian church should affirm its acceptance of the papal primacy, and should adopt certain reforms to show that this acceptance
was more than nominal. The reforms do not appear to have been
onerous: liturgical feasts, and specially that of Christmas, should
be observed in accordance with the western calendar; the
canonical hours should be recited by the clergy at the appropriate
times and not all together, immediately before Mass, as was the
Armenian custom; and the fasts on the vigils of Christmas and
Easter should be observed more rigorously. The legate demanded
that twelve Armenian bishops should swear to implement these
conditions, and the catholicus, Gregory VI, and St Nerses of
Lampron were among those who agreed to do so. The catholicus
was then invested with the *pallium* as a sign that unity had been
restored, and on the Epiphany 1198 Leo II was crowned at Sis by
the imperial chancellor.[1]

The Armenian historian Guiragos of Kantzag states that, when
the bishops expressed misgivings about the papal conditions, Leo
II persuaded them to take the oath by saying that they need only
give an outward sign of submission, but that they were not bound
in conscience by it.[2]   Tournebize disputes the validity of this
testimony and argues that the bishops were sincere in their profession of obedience to the Roman see,[3] but the evidence all suggests
that Guiragos was speaking the truth. The Armenians had
expressed reverence for the Roman see long before there was any
question of church union,[4] but western churchmen misinterpreted
the poetical language which they used and understood these
expressions of goodwill in terms of an acceptance of the papal
primacy as it had been defined by western canon lawyers, which
was alien to Armenian thought. There was also a more profound
misunderstanding between the two sides about the nature of the
church. The Armenian view is best seen in the thought of St
Nerses of Lampron, one of the signatories of the act of union,
and a man who was very sympathetic to the Latin church. He
had introduced some reforms after the Latin mode into his
cathedral at Tarsus even before the act of union, among which
were the use of ecclesiastical vestments, the communal recitation
of the Divine Office, the use of a proper form of monastic profession, the recognition of third marriages, and the organisation of
public charity.   Some of his opponents claimed that he was
latinising the Armenian church, but he defended himself against

1. Sempad the Constable, *RHC Arm*, I, pp 634—5.
2. Guiragos of Kantzag, *ibid.*, I, pp 422—4.
3. Tournebize, *Histoire . . . de l'Arménie*, p 269.
4. See chapter 8 above.

those charges in a letter which he wrote to Leo II after his coronation, and therefore after the endorsement of the union with
Rome.[1]

> It is self-evident to anybody who takes the trouble to think about it
> that Christian peoples differ from each other on some points, but God's
> grace has given me the strength of intellect to view their vain traditions
> with detachment, and only to value an exchange of brotherly love. As
> far as I am concerned, the Armenian is like the Latin, the Latin like the
> Greek, the Greek like the Copt and the Copt like the Jacobite ... By
> the grace of Christ I break down all the barriers which separate us, and
> so my good name extends to the Latin, Greek and Jacobite churches as
> well as to Armenia, while I remain immovable in their midst without
> ever bowing to their particular traditions.[2]

In St Nerses's view, which was that of the most pro-Latin wing of
the Armenian church, the church of Christ was made up of many
corporate churches, of which his own was one, whereas in the
opinion of Catholics there was only one visible church on earth,
ruled by the Vicar of Christ, and anybody who was not in
communion with it was in schism. Any union which was based
on such fundamental misconceptions was bound to be subject to
severe strains. In addition, the majority of Armenian bishops
lived in Great Armenia under Muslim rule and had had no contact
whatever with the Latin church, yet their consent was essential if
the reforms which the pope envisaged were to be put into effect.

The king of Cilicia tried to obtain the best of both worlds by
cultivating the Roman alliance which might afford him political
assistance against his Muslim neighbours, while refraining from any
attempt to implement the papal conditions of union which might
lead to a schism in his church. The claim of his great-nephew,
Raymond-Roupen, to the principality of Antioch, which was
recognised shortly after the union by prince Bohemond III, was an
additional inducement to Leo to remain on good terms with the
holy see.[3] On his side, Innocent III was anxious to preserve the
Armenian union which added greatly to the prestige of the
Roman see, since it was commonly supposed in western Europe
that the Armenian catholicus had jurisdiction over a far greater
part of Asia than was, in fact, the case.[4]

---

1. On the dating of this letter see the translator's note, *RHC Arm*, I, p 568, n 1.
2. St Nerses of Lampron, 'Letter to Leo II', *ibid.*, I, pp 586–7.
3. The legate, it would seem, persuaded Bohemond III to recognise Raymond-
Roupen as his heir, Cahen, *Syrie*, p 591.
4. WT, XV, 19, *RHC Occ*, I, p 687. Otto of Freising, 'Chronica', VII, 32, ed
Hofmeister, pp 360–1.

In 1199 Leo wrote to Innocent III asking for help against the Muslims and for papal support in the matter of the succession to Antioch. The pope did not side with him unreservedly: he demanded that the king should restore the castle of Baghras to the Templars,[1] and said that he would appoint legates to investigate the Antiochene succession. He also requested the king and the catholicus to implement the reforms which had been agreed to, but he sent the king the *vexillum* of St Peter, an honour reserved for distinguished Catholic rulers who were fighting against the enemies of the faith.[2]   There matters rested until Gregory VI died in 1203: his successor, John VI, had been archbishop of Sis, and one of the signatories of the act of union, so that his accession led to no change of official Armenian policy.[3] Cardinal Peter of S. Marcello, papal legate in Syria, invested the new catholicus with his *pallium*, and complained that no measures had yet been taken by the Armenian authorities to implement the reforms which the pope required. He also ordered the catholicus to make the *ad limina* visit in person or by proxy every five years and to attend general councils of the church.[4]

By this time the war of the Antiochene succession had broken out, and the legate tried to mediate peace between Leo II and Bohemond IV. Leo, however, made the tactical error of attacking Antioch while the legate was trying to arrange a truce, and the cardinal placed Cilicia under an interdict. But this was done without reference to the catholicus, the interdict was not observed by the Armenian clergy, and the catholicus complained to Rome that the legate's action was contrary to the articles of union by which the Armenian church should enjoy autonomy under the holy see. Pope Innocent upheld this objection, and appointed new legates to mediate peace in north Syria, but their intervention proved no more effective than that of cardinal Peter.[5]

Despite their quarrel with the legate the Armenians had, up to this time, worked in harmony with the local Latin hierarchy, led by the Latin patriarch of Antioch, Peter of Angoulême, who had taken the Armenian side in the succession dispute. This cooperation broke down after the patriarch's murder in 1208, for his successor, Peter II, was at peace with prince Bohemond IV and gave no open support to Leo.[6] Leo first behaved ambivalently to

---

1. Riley-Smith in Boase, *Cilician Kingdom*, p 101.
2. Innocent III, 'Reg.', II, nos 217–20, 252–4, 259, *PL*, 214, 775–80, 810–15, 819–20.
3. Guiragos of Kantzag, *RHC Arm*, I, p 423.
4. Letter from Leo II to the pope: Innocent III, 'Reg.', VIII, 119, *PL*, 215, 687–92.
5. *Ibid.*, 'Reg.', VIII, nos 2, 119–20, *PL*, 215, 557–9, 687–94.
6. Hamilton, 'Armenian Church', *ECR*, 10, 1978, pp 75–6.

the Latins by giving political asylum to the Greek patriarch of Antioch, Symeon II, when he was driven out.[1] He then, in the course of his war with the Antiochenes, confiscated the estates of the knights Templar in Cilicia and as a result was excommunicated by the pope's legate in Syria, Albert, patriarch of Jerusalem.[2] As a reprisal against the Latin church, Leo then expelled the Latin canons of Tarsus and replaced them with Greeks. When the pope was informed of this he threatened to cut off all military aid to Cilicia:[3] this threat worked, since Leo II was extremely dependent on the support of the Latin military orders, and in 1212, while quarrelling with the Templars, he had made an extensive grant of land in his kingdom to the Teutonic knights.[4] He therefore made his peace with the Templars and the excommunication was lifted.[5] In 1215 Leo's great-nephew, Raymond-Roupen, gained control of Antioch and, because the support of the Latin church was essential if the principality were to be successfully held, Leo II made full peace with the Latins: the Templars at last received back their castle of Baghras, and Latin archbishops were restored to their Cilician sees.[6] The union had, seemingly, survived a very testing period intact, although it is noteworthy that the catholicus John was not present at the fourth Lateran council in 1215 to which he was invited and which, by terms of papal decree, he was obliged to attend.[7]

Moreover, despite the preservation of formal unity, no attempt had been made, almost twenty years after the coronation of Leo II, to implement the reforms required by pope Celestine III. James of Vitry, who came to Syria at this time, remarked that 'although the Armenians promised obedience to the supreme pontiff and the holy Roman church . . . they have not shown any desire to change their ancient rites and their customary observances'.[8] He specified the ways in which they differed from Catholic practice, particularly in the matter of celebrating Mass with an unmixed chalice;[9] but the thing which most commonly distressed western observers about the Armenians was, in the words of Oliver of Paderborn, that 'they are very blameworthy in that . . . they do not celebrate the Nativity of the Lord on the same day as us . . . They keep the Nativity of the

1. See chapter 12 above.
2. Innocent III, 'Reg.', XIV, nos 64–6, *PL*, 216, 430–2.
3. *Ibid.*, 'Reg.', XVI, 2, *PL*, 216, 784–6.
4. Strehlke, pp 37–9, no 46.
5. Innocent III, 'Reg.', XVI, 7, *PL*, 216, 792–3.
6. See chapter 9 above.
7. Innocent III, 'Reg.', XVI, 30, *PL*, 216, 823–7.
8. James of Vitry, *HO*, c 79, p 155.
9. 'Aquam . . . cum vino in sacramento sanguinis Christi non ponunt: in quo ritu perpetuo non modicum errore convincuntur', *ibid.*, p 154.

Lord on the Epiphany and say that the Lord was baptised on the same date . . . '.[1]

The enthronement of a half-Armenian prince at Antioch, where the Latin church was established, was potentially a factor which should have led to greater stability in the union of the two churches, but it did not last long. In 1219 Raymond-Roupen was expelled from Antioch and when Leo II died later that year he had disinherited his great-nephew in favour of his own infant daughter, Isabel. The attempts which Raymond-Roupen made to seize the Cilician crown proved unsuccessful, despite the support he received from pope Honorius III who doubtless saw in this candidate a force for preserving the union of the churches, and Raymond-Roupen was killed in 1221.[2] The marriage of the princess Isabel to Philip of Antioch, son of Bohemond IV, in 1221 held out hope that a Catholic prince would rule the Armenian kingdom and would have a vested interest in maintaining the union with Rome, but the match was unpopular and Philip was murdered in 1225, leaving power in the hands of the regent, Constantine of Lampron who, in the following year, arranged the marriage of the widowed princess Isabel to his own son, Hetoum.[3] The lords of Lampron, who thus founded a new dynasty, were far less pro-Latin than the Roupenids, whom they succeeded, had been, and, moreover, the uniate catholicus, John VI, had died in 1221 and had been replaced, under the auspices of the regent Constantine, by the catholicus Constantine I who was less well disposed towards the Roman alliance. Further, the first and proper concern of the new dynasty was to unite all Armenians behind it: the union with Rome had few supporters and many opponents. One of Constantine of Lampron's first acts was to expel the Latin hierarchy from Cilicia once again, probably as a way of demonstrating to his subjects that he was anti-Frankish. The Latin archbishops were not readmitted so long as the Franks had any territorial hold on the Syrian mainland.[4] The prospects for the continuance of the union therefore looked very bleak in 1225.

Nevertheless, it did survive, chiefly because the Cilician kings had no alternative allies other than the Franks: western crusaders, and the Franks in Syria and Cyprus, would withdraw support from Cilicia if the pope ordered them to do so, and the pope would give

---

1. Oliver of Paderborn, 'Historia Damiatina', c 65, ed Hoogeweg, p 266.
2. Pressutti, nos 677, 2870, 3495, 3833; Hamilton, *ECR*, 10, 1978, p 77; Cahen, *Syrie*, pp 631–2.
3. *Ibid.*, pp 631–5.
4. Pressutti, nos 5222, 6027; *CICO*, III, pp 176–7, no 130, pp 199–200, no 151. See chapter 9 above. Date of Constantine I's accession: K.J. Basmadjian, 'Chronologie de l'histoire d'Arménie', *Revue de l'Orient Chrétien*, ser 2, 19 (II), 1914, pp 358–74.

such orders unless the union remained in being. In 1226 a Cilician embassy was sent to Rome, since it was known that the emperor Frederick was preparing a new crusade, and the Cilician kingdom had some call on his assistance, since it was technically a fief of the western empire.[1]   The union was maintained peacefully for the next eleven years, and was only put in jeopardy by the machinations of Bohemond V of Antioch who had a blood-feud with the Hetoumids because of the death of his brother Philip, and who succeeded in enlisting the powerful support of the Latin patriarch of Antioch, Albert of Rizzato. In 1237 the pope, at the prince's suggestion, ordered an inquiry into the marriage of Hetoum I and Isabel of Cilicia with a view to its annulment.[2] He also decreed that the Armenian church should be made subject to the Latin patriarch of Antioch,[3] and further, that all Armenians living in the diocese of Antioch should give canonical obedience to the patriarch Albert instead of to the Armenian bishop.[4]

The suggestion about the marriage was political dynamite, since the Hetoumid claim to the Cilician throne was derived from Isabel, and, were she adjudged free to remarry, her new husband would have the best claim to the throne. The new ecclesiastical regulations struck at the whole basis of the settlement of 1198, which had enacted that the Armenian catholicus should be subject to the pope *nullo medio*, and that Armenian bishops should have full powers of jurisdiction under him over their flocks. The Cilicians reacted strongly to the papal pronouncements, and Gregory IX gave way. He was already at war once again with the emperor Frederick and he had no wish to lose the prestige which the acknowledgement of his primacy by a large body of eastern Christians gave him. In 1239 he not only acknowledged the legitimacy of the marriage of Hetoum and Isabel,[5] the autonomy of the Armenian church under Rome, and the direct dependence on the catholicus of all Armenian churches in Frankish territory, which were not to be subject in any way to the authority of Latin bishops,[6] but he also extended the privileges which the Armenians enjoyed. No person might have the right to preach in Cilicia without the consent of the catholicus or of one of his bishops, unless he were expressly licensed to do so by the pope himself.[7]   In addition the pope gave a more explicit guarantee

---

1. Sempad the Constable, *RHC Arm*, I, p 648.
2. Auvray, no 3597; *CICO*, III, p 298, no 222.
3. *Ibid.*, pp 319–20, no 241; Auvray, no 4466.
4. *Ibid.*, no 4467; *CICO*, III, p 320, no 242.
5. *Ibid.*, pp 332–3, no 253; Auvray, no 4732.
6. *Ibid.*, no 4739; *CICO*, III, p 334, no 256.
7. *Ibid.*, p 334, no 255; Auvray, no 4734.

than any of his predecessors had ever done of the holy see's intention to preserve the traditional rites and customs of the Armenian church:

> We confirm to you and your kingdom the reasonable customs which have obtained there since the time of pope Sylvester . . . and of St Gregory, catholicus of the same kingdom, who are said to have been contemporaries, in so far as they do not contravene the rulings of the holy fathers or the canons of the church.[1]

The pope sent the catholicus Constantine the *pallium*, and further granted an indulgence to all Armenians who died in Cilicia fighting against the infidel in the defence of the Catholic faith.[2]

The union was preserved after pope Gregory's death. Innocent IV wrote to the catholicus about the mission of his legate, Lorenzo of Orte,[3] although Lorenzo himself does not seem to have had any direct dealings with the Armenians, but to have delegated this work to another Franciscan friar named Andrew.[4] While St Louis was living at Acre in 1251 a synod of the Armenian church met at the pope's request and affirmed their belief in the double procession of the Holy Spirit, a subject which does not seem to have been at issue at any time between Armenians and Latins, but which was a matter of bitter controversy between Latins and Orthodox.[5] The pope presumably found it useful in controversy to be able to claim that one of the eastern churches agreed with Rome on this subject.

It is noteworthy that although relations between the papacy and the Armenian church remained cordial, no attempt had yet been made by the Armenian authorities to put into effect the changes which the holy see had from the beginning required. This suggests that it was political self-interest rather than religious oecumenism which led the Armenians to seek to preserve the union, and the events of the following years tend to confirm this view. A third power had arisen in the near east in the middle of the thirteenth century besides those of Christendom and Islam, that of the Mongol empire. The Mongols first made an impact on Cilicia in 1243 when they invaded the Seljuk sultanate of Iconium and forced the Turks to become tributary to them. The Cilicians were obliged to enter into some relationship with these new and powerful neighbours and in 1247 Hetoum sent his constable, Sempad, to the court of the great khan to effect the only kind of

---

1. *Ibid.*, no 4733; *CICO*, III, p 333, no 254.
2. *Ibid.*, p 335, no 258; Auvray, nos 4735, 4740.
3. Berger, no 3046; *CICO*, IV (I), pp 74–5, no 32.
4. Golubovich, *Terra Santa Francescana*, I, p 216.
5. Tournebize, *Histoire . . . de l'Arménie*, pp 290–1.

alliance that the Mongols understood, that of submission. This brought Cilicia under the protection of the great khan and proved so effective in deterring Turkish raiders that in 1253 Hetoum went to the Mongol court of Karakorum in person to make his submission to the great khan Mongke. He was the first ruler ever to make a voluntary submission to the great khan and as a result was treated with great honour, and the khan freed the Armenian church throughout all his dominions from the payment of taxes. [1] By this time, of course, the great khan's dominions included most of Great Armenia, whose clergy had never been well-disposed towards union with the Latin church.

Thus when the Mongol horde invaded north Syria in 1260 Hetoum was already committed to their cause. Even after they had been defeated at Ain Jalut he relied on their protection against Mamluk reprisals. His alliance with them had, however, incurred the displeasure of the Latin church authorities in Syria. In 1261 the pope's legate, Thomas, bishop of Bethlehem, ordered the catholicus Constantine to attend a meeting with him at Acre. This must have been concerned with the Armenian attitude towards the Mongols, for such a summons was unprecedented in the history of Armenian—Latin relations. The catholicus pleaded that extreme old age made it impossible for him to make the sea journey, a statement which was almost certainly true, since he had ruled over the Armenian church for forty years. He was represented instead by the Armenian bishop of Jerusalem and the theologian, Mekhitar of Dashir. Mekhitar was an opponent of the union, and he must have been deliberately chosen, since, if the union had still had powerful supporters in the Armenian church at this time, it would have been an easy matter for the catholicus to have chosen his deputy from among their number. In the course of his discussions with the legate, Mekhitar attacked the papal primacy:

> Whence does the church of Rome derive the power to pass judgment on the other apostolic sees while she herself is not subject to their judgments? We ourselves [the Armenians] have the authority to bring you [the Catholic church] to trial, following the example of the apostles, and you have no right to deny our competence.[2]

Such plain speaking, which was not later repudiated by the Armenian authorities, effectively brought the union to an end. But

1. C. Cahen, *Pre-Ottoman Turkey*, London 1968, pp 270–1; Der Nersessian in Setton, II, pp 652–3.

2. 'Narrative of the Conference held between the doctor Mekhitar of Dashir, envoy of the Catholicus Constantine I, and the Pope's Legate at St Jean d'Acre', *RHC Arm*, I, pp 691–8 (the quotation is on p 697).

diplomatic links were maintained between the holy see and the Cilician court. Thus in 1265 pope Clement IV appealed to the king of Cilicia to help the knights of St John[1] and two years later he urged the Franks in Syria to aid the Cilicians whose kingdom had been savagely laid waste by the Mamluks in 1266.[2]

Pope Gregory X attempted to restore unity by inviting the catholicus Jacob I, who had succeeded the long-lived Constantine in 1267, to attend the council of Lyons in 1274, but he met with a refusal.[3] Whereas it might have been argued in 1261 that the Cilicians feared to offend the khan Hulagu by maintaining union with the Latins who, in the kingdom of Acre at least, had aided his enemies the Mamluks in the campaign which led to his defeat at Ain Jalut, such a view could no longer be sustained in 1274. Hulagu's son, Abagha, who had become ilkhan of Persia in 1265, was desirous of a western alliance and was on friendly terms with the papacy and, although a shamanist, was represented at the council of Lyons which his Armenian allies refused to attend.[4] The most obvious inference to be drawn from this is that the union had never commanded widespread support among the Armenian clergy, but had been forced on them by the rulers of Cilicia who saw in it a means of cementing a western alliance, and then when that alliance proved ineffective, as the failure of so many thirteenth-century crusades had proved it to be, and when new allies appeared who could afford protection without making any religious demands, the union was abandoned because it could serve no further purpose.

Ironically, it was during the period when the union was ended that the population of Great Armenia first came into direct contact with the Latin church, for the ilkhan Abagha allowed the Franciscans to open a house at Sivas and to work among his subjects.[5] Moreover, there was still considerable Latin influence in Cilicia itself. Many Armenian noblemen had intermarried with the Franks of Antioch and by the second half of the thirteenth century Frankish blood was fairly common among the Armenian aristocracy and with it came some tolerance for the Latin faith. Moreover, after the fall of Antioch in 1268, some dispossessed members of the Frankish nobility had taken service with the king of Cilicia.[6] Italian merchant colonies had been established in the

1. Jordan, no 919; Martène, Durand, *Nov. Thes.*, II, 170–1, no 111.
2. *Ibid.*, II, 469, no 468; Jordan, no 1200.
3. Basmadjian, *op. cit.*, p 340, n 4, above; Guiraud-Cadier, nos 304–5.
4. Hefèle, Leclercq, VI, p 174.
5. Golubovich, *op. cit.*, I, p 301. J. Richard, *La Papauté et les missions d'Orient au moyen âge*, Rome 1977, pp 115–16.
6. There was a long tradition of this: Sempad the Constable, *ann.* 1198, *RHC Arm*, I, p 639.

kingdom since the beginning of the thirteenth century and had been allowed to build churches of the Latin rite in some cities there.[1] The three great military orders all had property there[2] and therefore chapels for the use of their members. Finally, the Franciscans established convents there, and by 1292 were able to form a *custodia* in the kingdom.[3]

In the absence of corporate unity the Franciscans felt free to proselytize among the Armenians and to receive individual people into communion with the Roman church. This behaviour caused great resentment and in 1288 the catholicus Constantine II was deposed from office when it was discovered that he had clandestinely been reconciled to Rome three years before by the Franciscans of Sis.[4] A surprising *volte-face* took place in Cilician government policy towards Rome in the following year, for in 1289 the Franciscan, John of Monte Corvino, came to Rome with letters from king Hetoum II desiring union with the holy see.[5] John was not a member of the Cilician *custodia* but of the Franciscan community of Tabriz, and Hetoum had presumably employed him on the orders of the ilkhan Arghun, who had succeeded to the throne of Persia in 1285, and who was anxious to form a western alliance against Egypt.[6]

The pope, Nicholas IV, was also a Franciscan and welcomed this overture. He wrote to the catholicus, Stephen VI, urging him to promote the unity of the churches, and also sent letters in the same vein not only to the king himself, but to members of the royal family and of the nobility whom he believed to be sympathetic to the Latin cause, together with an encyclical letter on the same theme to all the faithful of Armenia. John of Monte Corvino was entrusted with this mission and was given legatine powers.[7]

The loss of the remnants of Frankish territory in Syria in 1291 and the death of the Francophile ilkhan Arghun in the same year meant that John's mission had no effect. Hetoum II's desire for unity seems to have been genuine enough, for when he abdicated in 1292 he took the Franciscan habit.[8] In view of this it is at first

1. Venetian churches at Mamistra, TT, I, p 384, no 94, II, p 428, no 307; and Ayas, *ibid.*, III, p 117, no 361. Genoese church at Mamistra, Imperiale, III, p 190, no 75.
2. Riley-Smith, *Knights*, pp 495–505; 'The Templars and the Teutonic Knights in Cilician Armenia', in Boase, ed, *Cilician Armenia*, pp 92–117.
3. Golubovich, *op. cit.*, I, pp 339, 355, II, pp 516–18.
4. Continuator of Samuel of Ani, *RHC Arm*, I, pp 462–3.
5. Langlois, no 2229; *CICO*, V (II), pp 152–3, no 85.
6. Golubovich, *op. cit.*, I, pp 301–9, II, p 440. See p 357, n 8, 358, n 1 below.
7. Langlois, nos 2222, 2229–34; *CICO*, V (II), pp 152–4, nos 85–6, pp 156–8, nos 88–9.
8. Golubovich, *op. cit.*, II, p 464; Der Nersessian in Setton, II, p 656, places these events in 1292, but the chronology of Hetoum II's reign is very confused.

sight surprising that he made no move to promote unity when he resumed the crown once again in 1294. The reason for this would seem to have been that he still relied on the protection of the Mongols of Persia against the power of the Mamluks and in 1295 the new ilkhan Ghazan embraced Islam and would have been unfavourable to a reconciliation between the Armenian church and Rome.[1] However, it was apparent after the Mongol defeat of 1303 that no real help could any longer be expected from that quarter, and Cilicia was driven back once more on the expedient of an alliance with the west, represented in the Levant by the Lusignan kings of Cyprus, but this, of course, entailed reunion with the Latin church. The catholicus Gregory VII summoned the council of Sis but died before it assembled in 1307. This council therefore met during a vacancy in the headship of the Armenian church and was under royal control. It accepted union with Rome and accepted all the papacy's demands: recognition of the authority of the seven general councils of the church; acceptance of the Catholic Christological definitions; the omission of the addition to the *Trisagion*; the use of a mixed chalice at the Eucharist and minor liturgical reforms.[2] The union was blatantly politically motivated, it commanded no widespread support, except among the latinised members of the Cilician court, and it led to schism in the Armenian church.[3]

Although it is arguable that in some sense the Armenian church remained in union with Rome from 1198 into the fourteenth century, that union can scarcely be considered a triumph for western oecumenism. It was imposed on the Armenian church by the kings of Cilicia for largely political reasons; it did not have the support of the clergy living outside Cilicia who made up the greater part of the Armenian hierarchy; and even among those who did favour it, it was based largely on misunderstandings about the nature of papal authority and of the church itself. No serious attempt was made before the fourteenth century to meet papal requirements about conformity to Catholic practices, and, as soon as an alternative political strategy could be found which did not involve subordination of the Armenian church to Rome, the union was hastily abandoned, only to be resurrected with equal haste when that alternative proved to be ineffective.

1. Ghazan was a Buddhist who embraced Islam reluctantly for reasons of state: J.A. Boyle, 'Dynastic and Political History of the Il-Khans', *Cambridge History of Iran*, V, pp 376–80.

2. 'Acta Concilii Sisensis Armeni', Mansi, XXV, 133–48, where it is dated 1305. For the preferred date of 1307, see Tournebize, *Histoire . . . de l'Arménie*, pp 309–11.

3. *Ibid.*, pp 311–88, 647–727, who tries to interpret the history of the union as favourably as possible.

One consequence of this policy was that a lasting prejudice against the holy see was created among those members of the Armenian church who were opposed to the union, and this displaced the older tradition of veneration for Rome which had been widespread among Armenian churchmen before the union. This is a matter for regret, since Armenians who had come into contact with the Latin church in the twelfth century had found much in it which excited their admiration, and which, in some instances, led them to adopt Latin customs, such as those introduced at Tarsus by St Nerses of Lampron.[1] Nor was this reaction by any means one-sided. Burchard of Mount Sion, who stayed in the palace of the catholicus at Hromgla, was full of praise for the piety of his host:

> I stayed with the catholicus for fourteen days . . . In his diet, his clothes and his way of life he was so exemplary that I have never seen anyone, religious or secular, like him . . . all the clothes that he wore were not worth five shillings sterling, yet he had exceedingly strong castles and great revenues and was rich beyond any man's counting. He wore a coarse, red sheepskin pelisse, very shabby and dirty, with wide sleeves, and under it a grey tunic, very old, and almost worn out. Above this he wore a black scapular and a cheap rough black mantle . . . He and all his prelates used to fast all Lent on bread and water, and so did the king and all his nobles.[2]

True piety, as in their different ways both St Nerses of Lampron and Burchard of Mount Sion found, is discernible in any tradition, however alien its outward forms may seem. Had the respect which began to grow up between the Armenians and the Latins in the twelfth century, when they began seriously to appreciate the spiritual values of each others' traditions, been allowed to grow naturally, unfettered by the trammels of an artificial union imposed for political reasons, the cause of true religious unity would have been better served.

The relations between the Latin church and the other main eastern Christian confessions, the Jacobites and the Nestorians, took a very different form.

The Franks had always been on cordial terms with the Jacobites, a substantial number of whom continued to live under Latin rule even after the conquests of Saladin. They had bishops at Acre and Tripoli,[3] and the Jacobite archbishop of Jerusalem preferred to live in Frankish Antioch after 1187 than to remain in his

---

1. St Nerses of Lampron, 'Letter to Leo II', *RHC Arm*, I, pp 599–600.
2. Burchard of Mount Sion, p 108.
3. Acre: James of Vitry, *Lettres*, pp 83–4, no 2. Tripoli: Bar Hebraeus, *Chron. Ecc.*, 710–14.

see under Muslim rule.[1] The Franks considered that the Jacobites, unlike the Orthodox, had remained loyal to them in their time of crisis, and the Jacobites were never accused of treachery by thirteenth-century Frankish writers as the Orthodox were.

The Latin bishops of Syria in the thirteenth century, many of whom had been well trained in theology in the schools of western Europe, were appalled by the ignorance and superstition of many of the Jacobites. Although some of their twelfth-century predecessors had shown an informed interest in Jacobite beliefs[2] none of them had expressed any criticism of Jacobite practice. The more rigorist approach of their successors may well reflect the more rigid attitude of thirteenth-century popes towards the importance of conformity with Roman norms of faith and practice among eastern-rite Christians. James of Vitry complained that the Jacobites circumcised their children, as the Saracens did; that they had abandoned the practice of sacramental confession; and that some of them branded their children at baptism with the sign of the cross, apparently in the belief that they were acting in accordance with St John the Baptist's prophecy about Christ that: 'He will baptise you with the Holy Spirit and with fire'.[3] That some of these abuses were fairly widespread among the Jacobites was admitted even by some of their own clergy.[4]

Significantly, James of Vitry was less well-informed about Jacobite theological opinions. This was not for want of trying to discover the truth about them. He did find some Jacobite theologians who stated that the human nature of Christ was absorbed in the divine 'as a drop of water is in wine'.[5] That was what they were all supposed to believe, and the Orthodox assured James that all Jacobites were of that opinion. They explained that that was why the Jacobites made the sign of the cross with one finger only, symbolising belief in one nature only in Christ. Yet when he talked to the Jacobites themselves about this they denied that they held such an opinion, and said that the one finger, with its three joints, symbolised the Trinity in unity. Some of them did, however, admit that the usage symbolised a belief in one will in Christ, since they considered that the human will was subordinate to the divine in the Lord.[6]

It would appear that it was historical accident rather than doctrinal conviction which separated many of the Jacobites from

1. MS, XXI, 8, vol III, pp 411–12.
2. *Ibid.*, XVI, 10, vol III, pp 255–6.
3. James of Vitry, *HO*, c 76, pp 144–6.
4. MS, XX, 8, vol III, pp 379–80.
5. James of Vitry, *Lettres*, p 96, no 2.
6. *Ibid., HO*, c 76, pp 146–8; *Lettres*, pp 83–4, no 2.

Catholic Christendom.   They were certainly willing to accept spiritual advice from Latin churchmen.   When James of Vitry arrived in Acre in 1216 he asked permission from the Jacobite archbishop to preach in his church.   Through an interpreter he exhorted his audience to adopt the practice of sacramental confession, and he upbraided them with circumcising their children.   So far from resenting his remonstrances many of his hearers assured him that they would do as he had suggested.   They seem to have been genuinely pleased that a Latin bishop should feel this kind of pastoral concern for them.[1]

In neighbouring Cyprus the small Jacobite community presented the Latin hierarchy with a different problem.   They had no bishop, and Eustorgius, Latin archbishop of Nicosia, complained to pope Honorius III that they wandered around like people without a ruler, practising their ancient errors.   The pope ruled that they were to be under the authority of the Latin hierarchy, which in effect meant that they had to accept the Roman primacy whether they wanted to or not.[2]   But the Latin church in Cyprus faced a special problem in that it was attempting to force union on an almost entirely Orthodox population against its will, and the presence of privileged eastern-rite communities, exempt from the authority of the Latin church, would have caused justifiable resentment among the Orthodox.   There is no evidence that any similar coercion was brought to bear on the Jacobites in Frankish Syria, where they seem to have continued to enjoy their traditional autonomy under their own bishops.

After the death of the patriarch Michael the Syrian in 1199 the Jacobite patriarchs had virtually no contact with the Franks for almost forty years.   His successors, Athanasius IX (1199–1207) and John XIV (1208–20), seem to have spent their reigns entirely in Muslim territory, and the same was at first true of the patriarch Ignatius II, who was elected at Pentecost 1222.[3]   But in 1236 Ignatius carried out a visitation of his churches in Frankish territory, going to Antioch, Tripoli and Acre, and then to Jerusalem, which was once again in Frankish hands.   He stayed in the Jacobite cathedral of St Mary Magdalen there, where he found a flourishing community of seventy monks.[4]   He was well received by the men whom Bar Hebraeus refers to as *Pherpherschuriae* who, as is clear from western sources, must have been the Dominicans.[5]   The consequences of this encounter are known from the

1. *Ibid.*, p 83, no 2.
2. Pressutti, no 3750; *CICO*, III, pp 117–18, no 87.
3. Grumel, *Chronologie*, p 449; Bar Hebraeus, *Chron. Ecc.*, 646.
4. *Ibid.*, 654.
5. Presumably, 'the brethren of Syria'.   The editors wrongly identify them as Franciscans.

letter which Philip, the prior of the Dominican province of *Terra Sancta*, wrote to pope Gregory IX. The Jacobite patriarch had discussed matters of faith with the friars and on Palm Sunday had taken part in their procession through the city. He had then sworn a solemn oath of obedience to the holy see, had abjured his errors, and had given the Dominicans a signed profession of orthodox faith written in both Arabic and Syriac. He had then received the Dominican habit.[1]

In the same letter the prior reported that he had received a similar profession of faith from 'the Jacobite archbishop of Egypt'. This would seem to refer to the Jacobite archbishop of Jerusalem, whose method of appointment was a matter of grievance to the patriarch Ignatius. The Jacobite church of Syria was a sister-church of the Coptic church of Egypt. Traditionally the boundary between the two was al-Arish in Idumaea and Jerusalem formed part of the jurisdiction of the patriarch of Antioch. The Coptic see of Alexandria had been vacant for nineteen years when a new patriarch, Cyril III, was appointed in 1235.[2] There were doubtless many vacancies to fill, and this is perhaps why he took it upon himself to appoint a Copt to be archbishop of Jerusalem. Ignatius objected to this, and complained that the right of consecration to the see belonged to him alone.[3] But this was the archbishop who seems to have made his submission to the Roman see at the hands of the Dominicans. This did not, of course, commit the rest of the Coptic church to a similar course, although prior Philip informed the pope that he had sent some of the brethren to Cyril III in Alexandria, who had expressed a polite interest in the possibility of union.[4]

This is the background against which Ignatius's relations with the church of Ethiopia must be interpreted. The Ethiopians, like the Egyptians, were Copts, and since the fourth century when they had first accepted Christianity they had received the head of their church, the abuna, from the patriarch of Alexandria. This was not very satisfactory, since the abuna was always an Egyptian, who did not know either the colloquial tongue of Ethiopia, or the liturgical language of its church, Geeze.[5] At the time of Ignatius's visit there was an Ethiopian community in Jerusalem, and one of

---

1. *MGH SS*, XXIII, pp 941–2; Matthew Paris, III, pp 396–8, cites the text of the copy of this letter sent by the pope's penitentiary to the Dominican priors of England, which contains minor variants.

2. Grumel, *Chronologie*, p 445.

3. Bar Hebraeus, *Chron. Ecc.*, 658–60.

4. *MGH SS*, XXIII, pp 941–2. J. Richard, *La Papauté et les missions*, p 57.

5. C. Santi, E. Cerulli, M. Gordillo, A. Raes, U. Monneret de Villard, 'Etiopia', *EC*, V, pp 684–708.

its members, a monk called Thomas, who was a member of one of the leading noble families of that country, asked the Jacobite patriarch to consecrate him as abuna, so that his people might have a head of their church who was of their own race. The Dominicans advised against this proceeding, but Ignatius, who was an obstinate man, went ahead with the consecration, thinking in this way to be avenged on Cyril of Alexandria who had infringed his rights in the matter of the see of Jerusalem. The consecration was viewed with horror by the Franks, and the patriarch was upbraided not only by the Dominicans, but also by the Templars and the Hospitallers. Not only might this act on the part of a visiting prelate, for whom they might justly be held responsible, jeopardise the negotiations for unity which the Dominicans were engaged in with the patriarch of Alexandria, it might also antagonise the Aiyubid sultan of Egypt. The Franks in those years lived in Jerusalem on Egyptian sufferance: the walls of the city had been demolished during the fifth crusade and had not been rebuilt and the Franks controlled very little of the hinterland. Ethiopia was considered important in Egypt since it was thought to control the waters of the Nile,[1] but the only control which the court of Cairo had over that distant kingdom was through the church, and if the Ethiopian church gained independence the Egyptian government could not be expected to view this as a friendly act on the part of the Franks under whose auspices it had happened. Quick thinking by a member of Ignatius's suite enabled the patriarch to pass the incident off as a matter of linguistic misunderstanding and he and the Franks parted on terms of cordiality.[2] Tantalisingly the sources do not relate what happened to the irregularly consecrated abuna, Thomas.

In 1237 pope Gregory IX wrote both to the patriarch Ignatius and to the Coptic archbishop of Jerusalem congratulating them on their reconciliation with the church.[3] But he was under no illusion that these were more than personal acts of submission to Rome: he did not regard them as corporate acts of unity which brought the whole Monophysite communion into union with the holy see, and he did not send the patriarch a *pallium*, the outward sign of corporate unity. Nevertheless, the patriarch's example was followed by at least some Jacobites living in Frankish territory, for in 1238 the pope granted the patriarch Albert of Antioch the faculty of dispensing Jacobites who had returned to the Catholic obedience from irregularities which they might have contracted in

---

1. E.A. Wallis Budge, *A History of Ethiopia*, 2 vols, London 1928, I, pp 279, 289.
2. Bar Hebraeus, *Chron. Ecc.*, 654—64.
3. Auvray, nos 3789—90; *CICO*, III, pp 303—5, no 227.

terms of western canon law while in schism; and he instructed the
bishop and archdeacon of Acre to protect Jacobites in that kingdom who had renounced their errors and acknowledged the papal
primacy.[1]   He also exercised what the Orthodox church would
have termed 'economy' when he informed Templars and other
Christian prisoners of war at Aleppo that if they could not receive
the ministrations of Franciscan missionaries they might make their
confessions to and receive the Blessed Sacrament from Jacobite
priests, though there was no guarantee that such priests had been
reconciled to Rome.[2]

It was Gregory IX's successor, Innocent IV, who clarified the
position of the Jacobites. Writing in 1244 to the Dominicans in
the province of *Terra Sancta* who were working to reconcile
eastern-rite Christians to Rome, he enacted that Jacobite clergy
who were received into the church should enjoy the privileges
granted to all clergy under western canon law; but he granted the
further faculty that the Dominicans might give the Jacobites a
special dispensation 'to dwell among their own people and to be
in communion with them'.[3]   Jacobite converts, in other words,
were not required to become Latin Christians or to form a
splinter uniate church; they might continue in membership of
their own church and work for union from the inside. There
was nothing clandestine about these conversions, which, like that
of their patriarch Ignatius, were matters of public knowledge.
Pope Innocent seems to have taken the view that if other Jacobites
did not object to remaining in communion with Catholic converts
the holy see had no objection either.

This policy produced results.   When Lorenzo of Orte was
appointed legate in 1246 his mission included negotiations with
the Jacobites.[4] These were conducted by the Dominican, Andrew
of Longjumeau, and met with success. The patriarch Ignatius
wrote to the pope submitting a profession of faith and renewing
his acceptance of the papal primacy. He also outlined a plan for
the corporate reunion of the Jacobite church with Rome, stipu-
lating four conditions: that the Jacobite patriarch should continue
to be freely elected; that the Jacobite hierarchy should not be
subject to Latin bishops; that the Latin church should not attempt
to tax the Jacobites; and that Jacobites who married Latin Christians should not be required to receive the sacrament of confirma-

1. *Ibid.*, p 312, nos 233, 233A; Auvray, nos 4138–9.
2. *Ibid.*, no 4404; *CICO*, III, p 318, no 239.
3. 'et hii qui ad catholicae ecclesiae redierint unitatem, ut inter suos habitent eisque communicent'. *CICO*, IV (I), pp 11–12, no 8; Berger, no 573.
4. *Ibid.*, nos 3046–7; *CICO*, IV (I), pp 73–5, nos 31–2.

tion again.[1]   The maphrian, head of the oriental Jacobites of
Mesopotamia, also sent the pope a profession of faith, but,
perhaps significantly, this contained no reference to the Petrine
office in the church.[2]   Nothing came of the patriarch's proposals
for corporate reunion, perhaps because they did not command
sufficient support from the rest of the Jacobite hierarchy.

Ignatius himself had in about 1238 moved his see to Antioch,
where he had built a palace on the slopes of Mount Silpius[3] from
which he administered the church.[4]   This can only have been
done with the concurrence of the Latin patriarch, Albert of
Rizzato, and was certainly a result of Ignatius's reconciliation with
Rome, for such a privilege of permanent residence had been
accorded to no previous Jacobite patriarchs, however cordial their
relations with the Franks had been. It may have been at this time
that a Jacobite bishop of Cyprus was appointed: one is first
mentioned in the account of the election of Ignatius III in 1264.[5]
Such an appointment, which would have freed the Jacobite
community in the island from the jurisdiction of the Latin clergy,
can only have been made with the consent of the Lusignan crown
and of the Latin hierarchy, and this must have happened at a time
when relations between the Franks and the Jacobites were at their
most cordial, which was during Ignatius's reign.

Ignatius died in 1252 having ruled his church for thirty years.[6]
His death was followed by a schism, but this does not seem to
have been attributable to a division between the pro-Catholic
bishops and the rest, but to have been a natural phenomenon
which plagued the life of the Jacobite church in the middle ages.[7]
The Syrian bishops elected Dionysius VII, former bishop of
Melitene, while the oriental bishops chose the maphrian, who took
the title of John XV.[8]   The Syrian bishops were certainly more
pro-Catholic, but it was the oriental candidate, John XV, who
came to Antioch to request permission from the Franks to be
ritually enthroned in St Peter's chair. The Latin dean of Antioch
reluctantly gave his consent in 1253, not, it would seem, because
the new patriarch had not taken an oath of obedience to the pope,
although he may not have done so, but because the Frankish
authorities wished to judge between the claims of the two rival

1. *Ibid.*, pp 99–101, 104–5, nos 53, 55; Berger, nos 3036, 3038.
2. *Ibid.*, no 3039; *CICO*, IV (I), pp 105–7, no 56.
3. Bar Hebraeus, *Chron. Ecc.*, 666–8.
4. *Ibid.*, 668–70.
5. *Ibid.*, 746.
6. *Ibid.*, 694.
7. E.g. Michael II had been elected in opposition to Athanasius IX in 1200, Grumel,
Chronologie, p 449.
8. Bar Hebraeus, *Chron. Ecc.*, 702, 708.

patriarchs and were unable to do so because Dionysius VII failed to present himself.[1] It is not known whether either patriarch was ever in communion with Rome, but some of the Jacobite bishops certainly were. Thus when the new maphrian abdicated in 1257 he chose to live in Tripoli, and when he died there his requiem was celebrated by Latin and Jacobite clergy.[2]

When the Mongol armies reached north Syria in 1259 Dionysius VII made his submission to Hulagu khan and was taken under his protection.[3] Given the hostility of the Latin church towards the Mongols this action might have been a setback for the cause of unity, but this was not put to the test, for while he was celebrating mattins in 1261 Dionysius was assassinated, and John XV was left as undisputed head of the Jacobite church.[4] He died two years later, and the synod which met to elect his successor assembled in Cilicia, still a safe Christian state, and chose the abbot of the Jacobite Cilician monastery of Gavithaca, Ignatius III. He ruled until 1282, and seems to have spent all his reign in the Armenian kingdom.[5] During those years there is no evidence of any communication between the head of the Jacobite church and the papacy.

Diplomatic relations were resumed again in the reign of his successor, Ignatius IV Philoxenus, who in 1289 received a letter from pope Nicholas IV urging him to submit to Rome, to adopt the Catholic faith, and to urge his people to do the same, and enclosing a Catholic profession of faith, *Credimus Sanctam Trinitatem*.[6] At the same time the pope wrote a similar letter to Jacobite prelates.[7] The pope also wrote to the emperor, the abuna, the clergy and people of Ethiopia, exhorting them to unity, though whether his letters were ever received remains conjectural; presumably they were delivered to the Ethiopian community in Jerusalem.[8] The pope did not make any overtures to the Coptic patriarch of Alexandria, realising perhaps that the hostility of the Mamluk authorities towards the Christian powers made such a move impractical. These approaches to the Monophysite churches produced no results, since within two years Frankish power in Syria had come to an end and the Jacobites were effectively cut off from communication with the west.

1. *Ibid.*, 710-12.
2. *Ibid.*, 728–30.
3. *Ibid.*, 734.
4. *Ibid.*, 738.
5. *Ibid.*, 742–50, 778.
6. Langlois, no 2218.
7. *Ibid.*, nos 2219, 2224.
8. *Ibid.*, nos 2223, 2227, 2235, 2237.

It seems doubtful whether any Jacobite patriarch after John XV was in communion with Rome, and even his case is hypothetical, although it is probable that some of the Jacobites living in Frankish Syria remained in communion until the Mamluk conquest. The holy see had not tried to impose corporate reunion on the Jacobites, but had encouraged individual conversions. The converts had not been required to leave their own church, but had been allowed to remain in its communion and to act, as it were, as a unifying leaven. Real religious unity might in time have been achieved by this method, but it was of necessity a much slower process than corporate reunion, and time was not on the side of the Latins.

The other major eastern church, some of whose members lived in Frankish territory, was the Nestorian. There had never been many of them in Frankish Syria and twelfth-century Frankish writers showed no interest in them at all. In the thirteenth century there were Nestorian communities at Antioch, Acre, and, by the end of the century, in Tripoli and the Lebanon also.[1] There were also a few Nestorians in Cyprus whom Honorius III placed under the authority of Latin bishops for the sake of ecclesiastical good order,[2] but nothing parallel happened to those on the mainland.

When James of Vitry came to Acre he wanted to preach to the Nestorians there, but they had no bishop and, being very conscious of the canonical authority of a bishop, he would not do so without their bishop's license. Clearly he did not regard them as under his own jurisdiction.[3] His attempts to find out about them were not very successful. He discovered that they used leavened bread at Mass, that their liturgical language was Syriac, and that they were considered heretical, but he only found out why that was so from a merchant who had travelled in further Asia, who told him that they believed in the separation of the two natures in Christ.[4]

James also remarked that they were found in the land of Prester John.[5] This was their main attraction for thirteenth-century Franks. Belief in this legendary potentate, which had

---

1. Antioch: Oliver of Paderborn, 'Historia Damiatina', c 66, ed Hoogeweg, p 266; Acre: James of Vitry, *Lettres*, p 85, no 2; Tripoli and Lebanon: Burchard of Mount Sion, pp 16, 26.

2. Pressutti, no 3750; *CICO*, III, pp 117–18, no 87.

3. James of Vitry, *Lettres*, p 85, no 2.

4. *Ibid.*, *HO*, c 77, pp 148–50; *Lettres*, p 96, no 2. The merchant added, it would seem falsely, that those in the land of Prester John had recently become Jacobites.

5. *HO*, c 77, pp 148–9.

grown up in western Europe in the twelfth century,[1] attained a new relevance at the time of the fifth crusade when news reached the Frankish armies of Genghis khan's attack on Khorezm, beyond the lands of the eastern caliphate, and they misinterpreted these rumours as evidence that Prester John was coming to their aid.[2]　Prester John proved attractive because he was thought to be a powerful Christian ruler living in the lands to the east of Islam and therefore well placed to help the Franks in their wars against the Muslims.　Any information that could be gained about the religion of his subjects was therefore of interest to western Europe in general.　Oliver of Paderborn reflects this interest in his *Historia Damiatina*, an account of the fifth crusade in which he took part:

> When visiting Antioch we made a careful study of the Nestorians who have their own church there.　They say that they believe that two natures are united in the person of Christ, and they confess that the Blessed Virgin is the Mother of God and man, and that she bore both God and man, which Nestorius denied.　But whether in their hearts they believe what they profess to believe, God alone knows.[3]

The Nestorians were a puzzle to western theologians who knew why Nestorius had been condemned at the council of Ephesus, because their beliefs did not resemble those of their eponymous founder.

When he wrote to the pope in 1236 about the reconciliation of the Jacobite patriarch, the Dominican prior Philip stated that he had also in the same way reconciled a Nestorian archbishop in Frankish Syria.　It is likely that this prelate had come to carry out a visitation of Nestorian communities there and had been reconciled while he was visiting Jerusalem, although it is possible that he had been converted by Dominican missionaries working in Muslim territory.　The prior added that a Dominican mission, led by William of Montferrat, had visited the Nestorian patriarch at Baghdad, and that he had expressed a desire to enter into communion with Rome.[4]

The reconciliation of the Nestorian archbishop was not an act of corporate reunion with Rome any more than that of the

---

1. F. Zarncke, 'Der Priester Johannes', *Abhandlungen der philologisch-historischen Klasse der k. sächsischen Gesellschaft der Wissenschaften*, 7, 1879, pp 827–1030, 8, 1883, pp 3–186.

2. E.g. James of Vitry, *Lettres*, pp 141–50, no 7.

3. Oliver of Paderborn, 'Historia Damiatina', c 66, ed Hoogeweg, p 266.

4. *MGH SS*, XXIII, pp 941–2.　Richard, *La Papauté et les missions*, pp 57–8. There was a Nestorian archbishop of Jerusalem. He does not seem to have lived there permanently, *CICO*, IV (I), p 97, no 52.

Jacobite patriarch had been. The pope wrote to congratulate the archbishop on his decision,[1] and he also issued the Frankish clergy of Syria with the same instructions about Nestorian converts as he did about Jacobite ones,[2] which shows that the archbishop's example was followed by at least some of the Nestorian community living in Frankish territory. Innocent IV in his turn granted the same dispensation to Nestorian converts as he had done to Jacobite ones: that they might continue to live among their own people and to remain in communion with them.[3]

Lorenzo of Orte, in his wide-ranging legatine commission of 1246, was empowered to treat with the Nestorians. He probably did so by proxy rather than in person,[4] but his mission produced some results. The Nestorian patriarch wrote to Innocent IV expressing polite thanks for his attention, and lamenting the sack of Jerusalem in 1244.[5] The Nestorian archbishop of Nisibin, however, sent a profession of faith to the pope, although he did not explicitly make his submission.[6] As a result of this work some at least of the Nestorians living in Frankish Syria recognised the papal primacy, but the main body of the Nestorian church was too distant from the Latin sphere of influence to be much affected by the papacy's friendly overtures.

The Nestorian church enjoyed the special favour of the Mongol khans: some tribes in the Mongol confederacy, like the Keraits, were Nestorians, and members of the ruling house married Nestorian wives. Thus when the army of Hulagu sacked Baghdad in 1258 the Nestorian patriarch and his flock were spared from the general slaughter.[7] When Hulagu's son, Abagha, became ilkhan of Persia in 1265 friendly relations were established between the Mongols of Persia and the holy see: the popes hoped to convert the pagan ilkhans, and the ilkhans hoped for western military aid against Egypt. Embassies were exchanged regularly between the two courts.[8] These exchanges culminated with the embassy led by Rabban Sauma, a Nestorian monk, which was sent to the west by the ilkhan Arghun, and received by pope Nicholas IV in 1288.

1. Auvray, no 3791.
2. *Ibid.*, nos 4138–9; *CICO*, III, p 312, nos 233, 233A.
3. Berger, nos 573; *CICO*, IV (I), pp 11–12, no 8.
4. *Ibid.*, p 73, no 31; Berger, no 3047. Lorenzo probably used the Dominicans of *Terra Sancta*, who already had dealings with the Nestorian patriarch, as his intermediaries.
5. Berger, no 3035; *CICO*, IV (I), pp 95–7, no 52.
6. Berger, no 3037; *CICO*, IV (I), pp 102–4, no 54.
7. A. Mingana, 'The early spread of Christianity in Central Asia and the Far East', *BJRL*, 9, 1925, pp 297–371; Saunders, *Mongol Conquests*, pp 111–12.
8. J. Richard, 'The Mongols and the Franks', in *Journal of Asian History*, 3, 1969, pp 45–57; *La Papauté et les missions*, pp 98–113.

Rabban Sauma celebrated Mass in the Nestorian rite before the papal court, and later received communion at the hands of the pope himself. According to Syriac sources the pope sent Rabban Sauma back with a set of vestments for the Nestorian patriarch Yabh-Allaha III and with a bull recognising him as patriarch of the church of the east.[1] This is not recorded in Nicholas IV's registers and the authenticity of the Syriac account has therefore been called in question,[2] but the fact that the pope admitted Rabban Sauma to communion seems to indicate that he found his profession of faith satisfactory, and there seems no reason to doubt that Nicholas IV did not consider that the Nestorian church was heretical, even though it was schismatic.

The pope followed up this mission by sending John of Monte Corvino back to the Persian court as his legate, with letters of recommendation to the Nestorian patriarch and to the faithful of his church, commending the legate to them and urging them to enter into union with Rome.[3] This project came to nothing, since the Christophile ilkhan Arghun died in 1291 and in 1295 his successor, Ghazan, embraced Islam.[4]

As papal treatment of the Jacobites and Nestorians in the thirteenth century shows, the holy see, through the work of Dominican and Franciscan missionaries, discovered that there was a great difference between these oriental Christians and the Orthodox and Armenians. The latter had well-trained theologians and a well-instructed clergy who were aware of the ways in which they differed from the Latin church in matters of belief and practice, and who were not willing to compromise about those matters. The Jacobites and Nestorians, on the other hand, were often poorly instructed in theological subtleties, and the majority of them no longer held the teachings which their churches officially professed and which originally had separated them from the communion of the orthodox.

Burchard of Mount Sion, a Dominican who had travelled widely in the east, but who wrote for a western public which understood heresies in western terms as movements which were dedicated and vocal in their opposition to the Catholic church, tried to explain to his readers that eastern heresies were not at all similar:

1. E.A. Wallis Budge, *The Monks of Kublai Khan*, London 1928, pp 165–97.
2. J. Richard, 'La mission en Europe de Rabban Çauma et l'union des Eglises', XII Convegno Volta, Rome 1957, pp 162–7, argues that the pope did recognise the Nestorian patriarch.
3. Langlois, nos 2220, 2236.
4. J.A. Boyle in *Cambridge History of Iran*, V, pp 372–9.

Many people are frightened when they are told that in regions beyond the sea there dwell Nestorians, Jacobites . . . and other sects named after heretics whom the church has condemned, wherefore these men also are thought to be heretics and to follow the errors of those after whom they are called. This is by no means true . . . but they are men of simple and devout life. Yet I do not deny that there may be fools among them, seeing that even the Roman church itself is not free from fools.[1]

It is very much to the credit of the thirteenth-century Catholic church that it made a distinction between Christians who differed from itself in belief, and insisted on dogmatic agreement before admitting them to its communion, and people who, for historical reasons, were estranged from it, but who did not hold the errors which had caused the estrangement centuries before. The Jacobites and Nestorians came into the second category: their faith was in most cases simply that which all western Christians held, without subtle Christological distinctions such as theological textbooks attributed to them. Having established this the papacy was content to treat them with generosity and not require that they should separate themselves from the communion of their fellow churchmen, but simply that they should make an orthodox profession of faith. This did not produce spectacular results in terms of corporate unity, but it generated great goodwill, in marked contrast to the arid, though necessary, theological arguments between the Latins and the Orthodox. The necessity of such arguments cannot be gainsaid, since both sides considered that issues of fundamental principle were involved and they could not be avoided with integrity, but the wisdom of the holy see is shown in its willingness to avoid generating artificial arguments with those oriental churches whose divergences in matters of doctrine were no longer a live issue.

But the very success of the initiatives for unity with eastern-rite Christians in Frankish Syria generated problems. These were two-fold: one group were practical. Normal papal policy allowed the bishops of eastern-rite churches in communion with Rome to exercise jurisdiction over their own flocks independently of the Latin hierarchy. Difficulties arose in areas where there were uniate congregations but no uniate bishops. One such area was the diocese of Tortosa where by 1267 the Latin bishop had appointed vicars to oversee Greeks, that is Orthodox, 'and members of other nations': the vicars were particularly charged to see that eastern-rite churches were constructed in an appropriate way.

1. Burchard of Mount Sion, p 107.

But the bishop also asked the help of the Hospitallers to enforce obedience to the Roman see, and to himself as bishop, on those eastern Christians and specially on 'any archbishop, bishop, abbot or member of their clergy'.[1] The bishops and archbishops referred to can only have been Orthodox, since there were no bishops of any other eastern-rite church in the diocese of Tortosa, and the Orthodox alone of the eastern Christians had always been subject to the authority of Latin diocesans. But the bishop also implies that all eastern-rite Christians in his diocese must be forced to accept the primacy of the Roman see. This reflects the second range of problems which the success of the initiatives for unity generated: the desire of Latin bishops to achieve uniformity in their dioceses. For, as large numbers of eastern-rite Christians entered into communion with Rome, dissident congregations became an anomaly, and there must have been a temptation to force unity on them. How common this tendency was is not known, but there is certainly no evidence that such a policy was practised before the second half of the thirteenth century, or that it was at all widespread even then.

Syria under Frankish rule was the meeting place of all the Christian confessions, and this was particularly true of Jerusalem where all the Christian churches were represented. In the course of the thirteenth century some measure of unity, though in varying degrees, was achieved between the western church and most of the separated eastern churches, although only the Maronite union has endured to the present day.

---

1. *CGOH*, no 3282.

14. THE SPIRITUAL WORK OF THE LATIN CHURCH IN SYRIA

Undoubtedly much of the history of the Latin church in Syria is unedifying: in this it resembles the history of most churches in most ages.   A great deal of what we know about its activities comes from accounts of litigation conducted by bishops and other church leaders about property rights, precedence and the collection of tithe and these have been preserved less through any random process of historical selection than because church-men themselves wished that they should be.   For when the Latin clergy finally left the Holy Land what they took with them were their titles to properties which they hoped might one day be restored to them, rather than liturgical or devotional books which they knew they could replace. Yet to leave the reader with the impression that the clergy of Latin Syria were worldly, career-minded men, intent solely upon amassing material possessions, would be partial and misleading.

The primary concern of the men who founded the Latin church in Syria was that the public worship of God should be properly performed in those places which had been sanctified by His bodily presence in Christ. They had to make provision for this virtually *ex nihilo*, for as a result of the fanaticism of the caliph al-Hakim and the subsequent decades of political unrest most of the holy places were in ruins when the crusaders arrived in the east.   Within a short time the great shrine churches of Jerusalem had been rebuilt, together with others elsewhere in the Frankish states: notably the basilica of Nazareth, the shrine of St George at Lydda, and those of St John at Sebastia, the Transfiguration of Christ on Mount Tabor, and Our Lady of Tortosa. At Hebron the Franks adapted an existing Muslim shrine, which itself incorpor-ated earlier work of the Herodian period, to the needs of Christian worship.[1]   In addition, in almost all the places where they found-ed bishoprics the Franks built new cathedrals, in many cases because there had been none there before; and they founded churches and chapels in large numbers in their cities, their castles, and on some of their rural estates, of which no systematic survey

---

1. L.H. Vincent, E.H.J. MacKay, F.M. Abel, *Hébron: Le Haram el-Khalil, sépulture des patriarches*, 2 vols, Paris 1923.

has yet been made.

The shrine churches and the cathedrals were all served either by monastic communities of men (and occasionally, as at Bethany, of women), or by regular or secular canons, whose responsibility it was to sing the day and night offices of the church and to celebrate the Eucharist with due solemnity. The churches were, in many cases, ornamented with frescoes and mosaics, and with carvings in the romanesque style, and even Muslim observers, hostile though they were to Frankish domination of their third holy city, were not insensible to the visual beauty of the Latin achievement. The cadi al-Fadl had this to say about Jerusalem after it had been recovered by Saladin in 1187:

> Islam received back a place which it had left almost uninhabited, but which the care of the unbelievers had transformed into a paradise garden . . . those accursed ones defended with the lance and sword this city which they had rebuilt with columns and slabs of marble, where they had founded churches and the palaces of the Templars and the Hospitallers . . .   One sees on every side . . . columns decorated with leaves, which make them look like living trees.[1]

The carrying out of so extensive a building programme and the endowment of clergy to serve these churches and cathedrals was a great expense in states which possessed little agricultural wealth, which were perpetually subject to invasion, and which had to maintain an expensive system of defence. The willingness of the Frankish landowning class to spend so generously on the establishment of the Latin church may not be a reliable index of their piety, but it does accurately reflect the importance which they attached to this work: the public performance of the Latin liturgy in the churches of Syria was the justification of the crusading movement. People in western Europe who sympathised with that movement were equally generous benefactors of the Latin church in Syria, but, as has been shown earlier in this work, the difficulties of transferring money from one part of the world to another in a society which was only beginning to develop the skills of international commerce placed the onus for the endowment of the Latin church squarely on the Franks of Syria, and it was a responsibility which they met.

If the primary purpose of the shrine churches and the cathedrals which the Franks founded was to provide for the public worship of God, their other main function was to be centres of pilgrimage. Every year, while the holy places remained in Frankish hands,

---

1. Quoted by Ibn Khallikan in 'The life of the Sultan Saladin', extracts in *RHC Or*, III, pp 421–2.

large numbers of pilgrims came from all over the western world to pray at those sites associated with the life and Passion of the Lord, and their presence was both a symptom of and a stimulus to the growth in devotion to the humanity of Christ which characterised twelfth-century Latin piety.[1]   But this phenomenon was by no means confined to the western world: pilgrims came also from the Orthodox commonwealth and from the churches of the east. Burchard of Mount Sion gives a vivid picture of these eastern pilgrims in the last century of Latin rule:

> Who could tell how many monks and nuns from Georgia, Great and Less Armenia, Chaldaea, Syria, Media, Persia, India, Ethiopia, Nubia, Nabatene, of the Maronite, Jacobite, Nestorian, Greek, Syrian and other sects, at this day roam over the land in troops of one hundred or two hundred each . . . and visit each holy place . . . Beating their breasts, weeping, groaning and sighing . . . this outward bodily show of the religious feeling, which they no doubt inwardly possess, moves many even of the Saracens to tears.[2]

By the time Burchard wrote most of the holy places were no longer in Latin hands, but the shrines which those pilgrims visited, though administered in most cases by eastern Christians, had been built by the Franks.

The Frankish rulers were concerned for the safety of the pilgrims, many of them poor and unarmed, who flocked to the Holy Land in such numbers.   Even in the time of Frankish rule many of the roads of the kingdom were unsafe because of robbers and Muslim marauders,[3] and it was to meet this need that in 1119 Hugh of Payens gathered together a band of followers who were trained knights and who placed themselves under a religious vow to protect the pilgrim routes.[4]   Within ten years this group developed into the order of the knights Templar, which became one of the chief bulwarks of the defence of the kingdom, but it never relinquished its early task, and the roads of Palestine are still dotted with remains of towers which the Templars built and garrisoned for the defence of pilgrims.[5]

The Franks were also concerned with the material welfare of pilgrims.   Many of them were poor people who often reached Palestine destitute, having spent all their money on the voyage

1. R.W. Southern, *The Making of the Middle Ages*, London 1953, pp 230–50.
2. Burchard of Mount Sion, pp 2–3.
3. *The pilgrimage of . . . Abbot Daniel*, pp 9, 59.
4. M.C. Barber, 'The Origins of the Order of the Temple', *Studia Monastica*, 12, 1970, pp 219–40.
5. These and the towers which the Hospitallers also built are described in Deschamps, *Défense du royaume de Jérusalem, passim*.

there; many of them were old and ill; and many succumbed to the diseases prevalent there to which they had no natural immunity. The Hospital of St John had been founded before the first crusade to care for poor and sick Latin pilgrims, but under the protection of Frankish kings it rapidly grew into the order of the knights of St John, who, together with the Templars, made up half the army of the Latin kingdom, but who never relinquished their charitable work.[1] They founded hospitals in other parts of the Latin states, as well as in the western world, but the most impressive of these was the hospital of the mother-house in Jerusalem which was the best-run and the largest in Christendom in the twelfth century, with the possible exception of some of those in Constantinople.[2] John of Würzburg who visited it in the 1160s records:

> When I was there I learned that the whole number of sick people amounted to two thousand, of whom sometimes in the course of one day and night more than fifty are carried out dead, while many other fresh ones keep arriving . . . This house supplies as many people outside it with victuals as it does those within.[3]

The order of the Hospital was not a unique instance of organised charity in the Frankish east. Other hospitals were founded by private individuals[4] and by religious communities, like that attached to Our Lady of Josaphat,[5] and this benevolent impulse was never lost among Latin Christians, for right at the end of the period of Frankish rule archbishop Gilles of Tyre founded a new hospital for Breton pilgrims at Acre.[6] The most striking example of religious dedication to the relief of suffering was the order of St Lazarus, founded for the relief of lepers, and run by members of the knightly class.[7] Nor were charitable works delegated simply to institutions: bishops considered it part of their normal duties to feed the hungry,[8] and during the drought of 1178 the patriarch Aimery of Limoges provided famine relief to the poor in his diocese of Antioch.[9] If the practice of the Christian life is to be evaluated in terms of performing the corporal works of mercy,

---

1. Smail, *Crusading Warfare*, pp 88–97.
2. D.J. Constantelos, *Byzantine Philanthropy and Social Welfare*, New Brunswick 1968, pp 171–84; T.S. Miller, 'The Knights of Saint John and the Hospitals of the Latin West', *Speculum*, 53, 1978, pp 709–33.
3. John of Würzburg, p 44.
4. E.g. William of Bures's foundation of St Julian's, Tiberias, later given to the Hospital of St John, Delaborde, pp 36–7, no 11.
5. *Ibid.*, pp 47–9, no 19.
6. Delaville Le Roulx, 'L'Hôpital des Bretons', *ROL*, I, 1893, pp 423–33.
7. de Marsy, 'Saint-Lazare', *AOL*, II, pp 121–57.
8. St Nerses of Lampron, 'Letter to Leo II', *RHC Arm*, I, p 600.
9. *MS*, XX, 6, vol III, p 375.

then the Latin churchmen of Syria had nothing of which to be ashamed.

The Frankish east under Latin rule attracted not only pilgrims, but also western Christians with a vocation for the contemplative life. The Cistercian foundations at Belmont in the Lebanon, Jubin in the Black Mountain of Antioch and St Sergius in the hills above Gibelet were not shrine churches, but were founded by men who wished to pray in solitude.[1] The dangers of invasion made it impractical for women with a similar vocation to live in equal isolation, but in Tripoli and Acre communities of enclosed Cistercian nuns devoted themselves to the cultivation of the interior life.[2] The eremitical life also flourished: a large number of hermits was found in the valley of Kidron outside Jerusalem in the twelfth century,[3] and in the Black Mountain of Antioch in the thirteenth.[4] One of these groups, the hermits of Mount Carmel, evolved into a new religious order in the early thirteenth century under the guidance of St Albert, patriarch of Jerusalem.[5]

The first western settlers in Syria came from a sheltered background in which everybody shared common religious assumptions and forms of worship in membership of the Catholic church. In their new home they found a bewildering variety of other Christian confessions and proved remarkably tolerant towards them at a time when tolerance was rare and when it was not regarded as a virtue.[6] In the thirteenth century the newly founded Dominican and Franciscan orders used Frankish Syria as a base from which to work among Muslims and eastern Christians in an attempt to convert the former and establish unity with the latter, but they were helped in their work for Christian reunion by the goodwill which the Latin Christians of Syria had established among their native Christian subjects in the previous century.

Of course, the history of the Latin church in Syria was not a record of unblemished success. The standards of religious observance declined sadly in the thirteenth century when the Franks were on the defensive and when their control of the holy places was intermittent, and the holy see had cause to complain that the Divine Office was no longer regularly sung in some of the cathedrals, while many of the clergy were guilty of drawing revenues

1. Hamilton in Pennington, ed, *One Yet Two*, pp 405–9, 414–15.
2. *Ibid.*, pp 411–12.
3. John of Würzburg, p 51.
4. Auvray, no 2660.
5. See chapter 10 above. James of Vitry, *HO*, c 52, p 86.
6. St Louis once said: 'A layman, when he hears the Christian faith impugned, ought only to defend it with the sword, thrusting it into the belly as far as it will go'. Joinville, c 10, pp 19–20.

in absentia and feeing ill-instructed vicars to perform their duties.[1]   Nor were the monasteries free from corruption: at the Cistercian house of Jubin in 1237 a dispute broke out among the brethren which culminated in the prior's using knights and mercenaries to drive out the subprior and thirty of the monks.[2] But even at that time the Latin church had not lost all its spiritual vigour: some of the ablest men in western Christendom were members of its bench of bishops, and they spent their lives in Syria, with little material reward or hope of improved circumstances, motivated by a sense of duty towards the ideal of serving the holy places.

At its best the Latin church in Syria excited the admiration of native Christians.   In 1177 St Nerses of Lampron, Armenian archbishop of Tarsus, wrote:

> In a few years the Franks have filled all the country with their piety. Having become masters of lands which had long been ruled by Armenian princes who had founded no churches or bishoprics there, the Franks' first care was to found an institutional church, as we have seen for ourselves . . . [3]

Twenty years later he explained to Leo II of Cilicia how he had been moved by the example of the Latins to adopt some of their practices, among which was the following:

> We have seen that they have charitable institutions for the relief of the poor and that they do not remain content with helping them in a haphazard way.   Wishing to emulate this praiseworthy zeal, which we are able to do because of your generosity towards our church of Tarsus, we have decided to distribute bread and beans to two or three hundred poor people each Wednesday and Friday.[4]

A genuine respect for Latin piety was certainly an important factor in helping to establish unity between the Latin church and the eastern churches.   And despite its failure to preserve unity with the Orthodox, which contributed to the worsening of the schism between the Roman and Byzantine churches, the Latin church in Syria has an impressive record of progress in the field of Christian unity.   In Innocent IV's reign the Armenians and Maronites, the Orthodox of Antioch, some Jacobites, including the patriarch, and even some Nestorians, were all in communion with the western church. A parallel degree of unity has only been achieved once since that time, during the later stages of the council

1. See chapter 11 above.
2. Auvray, no 4020.
3. St Nerses of Lampron, 'On the Institutions of the Church', *RHC Arm*, I, p 576.
4. *Ibid.*, 'Letter to Leo II', *RHC Arm*, I, p 600.

of Florence,[1] and in many instances that was more formal than real, nor has it ever been repeated. But without the formation of the Latin church in Syria, acting as a bridge between Rome and the eastern churches, unity of this kind could not have been secured at all.

Despite these impressive achievements the Latin church can be criticised in one very central way: it remained alien to the culture of Syria despite being established there for two hundred years. In part this failure stemmed from the lack of any desire to proselytize on a wide scale. As Riley-Smith has shown, there was a quite large number of individual conversions to the Latin church among the indigenous population, as is revealed by the presence of non-western names in lists of witnesses.[2] Nevertheless, there seems to have been a lack of any attempt at mass conversions on the part of the Latin clergy. During the twelfth and thirteenth centuries the majority of Muslim peasants in Sicily were converted to Catholicism, but nothing similar happened in Frankish Syria. The failure of the Latin clergy to attempt to use their social and political power to convert Muslim serfs will, in the present age, only be considered a virtue. That they made no wide-ranging attempt to latinise native Christians shows a considerable degree of wisdom when measured against later colonial experiments of that kind. But this is only a partial explanation of why the Latin church failed to put down roots during its long sojourn in Syria. The Frankish laity, after all, did become to some extent orientalised, a fact which excited unfavourable comment from western visitors.[3]

The church remained western, chiefly, it would seem, because throughout the period of Frankish rule the majority of Latin bishops were men who had been born in western Europe, while even some of those who were Syrian-born, like William of Tyre, received their education in Europe. The same was also true of many of the lesser Latin clergy, so that, although there were doubtless many priests born of Syrian Frankish parents, the hierarchy remained predominantly western and the church remained a branch of the western church set down in the Levant. This is reflected in its liturgy which, apart from the observance of the cult of a few local saints, is virtually indistinguishable from that of the church in western Europe.[4]

1. Gill, *The Council of Florence*, pp 304–48.
2. Riley-Smith, *Feudal Nobility*, pp 10 *seq.*
3. E.g. James of Vitry, *HO*, c 73, pp 133–6.
4. Ch. Kohler, 'Un rituel et un bréviaire du Saint-Sépulcre de Jérusalem (XIIe–XIIIe siècle)', *Mélanges pour servir à l'histoire de l'Orient Latin*, Paris 1900, pp 286–403. F. Wormald, in H. Buchthal, *Miniature Painting*, pp 107–34, (appendix on liturgical calendars in the Latin kingdom).

Thus when Frankish rule in Syria came to an end the Latin church ended with it: there was no native clergy of the Latin rite to perpetuate it, and only the Franciscan custodians remained by grace of the Mamluk government to minister in the holy places to the needs of western pilgrims. The long-term beneficiary of the Latin church in Syria was not the Holy Land, but western Europe, for the development of the western church as a whole was shaped in some important ways by developments which had their origins in the Latin patriarchates of Jerusalem and Antioch. The military orders, the Templars, the knights of St John and the Teutonic knights, all of which had been founded for the service of the Holy Land, diversified their activities and operated in other parts of the western world, and they also provided the model for other, strictly western European orders, like those of Calatrava, Alcántara and Santiago. The military orders had an importance in the political history of western Europe which lasted until the successful defence of Malta, and with it of the western Mediterranean, against the Ottoman Turks by the knights of St John in 1565; while the Catholic church in the later middle ages tried to persuade the feudal nobility to accept the ethical standards which the military orders had evolved in their practice of the Christian life.

The kingdom of Acre, where war was endemic, seemed a most unpromising setting for the formation of a contemplative tradition, yet the Carmelite order evolved there and rapidly spread throughout the western church. In the sixteenth century the reform of the order undertaken by St Teresa of Avila and St John of the Cross who restored the primitive rule first given by St Albert of Jerusalem, albeit with certain modifications, resulted in the enrichment of Catholic spirituality with a deeper understanding of contemplative prayer than had previously been available in the western church. The world of the crusades seems very remote both in time and in temper from that of the counter-reformation, but it was one with which St Teresa had a certain sympathy, for, as she relates in her autobiography, she and her brother Rodrigo, when they were children, resolved to set out and seek martyrdom in the land of the Moors.[1]

But the way in which the western church as a whole was most indebted to the Latin church in Syria was not through any of the institutions which evolved there, great though the influence of some of them was, but through the awareness it developed of the true nature of the church universal. Before 1095 western Christians had tended to equate Christianity with the Latin church, and

---

1. *The Life of Saint Teresa*, c 1, trans J.M. Cohen, Penguin Classics, 1958, p 24.

the more sophisticated among them, like the members of the papal court, would have added to this the Byzantine church; but the Latin church in Syria, through its contact with eastern Christians, altered the dimensions of western awareness on this subject. The holy see in particular, and educated western opinion in general, became aware that the Gospel had indeed been preached throughout the known world, and that any attempt to achieve Christian unity would involve not simply healing the breach with Constantinople, but establishing communion with all the churches of the east. Whereas the leaders of the first crusade in a mood of religious xenophobia had begged pope Urban to help them 'to root out and destroy' the Greeks and Armenians and Syrian Jacobites,[1] it became the aim of Urban's successors to gather these separated Christians into the unity of a single church. This is the true measure of the spiritual achievement of the Latin church in Syria.

1. Hagenmeyer, *Kreuzzugsbriefe*, p 164, no 16.

APPENDIX.

THE DATE OF RALPH OF DOMFRONT'S DEPOSITION

Ralph of Domfront was deposed by a legatine council convoked at Antioch on 30 November by Alberic, cardinal-bishop of Ostia,[1] but there is no agreement among scholars about the year in which this occurred. Röhricht placed this event in 1141,[2] but Cahen has dated it to 1139,[3] an opinion which is also shared by Runciman.[4] William of Tyre, who is the primary source for this event, gives no precise date, but places it towards the end of king Fulk's reign and after the first Syrian campaign of John Comnenus. He relates that when the legate arrived at Sidon he found that the Franks of Jerusalem were besieging Banyas, that he went to their camp, and that he was present when the city was handed over to them and when a Latin bishop was appointed there.[5] In November of that same year he presided over the council of Antioch at which Ralph was deposed[6] and the following spring he went to Jerusalem, where he kept Easter, was present at the consecration of the Temple and presided over a council which was attended by the Armenian catholicus.[7]

The one event in this sequence which can be securely dated from an independent source is the Frankish capture of Banyas. The Damascus Chronicle, a contemporary compilation, places the fall of Banyas at the end of Shawwal, A.H. 534, which in Christian terms is the middle of June 1140.[8] There seems no reason to doubt the accuracy of this evidence which has been accepted by most modern scholars,[9] but it would follow from this that the legatine council of Antioch opened on 30 November 1140, and that the legatine council of Jerusalem was held in Eastertide 1141. These dates are corroborated by two documents in the cartulary

1. WT, XV, 15, *RHC Occ*, I, p 682.
2. *RR*, I, p 50, no 203.
3. Cahen, *Syrie*, p 503.
4. Runciman, *History of the Crusades*, II, p 221.
5. WT, XV, 11, *RHC Occ*, I, pp 674–6.
6. *Ibid.*, XV, 15–17, pp 682–6.
7. *Ibid.*, XV, 18, pp 687–8.
8. *Damascus Chronicle*, ed Gibb, p 261.
9. E.g. Nicholson in Setton, *Crusades*, I, p 443; J. Prawer, *Histoire du Royaume Latin de Jérusalem*, 2 vols, Paris 1969–70, I, p 331; Mayer, *Crusades*, p 92, prefers the date of 1139.

of the Holy Sepulchre. The first of these, dated December 1140, is a grant to the patriarch of Jerusalem and the canons of the Holy Sepulchre by Raymond II of Tripoli of freedom of payment from all dues on goods imported in the port of Tripoli and on all produce grown on the Sepulchre's lands in the county of Tripoli and exported from that city. This was witnessed by archbishop Robert of Nazareth, archbishop Fulcher of Tyre and bishop Bernard of Sidon, who were therefore present in Tripoli at that time.[1]

In a second document dated 'anno . . . MCXL, mense ianuarii, indictione III', count Raymond amplified this concession, granting the patriarch and canons total freedom in the port of Tripoli from payment of dues on all goods 'que usibus suis necessaria fuerint'. He states that this privilege has been granted 'domni Willelmi . . . Iherosolymorum patriarche ab Antiochia revertentis ac suffraganeorum ipsius, Fulcherii, Tyrensis archiepiscopi, et Roberti Nazareni archiepiscopi, ac Bernardi Sydoniensis episcopi . . . petitionibus inducti.'[2] Röhricht dated this document to January 1140 and claimed that the December document was a confirmation of it.[3] Röhricht presumably preferred to date the January document to 1140 because the third indiction referred to that year, but since it was normal practice in Frankish Syria to date the new year from 25 March the document should be dated January 1139 if Röhricht's conjecture is correct. It seems more probable that in modern style the document should be dated January 1141, and that a mistake was made in the indiction either in the original document, or in the copy which was transcribed in the cartulary. Both grants were clearly made during a single visit to Tripoli by the prelates named in them; the January grant is an amplification of the privilege granted in the December document, not a simple confirmation of it; and it seems evident that the patriarch and his suffragans stayed at Tripoli from December 1140 to January 1141 on their way back to Jerusalem from the Antioch council.

One further piece of evidence which may confirm the 1140 date for Ralph of Domfront's deposition is that William of Tyre implies that his successor, the dean of Antioch, Aimery of Limoges, was appointed patriarch immediately after Ralph's deposition.[4] But Aimery is named as dean in two documents of April 1140[5] and therefore cannot have been appointed patriarch until after that date.

1. de Rozière, pp 186–7, no 94.
2. *Ibid.*, pp 184–5, no 93.
3. *RR*, I, pp 47, 49, nos 193, 198.
4. WT, XV, 16, *RHC Occ*, I, p 685.
5. de Rozière, pp 169–78, nos 88–9.

All the evidence therefore suggests that cardinal Alberic reached Syria in time to take part in the siege of Banyas in June 1140, that he convoked a legatine council at Antioch on 30 November of that year at which Ralph of Domfront was deposed, and that at Eastertide 1141 he presided over a legatine council at Jerusalem at which the Armenian catholicus was present.

ECCLESIASTICAL LISTS

I. POPES

Urban II	1088–99	Innocent III	1198–1216
Paschal II	1099–1118	Honorius III	1216–27
Gelasius II	1118–19	Gregory IX	1227–41
Calixtus II	1119–24	Celestine IV	1241
Honorius II	1124–30	Innocent IV	1243–54
Innocent II	1130–43	Alexander IV	1254–61
Celestine II	1143–4	Urban IV	1261–4
Lucius II	1144–5	Clement IV	1265–8
Eugenius III	1145–53	Gregory X	1271–6
Anastasius IV	1153–4	Innocent V	1276
Hadrian IV	1154–9	Hadrian V	1276
Alexander III	1159–81	John XXI	1276–7
Lucius III	1181–5	Nicholas III	1277–80
Urban III	1185–7	Martin IV	1281–5
Gregory VIII	1187	Honorius IV	1285–7
Clement III	1187–91	Nicholas IV	1288–92
Celestine III	1191–8		

II. LATIN PATRIARCHS OF ANTIOCH

Bernard of Valence	1100–35	Peter II of Ivrea	1209–17
Ralph of Domfront	1135–40	Peter of Capua	1219
Aimery of Limoges	1140–93	(patriarch elect)	
Ralph II	1193–6	Rainier	1219–25
Peter I of Angoulême		Albert of Rizzato	1227–46
	1196–1208	Opizo dei Fieschi	1247–92

III. LATIN PATRIARCHS OF JERUSALEM

Arnulf of Chocques	1099	Warmund of Picquigny	
(elect, not consecrated)			1118–28
Daimbert of Pisa	1099–1101	Stephen of Chartres	1128–30
Evremar of Chocques	1102–8	William I	1130–45
Gibelin of Arles	1108–12	Fulcher	1145–57
Arnulf of Chocques	1112–18	Amalric of Nesle	1157–80

III. LATIN PATRIARCHS OF JERUSALEM (Continued)

Heraclius	1180—91	Robert of Nantes	1240—54
Aimery the Monk	1197—1202	James Pantaleon	1255—61
Soffred, cardinal of	1203	William II of Agen	1262—70
Sta Prassede		Thomas Agni of	1272—7
Albert of Vercelli, St	1205—14	Lentino	
Ralph of Merencourt	1215—24	Elias of Perigueux	1279—87/8
Gerold of Lausanne	1225—39	Nicholas of Hanapes	1288—91

IV. ORTHODOX PATRIARCHS OF ANTIOCH

John IV, the Oxite		Symeon II	1206—post 1239
	1088/91—1100	David	c1245—ante 1258
John V	1106—c1134	Euthymius I ante 1258—c1274	
Luke	1137/8—1156	Theodosius V of	
Soterichus Panteugenus		Villehardouin 1278—1283/4	
(patriarch elect)	1156—7	Arsenius	1283/4—6
Athanasius III	1157—70	Cyril III	1287—1308
Cyril II	c1173—9		
Theodore IV Balsamon			
ante 1189—post 1195			

V. ORTHODOX PATRIARCHS OF JERUSALEM

Symeon II	ante 1092—1099	Mark II Cataphlorus	
John VIII	floruit 1106/7		1189/90—post 1195
Sabas	floruit 1117/18	Euthymius	
Nicholas	c1122—c1156		died at Sinai in 1222
John IX	floruit 1157	Athanasius II	floruit 1235
Nicephorus II		Sophronius III	
ante 1166—post 1171			dates not known
Leontius II	1174/5—1184/5	Gregory I	
Dositheus I	ante 1187—1189		ante 1273—post 1285
		Thaddaeus	floruit 1296

VI. JACOBITE PATRIARCHS OF ANTIOCH

Athanasius VII	1090—1129	Michael I, the Syrian	1166—99
John XII	1130—7	Athanasius IX	1199—1207
Athanasius VIII	1138—66	John XIV	1208—20

VI. JACOBITE PATRIARCHS OF ANTIOCH (Continued)

Ignatius II	1222–52	Ignatius III	1264–82
Dionysius VII	1252–61	Ignatius IV Philoxenus	
John XV (concurrently)			1283–92
	1252–63		

VII. CATHOLICI OF ARMENIA

Gregory II, Vahram		Gregory V	1193–4
	1065–1105	Gregory VI	1194–1203
Basil I of Ani	1105–13	John VI of Sis	1203–21
Gregory III	1113–66	Constantine I	1221–67
Nerses IV, the Gracious, St		Jacob I	1267–86
	1166–73	Constantine II	1286–8
Gregory IV	1173–93	Stephen IV	1288–c1293

ABBREVIATIONS

AA SS	*Acta Sanctorum Bollandiana.*
AHR	*American Historical Review.*
Anon. 1234, 'HC'	*Anonymi Auctoris Chronicon ad Annum Christi 1234,* 'Historia Civilis'.
Anon. 1234, 'HE'	*Anonymi Auctoris Chronicon ad Annum Christi 1234,* 'Historia Ecclesiastica'.
AOL	*Archives de l'Orient latin.*
'ATS'	'Annales de Terre Sainte'.
Auvray	L. Auvray, ed, *Les Registres de Grégoire IX* . . .
BEFAR	*Bibliothèque des Ecoles françaises d'Athènes et de Rome.*
Berger	E. Berger, ed, *Les Registres d'Innocent IV* . . .
BHCTH	*Bulletin historique et philologique du Comité des travaux historiques et scientifiques.*
BIHR	*Bulletin of the Institute of Historical Research.*
BJRL	*Bulletin of the John Rylands Library.*
Bourel de la Roncière	C. Bourel de la Roncière, et al., ed, *Les Registres d'Alexandre IV* . . .
BZ	*Byzantinische Zeitschrift.*
CGOH	J. Delaville Le Roulx, ed, *Cartulaire général de l'Ordre des Hospitaliers.*
Charon	C. Charon, *Histoire des patriarcats melkites.*
CHJ	*Cambridge Historical Journal.*
CICO, I	*Pontificia Commissio ad redigendum codicem iuris canonici Orientalis, Fontes,* series III, vol I, *Acta Romanorum Pontificum a s. Clemente I . . . ad Coelestinum III* . . .
CICO, II	*Ibid., Acta Innocentii papae III.*
CICO, III	*Ibid., Acta Honorii III et Gregorii IX.*
CICO, IV (I)	*Ibid., Acta Innocentii papae IV.*
CICO, V (II)	*Ibid., Acta Romanorum Pontificum ab Innocentio V ad Benedictum XI.*
CMH	*Cambridge Medieval History.*
CSHB	*Corpus scriptorum historiae byzantinae.*
DACL	*Dictionnaire d'Archéologie chrétienne et de Liturgie.*
DDC	*Dictionnaire de Droit canonique.*
Delaborde	H-F. Delaborde, *Chartes . . . de Notre-Dame de Josaphat.*

DHGE	*Dictionnaire d'Histoire et de Géographie ecclésiastiques.*
DOP	*Dumbarton Oaks Papers.*
DTC	*Dictionnaire de Théologie catholique.*
EC	*Enciclopedia Cattolica*, ed P. Paschini *et al.*, 12 vols, 1949–54.
ECQ	*Eastern Churches Quarterly.*
ECR	*Eastern Churches Review.*
EHR	*English Historical Review.*
EO	*Echos d'Orient.*
Ernoul	*La chronique d'Ernoul* . . . , ed L. de Mas Latrie.
Eubel	C. Eubel, *et al., Hierarchia Catholica* . . .
Gay-Vitte	J. Gay, S. Vitte, ed, *Les Registres de Nicholas III* . . .
GC	*Gallia Christiana.*
Gestes	*Les Gestes des Chiprois*, ed G. Raynaud.
Grumel, Regestes	*Les Regestes . . . du Patriarcat de Constantinople.* I. *Les actes des patriarches*, ed V. Grumel, I, *381–715*, II, *715–1043*, III, *1043–1206.*
Guiraud	J. Guiraud, ed, *Les Registres d'Urbain IV* . . .
Guiraud-Cadier	J. Guiraud, L. Cadier, ed, *Les Registres de Grégoire X* . . .
Hefèle, Leclercq	C.J. Hefèle, ed and trans, H. Leclercq, *Histoire des Conciles* . . .
Huillard-Bréholles	J.L. Huillard-Bréholles, *Historia diplomatica Friderici Secundi.*
Imperiale	C. Imperiale di Sant'Angelo, *Codice diplomatico . . . di Genova.*
Jaffé-Wattenbach-Löwenfeld	P. Jaffé, *Regesta Pontificum Romanorum* . . . , ed W. Wattenbach, S. Löwenfeld, *et al.*
James of Vitry, *HO*	James of Vitry, *Historia Orientalis.*
Jordan	E. Jordan, ed, *Les Registres de Clément IV* . . .
Kohler	Ch. Kohler, 'Chartes de . . . Notre-Dame . . . de Josaphat'.
Langlois	E. Langlois, ed, *Les Registres de Nicholas IV* . . .
Laurent, Regestes	*Les Regestes des Actes du Patriarcat de Constantinople*, I. *Les actes des patriarches*, ed V. Laurent, IV, *1208–1309.*
Mansi	G.D. Mansi, *Sacrorum Conciliorum nova . . . collectio.*
MGH SS	*Monumenta Germaniae Historica, Scriptores.*
Michelant, Raynaud	H. Michelant, G. Raynaud, ed, *Itinéraires à Jérusalem.*
MS	Michael the Syrian, *Chronicle*, ed Chabot.

MSAF	*Mémoires de la Société nationale des Antiquaires de France.*
Müller	G. Müller, *Documenti sulle relazioni delle città toscane coll'Oriente cristiano* . . .
OCA	*Orientalia Christiana Analecta.*
OCP	*Orientalia Christiana Periodica.*
Olivier-Martin	F. Olivier-Martin, ed, *Les Registres de Martin IV.* . .
Paoli	S. Paoli, ed, *Codice diplomatico del . . . ordine gerosolimitano* . . .
Pflugck-Harttung	J. von Pflugck-Harttung, *Acta Pontificum . . . Inedita.*
PG	J.P. Migne, ed, *Patrologia Graeca.*
PL	J.P. Migne, ed, *Patrologia Latina.*
Potthast	A. Potthast, *Regesta Pontificum Romanorum* . . .
PPTS	*Palestine Pilgrims Texts Society.*
Pressutti	P. Pressutti, ed, *Regesta Honorii papae III.*
Prou	M. Prou, ed, *Les Registres d'Honorius IV* . . .
QFIAB	*Quellen und Forschungen aus italienischen Archiven und Bibliotheken.*
RHC	*Recueil des Historiens des Croisades.*
RHC Arm	*RHC, Documents Arméniens.*
RHC Lois	*RHC, Les Assises de Jérusalem.*
RHC Occ	*RHC, Historiens Occidentaux.*
RHC Or	*RHC, Historiens Orientaux.*
ROL	*Revue de l'Orient Latin.*
de Rozière	E. de Rozière, *Cartulaire de l'Eglise du Saint-Sépulchre de Jérusalem.*
RR	R. Röhricht, *Regesta Regni Hierosolymitani.*
RS	*Rolls Series.*
SCH	*Studies in Church History.*
Setton	K.M. Setton, gen ed, *A History of the Crusades.*
Strehlke	E. Strehlke, *Tabulae Ordinis Theutonici.*
Thomas-Faucon-Digard	A. Thomas, M. Faucon, C. Digard, R. Fawtier, ed, *Les Registres de Boniface VIII* . . .
Tobler, Molinier	T. Tobler, A. Molinier, *Itinera Hierosolymitana.*
TT	G.L.F. Tafel, G.M. Thomas, ed, *Urkunden zur älteren Handels- und Staatsgeschichte der Republik Venedig.*
Ughelli	F. Ughelli, *Italia Sacra* . . .
WT	William of Tyre, 'Historia rerum in partibus transmarinis gestarum'.

BIBLIOGRAPHY

I. SOURCES

A. General sources

Bongars, J., ed, *Gesta Dei per Francos*, 2 vols, Hanover 1611
Devic, Cl., Vaissète, J., *Histoire générale de Languedoc*, ed A. Molinier, 16 vols, Toulouse 1872–1915
Dölger, F., ed, *Regesten der Kaiserurkunden des östromischen Reiches, Corpus der grieschischen Urkunden des Mittelalters und der neueren Zeit*, Berlin 1924
Echard, J., Quetif, J., ed, *Scriptores Ordinis Praedicatorum*, 2 vols, Paris 1719–21
Gallia Christiana, ed the Benedictines of St Maur, Paris 1715–1865
Mansi, G.D., ed, *Sacrorum Conciliorum nova et amplissima collectio*, 31 vols, Florence and Venice 1759–98
Martène, E., Durand, U., ed, *Thesaurus Novus Anecdotorum*, 5 vols, Paris 1717
— *Veterum Scriptorum et Monumentorum amplissima Collectio*, 9 vols, Paris 1724–33
Raynaldus, O., *Annales Ecclesiastici ab anno quo desinit Card. C. Baronius MCXCVIII usque ad annum MDXXXIV continuati*, vols 13–21, Colonia Agrippina 1694–1727
Les Regestes des Actes du Patriarcat de Constantinople, I. *Les Actes des Patriarches*, ed V. Grumel, I. *381–715*; II. *715–1043*; III. *1043–1206*; ed V. Laurent, IV. *1208–1309*, Paris 1932–71
Röhricht, R., ed, *Regesta Regni Hierosolymitani (MXCVII–MCCXCI)*, 2 vols, Oeniponti 1893–1904
Ughelli, F., *Italia Sacra*, 10 vols, Venice 1717–22

B. Chronicles and biographies

Abu-l-Fida, 'Annals' (extracts with French trans), *RHC Or*, I
Alberic of Trois Fontaines, 'Chronica a monacho novi monasterii Hoiensis interpolata', *MGH SS*, XXIII
Albert of Aix, 'Historia Hierosolymitana', *RHC Occ*, IV
Anna Comnena, *Alexiad*, ed with French trans B. Leib, 3 vols, Paris 1937–45
'Annales de Terre Sainte', ed R. Röhricht, *AOL*, II
Anonymi Auctoris Chronicon ad Annum Christi 1234 pertinens (comprising 'Historia Ecclesiastica' and 'Historia Civilis'), ed J.B. Chabot, *Corpus Scriptorum Christianorum Orientalium, Scriptores Syri*, ser III, 14, 15, Paris 1926, trans A. Abouna, introduction, notes and index J.M. Fiey, *ibid.*, 154, Louvain 1974
Baha ad-Din, *Life of Saladin*, trans C.R. Conder, *PPTS*, London 1897
Bar Hebraeus, *Chronicon Ecclesiasticum*, ed with Latin trans J.B. Abbeloos, T.J. Lamy, 2 vols, Louvain 1872–7
— *The Chronography*, ed and trans E.A. Wallis Budge, 2 vols, Oxford 1932

Bernold of St Blaise, 'Chronicon', *MGH SS*, V
Caffaro, *Annali Genovesi di Caffaro e de' suoi continuatori*, ed L.T. Belgrano, C. Imperiale di Sant' Angelo, *Fonti per la Storia d'Italia*, 5 vols, Rome 1890–1929
Choniates, Nicetas, *Historia*, ed J.A. Van Dieten, *Corpus Fontium Historiae Byzantinae*, 11 (I, II), Berlin 1975
The Chronicle of Lanercost, trans H. Maxwell, Glasgow 1913
The Chronicle of the Reigns of Henry II and Richard I, ed W. Stubbs, *RS*, 49 (I, II), London 1867. Published as the Chronicle of Benedict of Peterborough
'Chronique de Terre Sainte', see *Gestes des Chiprois*
Cinnamus, John, *Epitome rerum ab Ioanne et Alexio Comnenis gestarum*, ed A. Meineke, *CSHB*, Bonn 1836
Eracles. 'L'Estoire d'Eracles empereur et la conqueste de la Terre d'Outremer', *RHC Occ*, I, II
Ernoul. *La Chronique d'Ernoul et de Bernard le Trésorier*, ed L. de Mas Latrie, Paris 1871
FitzStephen, William, 'Vita S. Thomae', ed J.C. Robertson, *Materials for the History of Thomas Becket*, *RS*, 67 (I–VII), London 1875–85, vol III
Fulcher of Chartres, *Gesta Francorum Iherusalem peregrinantium*, ed H. Hagenmeyer, Heidelberg 1913
Geoffrey of Villehardouin, *La conquête de Constantinople*, ed E. Faral, 2 vols, Paris 1938–9
Gesta Francorum et aliorum Hierosolimitanorum, ed and trans R. Hill, London 1962
Les Gestes des Chiprois, ed G. Raynaud, *Société de l'Orient latin, ser historique*, 5, Geneva 1887, containing 'Chronique de Terre Sainte', 'Mémoires de Philippe de Novare', 'Chronique du Templier de Tyr'
Gregory the Priest, 'Continuation of the Chronicle of Matthew of Edessa', with French trans, *RHC Arm*, I
Guibert of Nogent, 'Historia quae dicitur Gesta Dei per Francos', *RHC Occ*, IV
Guiragos of Kantzag, 'History of Armenia', with French trans, *RHC Arm*, I
'Historia Belli Sacri', *RHC Occ*, III
'Historia Pontificalis', *MGH SS*, XX
Ibn al-Athir, 'Sum of World History', extracts with French trans, *RHC Or*, I
Ibn Khallikan, 'The Life of the Sultan Saladin', extracts with French trans, *RHC Or*, III
Ibn al-Qalanisi, *Chronicle*. Extract trans H.A.R. Gibb, *The Damascus Chronicle of the Crusades*, London 1932
al-Isfahani, Imad ad-Din, *La Conquête de la Syrie et de la Palestine par Saladin*, French trans H. Massé, Paris 1972
Itinerarium Peregrinorum et Gesta Regis Ricardi, ed W. Stubbs, *RS*, 38 (I), London 1864
James of Vitry, *Iacobi de Vitriaco libri duo, quorum prior Orientalis sive Hierosolimitanae, alter Occidentalis Historiae nomine inscribuntur*, Douai 1597, reprinted Gregg International Publishers, Farnborough 1971
John Dardel, 'Chronique d'Arménie', *RHC Arm*, II
John of Joinville, *Histoire de Saint Louis*, ed N. de Wailly, Paris 1868
Kamal-ad-Din, 'History of Aleppo', extracts in French trans, E. Blochet, *ROL*, 3–6, 1895–8
Matthew of Edessa, 'Chronicle', extracts with French trans, *RHC Arm*, I
Matthew Paris, *Chronica Maiora*, ed H.R. Luard, *RS*, 57 (I–VII), London 1872–83

Michael the Syrian, *Chronicle*, ed with French trans J.B. Chabot, 4 vols, Paris 1899—1924

Odo of Deuil, *De Profectione Ludovici VII in Orientem*, ed and trans V.G. Berry, New York 1948

Oliver of Paderborn, 'Historia Damiatina', ed H. Hoogeweg, *Die Schriften des Kölner Domscholasters, späteren Bischofs von Paderborn und Kardinalbishofs von S. Sabina, Oliverus, Bibliothek des literarischen Vereins in Stuttgart*, 202, Tübingen 1894

Orderic Vitalis, *The Ecclesiastical History*, ed and trans M. Chibnall, vols 2—6, Oxford 1969—78

Otto of Freising, 'Chronica, sive historia de duabus civitatibus', ed A. Hofmeister, *MGH SS rerum Germanicarum in usum scholarum separatim editae*, Hanover, Leipzig 1912

Pachymeres, George, *De Michaele et Andronico Palaeologis Libri Tredecim*, ed I. Becker, 2 vols, *CSHB*, Bonn 1835

Peter Tudebode, *Historia de Hierosolymitano Itinere*, ed and trans J.H. and L.L. Hill, *Documents relatifs à l'histoire des Croisades publiés par l'Académie des Inscriptions et Belles-Lettres*, 12, Paris 1977

Peter des Vaux-de-Cernay, *Histoire Albigeoise*, French trans P. Guébin, H. Maisonneuve, Paris 1951

Philip of Novara, 'Mémoires', see *Gestes des Chiprois*

Ralph of Caen, 'Gesta Tancredi in Expeditione Hierosolimitana', *RHC Occ*, III

Ralph of Coggeshall, *Chronicon Anglicanum*, ed J. Stevenson, *RS*, 66, London 1875

Raymond of Aguilers, *Le 'Liber' de Raymond d'Aguilers*, ed J.H. and L.L. Hill, *Documents relatifs à l'histoire des Croisades publiés par l'Académie des Inscriptions et Belles-Lettres*, 9, Paris 1969

Renaudot, E, *Historia Patriarcharum Alexandrinorum Jacobitarum*, Paris 1713

Robert of Torigni, 'Chronicle', in *Chronicles of the Reigns of Stephen, Henry II and Richard I*, ed R. Howlett, *RS*, 82 (IV), London 1889

Roger of Houedene, *Chronica*, ed W. Stubbs, *RS*, 51 (I—IV), London 1868—71

Roger of Wendover, *Chronica, sive flores historiarum*, ed H.G. Hewlett, *RS*, 84 (I—III), London 1886—9

Samuel of Ani, 'Chronography', extracts with French trans, *RHC Arm*, I

Sempad the Constable, 'Chronicle of the Kingdom of Little Armenia', with French trans, *RHC Arm*, I

Templar of Tyre, 'La Chronique du Templier de Tyr (1242—1309)', see *Gestes des Chiprois*

Wallis Budge, E.A., trans, *The Monks of Kublai Khan . . . or the History of Rabban Sauma, envoy . . . of the Mongol Khans to the Kings of Europe*, London 1928

Walter the Chancellor, 'De Bello Antiocheno', *RHC Occ*, V

William of Malmesbury, *Gesta Regum Anglorum*, ed W. Stubbs, *RS*, 90 (I, II), London 1889

William of Tyre, 'Historia rerum in partibus transmarinis gestarum', *RHC Occ*, I

— R.B.C. Huygens, 'Guillaume de Tyr étudiant. Un chapître (XIX, 12) de son "Histoire" retrouvé', *Latomus*, 21, 1962

C. Documents

'Actà Concilii Sisensis Armeni', Mansi, XXV, 133–48
Aguado de Cordova, A.F., Aleman de Rosales, A.A., Agurleta, I.L., eds, *Bullarium Equestris Ordinis S. Iacobi de Spatha*, Madrid 1719
Marquis d'Albon, ed, *Cartulaire général de l'Ordre du Temple, 1119?–1150*, one volume, Paris 1913
Benechewitch, V., ed, *Catalogus Codicum Manuscriptorum Graecorum qui in Monasterio Sanctae Catherinae in Monte Sinai asservantur*, St Petersburg 1911. Commentary in Russian
de Broussillon, B., 'La charte d'André II de Vitré et le siège de Karak en 1184', *BHCTH*, Paris 1899
—   *La Maison de Craon, 1050–1480*, 2 vols, Paris 1893
Chalandon, F., 'Un diplôme inédit d'Amaury I, roi de Jérusalem, en faveur de l'abbaye du Temple-Notre-Seigneur', *ROL*, 8, 1900–1
Codice Diplomatico Barese, publ. della Società di Storia patria per la Puglia, 18 vols, Bari 1897–1950
Cusa, S., ed, *I Diplomi greci ed arabi di Sicilia*, I, in two parts, Palermo 1882
Delaborde, H-F., ed, *Chartes de la Terre Sainte provenant de l'abbaye de Notre-Dame de Josaphat, BEFAR*, 19, Paris 1880
—   'Lettre des Chrétiens de Terre Sainte à Charles d'Anjou (22 avril 1260)', *ROL*, 2, 1894
Delaville Le Roulx, J., *Les Archives, la Bibliothèque et le Trésor de l'Ordre de St Jean de Jérusalem à Malte, BEFAR*, 32, Paris 1883
—   ed, *Cartulaire général de l'Ordre des Hospitaliers de St Jean de Jérusalem (1100–1310)*, 4 vols, Paris 1894–1906
—   'Chartes de Terre Sainte', *ROL*, 11, 1905–8
—   'Inventaire des pièces de Terre Sainte de l'Ordre de l'Hôpital', *ROL*, 3, 1895
—   'Titres de l'Hôpital des Bretons à Acre', *ROL*, 1, 1893
Hagenmeyer, H., ed, *Die Kreuzzugsbriefe aus den Jahren 1088–1100*, Innsbruck 1901
Hiestand, R., Mayer, H.E., 'Die Nachfolge des Patriarchen Monachus von Jerusalem', *Basler Zeitschrift für Geschichte und Altertumskunde*, 74, 1974
Holtzmann, W., 'Papst-Kaiser-und Normannenurkunden aus Unteritalien', *QFIAB*, 35, 1955
Huillard-Bréholles, J.L., ed, *Historia diplomatica Friderici Secundi*, 6 vols in 12, Paris 1852–61
Imperiale di Sant' Angelo, C., ed, *Codice diplomatico della Repubblica di Genova*, 3 vols, *Fonti per la Storia d'Italia*, Rome 1936–42
Kohler, Ch., 'Chartes de l'abbaye de Notre-Dame de la Vallée de Josaphat en Terre Sainte (1108–1291). Analyses et extraits', *ROL*, 7, 1899
Lamonte, J.L., 'A Register of the Cartulary of the Cathedral of Sancta Sophia of Nicosia', *Byzantion*, 5, 1929–30
de Marsy, A., 'Fragment d'un cartulaire de l'Ordre de Saint-Lazare en Terre Sainte', *AOL*, II
de Mas Latrie, L., ed, *Documents nouveaux servant de preuves à l'histoire de l'Ile de Chypre sous la règne des Princes de la Maison de Lusignan, Collection des documents inédits sur l'histoire de France, Mélanges historiques: choix de documents*, IV, Paris 1882
—   *Histoire de l'Ile de Chypre sous le Règne des Princes de la Maison de Lusignan*, 3 vols, Paris 1852–61
Mayer, H.E., 'Sankt Samuel auf dem Freudenberge und sein besitz nach einem unbekannten diplom König Balduins V', *QFIAB*, 44, 1964

Müller, G., ed, *Documenti sulle relazioni delle città toscane coll' Oriente cristiano e coi Turchi fino all'anno 1531, Documenti degli archivi toscani*, 3, Florence 1879

Nitti di Vito, F., ed, *Le pergamene di Barletta, Archivio Capitolare (897– 1285)*, vol 8 of *Codice Diplomatico Barese*, (q.v.)

Paoli, S., ed, *Codice diplomatico del sacro militare ordine gerosolimitano, oggi di Malta*, 2 vols, Lucca 1733–7

Petit, E., 'Chartes de l'abbaye cistercienne de Saint-Serge de Giblet en Syrie', *MSAF*, ser 5, 8, 1887

von Pettenegg, E.G., ed, *Die Urkunden des deutsch-Ordens-centralarchives zu Wien in Regestenform*, Prague, Leipzig 1887

Prologo, A. di G., *Le carte che si conservano nell'Archivio del Capitolo metropolitano della città di Trani dal IX secolo fino all'anno 1266*, Barletta 1877

Rey, E., 'Chartes de l'Abbaye du Mont-Sion', *MSAF*, ser 5, 8, 1887

—   *Recherches géographiques et historiques sur la domination des Latins en Orient*, Paris 1877

Riant, P., *Etudes sur l'histoire de l'Eglise de Bethléem: I. L'Eglise de Bethléem et Varazze en Ligurie. II. Eclaircissements sur quelques points de l'histoire de l'Eglise de Bethléem-Ascalon*, (published from the author's notes by Ch. Kohler), Genoa 1889, Paris 1896

—   'Indulgences octroyées par Galérand, évêque de Béryte, ambassadeur de Terre Sainte en Angleterre', *AOL*, I

—   'Six lettres relatives aux croisades', *AOL*, I

Richard, J., 'Le chartrier de Sainte-Marie-Latine et l'établissement de Raymond de Saint-Gilles à Mont Pèlerin', *Mélanges d'histoire du Moyen âge dediés à la mémoire de Louis Halphen*, Paris 1951, reprinted in Richard, *Orient et Occident*, no VI, (q.v.)

—   'Quelques textes sur les premiers temps de l'Eglise latine de Jérusalem', *Mémoires et documents publiés par la Société de l'Ecole de Chartes*, 12, *Recueil de Travaux offerts à M. Clovis Brunel*, II, Paris 1955, reprinted in Richard, *Orient et Occident*, no VII, (q.v.)

Riley-Smith, J., 'The Templars and the castle of Tortosa in Syria: an unknown document concerning the acquisition of the fortress', *EHR*, 84, 1969

de Rozière, E., ed, *Cartulaire de l'Eglise du Saint-Sépulcre de Jérusalem, Collection des documents inédits sur l'histoire de France*, ser 1, 5, Paris 1849

Santerano, S., ed, *Il Codice diplomatico Barlettano*, Barletta 1924

Strehlke, E., ed, *Tabulae Ordinis Theutonici*, Berlin 1869

Tafel, G.L.F., Thomas, G.M., eds, *Urkunden zur älteren Handels-und Staatsgeschichte der Republik Venedig mit besonderer Beziehung auf Byzanz und die Levante, Fontes rerum Austriacarum*, section III, 12–14, Vienna 1856–7

Zarncke, F., 'Der Priester Johannes', *Abhandlungen der philologisch-historischen Classe der k. sächsischen Gesellschaft der Wissenschaften*, 7, 1879, 8, 1883

Zimmerman, B., *Monumenta Historica Carmelitana*, one volume, Lirinae 1905

D.   *Papal sources*

Alexander III, pope, 'Epistolae', *PL*, 200

Alexander IV, pope, *Les Registres d'Alexandre IV*, ed C. Bourel de la Roncière, J. de Loye, P. de Cenival, A. Coulon, *BEFAR*, ser 2, 2, vols,

Paris 1902—31

Boniface VIII, pope, *Les Registres de Boniface VIII*, ed A. Thomas, M. Faucon, G. Digard, R. Fawtier, *BEFAR*, ser 2, 4 vols, Paris 1884—1939

Calixtus II, pope, 'Epistolae', *PL*, 163

Celestine III, pope, 'Epistolae', *PL*, 206

Clement IV, pope, *Les Registres de Clément IV*, ed E. Jordan, *BEFAR*, ser 2, Paris 1893—1945

Fabre, P., Duchesne, L., Mollat, G., eds, *Le Liber Censuum de l'Eglise Romaine*, 3 vols, Paris 1910—52

Gregory VII, pope, *Das Register Gregors VII*, ed E. Caspar, 2 vols, Berlin 1955, *Epistolae selectae in usum scholarum ex MGH separatim editae*

Gregory IX, pope, *Les Registres de Grégoire IX*, ed L. Auvray, *BEFAR*, ser 2, 3 vols, Paris 1896—1955

Gregory X, pope, *Les registres de Grégoire X et Jean XXI*, ed J. Guiraud, L. Cadier, *BEFAR*, ser 2, Paris 1892—1906

Hiestand, R., ed, *Papsturkunden für Templer und Johanniter, Abhandlungen der Akademie der Wissenschaften in Göttingen, Philologisch-Historische Klasse, Dritte Folge*, 77, Göttingen 1972

Hofman, G., 'Lettere pontificie edite ed inedite intorno ai monasteri del Monte Sinai', *OCP*, 17, 1951

Honorius III, pope, *Regesta Honorii papae III*, ed P. Pressutti, 2 vols, Rome 1888—95

Honorius IV, pope, *Les Registres d'Honorius IV*, ed M. Prou, *BEFAR*, ser 2, Paris 1888

Innocent III, pope, 'Regesta', *PL*, 214—17

Innocent IV, pope, *Les Registres d'Innocent IV*, ed E. Berger, *BEFAR*, ser 2, 4 vols, Paris 1884—1921

Jaffé, P., Wattenbach, W., Löwenfeld, S., Kaltenbrunner, P., Ewald, P., eds, *Regesta Pontificum Romanorum a condita Ecclesia ad annum . . . 1198*, 2 vols, Leipzig 1881—8

Lucius III, pope, 'Epistolae', *PL*, 201

Martin IV, pope, *Les Registres de Martin IV*, ed F. Olivier Martin, *BEFAR*, ser 2, Paris 1901—35

Nicholas III, pope, *Les Registres de Nicholas III*, ed J. Gay, S. Vitte, *BEFAR*, ser 2, Paris 1898—1938

Nicholas IV, pope, *Les Registres de Nicholas IV*, ed E. Langlois, *BEFAR*, ser 2, 4 vols, Paris 1886—93

Paschal II, pope, 'Epistolae', *PL*, 163

von Pflugck-Harttung, J., ed, *Acta Pontificum Romanorum Inedita*, 3 vols, Tübingen, Stuttgart 1881—6

Pontificia Commissio ad redigendum Codicem Iuris Canonici Orientalis: Fontes, ser 3,

    I.   *Acta Romanorum Pontificum a S. Clemente I (an. c 90) ad Coelestinum III (1198)*, Vatican City 1943

    II.   *Acta Innocentii papae III (1198—1216)*, ed T. Haluscynski, Vatican City 1944

    III. *Acta Honorii III et Gregorii IX (1216—41)*, ed A.L. Tăutu, Vatican City 1950

    IV(I).*Acta Innocentii papae IV (1243—54)*, ed T. Haluscynski, M.M. Wojnar, Rome 1966

    V(II).*Acta Romanorum Pontificum ab Innocentio V ad Benedictum XI (1276—1304)*, ed F.M. Delorme, A.L. Tăutu, Vatican City 1954

Potthast, A., ed, *Regesta Pontificum Romanorum . . . ab a. 1198 ad a. 1304*, 2 vols, Berlin 1873—5

Urban IV, pope, *Les Registres d'Urbain IV*, ed J. Guiraud, 4 vols, *BEFAR*, ser 2, Paris 1901—29

E. Travel and pilgrimage sources

Benjamin of Tudela, *Itinerary*, ed and trans M.N. Adler, London 1907
Burchard of Mount Sion, A.D. 1280, trans A. Stewart, *PPTS*, London 1896
Daniel, Russian abbot, *The pilgrimage of the Russian Abbot Daniel in the Holy Land*, trans C.W. Wilson, *PPTS*, London 1888
—   'Vie et pèlerinage de Daniel, hégoumène russe, 1106—1107', trans B. de Khitrowo, *Itinéraires russes en Orient*, I (I), *Publications de la Société de l'Orient Latin, Série géographique*, 5, Geneva 1889
Dawson, C., gen ed, *The Mongol Mission*, trans by a religious of Stanbrook, London 1955
Fetellus, circa 1130 A.D., trans J.R. MacPherson, *PPTS*, London 1892
Ibn Jubair, *The Travels*, trans R.J.C. Broadhurst, London 1952
John Phocas, *The pilgrimage of John Phocas to the Holy Land in the year 1185 A.D.*, trans A. Stewart, *PPTS*, London 1889
John of Würzburg, *Description of the Holy Land by John of Würzburg, A.D. 1160—1170*, trans C.W. Wilson, *PPTS*, London 1890
Michelant, H., Raynaud, G., eds, *Itinéraires à Jérusalem, Publications de la Société de l'Orient Latin, Série géographique*, 3, Paris 1882
Saewulf's pilgrimage to Jerusalem and the Holy Land, trans W.R. Brownlow, *PPTS*, London 1892
Theoderich's description of the Holy Places, circa 1172 A.D., trans A. Stewart, *PPTS*, London 1891
Tobler, T., Molinier, A., eds, *Itinera Hierosolymitana*, 2 vols, *Publications de la Société de l'Orient Latin, Série géographique*, 1, 2, Geneva 1879—80
William of Rubruck, *The Journey of William of Rubruck to the Eastern Parts of the World, 1253—5, with two accounts of the earlier journey of John of Pian de Carpine*, trans W.W. Rockhill, *Hakluyt Society*, ser 2, 4, London 1900

F. Miscellaneous sources

Balsamon, Theodore, 'Responsa ad Interrogationes Marci', *PG*, 138
Basil, Armenian doctor, 'Funeral Oration of Baldwin, Count of Marash', with French trans, *RHC Arm*, I
Bernard of Clairvaux, St, 'Epistolae', *PL*, 182
Brightman, F.E., Hammond, C.E., eds, *Liturgies Eastern and Western*, one volume, Oxford 1896
Canivez, J.-M., ed, *Statuta Capitulorum Generalium Ordinis Cisterciensis*, 6 vols, London 1933—
Golubovich, G., 'Disputatio Latinorum et Graecorum seu relatio apocrisarium Gregorii IX de gestis Nicaeae in Bithynia et Nymphaeae in Lydia, 1234', *Archivum Franciscanum Historicum*, 12, 1919
James of Vitry, *Lettres de Jacques de Vitry (1160/70—1240), évêque de Saint-Jean d'Acre*, ed R.B.C. Huygens, Leiden 1960
John of Ibelin, 'Livre', *RHC Lois*, I
Monachus of Florence, bishop of Acre, 'De Recuperatione Ptolemaide Liber', ed W. Stubbs, in Roger of Houedene, *Chronicle*, III, pp cv—cxxxvi
'Narrative of the Conference held between the doctor Mekhitar of Dashir, envoy of the Catholicus Constantine I, and the Pope's Legate at St Jean d'Acre', with French trans, *RHC Arm*, I

Nerses of Lampron, St, 'Letter to Leo II', with French trans, *RHC Arm*, I
— 'Reflections on the Institutions of the Church and Explanation of the Eucharistic Mystery', extracts with French trans, *RHC Arm*, I
Sanudo, Marino, 'Liber Secretorum Fidelium Crucis', ed J. Bongars, *Gesta Dei per Francos*, II (q.v.)
Sathas, C., *Bibliotheca Graeca Medii Aevi*, 7 vols, Venice, Paris 1872—94
Schlumberger, G., Chalandon, F., Blanchet, A., *Sigillographie de l'Orient Latin*, Paris 1943
Van Waefelghem, R., ed, *L'Obituaire de l'Abbaye de Prémontré*, Louvain 1913
'Versus de viris illustribus diocesis Tarvanensis, qui in sacra fuere expeditione', Martène, Durand, *Vet. SS.*, V, 539—40
de Vogüé, M., 'Achard d'Arrouaise, poème sur le *Templum Domini*', *AOL*, I
Wyngaert, A. van den, *Sinica Franciscana*, one vol, Quaracchi, Firenze 1929

II. SECONDARY WORKS

Abel, F.M., 'Le couvent des frères prêcheurs à Saint-Jean d'Acre', *Revue Biblique*, 43, 1934
Backmund, N., *Monasticon Praemonstratense*, 3 vols, Straubing 1949—56
Baldwin, M.W., 'Ecclesiastical developments in the Twelfth-Century Crusaders' State of Tripoli', *Catholic Historical Review*, 22, 1936
— 'The Latin States under Baldwin III and Amalric, 1143—1174', in Setton, II, (q.v.)
Barber, M.C., 'The Origins of the Order of the Temple', *Studia Monastica*, 12, 1970
Basmadjian, K.J., 'Chronologie de l'histoire d'Arménie', *Revue de l'Orient Chrétien*, ser 2, 19, 1914
Benvenisti, M., *The Crusaders in the Holy Land*, Jerusalem 1972
Boase, T.S.R., ed, *The Cilician Kingdom of Armenia*, Edinburgh 1978
— 'Ecclesiastical Art in the Crusader States in Palestine and Syria', in Setton, IV, (q.v.)
Boyle, J.A., 'Dynastic and Political History of the Il-Khans', in *Cambridge History of Iran*, V. *The Saljuk and Mongol Periods*, ed J.A. Boyle, Cambridge 1968
Brand, C.M., *Byzantium confronts the West, 1180—1204*, Cambridge, Mass. 1968
Bréhier, L., *L'Eglise et l'Orient au Moyen Age: les Croisades*, Paris 1928
Brincken, A-D.V. den, *Die 'Nationes Christianorum Orientalium' in Verständnis der lateinischen Historiographie*, *Kölnes Historische Abhandlungen*, 22, Cologne, Vienna 1973
Brundage, J.A., 'Adhémar of Puy: the bishop and his critics', *Speculum*, 34, 1959
Buchthal, H., *Miniature Painting in the Latin Kingdom of Jerusalem*, (with liturgical and palaeographical chapters by F. Wormald), Oxford 1957
Cahen, C., 'Indigènes et Croisés', *Syria*, 15, 1934
— *Pre-Ottoman Turkey*, English trans, London 1968
— *La Syrie du nord à l'époque des Croisades et la principauté franque d'Antioche*, Paris 1940
Chalandon, F., *Les Comnènes: Jean II Comnène (1118—1143) et Manuel I Comnène (1143—1180)*, 2 vols, Paris 1912
— *Histoire de la domination normande en Italie et en Sicile*, 2 vols, Paris 1907

Charon, C., *Histoire des patriarcats melkites*, 3 vols, Rome 1909–11

Cheikho, L., 'Les archevêques du Sinai', *Mélanges de la Faculté Orientale de l'Université Saint-Joseph, Beyrouth*, 2, 1907

Clapham, A.W., 'The Latin Monastic Buildings of the Church of the Holy Sepulchre, Jerusalem', *Antiquaries Journal*, I, 1921

Constable, G., *Monastic Tithes, from their Origin to the Twelfth Century*, Cambridge 1964

Constantelos, D.J., *Byzantine Philanthropy and Social Welfare*, New Brunswick 1968

Couäsnon, C., *The Church of the Holy Sepulchre in Jerusalem*, London 1974

Crawford, R.W., 'William of Tyre and the Maronites', *Speculum*, 30, 1955

Daux, C., 'L'Orient Latin censitaire du Saint-Siège', *Revue de l'Orient Chrétien*, 10, 1905

Delaville Le Roulx, J., 'L'Ordre de Mountjoye', *ROL*, 1, 1893

Der Nersessian, S., 'The Kingdom of Cilician Armenia', in Setton, II, (q.v.)

Deschamps, P., *Les Châteaux des Croisés en Terre Sainte*: I. *Le Crac des Chevaliers*. II. *La défense du royaume de Jérusalem*, 2 vols, Paris 1934–9

— *Terre Sainte Romane*, Paris 1964

Devréesse, R., *Le Patriarcat d'Antioche depuis la paix de l'Eglise jusqu'à la conquête arabe*, Paris 1945

Dib, P., 'Maronites', *DTC*, X (I)

Dichter, B., *The Orders and Churches of Crusader Acre*, Acre 1979

Dickinson, J.C., *The Origins of the Austin Canons and their Introduction into England*, London 1950

Donovan, J.P., *Pelagius and the Fifth Crusade*, Philadelphia 1950

Ducange, C. du Fresne, *Les Familles d'Outremer*, ed E.G. Rey, Paris 1869

Dussaud, R., *Topographie historique de la Syrie antique et mediévale*, Paris 1927

Dvornik, F., 'Constantinople and Rome', in J.M. Hussey, ed, *CMH*, IV (I) (q.v.)

Edbury, P.W., Rowe, J.G., 'William of Tyre and the Patriarchal Election of 1180', *EHR*, 93, 1978

Enlart, C., *Les Monuments des Croisés dans le Royaume de Jérusalem, Architecture religieuse et civile*, 2 vols, Paris 1925–8

Erdmann, C., *The Origin of the Idea of Crusade*, trans with additional notes, M.W. Baldwin, W. Goffart, Princeton 1977

Eubel, C., *et al.*, eds, *Hierarchia Catholica Medii et Recentioris Aevi*, 6 vols, Monasterii 1913–35, Patavii 1952–8

Every, G., *The Byzantine Patriarchate*, 2nd edn, London 1962

— 'Syrian Christians in Jerusalem, 1183–1283', *ECQ*, 7, 1947

— 'Syrian Christians in Palestine in the Middle Ages', *ECQ*, 6, 1945–6

Fedalto, P., *La Chiesa Latina in Oriente*. I. *La Chiesa Latina in Oriente*. II. *Hierarchia Latina Orientalis*. III. *Documenti Veneziani*. 3 vols, *Studi Religiosi*, 3, Verona, 1973–8

Foreville, R., 'Un chef de la première Croisade: Arnoul Malecouronne', *BHCTH*, Paris 1954–5

Forey, A., *The Templars in the Corona de Aragón*, London 1973

Forsyth, G.H., Weitzmann, K., *The Monastery of Saint Catherine at Mount Sinai: the Church and Fortress of Justinian*, Ann Arbor 1965

Frazee, C., 'The Maronite Middle Ages', *ECR*, 10, 1978

Funk, P., *Jakob von Vitry. Leben und Werke*, Berlin 1909

Furber, E.C., 'The Kingdom of Cyprus, 1191–1291', in Setton, II, (q.v.)

Gentile, M.L., 'Daiberto', *Enciclopedia Italiana*, XII, Rome 1949

Ghobaïra al-Ghaziri, B., *Rome et l'Eglise Syrienne-Maronite d'Antioche, 517–1531. Thèses, documents, lettres*, Beirut 1906

Gibb, H.A.R., 'The Aiyubids', in Setton, II, (q.v.)
— 'Zengi and the Fall of Edessa', in Setton, II, (q.v.)

Gill, J., *Byzantium and the Papacy, 1198–1400*, New Brunswick 1979
— *The Council of Florence*, Cambridge 1961

Golubovich, G., *Biblioteca bio-bibliografica della Terra Santa e dell'Oriente francescano*, 5 vols, Quaracchi presso Firenze, 1906–27

Grabar, A., *Byzantium. Byzantine Art in the Middle Ages*, London 1966

Grumel, V., 'Les Patriarches Grecs d'Antioche du nom de Jean (XIe et XIIe siècles)', *EO*, 32, 1933
— 'Notes pour l'*Oriens Christianus*', *EO*, 33, 1934
— *Traité d'Etudes Byzantines. I. La Chronologie*, Paris 1958

Hackett, J., *A History of the Orthodox Church of Cyprus*, London 1901

Hagenmeyer, H., *Chronologie de la première Croisade (1094–1100)*, Paris 1902

Hamilton, B., 'The Armenian Church and the Papacy at the time of the Crusades', *ECR*, 10, 1978, reprinted in Hamilton, *Monastic Reform*, no XII, (q.v.)
— 'The Cistercians in the Crusader States', in M.B. Pennington ed, *One Yet Two. Monastic Tradition East and West, Cistercian Studies*, 29, Kalamazoo 1976, reprinted in Hamilton, *Monastic Reform*, no X, (q.v.)
— 'The elephant of Christ: Reynald of Châtillon', *SCH*, 15, 1978, reprinted in Hamilton, *Monastic Reform*, no XIII, (q.v.)
— *Monastic Reform, Catharism and the Crusades, (900–1300)*, London 1979
— 'Rebuilding Zion: the Holy Places of Jerusalem in the Twelfth Century', *SCH*, 14, 1977, reprinted in Hamilton, *Monastic Reform*, no XI, (q.v.)
— 'Women in the Crusader States: the Queens of Jerusalem', in D. Baker, ed, *Medieval Women*, Oxford 1978

Hardwicke, M., 'The Crusader States, 1192–1243', in Setton, II, (q.v.)

Harvey, W., *Structural Survey of the Church of the Holy Nativity, Bethlehem*, Oxford 1935

Hefèle, C.J., ed with French trans, Leclercq, H., *Histoire des Conciles*, Paris 1907–

Hiestand, R., 'Zum Leben und Laufbahn Wilhelms von Tyrus', *Deutsches Archiv für Erforschung des Mittelalters*, 34, 1978

Hill, G., *A History of Cyprus*, 4 vols, Cambridge 1940–52

Hintlian, K., *History of the Armenians in the Holy Land*, Jerusalem 1976

Hodgson, M.G.S., *The Order of Assassins*, The Hague 1955

Holt, P.M., ed, *The Eastern Mediterranean Lands in the period of the Crusades*, Warminster 1977

Holtzmann, W., 'Die Unionsverhandlung zwischen Kaiser Alexios I und Papst Urban II im Jahre 1089', *BZ*, 28, 1928

Hotzelt, W., *Kirchengeschichte Palästinas im Zeitalter der Kreuzzuge, 1099-1291*, Cologne 1940

Hrbek, I., 'Egypt, Nubia and the Eastern Desert', in *Cambridge History of Africa*, III

Hussey, J.M., 'Byzantium and the Crusades, 1081–1204', in Setton, II, (q.v.)
— ed, *Cambridge Medieval History*, IV, *The Byzantine Empire*, part I. *Byzantium and its Neighbours*, Cambridge 1966

Janauschek, L., *Originum Cisterciensium*, one vol, Vienna 1877

Janin, R., 'Géorgie', *DTC*, VI (I)

Johnson, E.N., 'The Crusades of Frederick Barbarossa and Henry VI', in Setton, II, (q.v.)

Jordan, E., 'La politique ecclésiastique de Roger I et les origines de la légation sicilienne', *Le Moyen Age*, ser 2, 24, 1922, 25, 1924

Jugie, M., 'Monophysite. (Eglise Copte)', *DTC*, X (II)

Karalevskij, C., 'Antioche', *DHGE*, III

Khoury, P., *Paul d'Antioche, évêque melkite de Sidon (XIIe s)*, Beirut 1965

Knowles, D., *From Pachomius to Ignatius*, Oxford 1966

Kohler, Ch., 'Un rituel et un bréviaire du Saint-Sépulcre de Jérusalem (XIIe − XIIIe siècle)', in *Mélanges pour servir à l'histoire de l'Orient Latin*, Paris 1900

Krey, A.C., 'Urban's Crusade, success or failure?', *AHR*, 53, 1948

Lamma, P., *Comneni e Staufer. Ricerche sui rapporti fra Bisancio e l'Occidente nel secolo XII*, 2 vols, Rome 1955−7

Lamonte, J.L., 'To what extent was the Byzantine Empire the suzerain of the Crusading States?', *Byzantion*, 7, 1932

Laurent, J., 'Des Grecs aux Croisés, étude sur l'histoire d'Edesse', *Byzantion*, 1, 1924

Laurent, V., 'Le patriarche d'Antioche Cyrille II (1287−c1308)', *Mélanges P. Peeters*, II, *Analecta Bollandiana*, 68, 1950

Leclercq, H., 'Pâques', *DACL*, XIII (II)

Leib, B., 'Deux inédits byzantins sur les azymes au début du XIIe siècle', *OCP*, 9, 1924

− *Rome, Kiev et Byzance à la fin du XIe siècle*, Paris 1924

Lepointe, G., 'Dîme', *DDC*, IV

Marie-Joseph, P., 'Albert de Verceil', *DHGE*, I

Martin, J.P.P., 'Les premiers princes croisés et les Syriens jacobites de Jérusalem', *Journal Asiatique*, ser 8, 12, 1888, 13, 1889

de Mas Latrie, L., 'Histoire des archevêques latins de l'île de Chypre', *AOL*, II

− 'Les patriarches latins de Jérusalem', *ROL*, 1, 1893

Mayer, H.E., *Bistümer, Klöster und Stifte im Königreich Jerusalem, Schriften der MGH*, 26, Stuttgart 1977

− 'Das Pontifikale von Tyrus und die Krönung der lateinischen Könige von Jerusalem', *DOP*, 21, 1967

− *The Crusades*, English trans, Oxford 1972

− 'Studies in the History of Queen Melisende of Jerusalem', *DOP*, 26, 1972

Mayne, R., 'East and West in 1054', *CHJ*, 11, 1954

Miller, T.S., 'The Knights of Saint John and the Hospitals of the Latin West', *Speculum*, 53, 1978

Mingana, A., 'The early spread of Christianity in Central Asia and the Far East: a new document', *BJRL*, 9, 1925

Morgan, M.R., *The Chronicle of Ernoul and the Continuations of William of Tyre*, Oxford Historical Monographs, 1973

Müller-Wiener, W., *Castles of the Crusaders*, London 1966

Munro, D.C., 'Did the Emperor Alexius I ask for aid at the Council of Piacenza?', *AHR*, 27, 1922

Nasrullah, J., 'Le patriarcat d'Antioche est-il resté après 1054 en communion avec Rome?', *Istina*, 21, 1976

Nicol, D.M., 'The Byzantine reaction to the Second Council of Lyons, 1274', *SCH*, 7, 1971

− *The Last Centuries of Byzantium, 1261−1453*, New York 1972

Ormanian, M., *The Church of Armenia*, London 1955

Painter, S., 'The Crusade of Theobald of Champagne and Richard of Cornwall, 1239−1241', in Setton, II, (q.v.)

—   'The Third Crusade: Richard the Lionhearted and Philip Augustus', in
     Setton, II, (q.v.)
Powicke, F.M., *King Henry III and the Lord Edward*, 2 vols, Oxford 1947
Prawer, J., 'Colonisation Activities in the Latin Kingdom of Jerusalem',
     Revue belge de philologie et d'histoire, 29, 1951
—   'A Crusader Tomb of 1290 from Acre and the last Archbishops of
     Nazareth', *Israel Exploration Journal*, 24, 1974
—   *Histoire du Royaume Latin de Jérusalem*, 2 vols, Paris 1969—70
—   *The Latin Kingdom of Jerusalem*, London 1972
—   'The settlement of the Latins in Jerusalem', *Speculum*, 27, 1952
Riant, P., 'Invention de la sépulture des Patriarches Abraham, Isaac et
     Jacob à Hébron, le 25 juin 1119', *AOL*, II
Richard, J., *Le comté de Tripoli sous la dynastie toulousaine (1102—1187)*,
     Paris 1945
—   'La mission en Europe de Rabban Çauma et l'union des Eglises',
     XII Convegno Volta, Rome 1957, reprinted in Richard, *Orient et
     Occident*, no XXII, (q.v.)
—   'The Mongols and the Franks', *Journal of Asian History*, 3, Blooming-
     ton 1969, reprinted in Richard, *Orient et Occident*, no XXVII, (q.v.)
—   'Note sur l'archdiocèse d'Apamée et les conquêtes de Raymond de
     Saint-Gilles en Syrie du Nord', *Syria*, XXV, 1946—8, reprinted in
     Richard, *Orient et Occident*, no II, (q.v.)
—   'L'Abbaye Cistercienne de Jubin et le prieuré Saint-Blaise de Nicosie',
     Epeteris tou Kentrou Epistemonikon Ereunon, 3, Nicosia 1969—70,
     reprinted in Richard, *Orient et Occident*, no XIX, (q.v.)
—   *Orient et Occident au Moyen Age: contacts et relations (XIIe — XVe s)*,
     London 1976
—   *La Papauté et les missions d'Orient au moyen âge*, Collection de l'Ecole
     francaise de Rome, 33, Rome 1977
Riley-Smith, J., *The Feudal Nobility and the Kingdom of Jerusalem, 1174—
     1277*, London 1973
—   *The Knights of St John in Jerusalem and Cyprus, c 1050—1310*,
     London 1967
—   'Latin Titular Bishops in Palestine and Syria, 1137—1291', *Catholic
     Historical Review*, 64, 1978
—   'Some lesser officials in Latin Syria', *EHR*, 87, 1972
—   'The Templars and the Teutonic Knights in Cilician Armenia', in
     Boase, *The Cilician Kingdom*, (q.v.)
—   'The Title of Godfrey of Bouillon', *BIHR*, 52, 1979
Roberg, B., *Die Union zwischen der griechischen und der lateinischen
     Kirche auf dem II Konzil von Lyon, (1274)*, Bonner Historische
     Forschung, 24, Bonn 1964
Röhricht, R., 'Syria Sacra', *Zeitschrift des deutschen Palästinavereins*, 10,
     1887
Roquebert, M., *L'Epopée Cathare*. I. *1198—1211, L'Invasion*   II. *1213—
     1216, Muret ou la dépossession*, Toulouse 1970—7
Rowe, J.G., 'The Papacy and the Ecclesiastical Province of Tyre', *BJRL*, 43,
     1960—1
Rüdt-Collenberg, W.H., *The Rupenides, Hethumides and Lusignans: the
     structure of the Armeno-Cilician Dynasties*, Paris 1963
Runciman, S., *The Eastern Schism*, Oxford 1955
—   *A History of the Crusades*, 3 vols, Cambridge 1951—4
—   *The Sicilian Vespers*, Cambridge 1958
Salibi, K.S., *Maronite Historians of Medieval Lebanon*, Beirut 1959
—   'The Maronite Church in the Middle Ages and its Union with Rome',

Oriens Christianus, 42, 1958
— 'The Maronites of the Lebanon under Frankish and Mamluk rule (1099—1516)', *Arabica*, 4, 1957
Saller, S.J., *Excavations at Bethany (1949—1953), Publications of the Studium Biblicum Franciscanum*, 12, Jerusalem 1957
Santi, C., Cerulli, E., Gordillo, M., Raes, E., Monneret de Villard, U., 'Etiopia', *EC*, V
Saunders, J.J., *The History of the Mongol Conquests*, London 1971
Savignac, R., Abel, F.M., 'Neby Samouil', *Revue Biblique*, new ser, 9, 1912
Schwinges, R.C., *Kreuzzugsideologie und Toleranz. Studien zu Wilhelm von Tyrus, Monographien zur Geschichte des Mittelalters*, 16, Stuttgart 1977
Segal, J.B., *Edessa, the Blessed City*, Oxford 1970
Setton, K.M., gen ed, *History of the Crusades*.
    I.   M.W. Baldwin, ed, *The First Hundred Years*, Philadelphia 1958
    II. R.L. Wolff, H.W. Hazard, ed, *The Later Crusades, 1189—1311*, Philadelphia 1962
    IV. H.W. Hazard, ed, *The Art and Architecture of the Crusader States*, Madison, Wisconsin 1977
Sievert, G., 'Das Vorleben des Papstes Urban IV', *Römische Quartalschrift für christliche Altertumskunde und für Kirchengeschichte*, 10, 1896
Smail, R.C., *Crusading Warfare, 1097—1193*, Cambridge 1956
— 'The International Status of the Latin Kingdom of Jerusalem, 1150—1192', in Holt, ed, *The Eastern Mediterranean Lands*, (q.v.)
Southern, R.W., *The Making of the Middle Ages*, London 1953
Stern, H., 'Les représentations des Conciles dans l'Eglise de la Nativité à Bethléem', *Byzantion*, 11, 1936, 13, 1938
Strayer, J.R., 'The Crusades of Louis IX', in Setton, II, (q.v.)
Tekeyan, P., 'Controverses christologiques en Arméno-Cilicie dans la seconde moitié du XIIe siècle (1165—98)', *OCA*, 124, 1939
Thomson, W.R., *Friars in the Cathedral. The First Franciscan Bishops, 1226—61*, Toronto 1975
Throop, P.A., *Criticism of the Crusade: a study of Public Opinion and Crusade Propaganda*, Amsterdam 1940
Tisserant, E., *Eastern Christianity in India*, London 1957
— Amann, E., 'Nestorius. 2. L'Eglise Nestorienne', *DTC*, XI (I)
Tournebize, F., *Histoire politique et religieuse de l'Arménie depuis les origines des Arméniens, jusqu'à la mort de leur dernier roi à l'an 1393*, Paris 1910
Vailhé, S., 'Une "Notitia Episcopatuum" d'Antioche du Xe siècle', *EO*, 10, 1907
— 'La "Notitia Episcopatuum" d'Antioche du patriarche Anastase, VIe siècle', *EO*, 10, 1907
— 'Les recensions de la "Notitia Episcopatuum" d'Antioche du patriarche Anastase', *EO*, 10, 1907
Van Cleve, T., *The Emperor Frederick II of Hohenstaufen*, Oxford 1972
— 'The Crusade of Frederick II', in Setton, II, (q.v.)
Vincent, H., Abel, F.M., *Bethléem, le sanctuaire de la Nativité*, Paris 1914
— *Jérusalem, recherches de topographie, d'archéologie et d'histoire. I. Jérusalem antique, II. Jérusalem nouvelle*, 2 vols, Paris 1912-26
Vincent, L.H., Baldi, D., Marangoni, L., Barluzzi, A., *Il Santo Sepolcro di Gerusalemme*, Bergamo 1949
Vincent, L.H., Mackay, E.H.J., Abel, F.M., *Hébron: Le Haram el-Khalil, sépulture des patriarches*, 2 vols, Paris 1923

de Vogüé, M., *Les Eglises de la Terre Sainte*, Paris 1860
Wallis Budge, E.A., *A History of Ethiopia*, 2 vols, London 1928
White, L.T., *Latin Monasticism in Norman Sicily*, Cambridge, Mass. 1938
Yewdale, R.B., *Bohemond I, Prince of Antioch*, Princeton 1924
Ziada, M.M., 'The Mamluk Sultans to 1291', in Setton, II, (q.v.)
Ziadé, I., 'Syrienne. (Eglise)', *DTC*, XIV (II).

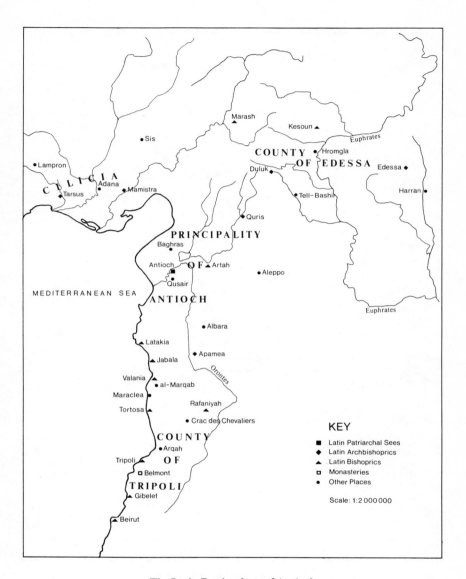

The Latin Patriarchate of Antioch

MEDITERRANEAN SEA

Gibelet ▲

Beirut ▲

Litani

Sidon ▲

Damascus ●

Sarepta ●

Tyre ▲

Toron ●

Banyas ●

KINGDOM

Acre ▲   Hattin 1187
                ✕

Haifa ●   Tiberias ▲
Mt Carmel ☐   Nazareth ◆ ☐ Mt Tabor

Ain Jalut 1260 ✕
Caesarea ●   Bethsan ●

Bosra ●

OF

Sebastia ▲
Nablus ●

Arsuf ●

Jordan

Jaffa ●   St Gilles
Lydda ▲

Ramla ●

Jerusalem ■   Jericho ●

Bethlehem ▲   St Sabas ☐

Ascalon ●

Gaza ●   Hebron ▲

Darum ●

Dead Sea

JERUSALEM

Beersheba ●   Kerak of Moab ●
                    Petra Deserti

al-Arish ●

KEY

■ Latin Patriarchal Sees
◆ Latin Archbishoprics
▲ Latin Bishoprics
☐ Monasteries
● Other Places
✕ Battles

Montreal ●

Scale: 1:2 000 000

To Mt Sinai
☐

The Latin Patriarchate of Jerusalem

INDEX

Prelates and rulers are listed alphabetically under the names of their sees or capitals, not under their personal names. Dates of office are given except where already listed on pages 373–375 above.

DATE DUE

FEB 0 8 2006			
FEB 1 4 2006			